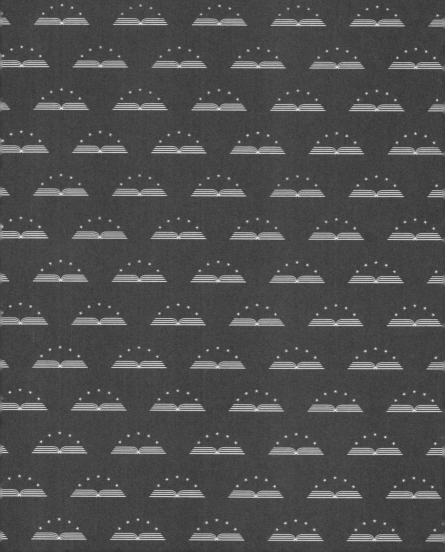

Library of America, a nonprofit organization,
champions our nation's cultural heritage
by publishing America's greatest writing in
authoritative new editions and providing resources
for readers to explore this rich, living legacy.

JIMMY BRESLIN

JIMMY BRESLIN

ESSENTIAL WRITINGS

Columns and Other Journalism 1960–2004
How the Good Guys Finally Won
The Short Sweet Dream of Eduardo Gutiérrez

Dan Barry, *editor*

THE LIBRARY OF AMERICA

Manufactured in the United States of America

Contents

HOW THE GOOD GUYS FINALLY WON:
NOTES FROM AN IMPEACHMENT SUMMER

COLUMNS 1976–2004

COLUMNS AND OTHER
JOURNALISM 1960–1974

Racing's Angriest Young Man

THE SHACK was on stilts so the floor wouldn't be against the ground in wintertime. But it didn't matter because when you went out to the creek for drinking water and brought it back in a basin, the way Bill Hartack had to before dinner every night, any of it that would drip on the floor quickly turned to ice. A pot-bellied stove was the only warm thing in shack number 371 and this does not constitute a heating system, even for a tiny three-room shack. But it was all they had because Hartack's father worked at soft coal in the mines around Colver, Pennsylvania, and there was no money in this. Nor was there much of a life in the shack. Hartack's mother had been killed when he was 7 and he had to raise his two sisters while his father dug coal.

You always remember this when you tell about Bill Hartack, the talented jockey who is one of the most controversial people in sports. It might make him easier to understand, you think.

But then Hartack will be at a race track, acting the way he did at Churchill Downs last May 7, and you forget everything because there is only one way to describe him. You say, simply, that his attitude is *to hell with everybody* and you have captured Hartack.

At 4:30 that afternoon, a guy in khaki work shirt and pants who is an assistant starter at Churchill Downs came up to Hartack's horse, a blaze-faced colt named Venetian Way. The guy took the horse by the bit, let him prance for a moment, then led him into stall number nine of the starting gate so they could begin the Kentucky Derby.

When the 14 horses all were locked into the gate, they slammed nervously into the tin sides and fronts of the stalls and the jockeys were calling "Not yet" and "No chance, boss" to the starter and there was a lot of noise and tension. Then the bell rang and the gate clacked open and, with riders yelping, the horses came out. Each made a leap first, because a race horse always is surprised to see the ground when the gate opens and he jumps at it. Then the horses started to run with the long, beautiful stride of a thoroughbred and there was a roar from the big crowd.

Hartack pushed Venetian Way into fourth, then took a snug hold on the reins. His horse was full of run, but Hartack wanted to keep him fourth, just off the leaders, and he stayed there until they were running down the backstretch. Then it turned into no contest. Bally Ache, one of the favorites, was leading. But not by enough. Tompion, the top choice, was in third position but he was creaking. On the final turn, Hartack let his horse out. Venetian Way made a big move and simply ran past Bally Ache as they swung by the five-sixteenth pole and headed into the long stretch.

With the thousands of people screaming from the three-decked stands, Venetian Way began widening the space. Hartack seemed to become frantic as his horse took over the race. He was whipping with his left hand and rolling from side to side in the saddle, the way the book says a jockey should not ride but the way Hartack always does. At the eight-pole Venetian Way had four lengths and Hartack was a wild, all-out jock giving the horse the kind of ride you must have when the purse is $160,000. Venetian Way won big.

After the winner's circle ceremonies, Hartack came into the crowded jockeys' room. At Churchill Downs, everything is a rotting, soot-covered mess and the jocks' room isn't much better. It is cluttered and steamy and, at this moment, was mobbed with reporters. It didn't look like much of a place, but it always has been one of the great sights in a jockey's life. You love everything when you win a Derby and it is all one big thrill of money.

But Hartack came into the room with that quick, long stride of his and his brown eyes flashed. He gave the reporters a dark look and said nothing as he went to his locker. He was obviously about to make a scene. There was no sense trying to relate him to a shack in Pennsylvania now.

The explosion came the moment the first newsman opened his mouth. "Willie," he began, "when did you think you had the race won?"

"Jeeez!" Hartack snapped. "Don't call me Willie. That's disrespectful. The name is Bill. And *that* is a stupid question. I stopped answering that one forty years ago. When you ask me an intelligent question I'll answer you."

People are encountered in all walks of life with a chip on

their shoulder because of harsh backgrounds. But you would have to be born of Murder, Inc. to be this angry after winning a Kentucky Derby.

For those who did not walk out on this blast, Hartack had a short description of the race, along with his usual course in journalism for those present. Reporters, he said, misquote him. And, he made it clear, newspapermen bother him. In fact, he didn't want to be bothered by anything except riding. Then he left to ride a horse in the eighth race. He finished second and was even madder after that. *To hell with everything, Hartack says, except getting home first on a horse.*

Winning horse races is something he can do. He has had two winners and a second in four Kentucky Derby rides. He won a Belmont Stakes, a Preakness, two Florida Derbys, the Flamingo, the Woodward, Arlington Classic. He has won virtually every major race the sport has and you can tap out that this is going to be the story for years to come. Just as big as the story they will go on making out of Hartack's behavior. For this is a kid who simply will not bend. It is either his way or you can go home, and most people don't like his way.

Two days after the Kentucky Derby, Hartack was sitting in the coffee shop of the Bo-Bet Motel, which is a short distance away from the Garden State Race Track in Camden, New Jersey. He had on a black sports jacket and gray slacks and a crisp white shirt which was open at the collar. He is 27, but he looks younger because he is only 5 feet, 4 inches and weighs 114 pounds. But when he toyed with the cup of coffee in front of him and started to talk you could see this was no little kid who could be moved around easily. And the guys at the table with him—Felix Bocchicchio, the old fight manager who owns the motel, Scratch Sheet Pestano, the jockey's agent, and a couple of newspapermen—did all the listening.

"There's only one thing that counts," Hartack was saying. "Words don't mean anything. They can misquote me all they want or write something bad about me, but the only thing that counts is the chart of last Saturday's race. It says Venetian Way, number one. It don't say nothing else. And nobody can change it. Everything else, they can have. The only thing I'm accountable for in this business is the race I ride. I have to stand up for the owner of the horse, the trainer and the people who bet on him. And I have to see another jock doesn't get hurt because of me. I don't have to worry about anything else. And I wish they wouldn't worry about me. Everybody is trying to run my life so hard they haven't got time to run their own."

He jammed a filter-tip cigarette between his teeth and started to light it. His speech was over. And he had left very little room for rebuttal. No matter what he was like, he had just brought home a 6–1 shot in the biggest race in America, and you had no argument.

You rarely do. Six weeks later, he came out of the gate in the Belmont Stakes aboard an 8–1 shot named Celtic Ash and for a half mile he held Celtic Ash back 10 lengths off the leaders. That was how he had been told to ride the late-running horse and Hartack followed instructions to the stride. First money was $96,785 and Hartack would get 10 per cent of it, but this didn't cause him to get jumpy and move up his horse too early, as nearly all of them do. He just sat there, way out of it. It took strong nerves. At the half-mile pole he moved to the outside to get a clear path in front of him. Going into the last big turn, he finally let Celtic Ash out. Then he started to slam and kick and push at the horse and it all worked out. Hartack came into the stretch with a live horse under him and won by five and a half lengths over Venetian Way—with whom Hartack had parted company after the Preakness because of a disagreement with the trainer. It's hard to argue against winners that pay 8–1.

Vic Sovinski, Venetian Way's trainer, found this out. He is a big ex-baker from Kankakee, Illinois, who has been accused of training a horse as if he were slapping together a tray of prune Danish. At Louisville, before the Derby, Sovinski was around knocking Hartack's brains out over the way Bill had ridden the horse in a warmup race the week before. Sovinski wanted the horse worked out an extra two furlongs after the finish. Hartack, who found the muddy going was bothering his horse, didn't push Venetian Way during the work. Sovinski said he loafed. Hartack thought he had saved the horse from being senselessly worn out. The press, always receptive to knocks on Hartack, trumpeted Sovinski's views. The Derby, of course, took care of that argument.

But after Venetian Way ran a poor fifth in the Preakness, Sovinski blew up again and yanked Hartack off him. The jockey promptly jumped on Celtic Ash. Then he explained the case of Venetian Way.

"Horses reach a peak, then they need a layoff," he said after the Preakness. "Venetian Way needed a freshener. He didn't get it. So he ran two races back in the pack. Then he was up again and ran second in the Belmont. Was I glad to beat him in the Belmont? What do I care? I don't have time to worry about particular horses I beat. I just want to beat them all."

In the Venetian Way case, Hartack was mostly silent for one of the few times in his career. This was because there was a steady stream of talk around the tracks that Venetian Way had been a sore-footed horse and only an analgesic called butazolidin had soothed him at Churchill Downs. It was ruled illegal at the Preakness and elsewhere. Hartack did not care to get into any discussion of this.

But in just about every other storm to come up during his career, he has been in there saying exactly what was on his mind. Because of this, people constantly compare him to baseball's Ted Williams. This is an untrue comparison. Williams is nasty, in general, only to sportswriters and spectators. When stacked against Hartack's style, this is like hating Russia. Anybody can do it.

Hartack goes all the way. He takes on anybody, from a groom to a steward or an owner of horses or a track itself and if he thinks he is right you can throw in Eisenhower, too, because while he can be tough and unmannerly and anything else they say about him he is not afraid.

He is a little package of nerves who has been suspended for using abusive language to stewards, for fighting with another jockey, for leaving the track and not finishing his day's riding because he lost a photo finish. He snaps at writers, agents, owners or anybody else in sight. The people who have anything good to say about him are few.

But nobody ever can say Hartack doesn't try. When he rides a race horse, he is going to do one thing. He is going to get down flat on his belly and slash whip streaks into the horse's side and try to get home first. Which is all anybody could want from a jockey.

But even those few people who have a good relationship with him will tell you that he is no fun when he loses. He is unbearable, no matter who is around. Since jockeys lose more often than they win, meetings with Hartack are on a catch-it-right basis. Most people don't like him because of this. But if there is anybody in sports who can afford to act this way, it is Hartack. He comes honest.

"Bill can walk on any part of a race track," Chick Lang, who used to be his agent, said one day last summer, "and he doesn't have to duck anybody. He can look everybody in the eye. There is nobody, no place, who can come up with a story on him about larceny or betting or something like that. How many can you say that about?"

Lang was extolling the rider while having a drink at a bar near Pimlico Race Track, where he now is employed. After six years of doing business with Hartack and taking down $50,000 a year for it, Lang found even the money couldn't soothe his nerves any more.

"It became just one big squabble," Lang said. "Bill would be fighting with me, then with an owner or a newspaperman or a trainer and it just got to be too much for both of us. He acts unhappy all the time. He acts as if he hates everything about what he's doing. I don't know what it is."

This drive, which makes Hartack a person who wants to win so badly he upsets you, comes from classic reasons. A boyhood in a Pennsylvania coal town during the depression does not make you easy going and philosophical about life. For a year and a half the family lived on the 50 cents a day credit at the company store which Bill's father earned by digging soft coal. For 50 cents a day, you lived on potatoes.

On December 13, 1940, Hartack's mother, father and year-old sister Maxine got into a battered car his father had borrowed so he could make the 30-mile drive to the mine company office where he was to be paid. By this time, miners were being paid money instead of potatoes. On the way, a trailer truck slammed into the car, throwing it down a hill. Bill's father was in the hospital for 10 weeks. Maxine, the baby, had to stay for a year. Bill's mother died on Christmas morning. He and his sister Florence, who was 6 then, were taken care of by neighbors. It was not a good day for a kid.

"I barely remember it," Hartack says. But you figure he carries it with him someplace, whether he knows it or not.

A year later, the Hartacks' shack caught fire and the four of them barely escaped the flames. They moved in with some other people while his father built a new house.

With his father working the long hours of a miner, Hartack took over the job of raising his two sisters. He saw they were up in the morning and had breakfast and made school. At night he cooked dinner for the family. As for himself, school in Black Lick Township was rough; Bill was small and the other kids, big-necked sons of miners, beat hell out of him.

So Hartack took it out on schoolbooks. He was valedictorian of his high school class.

When he graduated, at 18, Bill was thinking about an office job in Johnstown. Anything but the mines. When the office job didn't materialize, Hartack's father spoke to Andy Bruno, a friend who was a jockeys' agent. Bruno agreed to get Bill a job with horses. Hartack gave his son a dollar and let him drive away with Bruno to the Charlestown, West Virginia, track. Hartack picked up horses quickly. After he rode that first winner, he never stopped.

With this background, you'd think, it would be impossible for Hartack to miss. He had all the hunger and sorrow and hardness a kid ever would need to drive him to the top. It is the standard formula for successful athletes. But there have been fighters who have come out of the slums and they quit when you come into them and there are jockeys who had hunger and should be all out, but when it gets tough they shy away from the rail and take the easy way home.

Hartack, when he first came to the track, brought more than hunger with him. You can find that out by talking to his father. Bill Hartack, Sr., is a slight man with close cropped brown hair which has only a little gray in it, a thin mustache and a slight European accent. He was asked if Bill's early years were what made him so tough when he loses.

"Part of it," his father said, "but not all. I see him today how he acts and I don't say anything because he's just the same as I was. When I worked it was piece work. You got paid for the amount of coal you loaded. I set a record for soft coal that lasted until they brought in machines. I worked from when the sun came up to when the sun came down. And even when I was getting only that 50 cents a day for food I worked like that.

I'd come to work with only some water in my lunch pail, not even a piece of bread, but I couldn't let anybody dig more coal than me. Once, another fella dug more than me during a week. I was so mad that when I went home I couldn't sleep nights. I couldn't wait to get back and dig more coal than him. It had me crazy. You couldn't talk to me."

"The boy is just like him," Bocchicchio said. "When he first came to stay with me here, I'm looking for him one day. It's a Sunday. He ain't been out of his room for dinner the night before and now breakfast and lunch has gone by and I don't see him. It's getting dark and I'm worried. I go over to his room and knock on the door and he let me in. He was still in bed. He don't want to talk. So I leave him alone. But I get right on the phone with Bill here and I ask him what he wants me to do. He says, 'Did he have any winners yesterday?' I says no. So he laughs. 'He'll be all right in time for the track,' he tells me. That's what this kid is like. If he don't win, you can't talk to him."

"When I was young," Mr. Hartack said, "I had a terrible temper. I fight. In the mines I argue with anybody. But you find when you get older, you mellow and you're not so mad any more. Bill will be like that. It will take a little while, but he'll mellow. But he'll still want to win. That he'll never get over."

This win-or-shoot-yourself attitude of Hartack's comes out, during a race, in the form of a rail-brushing, whip-slamming kid who will take any chance on a horse to win. Regarded on form alone, Hartack seems to be a poor rider. The secret of being a jockey is to keep a good-looking seat on a horse. Hartack, on the other hand, does it all wrong. He rolls from side to side in such a pronounced manner that even an amateur from the stands can see it.

"The form doesn't look classic," Jimmy Jones of Calumet tells you, "but it really doesn't matter none, because he has a way of making horses run for him. And that's what the business is."

Horses ran for Hartack from the start. When Bill came to Charlestown, Bruno, the agent friend of his father's, turned him over to trainer Junie Corbin, a veteran trainer on the small, half-mile track circuit. Hartack had no particular interest in becoming a jockey when he arrived, but under Corbin he learned the business.

On October 10, 1952, with just two races behind him, he held onto a horse named Nickleby for dear life and came home on top to pay $18.40 at Waterford Park, West Virginia. Since then, he has never stopped. By 1954 he was one of the top jockeys on the half-mile circuit. A year later Corbin ran into trouble with his stable—a groom had given caffeine to a horse. When Corbin was suspended for this, his bankroll couldn't take the layover. So he sold Hartack's contract for $15,000 to the big Ada L. Rice Stable. Chick Lang was in the picture as agent now and at the first opportunity, a year and a half later, he and Hartack went free lance, meaning they could take whatever mounts were open. Calumet Farm asked for a first call on Hartack—and got it because of the horseflesh they were putting under Bill's rear end each day.

From then on he made it big. In 1957 his horses won a total of $3,331,257 in purses. This is a record for a jockey. He also won 43 stakes, which topped a mark set by Eddie Arcaro. As a rider he is in a special little class with Arcaro and Willie Shoemaker. And in three of the last six years Hartack has been off by himself as national riding champion.

He has taken his father out of the mines and put him on a farm he bought at Charlestown, West Virginia. He has his younger sister in college. And life for him has become a series of new hi-fi sets, a different date whenever he picks up a phone, plenty of money—and live horses.

Hartack, like most people who don't have to live with women, is not against them. "There must be 150 girls around Miami I can call up for dates," he says. The situation is similar in Louisville or Oceanport, New Jersey, or wherever else he rides for a living. But it is strictly on a spur-of-the-moment basis. Riding horses and winning on them is basically his whole life.

Money or acclaim never will change his attitude. A look at him in his own surroundings shows this. One warm Tuesday morning last February, for example, Hartack stepped out of his $50,000 brick-and-redwood ranch house in Miami Springs and walked across the lawn to a beige, spoke-wheeled Cadillac which was in the driveway. He keeps the car outside because the big garage has been turned into a closet to hold his 150 suits.

It was 11:45 A.M. when Hartack pulled away from the house and started for Hialeah. The street was lined with palm trees and expensive houses. Sprinklers played on the lawns and the sun glinted on the wet grass. Hartack was fresh-eyed. He had slept for 11 hours and when Paul Foley, a guy who stays with him, woke him up, Bill took a shower, swallowed orange juice and coffee and left for the job of riding horses. For the last five years he has been going to his business like this and making anywhere from $150,000 to $200,000 a year. For anybody who ever has had to go to work hours earlier each morning, packed into a train with nervous, bleak-faced commuters who spend most of their time at home two-stepping with bill collectors, Hartack's way of life is the kind of thing you would steal for.

Hartack didn't talk as he drove to the track. He was thinking about the horses he would ride that day. At night, he reads the *Racing Form* and carefully goes over every horse in each race and as he does this he tries to remember their habits. One will swing wide on a turn, he will tell himself, so if he gets a chance he will stay behind that one and then move inside him on the turn. This reading and remembering is something a jockey must do or he isn't worth a quarter. Hartack, as he drove to the track, ran over the horses in his mind. He was mute as he pulled the car into the officials' lot at the track. His face was solemn as he walked through the gate and into the jockeys' room. Inside, he undressed, put on a white T-shirt and whipcord riding pants, then sat quietly while a valet tugged on his riding boots. The other jockeys paid no attention to him except for a nod here and there and Hartack returned it. Then he took out the program and the *Racing Form* and began to look at them again.

"How do you feel," a guy asked him.

"Terrible," he said. "My stomach bothers me. It always bothers me." He kept reading the paper. It was the best you ever will get in the way of conversation when Hartack is on a track.

Outside, Chick Lang was standing on the gravel walk in front of the racing secretary's office. He was shaking his head. Lang is a heavy, round-faced, blond-haired guy of 32. He had been at the barns at 5:45 A.M. talking to trainers and owners and making deals with them for Hartack to ride their mounts.

"I don't know whether life is worth all this," Lang was saying. "You saw how he was today? Concentrating, serious. Nobody allowed to talk. That's fine. It's the way he wants it and that's the way it should be. But what about other people? Don't you think he should give them something, too? Last week, on Wednesday, he went to the coast to ride Amerigo in the San Juan Capistrano Handicap.

"Before he left we talked and decided that he wouldn't take any mounts here until Monday. That was yesterday. So I went out and booked him on seven horses. What happens? Sunday night he calls me from Las Vegas. 'I can't get a plane out of here,' he said.

"Well, you've been to Vegas. They run planes out of there like they were streetcars. But that's what he tells me. Now I've got to get on the phone and start trying to find trainers and tell them Hartack can't ride the next day. It embarrasses hell out of me. Here I make commitments and then I have to break them. It's terrible."

Trouble is something Hartack will take—or he will make—and he doesn't care about it. And while carrying around this winning-is-all-that-matters attitude he has had plenty of jams.

The business of newspapermen, for example. Hartack has one of the worst relationships any athlete ever has had with newspapers and he is not about to improve it.

Now many people do not like sportswriters, particularly the wives of sportswriters, and in many athletic circles it is considered a common, decent hatred for a person to have. But most sportswriters whom Hartack dislikes couldn't care less. And, the notion is, neither does the reading public. Ofttimes, the public is having enough trouble deciphering what sportswriters write without having to take on the additional burden of remembering that there is a feud between Hartack and the press box. But it is important to Hartack that he does not like the writers. And they put in the papers that his name is "Willie" and he blows up at them.

Hartack has troubles with officials, too, and these cost him. Suspensions dot his career. Last year, for example, he snarled at Garden State stewards—they insisted he cursed—and was set down for the remainder of the meeting. In 1958 he was set down for 15 days by Atlantic City stewards when he was first under the wire on a horse called Nitrophy. But Jimmy Johnson, who finished second on Tote All, lodged a foul claim against Hartack, saying his horse had been interfered with. The stewards allowed the claim and took down Hartack's horse. Hartack tried to take down Johnson with a left hand in the jocks' room. For his troubles both on the track and off it, Bill was given 15 days. In the last two years, Bill has been set down a total of 61 days. And he has been fined and reprimanded several times. At Hialeah in February he lost a photo with a horse called Cozy Ada and after it he was in a rage. "What do I have to do to get a shake here?" he snapped, walking out on the rest of his riding commitments. He was fined $100 for this. This is a kid who simply cannot stand losing, even to a camera.

His temperament does not make him a hero with other jockeys. There was a night last summer in the bar of the International Hotel, which is at New York's Idlewild Airport, and Willie Shoemaker and Sammy Boulmetis and some other horse guys were sitting around over a drink and Hartack's name was mentioned.

"I can't figure him out," Boulmetis was saying. "One day he seems nice to you. Next day he won't even talk to you."

Walter Blum, another rider, had an opinion, too. "You know," he said, "you can't live with him. He just wants to make you hate him. I mean, he really works at it."

Through all this, Hartack's outlook has been the same. "I do my job," he says. "I do what I think best. If I make a mistake, that's that. But the only place a mistake shows is the official chart of a race. If I don't win, that's a mistake. Nothing else counts. Not you or anybody else. Only that result."

To get down and wrestle with the truth, Hartack's attitude is, on many occasions, the only right one in racing.

Take, for example, the warm afternoon in February of 1959 at Hialeah when Hartack started jogging a horse called Greek Circle to the starting gate. To Hartack, the parade to the post is all important. He gets the feel of his mount by tugging on one rein, then the other and watching the horse's reaction. He tries to find out if the horse is favoring one foot or another or likes to be held tightly or with a normal pressure on the bit. Greek Circle responded to nothing. The horse seemed to have no coordination at all and that was enough for Hartack.

"My horse isn't right," he yelled to the starter. "He can't coordinate himself. He's almost falling down right now. I'm getting off him."

The starter called for a veterinarian and Hartack jogged the horse for the vet, Dr. George Barksdale.

"The horse is fine," Dr. Barksdale said. "Take him into the gate. He'll run fine."

Hartack's answer was simple. He stopped the horse and swung his fanny off him and dropped to the ground. The veterinarian shrugged. Across the way, in the stands, they were adding up figures and a neat little sum of $5,443.56 had been set aside as the track's share of the $136,089 bet on Greek Circle. Because the next race, the Widener, was on television and time was a problem now, the track stewards had to order the horse scratched and the money bet on him returned.

They knocked Hartack's brains out on this one. He was in headlines across the nation the next day as a little grandstander who should have been suspended for his actions.

But when the smoke cleared and you could think about it objectively, you could see who was wrong. Eddie Arcaro, over many glasses of a thing called Blue Sunoco in the Miami Airport bar a week later, talked about it. "Nobody in his right mind, the vet included, could knock Hartack for that. Do you know how many jocks have been killed because they were on broken down horses? And they tell me this horse has been sore all year. Bad sore, too. Hartack was right. It took a little guts, too."

Then on May 16, 1959, Hartack was aboard Vegeo at Garden State and as he got into the gate, the horse was nervous and reared up and Bill yelled to Cecil Phillips, the starter, that he wasn't ready to go. Phillips' answer was to press the sticks of wood in his hand together and they completed the electric circuit which made the gate open and the race start. Hartack's horse was rearing in the air and by the time he got him straightened out the field was up the track and the race was lost.

Hartack went to the track stewards with this complaint. Now Hartack coming off a loser is bad enough. But a Hartack coming off a loser that he felt is somebody else's fault is really something. This is a Khrushchev who rides horses. He called the stewards and snapped at them. Their version was that he cursed. They set him down for the remainder of the meeting.

"I get in trouble because of these things," Hartack tells you. "But I'm never going to stop because I'm right. I'm doing it honestly. The only reason I get my name around is that

I'm the only one who does it. When I have a horse under me
that's broken down, I won't ride him. And if the starter blows
my chances in a race, I yell about it. It doesn't just happen to
me. It happens to everybody else. But the rest of these riders
are afraid to say anything about it. They get on a horse that's
broken down and they keep quiet. Then they give him an easy
ride, so they won't take any chances of getting hurt, and when
they come back they give some ridiculous excuse to satisfy the
trainer. You know, 'The horse lugged in' or 'he propped on
me' or 'he tried to get out on me.' In the meantime, the public
has bet its money on the horse and they didn't get a fair shake.
But the jocks feel you don't have to make an excuse to them.
They don't count. Well, I look on it differently. I owe loyalty to
anybody who bets on my horse. The person who does that is
going to get the best I can give him. Nothing is going to stop
me from doing that."

If you have been around Hartack on race tracks, and watched
him as he tries to win, you would know how far he is willing to
carry his fight. Like the dark, rain-flecked Saturday in Louisville
in 1958.

The driver moved his ambulance slowly through the filth of
Churchill Downs' grandstand betting area and he had his hand
on the horn to make people get out of the way as he headed
for the gate.

Hartack was on a stretcher in the back of the ambulance. He
had a wooden ice cream spoon stuck between his teeth so when
the pain hit him he could bite into it. The stick doesn't help
take pain away, but you do not bite your lip when pain comes if
you have a stick between your teeth, so Hartack could grimace
and tighten his teeth on the wood each time the ambulance
hit a bump.

His body was covered with mud and his left leg was propped
on a pillow. He looked tiny and helpless, the way jockeys always
do when they are hurt. A few minutes before, a 2-year-old filly
named Quail Egg had become frightened in the starting gate
and she flipped Hartack. As he rolled around in the mud under
the horse, Quail Egg started to thrash at the ground with her
hooves. Then the horse fell heavily on Hartack and a bone in
his leg snapped.

As the ambulance moved into a main street, where it was

smoother riding, Hartack put the stick to the side of his mouth and muttered some words to Chick Lang.

"Nothing heavy on this leg," he said. "Don't let them put a heavy cast on this leg, Chick. We got to ride that horse next week."

The Kentucky Derby was to be run on the next Saturday and Hartack was contracted to ride Tim Tam. Now he was flattened out on a stretcher in an ambulance and his leg was broken, but he still was talking about riding the horse.

Then he called a company in Chicago which makes special braces. "I want a real light one. Aluminum," he told them. "Make it special. It has to go inside a riding boot. I need it by Wednesday."

"He won't listen to me," the staff doctor from the hospital in Louisville said quietly. "The fibula is snapped and there are some ripped ligaments around it. That leg will need a long time."

It did. Hartack was out for six weeks. But if you had seen him with a stick in his mouth and pain waving through his body and heard him talking about trying to ride a horse, then you had to say that he is a kid with something to him.

Every time Hartack has been hurt he has been like this. On July 10, 1957, he was moving around the last turn at Arlington Park on a horse called Smoke-Me-Now. The one in front, Spy Boss, had been running steadily, but he became tired and started to fall apart all at once and Smoke-Me-Now ran up his heels. With a thoroughbred horse in full motion, it only takes the slightest flick against his ankles to cause a spill. This time Smoke-Me-Now caught it good and he went down in a crash. Hartack was tossed into the air. His little body flipped in a somersault and he landed on his back. Nobody would pick him up until an ambulance came.

They took him to a hospital in Elgin, Illinois, and the doctors said Hartack had a badly sprained back and muscles were torn and he'd be out for a couple of weeks at a minimum. This was on a Thursday. On Saturday, Hartack was scheduled to ride Iron Liege, for the Calumet Farm, in the $100,000 Arlington Classic. Hartack likes $100,000 races.

At 8 o'clock on Friday night, Dogwagon, who is an exercise boy for Calumet, was sitting in a camp chair in front of the barn at Arlington Park and a guy came over and asked who was riding a stable pony around the area at this time of night.

"That is Mr. Bill Hartack," Dogwagon said. "Mr. Bill Hartack has a fine feeling for money and right now he is teaching his back to feel the same ways. He strapped up like he was a fat ole woman trying to keep the rolls in. But he goin' be ridin' Iron Liege tomorrow and he'll be therebouts when they pass out the money, too."

Hartack was jogging back and forth across the stable area on a painted pony. He came back to the barn, after 45 minutes of this. He hopped off and went to a phone to tell Calumet's Jimmy Jones that he could ride the next day. He was beat a nose on Iron Liege and he went into a rage because he lost the race.

In the tack room, somebody passed by and said, "You did a wonderful job getting second. I mean, you're lucky you can walk, much less ride."

"I don't care if I have one leg," Hartack snapped. "That's no excuse. I wanted to win the race."

Which is the whole game with Hartack. There isn't a thing in the world you can say is wrong with him except he cannot stand to lose. And he does not think anything else in the world matters except not losing.

Last June, for example, Hartack was at Monmouth Park and was due in New York to see Floyd Patterson fight Ingemar Johansson. Scratch Sheet Pestano, his agent, was at the bar in Jack Dempsey's Restaurant on Broadway, Hartack's ringside seats in his pocket.

"You meeting Hartack?" somebody asked him.

"When I get the race results, I'll let you know," Pestano said.

He went into a phone booth and called a newspaper office for the day's results at Monmouth. Hartack was on seven horses. As Pestano listened to the guy on the other end, his face became longer. He came out of the phone booth with the tickets in his hand.

"You meet him and give them to him," he told somebody with him. "He lost on seven horses today. Every one of them should have been up there. He won't be fit to live with tonight. I'm going home. I don't want to be anywhere near him. He just can't stand losing."

Mr. Harry (Champ) Segal, dean of Broadway horse players, was listening to the conversation.

"If all them jockeys was like that maybe you could cash a bet now and then," the Champ said.

Which is what everybody has to say about Hartack, whether they care for him or not.

November 1960

Worst Baseball Team Ever

I T WAS long after midnight. The bartender was falling asleep, and the only sound in the hotel was the whine of a vacuum cleaner in the lobby. Casey Stengel banged his last empty glass of the evening on the red-tiled bartop and then walked out of this place the Chase Hotel in St. Louis calls the Lido Room.

In the lobby the guy working the vacuum cleaner was on his big job, the rug leading into a ballroom, when Mr. Stengel stopped to light a cigarette and reflect on life. For Stengel this summer, life consists of managing a team called the New York Mets, which is not very good at playing baseball.

"I'm shell-shocked," Casey addressed the cleaner. "I'm not used to gettin' any of these shocks at all, and now they come every three innings. How do you like that?" The cleaner had no answer. "This is a disaster," Stengel continued. "Do you know who my player of the year is? My player of the year is Choo Choo Coleman and I have him for only two days. He runs very good."

This accomplished, Stengel headed for bed. The cleaner went back to his rug. He was a bit puzzled, although not as much as Stengel was later in the day when the Mets played the St. Louis Cardinals in a doubleheader.

Casey was standing on the top step of the dugout at Busch Stadium and he could see the whole thing clearly. That was the trouble.

In front of him the Mets had Ken Boyer of the Cardinals in a rundown between first and second. Marvin Throneberry, the marvelous first baseman, had the ball. Boyer started to run away from him. Nobody runs away from Marvin Throneberry. He took after Boyer with purpose. Marv lowered his head a little and produced wonderful running action with his legs. This amazed Stengel. It also amazed Stan Musial of the Cardinals, who was on third. Stanley's mouth opened. Then he broke for the plate and ran across it and into the dugout with the run that cost the Mets the game. (Throneberry, incidentally, never did get Boyer. Charlie Neal finally made the putout.) It was an incredible play. It also was loss No. 75 of the season for the Mets. In the second game Roger Craig, the Mets' starter, gave up so many runs so quickly in the seventh inning that Casey didn't have time to get one of his great relief pitchers ready. The Mets went on to lose No. 76.

Following this, the team flew to New York, where some highly disloyal people were starting to talk about them. There seems to be some sort of suspicion around that the New York Mets not only are playing baseball poorly this season but are playing it worse than any team in the modern history of the sport. As this week began, the Mets had a record of 28 won and 79 lost and seemed certain to break the modern record for losses in one season. This was set by the 1916 Philadelphia Athletics, who lost 117 games—an achievement that was challenged by the Boston Braves of 1935, who lost 115 games and were known as The World's Worst Team. But, by using one of the more expensive Keuffel & Esser slide rules, you discover that the Mets, if they cling to their present pace, will lose 120 games. You cannot ask for more than that.

Figures, of course, are notorious liars, which is why accountants have more fun than people think. Therefore, you just do not use a record book to say the Mets are the worst team of all time. You have to investigate the matter thoroughly. Then you can say the Mets are the worst team of all time.

"I never thought I would have an argument," Bill Veeck says. "I was always secure in the knowledge that when I owned the St. Louis Browns, I had the worst. Now it's different. You can say anything you want, but don't you dare say my Brownies were this bad. I'll prove it to you. There are still a few Browns in the major leagues and this is nine years later. How many Mets do you think are going to be around even two years from now? I'm being soft here. I haven't even mentioned my midget, Eddie Gaedel."

Reporting from Philadelphia is Pat Hastings, proprietor of the Brown Jug bar and a man who has sat through more bad baseball than anybody in America. For consistency, Philadelphia baseball always has been the worst. On nine occasions during Pat's tenure at old Baker Bowl and Shibe Park, both the Phillies and A's finished in last place.

But Pat, who has viewed the Mets on several occasions this season, refuses to put any team in a class with them. "The 1916 Athletics had Stuffy McInnins, you got to remember that," he says. "And some of them Phillies teams could hurt you with the bat pretty good. There was players like Chuck Klein, Virgil Davis, Don Hurst. I seen 'em all. Why, we used to make jokes about Buzz Arlett. He played right field for the Phillies in 1931. People used to go out and get drunk if they seen him catch a fly ball. I feel like writing the fellow a letter of apology now. Why he done more fielding standing still than some of these Mets I seen do at full speed."

In Brooklyn there is Joseph (Babe) Hamberger, who once associated with the old Dodgers and vehemently denies he ever saw a Brooklyn club as bad as the Mets.

"When Uncle Robbie [Wilbert Robinson] was managing, he didn't even know the names of the players," Babe says. "But he won two pennants and was in the first division a couple of times. Casey was over here, too. Ask him. He'll tell you. It got rough, but never like now."

Now all this is not being pointed out as an act of gratuitous cruelty. Quite the opposite. The Mets are so bad, you've got to love them. Name one true American who could do anything but root for a team that has had over 135 home runs hit against it. In New York a lot of people root for the Mets. They are mainly old Brooklyn Dodger fans and their offspring, who are called the "New Breed" in the newspapers. They are the kind of people who, as San Francisco Giant Publicist Garry Schumacher once observed, never would have tolerated Joe DiMaggio on their team at Ebbets Field. "Too perfect," Garry said.

The Mets are bad for many reasons, one of which is that they do not have good players. The team was formed last year when the National League expanded to 10 teams. ("We are damn lucky they didn't expand to 12 teams," Manager Stengel says.) The other new team, the Houston Colt .45s, has done a bit better than the Mets. It's in eighth place, 11½ games ahead of New York. For players, the Mets were given a list of men made available to them by the other eight National League teams. The list was carefully prepared and checked and rechecked by the club owners. This was to make certain that no bona-fide ballplayers were on it.

"It was so thoughtful of them," Stengel says. "I want to thank all of them owners who loved us to have those men and picked them for us. It was very generous of them."

Actually, the Mets did wind up with a ballplayer or two. First Baseman Gil Hodges was fielding as well as ever before a kidney ailment put him in the hospital. Center Fielder Richie Ashburn, at 35, is a fine lead-off hitter, although he seems to be on his way to setting some sort of a record for being thrown out while trying to take an extra base. If Jim Hickman, an outfielder, ever learns to swing at good pitches he might make it big. Here and there Al Jackson and Roger Craig produce a well-pitched game. And Frank Thomas can hit. But all this does is force the Mets to go out of their way to lose.

And once past these people, the Mets present an array of talent that is startling. Most of those shocks Casey talks about come when his pitchers throw to batters. There was a recent day in St. Louis when Ray Daviault threw a low fast ball to Charley James of the Cards. James likes low fast balls. He hit this one eight rows deep into left field for the ball game.

"It was bad luck," Daviault told the manager after the game. "I threw him a perfect pitch."

"It couldn't have been a perfect pitch," Casey said. "Perfect pitches don't travel that far."

One of Casey's coaches is the fabled Rogers Hornsby. Rajah was a batting coach during spring training and for the early part of the season. But all of his work now is done with prospects out on the farms. Which is good, because Hornsby hates to lose. Oh how he hates to lose! One day he was sitting in the dugout at the Polo Grounds before a game and you could see him seething. The Mets had been losing. So was Hornsby. He couldn't get a thing home and he was in action at three or four different major tracks around the country.

"You can't trust them old Kentucky bastard trainers," he confided.

The general manager of the Mets is George Weiss, who was let go by the Yankees after the 1960 season because of his age. He is 68 now. George spent all of last year at his home in Greenwich, Conn. As Red Smith reported, this caused his wife, Hazel, to announce, "I married George for better or for worse, but not for lunch." She was pleased when George took over the Mets this year and resumed his 12-hour working day away from home.

The Mets also have many big-name sports reporters who write about them. This may be the hardest job of all. As Barney Kremenko of the *New York Journal-American* observes, "I've covered losing teams before. But for me to be with a *non-winner!*"

There are some people, of course, who will not stand still for any raps at the team. They say the Mets have a poor record because they lose so many one-run games. They point out that the Mets have lost 28 games by one run so far. However, this figure also means the Mets lost 51 other games by more than one run.

One who advances the one-run theory is Donald Grant, the Wall Street stockbroker who handles ownership details for Mrs. Joan Payson, the class lady who put up the money for the Mets. It is Mr. Grant's job to write letters to Mrs. Payson, explaining to her just what is happening with the Mets.

"It is annoying to lose by one run, but Mrs. Payson and I are pleased with the team's progress," Grant says. "She is perfectly understanding about it. After all, you do not breed a Thoroughbred horse overnight." Grant obviously doesn't know much about horse racing.

Whether the Mets lose by a run or by 14 runs (and they have done this, too), it doesn't matter. They still lose. They lose at night and in the daytime and they lose so much that the only charge you can't make against them is that their pitchers throw spitters.

"Spitters?" Stengel says. "I can't get them to throw regular pitches good."

Basically, the trouble with the Mets is the way they play baseball. It is an unchanging style of walks, passed balls, balks, missed signs, errors, overrun bases and bad throws. You see it every time. It doesn't matter what day you watch the Mets play or if they win or lose. With this team, nothing changes. Only the days.

On July 22, for example, the Mets were in Cincinnati for a doubleheader. They not only lost both games, but they also had four runners thrown out at home plate in the course of the day. Nobody could remember when this had happened before—probably because it hadn't. What made it frightening was the ease with which the Mets brought the feat off. You got the idea that they could get four runners thrown out at the plate any day they wanted to.

In the first game Choo Choo Coleman was out trying to score from second on a single to left. In the second game Stengel jauntily ordered a double steal in the second inning. He had Cannizzaro on first and Hot Rod Kanehl at third. Cannizzaro took off and drew a throw. Kanehl broke for the plate. The Cincinnati shortstop, Cardenas, cut it off, threw home, and that took care of Kanehl. In the fourth inning Elio Chacon tried to score from first when the Reds messed up a fly in the outfield. But Vada Pinson finally got to the ball, and his throw home beat Chacon by a couple of steps. In the fifth inning Jim Hickman was on third. He broke for the plate as Rod Kanehl hit the ball. Kanehl hit the ball square at third. The throw had Hickman by a yard.

The day before that, Roger Craig, the team's version of a big pitcher, had gone over to Stengel and volunteered for relief pitching in the doubleheader, if he were needed. Stengel nodded. It was nice of Craig to say he would work between starts. And the next day the Mets certainly did need Craig. Going into the ninth inning with a 3–3 tie against the Reds, Stengel called on Roger to save the day. Roger took his eight warmup pitches. Then he threw two regular pitches to Marty Keough of the Reds. Keough hit the second one eight miles, and the Reds won 4–3.

Two days later in the first inning of a game in Milwaukee, the Braves had runners on first and second. Henry Aaron hit the ball hard, but Chacon at shortstop made a fine backhanded stop. As Chacon regained balance, he saw Roy McMillan of the Braves running for third. Chacon yelled to Felix Mantilla, the Mets' third baseman. He was going to get McMillan at third on a sensational play. Mantilla backed up for the throw. Then he backed up some more. By the time Chacon threw, Mantilla had backed up three yards past the base and when he caught the throw all he could do was listen to the crowd laugh. McMillan had his foot on third.

The Mets fought back, however, and had the game tied 4–4 in the 12th. Casey called on a new pitcher to face the Braves in this inning. He was R. G. Miller, making his first appearance as a Met. At the start of the season, R. G. was managing a car agency and had no intention of playing baseball. Then Wid Matthews, the Mets' talent scout, came around to talk to him. Miller, Matthews had found, needed only 18 days in the major leagues to qualify as a five-year man under the baseball players' pension. R. G. had spent a couple of years with Detroit before deciding to quit.

"Go to Syracuse for us," Matthews said, "and if you show anything at all we'll bring you up. Then you can put in your 18 days. When you reach 50, you'll get about $125 every month until they put you in a box."

Miller went out front and spoke to the boss. The job would be waiting for him after the season, Miller was told. So Miller went to Syracuse. He pitched well enough to be brought up. Now he came out of the Mets' bullpen to take on the Milwaukee Braves.

Miller loosened up easily, scuffed the dirt, looked down and got the sign and glared at Del Crandall, the Milwaukee batter. Then Miller threw a slider, and Crandall hit a home run. Miller, with his first pitch of the year, had lost a game.

"He makes the club," everybody on the Mets was saying.

Marvin Throneberry, the fast-running first baseman, has had his share of travail this year, too. In fact, anytime you meet some oldtimer who tries to bore you with colorful stories, you can shut him up quickly with two Marv Throneberry stories for every one he has about players like Babe Herman or Dizzy Dean.

Throneberry is a balding, 28-year-old who comes out of Memphis. He was up with the Yankees and once even opened the season as a first baseman for them. After that, he was with the Kansas City A's and the Orioles. Throneberry is a serious baseball player. He tries, and he has some ability. It's just that things happen when he plays.

Take the doubleheader against the Cubs at the Polo Grounds early in the season. In the first inning of the first game, Don Landrum of Chicago was caught in a rundown between first and second. Rundowns are not Throneberry's strong point. In the middle of the posse of Mets chasing the Cub, Throneberry found himself face to face with Landrum. The only trouble was Marvin did not have the ball. During a rundown the cardinal rule is to get out of the way if you do not have the ball. If you stand around, the runner will deliberately bang into you, claim interference and the umpire will give it to him.

Which is exactly what happened to Marv. Landrum jumped into his arms and the umpire waved him safely to first. Instead of an out, the Mets now had to contend with a runner on base—and that opened the gates for a four-run Chicago rally.

Marv had a big chance to make good when the Mets came to bat. With two runners on, Marv drove a long shot to the bullpen in right center field. It looked to be a sure triple. Marv flew past first. Well past it. He didn't come within two steps of touching the bag. Then he raced toward second and careened toward third. While all this violent motion was taking place, Ernie Banks, the Cubs' first baseman, casually strolled over to Umpire Dusty Boggess.

"Didn't touch the bag, you know, Dusty," Banks said. Boggess nodded. Banks then called for the ball. The relay came and he stepped on first base. Across the infield Throneberry was standing on third. He was taking a deep breath and was proudly hitching up his belt when he saw the umpire calling him out at first.

It was suggested to Throneberry on a recent evening that his troubles, and those of the entire Mets team, come from unfamiliarity. A year of playing together might help the team considerably, Throneberry was told. Marv took this under consideration.

"I don't know about that," he allowed. "They's teams been established for 30, 40 years and they's still in last place."

Marv has been rankled only once all year. It involved Ed Bouchee, whom Stengel put on first for a couple of games. In San Francisco, Roger Craig, who has a fine pickoff motion for a right-hander, fired to first and had Orlando Cepeda of the Giants clearly nailed. But Bouchee dropped the throw. Two wind-ups later, Craig again fired to first. He had Cepeda off the bag, with all his weight leaning toward second. It was an easy pickoff. The ball again bounced out of Bouchee's glove.

Back in New York, when Bouchee stepped out on the field at the Polo Grounds, the fans gave him a good going-over.

"What are you trying to do, steal my fans?" Throneberry complained.

It is a long summer, but the man who is probably finding

it longest is Weiss. He is a pale-eyed, bulky, conservative old baseball business man who, as he was saying a couple of weeks ago, is not used to losing.

"I've been in baseball since 1919," George said, "and this is only the second time I have had a second-division team. My first year in baseball I had the New Haven club and we finished seventh. That was in the Eastern League. This year is, I must say, a bit of an experience with me. No, it is certainly not a funny thing to me. But you could say I am not doing things halfway. When I finally get in the second division, I really get there.

"The job this year was simply to get a club started. Why, we couldn't even hire office personnel at first because we didn't have an office. Now we have what I think is the finest office in the majors. Of course we don't want to confine ourselves to leading the league in office space. The future depends on how hard we work now. The main thing is to build up our scouting staff. We had great scouts with the Yankees, Kritchell, Devine, Greenwade. We have Wid Matthews now, but we have to wait until contract time and some of the other good scouts become dissatisfied with their organizations. Then we can make moves. But right now all we can do is hope the players come along and it gets a little better. Anyway the manager is doing a fine job, isn't he?"

The manager certainly is. This is, everybody agrees, Casey Stengel's finest year. When he was running the Yankees and winning 10 pennants and becoming a legend, Casey never really struck you as the one they wrote of in the newspapers. His doubletalk was pleasant, but it had a bit of show business lacquer to it. And he could be rough on young players. Norman Siebern, at one time a tremendous outfield prospect, never really got over a couple of tongue-lashings from Casey. And Bobby Richardson and Clete Boyer were not the most relaxed players in the world under Stengel.

But here with the Mets, at age 73, Stengel is everything you ever read or heard about him. The man has compassion, humor and, above all, class. There is no grousing, and no screaming that players are letting him down. Mr. Stengel came to baseball this year ready to stand up no matter how rough it became. Well, it has become awful rough and he is standing up as nobody ever has. And trying. He talks to the players and he makes all the moves he knows. When they do not work out, he simply takes off his cap, wipes his forehead, then jams it back over his eyes and takes it from there.

In the rare instances when he does have the material to work with in a situation, that old, amazing Stengel magic is still there. Two weeks ago in St. Louis, the Mets won two of a five-game series against the Cards and one of the games was a result of Stengel's moves.

Curt Simmons, a left-hander, was pitching for the Cards, and Stengel sent up Gene Woodling, a left-handed hitter, to pinch-hit. Normally, this is not protocol. But Simmons had been coming in with a screwball as his best pitch. In a left-against-left situation, a screwball breaks toward the hitter and is easy to follow. Simmons had to go with a fast ball. Woodling hit it on top of the roof in right and the Mets had two runs and a ball game.

"I remembered another thing," Casey said after the game. "Once when I had Ford goin' for 20 games over with the Yankees Woodling beats him with a home run down in Baltimore. What the hell, don't tell me he can't hit a left-hander. I remember him doin' it, and that's why I put him in there."

A few lockers down, Woodling was talking about the manager.

"I was with him for five championships with the Yankees," he was saying, "and he and I had our differences. It's nothing new. Everybody knew that. But I've never seen anybody like him this year. This is a real professional."

You could see it a day later, when Casey and his Mets came into the dressing room after losing a doubleheader to the Cards. The manager had a wax container of beer in his hand and he was growling about a call that he said cost him the first game.

"The man don't even know the rules," Casey was saying. "My man was in a rundown between third and home and when he tries to go to home the catcher trips him right on the baseline. You could see the chalk was all erased. The umpire don't call it. Costs me a game. It was an awful thing."

He kept talking about this one play, as if nothing else had happened during the long afternoon. He was going to give "my writers," as he calls newspapermen, something to put in the paper the next day. And maybe it would give these 25 beaten players getting dressed in the room with him something to get mad about. Maybe it would help a little.

When he stopped rasping about the play for a moment, he was asked about a couple of particularly costly plays by Throne-berry and Charlie Neal.

"Aaahhh!" Casey said. "Bonehead. They was bonehead plays. Damn bonehead plays." His eyes flashed.

Then he leaned back and spoke in a soft voice. "Look," he said, "I can't change a man's life. I got four or five guys who are going to make it up here. The rest of them, we just got to get along with. I'm not goin' to start breakin' furniture because of them. It's the man and I got him and I can't change his life."

Then he got dressed and a guy named Freddie picked up his suitcase and led him out of the dressing room. They had a taxicab waiting across the street, in front of an old, one-story brick-front place named Gus & Marge's Tavern. Casey pushed through the crowd and got into the taxi. He was carrying on a running conversation with the crowd as he shut the door and the taxi started to pull away.

It was, you figured, the way it should be. For over 50 years now, Casey Stengel has been getting into taxis in front of old saloons across the street from a ball park. He has done this with great teams and with bad teams. Now he has the worst outfit anybody ever saw. But even if the players don't belong, Stengel does. He'll be back next year.

God help him.

August 13, 1962

The Old Indian's Last Stand

A T 8 o'clock in the morning Floyd, the night man at the Early
Wynn Steak House and Bowling Lanes in Venice, Fla.,
went into a narrow, windowless, cinder-block office and woke
up the old Indian, who was asleep in a T-shirt on the couch.
His name is Early Wynn and he sat up, ran a hand through
his Cherokee-black hair, and then reached for his dental plates.
They were on a cluttered desk, next to the bottles of pills he
uses for the gout.

The dental plates, which hold seven teeth, are the result of
being hit in the face with a line drive. The gout, which settles
in his right shoulder and elbow and gets bad at times, comes
from 25 years of traveling with baseball teams and eating rich
food in restaurants. Wynn also has a badly twisted ring finger
on his right hand. A couple of years ago a construction worker
at a local diner thought he could abuse the pitcher, so Wynn
tried to put his right hand through the side of the guy's head.
Everybody in Venice who saw it says it was a spectacular knockout. But Wynn hurt his finger with the punch and for a couple
of months he thought he would never pitch again.

When Wynn started to dress in his office on this morning he
found he had no clean socks. He put on sandals and went to
the car with a dirty pair of socks in his hand. He would wash
them at the ball park. He owns a $50,000 waterfront house
only a few minutes from his place, but after 18 years of marriage
he and his wife Lorraine have separated. Now Early sleeps on
a couch in the office of his bowling alley or in a trailer he has
parked nearby. Nothing is permanent for him any more—least
of all baseball.

Early Wynn is 43 years old now and he long ago established
himself as one of the best right-handers baseball has ever
known. He has won 299 games in the major leagues and wants
to be the third man in modern times to win 300 or more.
Only Lefty Grove and Warren Spahn, another left-hander, have
done it since 1930. Before them, only 11 others were able to
win that many. The select list includes hallowed names like
Grover Cleveland Alexander, Christy Matthewson and Walter

Johnson. There are no fluke 300-game winners. Because of today's revolving-door policy, which has pitchers in and out of games so quickly, Wynn may well be the last to come near the 300 figure. There is also a good chance that getting near 300 is all Early will be permitted to do.

Late last season Wynn missed three straight chances to get his 300th. After his 299th victory on Sept. 8, Lopez held him out of the lineup for 10 days so that he could pitch the big game before a home crowd. The Red Sox knocked him out of the box in the fifth inning and went on to beat Chicago, 10–5. The game became Wynn's 240th loss. His last two attempts of the season were against the Yankees, and both were heartbreakers: first they beat him 5–1 in an extra-inning game. Then, on his last chance of the year, Wynn's own mistakes cost him the victory. He threw a knuckleball to Clete Boyer of the Yankees that still hasn't bent. Boyer slammed it for a double. After that he threw a curve that did not curve to Joe Pepitone. This one went into the right-field stands.

After the game the White Sox players sat silently in front of their lockers while Wynn walked up and down in the dressing room. There was no cursing. No chairs or gloves were slammed around. There was only Wynn walking up and down and saying nothing.

"Don't go near him," Tony Cuccinello, the old coach, whispered. "If you go near him now, he'll kill you with his bare hands. This guy doesn't joke."

So Wynn came back this year to get what belongs to him. But he is a year older and it is not easy. On this morning, for example, he came out for a practice at Payne Park in Sarasota with two thick shirts on under his uniform to help him sweat off the fat. He did not have to look far for trouble. It was right in front of him. There were 25 other pitchers on the field, many of whom were not born when Wynn was already a big-leaguer.

Manager Al Lopez of the White Sox can keep only 10 of the 26 pitchers now on his roster. He is not going to keep Wynn just to give him a chance at his 300th victory. No professional baseball team that wants to do any good can carry a man for sentiment. Either you can pitch for a whole season or you can't and you get cut. This is the business.

So Wynn, after all those years and all those victories, was

out on a baseball field last week and Lopez and his coaches were giving him the same appraising look people have to face anywhere when they are looking for work.

If Wynn cannot make it, baseball will be the big loser. For Early Wynn—or Gus, as they call him—is the perfect ad for the sport. At 16, during the depression, he was an unschooled kid farming peanuts in Hartford, Ala. In country boy's uniform—bare feet and overalls—he drove a truck 400 miles to Sanford, Fla. where the Washington club was holding a minor league tryout camp. He was signed for $100 a month. That was in 1937.

Today Wynn is a handsome, well-dressed, soft-spoken, mature man who has pitched for three major league teams. He moves through the big restaurant in his bowling alley shaking hands, talking with customers and always reaching to light somebody's cigaret. His Indian blood comes from his grandparents, and his strong, ruddy features still suggest the farm boy he once was. But Wynn once wrote his own column for a Cleveland newspaper. He is a photography buff, flies his own plane and is one of the leaders of a political fight for better highways on the Florida west coast.

He has traveled through baseball on a first-class ticket since the day he cashed his first paycheck. With Early Wynn it is good talk and hors d'oeuvres and all the whisky they can take for any visitors to his hotel suite. But he is not a soft man. He weighs 218 pounds and if anybody pushes him, there is a distinct chance that he will push back. In baseball he is regarded as one of the two or three most competitive pitchers anybody today can remember.

When somebody reminds him he has a reputation for being mean, his face takes on a hurt look. "I never throw at a man's head," Wynn insists. Then he smiles and leans across to you at the bar and jabs a big hand into your ribs. "Right there, now that's a different story. That's where you put it when you sort of want the man to stop crowding that plate. You kind of put a board in his back."

When Wynn stands on the mound and works at his trade, he regards every batter as an enemy. Even his own son. A few years ago in Cleveland, Wynn pitched batting practice to his son Joe before a game. The boy was 15 then, but he could swing a bat. He hit two long ones in a row off his father. The ushers, standing around in the empty park, started to clap. Wynn's mouth thinned. From this point on, Early claims, the story has been distorted. He mumbles something about only wanting to teach the boy a lesson. But the fact remains the next thing anybody saw was Joe Wynn, age 15, flat on his back in the batting cage, scared stiff from one of Pop's knockdown pitches.

Last year Wynn was pitching batting practice to Joe Cunningham, the White Sox first baseman, and Cunningham slammed a line drive at the box. It missed Wynn by inches. Wynn said nothing. He took a new ball, wound up and threw. The pitch was right under Cunningham's chin and the batter fell onto his back getting away from it. Cunningham got up, dusted himself off, then stepped in again. The next pitch was also right at his chin, and Joe had to flop again. After the third knockdown pitch, Wynn let up. After all, Cunningham was a teammate.

"Early Wynn can put a ball any place he wants to, including in your ribs," Bill Veeck, his old Cleveland boss, was saying one night last week. "Now the rules have been changed so pitches around the shoulders will be strikes—that's a present for Wynn. He's always been a high ball pitcher, using fast, breaking stuff on the inside. Believe me, he's going to have a good year."

Wynn wants the good year, not just one good game. After one workout in the first weeks of spring training he sat in an old saloon behind the ball park in Sarasota and drank a couple of tap beers and talked about it. The saloon was the perfect place to talk about anything. It had a cement floor, a loud player piano, an old barmaid who had a hangover and a skylight that dripped rain onto the bar when a sudden shower developed.

"I want to win about 15," Wynn was saying. "Then someday somebody'll look at the record book and see I didn't just barely make it. The man'll see I really meant it. What's the sense of torturing myself like this just to come back for one game? If you do a job, do it all the way. I don't even think about not making it. I'm just here, period.

"I'd like to show up some people, too. When I was released by the White Sox last winter, this Finley, the man who owns Kansas City, called me up. 'I think you deserve the chance to win your 300th game,' he told me. Isn't that nice of him? I 'deserve' it. He is going to let me fill his ball park with people who want to see me win my 300th game. That's nice of him. Well, I don't deserve *that*."

Early shook his head. "I got my whole life put into this game. Hell, Goose Goslin was playing baseball when I first came up to Washington. Imagine that! I played with Goose Goslin. Hell, I belong in a rocking chair." He says it with a laugh, but the listener recognizes the old, poignant cycle of sports—a great athlete growing old in his job and trying to hang on until he gets all he wants; and then suddenly finding himself put in with young kids who try to move past him and take the bread out of his mouth.

You can see this during a White Sox workout. The club finally decided to give Wynn a chance to prove he could make the team—no contract, no promises. He is strictly a free agent. He stands out near the right-field fence, squinting in the sun. Then he puts his head down and runs a wind sprint of about 60 yards across the outfield grass. He has been running these sprints for 20 minutes. When he finishes this one, his chest is heaving. He stands and runs the back of his thumb across his forehead to keep the sweat from running into his eyes. Then he looks at the moisture on his thumb.

"Blood," he laughs. "Man my age shouldn't be out here like this. I'll drop dead. Then where we going to be?" He laughs again and then pushes off on his right foot and starts another sprint. He runs like an old cop.

A few yards away three or four of the young pitchers start to pull up after a sprint. They all move with the huge, wonderful, springy strides of the young athlete. When they stop, one of them, a towering kid with a crew cut, glances at Wynn. The kid is about 21 and he has an 18-inch neck. He is up from the minors someplace and he intends to stay. Now he stands with the others and keeps looking at Wynn. And you can almost hear him say it:

"You old bum, I hope you fold and go home."

Wynn has until April 8, when the roster is cut, to make it. He feels that is all the time he needs. And anybody who has been around Wynn finds it impossible to believe he is not going to make it.

"I'll tell you one thing," says Al Lopez, who has been Wynn's manager, at Cleveland and Chicago, for 11 years, "if heart has anything to do with it, Early'll be there. Take that business with Valdivielso. That shows you what he is."

Lopez was talking about a game in Washington in 1956. Lopez was managing the Cleveland Indians then and he had Wynn working. In the fourth inning, José Valdivielso, a Washington infielder, hit a line drive right back at Wynn. The pitcher never saw the ball coming. The liner slammed off the point of his chin and rolled halfway to first. Wynn staggered. Then he went for the ball. He couldn't see because he was knocked dizzy. But he ran low, with his hands out, groping for the ball so he could try and throw to first.

He never found the ball, and Lopez came out of the dugout on the run to look at him. Wynn buried his chin in his chest and wouldn't talk.

"Lemme see your chin," Lopez said.

"I'm fine," Wynn said.

"Come on, let me see the chin."

"No."

"Let me see the chin or I'll take you out without looking."

Wynn picked up his head. He had a deep gash and every one of his lower teeth was loose. Later it took 16 stitches to close the gash and he lost seven of the teeth. His mouth hurt and blood was splattering his uniform. But he didn't want to come out of the game.

"I want to pitch to him once more," Wynn said. He looked over at Valdivielso, who was on first. Valdivielso was worried. Lopez of course said no and yanked Wynn out of the game. Valdivielso felt a lot better when he saw Wynn go.

"He was scared to death of me staying in there," Wynn remembers. "He should have been. Nobody hits the ball back at me and gets away with it."

Off the field Wynn can be just as tough. There was one night last winter when Early noticed a car following him as he drove home after closing up the bowling alleys at 2 A.M. Wynn made a couple of turns and the car still followed. Early drove up a dead-end street, pulled into a driveway and then reached under the front seat for a little item which he's licensed to carry, known as a Magnum .357. This is listed as a pistol, but they could fight the next war with it and get a lot done.

The guy following Wynn took one look at the pistol in

Early's fist and tried to back out of the street in a hurry. But his rear wheels went into a ditch. Then he tried to get out and run, but he slipped and fell on his face in a puddle of water in the bottom of the ditch.

When he looked up he nearly fainted. The biggest gun he had ever seen in his life was pointing down at him. And behind the gun was a mean-looking man. Wynn said nothing. He just kept the guy in the water for 15 minutes.

Early finally said, "Where you from?"

"The circus," the guy said, thinking fast. The circus was indeed at its winter quarters in Venice at the time.

"Well, you go back and tell *everybody* that I don't take receipts out of the building at night," Wynn said. "And if I ever see you again, I don't know what I'm going to do to you."

Wynn got back into his car and drove away. The formalities of the situation—police calls and the like—did not interest him. He knew it would be the last time the fellow would follow him.

Wynn is one of the few baseball players around who didn't learn his trade until after he got to the major leagues. He came up to the old Washington Senators in 1939 as strictly a fast-ball pitcher. Washington had eight men who could hit .300 or better, but nobody could catch a ball. The pitching was terrible. Wynn, trying to get by with a fast ball only, was murdered. In 1944 he had lost 17 games by July. Then the Army drafted him.

"If they'd of left me alone, I'd'a' lost 50 that year," Wynn says.

He was traded to Cleveland in 1948, and it was the break of his life. Mel Harder, the articulate Cleveland pitching coach, took Early aside and showed him the mysteries of the curve ball and pitching to spots and in patterns. Wynn, working hard, came along fast. He became a regular 20-game winner and ran up the numbers big from then on.

"It hasn't all been nice, though," he says now, "off the field or on." He shut his eyes to remember. A game lost here, a game lost there—he remembers them all but a few stick out. "There's a game two years ago," he said finally. "Of all the ones I blew over all the years that's the one I think hurt me most. We're ahead of the Yankees by four runs in the sixth inning. I got the gout in my elbow. There is no way not to get the gout, the way I live. Always on the road someplace, eating steak and spaghetti and barbecued spareribs and French fries in restaurants. A little beer and Scotch and so forth. Well, the gout is in my elbow this day and the bases are loaded, and the score is 6–2. Bob Cerv is up. I fire. Nothing happens. My elbow hardly bends. Damn gout. The ball comes right up there. Cerv hits it 450 feet for a grand slam. We finally pulled the game out, but by that time I'd been yanked and someone else got credit for the win. You could say that game ruffled my feelings a little bit."

Wynn was waving a filter-tipped cigaret in his right hand as he talked. His wrist, after years of snapping off curve balls, is as thick as his ankle.

His world series record—one win in four starts—doesn't set too well with Early either. "There was this boy Dusty Rhodes," he said. He shook his head and called for another beer. "I don't even want to remember him. I'm going along fine against the Giants in the '54 World Series. It's the second game, fifth inning, and we're ahead 1–0. Up Rhodes comes. Pinch hitter. Two men on base. I throw him a pitch he still hasn't seen. He just swings. He gets a little piece of the ball. I still can hear that tinny ring. The ball drops in over the infield and it's a mess. He's a national hero. A couple of years later nobody could find him, he was so deep in the minors. And here I am, nine years later, still around. A guy like that beats you, it's got to burn."

Wynn looked at the clock up over the bar and said he had to go back to Venice. His place there had partner troubles for over a year and now Early is trying to push the business up to where it should be.

"I'll be back tomorrow," he said. "Donating more blood."

He thinks he is a cinch to make the team. But later in the day Al Lopez, the White Sox manager, sat at a candlelit table in the cocktail lounge of the Sarasota Terrace Hotel and he was saying he didn't think it was an easy case at all.

"I'm handicapped here," he said quietly. "I can only keep 10 pitchers. What can I do? I can't do anything. Early has to force his way in.

"I don't have to tell you what this does to me. Hell, I've had Early pitching for me since 1951. He's a friend of mine. I won a pennant with him in Cleveland. I come to Chicago and I win a pennant with him in 1959. The guy will do anything for you. He was the best pitcher in baseball and he'd come around and say, 'Any time you get a little short in the bullpen, I'll work relief between starts.' Where you going to find a man like this?"

Lopez shook his head sadly. "All these things don't count now. It's only what he can do now. He's old. In spring training he used to be out pitching batting practice the first day. Now he waited about a week before he thought he was ready. It's going to be real tough for him. The 300 games? It means nothing. That's just a figure. I've got to look to a whole season."

"Who has to tell him if it doesn't work out?" he was asked.

"Me," Lopez said.

"What do you tell a fellow after 25 years?"

He looked down at the table. "I don't know. I just don't know. I just thank God that he's the kind of man he is."

April 5, 1963

Whitey Revisited

S OMETIMES, NO matter how much happens, things do not change that much at all. Stillman's Gymnasium, which was the University of Chicago of boxing, now is a pile of broken brick behind a fence on Eighth Avenue. And in the few arenas left, fighters move around in front of empty seats and lead with their faces as if this is the way it is supposed to be done.

Everybody says boxing is gone. But Morris (Whitey) Bimstein looked just as he always has. Whitey had on a rumpled blue suit with three cigars jammed into the breast pocket, and his shirt was unbuttoned so that a T-shirt and a tuft of white hair showed at the collar. He spat on the floor and said it was damned hot and that he was going to go over in a minute and drink plenty of beer.

He was standing at one end of Bobby Gleason's Gymnasium, which is the big fight place in town these days, and he was showing a kid named Lucius Benson the same things he has been showing fighters for nearly 50 years. Benson was punching a heavy bag and Bimstein kept growling at him to turn his wrist when he threw a left hook.

"You do that, the punch goes right around the other guy's hand," Whitey was saying. "The bum thinks he got it blocked good and then, boom! You clip him right in the mush. Now do it again."

Benson, a middleweight with 12 fights, his body sopping wet, threw another punch at the bag and the wrist turned as he brought the punch across. Bimstein promptly began to lie about how good this kid was going to be. Once, he stood in Stillman's and talked about Billy Graham and Rocky Graziano. Now he is in the Bronx and talks about some kid named Benson.

There was only one fight in New York last week, over at Sunnyside Garden, and the biggest fighter training at Gleason's is Doug Jones, who lost to Cassius Clay, the great non-fighter. The rest of them in Gleason's the other afternoon were vague names and faces with dents in them. They are in a business which has been wrecked financially by electronics. Better pay on the docks and in trucking terminals has taken care of nearly all the talent, and most people feel the game is only a law or so away from being extinguished.

But for this one afternoon anyway, here in this hot room one flight up from crowded Westchester Ave., Whitey Bimstein, who never changes, took you back into the fight business as you always knew it. There was, most important, the promise of seeing a real war some night soon. This guy over there is going to fight that other guy, Whitey was saying, and it is going to be something to see. It'll be in the Garden, too.

And there was the ageless talk about managers of fighters and how bad they can be. This one guy, Whitey was saying, he don't know how to do anything in the whole world except cheat. And, too, there was the inevitable reminder about just how dangerous a business this can be.

The little kid was three years old and he had on a striped shirt and long pants and he sat on a folding chair in front of a mirror and his big dark eyes stared at Bimstein.

"This is my pet," Whitey said.

"What's your name?" I asked the kid. He didn't answer.

"*Dile tu nombre*," Caron, a trainer, said to him in Cuban.

"Benny Paret," the little kid said. He got up and stuck out a tiny hand. We took it and he shook with us as hard as he could.

"You knew the old man, didn't you?" Bimstein said.

I told him yes. And I told him the last time I had spoken to Benny Paret, he was shadowboxing in front of the mirror there, right where this kid of his is sitting, and it was the night before he was to fight in the Garden and yet they still had him out trying to lose three and a half pounds.

"I'm thirsty," Paret said through an interpreter that night.

I remember saying to the interpreter that the way they handle this kid, he is a cinch to get killed. Now I looked at Benny Paret's son and wondered what he was doing in this place.

"He comes always," Caron said. "I bring him. He loves the fighters."

"Let's get the beer now," I told Bimstein.

We went downstairs and walked across the street to a place on the corner. Whitey said it was his kind of a joint. There are apartments up over the bar. A red-haired woman in a house dress leaned out of one window and, hands cupped under the chin, watched what was going on in the street. The family dog sat on the windowsill beside her.

The bar was called O'Connor's and it was crowded. The tables were filled with housewives who were in old dresses and drank beer. Grocery shopping bags were on the white tile floor next to the tables.

The kids, all in T-shirts and sneakers, sat at the tables and drank Coke while the mothers had their beer. Or they stood around the juke box and watched the records change. A song called "Brennan on the Moor" was played often. At the bar, a red-haired woman in a black raincoat drank rye and shot a toy water pistol at her little girl, who was about six.

This is the kind of a place you used to get the good New York fighter coming out of. It is a family saloon in a neighborhood where people have to work hard for their money and any entertainment past a 15-cent beer is a problem.

Once, in the Irish neighborhoods, you had one of these places every couple of doorways. But now there are only faint traces of Irish neighborhoods left and this kind of a bar is rare. It is, Bimstein was saying over his beer, a shame.

"These is good people," he was saying. "I been with these kind of people all my life. They give you corned beef and cabbage and potatoes with the jackets on. And if I could only find one of them that could fight. Just one Irishman. Give me one big lug of an Irisher who could box a little bit and I'll turn this game upside down. These guys today, they fight like savages. If I just had a old Irish stand-up boxer."

"The Irish don't fight anymore," the owner, Mr. Dennis O'Connor said. Mr. O'Connor was standing at the end of the bar putting on his hat to go home. Mr. O'Connor's chin looks like it could take a pretty good belt.

"I'm from Sligo but I went to school in *Cark*," he said. "Presentation Christian Brothers on Wellington Road in *Cark* City."

"What do your kids do?"

"One is out of Iona, the other boy is in Fordham and I have a daughter who graduated St. John's and got married."

"You see," Whitey said. "All these people go to school now. We ain't got a chance of finding a good one."

But there always are going to be people who are poor and want to take a shot at life with their fists instead of washing dishes. Once, the Irish were like this. Now it is the Cubans and the Negroes and the Puerto Ricans and they want whatever boxing has left to offer.

And they were back upstairs in Gleason's boxing and sweating and hoping for a break and, thanks to Whitey Bimstein, it was good to be around them for an afternoon.

Except for one thing. Somebody had put a pair of tan punching bag mittens on little Benny Paret and when we got back from the bar here was this little serious-faced three-year-old kid standing directly under the heavy bag and throwing punches at it.

He always led with his left hand, the way you are supposed to, and everytime he threw the right he said "Ooohhhh," just like fighters do when they throw a hard punch.

His father was making the same sounds the last time I heard him talk.

June 2, 1963

The Wake for a Newspaper

THE COPY was on white paper and on top of it, in pencil, was the notation "2/12 lite indent nuts." This is a printing term which meant that this copy Selig Adler, managing editor of the New York Mirror, had in his hands was to be set in large type on two columns with some white space at each end so people could read it easily.

Adler walked down one flight of stairs from his office to the Mirror composing room and handed the copy to Marty Tanzer, who was in charge of distributing it to the type-setters.

"What's this?" Tanzer asked.

"Get it set in type and then go get yourself a job," Adler said. He took the cigarette out of his mouth and walked out of the composing room.

The copy began, "The Hearst Corporation announced yesterday that it will cease publication of the New York Mirror with the issue of October 16, 1963."

It was 8:15 P.M. and the New York Mirror, after 39 years, with a daily circulation of 882,822, which made it the second largest paper in the nation, and with a total of 1,600 human beings working for it as livelihood, and working in a business which is unlike any other, was no more.

Tanzer took the copy and walked over to a printer and told him to set it into type. And now, throughout the old brick loft building at No. 235 E. 45th St., a newspaper began to die. People do not start throwing things or running to bars or crying when a newspaper dies. They are just people working on a job and then somebody comes up and tells them the paper has just folded and then they simply get up and stand and talk, and they stay that way for a long time because they have nothing else to do.

It took only a couple of minutes for everybody in the Mirror editorial room to know that their paper was gone, and while the type was being set, the copyreaders and reporters and rewrite men stood on the black and white vinyl floor alongside their gray steel desks and, with nine long rows of fluorescent lights glaring down on them, they smoked cigarettes and talked aimlessly. They had not been told officially. This was still to be taken care of.

Two sets of proofs were taken into the private office of Glenn Neville, the Mirror's editor.

"It's lousy," he said.

"What's the matter?" Ed Markel, the executive city editor, asked.

"They changed it," Neville said.

"That's the way they wanted it," Adler said.

"Can they have it outside?"

"Yes, see that they get it."

Somebody took the proof out to Wilfred Alexander, a rewrite man, and he got up on top of a desk and called out, "All right, here it is," and he started to read it. Now, officially, the people who worked for a living on the Mirror were told that the paper was gone.

Manny Elkins, the picture editor, was on the phone in a little glass-inclosed office at one end of the editorial room. He is a lean, gray-haired man with sad eyes and he talked while he waited for somebody to come on the phone with him.

"I came here in June of 1924," he said. "The building was at 55 Frankfort St. and I was a boy. This is my whole life."

Then he put the phone to his mouth.

"Estelle, I've been on the phone trying to get you to tell you don't worry, dear.

"I know, dear, just don't worry.

"Look, it happened . . ."

He held the phone away for a minute and shook his head.

"She's all right," he said. "You know what the trouble is? I got two photographers assigned to the Valachi story in Queens tomorrow, Ab Fier and Bruce Hopkins. They thought I was home and they were calling there to find out if they should go to the Valachi thing tomorrow. So she was sitting in Elmhurst and trying to tell them what to do. I tried to tell her, but she just doesn't seem to understand. She's very busy worrying about covering Valachi."

He went back to the phone.

"Home? Yes, Estelle, I'm coming home."

Ray T. Morgan sat alone at one end of the horseshoe-shaped Mirror copy desk with a pencil in his hand and no copy on the desk to use it on. He sat erect. In a blue checked shirt, subdued red-striped tie and creased blue suit, he was the best-dressed man in the place. This one is old. He reviewed books for the New York Sun, which was a newspaper, and he was finishing out a career as so many newspaper men do, sitting at a horseshoe-shaped copy desk and writing headlines for stories that younger men collect and write.

Morgan took off his glasses with a slow, grand sweep when you came up to talk to him.

"I shall retire," he said. "I hope to get a, hum, a pension and, uh, some sort of terminal pay from here, and then just go and live out my life."

Over in a corner of the editorial room, in the part used by the sports department, George Girsch, a copy desk man, picked up the telephone. Toney Betts, the Mirror's racing writer, was calling from the press box at Aqueduct Race Track.

"What's this?" Betts asked.

"It's right, the paper is gone," Girsch said.

Then, "I better come up with a good daily double tomorrow," Betts said.

This man is a loss to anybody who reads papers. There are very few writers on newspapers who can make you smile, and Betts is one of them.

The people still were standing and talking in the editorial room and now Walter Winchell came in. He had no hat on, but his blue television shirt was flashy. Winchell put a foot up on a chair and began to talk softly.

"June 10, 1929," he said, "I walked right into this place and I was ready to swing."

"Tell me about the big one with Lepke," somebody said to him.

"It was on the corner of 5th Ave. and 28th St. between 10:20 and 10:30 P.M. and I got out of my car and took Lepke—that's Louis Lepke, the great killer, public enemy No. 1—I took him right by the wrist like he was a little boy and walked him over to John Edgar Hoover's limousine.

"Then I headed for the telephone. I had just brought in the biggest criminal in the country. I call the office and Hinson Stiles says to me, 'You and your scoops. Hitler just walked into Danzig. We don't have any room for it.'"

"What's left," he was asked.

"I'm 66," he said quietly. "I've had an awful lot of action over the years."

You don't have to worry about him. But the ones he was looking at, the ones who were standing by their desks and talking, they are the ones that were hurt when the Mirror went last night. Oh, they'll get jobs. But working for a newspaper can get to be a way of life more than a job, and now these people stood there and talked and their way of life was gone.

October 16, 1963

The Last Gallo Living at 51 President Street

THE LAST Gallo living at 51 President Street is the grand-mother, Mrs. Big Mama Nunziata, who is 77 and never scared easily before and sees no reason why she should start backing off now. She lives alone in a bare, four-room apartment on the second floor of the empty three-story building which once housed the Gallos, and their armed gang. The door to Mama Nunziata's apartment has a peephole cut into it so you can see if anybody is coming up the stairs to kill you, but she regards this as nonsense. Leave the door open, she tells you when you leave. Mrs. Big Mama Nunziata would spit at a forest fire.

She has seven children, 28 grandchildren and 22 great grandchildren, but she lives at 51 President Street, where all the trouble is, because three of the grandchildren, Joey, Larry and Albert Gallo, need the help, not the rest of the family. And to Mama Nunziata, help means only one thing. You come in and then you stand up no matter what happens.

There was this Sunday morning a while back when somebody in Brooklyn deliberately set off loaded rifles and two members of the Profaci gang, the Gallo rivals, were badly hurt. One of them was Carmine Persico. Since Persico had once tried to garrot Larry Gallo, the police, acting on a wild hunch, went looking for Larry.

They busted into 51 President Street, and for their troubles ran into Mama Nunziata, who was in a mood to fence with them. "Larry?" she said. "He watches the televeesh with me all night."

"Mama," one of the detectives said, "the guy who tried to strangle Larry got shot pretty bad and we want to ask him about it."

"Oh," Mama Nunziata said. "Is this boy, is he all right?"

"He's not dead, but he's hurt pretty bad."

Her eyes opened wide. "Oh, he's not dead," she said.

"So tell me, this boy. Is he a good boy or is he a bad boy?"

"Bad," the detective said. "Very bad."

Mama smiled in triumph. "Then it's better off he dies."

That ended the interview.

Later, when Larry came back to 51 President Street, Mama Nunziata sat quietly in the apartment and kept looking at him.

"What's the matter, Larry," she said, "you can't shoot straight?"

Right now, Mama Nunziata's three grandsons are out of action. Joey is in Attica prison and Mama sends him a food package every week. Larry is in the Federal House of Detention. He'll be out Dec. 22 and Mama will make Christmas for him. Albert, whom she calls Blast, is out dodging people who want to kill him. So Mama Nunziata sits alone at 51 President Street and holds the place together for them.

She was there last night. She sat on a chair and her old, strong hands kept moving as she spoke of her grandsons. She has gray hair pulled to the back of her wrinkled face and she wears the black oxfords that all old Italian ladies wear. At first, with her hair and her wrinkles and her shoes, you'd think that this is all Mama Nunziata is. But then she starts to talk, and her eyes widen and flash and the words come out shrewdly, and with humor, and as the night goes on you find you are with one hell of a woman.

She started with a good beef against stool pigeons.

"This Valachi," she was saying, "what does he do? He's with a *Genorovyse* for 30 years and all of a sudden he stool pigeons. And this Sidney Slater. He's a little rat. He was always here with Joey. It was Joey this and Joey that. Now he has the detectives all around him and he tells lies about Joey. He always lied. He told lies to me when he was around here.

"Look," she said, the hands out in front of her now, "what do these people want? Do they want to be a gangster, a thief and a stool pigeon all at the same time? That's no good.

"You got to stick to one thing."

Mama shook her head. "All the rest of my family has done well. The daughters all marry nice. One of them, she's even with the F. B. I. She's a good shooter, too." Mama said this with great pride.

"Out of all my family, only these boys turned bad. Joey and Larry. And they ruined Blast. It never happens with me. I raised them. Right in this house. Then they went back to their mother and I don't know what happens over there. But when they were with me, they were good. Joey and Larry would come in late. Ten o'clock at night. I sit here and wait. They sneak in back there and crawl under the bed when they hear me. I go right in after them and I grab Joey's leg and pull him out. Then, I had teeth then, I bite him right on the leg. He screams, 'Oh, please, Mama, we never do it again.'

"Huh. With me they never would of gone into trouble. But what are you going to do? They're mine and I'm with them.

"It used to be crazy here. They had the lion. Ooohhh, what a big head he had. He ate $5 worth of steak every day. We got him out on the leash walking down the street and this fellow comes up from the docks and he says, 'What a big head that dog got.'

"I say to him, 'Dog? That's no dog. What's the matter with you? That's a lion.' You should have seen him run back to the docks.

"We put the lion in the pool room window and he paces back and forth all the time and the kids never go to school because of him. Then Joey had the panel truck and he put the lion in the back and drove around. So the cops stop him one day. 'What are you got in the back of the truck?' they say. Joey says, 'Please don't open the back of the truck. It's very bad.'

"You know how nosey those cops are. This one goes right to the back and opens the doors to the truck. So here's the lion, with the big head, and the cop he yells and starts to run. Joey got to grab the lion before the lion chases the cop."

The lion, once the proud mascot of the Gallos, was shipped away when he made a bad mistake. Joey Gallo was using the truck to ride around and pick up slips from a numbers operation. One day he purchased a good hero sandwich during his rounds and shoved it into the paper bag holding a large amount of numbers slips. The slips never bothered the lion. But the hero sandwich did. And rather than sort out the hero sandwich from the slips, the lion simply opened his mouth and swallowed the whole bag. There was hell to pay in the Gallos numbers empire that evening. The next day, the lion was on his way to Jersey.

Mama was in the front room of the apartment last night. There is almost no furniture in the place—"the cops came in and wreck it when they look for guns or something," she says—and it is heated with a brown gas-burning unit in the middle of the floor.

Two windows look down on the blackness of President St. Once, anybody who sat by the window stood a fine chance of contracting holes in his head. The Gallos even had thick wire screens put over the windows so no bombs could be thrown through them. But last night, Mama sat right by the window.

"Afraid? Huh," she said. "I'm a mad, not afraid. The insurance company sends me back my check. They don't want to insure the building. They say somebody throws a bomb on me or something. How am I going to rent this building if they keep saying that? Nothing's going to happen. That's gone."

Outside, President St. was dark and shabby and empty. The Gallos, and their mob of 200, who had started the biggest crime war this city has had in 25 years, are gone. Only now and then do any of them come around. It is too dangerous a place for them.

But not for Mrs. Big Mama Nunziata, who sat upstairs alone by the window of 51 President St. She is 77 and the last of the Gallos and she stays because she is a little too much woman to be afraid.

October 22, 1963

The Talent Hunt

THERE HAD been rehearsing for a week. And right to the end, the singer was trying to get ready. He had paid money for one last vocal lesson at lunch time. Now, a girl with a blue card in her hand came out onto the stage in front of him and gave his name. Then she stepped out of the way and the singer spread his arms and started to sing the song he had been practicing for a week. He was out of it with three words.

"To the sea . . . ," he began.

"No good," Garson Kanin, the director, said.

Kanin was in the back of the theater, standing against a ladder painters had left against the wall.

Buster Davis, the vocal director, said the same thing without talking. He was sitting in a third-row orchestra seat and the minute the guy started to sing, Davis slumped in his chair and made a note on the yellow legal pad he had on a table in front of him. Two seats away, Carol Haney, the choreographer, turned around with a cigarette in her mouth and asked somebody for a light.

Up on the stage, the singer kept on. He was allowed 16 bars, and they were going to let him finish.

"He has no projection," Kanin was saying. "He's weak in the lower register."

When the guy finished singing, he looked down at Buster Davis. The singer's eyebrows were up. He was hoping. If there is one emotion that human beings seem to show strongest, it is hope.

"Thank you," Buster Davis said. "Thank you very much."

The eyebrows came down. In the theater, "thank you" is a way of saying "please go home." The singer nodded, and went to the piano to get his music.

Then the girl came out on the stage again with another blue card in her hand and another singer walked out behind her, and it went like this all yesterday afternoon at the Cort Theater. There were 250 male singers standing under the black fire escapes in the alley outside the stage entrance, waiting for their chance to come in and try for one of five jobs.

This was what is known as the "Equity Call" for chorus people. They were needed for a show called "Funny Girl," which
is booked to open in the Winter Garden Theater, Feb. 27.
"Funny Girl" is a $500,000 show based on the life of the late
Fanny Brice. It is to star Barbra Streisand and Sydney Chaplin.
Yesterday at the Cort, there were only singers you never heard
of, and they were trying for jobs that will pay small money,
$125 a week. But they were all out in the alley under the fire
escapes because this is a Broadway show, a big one maybe, and
kids who think they can sing take buses in from San Diego for
something like this.

And they come in for what is a cruel and yet maybe the best
way that there is to handle a person looking for work. "Thank
you," Buster Davis kept saying all yesterday afternoon and that
was all there was to it. There were no long applications to fill
out, no secretaries saying, I'm sorry, he isn't in just now, and,
above all, no glad-hander saying that he would keep you in
mind. Just Buster Davis saying "thank you." Maybe the theater
is rough, but yesterday afternoon at the Cort it was honest and
that is more than you get in most places.

"We try to make it a little nicer for them," Kanin was saying.
"Do you notice the lights?" There were 14 of them mounted
on the mezzanine. "Most of the time, they come on and there
is a bulb in a wire cage dropped down from the ceiling. Here,
we at least try to make them feel they look good."

Then the girl came on the stage again, and following her was
a guy with close-cropped hair and a gold jacket.

"I bet he can sing," Kanin said.

"Why?"

"I don't know him, but I bet he can sing," Kanin said. He
walked down the aisle and took a seat.

"And did I leave you . . . ," the gold jacket started to sing.

Kanin tapped you on the arm. "I told you," he said.

When the fellow finished his 16 bars of "If Ever I Should
Leave You," Buster Davis looked at Carol Haney and they both
nodded and then he called up to the singer, "Would you please
wait?"

The singer's name was Alexander Orfaly and he has a Ben-
sonhurst phone number, but when Davis asked him to wait
around the theater yesterday, he walked off that bare stage and

went out under the fire escapes in the alley as if he was the biggest thing on Broadway.

October 25, 1963

A Death in Emergency Room One

DALLAS—The call bothered Malcolm Perry. "Dr. Tom Shires, STAT," the girl's voice said over the page in the doctors' cafeteria at Parkland Memorial Hospital. The "STAT" meant emergency. Nobody ever called Tom Shires, the hospital's chief resident in surgery, for an emergency. And Shires, Perry's superior, was out of town for the day. Malcolm Perry looked at the salmon croquettes on the plate in front of him. Then he put down his fork and went over to a telephone.

"This is Dr. Perry taking Dr. Shires' page," he said.

"President Kennedy has been shot. STAT," the operator said. "They are bringing him into the emergency room right now."

Perry hung up and walked quickly out of the cafeteria and down a flight of stairs and pushed through a brown door and a nurse pointed to Emergency Room One, and Dr. Perry walked into it. The room is narrow and has gray tiled walls and a cream-colored ceiling. In the middle of it, on an aluminum hospital cart, the President of the United States had been placed on his back and he was dying while a huge lamp glared in his face.

John Kennedy already had been stripped of his jacket, shirt, and T-shirt, and a staff doctor was starting to place a tube called an endotracht down the throat. Oxygen would be forced down the endotracht. Breathing was the first thing to attack. The President was not breathing.

Malcolm Perry unbuttoned his dark blue glen-plaid jacket and threw it onto the floor. He held out his hands while the nurse helped him put on gloves.

The President, Perry thought. He's bigger than I thought he was.

He noticed the tall, dark-haired girl in the plum dress that had her husband's blood all over the front of the skirt. She was standing out of the way, over against the gray tile wall. Her face was tearless and it was set, and it was to stay that way because Jacqueline Kennedy, with a terrible discipline, was not going to take her eyes from her husband's face.

Then Malcolm Perry stepped up to the aluminum hospital cart and took charge of the hopeless job of trying to keep the thirty-fifth President of the United States from death. And now, the enormousness came over him.

Here is the most important man in the world, Perry thought.

The chest was not moving. And there was no apparent heartbeat inside it. The wound in the throat was small and neat. Blood was running out of it. It was running out too fast. The occipitoparietal, which is a part of the back of the head, had a huge flap. The damage a .25-caliber bullet does as it comes out of a person's body is unbelievable. Bleeding from the head wound covered the floor.

There was a mediastinal wound in connection with the bullet hole in the throat. This means air and blood were being packed together in the chest. Perry called for a scalpel. He was going to start a tracheotomy, which is opening the throat and inserting a tube into the windpipe. The incision had to be made below the bullet wound.

"Get me Doctors Clark, McCelland, and Baxter right away," Malcolm Perry said.

Then he started the tracheotomy. There was no anesthesia. John Kennedy could feel nothing now. The wound in the back of the head told Dr. Perry that the President never knew a thing about it when he was shot, either.

While Perry worked on the throat, he said quietly, "Will somebody put a right chest tube in, please."

The tube was to be inserted so it could suction out the blood and air packed in the chest and prevent the lung from collapsing.

These things he was doing took only small minutes, and other doctors and nurses were in the room and talking and moving, but Perry does not remember them. He saw only the throat and chest, shining under the huge lamp, and when he would look up or move his eyes between motions, he would see this plum dress and the terribly disciplined face standing over against the gray tile wall.

Just as he finished the tracheotomy, Malcolm Perry looked up and Dr. Kemp Clark, chief neurosurgeon in residency at Parkland, came in through the door. Clark was looking at the President of the United States. Then he looked at Malcolm

Perry and the look told Malcolm Perry something he already knew. There was no way to save the patient.

"Would you like to leave, ma'am?" Kemp Clark said to Jacqueline Kennedy. "We can make you more comfortable outside."

Just the lips moved. "No," Jacqueline Kennedy said.

Now, Malcolm Perry's long fingers ran over the chest under him and he tried to get a heartbeat, and even the suggestion of breathing, and there was nothing. There was only the still body, pale white in the light, and it kept bleeding, and now Malcolm Perry started to call for things and move his hands quickly because it all was running out.

He began to massage the chest. He had to do something to stimulate the heart. There was not time to open the chest and take the heart in his hands, so he had to massage on the surface. The aluminum cart was high. It was too high. Perry was up on his toes so he could have leverage.

"Will somebody please get me a stool," he said.

One was placed under him. He sat on it, and for ten minutes he massaged the chest. Over in the corner of the room, Dr. Kemp Clark kept watching the electrocardiogram for some sign that the massaging was creating action in the President's heart. There was none. Dr. Clark turned his head from the electrocardiogram.

"It's too late, Mac," he said to Malcolm Perry.

The long fingers stopped massaging and they were lifted from the white chest. Perry got off the stool and stepped back.

Dr. M. T. Jenkins, who had been working the oxygen flow, reached down from the head of the aluminum cart. He took the edges of a white sheet in his hands. He pulled the sheet up over the face of John Fitzgerald Kennedy. The IBM clock on the wall said it was 1 P.M. The date was November 22, 1963.

Three policemen were moving down the hall outside Emergency Room One now, and they were calling to everybody to get out of the way. But this was not needed, because everybody stepped out of the way automatically when they saw the priest who was behind the police. His name was the Reverend Oscar Huber, a small seventy-year-old man who was walking quickly.

Malcolm Perry turned to leave the room as Father Huber came in. Perry remembers seeing the priest go by him. And he remembers his eyes seeing that plum dress and that terribly disciplined face for the last time as he walked out of Emergency Room One and slumped into a chair in the hall.

Everything that was inside that room now belonged to Jacqueline Kennedy and Father Oscar Huber and the things in which they believe.

"I'm sorry. You have my deepest sympathies," Father Huber said.

"Thank you," Jacqueline Kennedy said.

Father Huber pulled the white sheet down so he could anoint the forehead of John Fitzgerald Kennedy. Jacqueline Kennedy was standing beside the priest, her head bowed, her hands clasped across the front of the plum dress that was stained with blood which came from her husband's head. Now this old priest held up his right hand and he began the chant that Roman Catholic priests have said over their dead for centuries.

"Si vivis, ego te absolvo a peccatis tuis. In nomine Patris et Filii et Spiritus Sancti, amen."

The prayer said, "If you are living, I absolve you from your sins. In the name of the Father and of the Son and of the Holy Ghost, amen."

The priest reached into his pocket and took out a small vial of holy oil. He put the oil on his right thumb and made a cross on President Kennedy's forehead. Then he blessed the body again and started to pray quietly.

"Eternal rest grant unto him, O Lord," Father Huber said.

"And let perpetual light shine upon him," Jacqueline Kennedy answered. She did not cry.

Father Huber prayed like this for fifteen minutes. And for fifteen minutes Jacqueline Kennedy kept praying aloud with him. Her voice did not waver. She did not cry. From the moment a bullet hit her husband in the head and he went down onto his face in the back of the car on the street in Dallas, there was something about this woman that everybody who saw her keeps talking about. She was in shock. But somewhere, down under that shock some place, she seemed to know that there is a way to act when the President of the United States has been assassinated. She was going to act that way, and the fact that the President was her husband only made it more important that she stand and look at him and not cry.

When he was finished praying, Father Huber turned and took her hand. "I am shocked," he said.

"Thank you for taking care of the President," Jacqueline Kennedy said.

"I am convinced that his soul had not left his body," Father Huber said. "This was a valid last sacrament."

"Thank you," she said.

Then he left. He had been eating lunch at his rectory at Holy Trinity Church when he heard the news. He had an assistant drive him to the hospital immediately. After that, everything happened quickly and he did not feel anything until later. He sat behind his desk in the rectory, and the magnitude of what had happened came over him.

"I've been a priest for thirty-two years," Father Huber said. "The first time I was present at a death? A long time ago. Back in my home in Perryville, Missouri, I attended a lady who was dying of pneumonia. She was in her own bed. But I remember that. But this. This is different. Oh, it isn't the blood. You see, I've anointed so many. Accident victims. I anointed once a boy who was only in pieces. No, it wasn't the blood. It was the enormity of it. I'm just starting to realize it now."

Then Father Huber showed you to the door. He was going to say prayers.

It came the same way to Malcolm Perry. When the day was through, he drove to his home in the Walnut Hills section. When he walked into the house, his daughter, Jolene, six and a half, ran up to him. She had papers from school in her hand.

"Look what I did today in school, Daddy," she said.

She made her father sit down in a chair and look at her schoolwork. The papers were covered with block letters and numbers. Perry looked at them. He thought they were good. He said so, and his daughter chattered happily. Malcolm, his three-year-old son, ran into the room after him, and Perry started to reach for him.

Then it hit him. He dropped the papers with the block numbers and letters and he did not notice his son.

"I'm tired," he said to his wife, Jennine. "I've never been tired like this in my life."

Tired is the only way one felt in Dallas yesterday. Tired and confused and wondering why it was that everything looked so different. This was a bright Texas day with a snap to the air, and there were cars on the streets and people on the sidewalks. But everything seemed unreal.

At 10 A.M. we dodged cars and went out and stood in the middle lane of Elm Street, just before the second street light; right where the road goes down and, twenty yards farther, starts to turn to go under the overpass. It was right at this spot, right where this long crack ran through the gray Texas asphalt, that the bullets reached President Kennedy's car.

Right up the little hill, and towering over you, was the building. Once it was dull red brick. But that was a long time ago when it housed the J. W. Deere Plow Company. It has been sandblasted since and now the bricks are a light rust color. The windows on the first three floors are covered by closed venetian blinds, but the windows on the other floors are bare. Bare and dust-streaked and high. Factory-window high. The ugly kind of factory window. Particularly at the corner window on the sixth floor, the one where this Oswald and his scrambled egg of a mind stood with the rifle so he could kill the President.

You stood and memorized the spot. It is just another roadway in a city, but now it joins Ford's Theatre in the history of this nation.

"R. L. Thornton Freeway. Keep Right," the sign said. "Stemmons Freeway. Keep Right," another sign said. You went back between the cars and stood on a grassy hill which overlooks the road. A red convertible turned onto Elm Street and went down the hill. It went past the spot with the crack in the asphalt and then, with every foot it went, you could see that it was getting out of range of the sixth-floor window of this rust-brick building behind you. A couple of yards. That's all John Kennedy needed on this road Friday.

But he did not get them. So when a little bit after 1 o'clock Friday afternoon the phone rang in the Oneal Funeral Home, 3206 Oak Lawn, Vernon B. Oneal answered.

The voice on the other end spoke quickly. "This is the Secret Service calling from Parkland Hospital," it said. "Please select the best casket in your house and put it in a general coach and arrange for a police escort and bring it here to the hospital as quickly as you humanly can. It is for the President of the United States. Thank you."

The voice went off the phone. Oneal called for Ray Gleason, his bookkeeper, and a workman to help him take a solid bronze casket out of the place and load it onto a hearse. It was for John Fitzgerald Kennedy.

Yesterday, Oneal left his shop early. He said he was too tired to work.

Malcolm Perry was at the hospital. He had on a blue suit and a dark blue striped tie and he sat in a big conference room and looked out the window. He is a tall, reddish-haired thirty-four-year-old, who understands that everything he saw or heard on Friday is a part of history, and he is trying to get down, for the record, everything he knows about the death of the thirty-fifth President of the United States.

"I never saw a President before," he said.

November 24, 1963

It's an Honor

WASHINGTON—Clifton Pollard was pretty sure he was going to be working on Sunday, so when he woke up at 9 A.M. in his three-room apartment on Corcoran Street, he put on khaki overalls before going into the kitchen for breakfast. His wife, Nettie, made bacon and eggs for him. Pollard was in the middle of eating them when he received the phone call he had been expecting.

It was from Mazo Kawalchik, who is the foreman of the gravediggers at Arlington National Cemetery, which is where Pollard works for a living. "Polly, could you please be here by eleven o'clock this morning?" Kawalchik asked. "I guess you know what it's for."

Pollard did. He hung up the phone, finished breakfast, and left his apartment so he could spend Sunday digging a grave for John Fitzgerald Kennedy.

When Pollard got to the row of yellow wooden garages where the cemetery equipment is stored, Kawalchik and John Metzler, the cemetery superintendent, were waiting for him.

"Sorry to pull you out like this on a Sunday," Metzler said.
"Oh, don't say that," Pollard said. "Why, it's an honor for me to be here."

Pollard got behind the wheel of a machine called a reverse hoe. Gravedigging is not done with men and shovels at Arlington. The reverse hoe is a green machine with a yellow bucket which scoops the earth toward the operator, not away from it as a crane does. At the bottom of the hill in front of the Tomb of the Unknown Soldier, Pollard started the digging.

Leaves covered the grass. When the yellow teeth of the reverse hoe first bit into the ground, the leaves made a threshing sound which could be heard above the motor of the machine. When the bucket came up with its first scoop of dirt, Metzler, the cemetery superintendent, walked over and looked at it.

"That's nice soil," Metzler said.

"I'd like to save a little of it," Pollard said. "The machine made some tracks in the grass over here and I'd like to sort of

62

fill them in and get some good grass growing there, I'd like to have everything, you know, nice."

James Winners, another gravedigger, nodded. He said he would fill a couple of carts with this extra-good soil and take it back to the garage and grow good turf on it.

"He was a good man," Pollard said.

"Yes, he was," Metzler said.

"Now they're going to come and put him right here in this grave I'm making up," Pollard said. "You know, it's an honor just for me to do this."

Pollard is forty-two. He is a slim man with a mustache who was born in Pittsburgh and served as a private in the 352d Engineers battalion in Burma in World War II. He is an equipment operator, grade 10, which means he gets $3.01 an hour. One of the last to serve John Fitzgerald Kennedy, who was the thirty-fifth President of this country, was a working man who earns $3.01 an hour and said it was an honor to dig the grave.

Yesterday morning, at 11:15, Jacqueline Kennedy started walking toward the grave. She came out from under the north portico of the White House and slowly followed the body of her husband, which was in a flag-covered coffin that was strapped with two black leather belts to a black caisson that had polished brass axles. She walked straight and her head was high. She walked down the bluestone and blacktop driveway and through shadows thrown by the branches of seven leafless oak trees. She walked slowly past the sailors who held up flags of the states of this country. She walked past silent people who strained to see her and then, seeing her, dropped their heads and put their hands over their eyes. She walked out the northwest gate and into the middle of Pennsylvania Avenue. She walked with tight steps and her head was high and she followed the body of her murdered husband through the streets of Washington.

Everybody watched her while she walked. She is the mother of two fatherless children and she was walking into the history of this country because she was showing everybody who felt old and helpless and without hope that she had this terrible strength that everybody needed so badly. Even though they had killed her husband and his blood ran onto her lap while he died, she could walk through the streets and to his grave and help us all while she walked.

There was mass, and then the procession to Arlington. When she came up to the grave at the cemetery, the casket already was in place. It was set between brass railings and it was ready to be lowered into the ground. This must be the worst time of all, when a woman sees the coffin with her husband inside and it is in place to be buried under the earth. Now she knows that it is forever. Now there is nothing. There is no casket to kiss or hold with your hands. Nothing material to cling to. But she walked up to the burial area and stood in front of a row of six green-covered chairs and she started to sit down, but then she got up quickly and stood straight because she was not going to sit down until the man directing the funeral told her what seat he wanted her to take.

The ceremonies began, with jet planes roaring overhead and leaves falling from the sky. On this hill behind the coffin, people prayed aloud. They were cameramen and writers and soldiers and Secret Service men and they were saying prayers out loud and choking. In front of the grave, Lyndon Johnson kept his head turned to his right. He is President and he had to remain composed. It was better that he did not look at the casket and grave of John Fitzgerald Kennedy too often.

Then it was over and black limousines rushed under the cemetery trees and out onto the boulevard toward the White House.

"What time is it?" a man standing on the hill was asked. He looked at his watch.

"Twenty minutes past three," he said.

Clifton Pollard wasn't at the funeral. He was over behind the hill, digging graves for $3.01 an hour in another section of the cemetery. He didn't know who the graves were for. He was just digging them and then covering them with boards.

"They'll be used," he said. "We just don't know when."

"I tried to go over to see the grave," he said. "But it was so crowded a soldier told me I couldn't get through. So I just stayed here and worked, sir. But I'll get over there later a little bit. Just sort of look around and see how it is, you know. Like I told you, it's an honor."

November 26, 1963

Holiday in Automat

THERE ARE no ash trays on the tables in the Automat. People who smoke sit too long at a table, and the Automat is a place for volume. So yesterday, in the Automat at 33d St. and Eighth Ave., the men used their empty coffee cups for putting out cigarettes during the long, deadening afternoon. They sat and smoked for a long time, most of them. They are faceless old men who dress vaguely and live in furnished rooms. Thanksgiving dinner at the Automat is a way of life for them. On a big holiday, it is depressing to see these men and their coffee cups cluttered with cigarette butts, but yesterday was so bad everyplace that it made no difference.

Three of them sat at a table by the revolving door. The attendant had cleared their trays and the dishes of their $1 special dinner. They were left with the coffee cups and crumpled paper napkins, and a long day in front of them. They talked of where they came from, not where they are going.

"The stores in this town? The stores here are all right," one of them said. He was thin and wore a gray hat and a gray suit with a blue sweater underneath.

"Good stores here," one of the others said.

"They got good stores in other places," the first one said. "Philadelphia. Gimbel's, Wanamaker's, Strawbridge's, I know all the stores in Philadelphia."

The third man had gray hair slicked straight back. He kept a blue topcoat on.

"Were you here in 1937?" he asked the one in the gray hat.

"I wasn't here in 1937," the gray hat said. "I was here just before the world's war."

"You were in Pittsburgh before that," the man in the topcoat said.

"No, I wasn't here from Pittsburgh. Reading. I lived at 513 North 5th St. I was in Pittsburgh before that. Lott St. I was at 515 Lott St. I remember all my addresses wherever I lived. Those two are the only 500 addresses I ever had. Now I live 300 West."

"I was never in Reading," the man in the topcoat said. "What do they have in Reading?"

"The railroad. The Reading Line. The shops were right on North 5th St. So was the YMCA. Both of them right on Fifth St."

"I was never in Reading. I was through Philadelphia a lot," the topcoat said. "Philadelphia has a beautiful railroad station."

"It sure does," the gray hat said. "This thing they say they're going to build across the street, that's no railroad station. What kind of a railroad station is it that has a big office building 60 stories high?"

Penn Station, huge, gloomy, but at least identifiable with railroading, was across the street. It is being torn down to make way for the inevitable plate glass this city goes in for.

"To me, a railroad station has to have hand carts that you can sit on while you're waiting for a train. Otherwise it isn't a railroad station to me," the blue coat said.

A lot of other people sat alone. Only one or two tables were empty. They came in and took trays and waited silently on line at the cafeteria steam tables for their food. There are very few coin slots left in the Automat these days. There were two banks of coin slots, with their little windows, for sandwiches, one for pies, another for cakes and one for bread and rolls. There was only one bank for the baked macaroni and cheese (three nickels), and beef pie (one quarter, three nickels) and other Automat specialties. Coffee still comes out of a spout with a silver handle. It costs 10 cents and still is good coffee.

Outside, Eighth Ave. was vacant. A few cabs moved by. Now and then, a bus. The few people on the street were old and alone. There were some postoffice workers. They were paid yesterday, and they scouted around Eighth Ave. for someplace open so they could cash the check. Otherwise it was a vacant day in the Automat.

Which was right. Yesterday was a day meant to be vacant. It seemed right to sit on Thanksgiving Day and put out butts in a coffee cup and, every once in awhile, have an attendant in white shirt and slacks, reach past your shoulder and take crumpled napkins from the table.

November 29, 1963

Feat of Clay: TKO in 7th

MIAMI BEACH—Cassius Clay landed a left jab and moved to his right and then nothing much was happening. The bell rang and Big Willie Reddish, sweat pouring from under his brown beret, swung into the ring and moved around Sonny Liston's left shoulder and started to talk to his fighter.

Liston cut him short and started complaining about something. Reddish started looking around and then, from nowhere, here it was. They called the referee over. He called for a doctor. Cassius Clay got up to start round seven and the bell rang for it. Liston remained seated. Then somebody called over to Clay and Clay let out a scream and started jumping up and down and all of a sudden everybody was making noise.

So much noise that your loud, resolute yelp for the cops was not heard. Or maybe it was, because soon the Miami Beach Boxing Commission was announcing that it was holding up Liston's purse until it could get a couple of doctors to examine Liston and the Miami Beach City Council was saying that it planned an investigation of its own.

Charles (Sonny) Liston gave up his heavyweight title while sitting on a stool with his head down on his chest last night. It was a tableau originally made famous by the late Marcel Cerdan, when he threw out his shoulder against Jake LaMotta in Detroit and set up a return match which only a plane crash prevented. Later on Willie Pep used this pose to great good in a featherweight bout with Sandy Saddler. This bad shoulder also produced a rematch.

This morning, then, the heavyweight champion of the world is Cassius Marcellus Clay.

As the fight started, the only mystery which seemed in need of solving was how Clay ever got himself together to get into the ring. Worry had made him one of the walking wounded for four days before this fight. The weigh-in yesterday qualified him for an asylum.

Then with all the talk and conjecture over, he was in the ring, waiting for Liston to knock his head off. This was not to happen. Liston won three of the six rounds fought, with one of

67

them even, in this book. But there was, as the sixth round came up, this crazy feeling that Mr. Liston had shot it all.

In the fifth, he had knocked Clay all over the ring and should have had him out of there at a number of points. But his clumsy punching style caught up with him and he chopped with the right instead of sending it in straight.

Now it was the sixth, and it was becoming hard to believe. Clay, dazed and reeling flat on his feet in the fifth, suddenly was standing straight up on his toes. His jab came straight out. He threw a right hand into Liston. A real good right hand. And Liston, old-man wrinkles showing in the back of his neck, looked clumsy and tired.

So as Liston came to his corner, you were about to think you were watching a fight. And a fight that was going to get better as they went along. Then all of a sudden here was Liston talking to Reddish and the shoulder thing was about to become boxing history.

It becomes a part of history right along with Frankie Carbo and the bad shoulders of Cerdan and Pep and the night Jake La Motta lost to Billy Fox at the Garden and the night Ray Robinson collapsed from the heat against Joey Maxim and, oh, you can go on with this for hours.

For Sonny Liston, just like every con who ever went before him, is stuck with his own reputation today and the reputation of the boxing business. Sure, his shoulder could have been thrown out, the guy might have boxed the sixth round in desperate pain. It is distinctly remembered here that he had Clay on the ropes in that round, threw one left hand, then for some reason, let Clay go. Maybe the shoulder was the reason. Maybe. But who was going to believe it?

Boxing's history is simply too bad to allow you to sit at ringside in Miami last night and say, yes, I'll believe it, Sonny Liston threw out his shoulder and this makes Cassius Clay the champion.

The facts are, at best, bad. Liston was a 7–1 favorite and had no challenger in sight—none for at least a year to come—with whom he could make any money. So at the end of the sixth round last night he sat in his corner and quit. And quit a fight that he should have won easily, no matter how well Clay fought last night.

Oh, while it went, it was a great fight to watch. Liston, blowing spit out of his nose and with five lines of blood dripping from a cut under his left eye, stalked Clay and Clay swiveled and moved and jabbed and tried to stay alive. But then came this thing in the corner and it was enough to make a person suspicious. It was almost like an afternoon spent in a saloon some time ago when a fish delivery truck pulled up onto the sidewalk, right over the saloon's cellar steps. The doors of the fish delivery truck popped open and two guys rolled a safe out of it. The safe fell into the cellar like a bomb. Everybody in the bar picked up burglary tools and rushed downstairs.

February 26, 1964

Fear and Hate—Sputtering Fuse

THE THREE cops got to the big colored guy in the tan shirt when he was in front of the dry cleaning store. The leather thongs bit into their white hands as they took a tight grip on their club and now they were on him. They did not hit the colored guy with these full-arm swings. It takes too long to pull back your arm for this. The cops hit with their clubs from whatever position their hands were in and the colored guy in the tan shirt went down on his back and the left side of his face cracked open and blood covered his profile.

They hit him again when he was down and he put his hands to his head and started to get up. When the colored guy was on his feet the cop in the middle gripped his club again and wanted to take another shot but the colored guy staggered back and kept going until he was safe, and he spit a curse at the cops and they cursed him back. Then a bottle came flying at the cops standing in the middle of Seventh Ave. "Look out," cops yelled to each other. Then the bottle smashed on the street and right away, a dozen of the cops ran at the crowd where the bottle had come from. The crowd was standing on the southwest corner of 133d St. and Seventh Ave. and the cops came at them with nickle-plated pistols shining in the streetlights. The cops started shooting into the air, but some of them were not shooting high enough. Then the crowd started to break and run down 133d St. and from the middle of the crowd you saw this little puff of smoke and this meant somebody had a gun and was trying to kill a cop with it.

Now bottles came flying from every place and police were running with their guns out and shooting and everybody was yelling "Look out" and the sidewalks were filled with colored people who were running and yelling and throwing things and now, with the shots and the bottles flying, you fell onto the street alongside a police car and the sickness came right into your mouth.

Here was the answer to all the talk and all the speeches and all the ignorance and all the history of this deep, vicious thing of black man and white man which they put down under the nice name of civil rights. The answer was right in front of you. Just lift your head up from the pavement you had it on and look around. This was a war. The colored people of Harlem against the white police. The battle lines were simple. The police stood on the tree-lined island which runs in the middle of Seventh Ave. The colored people stood on the street corners or hung from windows. There was no traffic. Between outbreaks, there was silence. A terrible silence, and the women hung from the open windows of the five-story buildings and looked and said nothing.

Kids were on the street corners. They were 14 or 15 or 18 or 21 and there were some adults with them, but age didn't matter because all of them were trying to hit a cop in the face with a bottle and if they killed a cop they would have cheered.

This was New York City you were in last night. It wasn't Mississippi or Alabama or any place else where these things are supposed to happen. You were in New York and right on the other side of the traffic island, on the east side of the avenue, was the big neon sign for Pauline's Interlude. You've been in the joint a thousand times. Frankie Moten owns it. The bartender sings songs for you. But if you tried to go from the island in the middle of the avenue to the sidewalk and into Frankie Moten's bar last night somebody would have leaned out a window and tried to kill you with a bottle. This is how far down we came in New York City last night. Civilization was gone. It was gone in a rash of guns and flying bottles and kids screaming, "We want Malcolm X. We want Malcolm X," and you saw all of this, saw it for hours, but it was so low and so degrading that it made you sick and you really couldn't understand it. The shots cracked and the bottles flew and you prayed for a rainstorm that would end it. The rain never came.

Three blocks down, on 130th St., it was terrible. There is a housing project, 14 stories high, and a darkened playground alongside it. The playground is next to the redstone Salem Methodist Church. On the sidewalk in front of the playground is a glass telephone booth. Two cops were using the telephone booth for a shield and they had their guns out and were aiming them up at the housing project. One of them shifted his feet a little to get better position. But he kept aiming the gun. They were not going to just shoot into the air. There was somebody up in that building that they wanted a shot at and if they got it these two cops were going to try to take this somebody's head off.

Then the whole place exploded. On both sides of the avenue, there was screaming and cops in white helmets racing at the people with their club in one hand and the gun in the other, firing into the air, and the people ran and screamed and threw bottles and then, from a crowd in front of the church, a black arm went into the air and a bottle came flying. It landed in the middle of the street and exploded into a five-foot-high flame. It was a Molotov cocktail and it had been thrown to kill.

"Bastards," a cop said.

From way up, from the 14th floor of the project, a woman hung out the window and screamed. "Die, you dirty white bastards. I hope you all get killed."

Then the cops raced for the playground. You couldn't see what they were after in the playground because of the darkness, but the cops were not shooting in the air. They were firing through the fence and firing as fast as they could. They were trying to kill somebody in the playground.

"Look out," the ones next to you shouted. Everybody crouched down behind a car. The bottle broke on the street in front of the car.

Then the store windows went. The crowd caved in a laundromat on the east side of the avenue. Then they hit a place next door to it. The glass broke with a loud sound. The crowd screamed in delight when it went.

The cops raced over to stop them from breaking any more. The crowd ran into hallways. The police went in after them with clubs and you could see the clubs catching the people in the hallways and now you felt 185 years old. For this is what it is all about. This is what a few people have been talking about and wanting something done about and nobody else ever did anything but call them nigger lovers. Call them nigger lovers and then go home to their neighborhoods and stay with their white friends and then get up in the morning and go to work on their white jobs with their white friends and they would wonder, what the hell do these niggers want, anyway. We have had Harlem and all the Harlems of New York through election after election and all the talk that goes with elections and these people live like pigs just as their parents lived like pigs and last night and this morning, in the heat of a Harlem night, they exploded while this country has a nominee for the office of President of the United States whose followers want to see this business of loving niggers come to a decent halt before it gets too far and something is done. Something that might mark us as civilized human beings, not animals who lie in the streets and shoot at each other.

The colored people, all of them, even the leaders, acted like small children yesterday. They have a deep, serious, legitimate, immediate case for themselves. A 15-year-old boy who weighed only 100 pounds was shot to death by an off-duty police lieutenant last Thursday. The case is being investigated. It has inflamed Harlem. The young kids, semi-illiterate most of them, who follow Malcolm X and other dangerous rabble rousers, used this to start a riot. They did not, these people milling from 125th to 133d Sts., last night, represent all of Harlem. They represented the part of Harlem that couldn't wait for trouble with white police. But they stood on street corners and hoped for trouble and when it came and the police hit them, the leaders promptly screamed "Police brutality."

Police brutality? Sure, there was brutality last night. Terrible, sickening brutality. But this was a mess, an absolute, incredible mess, and if you were on the street with the bottles coming down and who the hell knows what was going to come from the rooftops, there was only one thing to do. Go after these crazy bums on the street corners and knock their heads open and send them home with blood pouring all over them. The crowd was uncontrollable. They laughed when Bayard Rustin took a microphone and pleaded with them to go. They jeered and spit at policemen. They wanted everything they got last night.

July 20, 1964

The Last Great Statue

Lᴏɴᴅᴏɴ—In the morning rain and mist, the tan pebbles were unlittered in front of No. 28 Hyde Park Gate. A street cleaner moved over to the side to get out of the way of the blue car coming down the street. The old doctor in the front seat was fumbling with the door handle before the car stopped.

Up at the corner, a mother and her daughter, in black derby hats and short tan jackets, sat on white horses and waited for the traffic light on Kensington High Street. When it changed, the horses walked across the street and into Hyde Park. Then the daughter broke her horse into a trot under the leafless trees. The doctor was in the house now, white scarf and overcoat off, looking at the old man in the green bed jacket who was in the first-floor bedroom in the rear.

The rest of London was quiet and empty in the wet Sunday morning. Lord Nelson stood on his spire, high over the black lions and water fountains of Trafalgar Square. The Duke of Wellington glared down at the taxicabs and delivery wagons moving around his plaza. Queen Victoria sat grandly on her throne, surrounded by angels, her back turned on Buckingham Palace. The water dripped from Gladstone, who was stationed by Saint Clement Danes Church. And at 8:05 A.M., on January 24, 1965, in the rear first-floor bedroom of No. 28 Hyde Park Gate, the old man in the green bed jacket died with the curtains drawn and a lamp turned on and he became England's last great statue.

Sir Winston Spencer Churchill, who saved his nation; saved, perhaps, the entire English-speaking world, stepped into history with its scrolls and statues, and he will be the last who ever will do it as he did because the world never again can survive the things that had to be done in the years he lived.

He died wordlessly. He was a man who put deep brass and powerful strings into words, and then built them up to a drum roll to reach out and grab people and shake them by the shoulders and in their hearts. But he had not uttered a word for ten days when he lay dying in a coma, while his heart throbbed and struggled to throw it off.

There were ten people who watched him die.

"It was strange," one of them who was in the room was saying later. "One moment here was this ancient man, barely breathing. Then the years seemed to come right off his face and he died and he looked just as he did when he was running the country. He simply became younger in death."

A young naval lieutenant was on duty on the sixth floor of the Ministry of Defence building when his phone rang. He picked it up and said, "Sir," when he heard the voice on the other end, and then he reached for a yellow message pad.

"With deep regret," he wrote as the voice over the phone dictated to him, "the Admiralty Board learned today of the death of Sir Winston Churchill. All flags are to be lowered to half staff. The Admiralty Board has today also sent a message of condolences to Lady Churchill."

The lieutenant hung up the phone and signed the message, then put it into a Lamson tube near his desk. The message went through the tube to the fifth-floor communications center and from there it was wired to all commands of Her Majesty's Royal Navy.

Once, in 1939, the message to the fleet read: "Winston is back," and seamen cheered. But that was twenty-six years ago and Churchill was only sixty-four and he was just starting to teach his nation that great wartime lesson in heart. Yesterday the message called him Sir Winston Churchill and the seamen who heard it were too young to have served under him.

David Bruce was having breakfast. His silver hair brushed back, a tie and blue shirt on, he lounged over coffee in the high-ceilinged sitting room of Winfield House, the American Ambassador's residence.

"The phone, sir," somebody said.

He picked it up. It was the duty officer at the embassy telling him that Churchill was dead.

"I'll be in," Bruce said. Bruce has had a three-man group working on details for Churchill's death for some time now. Yesterday, with the death a fact, there was more to do. The United States is to show its respects, as it never has shown them for a foreigner before, at the funeral of Sir Winston Churchill on Saturday.

In a big wooden-floored living room of his apartment on Eaton Place, Sir John Langford-Holt heard the news on the radio and he looked down for a moment and then he told his wife he wanted to go to church immediately.

"I'm almost thankful it is over for him," Langford-Holt said. For the last two years Langford-Holt, a Tory MP, was assigned, by silent agreement, the task of seeing to it that Churchill had help if he needed it when he visited the House of Commons. Churchill was old and gone and he tottered down the gangway, gripping a cane, his arm motioning to people to get back and leave him alone, and Langford-Holt walked with him and all of Commons looked away. They did not want to see, if Winston Churchill ever fell down in their presence.

"I hated it," Langford-Holt was saying. "Here are we, insignificant people who never led or could hope to lead his life, and we were being patronizing to him. It simply was not right. Now this is no eulogy to the man. He had all the flaws of a human being, he was wrong many times and he was obstinate and temperish, but he was great and we are insignificant and I felt wrong."

He dressed and went to church. Inside, he remembered Churchill, as he always will remember him, the old man sitting on the green leather bench in Commons, holding his cane and tears coming from his eyes.

"They had such difficulty and hardships during the war," Churchill was saying aloud, "and now they are out in the streets worrying about housing and food and money. After all they've done for us. They are heroes and they should live as heroes."

He was crying and talking about the people who had to fight the war he ran.

"He was great because he cared," Langford-Holt was saying. "This is why he was so great. You see, the man cared so very much."

And now, at No. 28 Hyde Park Gate, there was nothing else to do. He was in the hands of history now, history and the carefully planned funeral arrangements which will give London its greatest spectacle in nearly two centuries. And Sergeant Edmund Murray, Scotland Yard, stood in front of the house with nobody to guard any more, and he wasn't sure about what to do.

"I guess I'll go home," he said. "I guess there's nothing else to do but go home." He looked around. "You know, when I'd help him near the end there, I might grab his hand a little too hard and it would press the ring on his finger and he'd give a little growl and say, 'Easy now,' and just for a moment you imagined him back running things again. Well, he's gone now. When the King is dead, you say, 'The King is dead, long live the King.' What do you say now? Who is there to talk of?"

He went home. And in the East End of London the people came out. He was an aristocrat and he lived with beef and champagne and cigars, but he stood in the streets with these people, stood in the smoke and ruins and watched the bodies being carried out and he bit his cigar and made a V with his fingers and the old ladies screamed at him their cockney and he would growl with them and they would go back and get ready to take another day and night of it.

Trafalgar Square was crowded and there was no more room to stand and people lined the steps of the National Gallery behind it. A group of ministers stood at microphones on the base of the statue of Nelson. They took turns reading prayers to the people. Hundreds of pigeons flew overhead. The people were silent, and only the noise of water spouting in the fountains, and red double-decked buses passing by on the street, mingled with the ministers' prayers. The huge black lions crouched at the bottom of the statue and watched everywhere.

"Oh, God, in all His majesty . . ." a red-robed minister prayed.

January 25, 1965

Malcolm X Slain by Gunmen as 400 in Ballroom Watch

U P IN the front of the ballroom, on the stage, somebody was saying, "Malcolm is a man who would give his life for you." Then the people, 400 of them, the best crowd Malcolm X has had in a long time, got up from their wooden folding chairs and clapped for 45 seconds while Malcolm X came to the rostrum and stood there, ready to talk.

The air was clear of smoke and the Sunday afternoon sun came through the thin drapes on the windows that looked out onto Broadway. Malcolm arranged some papers on the lectern, which came up to his chest. The applause stopped and the people sat down and Malcolm X's goateed face looked up and he said, "A Salaam Alaikem," and the crowd murmured its response of "peace be with you also," and then the two lead-off men made their move.

They were in a middle row and they stood up and started pushing each other and one of them was saying, "Get your hands out of my pocket. Stop messing with my pocket." Malcolm X's bodyguards started to move toward them to break it up and up on the stage, Malcolm stepped out from behind the lectern and he was saying, "Now, brothers, break it up. Let's cool it." He stood there, alone on the stage, with one hand up in the air and he was a perfect target and a man—police say he was Thomas Hagan—ran down the aisle with a shotgun and the ones with him were already shooting when the shotgun was right in front of Malcolm X and both barrels raked him.

Malcolm X went straight back and the sound of his head slamming onto the wooden floor was mixed with the screams and he lay on his back on the stage of an old ballroom on 166th Street and Broadway and he died while two others in the crowd fired their guns, a big-slugged .45 and a .38.

Malcolm X's people pulled out guns and began firing back and now bullets thudded into walls all over the room. It was a murder in front of 400 people, a murder done in afternoon sunlight in an old dance hall, and it was planned and executed with the help of people Malcolm knew and considered his followers.

Malcolm was the head of the Organization for Afro-American Unity. It is a small organization, but its goal is to fight against and try to lure members away from the Black Muslims. But Black Muslims, sworn to kill Malcolm X, had been trying to infiltrate his movement for some time. Yesterday, after months of waiting, they had him set up. Somebody let the Muslim murderers carry weapons and the bomb into the meeting. Malcolm's bodyguards were at the doors, even turning away white newsmen. But one of them did not turn away the people who came in with guns to kill Malcolm X.

It was carefully planned, with as many as five of them passing into the audience at the Audubon Ballroom. Three did the shooting. There was also a diversionary fire bomb which was lit and ready to go off in the back of the hall when somebody saw it and snuffed it out with a coat.

One of the murderers got away clean. He ran out a side door of the building. The others bolted for the back of the ballroom, firing guns and running. They started down the stairs to the street, followed by a crowd of Malcolm's people. Hagan, the only one anybody seemed sure of, was caught on the sidewalk. He was caught and shot and kicked and thrown to the ground and he was going to be killed on the sidewalk by a mob when police threw themselves into the crowd and saved his life. Hagan was taken to Bellevue Hospital where he was put in the prison ward, which was sealed off with a dozen uniformed police.

Police held Reuben Francis, of 871 E. 179th St., the Bronx, for illegal possession of a .45 automatic. They said Francis, one of Malcolm X's faction, drew the .45 and shot the 22-year-old Hagan in the leg, breaking his thigh bone.

Two spectators, William Harris, wounded in the stomach, and William Parker, shot in the foot, were taken to the hospital by police. The identity of the man who went out the side door and got away was known to police and they combed Harlem for him last night.

Whoever he is, and whoever was with him, accomplished exactly what they had been sworn to do. They had come to the

Audubon Ballroom, this old wooden-floored dance hall, and they murdered Malcolm X and then ran from the place while his 37-year-old wife Betty was screaming, "They're killing my husband." Then she turned and ran back to the stage and bent over him.

People were milling around and crying and moaning and out on the street there was a roar while the mob tried to overturn the radio car Hagan had been put into by police. Twenty minutes after the shooting, four policemen came in with a stretcher and Malcolm X was put on it. The stretcher had wheels and it was carried downstairs and out on the sidewalk. Malcolm X's followers surrounded it and they screamed, "Get out of the way or we kill you" while it was wheeled across Broadway and to the emergency entrance of Columbia Presbyterian Hospital.

At the hospital, white-coated interns came from everywhere and some of them grabbed the stretcher and pushed it onto an elevator and others bent over the body and began to work on it while they were walking. Upstairs, in the third-floor emergency operating room, more of them waited.

The white hands that Malcolm X had preached so much hatred about clawed at his blood-soaked clothes and touched his body. One of the white hands clamped an ether mask over his face. Another white hand, holding a scalpel, came at his chest. Other white hands worked at the chest as it opened and they massaged Malcolm X's heart. The operating room was filled with doctors and nurses, and they were all busy and working quickly, but it was all meaningless. The bullets had done the job on Malcolm X.

Downstairs, in an office in the hospital, a man came in and said, "The gentleman you know as Malcolm X is dead. I'm not sure of the time. He was dead or dead-appearing as he was brought in here. He was shot several times. In the chest. Once in the cheek. His family was present when he died. There were no words passed before he died."

Across the street, in the Audubon Ballroom, Thomas Renaghan, the inspector in charge of detectives for the North of Manhattan, chewed on a cigar and walked hurriedly around while police technical men crawled over the room. What was to become one of the heaviest homicide investigations this city has ever seen was under way.

For this was a murder within the radical Negro movement and one murder could lead to a round of them. Malcolm X was not dead one hour when police received a report that six of his followers had left New York City for Chicago so they could kill Elijah Muhammad, who heads the Black Muslims.

And then, right away, the word ran through Harlem about a Muslim named Captain Joseph.

"Captain Joseph is a popular man right now," one of Malcolm's followers was saying. "We just put him Number One on the hit parade."

Captain Joseph is heavy-set and he is a Muslim strong-arm man who frequents their restaurant, The Temple Number Seven on 116th Street and Lenox Avenue. The restaurant was closed last night and police were all over the area. They were all over every other area in Harlem, too. Green buses carrying Tactical Patrol Force teams rolled into Harlem immediately yesterday and by nightfall the streets were being patrolled in near-riot force.

On Seventh Avenue and 125th Street gatherings of any size were broken up immediately with Lloyd Sealey, the captain in charge of the precinct, walking the beat himself.

"All right, gentlemen," Sealey kept telling any group which tried to form, "please move on." The club in his hand spun on the end of the leather thongs and he stood there and the crowd would immediately melt.

"Oh, it's quiet," Sealey was saying. "You can see that for yourself."

"They don't want riots, they want revenge on individuals," somebody said to Sealey.

He shrugged. "We'll just keep working at it and let's get through the next couple of nights," he said.

Many people thought of this as impossible. Malcolm X was a leader without a following of any numbers. He was a 30-year-old ex-pimp, narcotics pusher and convict who preached violence against the white man but had not raised a hand in violence in years and his reputation came from white newspaper men who built him into an illusion. But he did have a group, however small, close to him, and last night that group was looking for revenge.

Leon 4X Ameer, one of his followers, called from Boston

and promised "massive retaliation." And everywhere else, Malcolm's followers kept saying, "Just stay on your toes and you'll be covering some good murders."

So the violence Malcolm X preached so much about came about with his own death, and if there is more violence, it was his death that set it off.

He was a shallow, uneducated guy who was known as "Big Red" around 125th Street and he was a nonentity until a television producer found him in 1957. He gave Malcolm a chance to talk, and if there is one thing Malcolm X could do, it was talk against the white man. His words, hitting a white nation which was just starting to put "Civil Rights" into its vocabulary, frightened people. Newspapers grabbed him up and made him a national name. In 1961 and '62, Malcolm X was hated and feared by whites. And loved by many Negroes. Not for his views. They wouldn't stand still for his establishment of a separate Negro state or for this violence he called for. But they loved him because he made the whites nervous and caused them to back off, and when they did this, it made it easier for the established Negro organizations, the Urban League and the NAACP, to strike bargains.

"Malcolm makes CORE look conservative," the Negroes would laugh.

February 22, 1965

On Highway 80

SELMA, ALABAMA—Patricia Anne Doss, ten, stood in the red dirt and twitched her black toes to brush away the ants crawling over her feet. She put her head between the strands of cattle wire and looked at the people walking on the road.

"I know why you marchin'," she said.

"Why?"

She smiled and looked down at her toes. "I know why you marchin'. I know it good."

Jesse Daniels, thirteen, wearing cut-down Army fatigues, was sitting up on the rotted wooden gate. "I knows why," he said. "'Stead of one goes to school this place, t'other go to the other place, everybody go to the same school. We get smarter. That's why they marchin'."

Back at the head of the long dirt path, their families stood on the porch of the tin-roofed shack and the women held babies on one arm and shaded their eyes with the other so they could look through the heat shimmers and see the people marching down the highway.

Farther along the road, at a rutted turn-off leading up to a construction site, workers in tin hats sat on the hoods of cars and displayed the best of local overalls culture.

"Hey, boy. You, boy. That's right. Coon-lover. Turn around here so's I can take your picture."

A bearded white marcher turned around and one construction worker stood up on the car bumper and took his picture with a small camera.

"Greenwich Village You-niversity," the worker said.

"New Yawk coon-lover," the one next to him yelled.

The pictures the worker took will be used to give visual aid when the children at home are taught that this civil rights march had nothing to do with these nice local niggers at all. It was a thing strictly for beatniks from New York.

"Coon-lovers," they yelled boldly.

Then they go back to their jobs and this line goes past them slowly, pushing up the road, silently eating away a method of life that has existed for a hundred years.

All day yesterday the civil rights march from Selma to Mont-gomery trailed along U.S. Highway 80, with the great Hook-worm Belt, Lowndes County, stretching out from both sides of the road. At the head of the line was Dr. Martin Luther King, the Nobel Peace Prize winner who walked like a sharecropper. Behind him, two abreast, were the marchers. And there was a line of cars, sanitary vans, water trucks, and jeeps. The road was clear, the walking easy, and it was a sparkling Alabama day. And all around were people who work for the United States government and carry guns.

Off to the side, Army helicopters sat with the cattle in the sweeping fields, then took off and flew low over the woods to watch for anybody who might be out to get himself a good nigger at three hundred yards or so. Jeeps blocked the red dirt side roads. MPs with slung rifles stood alongside. Truckloads of troops were parked under trees in spots where somebody thought there could be trouble.

On the highway, business-suited FBI agents and United States marshals walked near the marchers, or rode slowly behind them in rented cars. Generals stood on the road or came past in cars. They were looking, giving orders, looking down at clipboards, then looking up and giving orders.

This march doesn't look like much, really. It's just a rumpled line of people, many of them exhibitionists. But the generals have tight faces. One of them, the name Graham sewn on his fatigues, runs from spot to spot. He reports to Lyndon Baines Johnson personally if something goes wrong here.

There are a lot of people to protect. The marchers are limited to exactly three hundred. But this is a changing group, with new ones coming in from Selma and others shuttling back, and crews of workers up the road busy setting up a camp for the night. And there was Albert Turner, who was marching along at the end of the line yesterday.

He had on tan unfinished cowhide work boots, black pants, and a white sweatshirt. He is twenty-nine, but he has a little weight on him and he grunted while he walked along. Sweat showed on the two creases on the back of his neck. He is just a bricklayer from Marion, in nearby Perry County, and he marches with no ceremony, and with his head down, and he was the last one in line yesterday. But if Albert Turner wanted to make this march by himself he would rate every gunhand that the government had on the road. Albert Turner comes with a fairly legitimate beef.

On a Friday night in 1960, Turner came home from his job as a bricklayer and sat down with his wife at the kitchen table and began to match money with his bills. Oh, he had enough money. Turner was a bricklayer, and they get $3.00 an hour, $3.50 in some spots in Alabama.

Bricklaying always was considered niggers' work in the South, and it paid accordingly. But there was a building boom in 1947 and then a strong union came in, and the South found that it had figured wrong again. Here was a nigger job that all of a sudden was paying people like Albert Turner $150 a week.

What bothered Albert Turner on this night was the figures on his pay stub. It said that $27.52 had been taken out for income taxes. He looked at the stub and a strange thought ran across his mind: If the government can take $27.52 a week, then it can give back something to Albert Turner. Like a vote in an election.

"I'm goin' to go down to the courthouse Monday and register to vote," he told his wife.

"Albert, they'll throw you in the river," his wife said.

"I work almost a whole day for $27.52," Turner said. "How'm I gonna stand there and lay brick all day when I know I'm not gettin' anything for it? Somebody stealin' a day's work off me. That's it. They take the tax, then I vote."

On Monday he appeared at the courthouse, and a registrar, anxious to get back to his cows, growled when Albert stated his business.

"All right, boy," he said. "Sit yourself down and answer this here test."

He handed Albert a sheet which had twenty-five questions. They asked for name, address, place of employment, names of friends and relatives and their addresses and places of employment, and other pertinent information that would aid the White Citizens Council in times of anger. Turner filled it out anyway.

He has a degree in mechanical art from Alabama A & M,

and his penmanship was quite clear on the exam. He handed it to the registrar. The registrar took it from him and didn't look at it.

"You done failed, boy," he said. "You done failed on two of these here questions."

Then somebody came up and asked the registrar to sign something. The registrar reached for a pencil, curling his fingers around it as if it were a pneumatic drill, and went to work.

"I thought he'd hurt himself with that pencil," Albert was saying while he walked along yesterday.

From the time he failed that test, Albert Turner decided he was going to vote. He began to agitate, and he blew jobs and had to travel to be a bricklayer. But then people from the Justice Department began to come around and Albert got hope and he kept talking it up with people and going back again and again to register.

He was threatened. A few weeks ago he led a night march in Marion. The state troopers jumped them with clubs and gave Albert a going over. Then they went through the town and grabbed his friend, Jimmy Lee Jackson, in a place called Mack's Café. They beat hell out of Jimmy Lee. Shortly thereafter he was shot to death.

But Albert Turner kept agitating and showing up at rallies and yesterday he marched along Highway 80, grunting and sweating, and Tobacco Road doesn't know what it got itself into when that registrar told Albert that he had done failed his examination.

Here he came, walking along past the sign that says: "Welcome to Benton. Churches: Baptist, Presbyterian, Methodist." And then, up at the crossroads, was the Benton Service Station and Byrd's Lucky Dollar truck stop, and in front, parked at the roadside, were cars with white painting on their hoods and doors. "Welcome coons," the lettering said. "Go home, scum."

And the whites stood there, these real outdoor whites, with their sunglasses and tanned faces and thin lips, and MPs sat alongside the cars, and a helicopter flew very low overhead and back down the road where the truckloads of troops were parked. Albert had a lot of backing yesterday for this thing he wants.

John Doar, the Justice Department's man in charge of civil rights, stood in the road and pointed out Albert yesterday.

"We've known him a long time," Doar said. "He's a man. He's worth the whole thing."

March 23, 1965

Alabama Schoolhouse

SELMA, ALABAMA—The Rolen School sits in the dirt off United States Highway 80 in Lowndes County, Alabama. It is a public school of the State of Alabama for grades one to six. It has eighty Negro students and three Negro teachers. It is open from 8 A.M. to 3 P.M., but from the road it looks like a deserted shack.

The Rolen School is a wooden building that was a church when people in Lowndes County wore Confederate uniforms. It once was painted yellow. The building sits off the ground on small piles of loose red bricks. It has ten frame windows. Nearly all the panes are broken. Beaverboard, put up on the inside, covers the broken windows. The school has a tin roof. Yesterday part of the roof was flapping in the breeze coming through the fields. In the winter the wind comes strong and keeps blowing parts of the roof away and the students sit in class under the cold sky.

A shack in the dirt field behind the school serves as a bathroom. There is a small coal bin on the side of the school. A tin basin, used by students for carrying coal inside to the pot-bellied stoves, is on the ground next to the bin. A long-handled ax stands against the building. The students gather wood at lunchtime and chop it for the fires inside. The school has a church entrance, with five wooden steps leading up from the dirt. The steps are rotted and an adult cannot stand on them.

The principal, John Bowen, who also teaches the fifth and sixth grades, stood outside the school yesterday. He is forty and has gray-topped hair. He wore a long-sleeved dark blue sports shirt. His arms were folded in front of him and he spoke quietly.

"Nobody is allowed inside the school without a permit, we were told," he said.

"When did they tell you this?"

"Well, when all the people started coming around here they told me that."

"I see. They don't want us to get a look at the place."

"Well," he said, "I work for the county school system. You shouldn't work for a person, then give him bad publicity. But

88

I have to say you can't learn in this school. There's no way to learn here. It's just impossible."

"If you'll excuse me, I'm going to go into your school without this permit."

The inside of the school was divided into three rooms. The first and second grades were in the room on the left. There were eleven small black faces with big eyes sitting on benches around a wooden picnic table. A girl was on her stomach on another bench, looking up at the visitor. The teacher, Josephine Jackson, wearing a pink dress, sat at a bridge table in the corner, next to a big rusted stove.

Beaverboard covers the classroom window, but light comes in through large holes in the side of the building. The holes give the kids a view of the fields. The kids also can look through a huge hole in the floor and see coal ashes and empty pork-and-beans cans on the ground under the classroom.

"We use coal when we can get it, and wood in the winter," Miss Jackson was saying. "It run to, oh, 'bout twenty-five degrees here in the winter. We hardly ever get near zero. The children wear hair rags and overcoats. They don't have gloves. When it gets too cold they sit with their hands in the coat pockets."

"Can you get anything done here at all?"

"Well, I try as hard as I can."

"Do the parents know what's going on?"

"Oh, I don't think they understand, either," she said. "They went to the same kind of school as this and these children here will have to send their children to a school like this and, oh, I guess it never will come to an end."

The kids sat at the table and watched with big eyes. One girl put her head on the table and looked up, a finger stuck in her mouth.

Arthur Lee Williams, in overalls, red shirt, and sneakers, looked up, turned around, and looked at the visitor. Then he mumbled something and broke into a giggle and buried his face in the shoulder of the kid next to him.

"What'd you say?"

The kid next to him answered. "He say, 'Stop there, little preacher.'"

This should have been a big laugh, but there is nothing funny in the idea that any white man who would visit that school would have to be a minister.

Arthur had a torn, thumbed workbook in front of him. There was scrawling all through it. There was not one legible letter on page after page of scrawling.

"Do you have a bright one?" Miss Jackson was asked.

"That one," she said, pointing to a little girl in pigtails and white sweater.

The top of the girl's workbook said her name was Janice Cosby. On the first page she had printed, "See the kitten. The kitten says mew mew." It was neatly done.

"Do you like school?" she was asked.

Her eyes brightened and her head shook up and down. "Yop," she said.

"Do you do any writing at home?"

"Yop. In the back yard when I get home."

"Would you want to write something for me now?"

She grinned and picked up a pencil and, carefully, and neatly, and proudly, she printed, "Sunday is the day before Monday."

"That's very good," she was told. She beamed and began printing something else.

"What does her father do?" the teacher was asked.

"Farmer. Sharecropper."

"And what happens to the girl here?"

"When she gets old enough, she goes into the field and picks cotton and doesn't come to school any more."

A door with cardboard panels led to the next classroom, which was for the third and fourth grades. A Coca-Cola machine was in one corner of the room. A big blue metal gas-station sign, "Firestone Tires, the mark of quality," was nailed over a hole in the floor in the middle of the room. Old Alabama license plates were nailed here and there around the room to cover other holes in the floor.

A heavy woman in a striped dress stood against the wall and watched the seventeen students, who sat on benches and did nothing. She said her name was Lillian Pierce and that she was sixty.

"I been teachin' around between twenty-eight and thirty-nine years in this county," she said.

"Where did you go to school?"

"I went to schools right in this county," she said.

"This is awful," she was told.

"Awful?" she said. She looked surprised. She didn't understand.

The fifth and sixth grades were in the back room, a big bare place with cement blocks and pieces of charred firewood lying on the floor. A kid in a raincoat was hammering a nail into a bench that was falling apart. A small cluttered table, with an old blue globe on it, was in the front of the room. There were no blackboards or charts hanging on the wooden walls.

Seven or eight boys sat on the other benches, doing nothing. Two girls were standing at a door leading out to the back of the school. One boy, in a blue shirt with ripped shoulders, leaned against the wall in the other corner of the room.

"What grade are you in?" he was asked.

"Sixth."

"How old are you?"

"Twayelve."

"What do you want to be when you grow up?"

"What I want to do? I want to wait. Wait on tables."

"Is that a good job?"

He smiled. "Oh, my father he say that a very good job."

The books were on a shelf behind him. The flyleaves all carried the stamp: "This book is the property of the State of Alabama, County of Lowndes."

The books consisted of a Bobbs-Merrill reader put out in 1939, a book called *Conrad's Magic Flight*, also put out in 1939, and an arithmetic book whose title page was ripped so that its publication year could not be determined. But its approach to arithmetic was in the same small print, with no visuals, which the visitor remembered seeing in about 1939.

A hand bell tinkled in the next room and kids walked out the door into the yard. It was lunchtime. Most of them stood in the dirt or went in front of the building and sat on the top step. None of them had anything with them to eat.

"Hey," one of them was asked, "don't you have anything for lunch?"

He shook his head yes. "Light bread and hot sauce. I eat it on the way to school."

"Don't they get any lunch to bring?" Bowen was asked. He

shrugged. He could see the visitor did not understand Lowndes County, Alabama.

A little one sitting alone on the step watched the visitor carefully. The kid had on a sweatshirt with red lettering: "Four Seasons C.C." The shirt had not been washed in a long time. His dungaree pants had holes at the knees. There were no tongues in his little brown boots. His bare feet showed through the laces.

"What's your name?" he was asked.

His eyes narrowed and he moved his mouth. "Uh," he said.

"What did you say?"

His lips shook and he gurgled something again.

"He Akin Grant," one of the other kids yelled over.

"Let him say it himself. Come on, now, what's your name?"

The little kid's eyes narrowed and his lips moved and he tried to talk. And then his eyes filled and he sat there afraid, and crying, and then you could see that he had something the matter with his mouth and that he could not form words.

The visitor started to put his hands on the kid's shoulders, but the kid got up and ran, crying, over to the side of the porch and jumped off and went back behind the school.

"How much of this do you have?" Bowen, the principal, was asked. "This kid needs help. What is this, letting him come here like this?"

"I don't know how much of anything we have," Bowen said. "What do we call normal? How do we measure what is normal and what isn't when he have a situation like this? They're all so far down here. They don't have any hope particularly. The school building is here and a couple of teachers is provided. Then nobody cares whether these kids come or not. It don't matter. School for these kids is just a period between childhood and growin' up and workin' in the fields."

The lunch period ended and Bowen said good-by and went back into school with these little children who are being brought up as semi-human beings.

The visitor to the Rolen School got into the car and drove out onto the highway and back to Montgomery. The marchers were by the airport now, and the line was long, numbering in the thousands, and the people walked along and clapped hands and sang. They marched in the sun because of things like the

Rolen School, which stands for every step of every foot which has touched United States Highway 80 this week.

But farther up the road, the sunglasses-wearing state police stood by their cars and they sang, "The niggers are coming," and the white people standing on the sidewalk laughed. And in downtown Montgomery the great Tony Bennett, here to entertain the marchers, was told not to go out on the streets because everybody is mad about his being here and he is liable to get hurt. And in the State Capitol, which sits under a flagpole that has the Confederate flag flying over the American flag, the legislature yesterday passed a special resolution condemning the ministers who are in the civil rights march and calling attention to all "the fornicating" going on among the marchers. And the Governor of the State of Alabama, which, in the year 1965, in the United States of America, has the Rolen School as part of its great educational system, sits in his office and says he is not going to give in to this mob rule of Communists.

March 24, 1965

The Retreat

MONTGOMERY, ALABAMA—Fat Thomas, who in his retirement decided to see Alabama two weeks ago, rolled into the Jefferson Davis Hotel, Montgomery, Alabama, and registered as "Martin Luther Fats." The room clerk took this with a smile. The same kind of smile the sheriff of Dallas County gave when he saw Fat Thomas. And the same way Mr. L. B. Sullivan, Police Commissioner of Montgomery, smiled at Fat Thomas. In fact every place Fat Thomas went in Alabama, he made people feel good. They loved the idea of speculating on how many people it would take to carry Fat Thomas out of town on a railroad tie.

"You people don't have enough tar to handle me," Fat Thomas kept telling them.

As his daytime headquarters, Fat Thomas chose a back booth of the Selma Del, which is in Selma, Alabama. He spent much of the time ordering small snacks for himself. By the middle of the week, waitresses in the Selma Del were walking around with no shoes on. At dusk each day, Fat Thomas would come across the street and set himself up on the third floor of the Albert Hotel, where Bob Gay, proprietor, had a private saloon set up. Fat Thomas would drink gin at a white leather bar and Bob Gay would call up all his friends and they would come up to the saloon room and sit on a couch and watch Fat Thomas drink.

"Man down here, if he's big as you, can't get enough work to feed hisself," one of the locals observed one night.

"I've got a hard-working girl friend," Fat Thomas said.

Between meals, Fat Thomas toured the town a little bit, and what he saw on his tours disturbed him.

"All they do is sell guns down here," he said. "A guy goes into the store and orders a pound of baloney, a hundred rounds of ammunition, and a loaf of Wonder bread."

Fat Thomas, of course, was called on to take quite a bit of abuse from the loungers and state troopers around Selma, and from people in such places as Byrd's Lucky Dollar truck stop in Denton, Lowndes County. Fat Thomas said nothing in return, but he kept making notes in a little book.

Over in Montgomery, everybody in sight insulted Fat Thomas.

"You fat beatnik," they yelled.

Even the owner of the shoeshine stand tried to abuse Fat Thomas. "Don't you give that damnyankee no shine," the owner said to the Negro who was doing the shining.

"In Harlem they put two men on me and they sing for me when they give me a shine," Fat Thomas told the Negro kid.

"Don't you listen to him," the owner said. He came over to the shoeshine kid. "Don't I get you out of jail?" he asked the kid. The kid nodded yes. "Then don't you give this fat white trash no shine," the owner said.

"I'm gonna do something," Fat Thomas said.

"Sit in? We have a way to handle all you sit-ins round here," the owner said.

"I said sit down, not sit in," Fat Thomas said. He got up on the shoeshine stand, took a deep breath, and then sat down hard. The shoeshine stand was made of pretty old wood. When it splintered, one of the arms flew right out the door and onto the sidewalk.

However, because of Fat Thomas's size—he weighed approximately 485 during his stay in Alabama—the locals began to recognize him and regard him as a prime target. Evil rumors about what would happen to Fat Thomas if he showed again in Lowndes County began to make the rounds. Fat Thomas got riled at this and late one night, loaded with gin, he was mumbling something about going out to buy some Wonder bread and bringing his friend Bad Eddie down from New York for target practice.

Then there was a bit of trouble in the bar of the Jefferson Davis, caused when somebody called Fat Thomas the fattest nigger-lover ever to live, and the bar was closed to him thereafter. And everybody in town began to scream insults and finally Fat Thomas got on the plane and left for New York. He was relieved to be out of Alabama, but agitated by his treatment there. He couldn't wait to get to the Atlanta airport, where, over cold tap beer, he took out the little book he had been marking up all during his stay in Alabama and he jammed himself into a phone booth.

He started calling up every place that had abused him. He

told them all the same thing. "Go out and buy yourself a Dalmatian dog so he can bark when he smells the smoke," Fat Thomas yelled into the phone. "Get a good Dalmatian dog. And make sure he got no laryngitis. Because your joint is going to have an accidental fire in the middle of the night very soon."

Then Fat Thomas hung up, drank his beer, and got on the plane for New York, which is where he and everybody else belongs.

March 29, 1965

The Day I Company Got Killed

CHU LAI—Eighteen rifles, stuck in the hot sand by their bayonets, stood in a semicircle in front of a tent. A camouflaged helmet rested on each rifle butt.

The rifles were symbols of the men of the 3rd Battalion of the 3rd United States Marine Regiment killed at Van Tuong last week in the biggest American battle of the Viet Nam war.

Inside the tent, the battalion commander, Lieutenant Colonel Joseph Muir, knelt with his men at memorial services. Colonel Muir appeared to be holding back tears. Some of the Marines sobbed.

"They did not come back," said the chaplain. "O god, for those who fell in battle, we know you are with them. And for those who are here, we give you thanks."

The black mountains of Chu Lai come down to the sea with rice paddies in front of them and then a wide area of orange sand that is covered by lifeless bushes that are shoulder-high. The South China Sea, flat and lukewarm, begins where the land ends.

It was here, on the sand and in the bushes, and under a terrible sun, that the United States Marines fought a battle for the first time in this place in Asia called Viet Nam.

They fought all day Wednesday and into the night, and they fought again on Thursday. Their big American tanks and armored vehicles were useless to them. The enemy, these little Asians in black shirts, knocked the armor out right away.

The Marines were hit with shots coming out of the bushes in the sand. They fought with rifles and machine guns. When the Viet Cong were not on the sand any more, the Marines went into the mud of the paddies after them. The fighting was continuous and the dead were everywhere and now everybody knows that America is in a war.

The Marines say they killed 564 Viet Cong. The Marines do not give their own casualties because this is a war. But their dead were in the sand Wednesday and Thursday, waiting to be put in boxes and sent home to America. The broken bodies of the wounded were being taken to field hospitals. And the rest of them, the kids of eighteen, nineteen, and their early twenties, have had their lives changed forever by this day on the sands and in the mud in front of the black mountains of Chu Lai.

"A lot of boys came off that ship," Daniel Kendall, nineteen, a lance corporal, was saying, "and a lot of men are going back."

Kendall is from Boston and he is in I Company. He thinks I Company is the best company in the Marines and when it was put together in October, back at Camp Pendleton, San Diego, they got to know each other right away because they all knew they had thirty months to live together. And on Tuesday afternoon, when they were taken out of their tents at Da Nang and put on a cramped troop ship without being told where they were going, nobody in I Company was worried.

"We all know what we're doing," Terry Hunter, twenty-two, a corporal, said.

"We got the smartest officers and the best noncoms and the best men," George Kendlers, who is twenty, called out.

"India Company is the best in the Marines," another one of them called out.

"Yeah, we're the best," the kids started to yell, and the gray ship pulled out of Da Nang and went into the sea. They were given chili and rice and cold milk. They liked the cold milk. It was the first they had had since coming to Viet Nam.

"They give us this, they must have some wild operation planned for us," Kendlers said.

None of them had been in action before, outside of having a few stray shots thrown at their camp. After dinner, they were told where they were going. They were going to land on the beach twelves miles to the south of the town of Chu Lai.

"Intelligence says a lot of Viet Cong are dug in in the area," one of the officers said. "But this is one of those things. You may not fire a round. Or you might get your behinds shot off."

"Just remember what you've been taught," Bruce Webb, the company captain, told them. "When you're fired on, go down, then come up and shoot. Don't just lay there. After you shoot, move. Move even if bullets are all around you. You run up less casualties when you move."

They went to bed at 9 P.M. and were up at 4 A.M. and had eggs and pancakes for breakfast. At 6:50 A.M., with the sun breaking over the black mountains in the distance, I Company came through the water and onto the sand and bushes, and it was the first time they ever had been in action.

Walking quietly, with no talk, they went into a small cluster of filthy huts with dirt paths between them. They call these places villages here. The village was empty. On the paths leading from the village to the sand and bushes, they found women and children hiding. The women held their children and looked at the Marines and said nothing. The women knew where the Viet Cong were. But they would not tell the Marines. The Marines were the enemy.

A second village was approached. To get to it, they had to go over a small bridge. The front of the village was lined with bushes and shrubbery. I Company moved up to the bridge. They started to go across it when one of the bushes in front of the village moved and a machine gun began firing from a trench under the leaves.

The Marines and mortars dropped into the village. They called for an air strike. Armed helicopters lumbered in. Swept-wing jets dove at the village after the helicopters moved away. When the air strike stopped, all the bushes began to move and there was firing both ways and then black shirts were climbing out of the trenches under the bushes and running back through the village. I Company came after them. They came across the bridge and into the village and Captain Webb was talking with two corporals, a radio man and a runner, and they were going along one of the trenches with the bushes over it when the booby trap exploded. It killed the three of them. I Company now knew what war is.

"He's not dead," another officer kept telling them. "They're taking him out by helicopter. He's all right." The officer didn't want the men to know that their commander had been killed in the first half-hour of the first action of their lives.

Now they were out into this sand with the bushes and the fire was coming at them. Not concentrated fire. But a shot here, a shot here, a machine gun from somewhere else, and all of it coming from holes and bunkers as they came through this sand, with the bushes tearing at their hands. Every few minutes, Michaels, who was carrying the radio, would hear something on it and he'd call over to those around him.

"Smith got hit. He's dead."

"Smith," the one near him would say. He'd turn to somebody else. "Smith got killed." It would go down the line.

They moved over three Viet Cong bodies killed by their machine guns. A helicopter was downed in one of the rice paddies in front of them. A line of tanks and armored carriers was going in to get out the helicopter pilots. I Company was to go with them. There was a line of eight armored vehicles. The tanks went first. The first tank pitched through the sand and into the mud of the paddy and nothing happened to it.

The Viet Cong fired at the second vehicle. It was an armored carrier, and they tried to get it with a .57-millimeter recoilless rifle. The shot missed. The I Company Marines in the carrier were climbing out to fight. The second shot from the .57 hit and covered the carrier with black smoke and the bodies fell out of the black smoke and into the mud.

The water ran out at noon. Fire was too heavy for helicopters to land with supplies. The Marines of I Company went through the sand with the sun glaring at them and the shots trying to kill them and they were licking their lips and trying to forget about water while they fought. These should be stories from a book about 1944. They are about 1965.

In the afternoon, a young boy popped up in front of them. He had crawled out of a hole which had an opening so small you could walk by it and not notice it. He pointed down into the hole. The boy started running. A small hand came out of the hole. Then a black shirtsleeve. Then a rifle. The Viet Cong pulled himself out and started running. The I Company machine-gunners caught him in the middle and his body fell in two parts.

I Company dug in for the night. There was firing all night and all morning and Michaels, the radioman, kept calling out to the ones near him the names of buddies who were killed.

Friday, their faces orange from the sand, their lips encrusted with it, their eyes bloodshot, Terry Hunter, Daniel Kendall, and George Kendlers sat in a foxhole with their rifles and a 3.5 rocket-launcher and they were in with another outfit because I Company was not in the battle any more. I Company had been blown apart. The others who were left had been taken back to the beach.

"It's still the best company in the Marines," Kendlers said in the foxhole. "We just had bad luck. Up on the hill, when the captain got killed, I wanted to go right in. When they started shooting at me later, I felt good. I didn't want to be the only one who didn't get shot at."

"We're all real good buddies," Kendall said.

"We always went to the Pike together. Back in Long Beach. I Company always was together."

"The Pike? Is that a gin mill?"

"Gin mill? No. It's an amusement park. It's got rides," Hunter said.

"Dancing," Kendall said. "You know, an amusement park."

Somewhere close, artillery was going off. Jets screamed in the sun overhead. They sat with their chins down so the sand wouldn't blow into their eyes. They talked about an amusement park in Long Beach where young kids go. Then Kendall's eyes came up and he saw a guy walking toward them from another hole.

"What are you, soft?" he yelled. "You'll get shot right through the ass doing that."

The other two looked up. They all looked the same. Three kids in a foxhole with faces that are very old.

August 23, 1965

Four Funerals

SAIGON.—Four funerals were to be held on the little street in front of the theater on the air base. The pallbearers, who came from the units of the men who were killed, arrived early, at 9 A.M., in freshly ironed uniforms. They stood alongside sawhorses that had been painted black and were to hold the caskets when they arrived from the morgue.

Two trucks came around the corner and stopped. A Vietnamese military band climbed down. The bandsmen wore blue berets and had gold braid looped around their shoulders. They put their instruments down on the asphalt and walked over to the theater and went inside and sat down in the seats and fell asleep.

An old master sergeant, capless and wearing glasses, came out of the theater. He tapped a microphone to make sure it was on.

"All right," he called out through the microphone, "we're going to get a casket here for you men to drill with. We'll run this through a couple of times and get it down right. Let's put the cigarettes out."

The pallbearers shredded their cigarettes and formed around the carpenter's horses. They faced the theater, a high white cement building with a sun-bleached asbestos roof. The wooden marquee had been stripped of movie posters. Only the red letters "Theater" remained.

"We'll use the same *ve*-hicle each time in the drill," the sergeant said. "In the funeral itself each casket will come in a different *ve*-hicle."

Behind the pallbearers, Vietnamese teen-agers in shorts and with no shoes on pushed wheelbarrows filled with cement over to a walk they were building through the scrub grass. A barbed-wire fence separated the grass from the air base landing strip. The strip was busy, and F-101s taking off made it difficult to hear the master sergeant.

"When I say '*pre*-sent harms' that means everybody executes except the group moving the body," he said. "Now let's start with the carry-casket position."

The first group of pallbearers, officers from an Army helicopter unit, stepped in front of the black sawhorses. A blue
station wagon with an empty aluminum casket in the back came
down the street. It stopped in front of the helicopter officers
and they reached in and took the casket out and marched it to
the sawhorses.

"When you get it over to the sawhorses, do a right step," the
sergeant said.

The helicopter officers went through the drill and when they
were finished they stood in the sun and smoked cigarettes.

"Who are you waiting for?" a big warrant officer was asked.

"A man that flew with me. At Chu Lai."

"What was his name?"

"Radcliff. Major Radcliff. Donald G. Radcliff."

"When was he killed?"

"On the first day."

A colonel turned around. "He was here for 20 minutes less
than two weeks," the colonel said. "How do you like that for
some kind of a record?"

The warrant officer closed his eyes.

"Now we have about 20 minutes," the master sergeant called
out. "You can go get yourselves coffee if you want."

The warrant officer walked up the little street to the officers
club. He went to the counter and got two cups of coffee. Then
he sat down and introduced himself. His name is Dave Gehling
and he is from Avenue M in Brooklyn. He flew the armed
helicopter last Wednesday morning, the first day of the fighting
between the Marines and the Viet Cong in the sand and mud
south of Chu Lai. Radcliff sat next to him as a gunner.

The armed helicopter was escorting six Marine troop-carrying
helicopters into a landing area in the sand and bushes. The Viet
Cong waited until the helicopter was down to 300 feet. Then
they fired machine guns at it. One bullet came from behind and
it went through the arm of a machine gunner on the helicopter
and into Radcliff's neck in the back and came out the front
and smashed the windshield. Radcliff fell onto the controls and
the helicopter swerved toward the heaviest fire. The machine
gunner, Theodus David, could not unstrap himself because his
wounded arm was useless. He took out a knife and cut himself

free. With one arm he pulled Radcliff off the controls. David went back and fired his machine gun with one hand.

"Radcliff didn't even have to come with me," Gehling said. "He wanted to fly with me. So I said, all right, come on this one. It'll be nothing. Nothing ever happens down there."

"Did you know him long?"

"He was a friend of mine. I served in his unit back in Georgia."

"What was he doing over here?"

"He came here ahead of his unit. He didn't have to fly in combat. He could sit back and worry about supplies and housing and all that. He wanted to go out and fly everywhere. He wanted to know the problems so he could tell his unit about it when they got here. He thought he could save casualties that way."

"Was he married?"

"Yes. I know his wife. In fact my wife is down at Columbus, in Georgia, with her right now."

"Children?"

"Two of them. Cindy and Connell. You know what else I told him? The first thing I told him, I told him to have his gunners watch the rear. You see what they do, they let you come down low and go over them. They come up and shoot at you from behind. I told him that was the most important thing. Watch behind. Then the gunners are busy firing and the shot comes from behind and kills him."

There was water in his eyes and he was embarrassed. He picked up the coffee cup and held it to his mouth and looked down.

"We couldn't find the wound," he said. "We looked everywhere but we couldn't find it. Right in the back of the neck. Low. It came out the front and smashed the plexiglass. We saw the plexiglass. But we couldn't find the wound."

"What could you have done?"

"The doctor said nothing. But we didn't know that then. We thought he was alive. We went crazy trying to fly and look for the wound."

He ran a hand over his face. "How can I write about this?" he said. "Nina. That's his wife's name. I got to write her and I don't know what to say. I have five letters I wrote. I don't know which one to send. I don't think I say it right in any of them. I went to Dewey High School and Jamaica High School. I wish I went to a lot of schools so I would know how to write this letter."

"Nobody knows how to do that," he was told.

"What can I say? That I'm sorry? That I feel bad?"

"Don't write about him. She knows what kind of a man he was."

"What do I write then?"

"Just put down that he was killed because he was trying to find out some things that would save some other lives. Just put that down."

"Will that tell her enough?"

"That'll tell a lot about her husband."

"I'll try and write that tonight."

It was time for the funeral. He got up and went out onto the little street and took his place around the black sawhorses. The Vietnamese band was out on the street now, standing at attention with yellow-bannered instruments. Generals came and stood under the marquee of the theater. The master sergeant had his cap on. He stood in the middle of the street and shouted attention.

Then the caskets came from the morgue. They came around the corner onto the little street. They were in back of station wagons and had American flags draped over them. Everybody was standing stiffly. The two Vietnamese kids put down the wheelbarrows and stood behind the pallbearers and watched.

Radcliff's body came first, in a gray Navy station wagon. It stopped in front of the helicopter pilots and they marched out to the station wagon and reached under the flag and grabbed the aluminum handles of the casket. Then they marched Donald Radcliff's body to the black sawhorses and the chaplains came out of the theater and into the sun to start the funeral service.

August 25, 1965

Warm Air, Light Skin

SAIGON.—The rain came down on the dullness and squalor of Saigon and drove the people from the streets, the old men who use them for bathrooms, the naked children who crouch in the dirt in front of the shack houses, the women who are creased and wispy, the government clerks who ride bicycles and have only small lives in front of them, the American soldiers in short-sleeved shirts who come in washed and red-faced and try to make it a service town but are defeated by its dullness, the policemen who wear white uniforms with sooty collars, and the small round-shouldered men who are of military age but have been let out of the army after three years because the country has been at war for so long that there is no more urgency to it.

The rain was tropical, heavy and warm, but it could not wash the smell out of the air. The air in Saigon is hazy with the black smoke from the broken exhausts of the motorbike taxicabs which crowd every street. The smoke mixes with the smell of dead fish and damp wood and body odor and charcoal and opium and it all becomes the smell and the mood of Saigon, and of Viet Nam. . . .

The helicopter, deep brown, was tilted on its side and it circled the three gray wooden fishing smacks which sat in the water south of Da Nang. The faces in the fishing smacks looked up at the helicopter as it circled 100 feet over them.

The Vietnamese spotter who was riding between the machine gunners in the back of the helicopter became excited. "VC," he said. Then he pointed out the open door at the faces looking up at him from the fishing smacks and he began to yell. "VC," he kept saying.

He unsnapped the olive-drab safety strap around his middle and he got up and leaned over the shoulder of the pilot, Dave Cockett, a captain. "VC there," he said, "get VC."

Cockett looked at the fishing smacks while he kept his ship sweeping in a low circle over them.

"How do I know what they are?" he said.

The Vietnamese had his hand on Cockett's shoulder. "Le

boom," he said, "VC, le boom." He was excited. His fingers pulled imaginary triggers.

Cockett shook his head. "I can't shoot anybody," he said. "How do I know who I'm shooting at?"

"No," the Vietnamese said. "Le boom, VC . . ." He began to jab his finger onto the top of Cockett's hand.

"I'm flying a ship," Cockett yelled at him. "Stop that. No good. Number ten."

The Vietnamese kept jabbing the finger onto Cockett's skin. "Same," he said. "You look. Same." Cockett looked at his hand. Then he looked at the boats.

The light faces standing with the sun-blackened fishermen in the boats stood out now. The faces were light from staying in holes or in thick jungle where little sunlight gets in.

Cockett swung the ship around and said something into the black helmet microphone which was in front of his mouth. The two gunners pulled their machine-guns out of the way and put rifles into the slings at the door and the helicopter came around in a circle and hovered over one of the gray fishing smacks and the faces looked straight up at the helicopter and the gunner looked out the open door, right at one of the light faces which was looking up at him, and he fired from 75 feet away.

The bullet knocked the light face into the bottom of the boat. The people ducked down into a tangle and there was another light body which the gunner could not shoot at, and he said something into his microphone and Cockett moved the helicopter up to another one of these gray boats and there were three light faces in this one and the gunner picked out one and then shot.

He saw the light face disappear. A woman in the boat made a rush for one of the light faces. She had her hands on his neck and then the men came and helped her and they threw the two Viet Cong they had been hiding into the water. One of the Viet Cong came up on the side of the boat and tried to reach up and hold onto it. The men hit his hand with a board. The helicopter came in and the gunner started firing and the Viet Cong's hair jumped when the bullet went into his head. The other one floundered in the water and there were plumes all around him when both gunners shot at him, and when the plumes stopped the water was empty.

The people from the third boat were pointing straight out. The helicopter came over. There was nothing on the surface. Then black hair came up and then went under again and Cockett moved the helicopter right over the spot and when the Viet Cong came up for air again the helicopter made the water ripple and the guns hit him and knocked his head apart.

"Le boom," the Vietnamese in the helicopter kept yelling. Cockett kept circling the ship, looking for another one, and the gunners watched, the brass rolling around on the floor by their feet.

"There's another here someplace, isn't there?" Cockett said into the microphone.

The gunners said something back to him and he nodded. He kept circling the ship over the water, watching the green between the white foam for signs of black hair. Nobody saw anything.

"He's not in the boats," Cockett said. "He must have drowned." He moved the controls and the helicopter rose and headed for the shore.

"Tell him to put on his seatbelt," Cockett said. The gunner reached out and hit the Vietnamese and pointed to the seatbelts. The Vietnamese sat down and started to strap himself in. . . .

Chet Richardson sat over coffee in the morning heat in the empty mess hall in the Army barracks building in the town of Phan Thiet. He had on a plaid sports shirt. He is 49, has a weathered face and crew-cut graying hair. He was a major in the paratroops during World War II. Now he works as the United States Operations Mission field director for Phan Thiet. His organization is the one that tries to assist government on the local level. Richardson's job is to do it without shooting. He does not carry a gun. But this does not make him immune. Nobody is safe in Viet Nam.

"They tried to get me once in Binh Duong," he was saying. "I went out with this major and we were on the road when somebody came running up to us with a handkerchief in his hand. He stuck his hand into the jeep. The minute I saw it I yelled, 'That's a grenade!' I reached for the door with one hand. I reached down on the floor for the grenade with the other. All I got was the handkerchief. So I jumped out. The major just didn't react. He didn't get out. I got to the back of the jeep and it went off. I could see his head just rising up."

"What was his name?" Richardson was asked.

"Now what was his name?" he said. "I forgot his name. God, I thought I'd never forget the name."

"You don't know it?"

"By God, I really don't."

"How much," Richardson was asked, "of this stuff do you have to live with until you get to the point where you forget the name of a guy who got killed sitting next to you?"

"I don't know," he said. "I don't know what these things can do to you."

He brought up his coffee cup. "We have $5 million worth of schoolbooks being printed in the Philippines," he said. "These are the first schoolbooks they've ever had to work with in this area. We got the first set of them in December. The first book we gave them was on health. The books should last three years. Do you know how much good a schoolbook can do for you?"

He wanted to talk about this, not the other.

Outside, the town was hot and the smell came out of the streets.

September 14, 1965

Stork Club Closes an Era

SHERMAN BILLINGSLEY stood at Table No. 1 and waited for his customers. The numbers of the tables are important at the Stork Club and No. 1 is right as you come in and No. 28 is on the aisle where Connie Bennett sat. No. 50 is in the back, in the Cub Room, and the whole country knows that only one man sits at Table 50 in the Stork Club. Table 50 is Walter's table. W. W. would be in later on, at midnight. He always came. So did everybody else. And Billingsley waited at Table No. 1 for Morton Downey, Brenda Frazier, Gene Tierney, Ernest Hemingway and Doris Duke.

He waited two hours for these movie stars and big names of the thirties and forties and the early fifties. The door did not open once because the thirties and forties, and early fifties are gone. And Sherman Billingsley, old and stooped over now, had only three customers in his place on this night a couple of months ago.

Yesterday, he had a sign put in the door, "Stork Club closed . . . will relocate." So the night club which put the phrase Cafe Society into the language is gone.

A blond haired man in a white shirt answered the door yesterday afternoon. "Mr. Billingsley is not here," he said. "I don't know where he is. I can't tell you anything." He shut the door. Two empty packs of cigarettes were on the sidewalk under the canopy at 3 E. 53d St. Nobody else came along to try and get in the place.

Once, the doorman kept a rope across the door and only the select could get past him. Inside, the place was crowded and almost every customer had a name you would know from the gossip columns.

Sherman Billingsley came out of the 1920s when he worked as the general manager for five prohibition speakeasys owned by gunmen Owney Madden and Frenchy DeMange. One of the speakeasys, on 58th Street, was called the Stork. After prohibition, Billingsley relocated it and opened it as a fashionable night club. It became easily the best known night club in America. It was the place where a high roller got his hat and coat and

then said wait a minute to the hatcheck girl and he wrote out
a check for $2,000 and gave it to her. It was the place where
glamorous women wore the most expensive perfume and the
biggest orchids. It was the place that had an hour television
show of its own for six years on Saturday nights. It was the place
where Walter Winchell got so many of those notes he put in his
big column. And it was, everybody in the restaurant business
says, the best run place in the country. "He made an art out of
serving whisky," Dick Conlon, who worked for him and now
runs Gallagher says.

Then time began to pass the Stork Club. It began with the
movie industry changing because of television. The big stars
didn't pull into Grand Central Terminal on the 20th Century
and sit on their luggage and pose for pictures, and then be in
the Stork Club that night. The new movie stars are in Italy and
England and they don't even wear ties. The old movie stars died
or went away. Debutantes didn't mean much anymore. Gossip
columns went far down in importance.

The Stork Club turned into a relic of the time when men
held onto women when they danced. The place has been empty
night after night and the new generation is out shaking all over,
hair flying, nobody touching anybody, on the dance floor at
Arthur or the other discotheques.

In 1956, a union tried to organize the Stork Club waiters.
Billingsley, who felt he was above all aspects of such a thing,
decided to fight the union. It cost him hundreds of thousands,
but the fight still was going on when the place closed. Billingsley even had the front of the club wired so that he could record
a union picket saying something wrong about him.

"Let them slander me once," he kept saying. "I'll have it on
a record and I'll do something about it." He wasn't too sure of
what he would do. But it would be something, he promised.

So New York changed, and the Stork Club became silly and
old. Places like Arthur, which is silly and new, draw the people.
Billingsley, the last to know, closed up on Saturday night. He
told a friend he had sold the building and he would reopen
someplace else with a new kind of operation.

Actually, he isn't the last to know. "*Walter*? Oh, he's not
available right now," Walter Winchell's office said last night.
"He's around, but he's not *available*. He's having trouble with

his teeth and he's out getting them fixed. He's taking a week off from the column. But that's not news. Everybody knows about that."

October 6, 1965

The One Woman in the Operating Room

BETHESDA, MD.—The alarm clock went off in the darkness and Peggy Sue Heimberger's face came out of the pillow. Her hand went out for the clock radio. Then she remembered that she was not using it this time. The night before, she had decided the radio would come on too loud and it would wake up her mother, who was staying in the apartment with her. Peggy Sue Heimberger raised herself up on an elbow. She reached out with the other hand and hit the metal alarm clock which was buzzing on the night table. It was four o'clock in the morning. The President of the United States still was sleeping. He was under sedation and they would not wake him up for his operation until five.

Peggy Sue Heimberger turned on the lamp on the night table and got out of bed. She went over to the closet. Usually, she wears a sweater and a skirt to the hospital and she changes into her nurse's uniform when she gets there. But the night before, the head of the hospital had called and said the people involved with the operation on the President should report at 4:30 A.M. and have breakfast together in the officers' mess at the hospital. It must be a big official thing, she thought. She took out her blue dress uniform, with the gold braid of a commander in the United States Navy on the sleeves, and put it over the back of the chair.

She went into the bathroom to wash. While she was brushing her teeth, she began to think. *Routine. This is just routine. You've done it all your life.* Then she thought about Tuesday night. She had been sitting in her apartment watching the six o'clock news on television. The announcer said Lyndon B. Johnson was going to have an operation for gall bladder at Bethesda Naval Hospital on Friday. Peggy Sue Heimberger, the chief nurse for the hospital's operating rooms, knew she would have something to do with the operation. A little tight feeling ran through her. It was still there now, while she brushed her teeth and told herself it was all routine.

At 4:25, she parked her white 1965 Buick in the parking lot behind the towering white hospital building. It was chilly outside. The car radio had said 52 degrees. She went in a back door and walked into the officers' mess on the first floor. She is a tall thin woman from Rolla, Mo. She has short brown hair with a little gray in it. She wore no makeup. Four medical corpsmen already were at the table. They were in their blues and they felt a little strange being in the officer's mess. Peggy Sue Heimberger looked at them while she walked to the table. Woolridge, Glover, Largin, Gaylord. That was the four assigned to the operating room and they were on time.

"Good morning," one of them said to her.

"It isn't even morning yet, is it?" she said.

"It sure isn't," another one said to her.

She sat down at the table. There was no more conversation. The four corpsmen would work the operation. Commander Heimberger would be the only woman in the room. She was to be the circulating nurse. They had gone over this in meetings with the doctors on Wednesday night and again on Thursday night. And now they were going to be part of an operation on the President of the United States and they did not feel like talking.

They had bacon and eggs, rolls and coffee. They ate quickly and left to change into green surgical clothes. At 5 A.M. she came out of the nurse's room and walked down a hallway to a light brown door with a black sign over it saying "Operating Suites." Ann Fogarty, another nurse, was standing by the door in her lieutenant commander's uniform. Three young men with identical short haircuts and three-button business suits were standing with Ann Fogarty.

"This is Commander Heimberger. The nurse in the operating room," Ann Fogarty said.

One of the three men nodded and opened the door.

She went through it and down to a pale green walled operating room.

A strange face, in green surgical clothes, was at the door to the operating room. She did not know him. But he said good morning to her by name and opened the door. Inside the room, the four corpsmen were busy scrubbing down the room. There was one other man in the room. He was standing in the raised, glassed-in observation booth the cardiologist would use during the operation. Upstairs, in a suite of rooms two flights over the operating rooms, Elizabeth Chapowicki, another nurse, came up to the man who was asleep in the bed.

She touched his shoulder.

"Mr. President," she said.

And in the other rooms on the corridor, men were moving. There was James Cain of the Mayo Clinic, gray-haired, soft spoken.

He is Lyndon B. Johnson's personal physician.

And George Burkley, a Vice-Admiral and the White House physician, and Edward Didier, an anesthesiologist, and Willis Hurst, chairman of the Emory University Medical School and the heart consultant to the President. And Ormond Culp, a ureter specialist from Mayo Clinic. There was evidence of a kidney stone in the President's ureter and if it could be removed Culp would do it. And there was George Hallenbeck, also of the Mayo Clinic. His job was to make the incision and go into the body of the President of the United States and remove the gall bladder.

In the operating room, Peggy Heimberger was working. Clean surgical packs were out on the table. Good. The gloves, where are the gloves? Good. Gaylord was putting them out. She went over to the operating light and moved it around. Fine.

It was a little before 6:10 A.M. when she gave a last look and saw that all the work had been done. Then she nodded to Woolridge and the two of them left the room. Outside the door, Woolridge put his hand on a gurney, a rolling stretcher, and pushed it to the elevator. An elevator was waiting for them and they went onto it with the stretcher and the elevator door closed right away and took them to the third floor.

They went down a passageway to a room men were standing in front of. The men nodded and stepped out of the way and she and Woolridge, the corpsman, pushed the gurney into the bedroom and this huge figure sitting up in bed looked at them.

"Why, good morning," the man said with a drawl.

"Good morning, sir," Peggy Heimberger said.

"Good morning," a black-haired woman in a red robe said.

There was a young girl in a yellow robe in the room, too. She said something in a bright voice. Peggy Sue Heimberger heard it all. But she really didn't hear it. These faces, so familiar when you see them on the front page of a newspaper or on television, can strike you very hard when you are in the same room with them for the first time in your life.

At 6:15 A.M. Woolridge and Peggy Heimberger rolled Lyndon Baines Johnson into the operating room and nine doctors, in green surgical gowns, were waiting and the four corpsmen got ready to serve them and one of the doctors said, "Miss," to Peggy Heimberger and now she was the nurse on duty for the operation on the President of the United States.

Her job was to anticipate. More sponges. Have sponges ready. And lap tapes and sutures and go over and adjust the operating light to give the surgeon better visibility. Do it without being asked. Keep moving around the room and do everything. It came automatically to her. She had been a nurse since 1949. And this was another operation, another routine gall bladder removal. They had stressed this from the start. And she had listened and nodded and said, of course. But now as she moved around the room it was not routine at all because there was, under the glaring light, this long face. And the large ears and nose. A face that people are in awe of. And it was right in front of Peggy Heimberger wherever she went and it was in front of the doctors, too, and you could feel it in the room that they were conscious of it. And one Secret Service man watched them from the glass booth where the cardiologist worked and another Secret Service man outside, had his forehead pressed against the window in the door.

When the anesthesiologist stepped up to Lyndon Baines Johnson, one of the doctors went to the door and looked outside and nodded to the slim, dark-haired man who was sitting in a chair against the wall.

"We're starting, Mr. Moyers," the doctor said.

Bill D. Moyers, who has a title as press secretary but is really the main assistant to Lyndon Johnson, nodded and reached for a telephone next to him.

"Get me the Vice-President," he said.

Moyers held the phone in his right hand. He held up his left hand and he followed the second hand as it ran across the face of a Turler wristwatch.

He heard the phone begin to ring once. Then it was picked up and a voice said, "just a moment, Mr. Moyers."

Then another voice came on. "Bill?" Hubert Humphrey said.

Moyers looked at the watch. It had taken him seven seconds to get the Vice-President of the United States on the phone at his home in Chevy Chase.

Good, Moyers said to himself. His left hand dropped and he talked to Hubert Humphrey about the running of the nation while the President was under anesthesia.

The operation took two hours and 15 minutes. When it was over, nine doctors looked up and smiles were in the eyes over the green surgical masks and the President was taken off the table and rolled on the gurney off to the side of the room. The recovery room was in the operating room.

Peggy Heimberger stopped walking. And now she felt tired. She stepped outside the room. Moyers still was on a chair. A secretary sat next to him. The secretary held a dictation pad. Moyers was on the telephone.

"Mr. Vice-President," Moyers was saying into the phone.

Two attendants passed by rolling another gurney. A blonde woman was on it. She was Mrs. Karen Carrick, 20, the wife of a Navy enlisted man. Mrs. Carrick was going for a gall bladder operation. While they rolled her by, she could see the President of the United States asleep on a bed. She looked at him. Then she began to worry about her mother-in-law who was home in Lexington, Md., with seven-and-a-half-month-old Mark. *He pulls ashtrays off the table. He could burn the rug. I hope she watches for that. She's not used to watching a baby like this*, Karen Carrick thought.

"Yes, Mr. Vice-President . . ." Bill Moyers was saying.

And Peggy Heimberger walked down the hall and into the nurse's room and sat down. She took out a cigarette. One of the nurses brought her a cup of coffee.

"Oh, can I use that," Peggy Heimberger said.

She sat with the coffee. Nobody talked to her. They sat and looked at her, but they would not say anything to her. She took a sip of coffee, then put the cup down.

"It went fine," Peggy Heimberger said. "It couldn't have gone any better."

She was very tired now. It had been just a routine operation for gall bladder. But she was very tired.

October 10, 1965

Easter Rising

DUBLIN—Rain during the night had fallen on the street like a scrubwoman, leaving O'Connell Street washed and shining in the morning sun. New flags hanging everywhere made the street a long swatch of color. By the time the ten-o'clock masses were over, a crowd of about 250,000, probably the largest Dublin has ever seen, crowded on the clean cement to watch the parade which passed General Post Office in celebration of the fiftieth anniversary of the Easter Rising.

The parade was short. There were no speeches. The Irish felt the day was too important to be marred by oratory, of which there could have been very much. There were not even introductions of the people on the reviewing stand. The only words spoken came when old Eamon de Valera, in top hat and black overcoat stood up under a canopy on the post office steps and from behind him came a voice over the loudspeakers. The voice read the proclamation which the rebel Irish Republican leaders had posted when they started their revolt. The absence of speeches before, and the silence that came after, set the words of the proclamation off. The effect on the crowd, because of this, was marked.

"Irishmen and Irishwomen," the voice said. "In the name of God and of the dead generation from which she received her old tradition of nationhood, Ireland, through us, summoned her children to her flag and strikes for her freedom. . . . We place the cause of the Irish Republic under the protection of the Most High God whose blessing we invoke upon our arms, and we pray that no one who serves that cause will dishonor it by cowardice, inhumanity or rapine. In this supreme hour the Irish nation must, by its valor and discipline and by the readiness of its children to sacrifice themselves for the common good, prove itself worthy of the august destiny to which it is called."

The ones still alive who had started the uprising sat in rows on de Valera's left. They all looked alike. Craggy and creased, white hair showing among the deep lines that crisscrossed the backs of their necks, they sat in dark overcoats and they all wore drab hats old enough to have British bullet holes in them.

First man off the reviewing stand was Captain Frank Daly, B. Company, 1st Battalion. Timing his maneuver perfectly and executing it with dispatch, Captain Daly moved from the middle of a row and went down a flight of stairs at the side of the stand. At half past twelve, the legal opening hour, he came through the door of Tower Pub, across from the side entrance to the post office. The barkeep already had pints of stout and halves of whisky set out on the bar ready for the crush. Captain Daly said whisky. The barkeep pushed a half of Paddy's at him.

"Good healt'," the captain said.

"T'ank you and God bless you," one of the mob now in the pub called out.

Daly had four medals from the revolt pinned to the front of his black overcoat. He was asked what each was for.

"Probably for going to jail," he said.

"Oh, the British had you in jail too."

"A many of them."

The pub was packed now, and dark pints of stout were being passed overhead to the ones in the rear rank. Conversation was broken off and the celebration was gathering itself with every pint. It would go on all through the glorious day.

The kids on Sheriff Street had a celebration yesterday too. They scrambled up from the sidewalks where they had been sitting and they came running through the smoke from soft coal and wood which hung in the air, and they surrounded the two strangers in the middle of the street who had just given Christy Costello and Tony O'Driscoll two and six each to go to the show.

"Mister, me; me, mister," they said, hands held out, when they got around the two strangers.

"What's your name?" one of the kids was asked.

"Joe Moore. I'm twelve."

"What's the pin on you for?"

Joe Moore held out his striped shirt and looked down at the small red pin on it.

"It's the pledge in the Choich."

"What pledge?"

"For not to drink."

"Do they drink at home?"

"Me dad drinks. Just one after the job, he says. Keep himself fit. Only he doesn't stop drinkin' until the mother makes him go to bed."

"What does the father do?"

"He woiks odd days."

At first there were only five or six of them. But more kept coming at the two strangers. One of the strangers was Terry O'Neill, who owns two saloons in New York, and he was handing out the coins. In a matter of seconds he had a crowd of fifty kids around him. They were all ages, four and five and ten and eleven, and they were all dirty and they were all coming off the littered sidewalks in front of these long rows of attached stone houses on the street.

"Me, mister," they kept calling out. Dogs jumped among them. One kid held up a card that said he was a boxer in the Transport Workers' Club.

He wanted a reward for that. Another one, blond and smudged face, with bony, dirty legs sticking out of short pants, pushed close. He was looking up and yelling, "Me, mister," while he put his hands into Terry O'Neill's pocket.

"Get your hands out of there," Terry O'Neill called out. Then he swung his head around to catch the kid who was trying to pick his other pocket. Finally he flung a handful of coins into the air and the kids dove for them in a pack and he ran to the Raven Pub with the stragglers chasing him.

"Me, mister," they shrieked.

The oppression ended fifty years ago. But the product of it still is in Dublin. The kids on Sheriff Street and the blocks and alleys around it live in houses that have overflowing garbage cans inside the front doors and no baths inside the flats. Once a week everybody on the block goes to the Tara Street Public Baths, a couple of blocks away. Last year a movie with Richard Burton in it was filmed on Sheriff Street. The set was of a public bath. When the kids looked out the window and saw it, they streamed out of their filthy houses with towels over their arms and ran at the doors in the set and knocked it over.

"You go home and they talk about Harlem," Terry O'Neill was saying when he got into the Raven Pub.

The parallel is natural. The Irish Rebellion was the first successful ethnic revolt. And it started, the veterans were recalling yesterday, with only a few fighting in the post office and crowds of thousands taking advantage of it to smash into stores and loot everything in Dublin. Watts, then, would seem to have a precedent.

Later in the afternoon more official ceremonies were held in the ugly, cramped courtyard of the Kilmainham Prison, where the British executed sixteen of the Irish leaders. The executions inflamed the Irish and the revolt became successful. The Irish are restoring the prison, the cells included, as a national monument. Great issue is taken with this. Prisons are things men should tear down, not rebuild. So the rest of the day of celebration was spent in the Raven Pub. All afternoon, the kids crowded outside the door and called in, "Me, mister."

April 11, 1966

A Struck Paper, Famous and Needed, Goes Down

IT HAPPENED quietly. The New York *Herald Tribune*, which had a history in New York for 131 years, went under last week with only a little plume of water to mark what had happened. There was a headline in the New York *Times*, a few film clips on television, a few people looking up at the newspaper's building before they went down into the subway. Otherwise, nothing. And what was a very good newspaper now becomes just another thing for you to talk about someday when the past becomes important.

The *Herald Tribune* was a famous newspaper, and it always used the language well. But it was badly mishandled by some of the people who ran it during the last 20 years. And, at the bottom, the people who worked on the production had no regard for the newspaper at all. Their allegiance was to a union, not a newspaper. The *Herald Tribune* kept losing readers to the immense *Times* and, worse, to nowhere. The labor situation was implausible. There was a 114-day strike in 1962, a 10-day shutdown and threats of others in 1965. This spring, the *Tribune* was merged into a corporation with two afternoon papers, the *World-Telegram & Sun* and the *Journal American*. The corporation planned to publish the *Herald Tribune* in the morning, plus an afternoon and a Sunday paper. On April 24, another strike started. This one was 113 days old when the corporation announced it wouldn't bring back the *Herald Tribune*.

The paper came to an end at 5 P.M. on an oppressive, crowded Monday in Manhattan. The sidewalk outside the old *Herald Tribune* building on West 41st Street was cluttered with the television camera equipment and cables that workmen were running inside the building where the announcement of the paper's close was being made.

A woman paused at the subway entrance at the front of the building. "What's all this for?" she said.

"The *Tribune*," a man with her said. "Didn't you hear it on the radio before? The *Trib* is closing."

She looked at the Old English sign on the building. "Oh,

isn't that a shame?" she said. Then she began to talk about something else while she went into the subway.

Upstairs, on the ninth floor, John Hay "Jock" Whitney, the millionaire who had owned the paper since 1958, stood at a lectern in a steaming auditorium. His forehead was wet in the heat from the television lamps. His hands shook a little. His shoes kept shifting—the highly polished, black plain-toed shoes rich men seem to like. He spoke in a tight voice, "I have never been involved in a more difficult or painful decision. . . ."

It was the first time in his life that he had lost at anything big.

Actually, the newspaper was finished long before last week. Once it was a larger and far better-written paper than the *Times*. Over the years, its writers and reporters had been such as John O'Hara, St. Clair McKelway, Don Skene and Joel Sayre. You could find lines of writing in the *Herald Tribune* such as Joe H. Palmer's ". . . he was living in an apartment with a lady who may have been his wife."

The paper was then owned by the elder Ogden Reid. When he died in 1947, first his widow and then his two sons ran it. By 1957, the once highly readable, beautifully made-up newspaper looked as if it were being published in a flophouse. The paper was broke. The *Herald Tribune*, always considered the voice of the Republican party in the East, was important politically to Jock Whitney. He put the first millions from his complex fortune into the paper, then took it over.

He took over a newspaper that was down to running a gossip column on the front page and had a once-famous sports section now featuring a woman writer. The gossip columnist went. Stanley Woodward, the sports editor who had brought Red Smith and Joe Palmer to New York, and then had been fired by the Reids, was immediately reinstalled. "Well, I fired the broad," Woodward said proudly on one of his first days back at work.

Whitney, involved personally, ran the paper with great class and grace. The *Herald Tribune* still had Walter Lippmann, Joseph Alsop, Art Buchwald and Red Smith as writers. Whitney almost had a shot at success. With energy and money behind it, the *Herald Tribune* reached a circulation of 411,000 and was gaining a thousand copies a week by the fall of 1962.

Then cold, unimaginative Bertram Powers, head of the

printers' union, pulled a general newspaper strike. "To a printer," Powers says, "a newspaper is just another factory job. One is the same as the other." His strike lasted 114 days and settled nothing. When the *Herald Tribune* came back, its circulation had evaporated. It takes a long time for a newspaper to seep into a person's life and become a habit. The *Tribune*'s new readers had not been with the paper long enough. They forgot it over 114 days. The losses in money were huge, close to $5 million a year. A merger now was the only way out.

After three years, the *Herald Tribune* and the two afternoon papers announced the largest press merger in U.S. history. The new corporation was to begin publishing on Monday, April 25. The night before, during a steady rain, pickets of the New York Newspaper Guild came onto the street. Behind the Guild were nine other unions which had not signed contracts. There was no *Herald Tribune* the next morning. What Columnist Red Smith calls "the spectacular immaturity, the complete childishness of labor-management relations in the newspaper business" started.

The newspaper, which was a kind of person, was left in a big, empty office and by the time anybody came back to look for it, it was gone.

Right away, the staff began to break up. Fifteen reporters went to the *Times*. Doug Kiker, the Washington writer, came into New York with his hair slicked down and he went to NBC to have lunch. Andrew J. Glass was around Capitol Hill as a reporter for Newsweek. By the time the decision to close the paper was made, 65% of them had left.

While this was going on, the negotiations with the Guild went nowhere. Three newspaper staffs had to be merged into two. A total of 712 editorial employes was involved. The number had to be cut to somewhere around 500. The Guild insisted on a straight seniority system for picking those to be retained. But the *Herald Tribune*'s only asset, its young staff, would have been wrecked under a seniority system—its racing writer, Peter Axthelm, was a smashing 22.

But the Newspaper Guild in New York is comprised 70% of business department workers. The union's head, Thomas Murphy, is a former bookkeeper for the *Times*. His knowledge of the product of a newspaper—the thinking and writing—is by hearsay. He appeared at sessions for bargaining over reporters with a five-man negotiating team. None had ever worked in a city room.

And one morning, in the early part of the strike, James G. Bellows, the 43-year-old *Herald Tribune* editor, came into a third-floor room in the Hotel Commodore in Manhattan to make a fight for his newspaper. He spoke quietly to Murphy. "Now, we can't have straight seniority in the *Herald Tribune* editorial staff because our requirements are different from a circulation department."

"We're all the same in our union," Murphy said. "We're all just composing room helpers."

"No, you don't see it," Bellows said. "We need certain talent. We have to buck up against the *Times* every morning."

"That's your fault that the *Times* got ahead of you, not ours," Murphy said.

"What I'm talking about here," Bellows said to Murphy, "is survival of the *Herald Tribune*. Don't you care if this paper lives?"

"That's your worry, not ours," Murphy said.

Finally, with nine unions signed, the pressmen, the 10th and last, were demanding things given to them by no other paper. The union president, William J. Kennedy, a nondrinking bachelor, had political problems in his union. They were far more important to him than the *Herald Tribune*. While Kennedy sat, Matt Meyer, the president of the merged corporation, drafted a memo recommending that the *Herald Tribune* be dropped.

Last week, Whitney got up and read his statement and the paper was gone. Reporters kept asking questions. The people who had worked for the *Herald Tribune* sat bleak-faced and silent. For them, it was a wake. It's funny when a newspaper folds. It means your job is gone. It means you may never have things the same in your life again. For some of these people, the news editors in their 50s, it meant cold economic loss at a point in their lives when there is no way to make it up. These were the last things anybody was thinking about. All they wanted, the people in this room, was for this paper that had lived in class to go out in class.

"Good," Jim Bellows, the editor, said quietly to somebody with him. "He was worried about this and here he's doing it just beautifully."

Jock Whitney is the only millionaire I ever rooted for. The guy hired me while I was drunk at a bar. He seemed to think my conduct was a mark of excellent character. His behavior as an employer only improved from then on.

There was one day about two years ago when Whitney sat in an editorial conference and looked at a folder containing a large series of articles that were being worked up. The articles were about Republicans in New York State who were practicing the art of thievery while in office. Whitney looked through the copy. Names of people he knew, or who were associated with friends of his in Republican politics, kept appearing in the copy. He shook his head. In virtually any newspaper in this country, the shake of the publisher's head while he's looking at this kind of copy means the stories are dead. But Jock Whitney put down the folder and stood up and said, "Well, battle stations, everybody." He walked out of the room and the series ran.

Last week, when Whitney finished talking, I went down to where the city room used to be. It was dark and bare and filthy and boxes of telephone company equipment were scattered around the floor. Fred Shapiro, who was a rewriteman and now works for *The New Yorker*, walked over to the drinking fountain. He turned it on. The water splashed onto the floor.

"Now it works," he said. In the summer, or when you had a hangover, the only two times a human *really* requires water, the *Tribune* fountain was sure not to work.

In one corner of the city room was this big musty conference room. It was covered with soot which seeps in through the window frames. It used to be a helluva place. It had a carpet and a big couch and a private bathroom and walnut table desks put together to form a conference table. I weaseled into the place from a desk in the city room one day. Nobody threw me out, so I started to use it every day. After a while I began to believe it was mine and I went around telling everybody, "If you want me, I'm in my private office."

Right outside the door, Walter Kerr, the drama critic, would sit at the typewriter, coughing nervously, his hands moving back and forth while he tried to figure out which keys he wanted to hit. He had an hour and 10 minutes to make the paper. His wife, Jean Kerr, would sit on the couch in my personal office. Jim Bellows would come in with my copy in his hands and say, "Now look, I don't want you to make yourself look bad by going off here." Always with class. He would take a chance that would raise your hair, too. It was a beautiful way to work and now the room was dark and stuffy and I wanted to get out of there.

August 26, 1966

Hero of '54 World Series Watches '66 Epic from Prison Bench

HUNTSVILLE, TEX.—Henry Thompson, like all convicts, thinks only of the good days he had on the outside. Henry Thompson sits in the day room of the Ferguson prison farm of the Huntsville Penitentiary and watches the World Series on television and remembers the big days of his life so clearly that he begins to see them on the screen in front of him.

He sits there in his white prison uniform. It has "Thompson 174819" stenciled on the front of the shirt. He sits and he watches Junior Gilliam of the Dodgers and Brooks Robinson of the Orioles playing third base. But he keeps thinking about something else and, right in front of him on the screen another game comes on.

It is the ninth inning of the fourth game of the 1954 World Series and a player named Dale Mitchell is at bat for the Cleveland Indians. A left-hander, John Antonelli, is pitching for the Giants, they were the New York Giants then. Antonelli lifts his leg to throw. Mitchell swings. He hits a little pop fly into foul ground off third base. The Giants' third baseman is Henry Thompson. He goes for the ball. Thompson goes for it with both hands out and his body bent over and he skids on his knees and makes the catch. He jumps up and begins shouting and holding his hands up in the air. The Giants have won the World Series in four games.

Then Henry Thompson thinks of the plane ride home from Cleveland. Everybody was swallowing champagne and talking about the World Series money that was coming to them, $11,000 each for four games of baseball.

Then somebody in the day room says something. Henry Thompson's mind comes back to prison and he starts watching the ball game again.

Now Thompson is just a guy with a number, a holdup man serving a 10-year sentence, and if you want him, they send a guard after him and they walk him right into the prison office for you.

"How are you?" he was asked.

"I'm doin' real fine," he said. He shifted his feet. He had on white sneakers and he kept looking at them. He was a little nervous, a little embarassed, a little unsure of himself.

"Do you see the games?"

"We get to see them here. Uh huh, yes, we see the games."

"Did you see Willie Davis make all those errors?"

"He just lost the balls in the sun and got rattled, that's all," he said. "It could happen to anybody, you know that."

Finally he stopped talking and looked down at his hands.

"Hank's been a real good inmate," E. D. Hutto, the assistant warden, said. "We use him as an athletic instructor for the 17 to 21-year-olds who are in here as first offenders."

"I come up for parole next month," Thompson said.

"How long have you been here?"

"Thirty-three months," he said quietly.

This was a tough 170-pound third baseman who hit left handed. He came to the Giants in 1949. He was part of the great pennant finish of 1951. He started the World Series against the Yankees as a right fielder. By 1954, he was as good a third baseman as you could want.

The trouble, however, was whisky. The newspapers called him "Hammerin' Hank." But around the bars, he was "Sportin' Henry" and he went for everything he had in his pocket. By 1956, his hands shook and the whisky was in his legs and he was through. The big baseball salaries, $25,000 and $32,000 a year, were gone. Henry tried to keep sportin' it. He went to the gun to get the money. He was arrested for a stickup in Harlem. He wound up in Houston. On a Saturday afternoon, July 13, 1963, he walked into a liquor store and broke out a gun and took $270 out of the place. The detectives caught up with him that night.

Now, sitting in the office in the prison, he said there was no reason to feel sorry for him.

"I didn't even bother with a trial," he said. "I was guilty and that was that. When they said I could cop out to 10 years I did it. Don't make this out as any mistake. I'm here on account of I'm guilty . . .

"It happened at the right time," Thompson said. "The road

I was on, all messed up with drinking, I could've wound up anywhere. I got my head straightened out now. Everything's going to be all right."

He got up and shook hands. Later in the day, he'd watch the World Series and see himself on television, skidding on his knees with that pop fly in his hands. Guys in prison can sit there and see the good days of their lives very clearly.

October 9, 1966

Will All Those Kids Vote for Bobby?

NEW YORK—It is a very simple thing. In the next five years, there will be 26 million new voters in America. Twenty-six million voters who are 21, 22 and 23 years old. To see what this means, you do not have to know politics and its issues and its newspaper words, "pragmatic" and "dogmatic" and "his own particular brand of liberalism" and "power base." All you have to do is stand around where there are groups of these young kids growing up. And then put down "26 million" on a sheet of paper and remember what it means.

To see this, you can go anywhere. To the Greek theater at the University of California campus at Berkeley. Or to Des Moines or North Tonawanda, N.Y., or any of the places where they are being brought up recognizing the name of only one politician in this country. You can see it, as well as anywhere, on a cold fall afternoon in New York City.

Robert Kennedy's hands fidgeted with the folded sheet of paper. On top of the sheet, in IBM electric typewriting, were the words, "FRANK J. VIOLA, BRONX POSTMASTER." Kennedy unfolded the sheet. There was a short biography of Viola put into the form of remarks. Around Kennedy, in the afternoon gloom in the post office lobby, the politicians stood in a semicircle. People sat in front of them on wooden folding chairs.

A man was at a microphone talking to the people. "He'll make you a very, very fine postmaster of which the Bronx can be very proud," the man said.

Frank J. Viola, a carnation in his lapel, stood in the semicircle. Kennedy stepped up and spoke. His hands, red from the cold, had the hint of nerves in them. His voice had very little modulation. The lobby of the Bronx General Post Office was not Robert Kennedy's world.

Outside, Kennedy got into the front seat of a white four-door Lincoln convertible. He sat sideways. Bill Barry, a wide-shouldered guy in his late 30s, was driving.

Earl Graves, who works in Kennedy's New York office, sat in the back. A photographer was next to him. There always is a photographer from some place sitting in the back of a car Kennedy is in.

Graves took a sheet of paper out of his inside pocket. "SEN-ATOR KENNEDY'S SCHEDULE," the electric typewriting said. Under it was a list of times and places. Graves studied it.

"I'd like a milkshake," Kennedy said. "Can we find a Schrafft's? Where is the stop?"

"Manhattan and Nassau in Brooklyn," Graves said.

"You won't find a Schrafft's there," Barry said.

"Why Schrafft's?" the photographer said.

"I don't know; I like ice cream," Kennedy said.

His fingers began to drum on the dashboard. He talked about his Newfoundland sheepdog messing the late Sen. Harry Byrd's office rug. Barry drove the car across the Triborough Bridge and on an expressway into Brooklyn. The car came off the expressway and through factory streets and into Greenpoint.

"We're about 15 minutes early," Graves said. "And there's a place right over there—see?—where we can get a milkshake."

Kennedy was looking across the window at the park. The place was McCarron Park, a big stretch of soot-darkened grass and black dirt. Off on the other side, a football team was practicing.

"Bring me some tea over to the football practice," he said.

Barry got out of the car on the other side and walked next to Kennedy. At the low black iron fence, Kennedy did a skip step and hurdled it. On the grass on the other side, he began to trot. His hands were stuck in the pockets of a gray form-fitting topcoat. He trotted across the grass with the photographer running behind him.

It was 5:30 P.M. and the street lights around the park were on. The offensive team was in the huddle, the substitutes standing behind them.

One of the coaches turned around and you could see "St. Francis" printed on the back of the parka.

"This must be St. Francis Prep," somebody behind Kennedy said. "They're about the only school in the city that knows how to play football."

"Good," he said. "I like to see the good ones."

A head looked up from the huddle for a moment. Just the head. The eyes under the helmet looked at this person with his hands in the topcoat pocket and the bleak and bony face and the deliberately cut long hair falling up and down onto the forehead with the motion of his body.

The boy in the huddle stood straight up now and looked at Robert Kennedy. The boy's mouth came open. Then his hand automatically reached for the one next to him in the huddle. The other one straightened up and looked around. And now they all looked up, and the substitutes began pushing to see who was coming.

"Never mind me, let's see you run the play," Bobby Kennedy calls out.

The coach steps forward. "All right, let's get back to business," he says.

The heads go down into the huddle. On the defense, a linebacker calls out, "All right, come on, let's show him how we do it."

"They're very big," Kennedy says.

"Hut one," the quarterback says.

"Senator Kennedy, I'm Vince O'Connor, the coach," a guy wearing glasses and a baseball cap says.

". . . two . . . hut three."

The quarterback starts dropping back and there is a slap as both lines go into each other. The pass is sharp, and the right halfback grabs it in full stride and races past a linebacker.

"They're good," Kennedy says. He turns to the coach. "Who are the best ones?"

"We have a tackle, Anthony DiNardo, Senator. He's been all prep school twice. Ivy League schools want him."

"Which one is he?" Kennedy says.

O'Connor points to two thick legs in the huddle.

"Then we have a halfback who is going to break the all-time city record. Richie Szaro. He's only here three years from Poland."

"Really? Where? Which one is he?"

They run Szaro on a play that looks like an inside reverse. He comes slapping through the hole, spinning off a hand that grabs him and he flies over the black dirt and runs the play out.

"Terrific," Kennedy says. "What are his marks like?"

"He has the potential to go to an Ivy League school, Senator," O'Connor says.

Kennedy smiles. "Harvard spoke to us about him."

"Isn't that wonderful?" Kennedy says to Graves. "Only here three years from Poland and look at how he can play and what he has in front of him. I think that's terrific." A Kennedy immigration bill is what he is talking about.

It was cold, and it was becoming almost too dark to follow the ball. They did not talk to each other, these high school kids and the politician. There were no autographs or handshakes. There was just the high school kids running their football play and Robert Kennedy watching them and the thing that was there between them was so strong you could feel it.

It needed no words or handshakes or adulation. It was an attraction that is so basic it can never be broken, and it starts with the millions of color pictures of John Fitzgerald Kennedy hanging on the walls of the houses in this country.

Now nobody who started in life delivering magazines in a chauffeured car, as Robert Kennedy did, can ever really come all the way down to us and become one of the kids from the candy store in Greenpoint. Bobby Kennedy never had to make rent, or even meet a payroll, in his life. He comes with some of these things the rich have, a little cold, a little automatic, a little standoffish. After all, the guy is, despite the slobbering over him in print, the son of a millionaire.

But when he stands on a football field with kids, you can forget everything. Forget issues and names and faces and polls and surveys and anything else they base politics on. The thing Bobby Kennedy has and he is the only one who has it, is that strong.

Somebody came running across the field waving. "They're ready now," the guy called out.

Kennedy turned and shook hands with the coach and began running across the field to the place he had to be. The heads came out of the huddle and watched him go.

Later, in his 14th floor apartment in the U.N. Towers, Kennedy sat with his shirt sticking out of his pants and a vodka on the rocks in his hand.

"Weren't they good?" he was saying. "That boy from Poland. I can't get over him. Here only three years and he can play so well. He has all these marvelous things in front of him."

St. Francis Prep played against Chaminade High School on

Sunday at a place called Boys High Field, which is in Brooklyn. Richie Szaro kicked a 45-yard field goal and scored on that play which seems to be an inside reverse.

When the game was over, the St. Francis kids crowded into a narrow locker room that had a low cement ceiling. They had won easily. The kids grabbed the doors of the green metal lockers and began to bang them in rhythm.

"We're number one, we're number one," they chanted.

They stopped chanting and broke into a cheer when O'Connor, the coach, walked in. O'Connor was holding the game ball over his head.

"Senator Kennedy," the kids yelled. "The ball goes to Senator Kennedy."

They yelled it loud. Young faces, streaked with mud from a game, young faces of boys 16 and 17 and 18 and 19. The same young faces that are all over the country and the only name they know in politics is Robert Kennedy, the President's brother.

Young faces, and some of them will be 21 in 1968 and all of them will be 21 in 1972, and this is not a story about politics, it is a story about simple arithmetic.

December 3, 1966

Home Folks "Treat" a Hero Too Well

ALL DAY the helicopters came down out of the terrible sun to pick up the wounded who were wrapped in bandages with blood coming through and the dead whose bodies were in chunks inside ponchos. The red sand began to blow when a helicopter came low.

The men standing in the sand ducked their heads and squinted and tried to see the helicopter. The men had orange faces from the sand. Their teeth were coated with sand which could not be licked away by their tongues.

They looked to see if the helicopter had brought any water. There had been no water since noon the day before. It was 137 degrees and the Marines had no water,

They were 12 miles south of Chulai in a place where the black mountains come down to the sea. It was here, under this terrible sun, that the Marines fought the first sizable battle of the war in Vietnam.

The date was Aug. 18, 1965. The ones who fought had faces that were very old but spoke in voices that were very young. They were 18 and 19 and 20, but their eyes were deep in their faces and their faces were drawn and they had been changed forever in one day of heavy killing.

"How are you?"

"All right I guess," one of the two Marines in the foxhole said.

"There's only 50, 60 of us left out of company," the other one in the foxhole said. "There was nothin' and then we come up to this trench line and the sons of bitches was set in all around us."

"We lost guys bad. The captain was killed right away."

"We would of lost more guys except Cpl. O'Malley come off a tank and got into the trench."

"Where is O'Malley now?" they were asked.

"I don't know. He got hit and they took him out some place."

The next day, there was this lieutenant sitting on a cot in the sand, reading a note written in pencil on two pages of blue-lined school composition paper. The lieutenant shook the paper to get the sand off it.

"To whom it may concern:

Statement by LCpl. James H. Kremer 2097274 3d Squad, 1st Platoon "I" Co. 3d Bn. 3 Marines.

On the morning of 18 August, our sqd. was security force for the tanks attached to our unit, for support.

The 3 tanks we were on pulled ahead of the co. by 200–300 meters. We were brought under heavy enemy fire from a trench line a few feet away from where the tanks stopped. We were instantly pinned down by the enemy. We were in a tight situation, as we had one man seriously injured on a tank.

Our squad ldr. Cpl. R. E. O'Malley ran across a rice paddy while under heavy enemy fire and jumped into the trench line on our left flank, from where we were receiving heavy enemy fire. Within a matter of a couple of minutes, Cpl. O'Malley had stopped all fire coming from our left flank, along the trench line. Cpl. O'Malley was wounded in the arm during his actions along this trench line.

Cpl. O'Malley, showing his fine leadership abilities, kept our hopes built high when we were pinned down. In my estimation, Cpl. O'Malley is a fine leader and Marine, showing this, and more, during his squad's actions on this operation.

Last December, 16 months after the sand and the heat and the Marines with those old faces and young voices, the newspapers in New York all had front-page pictures of Lyndon Johnson placing the Medal of Honor around the neck of Sgt. Robert E. O'Malley of Woodside, Queens, New York City. After that, there were stories about a big beer party, with bagpipers, in the back room of a saloon in Woodside.

During the holidays, the Orange Bowl football game in Miami was on television and the announcer was saying that Sgt. Robert E. O'Malley, the Medal of Honor winner, was coming onto the field. On the screen, a Marine in full-dress uniform, with the blue ribbon and the medal around his neck, marched stiffly between rows of flags. Everybody cheered him. He saluted while they played the Star-Spangled Banner.

I got up and went to the closet in the bedroom and fumbled through the notebooks on the floor. In the middle of one notebook was scrawling which said, "To whom it may concern: Statement by LCpl James H. Kremer . . ."

I brought the notebook back and sat down and watched O'Malley drop his salute at the end of the Star-Spangled Banner. The crowd gave another big cheer. It was for O'Malley. But it was also because the crowd knew the field was going to be cleared and the college football players from Florida and Georgia Tech would come out.

The people were there for a college football game. Sgt. O'Malley and his medal were part of the pre-game show, along with four bands and a girl who was the Orange Bowl Queen. I looked at him marching on the television set and I didn't like it. I didn't know him. But I thought, this kid shouldn't be parading around a field before a football game. The notebook in my hand said he was too big for a thing like this.

I called Robert O'Malley's house two days later. "He should be back tonight," a woman's voice said. I called him for a couple of days and he still wasn't home from Miami. When I called on a Sunday night, he answered the phone.

"Well, we're having a christening now," he said slowly. "And later I have to meet somebody."

"Oh, you'll be busy then?"

"Well, I think I will. I told a girl I'd meet her at the Play Lounge."

"What time?"

"Later on. When I get there, I'll be there."

The Play Lounge is a place a couple blocks off Queens Boulevard in Woodside. It is a dim, barren place with a long bar and a dance floor with luncheonette tables set around it. The sign on the bandstand says, "The Four Peps Featuring Louis the Bird." The Four Peps come over the speaker system so loudly your ears hurt.

The bartender leaned over.

"Yours?" he yelled.

"Is O'Malley here? He's the Marine who . . ."

The bartender pointed at two young guys who were standing and drinking. Two girls with them sat on barstools with their backs to the bar and shook their heads to the music.

"Bob O'Malley?"

He nodded his head yes. He was short, with eyes that were set deeply into a funeral face. He held a green stirrer between his teeth. He snapped his fingers to the music. A drink of mixed whisky and four dollar bills were on the bar in front of him.

On the back bar was a picture pasted on cardboard of President Johnson putting the medal around his neck. Over the picture, black crayon printing said, "!!WELCOME!! TO OUR CONGRESSIONAL MEDAL OF HONOR WINNER SGT. ROBERT E. O'MALLEY."

He had on a severely cut, tight-fitting gray suit. A blue rosette for his medal was in the lapel.

"How was it in Miami?"

"Great," O'Malley said. "They give me a '67 Fury to use and then a '67 Dodge. The cops stopped me five times. I told them who I was. Shooo. They told me good luck."

"He said who he was only when he was going to get a ticket," Jimmy said. "That's the only time he said anything. Bobby don't capitalize right on what he got."

One of the girls, dark-haired and in tight slacks, leaned forward. "Tell him what the major down in Miami said to Bobby. The major said, 'You done a service to your country and you should never have to pay for anything again in your life.' That's what you told me the major said, isn't it, Jimmy?"

"That's what he said," Jimmy said. "But Bobby, he don't listen."

A dark-haired man named Nick, who owns the place, came up. "Hey, Bobby, let me buy you a drink for New Year's. Geez, I seen ya on the television."

"Did you?"

"Yeah, I was sittin' there and I says, geez, look who's on the television. It's Bobby. Did you have a good time?"

"They give me the key to the city," O'Malley said.

"How do you feel?" he was asked.

He made a face. "My chest, I got hit in the lung and it bothers me sometimes. The day we had all the smog here, 61 per cent smog or something, I couldn't get out of bed practically all day. The breathing was too hard."

"If he don't eat breakfast, he's all right," Jimmy said. "But if he eats, he has to go right in and throw up. He coughs so much in the morning he can't keep food down."

O'Malley kept lighting cigarettes with a big-flamed lighter he kept in the breast pocket of his shirt.

"The cigarettes won't do you any good," he was told.

He made a face and said nothing. He was telling you to keep your advice to yourself.

He and Jimmy and the girls began to look at each other. O'Malley nodded to the girl.

"We're going some place now," he said to me. "I'll see you someday in the week."

"Where will you be tomorrow?"

"Tomorrow I have to go to the veterans for an examination," he said.

"Then where do you go?"

"I think I'll go to the Allied Chemical office. They wrote me and told me to come in and see them and they would give me a job and send me to college."

He thought for a moment. "Do you know Frank Scott?" he said.

"The agent for ballplayers?"

"Yes. Somebody sent me to him. He is getting me on shows and things. Call him up. He knows the appointments I have to keep."

"Say, tell me," he was asked. "How long have you been home now?"

"Since April."

"April? April's a long time ago. What were you doing from April until the President gave you the medal last month?"

"I worked two days. I worked one day as a bartender. Then I shaped up another at a whisky distillery."

"What have you been doing with all your time?"

He pointed to the bar and smiled.

"This," he said.

The next morning, a man named Reilly checked all the departments in the Veterans Administration building on Seventh Avenue. He could find no record of an appointment for O'Malley. Frank Scott, the agent, said over the phone that O'Malley was due at the offices of Goodson-Todman, the television producers, at 1:30 P.M. He was to have a briefing and then go to a studio and tape the quiz show, "To Tell the Truth."

The Goodson-Todman offices are on the 10th floor of the Seagram Building on Park Avenue. At 1:30, a dark-haired girl sat at a reception desk at Goodson-Todman and looked at the appointment schedule, which said, "Robert O'Malley," and then she looked at the elevator bank.

A few minutes later, a man opened a door at one side of the reception room.

"No?" he said.

"No," the girl said.

At 2:30, Wally Segal, one of the producers of the show, came out and leaned against the wall. He watched the elevator bank in silence. A few minutes later, Willie Stein, another producer, came out of another door.

"Our first show in color and we've got to have this," Willie Stein said.

At 4:05 P.M., the doors opened and a man in a camel hair coat came out. It wasn't O'Malley.

Willie Stein thought. "Are you sure there isn't another Medal of Honor winner in New York?"

"Not as good as this one. How about a window washer?"

"I'd take that," Willie Stein said. "Guy washes windows at the top of the Empire State Building. Washes the 102d floor. I'd take that."

Willie Stein turned and went inside to his office. "The Medal of Honor story is out," he was saying to somebody. "We'll have a window washer."

Wally Segal gave one last look at the elevators. "This is the first time in ten years that somebody hasn't shown up," he said. "I can't understand him."

At 4:50 P.M. Robert O'Malley was in the White House, a saloon two blocks down from Queens Boulevard in Sunnyside. He had been there for an hour. Brendan Brick, the bartender, was passing a whisky sour out to him.

"You're missing that show," O'Malley was told.

"It's not today, it's next week," he said.

"It's today. They've been waiting all afternoon."

"No, it's next week."

"I don't want to argue with you. But why don't you let me call them and put you on with them and you see for yourself?"

"No, it's next week," he said.

That closed it. He is the withdrawn kind who uses very few words unless he wants to. Silent Irish.

O'Malley took out a cigarette. His hand shook while he put it in his mouth. He put his hand into his shirt pocket and brought out the lighter. The lighter shook badly while he manipulated it. He smoked the cigarette in short, nervous motions.

"What time did you get in last night?" he was asked.

"Seven-thirty this morning."

"What did you do after you left me in that Play Lounge?"

"We went to another place. The Pig and Whistle."

The Pig and Whistle is in the Inwood section of Manhattan, which is mainly Irish. If O'Malley got home late from the Pig and Whistle, his hands were not shaking because of a war.

He walked over to the window. Outside, 48th Avenue was getting dark.

"They won't miss me anyway," O'Malley said.

"But they were waiting for a long time."

"People take me here, they take me there, I'm tired of being supposed to be someplace. They made me go to the Ed Sullivan Show. They told me I was supposed to get paid for it. I go there and they have me stand up. I didn't get any money for it. I didn't say anything about it. But they shouldn't of told me I was going to get paid when I wasn't going to get paid. Somebody's always telling me something."

Men in working clothes came past the window. They were steamfitters like Jack McMahon, who came into the White House. Or bricklayers who went into the Command Post a block down. Or into the Green Castle, or any of the other saloons which line 48th Avenue. The place they call Sunnyside is a place where working Irish live. And the Irish use saloons as an extra living room.

Robert O'Malley has spent his life in Sunnyside. His father and mother came here from Newport, in County Mayo. The father works the 4–12 shift at Railway Express.

Robert O'Malley went to Aviation High School, a trades school. His marks were the marks common to nearly all the kids who go into the Marines when they are 18 and 19 and 20. But the Marines found that he could, casually and for hours, stand up and do the highest thing a human being is capable of: risk his life to save others.

He jumped into a trench where heavy Vietcong firing was coming from. Standing in a narrow space, with people who would kill him only feet away, he emptied his rifle into Vietcong in the trench. He jumped out to reload. Then he jumped back in, firing again. When he had finished, he had killed eight. A unit which had been pinned down and was having men killed by the firing from the trench was freed.

O'Malley was wounded in the arm and ankle. A piece of shrapnel went through his chest and into his lung. He kept firing at another trench line which had a Marine unit pinned down. He began helping to evacuate wounded. He refused to be evacuated himself until the last man in his outfit was taken care of.

"Tell me," he was asked one afternoon, "the one thing that comes to you right away about the whole experience."

He started talking automatically.

"When I couldn't save my friend who got shot off the tank. Two guys with him just jumped off and left him there. I went up to him and I was putting a battle dressing on him. He was shot in the ass, but the bullet went up inside his stomach.

"I was putting a dressing on the wound and he was asking me, 'Am I going to make it?' I was telling him, 'When you get home, all the girls will want to see your battle wound and you'll have to drop your pants to show them.' And then this chicken yellow bastard, one of the guys who had left him, come back and he started moaning, 'Oh, he's going to die, he's going to die.' I had to stop putting the dressing on and get up and give this yellow bastard a knock to keep his mouth shut.

"The corpsman came along and I told him the fellow needed plasma. The corpsman looked at him and said, 'No, he's all right.' He went away. I had to go. By the time somebody got my friend out of there, he was dead. That's the thing I remember. I couldn't save him."

While he spoke, he looked right at you and there was this little brightness in his eyes. A fire. And his voice was a tone different. It was hard. You looked at him while he talked and you could see that, yes, this must be one hell of a guy to be with when there is trouble. And there was something else. He was telling the story about winning the Medal of Honor, but the story was about somebody else.

The problem is that O'Malley is a man who has achieved greatness, and at the same time, he is a 23-year-old. People regard him as a man. They sit O'Malley next to Gen. Omar Bradley at a dinner, and they expect O'Malley to fit right in, and instead O'Malley sits there bored and silent.

He doesn't know who Omar Bradley is. Bradley was in a war that was being fought before O'Malley was born. O'Malley wants to do the jerk to the Four Peps and Louie the Bird. He doesn't want to sit with an old general he has never heard of.

"You've got to learn how to meet people better than you're doing," somebody said to O'Malley after the dinner. "Do you realize who that was you were sitting next to?"

O'Malley was irritated.

And O'Malley looks at most things with the viewpoint of a 23-year-old. When he received the medal, many firms wrote him letters offering jobs. He felt the letters indicated he would get something special from the firms. But when he went to see a couple of them, he found he was being offered jobs he felt anybody could get. Trainee's positions. And he was being questioned about what he was capable of doing. He didn't like it. He could not understand why they would write him, and then do this.

"He thinks people don't mean what they say," Tom Kelly was saying one day. Kelly is the president of the Congressional Medal of Honor club. He has been getting people he knows interested in O'Malley.

"He has all these people coming up to him," Kelly said, "and they shake his hand and say this and that, you know how people talk, and the boy has heard so many things that didn't happen the way he thought they should happen, he's starting to think people aren't sincere when they shake his hand. I think he's at crossroads right now. Somebody has to get things going the right way."

When he came home in April, he was unable to sleep for weeks. He stayed out as late as he could, hoping time, and a couple of drinks, would make him tired. Then April turned into June and July and August and there were places like the Hesch House in Long Beach, and Mann's in Rockaway Beach, and then it was fall and he was back in the White House in Sunnyside. And now it was winter and he was still there.

The old man had two teeth missing in the front of his mouth and he stood at the window of the White House and kept looking out. It was 2 o'clock in the afternoon, which is Robert O'Malley's time to check into the White House.

"Here's the hero now," the old man said. He went back to his barstool and put his hand on his money, ready to shove it toward Brendan Brick.

O'Malley walked in, and the man reached for his arm.

"Have a drink, Robert Emmet."

"Too early for me."

"Too early for you? No, you'll have a drink."

"I'll have a Coke."

"A Coke? A Coke for Robert Emmet? Never. You'll have a screwdriver, that's what you'll have. A large screwdriver."

O'Malley shrugged and said, yes, he'd have the screwdriver. It was 2 P.M. and somebody was putting vodka into him. And that night he went to Connecticut to a beer party in his honor. And on another night there was an American Legion affair, with a buffet and whisky, and the old Legion guys would give him a medal.

Then there was the United Irish Counties dinner-dance and the Custodial Engineers Union was planning a dinner in his honor. And there was something in Toots Shor's. He'd never been to Toots Shor's and he was going to go there, and the men there would give him these big drinks. And somebody from another Legion committee wanted him to attend a ceremony and the Medal of Honor Society had a function for him to attend.

For Robert O'Malley, everything has become a smoky hall with ice melting in the whisky while old men reach for his arm and say, "Here, son, come over here and have a drink at my table. You're a hero, you are. Have a drink with me on it."

"I don't like it," Brendan Brick was saying one afternoon. "Phony politicians and lobbygows takin' him around and pattin' his back and throwin' too many parties for him. The parties aren't for him. They're for the people throwing the parties who want to be hip by having Bobby come around."

"Have you ever read anything about other guys who have won the medal?" O'Malley was asked one day.

"I've read things," he said.

"Did you read about Ira Hayes?"

He nodded yes and said nothing.

"Yes, Ira Hayes," Brendan Brick said. "You tell him."

"Hayes was an Indian who was one of the Marines in the flag picture from Iwo Jima. They brought him back and took him around the country on a war bond tour. They kept getting him drunk, and when the war was over Hayes was helpless. He was a whisky bum. You know how he died? He drowned in his own vomit in the gutter."

O'Malley didn't say anything. He picked up some change and went back to make a phone call.

"He's smart," Dick Beyrer said. "He knows he has to go to college. He's spoken to me about going to college out of town. Ohio. He knows if he goes to college here, it'll be a party every day. Don't worry about him."

"The worry is the other people, not him."

O'Malley came back from a phone call. "I went up to Manhattan College and Brother James said he could give me some tests to see what my aptitude is. The Marines said they'd get me tutors. I need tutors for six subjects."

"When would you go to school, if you go?"

"Next September."

"That's a long time from now. That's time for a lot of parties."

He lives on the top floor of a two-family attached brick house ten blocks from the White House. His narrow bedroom is cluttered. A stack of color pictures of himself and Lyndon B. Johnson sits on the end of the bed. The President signed them, "To a great American."

In one of his bureau drawers, O'Malley has an ashtray. In it, among cufflinks and tie clasps, is a small piece of jagged, un-painted metal. It went into his lung in Vietnam. Doctors tell him it will be years before he is all right again. Right now, the lung can collapse on him any time.

Under a pile of papers on the bureau is a cardboard box with the stenciling on it saying, "Holder, One, Medal of Honor."

"They looked for me for weeks to tell me I was getting it," he said. "I was drifting around the country. They kept calling my house. When I called home here, they told me, 'Go to Washington. They want you for something.' I said I'd get there when I got there."

"Weren't you excited about the thing?"

"It was going on for so long. Sixteen months of —— over it. When I went to Washington and saw this major and some other people, they told me don't tell anybody about it because President Johnson wanted to announce it himself and if it got out first then I wouldn't get the medal. I said to myself I'll wait until I get it and then it'll mean something to me."

He picked up the box and took it with him. He had an affair to go to and the people had asked him to bring the medal with him so they could get excited over it and drink to its owner. He put it on the seat in his red Volkswagen and drove away for another night that would be late.

February 5, 1967

"Friendly Napalm" Changes Return Address on a Soldier's Letter

NEW YORK—The air mail envelope stuck into the mail box was smudged with light tan dirt that was very familiar. The return address was printed in pen:

> "SP/5 C. E. Schwartz,
> U.S. 51580424,
> B Co. 1/8 4th Inf. Div.
> APO S. F. 96285"

I didn't know the name of the sender, but the letter had an Army and Air Force postal service mark on it, and that and the dirt smudges showed it was from a soldier in Vietnam. I turned the letter over to open it. There was printing, in another hand, across the flap:

"THIS MAN DIE TODAY MAR. 22, '67."

A single sheet of paper was inside the envelope. The paper was smudged with tan dirt. A cigarette had nearly burned through the top of the paper. The first paragraph introduced the writer as being in the same platoon with a boy named Joe Grande, who had been killed in Vietnam a couple of weeks ago. The second paragraph read:

> "Joe Grande's death was an accident. Tragic as it may seem, one of our buddies died in a land none of us will understand. He died painlessly for a cause he was drafted to believe in. The question remains, why? But this as many others will have to wait for time to answer.
> Calvin Schwartz,
> And the Men of B 1/8."

A call was placed to the Pentagon in Washington. The operator gave the call to the Southeast Asia desk. A man who said his name was John Bellish answered the phone.

"Did you have an SP/5 Calvin Schwartz killed in Vietnam on March 22?" he was asked.

"Just a minute and I'll check," Bellish said.

He came back on the phone. "Yes, we have a man by that name. On March 22. We don't have any details. Just the next of kin listed."

"Who are they?"

"Mr. and Mrs. Frank Schwartz, address 1730 Carroll st., Brooklyn, New York."

"Thank you."

"Is that all you need?" Bellish asked.

"Yes, thank you."

A call was made to the Schwartzes. A woman answered.

"Is this the home of Calvin Schwartz?" she was asked.

"Yes, this is his mother," the woman said in a dull voice.

"Well, I have a letter here from your son and I thought maybe you'd want it."

"The boy died," she said.

"Yes, I know that. I don't know what to tell you."

"He died from our own napalm," she said. "Did you know that? He died from our own napalm. Why do they do it? Isn't it bad enough they get killed by the enemy? Do they have to die by our own mistakes?"

Her voice became very high and you could hear somebody talking to her, and then a man came on the phone.

"This is Frank Schwartz. I'm the boy's father," he said.

"How old was he?" he was asked.

"He was 20."

"Where did he go to school?"

"He went to P. S. 114 and he went to John Pershing High School. He was in the first class to go to the school, it was a new school then, and he was one of the ones who wrote the school constitution. Then he went to Rider College, in Jersey, you know. He was drafted, I know when he was drafted, too. He was drafted Nov. 22, 1965."

"How long had he been in Vietnam?"

"Exactly two months. He was due back here in August. Then on Friday morning, a sergeant came to the house and he said Calvin was missing. I said, oh, God forbid, but I had this feeling. Then Sunday night, the sergeant came back and said

Calvin was found. He was all burned up. He was caught by, ah, the, what do you call these bombs now . . ."

His voice went away from the phone and you could hear him calling out in the room he was in, "What was that thing they call about Calvin?" And you could hear a woman's voice, high and almost shouting.

He came back on the phone. "Yes, friendly napalm. You call it a friendly napalm bomb that killed my son. Burned him alive. I got this letter and he said, daddy, do me a favor and go to the optometrist and get me regular reading glasses and sunglasses. Then he said, daddy, I got the vitamins you sent me and they were swell and . . ."

He went off the phone for a moment. He came back on and said, "We don't know about the funeral yet. It's going to be at the Parkside Chapel on Coney Island Avenue, but we don't know when."

"Well, I can find that out when you have it," he was told.

"The letter," he said. "You could keep the letter if you would do one thing for us."

"Yes?"

"Put it in the paper that he was a very good son for us."

April 30, 1967

Namath All Night Long

THE BARMAID had long black hair and she was sitting on top of the bar with her chest coming out of her dress and her skirt useless against the amount of legs she was showing. She had her eyes shut and her hands held out in front of her.

"Excuse me," one of us said.

The barmaid didn't answer.

"Ah, may I ask you something?" I said.

The barmaid frowned. "Shhhhh. I'm driving my Jaguar."

"Oh," I said.

A girl in bell-bottom pants played the juke box and everybody in the place, Bachelors Three on Lexington Avenue in Manhattan, moved their heads with the music. Joe Namath is one of the owners of the place, and also one of its best customers.

"Well, I hate to bother you," I said to the barmaid, "but is Joe around?"

"Not now."

"Expect him?"

"He's at the Palm Bay Club right now. Here, get in. I'll drive you over."

The guy with me, a race track character whose name is Pepe, shook his head. "You know," he said to the barmaid, "I used to be considered a lunatic before kids like you came around."

Namath was found later at the Palm Bay Club. Later, because the Palm Bay Club is in Miami. In the world of Joe Willie Namath, location and time really don't matter. They are trying to call this immensely likeable 25-year-old by the name of Broadway Joe. But Broadway as a street has been a busted-out whorehouse with orange juice stands for as long as I can recall, and now, as an expression, it is tired and represents nothing to me. And it certainly represents nothing to Joe Willie Namath's people. His people are on First and Second Avenues, where young girls spill out of the buildings and into the bars crowded with guys and the world is made of long hair and tape cartridges and swirling color and military overcoats and the girls go home with guys or the guys go home with girls and nobody is too worried about any of it because life moves, it doesn't stand

still and whisper about what happened last night. It is out of
these bars and apartment buildings and the life of them that Joe
Willie Namath comes. He comes with a Scotch in his hand at
night and a football in the daytime and last season he gave New
York the only lift the city has had in so many years it is hard to
think of a comparison.

When you live in fires and funerals and strikes and rats and
crowds and people screaming in the night, sports is the only
thing that makes any sense. And there is only one sport anymore
that can change the tone of a city and there is only one player
who can do it. His name is Joe Willie Namath and when he
beat the Baltimore Colts he gave New York the kind of light,
meaningless, dippy and lovely few days we had all but forgotten.
Once, Babe Ruth used to be able to do it for New York, I guess.
Don't try to tell Namath's people on First Avenue about Babe
Ruth because they don't even know the name. In fact, with the
young, you can forget all of baseball. The sport is gone. But if
you ever have seen Ruth, and then you see Namath, you know
there is very little difference. I saw Ruth once when he came
off the golf course and walked into the bar at the old Bayside
course in Queens. He was saying how f'n hot it was and how f'n
thirsty he was and he ordered a Tom Collins and the bartender
made it in a mixing glass full of chopped ice and then handed
the mixing glass to Ruth and the Babe said that was fine, kid,
and he opened his mouth and brought up the mixing glass and
there went everything. In one shot, he swallowed the mixing
glass, ice chunks and everything else. He slapped the mixing
glass down and said, give me another one of these f'n things,
kid. I still never have seen anybody who could drink like that.
After that day, I believed all the stories they told about Ruth.

It is the same thing when you stand at the bar with Joe
Namath.

The Palm Bay Club is a private place with suites that can
cost you over $2,000 a month, and Namath lives through the
winter in one of the biggest, a place with a white leather bar
that many people say is the best bar in all of Miami, and a view
of sun splashing on blue water. When Joe Namath came to
his suite on this day, a guy he knew was taking up the living
room floor with a girl. Namath went politely past them into the

bedroom. Another guy he knew was there with a girl. Namath shrugged and left to play golf.

He walked around the Diplomat Presidential course in a blue rain jacket and with that round-shouldered, slouchy walk of the campuses and First Avenue. He had sideburns and a mustache and Fu Manchu beard and the thick, shaggy hair at the back of the neck which upsets older people so much, and therefore is a must with the young. I watched the Super Bowl game on television with 14-year-old twin boys, and Namath, slouchy and long-haired, came on after the game and said, "All these writers should take their notebooks and pencils and eat them." The two around me burst out of the chairs. "Yeah!" one of them yelled. "Yeah, Joe Willie! Outasight!" the other one yelled. It was Dustin Hoffman in *The Graduate* all over again. Screw the adults. I knew that Joe Namath was going to mean a lot more than merely the best football player of his time.

After he finished playing golf, Namath went right for the bar. He had his money up and was ordering whiskey while he kept looking at the people with him to make sure that they didn't get a chance to pay.

"I'm drinking a lot lately," he said.

"Do you drink a lot all the time?" he was asked.

"I might as well. I get the name for it whether I do it or not. In college, this fella Hoot Owl Hicks and I were out one night and we had two cans of beer in the car, that's all we had all night, and we're coming home in one of these four-door, no-door cars. Thing couldn't do over 35 miles an hour. But the Tuscaloosa cops stop us. They loved me. Huh. 'Hey, *Penn-syl-vania* kid.' I take the two beer cans and throw them out the car. There's a damn hill there and here come the two sonsofbitches rolling right back to the car. I grab the two cans and throw them back up again. They come rolling down again. The cop says, 'Hey, *Penn-syl-vania* kid, just leave 'em there. I said to the cop, 'You're a real piece of work. Now I know why mothers like you go on the police. Can't get a job nowhere else.' That did it. I got put in jail for being a common drunk."

"Do you drink during the football season?" he was asked.

"Just about all the time."

"What do you, taper off before the game?"

A grin spread from his mouth. His light green eyes had fun in them. "The night before the Oakland game, I got the whole family in town and there's people all over my apartment and the phone keeps ringing. I wanted to get away from everything. Too crowded and too much noise. So I went to the Bachelors Three and grabbed a girl and a bottle of Johnnie Walker Red and went to the Summit Hotel and stayed in bed all night with the girl and the bottle."

The Oakland game was in late December and it was for the American League championship. On Sunday morning, the Oakland Raiders football team, fresh-eyed from an early bed-check and a night's sleep, uniform-neat in their team blazers, filed into a private dining room in the Waldorf-Astoria for the pre-game meal. Meanwhile, just across the street in the Summit Hotel, Joe Willie Namath was patting the broad goodbye, putting an empty whiskey bottle in the wastebasket, dressing up in his mink coat and leaving for the ballgame. It was a cold, windy day and late in the afternoon Namath threw one 50 yards to Don Maynard and the Jets were the league champions. The Oakland team went home in their team blazers.

"Same thing before the Super Bowl," Namath said. "I went out and got a bottle and grabbed this girl and brought her back to the hotel in Fort Lauderdale and we had a good time the whole night."

He reached for his drink. His grin broke into a laugh. "It's good for you," he said. He held his arms out and shook them. "It loosens you up good for the game."

In the Super Bowl game, the Baltimore Colts were supposed to wreck Namath, and they probably were in bed dreaming about this all night. As soon as the game started, the Baltimore linemen and linebackers got together and rushed in at Namath in a maneuver they call blitzing and Namath, who doesn't seem to need time even to set his feet, threw a quick pass down the middle and then came right back and hit Matt Snell out on the side and right away you knew Baltimore was in an awful lot of trouble.

"Some people don't like this image I got myself, bein' a swinger," Namath was saying. "They see me with a girl instead of being home like other athletes. But I'm not institutional. I swing. If it's good or bad, I don't know, but I know it's what I like. It hasn't hurt my friends or my family and it hasn't hurt me. So why hide it? It's the truth. It's what the ___ we are.

"During the season, Hudson and I were drinking a lot and he said to me one day, 'Hey, Joe, we gotta stop all this drinkin'.' And I said, 'Jeez, yes. We'll stop drinking. Let's just drink wine.' Hudson said, no, we had to stop all the way. Well we did. So we don't drink and we go up to Buffalo and we lose, 37–35, and I got five interceptions. I go right into the dressing room and I tell Hudson, 'Jeez, let's not hear any more about not drinking.' Then before the Denver game, I had the flu and I didn't drink. Five interceptions.

"So we're in the sauna before the Oakland game, the first day we were working for the game and I'm saying, 'All right, fellas, this is the big one. Gotta win. Our whole season depends on it. Thinking about not drinking myself.' And Dave Herman yells, 'Jeez, don't do that. Do anything but don't you stop drinking. If you don't drink, I'll grab you and pour it down your throat.'"

Sonny Werblin, who had been on the phone, came back to the bar. He had been taking notes on a small pad. He showed the notes to Namath and spoke to him in a low voice. Sonny Werblin was the head of the Music Corporation of America and he was one of the five or six most important people in show business. He retired from MCA and bought into the New York Jets. In what clearly is the best move made in sports in my time, Werblin decided to base his entire operation on getting Joe Namath and making him a star. Last year, Werblin sold his part of the team. But Joe Namath still calls him "Mr. Werblin" and never "Sonny" and when something comes up in Joe's life, he asks Sonny Werblin about it.

Now, Namath sat and listened to Werblin.

"How much?" Namath asked.

Werblin said something and Namath nodded and they went back to their drinks.

A few minutes later, when everybody else was busy talking about something, Sonny Werblin said, "This thing I was showing him, it's about the movies. You see, I know he's a natural star. I mean, look at him. He's got the face and the eyes. Women'll tell you, bedroom eyes. He's got that animal sex appeal. I knew he was a star the minute I saw him. We'd been going around looking at All-American quarterbacks. They had one at Tulsa.

Jerry Rhome. He came into the room, a little, introverted guy. I said, nah, I don't want him. Never mind how good he is, I need to build a franchise with somebody who can do more than play. So we went down to Birmingham and the minute Joe walked into the room, I knew. I said, 'Here we go.' So what I'm doing now I've got picture offers for him, but I don't want any freaky thing just to cash in on him being a football player. I want to build a broad base for him. I heard about something just now. Paul Newman and Joanne Woodward are doing a film. We'll pay to get into it. We'll *pay* for the chance. I want him in with good actors, where he can look good. I don't want him over his head the first time with something we're doing just for the money. I couldn't care about money. I wouldn't touch a cent of anything I get for him. I just want to do it right for him."

We had to leave the golf club and drive over to a place called the Jockey Club. Before leaving, Namath ordered a round of drinks in plastic cups and everybody got into the car with the drinks. Joe Hirsch, the writer for the *Morning Telegraph*, was driving.

"I'm going up to Pensacola tonight," Namath said.

"Seeing Suzy?" somebody said.

"Yeah, I'll see her," he said.

"She is a lovely, very smart girl," somebody said.

"Is she your girl?" Joe was asked.

"I like her," he said. "She goes to college in Pensacola."

"What school?"

"Jeez, ah, Northern Florida something or other. It's a new college up there."

"Is she a senior?"

"I don't know. What is she, Joe?"

"She gets out this summer," Joe Hirsch said.

"Uh huh," Joe Willie Namath said.

There was a stop at a place with offices and Namath was walking through the hall and the elevator operator came after him and called out, "Mr. Namath, if you don't stop in this office, you'll break the heart of one of your biggest fans."

The operator led Namath to an office where a blonde in a pale yellow dress sat at a typewriter.

"Well, hi," Namath said.

"Hel-lo," the girl beamed.

"How are you?" Namath said.

"Fine," she said. "Do you remember me?"

"Of course I remember you." He repeated her name. She beamed. "You've got a good memory."

"Still got the same phone number?" She shook her head yes. "That's real good," Joe said. "I'll call you up. We'll have a drink or three."

"That'll be terrific," she said. "Like my hair the new way?"

"Hey, let me see," he said. He looked closely at her pile of blonde hair. She sat perfectly still so he could see it better. "It's great," Joe Namath said. She beamed. "See ya," he said.

Walking down the hall, Namath was shaking his head. "Boy, that was a real memory job. You know, I only was with that girl one night? We had a few drinks and we balled and I took her phone number and that's it. Never saw her again. Only one night with the girl. And I come up with the right name. A real memory job."

When the car got to the Jockey Club, Namath, who had been in the back seat, began to get out. Pulling himself by the hands, he got up, turned his body around and came out of the car backwards, hanging on, not moving for long moments while he waited for his two knees to adjust. Now you could see why Sonny Werblin worries about the right chance at the movies for him. All the laughs of Joe Namath are based, as laughs always are, on pain. And this is a kid who has made it to the top on two of the most damaged knees an athlete ever had. His next game could be the last. So today he swings.

In the Jockey Club, he drank Scotch on the rocks. When it was time for him to leave, he asked the bartender to give him a drink in a plastic cup so he could have something in the car. He shook hands and left to get the plane to Pensacola, where his girl friend goes to a school whose name he doesn't quite know.

April 7, 1969

The Baseball Encyclopedia

"THE BASEBALL ENCYCLOPEDIA" book is 2,337 pages of statistics that took two years to compile. The book is so heavy that the mailman bringing it to the house stumbled and suffered a severe groin injury. The statistics in the book are incredibly complete. On page 755, it shows that William Callahan DeKoning came to bat just once as a major league baseball player. That was in 1945, when he was a catcher with the New York Giants. All prior baseball record books show this fact. But "The Baseball Encyclopedia" goes even further. It shows that Bill DeKoning struck out in his lone chance at bat. Now, this is fantastic record keeping. And if you happen to be around the headquarters of Local 138, Operating Engineers Union, maybe you could stop Bill, who is the president of the union, and remind him that he struck out. And good luck to you, your statistics book and anybody who happens to be with you.

Baseball always has thrived on statistics, and on the arguments fans have about statistics. For years, my friend Charley Feeney would be at the bar in Mulligan's, conducting what he considered the ultimate test of a fan's allegiance to the sport.

"Give me the name of the major league player who committed suicide during a season," Feeney would say.

"That's easy," somebody would say. "Willard Hershberger, he caught with the Reds."

"What year?" Feeney would say.

"1940," somebody would answer.

"All right," Feeney would say smugly. "What was Hershberger's batting average when he died?"

I never knew anybody who could give the answer. Now, on page 970 of "The Baseball Encyclopedia" I see that in 1940 Willard Hershberger, may his soul rest forever, was in 48 games for the Reds, came to bat 123 times, had 38 hits—four doubles, two triples, no home runs—for a .309 average. Next to the "BA" for batting average, there is an "SA." I never heard of "SA" until I received this book. Upon diligent use of the directions in the front of the book, I find it means Slugging Average. Willard Hershberger had an "SA" of .374 when he died.

So the book figures to be of untold value to bartenders who have to settle arguments among customers. Although when I look through the pages, I don't examine the figures too much. I just use them to provoke memories. Slip through to the O's, and here is Mel Ott. Under his name there is this long table of figures, and I look at them for a moment and then I am not in a room with a book. I am on the stairs coming out of the subway stop at 155th Street. Up ahead, over the heads of all these men going up the stairs, is the street and I start squeezing and pushing through these men because the moment I get near the top of the subway stairs I can look around and see the ball park, the Polo Grounds, with the flags flying on the roof, and for me that was the best part of the whole day at a baseball game, coming up the subway stairs and seeing the park for the first time. Inside, I'd run up the ramps, then bend down so I could see the place in right field where the great Mel Ott stood and pawed with his spikes until it was bare of grass.

Go to the pages with the R's on them. Pete Reiser. Now I am on Bedford Avenue in Brooklyn, running down the hill to Ebbets Field. Right on the corner, there is a gate in the right-field fence. There is a space between the bottom of the gate and the sidewalk. I stop running and I flop onto the sidewalk and look under the gate and here, only a few feet away, is the grass of deep center-field. One of the pairs of legs moving around the grass in the pre-game practice belongs to Pete Reiser. Pistol Pete! Get up and start running for the general-admission gate on Sullivan Place.

Otherwise, I never had much interest in baseball records. I always found newspaper stories about baseball to be generally unreadable because of the torrent of numbers thrown into each paragraph. And I flinch when radio or television announcers begin to chant the ludicrous amount of figures they feel we must know about each player. The only baseball figures I ever enjoyed reading appeared at the start of the chapter on the Busher's Honeymoon in Ring Lardner's "You Know Me Al": ". . . yes Al I and Florrie was married the day before yesterday. . . . You was wise Al not to get married in Bedford where not nothing is nearly half so dear. My expenses was as follows: license $2.00, priest 3.50, carfair .45, new suit 14.50, flowers .50, candy .30, hotel 4.50, tobacco both kinds .25."

You see, I always thought a sport was supposed to be enjoyment and the talk about the sport based on humor rather than decimal points. See Joe Namath. But this is personal preference and it is not to take away from the completeness and the value of "The Baseball Encyclopedia" to those who like their baseball in figures. There never has been a book this complete.

But at the same time, I wonder if this book represents an era that is gone, and has been gone for a couple of years now, and so many, the older sports writers, the older bartenders, the older customers, are not aware of it yet. How would you like to try to interest the 400,000 young who were at Woodstock in a book of baseball statistics? Throughout the season, I kept asking four of the kids in my house if they'd like to go to a game with me, a Mets game no less. The answer always was the same. "Nope, we're going to bed early because we're getting up at 5 o'clock to go surfing at Montauk."

With the young, their music is fast, their dancing is fast, their cars are fast, their interests keep jumping ahead. And in a baseball stadium, a pitcher stands on the mound itching himself for 25 and 30 seconds before deigning to pitch and the games drag on to the three-hour mark.

I wonder how a sport this slow-moving can make it with these numerically huge, deeply aware generations coming up. Take the book I have here in front of me. It is 2,337 pages of the numerical history of a sport which is supposed to be our national game. Baseball people are enormously proud of this book. But tell these kids coming up, these kids who have been turning to drugs because of a dissatisfaction with things as we have them, go and tell these kids that you have this great, huge, official record book, but that because baseball would not allow a Negro until the great Jackie Robinson came to Ebbets Field in 1947, because of this slight matter, the book contains only the endeavors of white baseball players in the years before 1947. Tell them this, and they will tell you, why, your 2,337-page record book that took you two years to compile is nothing more than a big put-on with long division.

If you ever saw Josh Gibson catch a baseball game, you would have no defense. Josh Gibson was black and he was not allowed into the major league. If they ever had let him play a career in a small place like the old Ebbets Field or today's Fenway Park,

Josh Gibson would have forced baseball to rewrite the rules. "Gibson was, at the minimum, two Yogi Berras," Bill Veeck says.

But if you see it differently, and you want your baseball traditional style, with statistics, then "The Baseball Encyclopedia" is great. As my friend Jackie O'Neill, who batted .345 for Little Rock in the Dixie series in 1937, observes: "Look at this book, it proves baseball is the toughest business in the world. Your daily behavior gets printed up and they save it forever. How many bad days have you had that nobody knows about? You put your head under the pillow and it goes away. Bill DeKoning strikes out once 25 years ago and they still publish books about it."

While he was talking, I turned the pages to the D's. Joe DiMaggio. His record takes up 25 full lines, but I don't look at the numbers. I am thinking of something no record book ever will show. Joe DiMaggio running from first to third when the Yankee batter hits a single to centerfield. Joe DiMaggio running with these long strides, getting to second so quickly because he had broken the moment the ball was hit, Joe DiMaggio sweeping past second, running, running, running with his head up, proud, his body controlled and not heaving; the dignity of talent; and now Joe DiMaggio coming into third base standing up and there is no play on him. He has done it so casually that nobody points out that most runners either would have stopped at second, or been thrown out easily at third. This was one of his side abilities. If you want to know how good Joe DiMaggio was with the bat, you could look it up.

October 12, 1969

The Greatest Article I Read in My Whole Life

RICHARD NIXON'S Vice President, Spiro Agnew, writing about Attica under his byline in The New York Times newspaper the other day, said: "To compare the loss of life by those who violate society's law with the loss of life of those whose job it is to uphold it—represents not simply an assault on human sensibility but an insult to reason."

Beautiful. I think it was the greatest article I read in my whole life. Governor Rockefeller seems to feel the way Agnew does, but Rockefeller has a family background for things like this. The Ludlow massacre and all that. Agnew's terrific article came from the heart. Because of it I finally was able to brush off the last shreds of the stupid ideas Sister Anna Gertude outfitted us with in St. Benedict Joseph Labre School, Queens, New York City.

That silly Jesus Christ. The way that old nun made us learn it, Jesus spent the whole last morning of His life standing in Part XXXII with a real bum named Barabbas. Instead of making a deal to sink Barabbas, Christ stood around rooting for Barabbas to get his case severed and dropped. One description of Barabbas was that he was a boss of thieves in Jerusalem. The first Jewish button man. I used to sit in class and picture Barabbas as Lepke with a big beard.

Another thing I read said Barabbas actually was indicted for being the leader of a revolutionary movement, the Zealot Movement, which wanted to overthrow Rome. One of these demonstrations got rough and a guy died and the law grabbed Barabbas. Whichever version is right, Barabbas was under a heavy indictment and he was given amnesty and we were taught that it was a great thing, the way Christ was happy to see Barabbas get off. But now, reading Agnew, I can see what Christ really was. He should have figured, here, this guy next to Me is only a number and nobody is going to get excited if he goes. Then Christ should have maneuvered the judge and crowd so they would let Him go and make a party cutting Barabbas's head off.

Let's go to the afternoon. Here He is hanging on a cross all afternoon and what does He do? He spends most of His time talking to two thieves they have hanging alongside Him. Sister Anna Gertrude used to get tears in her eyes reading from Luke. And, look at the way this Christ, in a life-and-death situation, worried about thieves. Finally, one of the thieves, I put him down in my mind as a top hoodlum like Bumpy Johnson, said: "Lord, remember me when You come into Your Kingdom."

And Jesus Christ, in what I was taught was the last line He said on earth, turned to this thief, this Bumpy Johnson, and said: "This day you will be with Me in paradise."

How do you like it? How do you like what some backward nun put into my head? Here's a Guy has nails in Him and He is wasting His time giving amnesty to a thief, and they had me believing for a long time, Sister Anna Gertrude and the other nuns in St. Benedict Joseph Labre School, Queens, New York City, that this Jesus Christ was great because He died thinking of thieves. I should have spent my time looking at dirty pictures.

At least now, because of Spiro Agnew's terrific article, I know that thieves should be regarded in a crisis as ciphers to be killed and barely counted and never mourned. There are three real good prayer people who get their pictures taken with Richard Nixon and Spiro Agnew and it would be marvelous to hear them say something about Agnew's terrific article, just in case there are many people whose thinking has been crippled by faulty religious upbringing. It would help straighten this whole Attica question out if the three really good prayer people, Billy Graham, Norman Vincent Peale and Terence Cooke, would comment on Agnew's article, and how silly Jesus Christ was.

October 9, 1971

The Coach Who Couldn't Shoot Straight

THE FATHER, J. W. Chones, after 22 years of working as a moulder in a steel plant in Racine, Wisconsin, was in bed in the house, the life going out of him in the hollow dry cough of lung cancer. The mother made salads in a restaurant for $1.75 an hour. The six kids, confused, depressed, went through the form of attending school. The oldest and largest, James B. Chones, 18, six feet, 11 inches, played on the basketball team at St. Catherine's High School. It was hard for him, the months in the snow in 1969, with his father home dying and the men coming into the high school to talk to him.

Chones can recount almost everything that was said to him by these men from American colleges and universities. The first man from a college to talk to him said, "Your father's sick, that's too bad. We'll get him a nice house. Get you a car. How would you like that, a nice new car for yourself?"

Another one thought for a while when Jim Chones said his father was sick. "What we could do, we could get your mother a job. Real good job. Don't worry about what she'll get paid. Course, it'll really be your money, you know. You let us worry about how we give it to your mother."

"The father's sick," another one of them said, "Well, he can fly to all games. Doesn't take too much effort to get onto a plane, first class seat, and come and see your son play in the fieldhouse."

To the best of Jim Chones' recollection he heard from every college in the country that was interested in basketball. Except one. He had not received anything, a phone call, a letter even, from Marquette University in Milwaukee in his own state. The coach of Marquette was Alfred J. McGuire.

In April, when it was over, when J. W. Chones was gone, somebody from the high school asked Jim to stop into the athletic office.

"This is Al McGuire," the man said to Chones.

"I wanted to talk to you for a long time," Al McGuire said. "But we heard your father was sick and we didn't want to bother you."

He invited Chones to come down to the basketball banquet at Marquette. When Chones came to the banquet, Al McGuire spoke to him again. Spoke to him with those eyes locked on Chones. Big brown eyes that talk, question, laugh, challenge, get mad. Eyes that never leave you during a conversation.

"There is no money here," Al McGuire said. Chones mentioned some of the things he had been offered. "That's fine. You'll be just another hired hand for them. A field hand." Chones knew what that meant. Field nigger. "You listen to me, you can do it differently. You're big, you've got reactions, good speed. I think if you listen and work hard you have a chance to make big money as a pro. Big money for yourself. You can do whatever the hell you want with your life once you make it for yourself. You can be anybody you want, do anything you want. But make it on your own. You'll never get anything if you're just a hired hand for somebody. Listen to me and you'll make big money by yourself."

He also told Chones he had an important house rule at Marquette. A basketball player had to get a degree.

If you know Al McGuire for a long time, you smile when you hear about his rule. I sat with him when we were young and watching a college game at the old Madison Square Garden and during the warm up a ball bounced up to the seats and Al grabbed it and threw a shot, a two-handed set shot from his chest. It went into the flock of basketballs bouncing around the rim. "That's the first shot I ever took at the Garden," he said proudly. The shot had missed by a half-foot or so. Al would go home and tell everybody he put it right in. In college, he majored in defense. When he got out of school—rather, finished his time there—he announced that he was going for a master's degree. When he played with the New York Knickerbockers, he announced he could guard Bob Cousy so well that he owned him. Cousy used to score hundreds of points against the Knicks. The newspapers kept saying that Al McGuire owned Cousy. Al himself still was throwing up shots that were a half-foot wide. When he became coach at Belmont Abbey, a small school in North Carolina, he also had to teach history. The notion is his wife prepared the courses and Al did the talking in class. He remained approximately six pages ahead of the class. If a student asked him a question during class, Al said he would take that up with the boy immediately after class. At which point Al would flee out the front door of the classroom and hope the kid forgot what was on his mind.

Always, Al McGuire was growing. And what he didn't know he could cover with talk. His mind essentially was too quick for mere sports, which is why there is always so much more than sports going on when he talks to his players. Al McGuire wants college degrees for his players? Sure he does. It's a good show for Al, and a good show for the boy. The perfect way to obliterate these coaches who sell black basketball players on the theory that a car and three white broads is all they really want out of life. Al McGuire promotes things that last. And gets the players. See Maurice Lucas, this season's great sophomore. And then past the good show, past the fast talk, there is the knowledge that it not only looks right, but it is right. What better combination is there?

Al is Irish and Catholic, and he was behind a bar pulling beer at 108th Street in Rockaway Beach, in New York, before he was old enough to be allowed in as a customer. The background is supposed to produce conservative thinking. I sit with Al McGuire at dinner with business people from Milwaukee, and they are laughing about an open housing march led by a priest named Groppi. Al McGuire, the center of the table, said, "Fellas, you may think I'm losing my mind, but I have to tell you. I think the man is right." Silence fell. But not that sullen kind of silence. An embarrassed silence. They all seemed uneasy that they had said something stupid. I have been around people in a business called politics who try to sell unpopular ideas even to the smallest groups and all they ever receive is a grimace. I watched this guy talk. I had a small idea that Al McGuire is one of the few I know who can tell the bastards anything and make them like it. And maybe, as he thinks himself, it's time to try it out. But this is personal opinion. I know the guy a long time. See him through Jim Chones.

Chones came to Marquette in September, 1969. He found out a little bit more about his coach in the dressing room before a game with, he thinks, Creighton. He cannot remember it so well because he stayed in a corner of the dressing room in terror. One of the varsity players, Hugh McMahon, arrived late. The coach began screaming. McMahon started screaming back. Al McGuire was all over him so fast nobody knew what was happening. But Chones saw it clearly. The coach kneed McMahon in the groin. Then he hit McMahon in the face. He threw McMahon against the wall and was about to kick him in the groin. McMahon turned and started walking out of the dressing room, forever. It was one of the great goodbye scenes in sports. Then an arm came out and grabbed McMahon's collar and McMahon came yanking back into the middle of the room.

"All right, now get dressed and let's play," Al McGuire said to McMahon.

There was another afternoon when the team was practicing and McGuire decided Gary Brell, 6–6, wasn't in good enough shape. He had Brell running wind sprints from wall to wall in the gymnasium. Brell stopped in the middle of one of the sprints and stood in the middle of the gym, his long hair held out of his eyes by an Indian head-band. "Why don't you make some of the black guys do some of the running too?" Brell said.

McGuire said nothing. He loped out to the middle of the court and he spoke to Brell. He spoke to Brell by hitting him in the face. Brell began running again.

The Marquette varsity, on the floor before games, consisted of Brell with his head down in mourning for the war, a clenched black fist or two in the air and a coach who stood at attention while his mind was on the game. When somebody asked him about respect or style during the National Anthem, Al McGuire waved a hand. What the hell did he care about form in a matter as small as this? His team was here to play, not to pose. Patriotic Milwaukee, patriotic Roman Catholic Milwaukee, agreed. A weakling or somebody pompous would turn it into an incident. Al McGuire regarded the topic as a pain in the ass and he made everybody else think his way.

His black players came to him one day and said they were sorry, but the afternoon game with Detroit fell on Malcolm X day. At three o'clock, no matter what was happening in the game, they were going to stop playing and stand in silence for Malcolm X.

"You don't have to stop playing, I'll call a time out," Al said. "Don't worry about it. Now let's get on with getting ready to win the game."

When the time out was called, and the Marquette blacks stood in silence, fists raised, the Detroit coach, Jim Harding, nearly exploded. Which was understandable and even allowable. All coaches in all sports are not very smart, nor should they be expected to be very smart. They are in a business of games. Al McGuire is in another year, another century, from coaches of sports.

"Raise your fist, raise your ass, what do I care? Win the game, that's the only thing that goes into the book."

In his sophomore year, Chones was slow in early practices. He was not in the shape he had to be in, but he was blaming it on the floor, the heat, a cold, anything around him. The only ones tall enough to guard him in practice happened to be white players. Chones, irritated, pushed them around. In the middle of the practice Al McGuire walked onto the floor.

"Goddamn, why don't you swing for once at a black guy? Are you afraid one of them'll pick up something and break your head?"

Chones thought about that after practice. He never had heard a white man talk like that to him before. Completely uninhibited. As the months wore on, he began to see that his coach was the fairest white man he ever had heard of.

He also began to learn about a thing known as an Al McGuire promise. "You will make big money," Al McGuire told him.

And in Chones' sophomore year, Marquette came into New York to play Fordham and before the game, Al McGuire walked the streets.

"How's the boy doing?" he was asked. His son Allie was in the starting lineup.

"Fine, it's probably better for him that he would have gone someplace else, but at the same time it was better for me that he's here with me. He isn't the problem right now. I got to do something with Chones."

"What?"

"Well, the kid got nothing. The mother's working, he's got nothing. It would be a shame if the two leagues merge and you have no competitive bidding for him. Cost him a fortune, if that happens."

"What can he do, he's only a sophomore?"

"Supposing he doesn't play?" Al said.

Chones was inside Madison Square Garden, a nervous sophomore waiting to play his first game in New York.

And his coach walked in off the street and on the way to the dressing room he bumped into a sportswriter.

"I don't know if I'm going to be able to keep Chones," Al said. "They're after him already. He's the best big man in the country, can't stop him from doing what he has to do, either. I've looked in my refrigerator and I've looked in his."

"How imminent is this?" the sportswriter asked.

"The professional teams are crawling all over him," Al said.

At the end of the season, Jim Chones picked up the Milwaukee paper one day and he read an interview with Al McGuire. McGuire was quoted as saying, "I hope I can hang onto Chones for one more season." The words jumped out of the page at Chones. He went to see McGuire, but he couldn't find him. The season was over. Al McGuire has his own way of life. Nobody can find him unless he wants them to.

"I was looking all over for you," Chones said later.

"Maybe I didn't want to see you," McGuire said.

Throughout Chones' junior year, the practices were torture for Marquette. They had lost one game in '70–'71, and that by a point. They were perhaps the finest defensive team college ball had seen in decades. Through drill after drill, Chones worked on his pick and roll. The big man comes out and picks for a backcourt man and in the melee he hopes to wind up with the wrong man guarding him, at which point he immediately rolls to the basket. Or if his man does try to stay with him, the big man doing the picking hopes to wind up with the inside and, again, he rolls to the basket. It is the basic play of modern professional basketball. It also was the basic play for Al McGuire's big men.

In February, 1972, undefeated Marquette played Jacksonville. Marquette won by eight. Jim Chones scored 24, had 17 rebounds and blocked six shots. The next night, Chones was in his dormitory when he received a phone call from Gene Smith, a lawyer in Milwaukee. Gene Smith is Al McGuire's lawyer.

"Jim, I don't know what's going on," Smith said, "but I have some men here. They got my telephone number from Al. The men are from the Long Island Nets. They want to pay you, I don't know what it is, something like $2 million. You better come down here right away."

Chones went to the lawyer's office. Al McGuire was not there. Roy Boe of the Long Island Nets was there. Yes, he wanted to sign Chones to a three-year contract. No, he wasn't going to pay $2 million. That's way out of line. He would pay Jim Chones $1,800,000.

Chones called Al McGuire on the phone. It was midnight.

The phone was picked up on the other end.

"Uh."

"Coach?"

"Who the hell is this?"

"Jim Chones."

"Oh, yeah. Jimmy. I'm asleep. What's up?"

"Well these men are here from the pro team and they are offering me one point eight million dollars or something like that and I just wanted to. . . ."

"Well, good, Jimmy. I'll see you tomorrow. I'm going to sleep."

Marquette was undefeated, the tournaments were ahead, the coach was in line to be what the sports pages call "a basketball immortal."

When Chones hung up the phone, Gene Smith, the lawyer, shrugged. He knew what to do now. He took out his pen and handed it to Chones.

There was, of course, no flim-flam. It was announced the next day Jim Chones had become a professional and he could not compete for Marquette anymore. The team without Chones immediately lost a couple of games and the season quickly came to an end.

Al McGuire shook hands with Chones, and Chones left Marquette. "He has his diploma," Al McGuire said. "A big diploma."

In the McGuire family, there are three brothers. There is Al, successor to Adolph Rupp, Henry Iba, Phog Allen. There is Dick, probably one of the best backcourt men the game has ever known. He was the Knick coach and now he is the chief scout. And there is the oldest brother, John, who is famous for having received the largest and undoubtedly most needed

Western Union money order in the history of Hialeah race track.

I saw Chones recently. He was at Great Neck, on Long Island, after a Nets practice. He pulled up in a Cadillac car, and his sisters are in college and his mother is in a new house and she is not out making salads anymore. "She can't just stay home, she's so used to working," Jim was saying. "She's got to get a job. But a job doing something. Teacher's assistant, something like that. Not makin' any salads anymore. She can be useful."

"What money can do," he was told.

"But it's like he always told me," Chones said. "Coach McGuire always said to me, 'Jim, I want to take care of my family and live my own life. That's all that's important. I don't give a damn about anything else. I'm a happy man because I live my own life. I'm not dependent on somebody liking me or not. Now that's how I want you to be. Any hard work you do for yourself. You don't do it for me. And when you take care of yourself, you live your own life.'"

He got up to go. There was a team meeting upstairs.

"Everything he ever said to me came true," Chones said. "Everything. What else can I tell you?"

I said nothing, because what he was saying was an old story to me. I know the guy a long time.

1972

The Best Short Stories of Ring Lardner

IN OCTOBER, 1947, in the Senate Caucus Room, a special subcommittee of the House Un-American Activities Committee conducted public hearings. Present were subcommittee chairman J. Parnell Thomas and Reps. John McDowell, Richard Vail and Richard Nixon. Committee counsel was Robert Stripling. One witness was Ring Lardner Jr.

Chairman J. Parnell Thomas grew impatient with the questioning of witness Ring Lardner Jr.

THOMAS: All right, Mr. Counsel, let's get down to it. Go to the sixty-four-dollar question.

STRIPLING: Mr. Lardner, are you now or have you ever been a member of the Communist party?

LARDNER: I refuse to answer on grounds of the Fifth Amendment to the Constitution of the United States.

THOMAS: The counsel is to direct the witness to answer the question.

STRIPLING: I ask you again . . .

LARDNER: I refuse to answer on grounds . . .

THOMAS: You must answer the question or be in contempt of the Congress.

LARDNER: I refuse to answer the question . . .

THOMAS: You answer the question. Why, anybody in America would be proud to answer that question.

LARDNER: Mr. Chairman, I could answer it, but if I did I'd hate myself in the morning.

Heavyweights always do it with a flourish.

I could hear this line many times while going through this book of short stories written by the father Ring Lardner. As a collection it is the work of a stupendous genius; I do not believe I have been brought into the room to announce that. The 25 stories were written 50 and 60 years ago, and they are only good for another century or so. His style, wisdom comes from simplicity, produces a great many smiles until the terror wears you down. To me, a book of Ring Lardner stories all comes down to a man hanging over the Golden Gate Bridge and when grabbed by the police, telling them, shucks, I was only spittin' off the bridge. And in reading this book, you sense the power of the father, and the torment in which he lived, and you get an understanding of how the son performed so beautifully an act of high honor at a time in this country, 1947, when honor was considered the behavior of a traitor.

This doesn't put a lot of burdens and shadows on the son. For one thing he's too old for this. For another, he has his own success, an Oscar and cash for writing a movie called "M*A*S*H." All we are doing here is properly tracing royal blood.

Ring Lardner walked out of Niles, Mich., High School in 1901 with his final marks showing an A in everything but chemistry, and in that he received an A minus, undoubtedly because Lardner misspelled a word like salt. Lardner characters always blew the small words: "I don't suppose she had any *idear* how her face changed. . . ." His characters usually had other words spelled correctly. It was Lardner's theory that the people in his stories would go to the dictionary for any word of more than six letters. For anything under six letters, they would be on their own. Thus, "The four of us set around the lobby for a wile. . . ."

It was with this beginning, this fresh brilliance and fresh humor, that Ring Lardner came out of high school into the mid-America of 1901. His eyes were wide, with no college to corrupt and twist his innocent views. "I was goin' to tackle Cornell's but the doctor told me I'd have hay fever if I didn't stay up North." Ring Lardner went out into a place which proclaimed itself as America, but in 1901 it was a place for men on their way to making billions. The land was being stolen or scarred, the people manipulated and discarded and the Rockefellers, Goulds, Astors sawed and chewed their way through all rules of life. Their dishonesty set a tone for the nation, spread a stain on its people, which maybe we haven't been able to change yet.

Lardner, young, brilliant, believing in niceness and actually searching for it in people, found instead that his true gift was being able to see too many things, things others could not see. And so many of the things Ring Lardner saw were bad, so very bad, that it became too much for him to face the reality of it all and he went to the bar and tried to fight his misery with drink, and a lot of drink can kill you just as sure as anything in a gun. Ring Lardner was dead in 1933, at age 48, of an overdose of knowledge.

He had three brothers who did not last long, either. David Lardner was killed in the Spanish Civil War. James Lardner was killed in France in World War II. John Lardner, who was an exquisite writer—see "White Hopes and Other Tigers"—was killed in Bleeck's by drinking with Walt Kelly. Whereupon Kelly, who saw too many things himself, stepped up his drinking, anything in a glass would do, and now he is gone, too.

I know some people, purportedly well-read people, who are so stupid that they think Ring Lardner is a sportswriter or a humorist. A story in this collection is called "Who Dealt?" It is in first person, a wife talking during a bridge game, with no other voice disturbing her as she blithely, innocently details the scorched wreckage of her life and the lives around her. You want to drink for her, poor fool that she is, and for the others who have to live with her as part of their lives. The reason why you want to drink is that the story doesn't happen to be a story:

"What was I saying? Oh, yes, about Mr. and Mrs. Guthrie. It's funny for a couple like that to get married when they are so different in every way. I never saw two people with such different tastes. For instance, Mr. Guthrie is keen about motoring and Mrs. Guthrie just hates it. She simply suffers all the time she's in a car. He likes a good time, dancing, golfing, fishing, shows, things like that. She isn't interested in anything but church work and bridge work. . . .

"You take Tom and me, though, and you'd think we were made for each other. It seems like we feel just about the same about everything. That is, almost everything. The things we don't agree on are little things that don't matter. . . ."

In a story called "The Love Nest" you do not have to drink for the woman of the house. She does that alone, and the rages come up from the glass:

"Well off, am I? I'd change places with the scum of the earth just to be free! See, Barker? And I could have been a star without any help if I'd only realized it. I had the looks and I had the talent. I've got it yet. I could be a Swanson and get myself a marquis; maybe a prince! And look what I did get! A self-satisfied, self-centered ———! I thought he'd *make*

BEST SHORT STORIES OF RING LARDNER 175

me! See, Barker? Well, he's made me all right. He's made me a
chronic mother and it's a wonder I've got any looks left."

Oh, it must have been fun for him at times. He could take a
simple sentence, look at it, listen to it, I guess, and then somewhere inside him he would smile and rearrange the sentence.
And thus, in a story called "Alibi Ike" you read:

"I and Carey begin to lead him on."

With this to set the mood, he would do just about whatever
the hell he felt like. No reaching. Reaching for humor is a sin
he could not tolerate. The man just put down what he felt like:

"'What town in Idaho is your old man at?' I says.

"Ike thought it over.

"'No town at all,' he says. 'But he's near a town.'

"'Near what town?' I says.

"'Yuma,' says Ike."

Then there is the story called "Haircut." It is a story which I
think should be read every year of a person's lifetime.

"You know, in most towns of any size, when a man is dead
and needs a shave, why the barber that shaves him soaks him
five dollars for the job; that is, he don't soak *him*, but whoever
ordered the shave. I just charge three dollars because personally
I don't mind much shavin' a dead person. They lay a whole lot
stiller than live customers. The only thing is that you don't feel
like talkin' to them and you get kind of lonesome."

Lovely. Except the story "Haircut" is all about cruelty, about
a man who tortures the helpless, the village half-wit for one, and
the half-wit gets a shotgun and blows the man's head off. The
same with the story called "Champion." The main character,
Midge Kelly, at age 17, gives a beating to his brother, who is 14
and crippled. Midge Kelly knocks the younger brother down
and then kicks him in the crippled leg. He turns on the mother
and knocks her down. Midge Kelly goes on to throw punches
at the rest of the world, whether people had their hands up or
down. At one point Kelly, riding on top, receives three letters,
one from his wife, who tells him that his baby daughter is dying
and she has no money. She would like the $36 she sent Kelly
before he left her. Another is from his mother, who informs him
that the crippled younger brother hasn't been out of bed for
three years and even if Midge can't send a few dollars, would
he please write the boy a note? The third letter is from what

we once called a broad in New York who wants a couple of hundred. Midge Kelly fumed as he read them. "They're all alike," he said. "Money, money, money."

And now Lardner is taking you into the world he saw too clearly: the strong always abusing the weak and the afflicted. Abusing them, fooling them, making fun of them, robbing and cheating them. To make it worse, he was hoping that the strong would be decent. And always, the weak and the afflicted have a special dignity that the strong do not have, nor can they recognize.

The other night, Ring Lardner Jr. was at an impeachment rally and he was telling the crowd about the time he was in front of the H.U.A.C. in Washington. He mentioned the four members, McDowell, Vail, both dead; Richard Nixon and J. Parnell Thomas. Then he told how J. Parnell Thomas got his tail in trouble stealing; if there is one thing the right wing is known for it is an American flag on the lapel and stickum on the fingers. So J. Parnell Thomas was ushered into the main yard at Danbury Correctional Institution at the same time Ring Lardner Jr. was serving his sentence for not telling the Thomas and Nixon committee whether he was a Communist or not.

"So of the four members on that committee," Ring Lardner Jr. was saying the other night, "I already have seen 25 per cent of the committee go to prison. I now await the day when that number is raised to 50 per cent."

April 14, 1974

HOW THE GOOD GUYS FINALLY WON
FINALLY WON

NOTES FROM AN IMPEACHMENT SUMMER

For Jim Shanahan

"Guilty"

IT WAS as graceless at the end as it was at the start.
 The room was dim in the late afternoon and a heavy rain
beat on the smeared windows. The room, one of the witness
rooms on the second floor of the Federal Courthouse in Washington, was being used by defendants in the Watergate case
as they waited for the jury to come in. William Hundley, the
lawyer for John Mitchell, was standing in the doorway, taking
the quick last drags on his cigarette.

"A note," he said.

"A note?" one of the other lawyers in the room said.

"A note," Hundley said.

"A verdict?"

"All I know is the jury sent in a note."

The lawyer spoke in a low voice to Hundley. "I hope we
don't get a verdict today. My guy's not in shape to handle it."

"Well, you better go in there with him now," Hundley said.
Hundley knew it was a verdict.

The lawyer walked out.

"Who does he have?" someone asked Hundley.

He bent down, taking the final drag on his cigarette before
dropping it onto the floor.

"Mardian."

The hallway outside, empty all day, now was filled with
reporters running to get places in line at the doors to the
second-floor courtroom. As Hundley came out of the witness
room, John Mitchell, courtroom gray stained into his face,
passed by, his walk heavy. Hundley followed him. As we left
the dim waiting room, the windows suddenly became filled
with bright white light. Outside in the rain the television men,
plastic parkas and wet beards, were turning on their equipment.

It was 4:25 P.M. of an empty New Year's Day, 1975, and now
it was all coming to an end.

The windowless courtroom was too bright, the neon ceiling
lights glaring off the blond-paneled walls. This type of American ceremony has no richness to it; dark tragedies are played
out in flat, harsh civil-service surroundings. The five defendants

already were in the courtroom when the doors were opened for reporters. There were less than a dozen ordinary spectators. At the start of the sequence of trouble, there are large crowds of the curious and knots of close friends shielding you from the curious. As the case wears on, and next week becomes next month, the curious go elsewhere and the close friends live their own lives, and at the end you always are alone with fear.

The five defendants sit at separate tables with their lawyers. Haldeman. The forehead seeming a little too large for the rest of his head. A great deal of darkness about his eyes. Ehrlichman, thin-rimmed glasses, a bulging briefcase at his feet. He carries it with him every day, the sides of the bag swelling with each new proceeding, each new document. My case. The man in the most trouble in a courtroom always carries the most papers. Mitchell, sitting up against the wall, saying something to Hundley, who tries to smile. Mardian, lips pursed, eyes glaring, frightened. Parkinson, dull, clerkish, a cipher.

It was 4:35 and they waited in the courtroom. Along the wall in the front of the room were two easels used for exhibits during the case. One of the easels had been tipped over. The large white card on it carried a heading, "White House Chart." The squares showed which man was where in the times when they all thought the power they had was real and permanent. The card on the other easel said, "Committee to Re-Elect President." Titles out of the past.

The doorknob on the door in the front of the room, to the left of the bench, rattled noisily, metallically. The courtroom froze. A loud click. The door opened. A gray-haired clerk, carrying a sheaf of papers, walked in and sat at the table in front of the bench. Who knows what the papers were? Clerks in courtrooms always carry papers. Movement came back to the people in the harsh lighted room.

The doorknob rattled again. Movement in the courtroom froze again. Another loud click. Another clerk walked in carrying another sheaf of papers.

The defendants followed the clerk as he walked to his seat.

Minutes went by. It was 4:40 now. Reporters were standing, looking at the defendants, making notes of what they were seeing, their hands shaking in the tension.

The doorknob rattled again. Silence in the room. Now the

click. An immense black marshal, head shaved, looked into the room.

"All ready?" he said to the gray-haired clerk.

"All ready," the clerk said.

The marshal went out the door but did not shut it entirely. Now, without a sound, the door swung open. The marshal slammed his hand on the wood.

"All rise," the gray-haired clerk said.

Into the harsh light came the judge, John Sirica. He went to his seat quickly, his face expressionless. He sat down and immediately turned to the marshal.

"Bring in the jury."

The marshal leaned out into the hallway behind the court-room and stood there a moment, his hand on the door, and now there was another marshal in the hallway and behind him came the jury. They went to their seats with the shoes of the black women jurors sounding loudly on the wooden floor of the jury box. There was something pink around the neck of one of the women. There was an older woman, sparse gray wiry hair pulled straight back, hands folded in her lap. Old black woman sitting in a train station. Instead, she was passing judgment on a man who was the Attorney General of the United States. The foreman, somber, in brown, held a large brown envelope, a civil-service envelope.

The gray-haired clerk, James Capitanio, asked the foreman to rise.

"Has the jury reached a verdict?"

"Yes, they have." John A. Hoffar was the foreman.

He held out the civil-service envelope. The dark-haired clerk walked up and took it from him. The clerk took the envelope to the bench. It was 4:48. Everybody in the courtroom sat with mouths partly opened, breathing against nerves. The two clerks stood at the bench, backs to the courtroom, while Sirica opened the large envelope. He had trouble getting the papers out. He held the envelope up, reached into it, and began taking sheets of long white paper out. He put on his glasses and began reading the papers. One of the clerks shook the envelope to be certain it was empty. Sirica was saying something as he went over each paper, the clerks mumbling something back. At 4:49, Sirica still was reading and the clerks still mumbling with him.

The mouths in the courtroom became a little more open. At 4:50, Sirica nodded, his head came up, and he sat back. His face showed nothing.

"The clerk will read the verdict. Defendants stand."

James Capitanio turned around, the papers in his hands. There was only this slight movement of the papers to show Capitanio had any nerves about what he was doing.

And now, around the room, the five men stood up. Their wives, tight short hair, woolen suits, sitting in the first row. The five defendants who would have ruled a nation in their way, standing so that a clerk could tell them of their future. From where I sat, only Mitchell's, Mardian's, and Parkinson's faces were visible.

Capitanio began to read in a flat courtroom voice.

"Docket number seventy-four dash one hundred ten.

"As to the defendant John N. Mitchell:

"Count one. Guilty.

"Count two. Guilty.

"Count three. Guilty.

"Count four. Guilty.

"Count five. Guilty.

"Count six. Guilty.

"Signed, John A. Hoffar, foreman."

Mitchell's face had little flecks of white paste showing in the gray. He flinched, just slightly but enough to show it, as the guilty-guilty-guilty hit him in the face. He looked like a man who was starting to drown but was embarrassed by it and did not want anybody to think he needed assistance.

Capitanio went without pause into the next set of papers.

"As to the defendant Harry R. Haldeman:

"Count one. Guilty.

"Count two. Guilty.

"Count seven. Guilty.

"Count eight. Guilty.

"Count nine. Guilty.

"Signed, John A. Hoffar, foreman."

The papers switched around in Capitanio's hands.

"As to the defendant John Ehrlichman:

"Count one. Guilty.

"Count two. Guilty.

"Count three. Guilty.

"Count twelve. Guilty.

"Signed, John A. Hoffar, foreman."

Only an execution carries more formal pain, and disturbs more, than this scene of men standing and listening to their lives being ruined.

"As to the defendant Robert Mardian:

"Count one. Guilty."

Mardian's head moved from right to left, as if he had just been hit with a left hook. He looked at the jury and at the door and at the wall and at the people in the first rows. He looked for something, for somebody, to tell him that it never had been said, that this clerk in the front of the room had not said he was guilty. Face flushed, mouth open, eyes darting, Mardian looked for help.

Robert Mardian had stood on the balcony of the Justice Department in the gloom of the late afternoon in the fall of 1969, stood there behind John Mitchell and Richard Kleindienst. Sometimes Mardian was off the balcony and inside the office. But you always could see his face. Out on the balcony, inside the office, when the curtains parted. His face was red with anger and his mouth was contorted. He was pointing, the finger jabbing the air in anger, at the young people who were running through the tear gas in the street below. A huge antiwar demonstration had just ended at the Washington Monument. A couple of thousand, students mostly, many of them high-school students, had marched to the Justice Department. Some of them were looking for what they felt was trouble: climbing, window-breaking, raising a Viet Cong flag on the empty flagpole. They were the older ones, lost in the ridiculous dream of being Weathermen. Aside from these few—police could have easily handled them—the crowd was made up of students. And Mardian stood snarling and shaking with anger, and standing in front of him, Mitchell smoked a pipe. Kleindienst watched to see that his orders had been carried out—that the students were met with tear gas and United States Marshals. And here on the street in front of the Justice Department was a young girl, fourteen, laughing and skipping through the patches of tear gas. On the balcony, Robert Mardian's face became the deepest red. In front of Mardian, John Mitchell sourly sucked on his pipe. Later, over Scotch, he would say that they all should be arrested and deported to Russia. Next to Mitchell on the balcony was Richard Kleindienst, then the assistant Attorney General. Agents were tapped on the shoulder, orders were given to use more tear gas, to make more arrests, to go to the wooden clubs against these Communist hordes, these fourteen-year-old girls running through the tear gas. It was, on that late fall afternoon, a scene from another country—with the mean and powerful men standing on a balcony. And another country is precisely what John Mitchell's Justice Department attempted to make out of the United States.

And now, here in court, on New Year's Day, John Mitchell stood convicted of enormous crimes against the old America, the America that has a Constitution. And Richard Kleindienst already had pleaded guilty and had squirmed and cried his way out of a prison sentence. He went home hoping to be regarded as a man who was misunderstood. And Robert Mardian was looking wildly around a courtroom for help that was not to come.

Parkinson's verdict was read next. He was not guilty, the clerk said. Parkinson's lawyers slapped him on the back. John Mitchell looked across the room to him, his mouth forming the word, "Congratulations." Only Mitchell did this. The others stood in their own trouble. The defendants were told to sit down. Mardian sat heavily. His face came into his hands.

The jury was sent home after a couple of words from Sirica. James Neal, the prosecutor, slipped up to the bench. He told Sirica that he was leaving the job as of that moment. Neal had come up from Nashville to do what he had to do. He had disliked doing it. Neal does not prosecute for pleasure. Sirica said, "Thank you for your service to the country." Neal went back to his seat and stared at the table. He wanted what was coming next to be over as quickly as possible. He wanted to get out of the room, out of the building, out of Washington.

Sirica looked at the papers in front of him. He moved them away from him. He picked up something else, looked at it. Then his head came up.

"Now . . ."

With the one word—"Now . . ."—it was all different. No

longer was it a matter of guilt, of proving who was responsible for Watergate, for the attempted theft of something of national value. "Now" meant that this phase was over. And it had become time for the arrangements for punishment to be made, for dates to be set with probation officers, for pre-sentencing reports, for consideration of placing men into prisons.

Everything became dark. Once is too many times to be around things like this. The moment I could, I strayed out of the courtroom. Mardian was in his chair, motionless. His wife came up to place a hand on his elbow. Mardian brushed her off. In the prize-fighting business they used to call a guy like this a mutt.

I went back into an office they were using as a pressroom to pick up my raincoat. Ehrlichman came in with his wife. Reporters clustered around him and he answered questions, his finger jabbing out somebody whose hand was up. The finger motion was accompanied with a little compression of the lips. The German love for the mannerisms of authority is pervasive. I asked him if he didn't think it was time for Richard Nixon to come out of his house and take a little bit of the weight, assume the responsibility, in this matter that was wrecking so many lives. Ehrlichman listened to the question, looked up for a moment, nodded his head—Now I know what you mean—and began his answer. "I respect your opinion, but I just answered that question in words within the judicial framework. Ah . . ." He started down a trail which I did not understand. He was speaking in off-English, in words which seemed one half notch off true meaning. He spoke earnestly, affably, but with one foot out of bounds. In the White House one day, Ehrlichman had proclaimed that all government investigatory resources should converge upon Larry O'Brien so that O'Brien would be put into a prison before the 1972 election. Yet standing in the pressroom, trying to talk, getting a subordinate meaning out of anything said to him, Ehrlichman was a mournful figure. Why is it that the science of getting even always becomes desolate at the end?

Nixon's presence would have made things far gloomier. Apparently, Nixon was perfectly capable of being the worst defendant ever. Early in the going, Nixon is supposed to have mentioned something about committing suicide. And Haig supposedly said, "That might be an idea worth considering." And Nixon didn't speak to Haig for about a week.

I left as Ehrlichman droned on. Outside the building, H. R. Haldeman was standing in the rain in front of the television cameras. There was nothing profitable in listening to him. In the end, all convicted criminals are boring.

Back at the Jefferson Hotel, the bar and restaurant were closed for the holiday weekend. The only sound in the lobby was the desk clerk turning the pages of a newspaper. I went upstairs to pack. I left the door to my room open. From a suite down the hall I could hear a loud voice, a hysterical voice, and the sounds of other voices trying to calm everything down. Mardian in John Mitchell's suite. It was to take Mitchell two hours to get Mardian in some form of control of himself.

The voices were quite loud, drumming in the ears, while I waited for the elevator. It was a relief to step on the elevator, and have the doors close against the sound. I don't want to hear them, or hear much about them again. For there were too many decent people, people with honesty and dignity and charm, who were an important part of the summer of 1974 in Washington, the summer in which the nation forced a President to resign from office. And if we are going to talk about the end of Watergate, as we are about to do here, why don't we take a walk away from the convicts and step into the shafts of sunlight provided by some of the people who worked for their country, rather than against it. People who are so much more satisfying to know, and to tell of.

1

". . . impeachment is going to hit this Congress."

H E DOESN'T remember the date, he wasn't keeping notes on everything at the time, but Congressman Thomas P. O'Neill, Jr., does know that it was just after he had become Majority Leader of the House of Representatives in January of 1973 that he walked into Speaker Carl Albert's office and said, "All my years tell me what's happening. They did so many bad things during that campaign that there is no way to keep it from coming out. They did too many things. Too many people know about it. There is no way to keep it quiet. The time is going to come when impeachment is going to hit this Congress and we better be ready for it."

His opinion was not received with great warmth. The House of Representatives is not a place of positive action. It is an institution designed only to react, not to plan or lead. O'Neill had not often broken the rule. Albert's caution begins with breakfast. To speak of impeaching Richard Nixon was like asking him to use his shoetip to inspect for landmines. As O'Neill persisted in his conversation, Peter W. Rodino, Jr., was asked to the meeting. Through his years in Congress, Rodino had shown great natural cautiousness; he once took the grave risk of getting out front to pass a bill declaring Columbus Day a national holiday. And at this time, early in 1973, Rodino had just been made Chairman of the House Judiciary Committee, and thus was moving even more hesitantly than usual.

When you see Peter Rodino now, today, he sits in the back of a car, the windows open to the chill of a fall evening, and somebody in the car tries to close the window but there are so many people on the sidewalk pushing their hands and faces into the car to say hello to Peter Rodino that the window cannot be closed. The people are at the bus stop on Roosevelt Avenue, in the Flushing section of Queens, in New York City, and one of them, a woman, puts her head into the car and says she is Rae

Grossman. "For what you did for America," she says, "can I go get you a cup of coffee?" "Thank you," Peter Rodino says, "but we're leaving in just a moment now." "For what you did for this country just let me get a cup of coffee for you," she says. "No, thank you very much, but we're leaving," Rodino says. Outside the car, in the wind swirling up the block, the people coming home from work take a quick look at Rodino and then, talking excitedly, jam onto buses.

However, when it started, when Rodino was a Congressman from Newark whom nobody knew, Rodino regarded impeachment as a word that had danger hanging from it the instant it left the mouth. Rodino pointed out to O'Neill that there was absolutely nothing to go on. This irritated O'Neill. Of course he had something to go on. What was it? Why, he had what he just said, that an impeachment was going to hit this Congress and they all had better be ready for it.

There was one Sunday, in the summer of 1974, when O'Neill was talking about how it all started. O'Neill was at Harwichport, on Cape Cod, and the church traffic had the main street in town tied up. I got to O'Neill's long ranch house at 12:15, just as O'Neill was going out of the house into the early summer heat. The lawn was wet and trees were dripping. He got into a well-used Impala, put a pack of Daniel Webster cigars on the dashboard for the trip, and then we started driving to Boston, two hours away.

"I'll tell you how it happened, but of course you can't use any of this," he began. In the weeks to come, I would learn that he began practically every conversation with everybody in this manner, and those who heeded him, who did not write what he was saying, almost invariably woke up in the morning to find it printed in some other place.

"Now," O'Neill went on, "I was the Chairman of the Democratic Congressional campaign dinner in Washington, and because of that I got to know every big giver to the Democratic party in the nation. We had a guy everywhere to organize and to get you the money. You take New York, we got a dozen in New York. Jim Wilmot, Mary Lasker, Abe Feinberg, Gene Wyman did a terrific job for the party in California. And when he died his wife kept going for us. My job was to come in at the end and talk to them, and then to talk to anybody they had been contacting. I did the asking. Substantial contributors, I knew the majority of them in the country. You need them. There's no way it can be done without them until the entire system changes. As it is now, there are four parts to any campaign. The candidate, the issues of the candidate, the campaign organization, and the money to run the campaign with. Without the money you can forget the other three.

"Well, I can tell you that I started hearing from a lot of them. There would be a guy who always was a big giver and nobody was hearing from him. I'd go over the lists for our dinner and I'd say, 'Hey, where is so and so? He always was a helluva good friend of ours. Why haven't we heard from him?' So I'd call the guy and he'd call me back and he'd say, 'Geez, Tip, I don't know what to tell you. Nine IRS guys hit me last week and I'd like to stay out of things for a while.' I began getting that from a lot of people. Fellows like George Steinbrenner. He's a helluva guy. I called him up and I said, 'George, old pal, what's the matter? Why don't we hear from you any more? Is something the matter?' You bet I called him up. He was one of these guys who would get on the phone for you and raise up a half dozen other guys to come and help out. So what does Steinbrenner say to me? He said, 'Geez, Tip, I want to come to see you and tell you what's going on.' And he came into my office. He said, 'Gee, they are holding the lumber over my head.' They got him between the IRS, the Justice Department, the Commerce Department. He was afraid he'd lose his business.

"Believe me, when they start doing IRS audits on you, there is no way that they're not going to get something on you if they want to. No way. So I talked it over with Steinbrenner and what do you think he told me they wanted off him? He said Stans's people wanted a hundred thousand dollars for Nixon's campaign. And then they wanted him to be the head of Democrats for Nixon in Ohio. He told me he'd been in to see them and this is what they told him. Well, there was nothing we could do to help him at that point. These other guys had taken over the Republican party. They had set up independent financing. That would cripple the Republican party. And now they were going to cripple the Democratic party. I told George to do what he had to do. George said he didn't think he was going to give in. Then he left the office and I don't know what he did. He went over to see this Kalmbach or somebody like that. I guess he had no choice. This Maurice Stans. He has to be the lousiest bastard ever to live. Now, I was getting this from all over. Guys began to come in and see me and say, 'Tip, I'm having trouble with a contract. I never had trouble before. It's legitimate business. They tell me to see Stans. What can I do?'

"That's what it was like. All our old friends, our best friends, were afraid to come around. Well, you didn't have to draw a map for me to let me know what was going on. It was a shakedown. A plain old-fashioned goddammed shakedown. I can read pressure. I could see what they were doing. And then out comes this great big newspaper ad. Democrats for Nixon. And the ad had all the names of our people on it. The day the ad came out, they were calling me up saying, 'Tip, I had to sign the ad. They sandbagged me. It's either sign the ad or go into the soup.' Well, I kept saying to myself, this Nixon and Stans have got to be kidding. What they're doing is too big. You never can get away with a thing like this. Not in this country. But they were sure trying. Now I don't remember when I said it, but I know I said to myself somewhere in the 1972 campaign. I said, 'This fellow is going to get himself impeached.' The strange thing about it is that I never gave much thought to the Watergate break-in when it happened. I thought it was silly and stupid. I never thought it was important. I was concentrating on the shakedown of these fellas like Steinbrenner."

This ride ended in the rain in the parking lot of Suffolk Downs Race Track in East Boston. The occasion was the thirty-ninth running of the Massachusetts Handicap. They ran the 1974 Race on a Sunday and Thomas (Tip) O'Neill was going to be there no matter what. In his life, only a swearing-in is more important than Mass Handicap Day. Inside the track, on his way to the dining room, O'Neill shook hands with a headwaiter, with Joe Dugan, an old New York Yankee third baseman, and with Rip Valenti, the fight promoter. O'Neill sat at a window table and looked over the menu. "I'm going to eat something very light," he said. He put the menu down. "A New England boiled dinner and a bottle of beer," he told the waiter. When the food came, he looked at the scattered strips of corned beef on his plate. "Bring us a whole plate of corned beef on the side," he said. He put his glasses on and began making pencil marks on the program for the next race. "Class really stands out when there is no class," he said. This is a race track saying older than the race track we were sitting in. It was direct evidence of part of the higher education O'Neill received as a youth, training of inestimable value to a person who, someday, was going to push for impeachment of a President. For at the race track, where life is uncoated and speech is direct, there is an extraordinarily keen awareness of the possibilities of larceny jumping up at any moment, in any form. And a man who spent time at the paddock of a race track, as Tip O'Neill did, had no trouble at all in understanding exactly what was happening to people in this country like George Steinbrenner.

Early in 1968, at the big Democratic campaign fund-raising dinner in Washington, great anticipation ran through the room upon the appearance of George M. Steinbrenner III, the owner of a shipbuilding company in Cleveland, who was taking his first step into heavyweight politics. Steinbrenner was new money, which in politics is stronger than new love. Therefore, Steinbrenner had been given a great table, right down front, where he could be thoroughly exposed to attacks by the great names of Democratic politics. A tree facing a forest fire. But also a tree ready to join the fire: Steinbrenner owned a company which did business with the government.

On other counts, too, he was a natural to come into the game. He'd been active in Cleveland, saving the National Air Show for the city, walking through Hough at the time of the riot in 1966, and he also was interested in show business and sports, two distant cousins of politics. At the end of the 1968 campaign, Steinbrenner discovered how much of a natural for politics he really was. Nixon had just won the election and the Democrats were in debt $8.5 million nationally and there was no money left in the Democratic Senate and House campaign funds. At this point, Senators Daniel Inouye and Gaylord Nelson spoke to Steinbrenner, asking him to be the chairman of the 1969 fund-raising dinner. Steinbrenner accepted. In 1969, the dinner raised $800,000 for Congressional campaigns. The next year it brought in over a million. Great national heroes are as prominent as waiters when matched against a man who can raise big money for politicians.

The record also shows that from 1968 on, Steinbrenner was in continual difficulty with the government. How much of the trouble was for legitimate reasons—and how much of it was illegitimate (the Nixon re-election people at work)—is impossible to tell. Steinbrenner, over a gin at Shea Stadium in New York—he owns the Yankees—refers you to lawyers. The Nixon people, all either in prison or awaiting trial, also refer you to lawyers. It is understood, however, that there was an Internal Revenue Service audit of Steinbrenner and his businesses after 1968. So, as O'Neill said later, there is no such thing as an audit being done and nothing being found. If the IRS auditor doesn't find something amiss, his pencils are taken away from him and he has to write all reports with a buffalo nickel. Steinbrenner also had problems with the Commerce Department. In purchasing the American Shipbuilding Company in 1968, Steinbrenner inherited an obligation to build an oceanography research ship for the government. The ship was to cost, Steinbrenner claimed, $8 million more than originally estimated by the old owners of American Shipbuilding. Each department Steinbrenner went to, Commerce and then Defense, gave him either no action or no hope. After phone calls and letters, Steinbrenner finally was given word that Maurice Stans, then Secretary of Commerce, would see that there was a hearing. In November of 1971, a Department of Defense auditing team moved into the shipbuilding company. When the audits were finished, Stans sent word that the results appeared favorable. In February of 1971, Stans ruled against Steinbrenner. In 1972 he left the Commerce Department for the job of Chairman of the Finance Committee to Re-Elect the President.

On another front, Steinbrenner also was in difficulty with the Justice Department's antitrust division. Steinbrenner had entered into negotiations to purchase the shipbuilding division of Litton Industries. The Justice Department said the purchase would be in violation of antitrust laws. Steinbrenner became involved in the purchase of a tug company, Great Lakes Towing. Again, the Justice Department said it would be in violation. All during this period, industries of any size were being allowed and encouraged to use machetes on all rules and consumers.

The only anger Richard Nixon ever showed was at the least hint of a government agency preventing an industry from gouging the people of the nation. Yet all Steinbrenner, the Democratic Dinner Chairman, had was trouble. He began to entertain the notion that somebody was trying to tell him something.

Steinbrenner had in 1968 placed some of his law business with a college classmate, Tom Evans, an attorney in the firm of Mudge, Rose, Guthrie & Alexander—formerly Nixon, Mudge, Rose, Guthrie, Alexander & Mitchell. The law firm had offices at 20 Broad Street in Manhattan. Upon senior partner Nixon's election, branch offices immediately were opened in Washington, on Pennsylvania Avenue. This did not appear to be a move to discourage potential clients who had legal problems with government agencies. If you stumbled coming out of the Mudge, Rose Washington building, you wound up banging your head into the guard booth on the White House driveway. Evans does not seem to have been of any spectacular help to Steinbrenner at first. Somewhere in their relationship, Steinbrenner asked about a possible ambassadorship for his brother-in-law Jacob Kamm, a professor at Case-Western Reserve University. The price list Steinbrenner saw for ambassadorships was too high for him, brilliant brother-in-law or not. At the start of 1972, attorney Evans and client Steinbrenner began to discuss Evans' great desire to see Richard Nixon re-elected. Steinbrenner admitted he was not in love with the thought of supporting George McGovern, who at the time was methodically putting together the Democratic nomination. At the same time, Steinbrenner primarily was in love with the thought of getting out of his problems with government agencies. Nowhere has it ever been said that American business or politics is an amateur sport. During these conversations, attorney Evans told his client, "I'm setting up a meeting for you with Herb Kalmbach."

Steinbrenner asked who Herb Kalmbach was. Evans told him that Kalmbach was the man in charge of big donors to the Nixon campaign.

Steinbrenner saw Kalmbach in the offices of the Committee to Re-Elect the President. These offices were located in the same building on Pennsylvania Avenue as the Mudge, Rose law firm. One of the beauty parts of royalty is that you don't have to be subtle. At first Steinbrenner and Kalmbach talked good, pleasant Republican talk. Football. Steinbrenner once was an assistant coach at Purdue. Kalmbach knew the names of Southern California football players.

Kalmbach then said, "I understand from Tom Evans that you're interested in contributing to the campaign."

"Yes I am," Steinbrenner said.

"Well, if you're thinking of coming in here for under a hundred thousand dollars, don't bother," Kalmbach said. "We work up to a million around here."

"That's too steep for me," Steinbrenner said.

Kalmbach preferred not to hear. At this stage, Steinbrenner was in the exact position of a person who has lost on gambling to a bookmaker, and the bookmaker, seeking to get paid, has brought the gambler to a shylock with whom the bookmaker has an alliance.

"Do you intend to do this by check or by cash?" Kalmbach said.

"By check," Steinbrenner said.

Kalmbach took two sheets from his desk. Printed on them were the various committees formed to receive contributions to the campaign. Kalmbach said, "Now, here is what I would expect of you."

In the left-hand corner of the top page, Kalmbach wrote in black pen:

33 @ 3

1 @ 1

He pushed the paper across to Steinbrenner. The numbers needed no explanation: give $3000 to each of thirty-three committees on the sheets and give $1000 to one other committee. Steinbrenner could choose his committees. There were sixty listed on the sheets: Effective Government Committee, Dedicated Americans for Government Reform, Loyal Americans for a Better America, Stable Society Committee, United Friends of Reform in Society, Reform in Society Support Group. No matter which of the exotically named committees Steinbrenner preferred, the number would come out the same: thirty-three at three and one at one equals $100,000.

"You do a lot of business in Washington, you'd do well to get with the right people," Kalmbach told Steinbrenner. In other places, other men, better men than Kalmbach, tell you, "Pay or Die."

Kalmbach has admitted to Watergate investigators, Dave Dorsen for one, that, yes, he did have this way of speaking to potential contributors and he certainly could have spoken this way to Steinbrenner. As Kalmbach sees it, all he was doing was suggesting amounts and then sort of selling, prodding perhaps, the man into making the contribution. In a district attorney's office, this method he used is known as extortion.

When Steinbrenner left Kalmbach's office, he felt he was in trouble. He knew he had gone too far with Kalmbach, and now he was afraid to say no. And with the other side contacting him, with a Tip O'Neill calling him up, he decided he had, through design and accident, put himself into a great deal of trouble. While he was in Washington, Steinbrenner spoke to Tip O'Neill, Daniel Inouye, and Edward Kennedy. He told them of Kalmbach's demands. All of them said there was nothing that could be done at the time. Everybody was helpless. Steinbrenner went home to Cleveland. Where, immediately, the phone calls began from Herbert Kalmbach. If Steinbrenner was going to contribute, Kalmbach said, he was to be certain to do so before April 7. All campaign contributions were allowed to be in secrecy before that date. Steinbrenner had his treasurer, Bob Bartolme, make out the checks for Kalmbach. Seventy-five thousand dollars of it, Steinbrenner says, came from him personally. The other $25,000 was put together in the form of bonuses to executives, the bonuses immediately turned over to the Nixon Committee as personal donations. This was breaking all laws against corporate contributions. When the checks were in order, Bartolme sent a messenger to Washington with the $100,000 for the re-election of Richard Nixon.

That month, in April of 1972, Steinbrenner told the people around him that he finally was all right, that the lawyer Evans had told him that the three people running Washington were H. R. Haldeman, John D. Ehrlichman, and Fred Malek, and that he, Steinbrenner, was all right with all three of them. A lawyer from John Connally's Democrats for Nixon called Steinbrenner and asked if he would be head of Democrats for Nixon in Ohio. Steinbrenner resisted this. He did not make his new friends particularly happy with his resistance, but Steinbrenner felt he had done enough. He had. He was going to wind up with so many federal indictments against him that in August 1974 he pleaded guilty to a felony.

For at the start of 1973, instead of having such a smashing year with the Kalmbachs blocking for him, Steinbrenner wound up being tackled by James Polk of *The Washington Star-News.* Polk is first class. He spoke to Steinbrenner about the campaign contributions made by American Shipbuilding employees. Steinbrenner told Polk a story which Polk did not believe. Polk then went to American Shipbuilding employees. He found an accountant who earned $16,000 in salary had contributed $3000 to Dedicated Americans for Good Government and another $3000 to Dedicated Volunteers for a Better America. The accountant said they were personal contributions, not corporate contributions which of course were illegal. Polk learned that the employee had made out the campaign checks at the same time he had received a surprise bonus of $6000 from American Shipbuilding. Oh, no, the employee said. His contributions had been out of patriotism. Polk printed the stories. He also called the situation to the attention of the Watergate Special Prosecutor's office at the time it was established. The Special Prosecutor's office sent FBI agents out to interview Steinbrenner and his employees.

"Don't worry about it," John H. Melcher, Jr., American Shipbuilding counsel, told the employees. He, Steinbrenner, and the employees told the same story to the FBI that they had told to Polk. Subpoenas then were issued to the employees, calling them before a grand jury. "Don't worry," Melcher told them again. This time they did worry. "He would be saying 'don't worry' to me the day I got put behind bars for perjury," one of them said.

Out of their testimony came a sixteen-count indictment against Steinbrenner and Melcher. At this point, Steinbrenner dove into the offices of Edward Bennett Williams, Attorney at Law, Washington, D.C. Any criminal lawyer I've ever spoken to has told me that if he ever got into trouble he would try to retain Williams. Life became less complicated for Steinbrenner when Williams stopped his covering up and storytelling. With

Williams plea bargaining, the sixteen counts were reduced to two: illegal campaign contributions and aiding and abetting obstructions of justice.

Finally, in October of 1974, Steinbrenner entered a guilty plea in federal court in Cleveland.

Nothing ever happened on his claim of cost overruns on the oceanography research vessel. Steinbrenner has taken the case to the United States Court of Claims. He also was forced to suspend his activities as principal owner of the New York Yankee baseball team. Edward Bennett Williams asked Baseball Commissioner Bowie Kuhn, "Well, how do you explain baseball taking no action against Cesar Cedeno?" Cedeno plays centerfield for the Houston Astros, and in 1973 he was convicted in Santo Domingo of involuntary manslaughter when a gun went off in a motel room and shot a girl in the head. Kuhn said, oh, there was a difference. "After all, Cedeno did that in the off-season."

Nobody knows how many cases of this sort there were. Businessmen who were robbed would prefer to forget about it. The IRS agents burned files. They must have had a lot of burning to do, because the operation came from the top and almost nothing was considered too small. This can be attested to personally.

In the fall of 1971, a friend, Charles U. Daly, soon to be a vice president at Harvard University, had an enormously practical idea which involved Congressman Paul McCloskey, with whom Daly had served in Korea. Daly wanted to help McCloskey, a Republican, to run against Richard Nixon in the New Hampshire primary, in February, in order to bring some sort of pressure, if possible, on Nixon to stop bombing people in Vietnam. Daly and McCloskey agreed first to go to Laos and Vietnam, observe the bombing of unarmed people, then begin campaigning on that issue in New Hampshire. In order to raise funds for the trip to Asia and the start of the campaign, Daly and McCloskey came to New York, and writer Jimmy Breslin took them around for an evening of fund raising. We met in the Sherry-Netherland Hotel, which serves drinks strong enough to make a mule walk backward. We then went out into the night after money. At the third stop, an East Side cocktail party, I cornered Martin Fife, a plastics manufacturer.

Fife called a gray-haired man over and introduced him as Sam Rubin, an investor. Each said he would give $1000. I told Fife and Rubin that this was a great undertaking. "The public will listen more to a McCloskey, he's a Republican who fought in a war. This isn't some freaking New York peacenik going over there, like one of these trips this Cora Weiss takes." I walked away feeling great and reaching for another drink. How was I to know that Cora Weiss was Sam Rubin's daughter? The last stop of the night was at some high-class brownstone on the East Side. I came out of the house holding a full glass of Scotch and water, a fine crystal glass. I tripped as I hit the sidewalk. I held the precious glass up high as I went down, landing on my shoulder. The glass was safe. The butler came racing from the town-house doorway. He bent over me, snatched the fine crystal glass from my hand, then raced back inside the house. I was lying in the cold on the sidewalk and I heard the bolt clicking as the butler inside the house locked the door.

Sometime later there was a prominent newspaper story which mentioned that James Breslin, the writer, had helped raise money for the McCloskey venture. Days after the article appeared, the IRS announced in the mail that it had discovered I owed $7500 in back taxes. This was or was not a coincidence. I paid, McCloskey tried and failed to make an appreciable dent in New Hampshire, and that was the end of it.

And then in the middle of 1973, during the Ervin committee hearings, a committee staff worker handed McCloskey three sheets of paper, Xerox copies of evidence being compiled by the staff. McCloskey showed them to me. The first said:

FOR: *Attorney General*
FROM: *John Dean*
Attached is some additional information which Jack has collected re: McCloskey operation. I've passed a copy along to Jeb Magruder.

bcc Gordon Strachan

The second Xerox was of a White House Inter-Office memorandum form:

TO: *John Dean*
FROM: *John J. Caulfield*

Under the space for "Remarks" it read, "AG should see these. They are very consistent with my report."

Attached to the memo were a group of clippings, including *The New York Times* article about the McCloskey operation.

The third Xerox copy read:

TO: *John Dean, John Mitchell*
FROM: *John J. Caulfield*

On the East Coast, McCloskey has sought and has accepted what is described as "New York Peace Money." At a New York City party McCloskey raised $11,000 which was used to finance a trip to Southeast Asia. Some attending party were: Stewart Mott, left-wing philanthropist; Howard Steen, Dreyfus Fund; Sam Rubin, investor.

It was learned that writer Jimmy Breslin and former Kennedy staffer Charles Daly were instrumental in this particular effort. Daly accompanied McCloskey on the trip.

They were playing, therefore, a game that was extensive as it was dangerous. The fact that a Tip O'Neill could be aroused shows that. The man knows better than anyone else that this nation has yet to hold its first canonization of somebody who remained in a State of Grace while campaign fund raising. During the 1960 Presidential campaign, O'Neill was an advance man in Missouri for John F. Kennedy and in the course of his duties he came upon August Busch, who offered to round up thirty people for a $1000-a-head breakfast meeting if Kennedy would show up. O'Neill called Kennedy, who quickly asked the crucial question about the proposed meeting. "What time should I be there?" The breakfast was arranged at an airport motel and Kennedy arrived, stepped into the room, received the money nod from O'Neill, and then said to the guests, "If you'll excuse Congressman O'Neill and me for a moment."

The two of them went out and jammed into what O'Neill remembers as the world's smallest men's room.

"Now I have twelve thousand in cash and seventeen thousand in checks, what do you want me to do with it?" O'Neill said.

"Give the checks to Kenny O'Donnell. I'll take the cash."

O'Neill handed Kennedy the cash and watched it disappear into the inside jacket pocket.

"Geez, this business is no different if you're running for ward leader or President of the United States," O'Neill said to Kennedy.

Kennedy said nothing and the two of them went back to the breakfast.

2

"The reputation of power is power."

AFTER THE first meeting in which O'Neill remembers the word impeachment being used, the three of them, Albert, Rodino, and O'Neill went back to their businesses with nothing agreed upon. A few weeks later, Rodino mentioned the matter to the chief counsel of the House Judiciary Committee, Jerome Zeifman. Zeifman is the only person I ever have met who spent fifteen years in government and wound up a radical. The moment he heard impeachment the blood rose to his mouth. Zeifman already had a file on impeachment precedents put together. He had been forced to do research when the House Minority Leader, Gerald R. Ford of Michigan, acting as he always did even upon the whim of Richard Nixon, had called for the impeachment of Supreme Court Justice William O. Douglas. Zeifman gathered background and precedents for impeachment on the vague chance that the question would reach the Judiciary Committee. Which it did not. The files, however, remained, and now Zeifman could not wait to put his files to work against Richard Nixon. Somewhere in Washington there was a squealing, grinding sound. The hugest wheel in the country, bureaucracy, was starting to turn.

The problem was that there wasn't even a shred of documentation, only a race-track suspicion by one Congressman. Also the Chairman of the Judiciary Committee, Peter Rodino, had been raised by an immigrant father who taught him to hold the Presidency in respect second only to a statue in church. As Peter Rodino's father told him of the President of the United States, blue smoke appeared high in the sky over Newark and young Rodino saw enormous things appear in it. From the start of our history, most of this country lived in this manner. The Office of President is such a bastardized thing, half royalty and half democracy, that nobody knows whether to genuflect or spit. At the start, George Washington wanted to go to his first

inauguration in a gilded carriage drawn by twelve white horses
and insisted upon being called "His Excellency." Thomas
Jefferson caused him to settle for less horsepower and less
title—"Mr. President." Which accomplished nothing because
now, two hundred years later, in the Rayburn Office Building,
Washington, D.C., Peter Rodino was frozen by the illusion his
father had created for him.

Impeachment, Jerome Zeifman said to himself. Impeachment, impeachment, impeachment. Jerome Zeifman knew
John W. Dean III from the period when Dean was an assistant minority counsel on the Judiciary Committee. Zeifman
knew Dean as a person who took no chances on his own; at
all times John Dean wanted the full authority of everybody
over him. If Dean was performing any questionable acts, then
Zeifman knew automatically that Nixon knew of all of them.
And of course Dean had to be doing something wrong. Had
to. Impeachment, impeachment. It came to Zeifman what he
could do. He called Gary Hymel, legislative assistant in the
Majority Leader's office. Hymel came around to the Judiciary
Committee's offices. Zeifman worked in a space that was not
enclosed. He looked around, told Hymel they could not talk in
such surroundings. He led Hymel to a vacant room and locked
the door.

Zeifman is short, with thinning sandy-gray hair and a slow,
measured way of speaking. He will begin a sentence with a
word and then stop completely as if what he is going to say
next will cause a corner of the world to come to an end. He
comes from East Third Street in Manhattan. Gary Hymel is
tall, dark-haired, with the face of a boy who is just changing
into a man. He does not look like his experience, which is long.
Hymel is from New Orleans, and his predominant talent, a
great one, is that of listening.

"Gary, I am convinced . . ." Zeifman paused and looked
intensely at Hymel, ". . . by everything I see that there is going
to be an impeachment."

"I better tell Tip about it right now," Hymel said.

He left the room and went on the subway from the Rayburn
Building to the Capitol. He walked into the Majority Leader's
offices and found O'Neill. He shut the door so nobody would
disturb them. Then he told O'Neill of what Jerome Zeifman,

chief counsel, House Judiciary Committee, had told him. *Impeachment.*

"I knew it," Tip O'Neill said.

Dammit, now we better hurry up; the thing is starting without me. I better get right onto it. Impeachment. You bet he's going to be impeached. Why, they must have it in their heads to get going right now.

As he sat in his office, Thomas P. O'Neill, who is called Tip by most people and Tom by those who know him well, never noticed that he had his hand on a huge mirror that did not exist but did exist.

Tip O'Neill at all times has one great political weapon at his disposal. He understands so well that all political power is primarily an illusion. If people think you have power, then you have power. If people think you have no power, then you have no power. This is a great truth in politics that I was able to recognize in O'Neill's ways, because I had taken the enormous trouble to go out and learn this in the streets and clubhouses of the City of New York and particularly as a candidate for citywide office in 1969, an adventure which left me with the deep-lasting scars of one who went and learned the hard way, thus learning forever. For those who take their politics from a book, an easier but much less effective way of learning than mine, this same proposition has been advanced in print by Thomas Hobbes, who wrote in England in the 1600s: "The reputation of power is power." Power is an illusion.

Illusion. Mirrors and blue smoke, beautiful blue smoke rolling over the surface of highly polished mirrors, first a thin veil of blue smoke, then a thick cloud that suddenly dissolves into wisps of blue smoke, the mirrors catching it all, bouncing it back and forth. If somebody tells you how to look, there can be seen in the smoke great, magnificent shapes, castles and kingdoms, and maybe they can be yours. All this becomes particularly dynamic when the person telling you where to look knows how to adjust the mirrors, tilt one forward, walk to the other side, and turn one on its base a few degrees to the right, suddenly causing the refractions to be different everywhere. And then going to the blue smoke, lessening it, intensifying it, and all the time keeping those watching transfixed, hoping, believing himself. Believing perhaps more than anybody else in the room. And at the same time knowing that what he is believing in is mirrors and blue smoke.

This is the game called politics and power as it is played in the Legion Halls and Elks Clubs and church basements and political clubhouses throughout the country, throughout the world, while men try to please and calm others in order to maintain and improve a public career. Always, no matter what country you are in, the culmination of politics is considered to be the men who are in Washington and who are the best in the world at taking an illusion and telling you, and telling themselves, that it really is power.

This thesis, this truth, never was clearer than it was in Washington in the summer of 1974. Thomas P. O'Neill, Jr., had power, great power at times, because nearly everybody in Washington thought of him as having power. In the book, *Rules and Practices of the House of Representatives*, mention is made of every rule and roost in the House. There happens not to be one single mention, direct or indirect, of a position known as Majority Leader. By law, there is no such post. There is custom for it. There also is a line in the appropriations to pay for staff salaries for the Majority Leader. The holder of the job has large offices and is driven in great limousines. But by law or custom, there is no exact definition of the duties of the Majority Leader.

When Tip O'Neill decided that his primary duty was to make rapid the removal of Richard Nixon he took on great power. Because everybody began to regard him as being quite powerful. And meanwhile, each day, these little pieces of trouble dropped on the floor at Richard Nixon's feet and more and more people noticed it. As the level of regard for Nixon's power dropped, the level of danger for his career rose. At the end, Nixon had not the personal political power of a city councilman. He sat in the Oval Office, but he might as well have been in City Hall, in Dayton.

The ability to create the illusion of power, to use mirrors and blue smoke, is one found in unusual people. They reach their objectives through overstatement or understatement, through silent agreements and, always, the use of language at the most opportune moments.

The night Nixon introduced Gerald R. Ford as his nominee to replace convicted Spiro T. Agnew as Vice President, there were strolling strings and champagne in the White House. The notion was to put Watergate behind us; you have won, you have gotten Agnew, now let us forget about it and go on as before. In the pleasure of the evening, James Lynn, the Secretary of Housing and Urban Development, spoke with Thomas P. O'Neill.

"Tip, did you ever think we'd be standing here in the White House with history being made, the Twenty-fifth Amendment working for the first time. There's probably never going to be another night like it in the country's history."

"Not for about eight months," Tip O'Neill said.

Lynn's mouth opened. Tip O'Neill gave this great street laugh of his and jammed a Daniel Webster cigar in his mouth. James Lynn went away from the night with cement in his stomach. When people around him would say hopefully that Watergate was finished, Lynn would tell them it was not finished. Not anywhere near finished.

Once, for Richard Nixon, there were only two kids on *The Washington Post* newspaper who were causing trouble. Journalism, no matter how skilled, how brilliant, is a passive trade. Words command only when used by someone in command. Words written by a writer cause little immediate change. The full weight of nearly all the newspapers and nearly all the television had been used for eight years to make horrible the war in Vietnam. The war went on, more intensely at the end than it had at the beginning.

Another threat, another enemy for Richard Nixon now sprang up from another area. A judge, John Sirica. He was painstakingly honest. Lawyers and law professors will point to him forever as a reason for the law triumphing in Watergate; that in the end the actions of no other institution was needed: the law handled the matter. Senator Sam J. Ervin, Jr., thundered about the sanctity of the Constitution and Judge Sirica quietly, decisively applied it. And always, there was the Supreme Court ready to make honest rulings. All of which is beautiful for speeches at a Bar Association dinner or a law-school seminar. Yet all those associated with the law, from Sam Ervin and his committee to John Sirica, crept and probed and yet never took the decisive step, never reached out to grab anyone in the name of the law. The committee subpoenaed. The court ordered. For months Nixon surrendered nothing. Always, he held up the results of the election: 61 per cent of the country voted for him. The Ervin committee said it was sad that the President did not cooperate. The court coughed. The law crumbled in the face of an election certificate. There was no evidence suggesting that Nixon planned the Watergate affair. All he did was enter into a conspiracy to obstruct justice in the aftermath. Where I come from, this is only a misdemeanor. The law says nothing about the true crime committed: that of repeatedly lying to 250 million people. All the law could produce was a minor complaint, and as the time dragged, and time could help Nixon, it began to appear that nobody truly was going to press and attempt to destroy a President for a misdemeanor. For if somebody wanted to treat Nixon as a citizen and apply the law to him, the time element would have been minimal.

Once, in a federal courthouse in Newark, in New Jersey, I saw a businessman, ordered to produce his books as evidence, tell a judge named Whipple that the books were lost. Whipple said that was all right with him; the man could just go in the back there, go into the cells, and sit there until the books were found. The businessman sat in a cell for three days. On the fourth day he was joined by a large gray rat which came out of a crack under the base of the toilet. The next morning, Judge Whipple, busy on the bench reading a motion, heard the doors in the courtroom squeak loudly. Whipple looked up. Staggering into the courtroom, unable to see over the huge pile of blue ledger books he carried, was the partner of the businessman. Your honor, we have just been able to locate the books you requested. Now can my friend get out of jail? This is how it works every place there is a courtroom.

But it did not work this way in the Senate Watergate hearing room and, despite the lore of Sirica, it did not work in his courtroom.

Citizens would have been thrown in the slam for contempt. But the half-royalty of the White House held everybody off. Even when John Dean shook a nation with his testimony, there were only a few who felt anything ever could happen to Richard

Nixon. Clearly, then, journalism and the law were not enough to do anything about the crimes of Richard Nixon. But this is only natural. This is a country of men, not laws, and therefore the situation at this point needed a man; a working politician; a professional; a drinking, eating, handshaking member of the Elks, Knights of Columbus, Knights of St. Finbar; trustee of Boston College; Man of the Year 1962; National Conference of Christians and Jews; a director of the United Appeal; a ten-term Congressman who had spent 4000 nights at dinner tables everywhere in the city of Washington. Only a working politician could challenge and erode the one thing Richard Nixon could not afford to lose: the support of political people. And now, early in the game, so early in the game, Richard Nixon had a new opponent who was a popular politician.

This art which O'Neill pursues, this art of mirrors and blue smoke, is not fraudulent. Rather, it is how all of life works: in politics, life is compressed into a small number of people who spend a short period of time in a circle with a stunted radius. The practice of art can only be done successfully, and for the good of others, by human beings who bring with them a little intelligence, a little wit, a little honor—a seascapist must love an ocean before he can make its movement stand still.

And throughout the quest for justice in the nation in the years 1973 and 1974, Thomas P. O'Neill stood in the full nobility of his profession: a politician of the Democratic party.

As such, the man has no visible means of support. There is no badge, no tool kit, no license that says you are allowed to be a politician. There is only your word: I will do it; I will not do it. And if there is one thing that makes Tip O'Neill so effective in his business, made him so effective against Richard Nixon, it is his belief that a commitment—his word given—is an extension of his religion.

Go to any time in his career, pick out a situation and inspect O'Neill's conduct in it, and always you will see the worth of his word. Go to early 1946, the night a Cambridge politician named Chick Artesani came to Tip O'Neill's house with a skinny young man named Jack Kennedy, whom Artesani introduced as the next Congressman from the area.

"I want you to be with us, Tip," Artesani said.

"Well, I'm delighted to meet you, Jack, but I'm sorry I have to tell you and my old pal here that I'm already committed to Mike Neville."

O'Neill had served in the state legislature with Neville for eight years, and O'Neill's word of support for this particular Congressional race had been given to Neville some time back.

Artesani shrugged, Kennedy and O'Neill shook hands, and the meeting ended. When the primary race for the Congressional seat began some weeks later, O'Neill went out onto the streets with Mike Neville. He toured his district, Russell Street, Orchard Street, Blake Street, and rang doorbells and chatted with people.

"Hello, I'm Tom O'Neill. I'm a member of the state legislature and I see you're new in the neighborhood here, and I haven't had a chance to meet you yet. I just want to say I've lived here in the neighborhood thirty-odd years and I'm not busy in the legislature at this moment because the legislature is not in session. So I'm just coming around to point out to you, if you don't mind, that I think Mike Neville will make a great Congressman from this area; he'll give us the type of voice in Washington we deserve. I hope you'll give him your consideration when you vote on primary day."

And the woman he was speaking to excused herself and went to the dining-room table and brought back a pamphlet with a picture of a PT boat on the front. "Is your Mr. Neville running against this brave young Kennedy?"

Tip shook his head and went on to the next house. And then he began to work the people he knew. He came into Mrs. Murphy's house on Orchard Street, and she took him by the arm and led him into the kitchen for a cup of tea.

"Tip, how are you?"

"Well, Nellie, I'm just great. I just came in to say hello. I'm running again for re-election as you undoubtedly know, but I don't have any opposition, so I want to come here and talk to you about Mike Neville . . ."

Nellie Murphy said, "You don't have any opposition? Isn't this young fellow Kennedy running against you?"

"No, Nellie, he's running for Congress in Washington against my friend . . ."

"Oh, thanks be to God, Tom, I thought he was running against you. What a wonderful boy. We've got all this literature.

Oh, what a beautiful story about the PT boat, getting lost in those islands. Dear God, I don't know how I could have voted even for you against such a wonderful, brave young man."

When O'Neill got home that night, there was a phone call from candidate Mike Neville.

"What are you doing?" Neville asked.

"I'm taking a shower and you better do the same thing," O'Neill said.

As the campaign went on, Chick Artesani called O'Neill again. "I'm with Mike Neville, and that's it," O'Neill said. Jack Kennedy then called. The answer was the same.

One night, a next-door neighbor, Joe Healy, called O'Neill. "I've got Jack Kennedy here and I'm bringing him over to see you."

"Don't bring him here, it'll only embarrass him, and you'll embarrass me too," O'Neill said. "I'm with Mike Neville and that's it."

"Kennedy is going to win," Healy said.

"That doesn't have anything to do with it," Tip said.

A few minutes later the doorbell rang. It was Healy and Kennedy. O'Neill stood in his living room and said, "There's nothing I can do for you, Jack, I'm with Mike all the way."

From O'Neill's house, Healy and Kennedy went up to the home of Leo Diehl, O'Neill's closest friend. Diehl was delighted and flattered by the young Kennedy's attentions. But there was no way he could help. "I gave my word to Neville," Leo said.

On primary day, wherever Tip O'Neill looked, he saw coming down off the porches of their frame houses, coming down to vote, hundreds of housewives with pictures of PT boats in their hands.

The day after the election, the first phone call Tip O'Neill received was from Jack Kennedy. "Tip, I want you to know that the next time I do anything, I want you to be with me. When you have a friend, when Mike Neville had a friend like you, a trustworthy friend, then I want you to know I appreciate the position you were in and I will never forget how you acted."

And in 1974, when it all began in Congress against Richard Nixon, most politicians did not want to hear of impeachment. What is this impeachment? Freak John Dean, who elected him? What the hell does a courtroom have to do with our business? Let the judge go out and run for office. We're elected officials. If you can impeach Nixon, then you can impeach any of us. Translated into newspaper stories, this became a cry for national stability. But when a Tip O'Neill began using the word impeachment on the floor of the House of Representatives, this changed the issue. For he was no frivolous dreamer from the West Side of New York. This was a bone politician, a man with a word, and he gave great believability to the prospects of impeachment merely by saying it.

And this, Richard Nixon could not stand. He was too removed, too isolated, to watch the mirrors being arranged and the blue smoke rolling over them. You can't play baseball unless you get a baseball field and play baseball. Richard Nixon could not play politics if he was not going to be in the room where they had the smoke machine going. The game therefore began in his absence, and you had this first quiver, not a shudder, just this slight quiver, which ran across the floor of the House of Representatives. Something was happening. But you had to be there to feel the vibration on your feet.

In June of 1973, when John Wesley Dean III slipped into the witness chair at the Senate Watergate hearings, among those watching television closely was Jerome Zeifman. Zeifman's original suspicions hardened: Dean admitted a number of illegal acts; it followed that Nixon was involved in each of them. Zeifman saw O'Neill.

"Mr. O'Neill, there is one thing you ought to know, Nixon has committed a variety of crimes."

At the time, most people seemed to see it as a matter of John Dean's word against the word of the President of the United States. And that while a majority of the public might believe John Dean, there was general agreement that this still was hardly enough to ignite Congress into impeachment.

Tip O'Neill saw it differently. Steinbrenner alone had been enough justification for O'Neill to consider impeachment. With Dean's testimony in front of him, O'Neill couldn't see how much more was needed. Not being a lawyer, he was stuck with his good sense, which told him that Nixon was through.

* * *

At the end of July in 1973, Congressman Robert Drinan sat in his office late into each evening, hair matted with sweat, blue eyes concentrating on the piles of papers about him. He was preparing a resolution for the impeachment of Richard Nixon. This one was different. He was not using mirrors and blue smoke. He was using logic and reason and right. Which is why the impeachment resolution was not only ludicrous, it was dangerous: it could screw up the serious work that was already being done. The bill would have lost badly, with damaging public effect. They refer to Drinan as the Mad Monk. He is a Jesuit law professor out of Boston College and was one of the leaders of the antiwar movement. A McGovern man. What more do you have to say? Drinan also happens to be a brilliant law professor. His resolution called for Nixon to be impeached over the Cambodian war. But, shrewdly, Drinan did not take up the issue of whether the war was wrong or not. He called for Nixon's impeachment on the basis that Nixon should have informed the Congress that he was conducting a war in a country called Cambodia. As evidence of Nixon lying to Congress on this matter, Drinan had this quote from April 30, 1970: "We have scrupulously observed the neutrality of Cambodia for the last five years." Drinan then showed that over 3700 bombing raids had been conducted over Cambodia.

Word of Drinan's resolution reached Carl Albert, who immediately called in O'Neill. Albert pointed out the danger to all their hard work represented in Drinan's proposal. O'Neill spoke to Drinan. There was, of course, no way to talk Drinan out of it.

O'Neill took one last stab. "Well, you know, it's a little premature."

The use of the word surprised Drinan. He looked it up in the dictionary. The definition was "coming a bit ahead of its time, a premature time."

Drinan told himself that he had touched a nerve end with his idea. He informed other people of the use of the word "premature." More mirrors were moving.

On July 31, 1973, Drinan stood on the floor of the House of Representatives and began. "Mr. Speaker, with great reluctance I have come to the conclusion that the House of

Representatives should initiate impeachment proceedings against the President."

An impeachment resolution is a privileged resolution—it must be heard and voted on. Upon Drinan's speech, Carl Albert hurriedly called Tip O'Neill over.

"The floor must be guarded at all times," Albert said.

"Absolutely," O'Neill said.

"One of us has to be here at all times," Albert said.

A Republican could move at any time to have the Drinan resolution brought up for vote. At this time, the most votes an impeachment resolution could possibly get would have been twenty-five. Such a vote would appear in the newspapers as a vindication of Nixon by Congress.

"That would have been very bad psychologically," Carl Albert explained.

So each day, from noon until 7:30 and later at night, either Albert or O'Neill or Whip John McFall sat on the House floor, sometimes with only fifteen others present, in order to prevent any sudden Republican move on the Drinan resolution. Albert and O'Neill had agreed that the Democratic move would be to vote to have the resolution tabled. But as they took turns standing guard duty each day, they became tired. It was late in the year for Congress, they were heading for an adjournment, and the hours dragged particularly slowly. Finally, O'Neill ambled around the chamber to speak to Jerry Ford, the Minority Leader.

"Jerry, you know the walls have ears around here, and I've heard that some of your people want to bring this Drinan resolution up for a vote. Is that so?"

Ford said, "Tip, I've checked with the White House on that. They said it would be foolish for us to force a vote now. Somebody would just put up another resolution tomorrow. It's not the most important thing in the world for us."

"Thanks, Jerry."

O'Neill left the floor smiling. He now had some freedom of movement. And he also had established on the floor of the House this little bit of tension. The word impeachment had been in the room, not as part of a move by the lunatic Left, but as part of the normal business conducted by the Democratic leadership. Of course there were only twenty-five votes in favor of it right then. But what the hell, how many people had been exposed to the smoke? One other item of the day comforted him. Ford had not seemed distressed by the topic. He listened to the White House. Obviously they were not even regarding the possibilities of impeachment.

3

"He never even told his own family."

TIP O'NEILL lives at 26 Russell Street in North Cambridge, the part of Cambridge where people did not go to Harvard. He lives three houses away from the two-family house in which he was born. The house is a gray three-story house on a block with houses that are scarred from the years, a block that has a driveway entrance to Salvi Ford Sales and, down at the corners, the Cambridge Nursing Home, the Veterans of Foreign Wars post, and the Di Anthony School of Hairdressing. A couple of black families live on the block. The cab driver taking you there slaps the dashboard as the dispatcher's voice snarls over the radio, "Junior, don't you yell at me no more over the radio or you'll be sorry." In a lunch counter on the main street, Massachusetts Avenue, the waitress stands behind the counter shaking her head about her boss. "He'll give me," she says to the painter at the counter. "He'll give me all right. He'll give me, he'll give me drachmas. No, that's Greek. What is it in Italy they give you? Christ, it's the same thing, anyway. He'll give me nothin'." It is here at places like the Star Market, and with constituents like Red Fitzgerald, that Tip O'Neill's life and career are one.

Two miles away on Massachusetts Avenue begins the part of Cambridge where Harvard rules. Old red brick, old trees, old ivy, and old attitudes about the people in government who look like O'Neill does. At six-foot-two, and weighing anywhere from two hundred sixty-two to two hundred eighty-two pounds, with a great nose, Tip is not trim enough, nor does he have the outward elegance to cause people to use Latinate words in describing him. "I have an agreement with John Kenneth Galbraith," Tip says. "I don't say anything bad about him, and he doesn't endorse me in election years." But O'Neill knows Harvard. And he knows Radcliffe and Boston University and Suffolk Law and Massachusetts Institute of Technology and Boston College and the other schools in his district, the Eighth Congressional District of Massachusetts, an area with the greatest concentration of schools and students in the nation. Tip O'Neill lists over 100,000 students and teachers as constituents. Just as he does not have to be told what the waitress on Massachusetts Avenue believes, while she gropes for the word "lire," he also does not have to be told where Derek Bok of Harvard or John Silber of Boston University stand on an issue. And by this time, by the summer of 1973, Tip O'Neill knew it was right to be calling for an impeachment investigation of Richard Nixon. And he also knew it was not going to hurt him a bit in his district to have the matter go all the way through. There were no meetings at Harvard to pressure Tip O'Neill. Raoul Berger never cornered him over sherry and implored him to act. O'Neill's race-track instincts had him there ahead of all of them. But through the months that were to come, when he would become known as one of the strongest people in Washington pushing for impeachment, Tip O'Neill would always be able to turn the mirror if he felt like it and have people see that he had no other choice; it wasn't personal, it was a matter of serving the people of his district, reacting to them, surviving as a politician.

There were many people and many forces responsible for the end of Richard Nixon in the summer of 1974. It is difficult to determine which set of men and circumstances were most responsible. The full story never will become altogether clear in our time. Who becomes famous so often depends upon the politics of the academic world years later. Some historian will gain access to bundles of dusty letters, and the historian promptly announces that the author of the letters is a great force in history. He will receive the Sumner Prize for Originality. It usually matters not how much actual value the man had in his time.

The historian can produce the legend and the supporting evidence, and sell it throughout the academic world. In the small of the night, working with his subject, beginning to live with a man he never saw and knows only through letters and other papers, the historian naturally begins to make his subject larger and to prove his theme of how crucial the personality was to great events of history. There was a back-room politician in the Whig party named Thurlow Weed, who was active in the 1830s to 1850s, active as far as the record shows. Thurlow left great batches of letters extolling himself and all that he said he had done. The letters were discovered over a hundred years ago by Glyndon Van Deusen, University of Rochester, who proceeded to write a full-length biography of Thurlow Weed.

There should, however, be no difficulty in placing O'Neill. He appears to have done the most to gather and pack together the first particles of the bureaucracy, the particles squeezed together so tightly that pressure forced them to tumble over each other, tumble forward in the granular motion of a glacier. A bureaucracy under way, just as a glacier, does not halt upon command or obstacle. The bureaucracy takes on a life of its own and determines its own finish. O'Neill, who was the first to start the bureaucracy off, the first to see its initial imperceptible motion, also became the first to foresee its result. In October of 1973, when all available experts counted one hundred twenty-five votes at most against Richard Nixon if impeachment ever came to the floor of the House, O'Neill sat over Sunday brunch on Cape Cod and assured family and friends that the votes would be there.

Weighing as much as he does, O'Neill does not look like a figure who has had anything to do with history. The thinness, the austerity, and the haughtiness that glare at you from oil portraits of such men is totally absent in O'Neill. He comes with the full blood of Cork City in his face. A great head of silver hair allows O'Neill to be picked out of a crowd at a glance. He has a large bulbous nose that is quite red. Large blue eyes sometimes seem to be sleepy-slow and have led a thousand victims into thinking that they were on the verge of winning. When he has a thick Daniel Webster cigar stuffed into one corner of his mouth, O'Neill appears to be a backroom politician who always has a drink or a contract in his hand. Someday, when he gets very old, I think O'Neill might say that no matter how far he went in life, how powerful he became, this appearance, as interpreted by so many others, prevented him from going even further, from going to the places where his talents belonged. Because if you see in a man and say of a man only that he is a big, overweight, cigar-smoking, whisky-drinking, back-pounding Boston politician, then somewhere over the years the man himself, somewhere deep down under the winces, could begin believing some of this himself and his momentum would become diminished. In this case, the Protestant ethic has robbed us of our eyes. For if you see Tom O'Neill as he is, not as comformity forces us to see, then there is coming into the room a lovely spring rain of a man.

He is not gruff; he is courtly. He is not cunning; he is open. His choice of words and the rhythm with which he uses them are many levels above most people who are great successes in private and public life. He does not become mesmerized with the sound of his voice; he is a spectacular aural learner.

However, he most certainly is one of those old-fashioned politicians that most people prefer to detest. So much of his life has demanded caution, waiting in line behind others, that he can often make going along sound like accomplishment. In 1967, speaking at Boston College, he told a crowd why he was in favor of the nation's policy in Vietnam: "I've been briefed forty-four times by the President, the State Department, the CIA, and the Department of Defense," he said. "I know more than you." He then went into the light-at-the-end-of-the-tunnel speech. A student named Pat McCarthy stood up and asked one question: "You've been briefed by the people in favor of the war. Have you ever been briefed by people on the other side of the question?" O'Neill was shot down by the question, and he knew it. He began to go around asking second-level Pentagon and CIA people about the war. They told him it was a disaster, that the country was being lied to. In August of the same year, in the 150,000 copies of his newsletter to constituents, O'Neill came out against the war. He informed no one else of it, however. It wasn't until October that *The Washington Star* heard about it and printed the story. That night, Lyndon Johnson had Secret Service men pull O'Neill out of a card game. Johnson asked O'Neill why he had done it. O'Neill said because he felt everybody was lying, even to Johnson, about the way the war was going. "Well, I've one request of you," Johnson said. "Just don't go around giving interviews about it."

"Why?" O'Neill asked.

Johnson then leaned on old friendships. He said that O'Neill had been allowed into Sam Rayburn's old "Board of Education," that John McCormack was the one who had brought him into such an inside society. Somehow, Johnson saw this

as an obligation. Somehow, O'Neill saw the same thing. He
left the office and did not become one of the major voices
against the war. His instinct might have taken him to the right
decision, but his talent was betrayed by the life he had lived.
Which makes his actions against Richard Nixon all the more
important. We leave his full career for others to evaluate. Much
more important is that here, in this single rare instance, O'Neill,
and all these other politicians we scorn, stood up, stood apart
from their pasts, and took us to heights we as a nation never
have seen before.

Because of this, I decided to spend the summer of 1974 in
Washington, in the office of the Majority Leader of the House,
and watch the daily picture that would reflect and suggest the
whole of what was going on. At the same time there would be
as both company and subject a participant in the impeachment
who had all the things that were missing so badly from the
whole. In a time of lies and fear and weakness and hypocrisy, in
a time when evil was matched against evil and the results were
pronounced as good, O'Neill provided a few shafts of sunlight,
of charm and humor and mature compassion. Nobody ever said
you have to torture life to produce history.

We are not going to learn what happened to the Administration of Richard Nixon for many years; those who would
attempt to tell the story now are only frauds in search of hasty
profits. But from the bits and pieces gathered over a summer,
from what was seen and heard, some important impressions
were drawn. Many people feel that Republican politics in California—twisted, religiously negative—is responsible for much
of Nixon's personality. Perhaps. And all the more reason to tell
of real politicians on the other side, who are involved in a hard
business, a devious business, but a business that still tries to
work for people instead of against them. The people who come
from real politics, from the politics with a tradition of a Boston
(supposedly the rowdiest in this country), have qualities that
should be examined before anybody from another area, from
a California, is allowed to use his business as an excuse for his
tactics.

O'Neill, one of the first to call for impeachment, was, at the
end, the only man I knew who felt that Gerald Ford was correct

in pardoning Richard Nixon. On the Sunday afternoon of the pardon, O'Neill was in a hall in Cambridge. With the crowd calling for blood, O'Neill stood in the back and said to Walter Sullivan, the Mayor of Cambridge, "I don't want to ask you where you stand, but it looks to me right now like I'm the only vote in the place in favor of the pardon."

Secular writers would make a mess of this, as they made a mess of most of the reports on the demise of Richard Nixon. For it takes a belief in, and some comprehension of, Original Sin before you can see enough of Richard Nixon to both remove him and then ask that he be attacked no more. Original Sin is a cruel and vicious doctrine, subscribed to mainly by conservative members of the Catholic Church, but a doctrine which at this time appears needed by all human beings. For a belief in Original Sin is constant acknowledgment of the dark side of man. Born with it, he walks with a darkness always in his nature. The Catholic form is to search for forgiveness of Original Sin, and for a means to control it over a lifetime, through the Grace of Confession. These ceremonies of the religion—the Confession, the liturgical services—form a third-party intermediary; but with no way to externalize his evil, Nixon had only himself. Therefore, with no outward doctrine calling for the continual planning for failure, for sin, Nixon was unprepared for failure. Always, secular writers point out that Richard Nixon was a born loser and that he continually acted as such. This theory is in opposition to reality. Nixon's true fault was that he had no way to plan for failure, no way to externalize his evil.

In the 1970s, there are nuclear physicists who write of uncertainties, of indeterminate action, all coming from complicated third-party actions. In trying to understand this, in chasing the notion, they are merely drawing abreast of ancient religious writings which called for man to externalize his sin, his evil, to establish a third-party intermediary.

It is depressing that Nixon never dealt with any of this. Despite all the hysteria, he is not particularly different from anybody else. To look at him objectively, as now you must, is to understand that Richard Nixon, not the Kennedys, is the greatest American story—he ranged the furthest, from grocery store to world leader, and he ended in enormous, self-inflicted tragedy. Keeping his evil internal ruined him. With him being judge and jury of his own sins, a self-hatred was produced, resulting in continual accusations against others: "Nobody drowned at Watergate." A jury decision in a case against John Ehrlichman was a "blot on the criminal justice system." He twisted everything into instruments of revenge: send draft evaders to prison in the name of those who died in the war. If he had had a method of externalizing his evil he would have had a somewhat better chance against the life he led. It does not cure to externalize, but it provides for a bit more mercy, a little more ability to face the truth.

On the day that Richard Nixon left the White House, stepped into the helicopter on the lawn, and was gone forever, one of his chief defenders in the final months, Dean Burch, went home and had a drink. "He never told me the truth about the thing," Burch said. "He never even told his own family. That was why they were fighting so hard right to the last minute. They were the last to give in on resignation. They thought he was being screwed. He never told them the truth. I think that was his major failure, being so cynical. The man didn't believe in anything. He didn't believe in a religion or principle of anything. He was totally cynical."

This cynicism is one reason why Nixon had his taping system.

Late one day, on one of the last days of the summer's travail, O'Neill came into his office and watched the evening news on television. He almost never sees the news on television, weekends once in a while, but for the past few days the set had been on constantly. The newsmen on this night were talking, again, of Nixon's tapes.

"I'll tell you a story about these tapes," O'Neill said. "Say, I'll have Canadian Club and Fresca, I'm on a diet. Thank you. Now, the night the Vietnam war ended, Nixon had a few of us over for dinner before he went on television to tell the country that there was a peace agreement. We were over in the Executive Office Building. They have a beautiful place there. There was Nixon, Kissinger, Mansfield, Scott, Griffin, Rhodes, Byrd, and myself. We got there at six thirty and we had a couple of drinks. Nixon was to go on television at nine. At seven o'clock we sat down to eat. Naturally, we all were talking over dinner about the end of the war, and I had a question to ask. I said,

'Mr. President, I'm not going to address this question to you. I don't want to embarrass you and have you give an answer that perhaps you don't want to. So I'll address this question to Henry Kissinger. My question is: you ended the war by bombing Hanoi and mining Haiphong harbor. I happen to have been very close to Lyndon Johnson and I heard these same tactics discussed many times. Bombing of Hanoi and the mining of Haiphong harbor. But President Johnson could not get an off-the-record agreement with Russia and China, so he was afraid that if he did combine the bombing of Hanoi and the mining of Haiphong harbor it might end up with World War III. Five years later, we bomb Hanoi and mine Haiphong and the war is over. Therefore, you must have had an agreement with Russia and China that allowed you to do it.'

"And Nixon says, right away, 'Henry, I'll answer that question. I'll take this one myself.' And then Nixon says, 'There was no implied agreement with Russia and China. No implied agreement that allowed us to bomb Hanoi and mine Haiphong harbor. The President made this decision himself. It was the President who decided it had to be done, that it was worth the risk to end the war. There was no implied agreement with Russia and China.'

"As he's saying this, he first has raised his voice. Then I see he's looking upward, at the chandelier or whatever was there. 'No implied agreement with Russia and China. The President made this decision himself. It was the President who decided.' Now I see he's not only looking up, but he's pointing with his finger, as if he's talking to somebody up there. And I say to myself, You've got to be kidding. He has this place bugged. So now that night is over. That's in January of 1973. Later that year, in October, the Israeli war ended and the President had us over to his office in the White House to tell us about how the war came to an end and what it was to mean. Remember, he had no tapes going this time. The tapes had been discovered back in July and the system had been taken out. So now Nixon is sitting there, with no tapes going, and he says that the major obstacle had been the Russian propaganda machine in the Middle East. The peace settlement couldn't have been made without the help of the Russians. Nixon said, 'We needed their help. It was the same with Vietnam. We couldn't have done anything unless we had been able to make an agreement with Russia and China before we went ahead at the end.' I'm taking down notes while he's talking and I just say to myself, Oh, boy!

"Now that tells you what he was going to do with those tapes. He was going to take them with him when he left and spend years editing them, and then he could string together a record of his own which would show that he was the greatest man ever to live. He'd be able to prove it with tapes. You never would have known about any of the other stuff. That would have been thrown away. They would have only given you all these tapes with him making a hero out of himself. 'There was no implied agreement with Russia and China. The President made this decision himself.'"

"There is," wrote Kierkegaard, "no temple-robber, toiling in shackles of iron, so vicious as those who pillage among sacred things; and even Judas, who sold his Master for thirty pieces of silver, is not more despicable than those who traffic in great deeds."

On September 25, 1973, at 3:45 P.M., Carl Albert, Speaker of the House of Representatives, waved to O'Neill, who came to the rostrum.

"I've just received a call from the Vice President. He said he wanted to see me at four. He'll be in my office. Will you be here?"

"I'll be right here," O'Neill said.

At 4:10, one of Albert's aides came onto the floor and told O'Neill that he was wanted in the Speaker's office. The aide then went over to the other side of the chamber to find Jerry Ford.

O'Neill and Ford walked into the Speaker's brown-tiled office to find Spiro Agnew sitting stiffly, tensely waiting for them. Secret Service agents moved in and out, ear radios squawking.

"The Vice President has a matter he'd like to discuss with you gentlemen," Albert said.

"My problem, gentlemen," Agnew began, "is that in Baltimore we have a young United States Attorney named George Beall. He is mean and ambitious. His father was my great friend. This young man would not even have his own job today if I had not gone along with it. The father would be spinning in his grave today if he knew what the son was trying to do to me. I helped get this boy his job and here he is harassing me."

O'Neill remembered that he knew the father, former United States Senator Glenn Beall. O'Neill had been introduced to Beall by Paul Dever, the former Governor of Massachusetts. The meeting took place when O'Neill first came to Washington, in 1952. They were all together in Maryland politics, the Bealls and Agnew, O'Neill reminded himself. He does this all the time, goes over the players. He is a man who likes a score card at all times.

"I am being framed and harassed over campaign contributions," Agnew said. "I am clean. I have nothing to hide. But with this Beall, the way he is going about it, why, gentlemen, no politician living in the greater Washington area is safe. Let me explain what he is doing to me."

Agnew started outlining what he thought were new immunity provisions of the criminal law put together by John Mitchell. Actually there had been no change. Federal law gives a person immunity for testifying in a case only for those facts the person himself deals with. If the government can prove by independent sources that the person is involved in the same crime, the immunity does not protect the person. Agnew told the people in the room that this new immunity law was designed to help the government break up narcotics rings. Now, horror, it was being used against him.

Agnew read part of the letter which said there were great Constitutional precedents, involving the case of John C. Calhoun, which made it impossible for a President or a Vice President to be criminally tried in court while in office. He was absolutely certain of this as he spoke. O'Neill is not a lawyer, so he is unencumbered with such certainties. *What the hell ever happened to "No man is above the law"*? he thought. Agnew also said he was turning over in the morning all materials and records applicable to his case. He would send them to the Clerk of the House.

"If all these people being offered immunity by Beall were telling the truth, then I'd be a rich man," Agnew said. "This Beall is inviting people to come in and build a case against me. People that I never saw or even heard of are being offered immunity. Now, gentlemen, as Vice President I am presenting to the House, delivering by hand to the Speaker now, a request in writing for the House to make an inquiry into my case. I request that my matter be turned over to the Judiciary Committee for a complete investigation, an open investigation, gentlemen, on television, so I can prove my innocence to the people of the United States. Gentlemen, I am being robbed. My life, my career, my family, we are being threatened by young zealots. My God, I don't want to be the first Vice President of the United States indicted for a felony. It is unconstitutional for them to do it. But I have no chance against these young zealots. They will do anything to destroy me. Destroy us all. I don't know whether it is out of jealousy or insanity. But they are ready to do it to me. I will be ruined forever, and the name of my family ruined forever. I ask, I implore you for help."

While the words were deferential, his attitude was not. Haughtiness came out of him as he sat there, stiff-necked, slick-haired, smoldering eyes. But voice throbbing, he had touched a common chord. They were of a trade, politics, which places everything on the word survival. And here was Agnew, a fellow politician, whose survival was threatened. And threatened by the one subject with which they were all too familiar, campaign contributions.

Albert decided that more people had better hear the story. He asked for Majority Whip John McFall, Les Arends, the Minority Whip, and Lew Deschler, who at the time was the House Parliamentarian. When they arrived, Agnew again told his story. As he was telling it, the door opened, and Albert's aides placed more chairs in the room. Barry Goldwater and Hugh Scott arrived; the hallway outside Albert's office was crowded with reporters and cameramen. It was decided by everybody in the room that Albert would go to the rostrum, read Agnew's letter, and take no action. On the floor at this time, a debate over an immigration bill was taking place. Albert walked into the pale light of the chamber, indicating the debate should halt.

"I have a communication from the Vice President of the United States," Albert said. He read the letter.

"'I respectfully request that the House of Representatives undertake a full inquiry into the charges which have apparently been made against me in the course of an investigation by the United States Attorney of Maryland.

"'This request is made in the dual interests of preserving the Constitutional stature of my office and accomplishing my personal vindication.

"'I cannot acquiesce in any criminal proceedings lodged against me in Maryland or elsewhere, and I do not look to any proceedings for vindication.'"

Precedents involving Calhoun, bits and pieces of used hocus-pocus assembled into legal language by lawyers without a case. The letter ended with Agnew saying, ". . . no grand or petit jury could fairly consider this matter on the merits. I therefore respectfully call upon the House to discharge its Constitutional obligation. I shall of course cooperate fully. As I have said before, I have nothing to hide."

Albert walked off the rostrum and returned to his office.

Tip O'Neill said, "I think the Vice President should be allowed to leave now so that we can discuss the matter."

Agnew rose and left. The room was tense because of him. It was one thing to say, with ease, that Agnew had done something and thus had to be removed. But Spiro Agnew also had run on a ticket elected by one of the largest margins in history, he was a man with a great natural constituency, a group powerful enough to gain for him the Republican nomination for 1976. Nobody plays light with these circumstances.

Albert immediately sent for Peter Rodino and Edward Hutchinson, the senior Republican on the Judiciary Committee.

Ford, Arends, and Hutchinson took over the conversation. Ford said he felt great sympathy for Agnew, and he thought the House should proceed with his request. Hutchinson and Arends agreed. Scott and Goldwater nodded. Ford then went on to discuss the method of taking the Agnew matter to the Judiciary and also the public hearings on television. Perhaps somewhere, in old high-school papers in East Grand Rapids perhaps, the record might show Gerald Ford as taking a stand on the merits of a matter, rather than on interests special to him. Perhaps there is a record of such a thing happening. So far the record is not to be found in his long, bland career in Washington.

O'Neill made notes on a small pad during the conversation. The letters grew larger as he scrawled, in agitation, that the Republicans were speaking as if the matter had been settled. If they allowed Agnew to bring his case into the House, the matter would take months. A year. And where would this leave them with Richard Nixon? For months now, O'Neill had been telling Albert and Rodino that an impeachment of Richard Nixon was going to hit the House and they had to be ready for it. How were they ever going to handle the Nixon matter if the House, the people, the machinery were groping through the matter of Spiro Agnew?

The ready smile, the quick warmth, the fellowship were gone when O'Neill stopped writing his notes and looked up and said, "I don't go along with this at all. We're Democrats and we're in the majority. Now, Jerry, why don't you people go to your office and we Democrats will stay here and discuss this thing. For, frankly, I'm bitterly opposed to this right now."

The Republicans—Scott, Goldwater, Ford, Arends, and Hutchinson—left. Remaining in the Speaker's office were Albert, McFall, Rodino, and Lew Deschler. Rodino called for his chief counsel Jerome Zeifman.

As Zeifman came into the office, Albert said to him, "What do you think of the Vice President's letter?"

O'Neill said, "Hey, let him read it first."

Zeifman read the letter. It was a move he had been expecting. Agnew was being represented by Jay Topkis, member of a New York law firm headed by Judge Simon Rifkind, the same New York attorney whose firm was retained by Justice William O. Douglas, when Jerry Ford called for his impeachment. For the Douglas case, Rifkind, who is as nonpolitical as an alderman, wanted full hearings, counsel present and on television, in the House Judiciary Committee. Rifkind's philosophy was that any matter placed in Congress automatically disappeared. Now, as Zeifman saw, Topkis was trying the same strategy with Agnew. Zeifman read the letter and looked up. He of course was against it. He looked at O'Neill. Zeifman knew he had one vote with him anyway.

"I'm against this," O'Neill said. "The matter is before the courts, and Agnew is going to court to get an injunction to prevent the bringing of evidence before the grand jury. Now he

says the Constitution protects the President and the Vice President from criminal action. This is what *he* says. I don't know
that at all. I think we ought to leave that up to the courts."

The meeting broke up with no decision. It was agreed that
there would be a meeting the following morning.

At 9:30 the next morning, O'Neill was in the House restaurant having hash and eggs when Gary Hymel came in to tell
him the meeting would be at 10:30 in the Speaker's office.
O'Neill finished breakfast and went down the hallway to his
office. It was ten o'clock. McFall came in. He said the Speaker
was having the meeting at that moment. O'Neill reached for
the phone.

"Peter and I have it all worked out," Albert told him on the
phone. "But you can come up if you want to."

O'Neill went up the one flight to Albert's office. Albert, at
his desk, handed O'Neill a press release stating that the House
Judiciary Committee would begin inquiries into Vice President
Agnew's conduct.

"No," O'Neill said.

Albert and Rodino asked him why.

"Because the man is lying. He says he's innocent and he's
being framed. I don't know about that. I think he's worried
about going to jail, but he won't tell you that. He can't tell the
truth. If we put this into the Judiciary Committee, we're doing
exactly what Agnew wants. He'll have this stalled and delayed
for so long that the court would wind up having no rights in
the matter. And another thing, and I can guarantee this, if you
let the man get away with this, then the Democratic caucus will
skin you alive."

Peter Rodino sided with O'Neill. Zeifman came into the
room with Lew Deschler. Deschler spoke up in favor of the
House accepting Agnew's request. Deschler is one of those
creatures of large government, elected by nobody, yet holding
the illusion of power. Deschler began under Sam Rayburn and
lasted through the McCormack years. Now he sat in this meeting, conformist, royalty-leaning, he whose power is threatened
is to be aided—for mine could be diminished next—and he
argued that Spiro Agnew should have his case examined here,
in what he regarded as the most important place on earth, the
House of Representatives. Here, where old politicians, not

young prosecutors, would know how to inspect allegations against the Vice President of the United States.

"I couldn't disagree more," O'Neill said. McFall, Rodino, and Zeifman agreed with him. Albert looked at the press release. His pen began to go over it; go over it and make the words come out that Spiro Agnew's request for an inquiry—the start of a long impeachment process—was being turned down.

One problem was left. At the meeting of the night before nobody had focused on the delivery of Agnew's material, his records, to the House. If Agnew was able to get all his materials to the House, it would be similar to a criminal getting rid of his weapon. Zeifman told Rodino he felt the House should not accept the records. When this was told to W. Pat Jennings, the Clerk of the House, bureaucracy rose to its highest form.

"I can't do this on my own authority," Jennings told Zeifman. "I'm supposed to accept any materials given to me."

Zeifman argued with Jennings. Jennings took the problem to Lew Deschler, and came back to say, "Lew says I'm supposed to accept it. He says that any person has a right to petition Congress, most certainly the Vice President."

Zeifman made it plain that forces larger than Jennings' career were involved. But Jennings, a bureaucrat refusing either to lose face or depart from the rule book, needed a way out.

"Tell him he's sick and he ought to go home for the day," O'Neill said. "He looks a little tired anyway."

Jennings kept his office closed all day.

Agnew now was left for the prosecutors. His chance to take a criminal case and stall it in Congress, as if it were another appropriation to build a bridge, was gone. He told his staff it was O'Neill's fault.

4

"Peter is the perfect man for this job."

EARLY IN the morning of October 10th, the Congressional
leadership was called in for a briefing by Richard Nixon;
the Arab-Israeli war had erupted on the 6th. Those arriving
at the White House were tense. O'Neill walked into the Oval
Office, nodded hello to Nixon and Henry Kissinger, and sat
down. He took out his pad of white paper so he could keep
notes.

Kissinger began to explain what had happened. The Arabs,
taking advantage of the Yom Kippur holy day, had crossed the
Suez and . . .

"Ah . . . we had trouble finding Henry. He was in bed with
a broad," Nixon said. He began giggling and rolling his head
around.

Kissinger went on with the details.

"Henry, which girl was it that you were with?" Nixon said.

Kissinger kept explaining the war.

"It's terrible when you have a girl and the Secret Service has
to break in on you," Nixon said. He leered and winked.

On his notes, O'Neill wrote, "President is acting very
strangely."

When the meeting broke up, O'Neill rode back to the
Capitol with George Mahon of Texas and Thomas E. Morgan
of Pennsylvania, the only Congressman who is a physician.
Morgan said he thought Nixon was sick. Laughter while others
are being killed has a way of being disturbing.

O'Neill walked into his office, saw Bob Healy of the *Boston
Globe*, then went up to the floor. A messenger came and handed
him a letter. Somebody called to Tip. He put the letter into his
pocket while he was talking. When he was finished, he went into
the back of the chamber and had a cigar. He was thinking over
the morning. Nixon had acted loony. Then he remembered
the letter and he opened it. It was from Agnew. The letter said
that he had resigned. As O'Neill read the letter, Agnew was on
his way to federal court in Baltimore, where Eliot Richardson

would ignore equal justice and whisk Agnew in and out in a matter of minutes.

O'Neill's chest was now tingling with excitement and nerves, and it showed in his flushed face when he walked into his office.

"This must be what it's like when history is being made," he said.

He had dinner that night with Leo Diehl, who is listed as his administrative assistant but is much more than that. He and Tip O'Neill have been together since 1932. Leo Diehl caught polio when he was seven and it ravaged his legs. Thirty pounds of aluminum braces encase his legs. It is terrible work for him to move on crutches. He has a powerful chest, upper arms, and thick shoulders from supporting himself, body swinging in the air; the feet never touch while he works his way on his aluminum crutches. He has fallen and split his face open when he's misjudged curbs. Many times he has tumbled down flights of stairs. Never is anyone allowed to help him up, or even offer a handkerchief to wipe the blood. And never has he done anything but smile once he got up. He has a sharp nose, gray hair, pleasantness in every line of his face, and Massachusetts politics in his blue eyes.

"No wonder Nixon was so happy," O'Neill said to Leo. "He thinks he's free and clear now with this guy gone."

"He thinks," Leo said.

"You know, Leo, if the guy only would've said to us, 'Look, I've got a family. I'm afraid of going to the can.' Geez, that's all you have to tell me. I don't want to see any man go to jail. I don't have it in me. Maybe something could have been done for him. Give him some kind of hearing so he could kill a little time and then disappear. But the way the sonofabitch lied to us. And he acted as if it was our duty to believe him. He's got to be kidding. I don't like to be played for a sucker."

At the end of the night, Diehl pulled himself up and headed for the car, body swinging between the two aluminum crutches. They are a hardship, but it has been worse for him. For many years his crutches were made of rosewood. Back in 1944, he worked in an Army accounting office on Commonwealth Avenue in Boston. The officer in charge of the building was a general named Sherman Miles, an old-line Yankee who also was in politics. General Miles went about as if he were in the Ardennes Forest instead of an office building a few miles from his home. Among Miles's trappings were two huge mastiff dogs, which were walked each day by an aide. One afternoon the aide brought the mastiffs to the elevator to take them out for a lunchtime stroll. The elevator doors opened and the dogs rushed on, overjoyed to find Leo Diehl and his two fine rosewood crutches in one corner of the elevator. Immediately, as the elevator went down, one of the mastiffs sniffed the rosewood crutch, then began to turn around. "Get away," Leo said. The dog raised his leg.

"You dirty sonofabitch," Leo Diehl hollered.

Words were too late. The dog was peeing all over the rosewood crutch and all over Leo Diehl's legs.

Diehl put one shoulder up against the wall for leverage. He put all his weight on the crutch the dog was peeing on. The other crutch came around so hard it whirred. Here came the crutch whipping under the animal's raised leg and into the testicles. The animal went up in the air, giving an enormous howl, then flopped down in such obvious distress that the injuries seemed permanent. The general's aide, catatonic, saw himself reassigned to the Battle of the Bulge.

At the beginning of October 1973, Dwight Chapin announced that if anybody dared bring him in front of the Ervin Watergate committee, he would take the Fifth Amendment. And Jerome Zeifman, his impeachment precedents piled high, asked Rodino if the material could be printed and distributed to Congress. Rodino said this would be regarded as a direct attack upon Nixon. Zeifman had stacks of Calhoun, of Colfax, of Andrew Johnson and the Journal of James Madison. Over the summer he and Don Edwards, member of the Judiciary Committee from California, had gone to London, where Zeifman, catechist at work, sifted the impeachment files kept by Parliament. Before coming home, Zeifman sat in a hotel room for a week, reading the material until his head hurt. Now he shuddered when Rodino announced they would wait.

The amount of annoyance kept rising; on October 5th, the American Civil Liberties Union had called on the House to begin impeachment proceedings. On the 9th, Rodino sent

the impeachment material to the printer. All the printing is
done by the Government Printing Office located in a set of
gloomy brick buildings in the northwest section of the city. It
employs 7400 people who work on machines that run from
turn-of-the-century, hand-operated linotypes, matrixes jingling
through the smell of hot lead, to a silent light blue cabinet, a
Linotron Model 1010, one of five in the nation, which sets 1000
characters per second. Copy for the daily *Congressional Record*,
running up to 344 pages, reaches the plant after 8:00 P.M.
By 6:30 A.M., there are 55,000 sets of copies on Capitol Hill.
Jerome Zeifman's impeachment papers reached the printing
plant as part of the night's work of October 9, 1973. The report
ran 718 pages of the size used in a quality paperback book. It
did not disturb the flow of work in the plant that night. Copies
of the book, 1500 bound in a tan paperback cover, arrived at the
Judiciary Committee on the morning of October 10.

House Document No. 93–7
IMPEACHMENT
Selected Materials

The foreword was by Peter Rodino: ". . . to promote familiarity with a critical point of American law, I am pleased to
transmit this document as a committee print. It is my hope
that these materials, some of them previously scattered in select
libraries and in some cases out of print for more than a century,
will be more readily accessible to members of the Congress and
to a larger segment of the American Community."

A copy of the book was placed on the desk of each Congressman; a loaded gun for use in a duel. When Tip O'Neill came
in, he picked up his copy, thumbed it, turned to the last page,
saw to his surprise that it was 718 pages long, and announced,
"Peter did a hell of a job."

He walked out onto the floor of the House. "Did you see the
book Peter put together? Isn't that some job he did? Geez, that
Peter is something. What a job he did. Did you see it?"

"I have it in my office, Tip."

"Well, geez, you ought to read it. Peter did the best research
on impeachment that's ever been, they tell me. You ought to
see the calls I've been getting."

"Who from?"

"All the Constitutional law professors at Harvard. Christ, I'm going to wind up without a copy of the book for myself. The President of Boston College called and asked me and I only had the one and I had it sent to him. We have to get more of these printed."

"It's that good, Tip?"

"Hey, you got to be kidding. It's a fabulous work. Hey, there's Peter now. What a job he did. I want to go over and congratulate him."

There was now a book on impeachment. It wasn't an undefinable topic any more. Now it was right there, in a book, that Congressmen could lift and feel and thumb through. And on the cover it said, "Impeachment." It was 718 pages long. Jeee-zus! Goddam big book! Seven hundred and eighteen pages long. Keeerist! This is gettin' to be important business now.

Nobody read a line of the book, but everybody held it and looked at the last page to see that it was 718 pages long.

On Tuesday, October 23, 1973, representatives of the White House were due to be in court to answer a court order calling for the tapes and other documents to be turned over to Judge John Sirica who would give them to the Watergate Special Prosecutor. This Nixon did not want to do because the tapes would show among other things that he was very guilty. Nixon had at this time a lawyer named Charles Alan Wright, a professor, a scholar from Texas. Wright had done nothing to stop the rumor that he was the nation's most brilliant Constitutional authority. Charles Alan Wright sat in the White House while Eliot Richardson quit and Archibald Cox and William D. Ruckelshaus were fired. Don't think nothin' of it, Professor Wright informed Nixon.

On Saturday, October 20, while it was all going on, Tip O'Neill was closing up his house at Cape Cod for the winter. The phone started ringing. One caller was Carl Albert, who said he would wait twenty-four hours before doing anything. The newspapers and television became hysterical. O'Neill kept moving wicker in from the lawn. He knew at that moment, there were 434 other guys reminding themselves to take another look at that

718-page book on impeachment that they had received ten days before.

By Monday, October 22, most people who knew Congress assumed there would be an investigation of the Saturday-night firings. Right away maneuvering began by Congressmen who wanted to be a part of any special committee. There were those who wanted to get the President, those who wanted to defend him, and those who simply wanted to be a part of any history that might happen. Which was all normal. It was the other calls concerning the matter which bothered Carl Albert. Industry people were calling him on behalf of Congressmen who wanted to be placed on the committee. Albert says nothing about it, but it is presumed that at least some of the calls were from oil and natural gas people in his home state of Oklahoma. It was obvious to Albert that the White House was behind the calls, a point he made to O'Neill at a morning meeting. A special committee would be best for Nixon. By custom, the Republicans would be able to name their own members to the committee, in this case men religiously sworn to uphold their own and obstruct all else. There would be no Caldwell Butlers or Tom Railsbacks. Therefore, Albert shut off his phones and told O'Neill that the investigation would be conducted by the Judiciary Committee and that sentiment for any other form must be thwarted. O'Neill walked out of Albert's office and began looking for his people. Already, Bob Eckhardt of Texas was saying that he regarded Rodino as incapable of handling such a major assignment. Eckhardt spoke of Richardson Preyer of North Carolina as a man suitable to run a special committee investigating the conduct of Nixon.

O'Neill ran into another thing out in the halls, the rumors that Rodino somehow was connected to the underworld in Newark, the Mafia, and would be a disgrace to the Congress as chairman of a committee conducting hearings on the President. "Sometimes the minds of men run bad," O'Neill says. "And somebody had to be feeding some kind of nonsense. Somebody from the White House, you can bet your life on that. All I kept hearing about was Neil Gallagher and Hughie Addonizio, and Peter being involved with them."

Cornelius E. Gallagher, a Congressman from Bayonne in New Jersey, who had been convicted of income-tax evasion and was in prison. A magazine story in 1971, pushed by Charles Colson, had pictured Gallagher as a front for gangsters. Addonizio was from Newark. As a Congressman, he had roomed with Peter Rodino in Washington. One day Addonizio announced he was going back to Newark to run for mayor. "Hughie, what the hell are you doing that for?" O'Neill asked him. Addonizio said, "Christ, do you know what the budget for the City of Newark is? Take one per cent of that and I'm going to have something." O'Neill remembers saying to him, "Hughie, you got to be kidding. The game isn't played that way any more." Addonizio shrugged, went to Newark, and not only began stealing but, worse, was caught. At his trial, names of several hoodlums came up. Addonizio was given a ten-year sentence. In the White House on this Monday in October, the normal move was to connect Rodino to Addonizio and Gallagher—and then take the story over to the House of Representatives and try to sell it, just as you sell a transit bill.

O'Neill heard the stories. He also knew about the phone calls Carl Albert was getting from the big money interests on behalf of the White House.

"Peter is the perfect man for this job," O'Neill kept saying. This is known as an official word. He wanted to put this one together in a hurry.

On Monday the House Judiciary Committee also had a regularly scheduled meeting. As Peter Rodino walked up to Room 2141 in the Rayburn Building, shoulders swinging, big thick heels clicking on the marble hallway, he felt excitement. The newspaper reports the next day said that "Whether the discussion of impeachment becomes more than talk depends upon the cautious chairman, Peter W. Rodino, and the equally cautious House Democratic leadership. Of nine committee members contacted yesterday, six said they favored moves leading to impeachment and three said they were opposed." Excellent. Nobody even mentioned the possibility that the Judiciary Committee had not been given the impeachment matter by the full Congress.

On Tuesday, October 23, Charles Alan Wright dressed himself in the Madison Hotel, his mind concentrating on lofty Constitutional principles he would place before the court—issues that turned to glue when you touched them. He would

have lawyers, clerks, judges stuck together like wolves in heat
for so many months that nobody would know what was going
on. Wright did not include Congress in his calculations. Nor
had he actually sat down and listened to Nixon's tapes.

The problem was, Washington on this day was like an
electric wire downed in a storm, snapping in the high wind,
bolts of electricity sizzling and exploding out of its soaking
frayed ends. Constitutional principles or not, if Nixon defied
the court order—on top of the Saturday-Night Massacre—an
authentic accident just might have occurred: rapid history.
The White House asked for a delay—from noon until 2:00
P.M.—before Professor Wright appeared before Judge Sirica.
When Congress opened at noon, they were waving and calling
out for a chance to get up and offer impeachment resolutions.
O'Neill called for the matter to be given to the House Judiciary
Committee. Throughout the chamber and in the cloakroom,
more Congressmen were calling for a special committee to be
set up. O'Neill said in his speech on the floor, ". . . to the House
Judiciary Committee for speedy and expeditious consideration.
The House must act with determined leadership and strength."

Over at the White House, Richard Nixon sat and brooded.
He knew two things that his lawyer did not. One, that he,
Nixon, was a liar. And, two, the Congress was in a turmoil.
Who needed more trouble because of these freaking tapes?
Nixon said something which interrupted Professor Wright's
preparations. Professor Wright's face got about six inches
longer.

At two o'clock Charles Alan Wright walked into Sirica's
courtroom. Tall, large, sharp nose, hair slicked back. Watching
Wright as he walked, particularly his stride and head carriage,
one had enormous admiration for the long hours Wright must
have spent in front of mirrors learning to look just like John
Wayne. On this day Wright wore a brown suit, lime shirt, and
lime tie. He was impressive as hell. Only the moment Charles
Alan Wright sat down, his hand went right for the water pitcher.
He gulped a paper cup of water, filled it again, and gulped some
more. One thing about John Wayne, even when he was in the
middle of it all at Wake Island with the Japs crawling onto
him and the sun glaring, even when it was this tough, John
Wayne didn't take a drink of water. Next to Wright sat Leonard

Garment of the White House staff. Garment ran a hand over his face. Now he ran the hand through his hair. The hand went back to the face again. Garment's entire weight shifted in his chair.

There was a slap on the desk for attention as Judge Sirica came in. There was a bit of red in Sirica's face. His head had this little irritated nod as he sat down. Charles Alan Wright went to the water pitcher. Then he walked to the lectern. Head bowed to the judge, Wright spoke in a low voice. He said that "this President obeys the law." After weeks of high-sounding, confident talk about the separation of powers, Professor Wright was quitting in the pit in front of the judge. At noontime that day with client Richard Nixon, Professor Wright had discovered a thing he never learned about in all his reading of *Marbury* v. *Madison*: when the client is a liar and you believe him, he takes you down with him.

At the end of the day, O'Neill was at a party at the Congressional Hotel, down the street from the Capitol. It was a campaign fund-raiser for Charles Wilson, a Congressman from California. Wilson proudly took O'Neill around the room. When they stopped, O'Neill said to Wilson, "You know, Peter will do a very good job with this."

"If you say so, Tip, anything you say," Wilson said.

Hugh Carey was in the next room, which is the bar of the Democratic Club. O'Neill and I went in and had a drink with him. Carey was then on the strong, influential Ways and Means Committee.

Carey was telling a story about somebody's wife who was flying from Boston to Ireland on a Saturday night and had neglected to bring a passport with her.

"Seamus calls me and says, 'Geez, I got my wife at Logan Airport and they won't even let her on the plane.' So I said to him, 'Well, let me see what I can think up here.' And Seamus says to me, 'Of course, I'm not in any trouble if you don't deliver.'"

"I know just what you did," O'Neill said.

"Sure," Carey said, "I called Gene Krisak."

"That's right, Gene Krisak. He's a good fella."

"And I told Gene, 'Look, this woman has absolutely got to get to Ireland tonight and the plane is due to leave in a half-hour.' And of course you know only on matters of life and death are they allowed to do it. So I said it was absolutely a matter of life and death."

"And you weren't lying," O'Neill said.

"Absolutely not. It was going to be her life if she got to Ireland, and it was going to be Seamus's death if she didn't get there."

"That's good," O'Neill said. "Say, Hughie, we got to have Peter do this."

"Absolutely, we can't give it to anybody else."

"They've got to be kidding if they think they can put it anyplace else," O'Neill said.

"No question," Carey said.

Elizabeth Holtzman came over from her office to have a drink with us. It was more to say hello than have a drink—a Bloody Mary at eight o'clock at night is not drinking. She is a friendly woman, an intense woman. She talked about the people in her office who were going to stay on through the night working on impeachment material. A New York lawyer, active in reform politics, overheard her and cut in with a display of his great knowledge of the phrases and clauses that make up the books on impeachment law. The man would not stop talking. Elizabeth Holtzman listened with great courtesy. Carey made a face. O'Neill cocked his head so he could appear to listen most attentively. The cigar moved from one side of his mouth to the other as the lawyer from New York talked on.

O'Neill reached out and took my arm. "I was just thinking," he said. "What was the greatest fight you ever saw?"

"Two guys you probably never heard of," I said. "Heavyweights. Joe McFadden and Nino Valdés. They fought in a place called the Sunnyside Gardens around where I come from in New York. Eight knockdowns in six rounds. I never saw anything like it."

"Do you remember when Tony DeMarco fought Carmine Basilio?" O'Neill said. "Do you remember that one, do you? Geez, what they did to each other! You must be kidding, you don't remember that fight? Poor Tony, he was from the *Narth* End, you know. I used to see him all the time. Well the poor guy ran out of gas in the last couple of rounds and, geez, this Basilio, what a job he did on him. But until then, I never saw a fight like it in my life."

Then we went to dinner and he talked about Rocky Marciano. He never mentioned impeachment.

At noon the next day, O'Neill was on the House floor slipping into a seat in the front, then a seat in the back, moving in and out of the cloakroom, going behind the rail to have a cigar. Talking, talking, talking. In two spots he heard the same thing: "Why should we let Rodino get all that national television time? I've been heading up a committee a lot longer than Rodino has. Let's get somebody we know better in there."

O'Neill chewed on his cigar and thought about the argument. Later he got into a conversation with Gillis Vanderbilt (Sonny) Montgomery of Mississippi. On impeachment, Sonny Montgomery had taken his stand and never was to leave it: "Ah'm the first mate on the *Sequoia* and I intend to stay that way." Yet virtually nobody in Congress dislikes Sonny Montgomery personally. In the market place of legislating, he is one of the men you always go to, no matter how opposite his views.

"You know, Sonny," Tip said, "about this impeachment business going to the Judiciary Committee. Don't you think it would be a wonderful thing to give Peter Rodino a chance to finally get a little television exposure? Let people see what a great guy he is. After all these years of being on the bottom, nobody knowing him, wouldn't it be nice to give him his little chance?"

"Sure, he deserves a chance," Montgomery said. "Thing isn't going to go any place, so we might as well give Peter a little publicity." Montgomery would tell this to others. O'Neill went on to somebody else.

At this point, Peter Rodino decided it would be very good to have another meeting of the House Judiciary Committee to discuss impeachment. In going through the envelopes dealing with Mr. Rodino's career, as recorded in the reference library—the morgue—of the Newark *Star-Ledger* newspaper, I came across a yellow clip, the paper falling into pieces between your fingers, which showed that in 1940 an attorney from Newark's First Ward, Peter W. Rodino, candidate for the New Jersey State Legislature, had been endorsed by Mrs. Eleanor Roosevelt. I am told that Mrs. Roosevelt came to Newark on behalf of her husband, and posed for pictures. At which point the young lawyer from the First Ward, Mr. Rodino, came slicing through a wall of people and he stood, beaming, alongside Mrs. Roosevelt. Pictures were taken. When one of the pictures appeared in the Newark newspapers, Rodino said, of course, the picture speaks for itself; he had been officially endorsed by Eleanor Roosevelt. Blue smoke rose high in Newark that day.

And now, thirty-four years later, in the hall of Congress of the United States, Peter Rodino slipped through the doorway into the Judiciary Committee room. As he was going through, Rodino put his hand out and tipped a huge mirror a few degrees forward.

A vote was taken at the meeting which gave Rodino the power to subpoena any agent of the government, and his papers, public and private, for examination by the Committee. The vote was on straight partisan lines. But there had been a vote. What the hell, if they were voting on it already, then they must be in charge. There also appeared in the newspapers at this time a syndicated column by Charles Bartlett which told of how Rodino would handle the impeachment hearings.

Among the first to believe this was Tip O'Neill. He asked Rodino what he was going to do about a counsel for the hearings. That's the first question you ask. Christ, the counsels for big publicity committees have become famous and if you're in politics you want to know who has a chance to become famous. Kill the baby in the crib if you think he'll grow up to be an enemy. Rodino said he was going to bring in a big name from the outside. He ruled out his staff, including Jerome Zeifman. O'Neill went back to his office and began sending Rodino the names of prospects for the job. Rodino said thank you, but did not bite. Others suggested names to him. Rodino took none of them. Days turned into weeks. In November, O'Neill stood behind the railing in the House, smoking a cigar, muttering about the mail and phone calls from his home district. He put the cigar into the brass ash stand and walked onto the floor and sat alongside Peter Rodino.

"Now, Peter, when can we get this counsel and get going on this thing?"

"Well, I have to take my time, I want this done, I want this to be very carefully done."

"Now, Peter, for Christ's sakes, you have to get it done before we go home for Christmas."

Rodino began to talk about his problems. Like any successful politician he has several styles of speech, all of which must be calibrated in terms of how direct he cares to be at the moment. A Rodino answer can run from one word to six pages. For this moment, Rodino chose a long, rambling answer about the proper counsel for such a massive job.

O'Neill cut in. "Hey, Peter, we have to have a guy by Christmas."

Rodino writhed in the seat. "Hey, Tippy! Do you know how hard it is to find a counsel? Look at the names you sent me. Do you know what one of them was? This, this Cronin. He was a disciple of Father Berrigan. They'd kill us if we had a guy like that around."

"I gave you names so you could look at them. You look at one, you get an idea for another. I don't care. We have to get the man by the time this Congress goes home for Christmas."

"You're not a lawyer, you don't understand."

"Hey, I can read the calendar." They sat in the brown leather seats, in the high-ceilinged old chamber, and they talked about getting started on the impeachment of the President of the United States. Neither had a ruling or a license to do what he was doing. They were surrounded by mirrors and fighting with both hands over what each thought he saw in the blue smoke.

It was lunchtime as the two argued. In the White House, Richard Nixon sat alone, as he did every day, in a small sitting room off the main office—the Oval Office—and he had the same cottage cheese and apple that he had every day that he was in Washington. He never deviated. Alone with cottage cheese. The word impeachment had not even been mentioned inside the White House, and it would not be for months. Nixon never thought about it. The cover-up was a necessary, aggravating political job. There was nothing beyond it. To the nation at this time, and even to most of the men prowling the floor of the House of Representatives, impeachment was totally improbable. But Tip O'Neill and Peter Rodino saw it as a thing that was very real. Nothing, O'Neill knew, was as improbable as the way in which the two of them got to this afternoon in November when they could argue about getting rid of a President.

5

"I know one Republican . . . John Doar."

FOR TIP O'NEILL, his steps to the Majority Leadership began with problems others got into.

On January 12, 1970, in Room 902, United States Courthouse, Foley Square, New York City, Clifford Sanders, foreman of the grand jury meeting in the windowless room, called for a vote. Under consideration on this wet chill day were the possible criminal activities—fixing an SEC case—of Nathan M. Voloshen, a Washington lobbyist, and Martin Sweig, administrative assistant to John McCormack, Speaker of the House of Representatives. A quorum of jurors was present—sixteen of the twenty-three must be seated—and when Sanders asked for a show of hands on whether there should be an indictment against Voloshen, all were raised. He asked for a show of hands on Sweig. Again, all were raised. Sanders pressed a buzzer. Into the room came a short, dark-haired man who in those days always was first taken for a student, or a well-dressed messenger boy. He was an Assistant United States Attorney named Richard Ben-Veniste, and he was learning about crime by politicians, knowledge which would not hurt him four years later. Sanders gave Ben-Veniste the tally. Ben-Veniste watched the indictment placed into the grand-jury log. The grand jury left for home, and Ben-Veniste went downstairs to the fourth-floor offices of United States Attorney Whitney North Seymour. "I want to tell the Speaker about this myself," Seymour said.

After his phone call, the federal indictments of Nathan Voloshen and Martin Sweig were released to the public. Voloshen had backslapped and smiled his way into the company and confidence of Martin Sweig, whose life had been spent as assistant to the Speaker of the House John McCormack. Out of this great friendship between Voloshen and Sweig grew a few small schemes, all of which were conducted over the telephones in the Speaker's office. In an office such as this, in the Capitol Building itself, a telephone trumps a machine gun. Sweig and Voloshen, most unpardonable sin, were caught.

This was the first of two accidents which brought Tip O'Neill to the Majority Leadership of the House of Representatives, to a position from which he could, in 1974, do much to influence the course of a nation. But until you tell the story of the accidents, you cannot properly tell of O'Neill in Washington in 1974.

For the House of Representatives is not an active, thoughtful body. It never acts; it always reacts. Any strong, definite course taken by Congress in the spring and summer of 1974 was a rare instance in the history of the House.

"Nothing would have happened without O'Neill," my own Congressman, Benjamin Rosenthal, was saying one day. "If Hale Boggs was there, as much as I liked him personally I just know that Nixon still would be President. The same thing with Peter Rodino. We never would have had an impeachment vote in the Judiciary if Manny Celler were still in charge."

At the time when Nate Voloshen and Martin Sweig began manning the phones, O'Neill under normal progression of House politics did not seem to have much of a chance ever to get as high as Majority Leader. The Speaker, John McCormack, a wiry, frugal New Englander—"Is the pudding fresh today?"—was perfectly willing to live forever. Majority Leader Carl Albert waited behind McCormack. Third in line was Majority Whip Hale Boggs of Louisiana. Below them, all waiting, all with much strength of their own, were such as O'Neill, Hugh Carey of New York, Morris Udall of Arizona, Edward Boland of Massachusetts, and Daniel Rostenkowski of Illinois.

In the working of Congress—up to January of 1975—there is no such thing as a man jumping over another. Certainly not for such posts as Speaker or Majority Leader.

As John McCormack explained it to me, "One day, Mr. Sam told me that, 'Someday you're going to be the Speaker of the House.' And I stayed in the House and waited. And then one day I *was* the Speaker of the House. Pray to God that it always will work the same way."

By September the judge in the case was recommending that Sweig and Voloshen go home and get toothbrushes for the trip to Allenwood Prison camp—John McCormack's time was done before he wanted it to be.

He announced he was leaving Congress at the end of his

term, in November of 1970. The House elections for Speaker
and Majority Leader—House Democrats vote in caucus—
would take place in January of 1971. It was assumed that the
chain would move smoothly, that Carl Albert would become
Speaker and Hale Boggs the Majority Leader. The chain clicked
once: Albert was going to have no trouble. Then it clanked and
went off track. Hale Boggs had opposition. Morris Udall was
going to run against him, as was James O'Hara of Michigan.
The main reason they would run against Boggs was Boggs's
own behavior over the past year. He took a drink, old Hale
did. He once held a press conference that lasted two hours and
consisted mostly of him reading from news clippings, the Bible,
and from his personal appointments book. When a reporter
would arrive, Boggs would rush back to seat the reporter, then
resume reading. But when his living was threatened, Boggs
shook his head, buttoned his jacket, and went to work. He
gave a large party and walked about sober and affable. Udall
still seemed well ahead, but in Hale Boggs's office, Gary
Hymel carefully went over the list of freshmen Congressmen
due to arrive in Washington in January. Boggs began calling
them. When the newcomers arrived in Washington, they came
around to Boggs's office. Could he help them? The newcomer
mentioned some personal problem with finding an apartment
or a school for his children. Boggs pressed a buzzer. An aide
came in, and Boggs told him to handle the problem. The votes
turned the election around for Boggs.

In January of 1971, new Speaker Carl Albert and new Majority Leader Hale Boggs sat down and discussed who would be
named Whip. The candidates were Hugh Carey of New York
and Tip O'Neill of Massachusetts. Carey had bitter opposition
from Brooklyn Congressman John Rooney, an important man
on the major Appropriations Committee. Rooney was from
Red Hook and spoke like it. He considered Carey, who lived
on Prospect Park West in Brooklyn, as being "Lace Curtain
Irish." It was a bitterness that started long before 1970, 150
years before at least, and it damaged Carey's chances. O'Neill,
on the other hand, was liked by everybody and had the mantle
of John McCormack still about him. O'Neill was chosen Whip.

Now, in January 1971, Tip O'Neill was the third-ranking
Democrat in the House of Representatives. Fine. But still a

long way from the posts from which the illusion of power could be used against Richard Nixon.

In October of 1972, Hale Boggs went to Alaska to assist in the campaign of Congressman Nick Begich. Boggs went this far because Begich had voted against him in the 1970 election for Democratic Majority Leader. The theory of Hale Boggs, and any other politician who has more than a cabbage for a head, is that you immediately try to win over the man who voted against you. Go to any lengths. In this case, Anchorage, Alaska. On the night of October 15, 1972, Boggs, exhausted from a full day's tour of that part of the territory, decided he was not going to punish himself and get up at 7:00 A.M. to catch the commercial flight from Anchorage to Juneau. Begich chartered a private plane. The pilot, Don Jonz, flew down from Fairbanks on the night of the 15th. He called the weather bureau before he went to bed. "Looks like I'm not going to Juneau," he said. When he woke up in the morning, the weather was still bad. Jonz went to the airport anyway. He fueled the plane and taxied over to the terminal. His plane was a twin-engined Cessna 310. The destination, Juneau, was 560 miles to the southeast, a long, tiring flight in such a small plane. Jonz didn't expect anybody to be at the terminal. He was surprised therefore to see Begich and Russell Brown, his administrative assistant, talking forcefully to a tired, thoroughly wary Boggs. There were, Begich said, television commitments in Juneau and the dinner was a sell-out because of Boggs's appearance. Boggs shrugged and got into the plane. Jonz took the plane out to the runway. It was nine o'clock. He had not expected to be flying in the cold, murky weather. But it did not necessarily disturb him. At thirty-eight, Jonz had been flying in Alaska for ten years. "You gotta be willing to cheat the devil," he told people. He wrote an article for a flying magazine which was entitled, "Ice Without Fear." He flew this time without a personal emergency locator transistor. He had left it at home, in Fairbanks. As the plane left the runway, the weary, uncomfortable Boggs looked at the cold rain streaming down the windows.

The plane was heard from once, just before it went through a mountain pass. Then never again. At nine that night Mrs. Lindy Boggs was notified in Washington that her husband was missing. She called Gary Hymel, Boggs's administrative assistant, who was home watching the Monday-night football game on television. They left for Alaska the next day. The military meanwhile put on an exhaustive search—private and military planes spent 3600 hours covering 325,000 square miles. There was nothing.

On November 7, Tip O'Neill voted in North Cambridge, then slipped off to the airport with Leo Diehl. They flew to Washington. That night, in the Whip's office, they began taking election returns. Thomas Hale Boggs, Jr., and Gary Hymel joined them. Throughout the night, O'Neill made casual calls to friends who had won elections. He also made calls to the new Democratic Congressmen. All the new winners were flattered and some awed by receiving a call in their local headquarters from the House Democratic Whip. As the night went on, O'Neill, Boggs, and Hymel talked about the Majority Leader's position. On Wednesday morning, Tommy Boggs arranged for O'Neill to call Mrs. Lindy Boggs. Tommy Boggs sat next to Tip O'Neill as he spoke to Mrs. Boggs about the post her husband had held. "Well, all I can tell you is that we have to be practical," she said. "If Hale were around here in a similar situation, he'd be about to want to get started."

When O'Neill hung up, Leo Diehl began punching phone buttons. Three people began to help him place calls to the Congressmen scattered all over the country. Leo knew from the start that it was going to be all right. He had John Brademas of Indiana talking to O'Neill, and the laughter told Leo that it was better than all right. And Leo was holding Teno Roncalio of Wyoming.

"He's talking to Brademas, Teno, and the second he gets off, I'll put you through."

"Is this for the Majority Leadership?" Roncalio said.

"Yes, it is, he wants to ask for your vote," Diehl said.

"Oh, hell, I'm voting for him anyway. Let me hang up and get off your back. He doesn't have to ask for my vote."

"Yeah, but he's going to ask you anyway," Leo said.

By Wednesday night, O'Neill had sixty-three committed votes. On Thursday, he put together forty-six. On Friday, they came up with eleven more. This gave him a hundred twenty votes. He was one shy of a majority of the Democratic caucus.

In New Orleans, Gary Hymel went to a gathering for Mrs. Lindy Boggs at the home of Hale Boggs's brother, Archie Boggs. Congressman F. Edward Hébert of Louisiana was there. Hébert had been the city editor of the *New Orleans States* when Gary Hymel was a reporter. At the reception, Hymel said to Hébert, "Eddie, you always said to call you if I needed something. And I need you now." Hébert listened. "Tell Tip he has my vote," he said. Hymel went to the phone. He caught O'Neill in Logan Airport in Boston. O'Neill got the news at the airport counter that he was Majority Leader of the House. He and Leo Diehl left the airport singing.

Congressman Sam Gibbons of Florida announced that he too would run for Majority Leader. He made no impact and withdrew on December 26. On January 2, 1973, the 93rd House Democratic Caucus re-elected Carl Albert as Speaker. Then Sam Gibbons got up and said, "Tip, I am going to tell you something that nobody else in this room can. You haven't got an enemy in the place."

It came another way for Peter Rodino.

One night in February of 1972, I was starting to fall asleep on the Eastern Airlines 10:00 P.M. shuttle from Washington to New York when a hand grabbed my shoulder and shook it. Standing in the aisle was Meade H. Esposito, the Democratic leader of Brooklyn.

"Hey, where were you tonight, you should have come to the party," he said.

"What party?"

"The party they gave for me. Manny Celler threw a party for me. He had two hundred and fifty Congressmen and Senators come around to meet me. He said I was the greatest political leader in the country. Manny gave it for me in this big room the Judiciary Committee has. You ought to see the size of the room Manny has."

Esposito took a seat. In front of him sat Eugene Gold, the Brooklyn District Attorney. Esposito slapped Gold on the head.

"Look at this guy, I make him District Attorney and what does he do? Arrests two Italians a day and says he's doing his job."

Meade then held up a plaque.

"Here, see what they did for me? They gave me a plaque.
That's Manny Celler's work. He has all the Congressmen and
Senators give me a plaque for political leadership. Isn't that
something?"

Meade held the plaque and looked at it for a full minute.
Then he shrugged and put it down.

"One thing about the plaque that's good, it's a small plaque
so I can shove it up my ass like I'm supposed to."

"What was the whole thing about?" I asked him.

"This is how Manny runs a campaign," Meade said. "He
gives me a plaque and I'm supposed to make sure everything
is all right in his district. He never comes around. Well, what's
the difference? I'll take care of things for him."

"He has no trouble, has he?"

"Well, there's some broad says she's going to run against
him in the primary or something. You know these freaking
broads. Who knows what she wants? It don't matter. How the
hell can you run against the Chairman of the House Judiciary
Committee? Manny's a national landmark."

On a morning a month later, I stopped into Woerner's Restaurant on Remsen Street in Brooklyn, just downstairs from
Esposito's headquarters, and Meade, in a back booth, waved
for me to sit down.

"I don't know what to do, I can't get this freakin' Liz Holtzman out of the race."

"Who is that?"

"The broad running against Manny Celler."

"Well, is it a fight, or what?"

"Nah. Shouldn't be a fight. It's just that this Manny, you
know, he never comes around. And I hear this girl, she's got all
kinds of young girls running around for her. Indians. Freaking
squaws. I've tried to talk her out of the race, but it looks like
I can't do it. Maybe Manny better get his ass up here and see
some people. That plaque he gave me can't go out and campaign for him."

On March 29, Elizabeth Holtzman, a thirty-year-old attorney, announced she was running in the Democratic primary
against Emanuel Celler, eighty-four, the famous Chairman of
the House Judiciary Committee.

"As far as I'm concerned, she doesn't exist," Celler announced.

The years had destroyed Celler's ability to see. By this time he thought of himself as actually holding power, rather than holding the illusion of power.

The next morning, Ms. Holtzman was on the subway platform handing out literature describing Celler's interest in legislation that helped Fishback & Moore, a company he held interest in.

Only 23 per cent of the people in the district voted in the June primary. Elizabeth Holtzman received 15,596 votes; Emanuel Celler had 14,986. By the margin of 610, she was in Congress. The fabled Celler was retired, and in a Washington apartment on the morning of June 21, a virtually unknown Congressman, Peter Rodino of Newark, New Jersey, found he was the next Chairman of the House Judiciary Committee.

The primary election between Holtzman and Celler could be considered one of the most meaningful elections the nation has had. If Celler had won, he would have dominated the impeachment process with the Judiciary Committee, as he dominated everything about the Committee for his thirty years as Chairman. Brilliant but egotistical, he would have been quite abrasive in such a delicate process. Particularly to needed Republican votes. Celler's large private law practice certainly would have been brought up, much more searchingly than Elizabeth Holtzman had been able to do in Brooklyn. For so many years, Celler had regarded himself as both brilliant and above the normal rules. Any detailed accounting of his personal business would have badly damaged the impeachment process in the Judiciary.

One day, while the Judiciary was studying the case behind closed doors, I ran into Celler, coming off a shuttle at Washington. "What do I think of how they're doing?" he said. "They're taking too much time. They're trying to get it bipartisan. That can't be done. The other side is only going to make it a partisan issue at the end anyway. So you might as well just go right ahead and call them on it. What was it Macbeth said, 'If it is going to be done at all, better it be done right away.'" He was stooped and his legs seemed unsteady. But his voice was strong. He certainly could have run impeachment hearings. But I kept wondering about his idea of shoving the vote down Republican throats. At that moment, Peter Rodino was carefully, delicately, trying to put together the group of Republicans and Southern Democrats that would give him the vote he needed to convince Congress and the country.

Later that November afternoon, Rodino complained about the pressures to Francis O'Brien, his administrative assistant. O'Brien is small, dark-haired, and with a serious face. He had worked for Mayor John Lindsay in New York; at the time of widespread prison riots O'Brien was assigned to be the Mayor's liaison with police who were lined up at the House of Detention in Kew Gardens, in Queens. The police inclination was to storm the prison. O'Brien's was to wait. In a prison riot, time never killed anybody. The disturbance ended without a death. When the Lindsay term of office was running out, O'Brien, through his brother, and relatives in Newark, found there was a position open on Congressman Rodino's staff: Rodino, Washington and, in the background, possible impeachment of a President. This dictated an energy and enthusiasm in O'Brien which was visible almost immediately to Rodino. Francis O'Brien also has a mother who is Italian, which was not considered a deterrent by Rodino. Now, as O'Brien listened to Rodino complain about his arguments with O'Neill, he kept thinking of one name.

"It must be a Republican," Rodino said.

"I know one Republican," O'Brien said. "John Doar."

On November 20, John Doar was in his office at the Bedford-Stuyvesant Restoration Corporation on Fulton Street in Brooklyn, in the center of the largest nonwhite area in the northern part of the country. Doar's phone rang with a call from Abraham Goldstein, Dean of the Yale Law School.

"There's a funny question I have to ask you," Goldstein said. "Would you be interested in being the special counsel to the Chairman of the House Judiciary Committee?"

"Yes, I would."

"Well, that's all I have to ask you," Goldstein said.

"Well, good-by," John Doar said.

He knew enough to go back to his work and not let the possibilities plague him. The Bedford-Stuyvesant, two- and three-story scarred brownstones and ramshackle wooden houses, rags stuck in broken windows against the winter, sprawls for miles. The Restoration Corporation, private and public money, was an idea of Robert Kennedy when he was the Senator from New York. Restore entire blocks, with local labor, and have the streets stand there as an example and inspiration for what can be done in the ghetto if an orderly attempt is made. You drive through the broken streets and the heart suddenly is lifted by a swatch of pastel-colored fronts, gleaming black iron railings, gas lamps on the stoops, brightly painted window frames. John Doar came to the Restoration Corporation in 1968 from the Justice Department. He had been in the Justice Department since 1958, arriving as an Eisenhower Republican from Wisconsin. In 1961, new Attorney General Robert Kennedy was afforded one look at John Doar's work. Bobby Kennedy's blue eyes flashed. "Isn't there some way that we can have his door locked so he can't leave us?" Kennedy said. "It wouldn't look terribly nice for me to be chasing after him down the street, would it?"

By the end of the summer of 1973, John Doar felt he had little more to give to Bedford-Stuyvesant. After nearly fifteen years of long hours and low public-service salaries he had college educations to worry about. He decided it was time to earn money and intended to leave before Christmas. That was before the phone call from Yale, and the one that followed some days later from Francis O'Brien.

"Would you like to come down one night and talk to the Chairman?" O'Brien said.

Doar said he would, and a date was made. Francis O'Brien had never met John Doar, but he knew him. John Doar is a legend to anybody who has worked the streets of this country and has had to work with the tensions and fears brought about by the divisions of race and class.

Doar came into the Rayburn Office Building at seven at night. In the Judiciary room, Peter Rodino was conducting the hearing into Gerald Ford's nomination as Vice President. When O'Brien slipped up to Rodino and told him Doar was in the building, Rodino left the hearing.

"I have eight people I'm talking to," Rodino said.

"I understand," Doar said.

"Have you made up your mind on whether there should be an impeachment?" Rodino asked.

"I have not," Doar said.

Doar mentioned that he just did happen to have read *The Federalist Papers* before coming down to see Rodino. "The real important thing is the language of the articles of impeachment, if it ever comes to that," Doar said. He began to tell Rodino how careful wording had produced indictments of three law-enforcement people in Mississippi arising from the murders of three civil-rights workers, Andrew Goodman, Michael Schwerner, and James Chaney.

Doar sat in a chair alongside Rodino's desk. This tall, somber-faced, monotone-voiced man impressed Rodino as he has impressed anybody else who ever has spent five minutes alone with him. There is in John Doar, under his silence and under his mixture of propriety and informality, a terribly fierce fifteen-round fighter. Peter Rodino, who grew up in a tenement in the First Ward of Newark, sensed this immediately. For all purposes, Rodino was risking everything he had or hoped to have upon his selection of a special counsel. If he was going to go down, Rodino kept telling himself, he at least wanted to go down with a strong guy.

At eight o'clock, Rodino went back to the Ford hearings. As Doar left the office, Francis O'Brien said to him, "If you take this job you're going to be hit. Are you prepared for public exposure?"

"Sure I am," Doar said. "I've been divorced, but that's no problem."

He went back to the Congressional Hotel and sat in the room and thought. In the morning he called O'Brien.

"Nothing I heard last night changes my mind about this job. This is no job you volunteer for. I won't lift a finger to get it. I'm not going to call you or anybody else. I'll wait to hear from you. If I do hear from you."

Doar went back to Brooklyn.

6

"The President talked with Mr. Haldeman."

IN WASHINGTON one afternoon, Frank Thompson, Jr., a New Jersey Congressman who is Chairman of a House Administration subcommittee handling contingency funds, looked over a typed resolution that was about to be sent to the Government Printing Office. The resolution called for an appropriation of a million dollars to be given to the House Judiciary Committee. Thompson handed it to an assistant who then had it sent to the Printing Office. Later, with the House about to shut down, Majority Leader O'Neill took the floor to announce the business to be conducted on the next day. O'Neill read from a list which included such as H. Res. 8053, to establish within the Bureau of the Census a Voter Registration Administration for the purpose of administering a voter-registration program through the Postal Service. O'Neill finished and everybody went home for the night.

The next day, freshly printed copies of the House Administration subcommittee's resolutions were passed to members at the start of the day. There was a resolution calling for funds for the printing of the record of the proceedings unveiling the portrait of the late Philip J. Philbin; another resolution—H. Res. 605—was to authorize markers in Statuary Hall for the location of the desks of nine former Members of Congress who became President. And then there was H. Res. 702—H. Res. 702—which was "to authorize that the further expenses of the investigations and studies to be conducted pursuant to H. Res. 74 by the Committee on the Judiciary, acting as a whole or by subcommittee, not to exceed $1,500,000, including expenditures for the employment of investigators, attorneys and clerical, stenographic, and other assistants and for the procurement of services of individual special consultants or organizations thereof."

The bureaucracy, in all its language and totally hidden meanings, was about to enter full motion against Richard Nixon.

"Tip, what do they need all that money for to go after an

innocent man? Goddam, we can't be investigating the President," O'Neill remembers one Congressman saying.

"Well, you're not against the House looking into the situation, are you? Hey, you must be kidding. Nobody likes it. But we've got to show the public we're doing something or they'll be bullshit."

Wayne Hays, the Chairman of the Committee on House Administration, came to the front of the House to introduce the resolution. The clerk sitting behind him was ordered to read the bill. The clerk's flat dull tones went out into the chamber and became lost in the talking and laughing of the few members in the chamber.

During the reading, Hays called out, "Mr. Speaker, I ask unanimous consent that further reading of the resolution be dispensed with, and that it be printed in the *Record*."

Carl Albert called out, "Is there objection to the request of the gentleman from Ohio?"

No voice was raised.

John Wydler, a Republican, got up. "Mr. Speaker, I make the point of order that a quorum is not present."

Albert said, "Evidently, a quorum is not present."

O'Neill stood. "Mr. Speaker, I move a call of the House."

Each Congressman has a large electric clock in his office. On the rim of the clock there are twelve amber light bulbs. Now in each office, and in the dining rooms and committee hearing rooms, the clock gave three loud buzzes and three of the amber lights came on. Quorum call on the House floor. Members have fifteen minutes to get to the floor and be recorded present. There are many different combinations of lights and noises to summon Congressmen, from one buzzer and light to a civil-defense test warning of all the way up to twelve, which are rung at two-second intervals at eleven o'clock on the second Wednesday of each month. This time, the three bells brought 398 Congressmen to the floor. As they walked into the chamber, they inserted small plastic IBM identification cards into slots on the back of seats. Immediately, on a huge electronic scoreboard, over the press gallery, a dot appeared next to the name of the Congressman, showing he was present.

With a quorum present, the slowest dance began.

MR. WIGGINS: *Mr. Speaker, I have a parliamentary inquiry.*

THE SPEAKER: *Will the gentleman yield for a parliamentary inquiry?*

MR. HAYS: *I yield to the gentleman.*

MR. WIGGINS: *I thank the gentleman. Mr. Speaker, was the committee amendment agreed to?*

THE SPEAKER: *It was not.*

MR. WIGGINS: *The issue under consideration is the committee amendment?*

THE SPEAKER: *The gentleman is correct.*

On the floor, they walked about, slumped into seats, leaned over, talked with the next one, got up, ambled to the back, lit cigarettes and cigars, talked, laughed, disappeared into the cloakrooms, came back, wandered up and down the aisles. The press gallery had only two or three drones at work. Congress is rarely covered by newspapers or television, and this most certainly did not appear to be a day with any import to it at all. The spectators' galleries were half-empty. Sitting in one narrow section on the Republican side were three White House people in charge of Congressional liaison. Dark suits, blond hair, cipher faces. They watched, unconcerned. After all, this was just some more dull, ceaseless, meaningless, dragging House business.

David Dennis, the picture of a country lawyer from Indiana, took the floor to fight for the White House. "Is the gentleman aware of the fact that this Committee on the Judiciary already has an active impeachment investigation under way? That we have nineteen people working full time on that subject? Is the gentleman aware that we have two hundred thousand dollars left in the account for this session, and that, in the regular course of events, at the first of the year, we will get at least another six hundred thousand dollars, without getting a penny under this resolution?"

He was starting on the road he was certain was the safest, supporting the President, and he never was to leave it for a full year.

Dennis of Indiana, Dickinson of Alabama, Hays of Ohio, Thompson of New Jersey stood on the floor and bickered over the commas and periods of a resolution. Halfway through the debate, Hays announced, "Mr. Speaker, I yield five minutes to the gentleman from New Jersey, the Chairman of the Judiciary Committee, for the purposes of debate."

Rodino stood up. "Mr. Speaker, I regret sincerely that while our esteemed colleagues on the Republican side protest against partisanship, they have raised that very issue . . ."

Now Rodino got into the gut of the issue: ". . . I have treated the members of that Committee and especially the ranking Republican members with the utmost fairness, not because I just wanted to be fair but also because one must be fair, especially in this matter. The Committee on the Judiciary has presently a staff of twenty-six attorneys. Of them, nineteen were selected by the Democrats and seven by the Republican. That is better than a one-fourth ratio. I have never rejected or refused a request on the part of the ranking Republican member, the gentleman from Michigan, Mr. Hutchinson. We hired mail clerks, seven or eight mail clerks, to open the mail on this alone. The five GAO investigators were not hired by the Committee investigation funds. We requested them from the GAO. We have one office manager that we hired in order to be able to supervise the personnel. . . ."

At the end, Dennis still was complaining about the Democrats controlling all that money, and besides, it was just too much to waste on this matter.

MR. O'NEILL: *Mr. Speaker, will the gentleman yield?*

MR. DENNIS: *I yield to our distinguished Majority Leader, the gentleman from Massachusetts.*

MR. O'NEILL: *I thank the gentleman for yielding. Mr. Speaker, if it were not for the scandalous action on the part of this Administration, it would not cost anything.*

The vote then was ordered. Throughout the offices, buzzers sounded and lights gleamed again and Congressmen walked down hallways, were in elevators, the subway from the office buildings to the Capitol was closed for use by anybody but

Congressmen on their way to vote. On the floor, the cards went into the slots and the yellow lights on the big scoreboard over the press gallery showed how each man had voted. And on a wall on the Republican side, a small yellow scoreboard showed the tally as it rose. The final vote was 367 in favor, 51 against. The House Judiciary was to receive one million dollars for its bureaucratic life.

Congress immediately did what it always does best: recessed for the Thanksgiving holiday.

While everybody was at home for the holidays there was sent to Peter Rodino's office a single piece of white paper, stationery from the Speaker's office, upon which was typed the message that there was this day deposited in the office of the Clerk of the House the sum of one million dollars as per the resolution passed on the floor of the House. The piece of paper was thick and crackly. If you rubbed your thumbs across its surface, the paper produced a loud, satisfying sound. The edges of the paper, however, were firm and sharp. If you were to run a finger quickly down the edge of the sheet of paper, the finger would burn. A nick from a paper razor.

In the newspapers, only three paragraphs were devoted to the special appropriation of one million dollars for the Judiciary Committee. But everybody who had been in Congress for any length of time knew that the story was so much more important than that. The committee would spend most of the million dollars on paper; stacks and reams and tons of thick white paper, the edges burning, nicking and, in time, taking on the properties of tempered steel. The burns would become slashes; the nicks would become mortal wounds. In Washington, a million dollars' worth of paper will slash to pieces the life and career of any man who so much as brushes against its edges.

On the Monday after the recess, Tip O'Neill spent the morning hearing Confessions, as he calls it. Congressmen who had been home in their districts came onto the floor to tell him of unrest over the question of impeachment. "Tip, everybody asks me when are we going to do something? What am I supposed to tell them? Damn, but they all want to know about it."

O'Neill took a seat beside Rodino. He asked again about

progress in hiring a special counsel. This irritated Rodino; he wanted to work at his own speed; it was his life which had to be put up. He had been asking people throughout the legal world about John Doar. So far, nearly everything had been positive. Still, Rodino wanted to take his time.

"It has to be before Christmas, we absolutely have to have the man by then," O'Neill said. Rodino exhaled in disgust. He wanted to be left alone.

On the 14th of December, Francis O'Brien decided on one of the surest ways to make something either happen or not happen. He called the Washington bureau of the New York *Daily News*. The next morning, in Brooklyn, John Doar saw his name in the morning *Daily News* story. The piece, out of Washington, said that Doar was one of eight people being considered for the job of special counsel to the House Judiciary Committee. Doar's phone began ringing. "Oh, that?" John told callers. "My name always makes any list that has eight or more names on it. Once they get below eight, my name doesn't appear any more." The calls also came to Washington. Favorable calls. Doar would be very good.

At this point, *The New York Times* discovered that John Doar was leaving his position at Bedford-Stuyvesant. Doar did not inform the *Times* of this; he is not a politician. But the story did originate in New York City. While Doar is no politician, he knows one hell of a lot of people who are. None of Doar's people ever will admit that he had a hand on the mirror, although when the *Times* story got around Washington, everybody took it as fact that Doar was leaving Brooklyn to become Peter Rodino's special counsel. Francis O'Brien said he could say nothing. All he really knew about it was that Chairman Rodino and Mr. Doar had spoken to each other. Blue smoke, thank you, good-by. It now was a matter of a day or so before Peter Rodino sat in his office and asked his secretary to place a call to John Michael Doar in Brooklyn.

So far in this account, when the mirrors and blue smoke have been properly worked, when they are being touched and handled by politicians with ability, by human beings of some substance and honor, the formula has not come close to failing.

And so John M. Doar came to Washington. Melvin Laird

assured people in the White House that Doar was a fine choice. "He will not find anything if there is nothing to find," Laird said. "We couldn't ask for anything more."

Which was a proper determination, providing that Richard Nixon was more or less innocent, as Laird at the time believed. The one who knew differently, Nixon, said nothing. He should have. For John Doar believes in everything that Richard Nixon does not. And John Doar is a fearsome opponent.

In 1965, Doar was assigned by the Justice Department to be in over-all charge of the Reverend Martin Luther King's march from Selma to Montgomery. On the final day, a warm overcast afternoon, Doar walked slowly up Dexter Avenue in Montgomery, up the hill toward the State Capitol, where Governor George C. Wallace had the Confederate flag flying over the American flag. Behind Doar, minutes away, just starting into the main part of town, were Dr. King and the first ranks of his huge parade. Doar was walking alone to check the streets. The sidewalks were lined with hesitant, curious whites. In the window of a second-floor beauty parlor, a woman sat under the hair dryer, two beauticians alongside, all craning to see the beginnings of the horror of black masses who came walking to bring down a way of life that was hundreds of years old. The woman under the dryer pointed to John Doar, who was walking in the middle of the street, eating an apple. She said something. The beauticians sneered.

"It's a beautiful day," John Doar was saying as he walked.

He did not notice the three white men standing on the sidewalk under the beauty-parlor window. They looked at John Doar and spit. They were Collie Leroy Wilkins, William Eaton, and Eugene Thomas, members of the Ku Klux Klan from Birmingham. That night, on the highway from Selma to Montgomery, their car pulled alongside a car driven by Mrs. Viola Liuzzo, a white woman from Detroit, who had been part of the march. Collie Leroy Wilkins leaned out the window and shot Mrs. Liuzzo in the head. The FBI investigated the case and arrested the three, turning them over to local authorities. In Washington, John Doar was told that the three had been on the sidewalk in front of the beauty parlor and he had walked past them. Doar's face showed nothing. Inside, it was different.

The murder trial of the three Klansmen was held in a

second-floor courtroom of an old white courthouse in
Hayneville. When the jurors were given the case to deliberate,
they sat in a room that had two windows looking down on
the side and rear of the courthouse. The jurors leaned out the
open windows. The local people stood on the grass and looked
up and talked with the jurors. One man—"Just put down that
ah'm the Presbyterian preacher, Hayneville, Alabama"—whit-
tled a tree branch. He looked up at the jurors. "Now you boys
do your duty," he said. Everybody giggled. One of the men on
the grass called up, "Can't see why there's so much of a fuss. Ah
done shot a big buck nigger myself once. Nobody said a damn
word of it. She was out with niggers." The jury waited a day
and came back to tell the judge they could not reach a verdict.

In Washington, John Doar began to have papers made out
that would bring the three men in federal court in Montgomery on charges of violating Mrs. Liuzzo's civil rights.
After the papers were filled out, Doar went home and packed
a suitcase. He prosecuted the case himself in Montgomery.
The federal judge on the bench was Frank Johnson. As Doar
methodically laid out his case, his eyes smoldering, Judge
Johnson began to stiffen. Johnson began to explain things to
the jury, shaping them for what he was going to insist that they
do: convict the three. The night the guilty verdict came in,
Doar's taut face relaxed. The three Klansmen would be sent to
maximum-security federal penitentiaries for years. Doar went
to dinner at the Elite Restaurant on Dexter Avenue. The Elite
always was George Wallace's hangout. George C. Wallace once
was quoted as saying of John Doar, "Somebody should get a
shotgun and blow Doar's head off." Do not miss.

Out of the months of irritation, arguments, pressure, and
resistance between Tip O'Neill and Peter Rodino, politicians
from local clubhouses, there came a John Doar as the man
who would sit and examine and sift the possibilities of Richard
Nixon.

On December 20, 1973, John Doar walked into the barrooms
of the second floor of the Congressional Hotel. The building
had just been taken over by the House as a supplementary
office building. Doar had been given the entire second floor.
He would staff the rooms with 106 people. Guards were posted

at the lobby elevator entrances, and at the elevator doors on the second floor. Doar chose one long large room for the library. The windows looked out over what had been the hotel parking lot. Prison bars were sunk into the window ledges. Thick wire grating was bolted on top of the bars. Special locks were put on the door, which was reinforced with steel. The room took on the feel of a penitentiary; there was no way in or out. Bolted to the top of the wall at one corner of the room there was what appeared to be a stereo loudspeaker. A box covered with black fabric. It was a motion detector. Once this room would be locked for the night, the motion detector automatically would go on. Any movement in the room, if the door came ajar even slightly, would activate alarms in the offices of the Capitol Police, the Washington Police, and the Federal Bureau of Investigation. By the time a prowler coming into the room took his second step, half of Washington would be surrounding the building. On the ceiling in the middle of the room was the silver nozzle of a smoke detector. A cigarette left in an ashtray would precipitate howling alarms throughout Washington. The room became a silo for the weapons that were to be stored there.

On a Saturday afternoon in that week, December 21, Larry Kieves of West Seventy-ninth Street, New York City, another former neighborhood task-force worker in the Lindsay administration, took a White House press release dealing with President Nixon's personal finances, and he sat down at a table in the library. He reached over and ripped open a cardboard box containing seven-ply index cards. The top card was yellow. Under the first sheet of carbon was a pink card. Next were four green cards and their carbons. The last card in the packet was a blue one. Kieves typed the subject on the cards. He placed a double asterisk at the end. At the bottom of the card the asterisks were explained: "**PF-I-IG." Go back to personal finances, number one, inquiry general file.

Kieves was starting on a manual information-retriever system which was to be used in place of computers. John Doar does not like, nor believe in the use of computers. He says they are useless in any matter involving security because anybody can punch a computer and find out what it knows. He also feels computers break down so continually as to be useless in this, the most important matter the nation ever had been in. A computer is marvelous for a bank. If the computer breaks down, interest computations can be done when the computer is fixed. Checks can pile up for a day. Checks even can be sent back by mistake. The only damage is embarrassment. But here, in this wired, barred room on the second floor of an old hotel in Washington, what John Doar regarded as the future of the nation was going to be processed.

"I have two rules," Doar said. "The first is, I don't want anything done by machine that can be done by a human being. The second rule is, never delegate anything that you can do yourself."

Larry Kieves finished typing his seven-ply cards. He separated them, got up, and began to insert them into file drawers. They were the first of 500,000 index cards which would be filed in this room and which would become a cross-filing system with a level of precision that approached life. As Richard Nixon inhaled, somewhere in the file cabinets, seven cards would breathe with him.

The system had been devised when Doar was in charge of the Civil Rights Division of the Justice Department, during years when young lawyers in the department spent all their time legally ending barriers to registration and voting of blacks in Southern states, particularly Mississippi. Voters were being required to take a two-question exam, one question asking for a statement of the duties of a citizen, the second asking for an interpretation of a section of the Mississippi constitution. By cross-filing index cards of white and black voters, the lawyers were able to prove that if a black man and a white man gave exactly the same answers to the questions, the black man failed and the white man passed. In cases where the black man's answer was better, his exam was lost. The card system had also been put into use during investigations of the murders in Neshoba County, Mississippi, of Andrew Goodman, Michael Schwerner, and James Chaney, and they also were used in re-creating the movements of James Earl Ray, who pleaded guilty to killing Martin Luther King.

The system, then, was designed to protect the rights of black citizens, the same rights that Richard Nixon had been helping erode through his five years in office. And now this system, once used against old sheriffs in Philadelphia, Mississippi, was simply being turned around to face Pennsylvania Avenue. As Larry Kieves placed the first file cards in the first drawers, Richard Nixon never felt the first burning, the first nick on his finger.

For now, in December of 1973, the ultimate weapon of the bureaucracy, paper, was being used to end the career of Richard Nixon. Paper does not lose interest, nor does it get tired. Paper never goes away. With men, climates change, perceptions alter. What is on paper remains constant. The paper is in files, its carbon copies in other files. A subpoena. Thick, folded legal-bond paper. The prosecutor's office has a copy, the court clerk has two copies filed, the lawyer of the person receiving the subpoena has a copy. Destroy one copy and three remain. Destroy two copies and still two copies remain. Postpone the hearing, protest it on legal technicalities, tie it up in the courts. Become sick and apply for further postponements. Take months, take years, it does not matter at all. The paper does not go away. It is there and everything is on it and there always is somebody ready to pull the paper out of the file and cause it to be acted upon. Paper defied the law of bribery.

Into the second-floor offices of the Special Counsel to the Chairman of the House Judiciary Committee came thirty typists. Most of them had been picked because they were graduates of Catholic high schools. They were trained by nuns to believe in causes, and now they were to work on another cause, the greatest search for justice in the nation's history. Doar's notion was that their work on a cause would reflect their backgrounds. Jane Ricca, thirty-nine, of Our Lady Queen of Martyrs parish, Forest Hills, Queens, New York City, one day typed for twenty straight hours. Lawyers working on documents gave them to her, took them back for changes, handed the papers to her again, took them back for more changes. Six and seven times her work on one document had to be completely retyped. Jane Ricca never shook her head or sighed. She typed. Each day, the amount of paper rose. Cartons came from the Ervin committee. Barbara Campbell, a typist, came down the street from the Cannon Office Building, swaying from the huge stacks of

Xerox paper she was carrying to Doar's offices. This was the first of the 1.5 million sheets of Xerox paper used to make up the notebooks of the members of the House Judiciary Committee. The files grew, the library room began to resemble a newspaper city room, with desks jammed together to form one long desk, and paper piled all over the desktops. The architect for the Capitol had to be brought in. Workmen reinforced the library floor to accommodate the weight of all this paper. Two-drawer file cabinets became six-drawer file cabinets. And everywhere, on every typewriter, on every carbon, on every card and paper in every file drawer, there were notations such as, "AP-26-A." This particular one had to do with White House media relations. But it really had to do with Richard Nixon, as did every other card and piece of paper on the second floor of the Congressional Hotel. Nixon could fly to San Clemente. He could have his lawyers protest and delay. He could ignore what was going on. He could rail and sulk. He could fly to Moscow, to Tel Aviv, to Cairo. There would be sun and service—the President does not make a phone call by himself—and the days would become weeks and the weeks would become months. The public would tire of Watergate, the newspapers would begin to write of other things. The President would say it was over: let us go on to something else. And always the paper mounted and the files grew thicker and higher and the typists typed. The paper grew, the edges becoming sharper, sharper, sharper. Soon Richard Nixon would feel the pain as the paper began to cut his life away.

Among the bales of paper received from the Ervin Watergate committee were many copies of Richard Nixon's daily diary. The copies had been surrendered peacefully by the White House. They were strange documents, detailing Richard Nixon's day to the minute. Doar read them himself, as did nearly all of the staff. There was something basically so twisted in a man who would detail his whereabouts this precisely that the effect of reading it was stunning. A typical account would be the day in Richard Nixon's life, shown on pages 116–117, Thursday, July 6, 1972, at what was called the Western White House at San Clemente.

The gossip in people drew them to the amount of time Nixon spent with his wife. From 2:50 to 2:51, he spoke to his wife. At 4:48 he met Mrs. Nixon at the pool area. By 5:02 he was returning to the San Clemente Compound residence. At 5:47 he went with her to the oceanside patio. By 6:19 he was back at the residence. This pattern repeated itself throughout all the diary pages. Through the days and nights of his life his diaries showed he spent a half-hour, at the most up to an hour, a day with his wife.

Doar was more interested in the obvious implications. That Nixon would chronicle each movement of his life so thoroughly—all that was left out was his bathroom habits—meant that the man was so obsessed with the notion of his greatness that he wanted it recorded forever. The diaries were to be the basis for Nixon's New Testament.

The diary pages were piled up on desks in the typing rooms. As the diary pages were copied onto seven-ply cards, the people were too busy to notice that when the overhead light came onto the pages, the edges of the daily diary paper glistened more than any other paper in the room. The finely ground steel—whitened by sharpening—of a terrible swift sword.

John Doar began to show lawyers on the staff a method used in the old days at the Justice Department. Doar took all the cards for a particular day out of the files, spread them on a desk, and began to examine them and move them around into different positions. "Sometimes you get to moving them around and you find the cards are telling you a story you didn't know," Doar said.

One lawyer, Bob Owen, was more than familiar with the card game. He had spent twelve years with Doar in the Justice Department and he had been through everything. In Brownsville, Tennessee, someone walked into a meeting at a black church and asked to see Owen outside. As Owen came outside, five men with shotguns stepped out of the woods. Owen stared at them. "Put those guns down, I'm a federal official," Owen said. Confused, the men did not shoot him as they were supposed to. Owen walked back into the meeting.

In Neshoba County, Mississippi, a man reached into the car and put a .38 to Owen's head. Owen again said he was a federal

PLACE DAY BEGAN				DATE (Mo., Day, Yr.) JULY 6, 1972
THE WESTERN WHITE HOUSE SAN CLEMENTE, CALIFORNIA				TIME DAY 8:20 a.m. THURSDAY

TIME		PHONE P = Placed R = Received		ACTIVITY
In	Out	Lo	LD	
8:20				The President had breakfast.
8:21	8:23			The President motored by golf cart from the San Clemente Compound residence to his office.
8:28	8:33		P	The President talked long distance with Acting Director of the FBI L. Patrick Gray III in Washington, D.C.
8:40	8:41	P		The President talked with his Press Secretary, Ronald L. Ziegler.
				The President met with:
8:41	9:08			John D. Ehrlichman, Assistant
8:58	8:59			Alexander P. Butterfield, Deputy Assistant
9:10	9:15			The President met with his Personal Secretary, Rose Mary Woods.
				The President met with:
9:15	10:08			Henry A. Kissinger, Assistant
9:25	10:08			Sir Robert Thompson, author
9:25	10:08			Maj. Gen. Alexander M. Haig, Jr., Deputy Assistant
10:10	10:11			The President met with Mr. Butterfield.
				The President met with:
10:11	12:05			Mr. Ehrlichman
10:18	10:22			Mr. Kissinger
10:40	12:06			H. R. Haldeman, Assistant
10:40	12:06			Clark MacGregor, Campaign Director for the Committee for the Reelection of the President
10:40	12:05			Frederic V. Malek, Assistant Campaign Director for the Committee for the Reelection of the President
10:44	11:01			William E. Timmons, Assistant
11:00	11:01			Mr. Ziegler
12:06	12:08			The President met with: Mr. MacGregor Mrs. Clark MacGregor Ollie P. Atkins, White House Photographer
12:08				The Presidential party went to the lawn behind the President's office.
12:08	12:11			The Presidential party held a photo opportunity.
12:11				The President returned to his office with Mr. and Mrs. MacGregor.
12:11	12:12			The President met with Mr. and Mrs. MacGregor.

PLACE DAY BEGAN				DATE (Mo., Day, Yr.)
THE WESTERN WHITE HOUSE SAN CLEMENTE, CALIFORNIA				JULY 6, 1972
				TIME DAY
				12:13 p.m. THURSDAY

TIME		PHONE P = Placed R = Received		ACTIVITY
In	Out	Lo	LD	
12:13	12:14			The President met with:
12:13	12:25			Mr. Butterfield
				Miss Woods
12:26	12:30			The President met with:
12:26	12:32			Miss Woods
12:30	12:31			Mr. Butterfield
12:31	12:34			Miss Woods
				Miss Woods
12:37	3:00			The President met with:
12:39	2:36			Mr. Haldeman
1:33	1:38			Mr. Ehrlichman
1:37	2:23			Mr. Ziegler
				Miss Woods
2:50	2:51	P		The President talked with the First Lady.
3:03	3:05			The President motored by golf cart from his office to the San Clemente Compound residence.
1	3:24			The President motored from the San Clemente Compound residence to Red Beach with his valet, Manolo Sanchez.
3:26	3:31	R		The President talked with Mr. Ehrlichman.
4:26	4:46			The President motored from Red Beach to the San Clemente Compound residence with Mr. Sanchez.
4:48				The President and the First Lady went to the pool area.
5:02				The President returned to the San Clemente Compound residence.
5:24		P		The President telephoned Mr. Haldeman. The call was not completed.
5:28	5:29	P		The President talked with Miss Woods.
5:30	5:43		P	The President talked long distance with his Special Counsel, Charles W. Colson, in Washington, D.C.
5:47				The President and the First Lady went to the oceanside patio.
6:19				The President returned to the San Clemente Compound residence.
8	7:04		P	The President talked long distance with Secretary of Defense Melvin R. Laird in Washington, D.C.
7:10		P		The President telephoned Mr. Kissinger. The call was not completed.
7:15				The President and the First Lady had dinner.
10:23	10:25	P		The President talked with Mr. Haldeman.

official. "If you can't prove it, you're a dead man," the guy with the gun said. Owen slowly went through his pockets and came out with the card. The gun came away from his head.

When John Doar called him in January of 1974, Owen was in private practice in the firm of Patterson, Belknap & Webb, in Rockefeller Center, in New York. He made an arrangement with his firm which allowed him to take some time off to work with Doar in Washington. Owen also spent his weekends working with Doar.

Doar had made two major decisions about how the case should be conducted. He decided not to do any investigating of his own, but to simply pick up the materials gathered by the Ervin committee and the Special Prosecutor's office and work from there. He thought that an investigation, interrogating witnesses—on television—would give the public the idea that everybody was doing the same thing over and over and the entire idea of impeachment might lose its effect. Doar also decided to try to place Richard Nixon in the heart of the cover-up conspiracy, from the very day after the Watergate break-in occurred. The Watergate Special Prosecutor's office seemed to be concentrating on Nixon's activities from March 21, 1973, the day John Dean informed him of the "cancer growing on the Presidency." All of Nixon's defenses were based on the belief that the March 21 conversation with Dean was when the fight had to be made. And it was regarded in the White House as a fight that could be won. But over in the Congressional Hotel, John Doar was starting his attack from another direction. He was patrolling the streets of a year earlier, starting with June 18, 1972. When Doar first began working with his own staff, in January of 1974, one of his staff people, Evan Davis, who is confined to a wheelchair, told Doar, "From what we've got already, I think the one tape I want to hear, if I had to hear any tape, is for June twenty-third."

As Bob Owen began on the project, he went through stacks of reports for that period. He took the cards for June 17 out and spread them on the table. Owen was looking for some great flash to come to him. It had happened once before, during the investigation of the murders of Goodman, Schwerner, and Chaney. One of the suspects was named Cecil Price. When Owen spread the cards out onto the table one day he began to re-create Cecil Price's day. As he moved the cards, Owen suddenly realized that Price could not have been able to drive five miles and catch up with a car in the amount of time he said it had taken him. Owen called the FBI and had them go onto the road in Philadelphia, Mississippi, and do exactly what Price had claimed to have done. The agents reported back that Price had to drive at a hundred and fifty-five to cover the ground he claimed. And Price's twelve-year-old car couldn't do any more than eighty-five.

Now, as Owen looked down at the cards for June 17, then June 18, he was hoping that some place along the line he would see something. He worked in the crowded library room, smoking True cigarettes and drinking coffee out of a paper cup in a plastic holder. He has less sandy hair now than when he went up against shotguns in the 1960s. He has the deep lines in his face and the roll in his voice of an Albany, Texas, dirt farm. Owen knows it spoils everything when people find out he went from Albany on scholarships to Choate and then Princeton. Therefore, at times his speech—"Well now, you just ain't goin' to hardly make it that-a-way"—is used as a disguise.

"McCord," Owen said as he looked at the cards. "McCord is fired from his job at the Re-Election Committee. Fine. But now where is Liddy on the eighteenth?"

"He is still listed as working for the committee," Maureen Barden said to him.

"When did he leave the committee then?" Owen asked.

"Not till the twenty-eighth. He refused to talk to the FBI and they fired him."

"Not till the twenty-eighth? And only when they had to get rid of him?"

"I'll get it for you," she said. People like Maureen Barden working in the library were so obsessed with the subject matter that they sometimes used the files only to verify oral answers. As Bob Owen got into the work, he, too, could feel the heroin effect of the stacks of paper in the room.

Maureen Barden's records showed, of course, exactly what she had told Owen.

Owen decided that the White House was trying from the start to contain the investigation. McCord was fired right away. The entire re-election group, and the White House, knew the

Watergate break-in was a G. Gordon Liddy operation. Yet they never fired Liddy until nine days later, when they absolutely had to. Doar was right. Nixon had to be in on it from the start.

Owen began to work on the files and cards. Haldeman. Ehrlichman. Dean. Mitchell. And Nixon. Immediately after the 1972 election, Owen's eighty-six-year-old father wrote him a letter. One sentence of the letter stuck with Owen forever: "Richard Nixon is the most dangerous man in the history of the world."

Typewriters clicked. Drawers were pulled in and out. Winter rain lashed the parking lot under the library room windows. The noises and movements in the room would be the same when the first spring sunlight appeared. Everything moved slowly and there was no way to stop it.

7

"The night-school students are saving the country."

THE HAND that rocked the bureaucracy into motion was found, of a Saturday night in June 1974, wrapped around a glass.

"Will you drink a Manhattan?" Tip O'Neill asked a man joining the party.

The man thought about it.

"I asked you, will you drink a Manhattan?"

The man thought more about it. Agitation showed in O'Neill's face.

"The reason I'm asking you if you take a Manhattan is that there's no bar here and it takes them too long to bring us back a drink. So I ordered two Manhattans for myself and you can have one of them if you want."

This was in the early part of the evening, when more than forty people came into the private dining room of the Wayside Inn, at Chatham, on Cape Cod, the people gathering there in celebration and admiration of the thirty-third wedding anniversary of Tip and Millie O'Neill and simultaneously the sixtieth birthday of Millie O'Neill, that number being loudly announced to all by her husband.

O'Neill was standing in a circle of people, everybody talking, O'Neill talking back to everybody, when his son Tom—who was running, successfully it turned out, for Lieutenant Governor of Massachusetts—placed a hand on his father's elbow. "Dad, I just want to tell you this one thing."

O'Neill, looking straight ahead, the eyes taking in the entire room—politics is for backcourt men—said out of the corner of his mouth to his son, "Hey, I can listen to five conversations at once. Just keep telling me what you want me to know."

His father went back to the group. "Chuck, is the weather really that bad? I thought Bantry was part of Cork. Cork's not supposed to be that bad. Oh, it's in West Cork? Oh, they have bright spells. That's good. Bright spells. Dick, old pal, you look good. Mary, darling! How are you? What will you have to drink, dear? Are you playing any golf, Paul? Well, I played today. You know what happened the other day out there? I'm on the third hole and there's a ball on the fairway and I don't know where the hell it came from. And here coming through the woods from the other fairway is Jim St. Clair. I said to him, 'Hey, Jim, what are you doing over here?' He just gave me this shrug and I kept on going my way. Stop to talk to him? Oh, I wouldn't do that. It just so happens that we're both members of Eastward Ho. Do I know him? I'll tell you a story about Jim St. Clair. One day a long time ago I got a call on a Sunday morning from a man whose son was arrested for drunken driving the night before. The boy was a senior at West Point. He was taking a summer course at MIT. The boy had been out and he'd had a few and the officer arrested him in Central Square for drunk driving. Well, I get a call from the father. He said the son'll be thrown out of West Point. Could I help? Well, geez, a kid goes to his last year in the Academy. I'm not going to let him get into trouble over a few drinks. Of course, I'll try to help. I told him I'd get my brother Bill, who was alive then. Practicing law, you know. Well, Bill calls the guy and the father says there's ten thousand in it if you could get my son off. My brother says, no, one thousand will be the charge, and I *cahn't* guarantee you anything but a pretty good try. The father said, no, it has to be ten thousand. My brother Bill says, no, I'll charge you a thousand. So on a Sunday morning we all come to court. I take a seat and the clerk comes up to me and says the judge wants to see me in the back. So I go back there and the judge says, 'Tip, what are you doing in here?' So I tell him the story of this West Point lad. When I finish I go outside and by now the father and the boy are in court. And with them is Jim St. Clair. During the night, it seems the father had gotten nervous after he arranged to have my brother Bill. And the father asked for the name of the biggest lawyer in Boston and they told him Jim St. Clair. So Jim St. Clair sees Bill and I starting to leave and he says to the father, 'You know, I'm not as experienced in a city court like this one. I think you're better off with Bill O'Neill here.' So the father said all right, and Jim St. Clair went off to play golf and my brother handled the case. Well, it was in Cambridge, and you got to know Cambridge. The policeman got up on the stand and my brother asked him, 'Did you know that this boy was a senior at West Point and that he is taking summer courses at MIT in order to better prepare himself to defend his country, and that he just pulled off to the side of the road on Saturday night to sleep off the exhaustion?' And the cop said, 'No, I didn't. If I had known it, I never would have allowed the court clerk to issue the summons.' Now you see, in Cambridge at the time the cop did not issue the summons. The court clerk did. So now the cop decided not to press the matter any more. At the same time he himself didn't have to rip up any ticket or anything. It was up to the court clerk to revoke the summons. Which of course he did and the case was over. And now I'm going to show you where Jim St. Clair is so smart. Remember the father telling my brother Bill about ten thousand dollars for the case? Well, he gave Bill three hundred dollars on the first day. Now for the rest of the bill, seven hundred, it was pulling teeth to get it out of him. Anyway, Paul, old pal, you look marvelous. Hey, what about all this food? Come on now, let's eat." He began steering people toward the buffet table.

At the end of the night, on his way to the car, O'Neill led his wife into the crowded smoky taproom of the Wayside Inn. He waited until George McCue, who plays the piano, finished a song. Then he came through the tables and up onto the small bandstand. He wanted to do one thing before the evening was over.

"My name is Tip O'Neill and I fool around in politics. I just want to sing a song for my wife, Milly, on her thirty-third wedding anniversary. I want to sing the song they played on the day we were married. The name of the song is 'Apple Blossom Time.'"

George McCue began to play the song on the piano and O'Neill's barbershop voice boomed out the start of the song.

> *I'll be with you in apple blossom time,*
> *I'll be with you*
> *To change your name to mine. . . .*

He sang through the smoke to his wife, selling her a love song in front of strangers. You thought automatically of Nixon and his Haldeman and Ehrlichman, standing in the doorway of the amber light of the room, smirking and starting to leave,

secure in the absolute belief that no such open, old-fashioned
people could be dangerous. If O'Neill was Congress's idea of a
leader, how could they be hurt? How could a man who sings to
his wife in public ever qualify as an opponent? At the last note,
O'Neill broke into a neighborhood cheer, his voice coming up
from the sandlots:

"Milly Miller O'Neill! Yeah!"

The next day he went to Washington, taking with him in all
his mannerisms and speech the loud, crowded life of the streets
and of the frame houses of Cambridge and Boston, and the life
as a politician that is much a part of the area. There is no way
to understand what went on in Washington in the summer of
1974 unless you realize that what happened was because of
politicians. Ask Peter Rodino what was the single most important thing he had to do to bring about the impeachment vote
against Richard Nixon and watch the Constitutional scholars
pack around to hear his answer:

"When I was able to hold Mann, Thornton, and Flowers,
then I knew it could be done," Rodino tells you. "I had to have
them. Once I had them I could start to put it together."

Put it together. A vote. The basics of clubhouse politics. He
had to know that he had the votes of James Mann of South
Carolina, Walter Flowers of Alabama, and Ray Thornton of
Arkansas. With these Southerners for impeachment, the needed
Republican votes would not be impossible to obtain. Let the
scholars debate the narrow versus broad interpretations of the
Constitution as the most meaningful thing to come out of the
impeachment. Peter Rodino knew it was the votes that did it.
The politics, not the scholarship of the matter.

And, from his position, Tip O'Neill knew it was the job
of causing the bureaucracy to move that enabled everything
else to happen. He knew this because he was a professional
politician, and you might as well know a little bit of what these
people are and where they come from.

For a little island, it has caused so much pain. In 1845, there was
a great potato famine in Ireland, people in remote areas trying
to subsist on yellow winter grass and, finally, crazed, entering

the black torture of cannibalism. Everywhere in the country there were children unable to close their mouths, the lack of calcium in their bones preventing their jaws from working. Three O'Neills—Pat, John, and Mike—left Cork City for the terrible ocean crossing to Boston, and the promise of jobs with the New England Brick Company. In Boston, the first money the brothers gathered that was not needed for food went directly into the Irish stock market—cemetery plots. The next money Pat O'Neill had—in 1855—was spent going home to Ireland and bringing back a wife to America. A son from this marriage was Thomas P. O'Neill, Sr. He was raised to be a bricklayer. In 1900, he won a seat on the Cambridge City Council. On the day his son was born—Thomas P. O'Neill, Jr.—the father was picketing Harvard with people from the bricklayers' union. The only thing better a man from Cambridge could say about his father is that the father was elected President on the day he was born. For Harvard, until it began to grow up in the last fifteen years, always regarded the people outside its gates as leaves upon the streets.

In 1914, Thomas P. O'Neill, Sr., received the highest mark in a Civil Service test for the job of superintendent of sewers and sanitation for Cambridge. There were 1700 men on the payroll, none of them Civil Service, which meant that O'Neill was in charge of hiring and firing. His hand immediately reached out to touch more jobs. He married the executives of the Edison Cambridge Gaslight Company, a joining together worth hundreds of jobs to O'Neill, Sr. In North Cambridge, he became known as "The Governor." He ran the North Cambridge Knights of Columbus baseball team, was President of St. John's Holy Name Society and—strict Irish rather than dreaming Irish—head of the St. Matthew's Temperance Society. Nobody in his house was allowed to wear anything that did not have a union label on it. No clothes were ever thrown out—there always was a society for the needy. And all the children in the household were brought up to regard the first Tuesday after the first Monday in November as the most important day of the year. When Tip O'Neill was fifteen, he was out ringing doorbells to pull people out of their houses to vote for Al Smith for President and Charley Cavanaugh for Massachusetts

State Representative. Tip O'Neill, in charge of half a precinct, reported at the end of the day that only four people in his area did not vote, and they were out of town.

Tip O'Neill hung out with a large crowd of kids at a place called Barry's Corner, and without anybody mentioning the fact, O'Neill was the leader. One of them, Red Fitzgerald, remembers his mother saying that Tip O'Neill was going to be a bishop. "He never pulled a dirty trick in his life, so how could he miss?" Red says. O'Neill always had a way to keep the crowd around him, and also to be useful to them. He had a job as a night watchman at a brickyard, and he fixed up the outdoor telephone pay station with a nail into the contact so that his nightly crowd of visitors had free phone service. It was in the middle of the Depression and nobody had the nickel for a call.

By 1931, O'Neill was out of high school and earning $21 a week as a truck driver for a brick company. November of that year was cold and work was slow. O'Neill took courses at Boston College High School at night, then entered Boston College. Neither the college nor the O'Neill family publicizes his scholastic achievements, although Boston College prints his picture on its literature and considers him as perhaps the school's most important alumnus. Meanwhile, if Boston College ever were to falter, Harvard would be more than happy to claim O'Neill as its own. The matter of academic brilliance was brought up over the summer in Washington, when Peter Rodino (who never went to college) and John Sirica (scholastic background at best vague) were busy showing the nation that honesty might be important.

"The night-school students are saving the country," Mary McGrory, the writer, was saying one day. "I don't think Sirica or Rodino spent a day in a regular undergraduate school. And I'm certain that Tip did not."

"Oh, no, he went to Boston College," she was told.

"Oh, yes, but thank God it wasn't serious," Mary McGrory said.

In his education O'Neill did himself and the country a favor by not following the traditional path of entering law school before going on to politics. During the early months of 1973, a Tip O'Neill, attorney at law, trained in the deviousness and tiny facts of the law, never would have come walking into

Carl Albert's office saying that Richard Nixon was going to be impeached. That was too outrageous, and also too true, for a lawyer. Tip O'Neill, attorney, would have had instilled in him by professors the knowledge that he had not a scintilla of evidence upon which to base any judgment at all of Richard Nixon's status in February of 1973. O'Neill, not being a lawyer, did not know that he was using such terribly unsure methods as instinct, a little anger, and a boxcar full of common sense.

The fact that O'Neill is not a lawyer gives singularity to his success. It always has been extremely difficult for legitimate people to get into politics because the base of the American political system has been built on the needs of lawyers. They come out of offices that are one flight over a drugstore and have gold lettering on the windows that says "Attorney at Law," and they come into the political system because time and occupation make it the place to be. Lawyers are not lashed to a normal person's work schedule. Always, a lawyer can switch his schedule around so he may attend a City Council meeting at one-thirty on Thursday afternoon. Also, as the nation grew and started its sprawl at the turn of the century, the lawyers then in command drew up codes so intricate, so tangled that no citizen could ever do business with a government agency of any size, from town to federal, without the service of a lawyer. Particularly a lawyer involved in politics. Many of the rules and regulations adopted throughout the country, most still in effect today, carried with them the unwritten admonishment, "Bring Extra Money!" This, in envelopes, for sliding under the table. Corruption to benefit lawyers was built into the government structure as if it were notarized. Today in politics, at the place where most men must start, it seems to be almost solely a place for lawyers. Judges appoint referees, lawyers, for mock-auctions of foreclosed properties. The judges appoint lawyers known in the business, and politics is the business of judges. The items spiral upward to a point where you have foreclosure proceedings on multimillion-dollar mortgages and the judge appoints a referee, a monitor, again a clubhouse lawyer who receives as high as $30,000 on a million-dollar matter; receives the $30,000 for doing approximately nothing. How much of this does the lawyer keep for himself and how much does he hand back to the judge? That depends upon the bargaining ability of both. If they were to strike a poor deal, a quarrelsome deal, somebody might hear of it and a district attorney would consider the subject a prime opportunity for career advancement. Other matters between lawyer and judge can be settled in ways that almost can be traced; the judge has a son and daughter who attend expensive colleges, all bills paid from a sort of scholarship set up by a lawyer.

Because there is money to be made from the system, lawyers get into politics as a business necessity. The reasoning is that lawyers are necessary in government because government makes and deals with laws, and lawyers are best equipped for this. But laws are things to be understood and obeyed by everybody, so why should the making of laws be left to a small inbred system? The major reason for the presence of so many lawyers in government is, of course, the economics. Less than 5 per cent of the lawyers in the nation ever stand on their feet in a courtroom. That is too unsure a life. A public payroll, however, is very sure. Representing a contractor who does business with government agencies—where the lawyer knows many people through his political life—also can be considered a certainty. And then the financial structure of public life makes office-holding a dream for a lawyer. Most local and state and many federal elective posts allow a person to practice law on the side. Senator Jacob Javits has a law firm on Park Avenue in New York City. State Representative Michael LoPresti has a law practice in Boston. The rewards produced by the situation cannot be counted. Therefore, at the start of a career, it bothers not a politician to have to live in the state capital for four or five months a year, at a salary of perhaps less than $15,000, because his law office in his home district is producing a living for him. But for a college teacher with ideas, or a steamfitter with ideas, it is financially impossible to serve in a state legislature. Some think or dream or even try. Always the result is the arithmetic of family bills makes politics impossible.

Left mainly to lawyers, then, the pursuit among most politicians on a local level is for the great prize: a judgeship. Judges receive excellent money, serve lengthy terms, and have short working hours and long vacations. In New York, higher courts pay up to $49,000 for terms of fourteen years. Foraging rights appear to be limitless. The scramble for a judicial vacancy becomes so intense that the entire political structure of a county can be frozen while councilmen and assemblymen and leaders push and swirl and bargain—often openly passing money about—for the judgeship.

Tip O'Neill represents the ones who came another way. If you see the system work on a local basis, you wonder how anybody worth while ever lasts through it and gets anyplace. But for O'Neill, there was no way he could not be a lifetime politician. Clearly, the viral containers in his genes held, who knows, a couple of thousand years of the ability to control, to calm others, to decide without being abrasive, to be affable while the insides boil. For good politicians, real politicians, are not created in law school or in bank vaults. They are born, as their fathers were born, and the father of the father before them, and then back through the ages, with this viral container of public life in the genes. Just as the ability to play a piano in concert or to write a lasting novel is present at birth.

As a senior at Boston College he ran for Cambridge City Council. His father did virtually nothing to help him, and he lost the election by a hundred and fifty votes. The arithmetic still is fresh. "I got four thousand votes," he says quickly, "and thirteen hundred of them were from North Cambridge. I should have gotten eighteen hundred votes there. That's if I pulled what I should have in wards seven, eight, nine, ten and eleven. What happened? My father said to me at the end of the election, 'You know, you never asked me for help.' The woman across the street said the same thing to me on election day. Her name was Mrs. Elizabeth O'Brien. She was an elocution teacher. She called over to me in the morning, 'Good luck, Thomas. I'm going to vote for you even though you didn't ask me.' I told her I'd known her all my life. 'Mrs. O'Brien, I used to run to the store for you. I didn't think I had to ask you.' And she said to me, 'Tom, people always like to be asked.' Well, you could of punched me right in the nose and I wouldn't of felt it."

The next time he ran he was working in a small insurance brokerage and real-estate office in Harvard Square. The insurance business can serve the same purpose as a law degree to a politician, but he never did very much with it. In the election this time, there was a candidate named Tierney who had to be beaten for a seat in the State Legislature. A few days before the election, an old pro named Foley said to O'Neill, "You've done well for a beginner. I don't want you to feel bad when you lose." O'Neill began to come continually late to street-corner rallies. He was too busy working the side streets and asking housewives to vote for him.

On election night, Tierney took a hotel room, had a few drinks, then slept for an hour. He showered and changed his clothes in order to look fresh and vibrant when acknowledging the cheers later on. Tierney came to his headquarters and, whistling softly, asked to see the results from his prime area, Ward 11, Precinct 3. Eleven-three contained St. John's School, its rectory and convent. Tip O'Neill had worked the area so thoroughly he owned it. The slip of paper for 11-3 was handed to Tierney. Tierney's soft whistle stopped, as did his heart. The results from 11-3 showed O'Neill with 712 votes and Tierney with 163. Rested, showered, Tierney went out in search of a pulmotor. And in his own headquarters, a rumpled, sweaty, flushed Tip O'Neill let out the first of what were to become a lifetime of election-night laughs.

Some years later, 11-3 was given a thorough campaigning by Congressional candidate John F. Kennedy. The area is changing now, with college students moving into houses that have been cut into small apartments; but if you walk into the kitchen of a house where lifelong residents live, the woman will point to a chair at the kitchen table and tell you, "He came in here and he sat right there. God rest his soul."

One day after the 1962 Congressional elections, Jack Kennedy saw O'Neill in the White House, and he said, "Say, Tip, how did you do in eleven-three?"

"You know, only thirty-four people voted against me," O'Neill said.

"And I'm sure you have the names and addresses of every one of them," Kennedy said.

In 1935 O'Neill was almost twenty-three when he won this first election. Also in that election, up in another section of Cambridge called Greasy Village, Leo Edward Diehl, twenty-two, won a seat in the legislature. He won as much by his powers of observation as anything else. One morning, at the start of the campaign, Leo was out in the streets in time to see one Father

John Geoghegan driving a woman named Peggy Dolan in the general direction of Peggy Dolan's job in Boston. You would have had to cut off Leo Diehl's head to make him forget this.

Some mornings later, Leo Diehl was on the same street at the same time and here was Father Geoghegan again driving Peggy Dolan to work. Leo grunted.

It then happened that in the core of the campaign, Leo Diehl heard that Father Geoghegan was going door to door on behalf of Leo's opponent, a man named Hillis. When this news was brought to Leo Diehl, the candidate showed no outrage. He simply asked for somebody to give him a lift. As the car pulled away, everybody on the sidewalk was surprised at the calmness with which Leo received the news, very bad news for his campaign because in Cambridge a priest's word had power second only to money.

The friend driving Leo Diehl said to him, "Where are we going?"

"I want to drop by and say hello to Peggy Dolan."

Peggy Dolan was shocked by Leo Diehl's accusations. "I do not go out with Father Geoghegan! I just let him drive me to work.

"Besides," she said, "Father Geoghegan goes steady with Theresa MacNamara."

Theresa MacNamara was a local dance instructress who had danced the parish to death. Leo immediately had his friend drive over to Theresa MacNamara's dance studio.

"We do not!" Theresa MacNamara squalled. "All we do is the Texas Tommy together."

Leo Diehl persisted. Soon, in tears, Theresa MacNamara said: "He calls me Pussy Cat."

Later that night, grunting, grimacing, Leo Diehl pulled himself up the rectory steps and rang the doorbell. When Father Geoghegan appeared, Leo Diehl said, "I just wanted your permission for Theresa MacNamara to come around with me tonight and tell all the people that she's your best girl and that she wants them all to vote for me."

Father Geoghegan started to faint. He pulled himself together long enough to agree that he would make the rounds on behalf of Leo Diehl himself.

"Make sure you do," Leo said. "By the way, I don't know what's the matter with you. I'd rather jump on top of Peggy Dolan than Theresa MacNamara any day."

In January of 1936, O'Neill and Diehl entered the State House for the first time. It was the beginning of a relationship which is closer today than it ever was. And it also was the true beginning of a political career for Tip O'Neill.

There is in this country no place that could even be suggested as being anywhere near the Massachusetts State House for bone politics. Throughout the nation, the complaint with state legislatures is that they are part-time bodies. Not even that in many places. New York, supposedly so efficient, has a state legislature which meets in January and averages three days a week until the late spring. After which it is regarded as a criminal offense for the legislature not to be recessed well in advance of the closing days of the school year, thus giving legislators time to open summer houses, pack their kids' clothes for camp, and plan vacation trips. In Massachusetts, the legislators prefer to sit forever. They usually have to be driven out of the building, practically at gunpoint. If a Massachusetts legislator is removed from his game, his sport, his very life, then all that is left for him to do is return home to his wife and family, and in Massachusetts anybody can have a family but the true goal of life is to be a politician; or, true term, a Pol. It is not uncommon for the Massachusetts Pols to sit in the State House throughout the summer, arguing, spreading rumors, using the phones, and—true glory—plotting against each other.

But in this they are so right. For who would leave a building, and what possible reason could he give, where the life in its halls is dedicated to the memory of the actions of such as former Governor—among other things—James Michael Curley? Ask anybody in Boston about Curley and they will grope for a place to begin; there is so much to tell. Well, in 1933 new President Franklin D. Roosevelt offered Curley the post of United States Ambassador to Poland. From the State House there came a great cry, "He'll pave the Polish Corridor." And from James Michael Curley himself, in a face-to-face meeting with Roosevelt, there came, "If Poland is such a great place, why don't you resign and go there yourself?"

8

"I hear you play tennis."

AT THE start of the summer, Richard Nixon sat at his desk in his Oval Office with the political people, Anne Armstrong, Dean Burch, and William Timmons, seated across from him.

"How's Goldwater?" Nixon asked.

"He seems fine, but you know, Mr. President, I couldn't control one minute of his life," Burch said. Burch, from Arizona, had been one of Goldwater's chief campaign aides in 1968.

Nixon said, "Oh, the President knows that you couldn't do anything like that with Goldwater."

Nixon then said, "How's it look on the Judiciary?"

"Well, Railsback is on the fence."

"Railsback. Well, there's time."

"Smith is okay."

"Fine."

"Flowers is all right."

"We're heating him," Burch said. "We're talking to people at home. Newspaper editors. Radio and television."

"Sure. The people at home are behind the President," Nixon said.

"Mann," Burch said.

"Heat him up, too. All of his people support the President. Loyalty. They're loyal to the President."

The matter always was discussed in the abstract, Nixon referring to himself only in the third person. There were times during the years of Watergate that the thing grabbed him inside and threw everything around: when Haldeman and Ehrlichman had to resign on April 30, 1973, Nixon became an aimless drifter, flying everywhere, doing nothing. People in the White House say he was unable to function and the country had no true leader. But then there were times such as this meeting, when he sat in his office, discussing everything in the abstract, certain that he never had done anything wrong.

"He was the President," Dean Burch says, "and the President never does anything wrong because he is the President."

None of the political people talking to him—before leaving to defend him—ever had asked Nixon about the facts of the Watergate case. One simply does not go up to a President of the United States and say, "What about this? Are you guilty?" It has been our system up to this point. Most human beings who reach the White House, in any capacity, immediately become so royalty-prone that there appears to be no way for the situation to change.

After the meeting, Burch and Timmons sat down to discuss their defenses in the House and Senate. Timmons was a Congressional liaison man, a White House lobbyist on Capitol Hill. Burch was much stronger. He is listed as a Conservative from Arizona, but he is much broader and smarter than the connotations of any label. As an FCC Commissioner, he became known as the most independent of the commission. He kept saying that he saw no reason why in this country a newspaper should be allowed to own a television station. This belief—big communications is as dangerous as big government and big labor—brought choking sounds from the throats of the nation's finest liberal and conservative newspaper publishers who also owned television stations.

Burch and Timmons talked about their problems with a defense based on executive privilege regarding the President's tapes.

"I see something like this as only a last resort," Burch said. "I'd rather just let everything come out. It won't be all that bad. Now the whole thing is March twenty-first. All right, there's some things in there not so good. But on balance, you can come out of that all right. It's just a strong circumstantial case. Hell, you don't throw a President out on circumstantial evidence. No, we're all right on that March twenty-first. So I just don't see why we keep stonewalling it on the rest of the tapes. Let them out."

"It's about the end of the line for talking about executive privilege," Timmons said.

"We'll wind up sounding as bad as O'Neill," Burch said. "Save me from any more of this 'The future of the nation' that he keeps telling everybody. He's just playing plain old hardball politics."

* * *

Tip O'Neill made the fight out of his lair, the Democratic cloakroom of the House. Two double-hinged doors on the Democratic side of the chamber, doors with dull stained-glass windows, lead into the cloakroom. It is a long, narrow windowless room with a curved railroad-car ceiling. Brown leather couches and armchairs are set against the wall, linen handtowels covering the tops of the chairs. Brass ash stands are alongside the chairs and couches. The far end of the room is kept in darkness; somebody is always stretched out for a nap.

As you come into the room from the floor, there is a sink and an aluminum lunch counter. Lemon-meringue pies sit on racks inside tall circular plastic containers. The only thing missing from the scene is a couple of flies buzzing the meringue pies. The lunch counter is run, of course, by a black. His name is Raymond and he is quick to say, "I don't know nothin', I don't see nothin', I don't hear nothin'." In a cabinet on the wall there is a first-aid kit and a Life-O- Gen oxygen inhalator. The carpeting, wine with yellow and black speckles in it, is worn in spots. There should be much more dust in the carpet to emphasize the age from which its pattern is derived. The thought immediately occurs to you as you walk into the cloakroom that Congress is afternoon baseball.

The only thing to contradict this is a switchboard in an alcove, and fourteen phone booths. A red wall-phone next to the page boy who runs the switchboard is the one used to contact O'Neill.

He came into this room in June with a new weapon, another mirror, a forty-page notebook put together by William Hamilton and Staff, pollsters, for William Welsh of the American Federation of State, County, and Municipal Employees. The topic sentence of the report said, "In April our study shows 43 per cent will vote for a Congressman who is inclined to vote for impeachment; 29 per cent would vote for a Congressman who would not be so inclined and 28 per cent feel the Congressman's stand on impeachment would make no difference at this time."

A further interpretation of the figures showed that "50 per cent of Republican voters will vote against a Congressman who is inclined not to vote for impeachment, while only 7 per cent of the Democrats will vote for a Congressman who is inclined to vote against impeachment."

Into the cloakroom at this point came Dan Rostenkowski of Illinois. Cook County, Illinois. Rostenkowski is six-foot-two and he weighs about two hundred and twenty pounds. Dan Rostenkowski always says to people, "Do you know what is black and blue all over and is found floating in the river?"

"What?"

"A person who tells Polish jokes."

Rostenkowski had an opinion on impeachment. This was formed when he heard a number of fine, compassionate liberals demanding that Richard Nixon be both impeached and then thrown into jail for income-tax evasion. Rostenkowski did not like impeachment so much to begin with. When he heard income taxes mentioned, he nearly put his hand through the table. Income taxes! One sixth of Chicago would have to go to jail if they started a push on income taxes. In Chicago, the form always has been that the politicians receive huge, scolding headlines when they are caught stealing and selling high-rise sites and parking-lot locations, all in cash, all unreported. The public reads the headlines and then, joyously, gives the politicians in question the largest votes ever recorded. And that ends it. The other word the liberals were using—jail—is such a bad word in Chicago that Rostenkowski could not even get himself to mention it. He simply gave off a feeling of cold death and let it go at that.

O'Neill went right to Rostenkowski, because Rostenkowski is Mayor Daley's play-caller with the Illinois Democrats in Congress. A word from Danny is a word from the Hall. Deviation? Try Russia, not Cook County.

"Danny, old pal, did you see this poll yet?" Tip O'Neill said.

"What poll?" Rostenkowski grumbled. He despises polls, but he had to ask about a poll because he is in politics and he is supposed to ask about a poll.

"It shows here that we could pick up as many as eighty seats the way it's going now," O'Neill said.

"Whew."

"And it shows here that there is no way for a Congressman in an urban district to win an election against anybody if he doesn't vote for impeachment."

"Where does it show that?"

"Here, look. Only seven per cent of the Democrats will vote

for a Congressman who is against impeachment. That means a Republican could beat a Democrat in a city if the Republican is for impeachment and the Democrat is against it. Can you imagine that? Say, that's right. You represent a city, don't you, Danny?"

O'Neill began to show the poll around. He told Thaddeus Dulski, who comes from upstate Erie County in New York, that the poll showed all rural votes being lost to a Congressman who is against impeachment. "But you don't have any farms in your district," he told Dulski. Dulski grumbled. He had a religious belief in the Presidency. He also had a lot of farmers in his district. Out on the House floor, when O'Neill saw Angelo Roncallo, a Long Island Republican, he said, "Hey, Angie, old pal. Geez, but you really love it down here, don't you? Angie, I want you to know something. My door is always open to you, as you know. And to show you how much I think of you, Angie, my door is still going to be open to you next year when you're not going to be in the Congress because of this impeachment." O'Neill gave a great, fun laugh. Roncallo laughed with him but not as much.

It was like the first round of a fight. He jabbed, stepping in with the jab, and found the other guy went back right away. Then he bent down and tried a left hook to the body. The guy was right there for him. He always had said that the other guy was going to get knocked out. Now, after the first couple of punches, he was certain of it. There would come a time in this fight, probably on a hot afternoon sometime after the middle of August, with everybody out on the floor, and he would load up, hook off a jab, and Richard Nixon would go home in a blanket. No question. As far as O'Neill was concerned, the fight was off the boards.

At lunch one day in the House dining room he showed me why there was no other way.

"Here, look at the door and then you'll know as much as I do," he said.

In the doorway, looking around for a table was Congressman Joseph Moakley. Moakley was swinging his arms, clapping his hands in front of him, beaming and laughing, a hand reaching out to slap somebody on the shoulder.

"He just learned he has no opponent in the primary. Louise Day Hicks decided that she didn't want a primary. Now look at the other guy behind him."

The other guy was Congressman James Burke. He was motionless. He is an old Irish fox who keeps everything behind a straight face. But this time, a bleakness, a physical pain, was set in his face.

"He's got an opponent," Tip said. "Some young guy from the Milton City Council filed to run against him in the primary. There is no bad news like that news."

Moakley came past the table. Shaking hands, slapping shoulders.

"You must feel pretty good, old pal," Tip said.

"Thank God and anybody else who had anything to do with it," Moakley said.

Burke came by. "Hello, Tip," he said quietly.

"James, you look disturbed."

"Not at all, I'm fine."

"What are you going to be doing this weekend?" Tip asked him.

"I've got to go home. I've got a couple of parades I've got to go to."

"When was the last time you went home for a parade?" Tip said.

"Oh, I don't know."

"It doesn't matter because this year you'll be carrying the flag for the whole time," Tip said.

He laughed and Burke did not.

When Burke was gone, O'Neill said, "You see what an opponent can do to you? I think Jim can win all right. But the money kills you. Cost you a hundred thousand dollars. Now if an opponent you can beat is this disturbing, imagine what it's like to face one that you might not be able to beat. Imagine what it must be like for some of these Republicans. You're facing an election in November and the only issue in the country is how you stand on impeaching the President?"

There were two occurrences at the beginning of July, occurrences which had been taking shape for many weeks. When they arose, they added to the tension of the situation. One was more revealing of the enemy than it was dangerous. The second appeared, for a brief moment, a direct threat to the success of the impeachment process of the House.

The first occurrence, the one that revealed, began its life on June 4, 1974, when Jeb Stuart Magruder came up the dirt hill to the steps of the administration building at Allenwood Prison camp in the dull, working hills of central Pennsylvania. Loitering by the front door were two inept thieves from Brooklyn, their presence dictated by their performance with stolen treasury notes.

"It could get hot here this summer," one of them, Mr. J. G., said to Jeb Stuart Magruder. It was the first time J. G. ever had spoken to a man from Washington who was not part of the FBI.

"And it gets good and fuckin' cold in the winter," the second thief said to Jeb Stuart Magruder. Thus he, too, spoke for the first time in his life to somebody from Washington.

Magruder mumbled something and then looking around, in a first-day daze, he said, "Neil Gallagher here?" Magruder walked on without waiting for an answer. He knew what he was looking for. Out in the world, at the end, Jeb Stuart Magruder was confessing and repenting in a book and in newspaper interviews. He even went so far as to get his wife on television to dispense wisdom and gather sympathy.

Neil Gallagher—former Congressman Cornelius E. Gallagher of Bayonne, New Jersey—had in December of 1972 pleaded guilty to charges of income-tax evasion and had been sentenced to two years. On June 16, 1973, he appeared at the Federal Courthouse in Newark and turned himself in for the start of his sentence. Gallagher was slapped into handcuffs, leg irons and chains, and taken through a fence of cameramen to the Federal House of Detention on West Street in Manhattan. Two weeks later, he was shipped to Allenwood, a group of four dull brick buildings sitting in the businesslike hills of central Pennsylvania. Allenwood is supposed to be a country club as prisons go. There are no walls or guard towers. Fifteen miles away, Lewisburg Penitentiary rises out of the corn fields, a terrible rust-brick and iron smokestack of a place. All of which is a matter of degrees. A jail is a jail, and at eight o'clock of a night at Allenwood, with the mind becoming a scrambled egg, what does it matter whether or not the place has a wall and guard towers? Petty regulations in a minimum-security institution are so numerous and unnerving that many prisoners prefer the places with walls and guard towers because rules are less intricate.

At the end of six months in Allenwood, Gallagher applied for community visits with his wife and family and was turned down. Egil Krogh of the Watergate case came to Allenwood, was in the place for three months, and then was allowed off the grounds with his wife for twelve hours. Gallagher then had a disbarment hearing in New Jersey. A court order was delivered to Allenwood calling for Gallagher to be furloughed for purposes of the hearing. Usually, a minimum-security prisoner is furloughed for purposes of a hearing such as this. The authorities suddenly decided that Gallagher would be shipped in handcuffs and chains. When the Federal Bureau of Prisons in Washington was asked about this, their answer was that Gallagher never had applied for a furlough for the disbarment hearing.

At a parole hearing, a caseworker for the parole board looked at Gallagher's applications and said they were fine, but there were some areas where it was plain to the parole people that he was not cooperating.

"Where?" Gallagher said.

"Well, we know you took a beating on your supposed association with Joseph Zicarelli. But, ah, Mr. Rodino, for instance, certainly has an awful lot to hide and you probably could show us the way to get at it. So far we have received no help from you."

It became plain to Gallagher that he was going to do the maximum time on his sentence. This is so rare for a person in Gallagher's circumstances—nonviolent crime—as to be remarkable. Gallagher began to concentrate on his physical condition, running three miles a day. He worked in the prison office as a typist—"I'm training to be a Kelly girl," he wrote friends—he was elected head of the inmate grievance committee. However, the days would not let his mind rest. Agitation began to cause the skin on his cheeks to tremble.

Gallagher had been in Allenwood for a couple of weeks short of a year, and he knew he was facing at least another six months, on the day that Jeb Stuart Magruder came up the steps looking for him. At dinnertime on his first day as a prisoner, Magruder came up to Gallagher. "I hear you play tennis," he said. The inmates had cut a tennis court out of the dirt of the camp grounds; Gallagher was one of those who played on it.

The first time Gallagher went on the tennis court with Magruder, it was plain Magruder was not interested in tennis. He stopped the game and went off to the side of the court and spoke to Gallagher.

"If you could do anything to help, the President really would be able to do something for you," Magruder said.

"Like what?" Gallagher said.

He remembers Magruder saying to him, "Peter Rodino is going to be wiped out. We've got plenty on him. If you could help, that's all we need. When we come up with something on Rodino, the public will be so revolted that the President could make it through. And then you, you'd be out of here clean. With a pardon. You could practice law."

Gallagher said nothing to him. At this time, he had received notice that his home in Bayonne had been foreclosed, and the court was going to issue an eviction notice. He was worried about his younger children having to leave house and school, the only security they had in these times. And the idea of six more months in Allenwood gnawed at Gallagher. One day in prison is an awfully long time. Magruder, whose right hand is full of bribes, drew visions of success again for Gallagher.

Some days later, Magruder had a visitor. He said it was his lawyer. The two sat on the rough cement patio outside the prison's crowded indoor visiting room. Gallagher, working in the office, saw the two of them talking. Afterward, Magruder told him the lawyer had said they were just about to ruin Rodino.

"He'll be here again, and if we have anything for him, he can go right back to Bill Timmons," Magruder said.

Neil Gallagher went to the office and placed his name on the list requesting permission to use the phone. There is one pay phone in Allenwood. It takes about three hours to gain permission to use it, and then an inmate must stand on line waiting his turn.

Neil Gallagher called Congressman John Murphy in Washington. It now was almost the end of June 1974, and the House Judiciary was deep into the closed presentation of evidence.

John Murphy let O'Neill know about it. O'Neill went directly to Peter Rodino.

"Peter, there is an awful lot going on. There is nothing that can come out of the woodwork on us, is there?"

Peter Rodino shook his head violently. "Absolutely nothing." O'Neill nodded and the conversation was over.

"That's all you had to say to him?" O'Neill was asked later. "Yes."

"He didn't want to hear more about it?"

"No. He hated what he heard."

"And the answer was all it took to end the whole thing?"

"Yes. We had to believe each other. He knew what we were into as well as I did."

People in Rodino's office had heard that Nixon people were around Newark asking questions about him. And they also heard that in Washington Patrick Buchanan of the White House staff was trying to sell the line to reporters about Rodino being connected. In the minds of so many of the people in the White House, starting with Nixon and going naturally to the Buchanans and on down, all Italians were out of the fraudulent movie, *The Godfather*.

There also was much talk about immigration bills—all immigration bills go through the House Judiciary—which would show that hoods were being brought into the country. The last thing a criminal from a foreign country wants is his name on anything: a passport, visa, official document of any type. As for gaining admittance to the country, there are perhaps two hundred places on the border of New York and Canada where a person can drive a car back and forth and see nobody in charge of anything. In the small world of the defendants and accomplices inside the White House, these things were not known. Because, after all, there had to be something, someplace. Nobody ever would think of an Italian like Rodino gaining greatness.

Nobody knew how they thought better than Peter Rodino himself. When the tapes subpoenaed from Nixon began to arrive at John Doar's offices on the second floor of the Congressional Hotel, Rodino and Edward Hutchinson, the senior Republican on the committee, sat and listened through headphones. One day Rodino listened as the voice of Richard Nixon, speaking to John Ehrlichman, said:

"The Italians. We mustn't forget the Italians. Must do something for them. The, ah, we forget them. They're not, we ah, they're not like us. Difference is, the . . . they smell different, they look different, act different. After all, you can't blame them. Oh, no. Can't do that. They've never had the things we've had."

"That's right," Ehrlichman said.

Nixon's voice dropped. "Of course, the trouble is . . ." Now his voice went even lower. "The trouble is, you can't find one that's honest."

A great sadness came over Peter Rodino. He made sure Hutchinson heard it. Then he asked Hutchinson if Hutchinson would agree to leave out this part of the tapes for hearing by the full committee and, perhaps someday, the public. Rodino knew it would inflame Italians who had voted almost to a man for Nixon, and thus materially damage any support Nixon had left. But Rodino simply wanted the remark to go away. Hutchinson said he would do what Rodino wanted. Rodino said thank you, and the remarks about Italians did not get beyond the room. They did tend to remain, however, in Peter Rodino's heart.

There was one afternoon when Rodino was sitting for a television interview and, while the cameramen were changing film, Rodino was talking about what it was like to be an Italian-American and in his position.

"You know, all these things that have been written, all these movies, things like *The Godfather*, and they have concentrated so much on this business like . . . the Mafia. And here we see . . ." Rodino held his hand out as if he were supporting something. His eyes gleamed. "And here we see Sirica and Rodino upholding the institutions of the country. I just can't tell you the pride I feel in being an Italian-American. And I know how John Sirica feels about it, too."

Vernon Hixon, one of the television men, said, "That's beautiful. Now when we start the cameras this time, try to say it exactly the same way."

The cameras came on and Rodino was asked a question about his Italian heritage. A glaze of formality came over his eyes. Two expressive hands clasped into schoolroom propriety.

"I am naturally proud of being an Italo-American," Rodino said. "But we must remember that the heritages of all the people of the world are in our Constitution and it is our duty to uphold the Constitution regardless of what our individual backgrounds are."

"Stop for a minute," Vernon Hixon said to the cameramen. Then Hixon said to Rodino, "Congressman, that was very nice. But would you please say exactly what you said before, the thing about being abused by people using this word Mafia."

Rodino's chin went from side to side, slowly. He said in a near-whisper, "That wouldn't be appropriate."

"Oh, but you said it beautifully."

Rodino went into himself a little bit more, leaving behind a little smile. "No," he whispered, "I couldn't say a thing like that. Not when I'm dealing with the Constitution."

The second occurrence, the dangerous one, first began to take form months before. It grew out of the nature of the political business. On one hand there was John Doar, unelected, with working methods that were as strict and severe as they were successful. Security is a rather simple word to Doar: it means you say nothing to anybody. As politicians essentially are elected washerwomen, information often their only visible means of support, this secrecy made some members nervous. "We're so damn secretive that we're going to impeach Nixon in secret and he'll never know it," William L. (Bill) Hungate of Missouri complained. There also was impatience with Doar on the part of Jack Brooks of Texas, Jerome Waldie of California, Joshua Eilberg of Pennsylvania, and Robert Drinan of Massachusetts. And underneath this, the problem of Jerome Zeifman, who had been bypassed for the special counsel role in favor of Doar.

Zeifman began saying that Doar's presentation was stripped of all human ingredients. He said Doar had taken the case apart like some gigantic erector set, left it on the table completely disassembled, and never commented on how it should be connected. Doar and Francis O'Brien, Rodino's administrative assistant, regarded Zeifman as a destructive element, and the complicated matter of keeping thirty-eight human beings in some sort of harmony became even more trying.

During the long hours that Doar sat in the Committee, purposely dull, daring never to go near the advocate's role, David Dennis of Indiana—briefed, primed, prepared by James St. Clair and totally committed to Nixon's defense—hammered away at Doar. Let's get to March 21, 1973, Dennis was saying. Prove to me what the President did wrong. You've got a lot of circumstantial evidence here. Where is your proof, where is your proof, where is your proof? Dennis, too, did not notice it when Doar, in the midst of a dreary afternoon, poked through the material regarding Nixon, Haldeman, and Ehrlichman on June 23, 1972. Later, it was to cost Dennis his seat in Congress—he was defeated in the 1974 election. But at this point, with the first heat of a Washington summer making the days longer and more dragging, Dennis's continual table-thumping was effective.

At which point Zeifman and William Dixon, a counsel working for him, took their own course inside the committee. Dixon, working with Waldie, Eilberg, and Drinan, prepared a series of twelve memos which he felt would put some fire into the presentation. The memos pointed out the differences between the edited tape transcripts released by the White House, and the flat material read by Doar. One Dixon memo concentrated on Dennis's and St. Clair's defense of Nixon's conversation with John Dean on March 21. Dixon's memo said the conversation showed clearly that Nixon had told Dean that they had to buy time making a $120,000 payment of hush money to E. Howard Hunt. The memo circulated in the second week of June. By the 14th of June it had been leaked to the newspapers. Zeifman and Jack Brooks, meanwhile, were pushing to have Richard Cates, another staff counsel, present information to the Committee. Cates would have the fire they thought they needed.

The result was problems inside the Committee, and a major problem on the outside when the leaks appeared in print. The White House jumped on the leaked memos as an attempt by anti-Nixon people on the Committee to destroy the President. A number of voices quickly were raised in agreement. Newspaper columns—particularly Joseph Kraft in *The Washington Post*—began saying that the process had gone too long, that it was in danger of losing all momentum. A cartoon showed the impeachment ship sinking.

One evening Doar met Congressman Wayne Hays at the elevators in the Congressional Hotel. Hays had an office for his House Administration Committee on the sixth floor of the building.

"You blew it," Hays said to Doar. "You're never going to get the votes now. You had 'em and you lost them. You've taken too much time."

The conversation was more than a passing one to Doar. Hays headed the committee that provided the funds for the impeachment staff.

The talk, of course, came to the House. "I don't know, they tell me that Doar is an archivist, not a prosecutor," O'Neill said one morning. "I don't know what to say. I know it's taking too much time. Everything is timing, and these delays are starting to get me worried. They've got that Johnny Rhodes working for them here and, believe me, he is about the best you'll ever see."

On June 25, a Monday—Monday is the day party leaders such as O'Neill set aside for hearing "Confessions"—O'Neill began to hear complaints from too many about the slowness of the hearings. J. William Stanton of Ohio said, "We need action one way or the other. Can't you get it off our backs? Instead of the impeachment being an asset to us, now it's starting to hurt us. I heard it everywhere over the weekend. They're not only disgusted with Nixon, they're disgusted with me, too. They don't think anything is happening."

"It was the same from everywhere," O'Neill recalls. "'Tell us where we are; tell us where we're going to be,' that's all I was hearing."

He sat down next to Peter Rodino and began leaning on him.

"Will you get off my back?" Rodino said.

"Hey, I have two hundred and forty guys on my back," O'Neill said.

O'Neill wanted a definite schedule set for the hearings, the vote in Committee, the start of debate on the House floor. Rodino, who had been spending long hours in seclusion, poring over the rafts of paper, did not see how he could set a date. He reminded O'Neill again that O'Neill was not a lawyer, that he did not understand. O'Neill pressed for a date to be set. Rodino resented it. But at the end of the long, tortuous day, at one o'clock in the morning, Rodino sat in his office with John Doar and Francis O'Brien and told them that they had to set a schedule for the rest of their work.

O'Brien and Doar were against it. They wanted nothing to interfere with what they felt was a satisfactory pace.

"You don't understand, the leadership is on me," Rodino said.

"What leadership?" O'Brien asked.

"Well, Tippy is on me and they're on him and we've got to do it."

"What does Tippy O'Neill got to do with it?" O'Brien asked.

"You don't understand, it's the leadership," Rodino said.

"Wait a minute," O'Brien said. "Tell me one thing. What has Tippy O'Neill got to do with you? You're a committee chairman. Tell me where he can start telling you what to do."

"You don't understand," Rodino said.

"No, Francis has raised something," Doar said. "What right has O'Neill got interfering with your business?"

Rodino looked up at the ceiling and thought. As he thought, the blue smoke and mirrors disappeared. All that was left was the pages of a rule book. He, Peter W. Rodino of New Jersey, was Chairman of the House Judiciary Committee, and as such, under law, he was in charge of hearings into the possible impeachment of a President. As for Thomas P. O'Neill, Jr., of Massachusetts, he was the Majority Leader of the House. There is not one thing in law or House Rules that says the Majority Leader has the right to do anything.

Rodino's head came down and his hand hit the desk. "You're right! He has no business bothering me at all, and I'm going to tell it to him tomorrow."

In reconstructing the late-night conversation, both O'Brien and Doar are proud of the manner in which Rodino took on the matter. Doar adds, "And that was the night we set the date. We said we'd be ready for Committee debate on July fifteenth and we'd have a vote by July twenty-seventh. And we kept pretty close to that schedule, didn't we?"

Apparently, after Rodino brought his head down and slapped the desk, he not only summoned his anger, but he summoned a full complement of mirrors and blue smoke back into the room.

For, the next day, along with an angry rebuke to O'Neill, Rodino also gave him a timetable for the impeachment. O'Neill had the dates typed in his office and shown around the floor. The effect was sharp. Again, the moment you particularized the matter of impeachment, showed anything on paper, there was an immediate tightening of people. The more you made impeachment a reality, the more people were inclined to accept it.

With the schedule set, O'Neill went to dinner that night at Duke Zeibert's Restaurant. He told a table full of people, "I got on Peter's back and he resents it. He should. When the rest of us are all forgotten, Peter is the guy who is going to be in history. Remember what I tell you."

In the Committee, Rodino's hand also came down. Zeifman and Dixon were rebuffed. The danger passed, and the momentum of the paper, which never had slowed, again became apparent. The staff would compile, before it was to finish, forty-two books of information. The normal Xerox paper had a tendency to stick together and there was so much copying to be done that separating the paper was a major job in itself. They switched from Xerox paper to expensive bond paper in order to speed the process. The workload became so heavy that one night, at two in the morning, girls coming to a Xerox machine in the Rayburn Building, found Peter Rodino, in shirtsleeves, running the machine himself.

9

"Now, let me tell you what is going to happen."

BOB OWEN was coming down from New York on a Thursday now, and staying in the library until Monday morning. He would sleep a half-hour a day on a couch in Doar's office. In the early evening he would walk up to Pennsylvania Avenue, have a couple of martinis and a steak, and then return to the office and work through the night and through the next day. Coffee and cigarettes—he was onto three packs a day—took care of the rest of him. Owen would read the cards and other evidence pulled out of the files during the day. Then at night, after dinner, he would dictate his notes, which were to form parts of the "Statement of Information" book being worked on. Owen worked on thirteen of the first thirty-eight volumes put out by the group.

Owen was scheduled to go on vacation in July from his law firm. He couldn't wait. This would give him the chance to work full time in the second-floor library.

Up the street, in the Capitol building, Tip O'Neill began to think of gathering votes. He told the newspapers he was keeping no lists. Which was true. He was not keeping lists on paper. He was keeping them in his head.

When Congressman Teno Roncalio of Wyoming asked O'Neill to come out and speak at a dinner in Cheyenne, O'Neill said absolutely yes. Roncalio's district voted over 75 per cent for Richard Nixon in 1972 and now that Roncalio was going to be voting to impeach Nixon, any and all help he could get would be appreciated. O'Neill and Roncalio flew out of National Airport in Washington at eight o'clock in the morning, landed in Wyoming in midafternoon. On the way from the airport to the motel, the driver took O'Neill on a tour of Fort Custer. Great cottonwoods and Austrian pines, trees that can take the Wyoming winters, lined the roadway.

"Pershing lived in that house," the driver said, pointing to a brick house set back on lawns.

"Geez, it's beautiful," Tip said.

"Here's the parade ground," the driver said.

"Geez, what a parade ground!"

"Smell the air," the driver said.

Tip sniffed the light, sparkling early summer air.

"Geez, it's terrific. Say, where do you run the rodeo?"

"Oh, it's right across the way there."

"Do they make any money?"

"I guess so."

"Much Indian fighting out here?"

"Sandhill massacre was near here."

"Where was Custer massacred?"

"That was three hundred miles north of here."

"See the tepees over there," the driver said.

"Look at the Indians!" O'Neill said. "You mean they're actually living there?"

"Yessir."

"Wow!"

"You enjoy it out here?" the driver said.

"Well just look at it," Tip said.

Blue mountains sat against a blue sky with moving white clouds, the mountains appearing very close in the clear air, but they were actually twenty-five miles away.

"Geez, beautiful," Tip said. "What a place."

He pulled on his cigar and looked out the window.

"I could last about a day out here," he said.

At the motel, I was standing at the bar having a drink when the pilot of the plane, on his way to his room for a nap, stopped by to say hello. He had a Coke.

"Well, what do you think about Nixon getting impeached?" he said.

"Oh, I wouldn't know. I just flew out here with Congressman O'Neill. I wouldn't dare ask him what he thought, I wouldn't do that."

"That's funny," the pilot said. "Just before we were getting off the plane I asked him and he told me that Nixon was going to get his ass thrown out."

The dinner drew a crowd of 500 people, the backbone of

influence in Cheyenne. Roncalio told the audience that it was the first time a Majority Leader of the House was ever in Wyoming. He made that sound important. Roncalio then said, "He is one of the two or three men in whose hands rest the impeachment process in the House of Representatives."

O'Neill went right to his William Hamilton and Staff poll. The numbers had grown somewhat during the flight from Washington.

"In the 1948 election, ninety-two per cent of the Democrats voted for Democrats, and ninety-two per cent of the Republicans voted for Republicans," he said. "But now there is a thirty-nine-per-cent breakaway from the Republican party because of the impeachment matter. And the poll shows that eight-five per cent of the breakaway will vote Democratic."

That set the audience up. He went into economy and inflation for a moment. Then he stopped and put on black-frame glasses and arranged paper on the lectern in front of him.

"And now we come to the important topic of the hour, and probably in the entire history of the country. Impeachment. I try not to speak off the cuff on this matter. I use prepared notes for this."

You could feel the tension run through the room. Ranchers who had flown in for the meeting, big, long-armed Westerners, put the coffee cups down without causing the slightest clinking sound. Bankers held their cigarettes near the ashtrays and leaned forward. The woman seated next to me held her breath. It was the first time any audience in Wyoming had heard impeachment discussed by anybody involved in it. Now it wasn't a story in the newspapers anymore. And now on the dais O'Neill was not a likable storyteller any more. He became erect, careful. A major leader of government. His face was set and his voice did not come soft and easy. In slow, measured terms he began by saying:

"Justice Brandeis said, 'Decency, security, and liberty alike depend on the system in which no man is above the law. This mandate is a daily thing, answerable at all time on all matters.'"

Heads nodded every place in the room. O'Neill carefully scanned the room from left to right. He gave side glances at the dais. There, too, heads nodded in agreement.

You've got to be kidding, O'Neill told himself. *Nixon doesn't have a vote in the room. If he doesn't have a vote here, how the hell can he hope to get one from anywhere.*

". . . base men will drive out honorable men."

Again, the heads nodded.

"Now, let me tell you what is going to happen."

The feeling was the same as being in a courtroom waiting for a jury verdict.

"I doubt if forty Congressmen have openly said what they'll do. I, of course, never have said anything. Now when the witnesses are finished in the Judiciary, there will be three days to review the case. There will be a markup of the bill. On the twenty-sixth of July, the Judiciary Committee will have voted on the bill and reported to the full House. On August fifth, the bill will go to the Rules Committee. There then will be two weeks of full debate on the floor of the House or a hundred hours of debate, whichever comes first. The Republicans feel sixty hours will be sufficient. The vote in the House will come on August twenty-third. If the Judiciary Committee votes to impeach the President, then the President will be impeached by seventy-five votes in the House. If the President does not obey the Supreme Court order to turn over the tapes, the number will be much greater. In my opinion, if the House of Representatives votes to impeach by the seventy-five votes or more, then the Senate will convict the President in a trial, if there is one.

"We are not happy. But we are strong in our hour of sadness. Our country is strong enough to survive. Jerry Ford will give this nation the stability it needs."

He reached down and brought up a big ten-gallon hat he had been presented with earlier. He put it on.

"The rest of the nation isn't wise to Wyoming, and I won't tell them what you've got here," he said.

They laughed, got up, and applauded. Three quarters of the room had voted for Nixon, but there was not a mumble or a disgusted look.

Later, as the plane flew back through the night to Washington, Teno Roncalio tried to sleep, and O'Neill sat in the darkness and smoked a cigar and looked out the window. He said it just once.

"Wyoming," he said. "He doesn't have a vote in Wyoming. This thing has been over for months."

* * *

July. Bob Owen had not been to bed for three days. His teeth were stinging from cigarettes. He was up to four packs of True cigarettes a day. It now was the 15th of July and the House Judiciary Committee was coming to the end of its closed hearings. The full committee meeting, the debate and vote on impeachment, was now scheduled to start on the 20th. John Doar was driving to complete his final summary of information. This was the book that was to change his role. It was not a statement. He would not read it as a neutral. It would be his summation, his position on the matter. He would come out for the first time as an advocate. He would sum up his facts, give his interpretations, and he would take on James St. Clair's defense theories. Take on St. Clair and take on Nixon.

Owen worked with the cards of June 17, 18, 19, 20, 1972. They were filed by time, subject matter, and people—asterisks for cross-references everywhere. As Owen put the cards out, moving them, matching them, he could see a pattern of arrangements for a meeting on June 20th. Phone conversations, gained from logs and long-distance toll tickets, showed John Dean being called on the 18th and brought back from a trip to the Far East. The group in California—Mitchell, Mardian, Magruder, LaRue—came back from California. Attorney General Richard Kleindienst, in Washington, called L. Patrick Gray III of the FBI on the morning of the 19th and said that he must be briefed on the Watergate burglary. The President, in Key Biscayne, Florida, was coming back to Washington on the evening of the 19th. It was clear that everybody was to meet on the 20th.

John Doar lived in a basement apartment of an old brownstone house a block down from the hotel. The apartment had a kitchenette, a bedroom with no door, a living room with a pull-out couch for sleeping. Doar and his daughter stayed in the apartment. Doar left the front door open all night in case Bob Owen finally caved in and came down for a nap. The Capitol Hill section at night is a place of triple locks and guard dogs.

In the middle of the second night of working with Owen, Doar slipped down the block for a nap of his own. He was awakened by the sound of somebody padding around the living room. Doar looked up and saw enough in the darkness to tell that it was a prowler, not anybody he knew.

"Get the fuck out of here," Doar said.

The prowler walked out and Doar went back to sleep.

At 6:30 P.M. on his third day, Bob Owen stopped work and walked down to Doar's apartment. He slept for three hours. He went back and began dictating his notes for the summary. As Owen dictated, something was bothering him. He stopped, had a cup of coffee, lit a cigarette, and thought. He wanted to go back to the cards again. File drawers banged open and fingers went through the files, pulling out the index cards. Owen spread them out again and began looking.

"Now this is awfully peculiar," he said. He began to arrange them. His arrangement showed that on the morning of June 20, 1972, Richard Nixon had breakfast at 8:40. At nine o'clock he was in his Oval Office. From 9:01 until 9:04, Alexander Butterfield came in. Then from 9:04 until 10:20, the President sat alone in his office. He neither received nor placed any phone calls. Upstairs, in the office directly overhead, H. R. Haldeman met with John Ehrlichman and John Mitchell at 9 A.M. John Dean and Richard Kleindienst joined the meeting. The meeting lasted for an hour. The burglary had taken place early on the morning of June 17. This was the President's first day back in the White House since the burglary. It was the first day his staff had assembled and held a meeting since the burglary. Nixon knew they were meeting about the burglary. Yet from 9:04 A.M. until 10:20 A.M., the cards in front of Bob Owen showed, Nixon never once picked up the phone to ask his people upstairs one question about a burglary that was all over the front pages of the newspapers. And this was a President who interfered in even the most minor of matters—picking the color of a rug for an assistant's office.

It was clear what Nixon was doing in his office on the morning of June 20. He had ordered his people to fix the Watergate mess—can it, kill it, bury it—and he was taking the position that he did not want to know anything about it. This is the pattern and behavior of any boss-thief: you go do it, but don't tell me about it.

Owen called Doar in to look at the cards. Others crowded

into the room. The cards showed it was not until 10:20 that Nixon spoke to anybody. And then he spoke to Ehrlichman. Both Nixon and Ehrlichman were claiming that they never had spoken about the Watergate. Ehrlichman was just coming out of the big meeting about the mess and he and Nixon, who dealt in colors of rugs, never mentioned the biggest story in the country. Then from 11:26 until 12:46, in his office in the Executive Office Building, Nixon spoke with H. R. Haldeman. There was a tape of that meeting. Eighteen and a half minutes of the tape had been erased. Nixon had sent his attorneys into court with all sorts of theories about how the tape was erased. The good General Alexander Haig said he thought it was the work of the Devil. Secretary Rose Mary Woods said she might have done it with her foot while leaning across the desk to answer a phone. She posed for a picture to justify this theory. In the picture she appeared to be sliding into third base. Meanwhile, anybody with any sense in the White House knew who had erased the tape. Nixon had erased the tape. "He was the only one could have done that," Dean Burch says today.

So now, as Doar and Owen and the others stood in the organized litter of the library, with its barred, wired windows, with its red eyes and cigarettes and coffee, they knew they had it put together.

For much earlier, back on May 14, John Doar had presented to the Judiciary Committee the first piece of his information about Richard Nixon's activities on the first few days immediately following the Watergate break-in. It turned up in Book II of Doar's series of presentations to the Committee. The title of Book II was, "Statement of Information; Events Following the Watergate Break-In. June 17, 1972–February 9, 1973." He read the book aloud with the same verve used in writing the titles. Doar read to the Committee behind locked doors and under strange, delicate, intricate rules. He was counsel for the entire Committee and therefore an impartial voice, not an advocate. He was careful to have no opinion in word or tone. Doar also was an employee of the Committee, not an elected Congressman. The distinction has no subtleties. Congressmen often view the people working around them as primarily chauffeurs and errand boys. No matter how unobtrusive Doar became, how silently diligent, some Committee members still glared at him as if he had stepped across the line drawn by the ballot box. Rodino is specifically excluded here. But the attitude on the part of some of the others would produce sharp trouble later on.

On May 14, during the afternoon, Doar read to the Committee with his dead voice and when he came to page 36, his voice had even less in it.

"On June 23, 1972, H. R. Haldeman met with the President and informed the President of the communication John Dean had received from Acting FBI Director Gray. The President directed Haldeman to meet with CIA Director Richard Helms, Deputy CIA Director Vernon Walters and John Ehrlichman. . . . The President directed Haldeman to discuss White House concern regarding possible disclosure of covert CIA operations and operations of the White House Special Investigations Unit [the 'Plumbers'], not related to Watergate, that had been undertaken previously by some of the Watergate principals. The President directed Haldeman to ask Walters to meet with Gray to express these concerns and to coordinate with the FBI, so that the FBI's investigation would not be expanded into unrelated matters that could lead to disclosure of the earlier activities of the Watergate principals."

In footnotes, Doar had listed his sources and on which page of their thick notebooks Congressmen could locate them:

31.1 *H. R. Haldeman testimony, Subcommittee of the Senate Appropriations Committee, Hearings on Purported Attempt to Involve the Central Intelligence Agency in the Watergate and Ellsberg incidents, Executive Session, May 31, 1973, 353–54*
PAGE 356

31.2 *President Nixon statement, May 23, 1973, 9 Presidential documents, 693,696*
PAGE 358

31.3 *H. R. Haldeman testimony, 8 SSC 3040–41*   PAGE 360

31.4 *H. R. Haldeman testimony, 7 SSC 2884*   PAGE 362

James St. Clair, Nixon's lawyer, sat in the room while the reading went on. There was no way to miss what it was about:

Doar was showing that an obstruction of justice occurred on June 23, 1972, and that it was started by Richard Nixon. That on this date, in 1972, he knew everything about the Watergate break-in. St. Clair sat in his chair. His defense for Nixon was based on the President never learning anything until March 21, 1973. St. Clair gave no indication that he realized the danger in Doar's approach. Nor did he subsequently realign his defenses. The man was spread too thin to do much about it anyway, and he appeared to like the television lights too much to have any confrontations with his client that might lead to a new lawyer.

At another point in the reading, Doar droned out this: "At approximately one-thirty P.M. on June 23, 1972, pursuant to the President's prior directions, H. R. Haldeman, John Ehrlichman, CIA Director Helms, and Deputy CIA Director Walters sat in Ehrlichman's office. . . . Haldeman stated that it was the President's wish that Walters call on Gray and suggest to him that it was not advantageous to push the inquiry, especially into Mexico. According to Ehrlichman, the Mexican money or the Florida bank account was discussed as a specific example of the kind of thing the President was evidently concerned about."

As he read the Ehrlichman material, Doar could almost hear a cheer going up from the people back in his library. It was a burial job. The footnote on the page directed Committee members to Ehrlichman's testimony before the Ervin committee. At that time, all newsmen reported that Ehrlichman had put on a great show, sneering and fighting right down the line. But Ehrlichman had a habit of sometimes forgetting what he was talking about and when somebody brought up the checks from Mexico, Ehrlichman said, of course, the Mexican money. Yes, that's exactly what the President was concerned about. Nobody noticed what he was saying, and the day passed. But when they sat in John Doar's library and began chopping up Ehrlichman's Ervin testimony, they thought his statement about the checks was absolutely marvelous. With other material they could prove that on June 20, 1972, Maurice Stans had conducted meetings about covering up the Mexican checks. Ehrlichman, the perfect stonewall, had added greatly to the story.

When he was finished reading, Doar asked the Committee to subpoena the White House tape of June 23, 1972, which, his cards showed, featured Nixon and Haldeman in another discussion. This was the tape which Evan Davis, in his wheel-chair, had wanted. There was a drawerful of blank subpoenas in Doar's office, presigned by Pat Jennings, Clerk of the House. One of the blanks was typed up, carbons everywhere, and signed by Peter Rodino. Ben Marshall, a Committee employee, carried it over to the White House.

At this time, Nixon still was not listening to the tapes himself. Only one man had heard all the tapes, Haldeman. When Nixon checked with Haldeman, in California, on this latest subpoena of a tape, for June 23, a tingle of fear had to run along the telephone lines. Somebody over in the Judiciary was onto the game.

Doar was convinced that the White House never would give the tapes to his group. But at the same time he was beginning to become convinced that he was going to be able to build a case without any of the tapes at all. He was confident that he was going to prove it all with paper, prove that the President knew of Watergate and initiated a cover-up on June 23, 1972. If the Special Prosecutor's office went through the courts and was given the tape, fine. The House Judiciary Committee neither recognized any court's authority nor had the time to wait.

So the paper rustled, and Richard Nixon, never hearing it, kept up his public lie. In his office one day he jumped out of his chair and began pacing up and down, throwing his arms out, and saying to Leonard Garment, one of his counsels, "I go to China, go to Russia, we're trying to stop war in the Middle East. And to get tripped up by this . . . by this piece of shit!"

And now there was more. As Doar and Owen looked at their cards, they saw a clear picture of why and how Nixon operated from the very start, the first full day of the cover-up of the Watergate break-in. There had been a crime committed by people working for the President and the President says he did not inquire about it. He met with Ehrlichman. He did not ask. He met with Haldeman. He did not ask. Nixon maintained that it was not until nine months later, on March 21, 1973, that he first learned the facts of the Watergate break-in, learned them from John Dean.

As Doar and Owen looked at the cards, small sarcastic voices seemed to be everywhere:

Come on!

They knew the same voices would run through the minds of most of the Committee members as they began to hear the last of the evidence.

It was morning now. Owen walked down the street to Doar's apartment and took a shower. He came back to the library and started dictating notes. On his fourth straight day of work, sitting amidst a sea of paper, he was dictating more dangerous words onto paper, whose edges twinkled as the light hit its honed edges. This time Richard Nixon did not feel it as his head was being cut off.

On July 20th, 1974, on the day that John Doar really showed his teeth in the Judiciary Committee room, he came at them with this:

"On that morning of June 20th [1972], Mr. Haldeman, and you have got this all in your books, the logs, and everywhere, Mr. Haldeman meets with Ehrlichman and Mitchell at nine o'clock in the morning. Dean and Kleindienst joined that meeting, and they meet from nine to ten o'clock. This is the first day that the President has come back faced with a possibility of certainly a very serious scandal within his Administration.

"What does the President do while his people, his key advisers are discussing this matter? The President is alone in his office, except for a three-minute talk with Mr. Butterfield during that morning until John Ehrlichman comes in and talks to him about ten-twenty. He does not participate, does not inquire, does not question, does not search out for facts from John Mitchell or Richard Kleindienst, his Attorney General, or Mr. Ehrlichman, who has been assigned to the case the day before to make an investigation, or two days before, or from John Dean, who had been called back to get into it. . . ."

James Mann read. Tom Railsback read. Hamilton Fish, Jr., read. Caldwell Butler read. Ray Thornton read. Walter Flowers read. Harold Froehlich read.

10

"God save the United States of America."

ON JULY 24TH, at 11 A.M., two college students from Cambridge, Charles Sheppard and Fred Hyatt, leaned forward in their seats inside the Supreme Court, eyes fixed on the front of the room, four white pillars with red velvet behind the pillars, sculpturing of Romans above a clock. The Supreme Court in a minute or so was to issue its decision on whether President Nixon had to release a batch of sixty-four tapes subpoenaed by Special Prosecutor Leon Jaworski. One of the tapes was for the day of June 23, 1972. John Doar was going it without the June 23 tape, the one Evan Davis, in the wheelchair, had wanted to get at the day he began his job. But Jaworski's office was not going without the tapes. The case had gone to the Supreme Court and now these two college students, people whom Nixon hated when he was on the top, were waiting for the decision. At 11:03, a voice called out, "The Honorable Chief Justice Burger and the Associate Justices of the Supreme Court of the United States. Oyez, oyez, all having business before this honorable court draw near. God save the United States of America."

The minute William O. Douglas came out, the two college kids poked each other. You did not have to be a courtroom buff to see that Douglas was relaxed, a near-smile on his face. Of course the kids looked at Douglas first. For so long, in this country, Douglas was about all they had going for them. Burger ruffled papers in front of him. Docket number 731766, *United States* versus *Richard Nixon*; Docket number 731834, *Nixon* versus *United States*. Nixon's entire case was whether executive privilege allowed him to keep the tapes confidential. When Burger began reading, Douglas looked even better. The knockout was coming.

The courtroom was filled. Since dawn there had been long lines waiting outside on the marble steps. Gold grillwork separated the press, crowded onto the side of the huge old room, from the audience. This was an important day, a regal day. The lawyers and more scholarly writers tend to deify the Supreme Court. And at this time they looked at the Court as the place which would finally destroy Nixon. Which was fine, but the Supreme Court not only reads the newspapers, it attends cocktail parties and eats dinner out in restaurants, and all members have phones and visitors at home. As they sat in their robed splendor, they had to know the way things stood across the street, in the Senate and House, and in the House Judiciary, as well as anybody. "The vote will be eight to zero," O'Neill told me the day before. I asked him how he knew. "Constitutional lawyers at Harvard told me," he said.

Now, as Warren Burger read his decision, he came to his first "however," and this is a word, this "however," which has killed more people than field artillery. It is listed as a conjunction, but it should be assigned a number, like .155.

"However, the special prosecutor . . . has authority to represent the United States as a sovereign. . . ." From the "however," Burger went into *Marbury* versus *Madison*. This is a decision which set the supremacy of the Court in legal matters—no man is above the Court. Since Special Prosecutor Jaworski was sitting there with all the Court orders in his pocket, it was reasonable to assume that the remainder of Mr. Burger's reading was to be as bad for Mr. Nixon as it turned out to be.

Nixon had to turn over the sixty-four tapes, including the tape of June 23.

As Jaworski went down the steps of the Supreme Court, with the young people crowding around him and cheering, and the reporters guiding him to live network-television cameras, it was one of those days when people in the profession say proudly that the law has prevailed. The jealous mistress had triumphed again. Perhaps, or perhaps it had triumphed because the people conducting the business of the law had an essentially abstract matter on their hands, and it also had about three hundred votes going for it across the way in the House of Representatives. Historically, the Supreme Court always functions beautifully at these times. And nowhere in the decision was it stated that if the Supreme Court did not come out unanimously for Nixon to give up the tapes, if the Chief Justice, appointed by Nixon, did not read the decision himself, then the Court, as an institution, would have been irrelevant at a great moment in the nation's history and damaged forever. For Nixon was going out of his job, no matter how the Court voted. And the Chief Justice himself would have been suspect and a personal laughingstock if he himself did not read the decision.

Supportive evidence for this theory can be found in the activity of the Court on the very next day, July 25th. When, with virtually no publicity and with no strong sense of what Congress wanted, the Court made a ruling on an important human matter, the Detroit metropolitan school-busing case. In this case, the city of Detroit had asked to be allowed to bus, for integration purposes, blacks from the city of Detroit across the city line and into metropolitan suburbs. The Supreme Court voted against the busing plan. The Burgers, Blackmuns, Rehnquists—the white men appointed to the bench by a white crook—were in the majority. Dissenting was, of course, Douglas:

> *Desegregation is not and was never expected to be an easy task. Racial attitudes ingrained in our Nation's childhood and adolescence are not quickly thrown aside in its middle years. But just as the inconvenience of some cannot be allowed to stand in the way of the rights of others, so public opposition, no matter how strident, cannot be permitted to divert this Court from the enforcement of the constitutional principles at issue in this case. Today's holding, I fear, is more a reflection of a perceived public mood that we have gone far enough in enforcing the Constitution's guarantee of equal justice than it is the product of neutral principles of law. In the short run, it may seem to be the easier course to allow our great metropolitan areas to be divided up each into two cities—one white, the other black—but it is a course, I predict, our people will ultimately regret. I dissent.*

But on the previous morning, July 24th, with a decision involving tapes and principles, neither of which has blood running through the arteries, the Supreme Court could afford to be an anchor of civilization. The inscription on the outside of the building, running across its eight pillars, "Equal Justice Under Law," nearly seemed real on this day.

Across the street, across the square of dripping trees and

damp grass, there sat on the steps of the Capitol the only demonstrators seen in Washington during the entire time of impeachment and resignation. The young, sadly disciplined followers of Sun Myung Moon stood in vigil in the muggy air, holding a sign announcing which member of the House each was praying for, to save his soul from certain damnation if he chose to vote against Nixon. One of the young people, who came from Alaska, did not know how to spell Moon's name. "I never had reason to spell it before," he said. He was living in one of Moon's religious dens in Tarrytown, New York.

Aside from these demonstrators, who had the effect of depressing all who saw them, there was nothing.

It was strange to be around when it happened, because it was an enormous thing and it had never happened before; but there still was so very little to see in Washington in the summer of 1974. White marble sitting in swamp heat. On this day, on the 24th, the news of the Supreme Court decision should have "rocked" the White House and the nation. It did no such thing. Oh, it wasted Nixon some more. The flesh turned pasty and the eyes hollowed and the flesh under the chin fell through the muscles. He was out at San Clemente when the news of the decision was announced. The story circulated that Nixon had attempted to walk into the ocean and drown himself. The great scene from *A Star Is Born*. James Mason going into the ocean while Judy Garland sings. The story was untrue. General Haig, however, apparently did get his hands on Nixon's tranquilizers. The essential Roman Catholic mind: die by the gun if you must, but an overdose of narcotics is sinful; that's for the weirdos.

But, otherwise, there was no turmoil, no racing through corridors, no people screaming out windows. In the White House, people for the first time began to glance out the windows to see that the avalanche of paper had started to pound the ground away from the building much as the ocean washes out the underpinnings of a beach house. It was only a matter of time. By now it was coming from so many places—from the Court, from Jaworski, from Sirica, from Congress, from the newspapers and television, over the phones, in the mail—that it was just a matter of which method did the job first. Yet nowhere in Washington were there voices raised. The hallways and cafeterias of the Capitol were crowded with tourists from America. Cameras, bare, tan springy legs, cut-off jeans. Children running down a marble hallway ahead of parents. Don't want to look at the statue, want to go down and look out that window. The young ones, boys and girls alike, all seemed to wear short-sleeved replicas of football jerseys worn by professional teams. Through the swirl of cameras and jeans and football jerseys, here was Hugh Scott walking to meet Barry Goldwater.

At the House end of the building one day, O'Neill came out of his office and a boy with American short blond hair and wearing a replica of a Pittsburgh Steelers jersey bumped into him. Gulliver plays football. O'Neill went down the hall, picking his way through the tourists, to attend a meeting at which John Rhodes, the Republican leader in the House, gave it one last try for Nixon. Rhodes said he wanted the impeachment resolution recommitted with instructions that there should be a vote on censuring the President.

"I'm bitterly opposed to that," O'Neill said.

"But you wouldn't be opposed to us having a vote on censure, would you?" Rhodes said.

"Yes, I would," O'Neill said.

On the night of the 24th, the House Judiciary Committee began its televised hearings. The moment Peter Rodino began to speak directly into the camera, speak solemnly, powerfully, there was nothing left. There were thirty-eight members of the Committee. There were not at this time thirty-eight people from any walk of life in the nation—take any thirty-eight executives earning over a half-million a year—who could have stayed abreast with this group, for accuracy, for style, for perception, for understanding of what it was that they were doing. Sometimes, each said the same things, but each was saying it in his own way, and you wanted to hear more of what each had to say, not less. When James Mann of South Carolina spoke, he caused the eyes to go out of focus, the mind to sway. He became distant, a figure from a painting, from a page in a history book, a figure who had lived a couple of hundred years ago.

On the way home to the Shoreham Hotel from a Chinese restaurant that first night, Roger Brooks, O'Neill's chauffeur, drove us slowly past the Capitol. The great white dome, washed in brilliant and yet subdued lighting, looked magnificent.

"No matter how many times I pass by it," O'Neill said, "I still get a feeling right in here." He punched his stomach with his fist. "It stands for stability. You see that dome up there, you know that nobody is going to let anything bad happen. You die before you let this country down."

On July 29th, O'Neill sat with the Republican Whip, Les Arends, in the back of a plane at National Airport, waiting for Vice President Ford to arrive. They were flying to a golf tournament in Massachusetts.

"Tip, you don't have all those votes," Arends said.

"Les, we're friends talking now. We're going to have three hundred votes in the House. Now we're talking as friends. And let me tell you something else. He's dead in the Senate. He doesn't have twenty-four votes in the Senate, I can tell you that right now."

"Where are you getting this from?" Arends said.

"Hey, I'm getting it from the floor. I'm out there every day. I get it from the members."

"Well, that isn't the figures we're getting," Arends said.

"Well, where are yours coming from?" O'Neill asked him.

"From the White House," Arends said.

"You've got to be kidding," O'Neill said.

When Ford came on the plane, Arends went to him and had him listen to O'Neill's figures. Ford had said he did not want to hear anything about being President. A politician, however, will listen to arithmetic. As Ford heard O'Neill's figures, his face changed.

O'Neill relaxed on the plane and decided to tell a story about Elliot Richardson. After all, Ford would need a Vice President and there was no harm in telling him about Elliot Richardson.

"When Richardson was the Attorney General of Massachusetts he went after a man eighteen months after the fella died, I never heard anything like it in my life," O'Neill said. "Bill Callahan. He was the Commissioner of the Massachusetts Turnpike Authority. When Bill died, his secretary, Helen Healy, emptied the contents of the wall safe in Callahan's office. So Richardson has her subpoenaed before the grand jury which was going after Callahan, who has been dead for eighteen months now. So they put Helen Healy on the stand and the prosecutor asks her, 'Did you not empty the contents of the Commissioner's safe?'

And Helen Healy says, 'Yes, I did.' And she is asked, 'What did the contents consist of?' And she says, 'Oh, I couldn't tell you that.' The prosecutor says, 'I direct you to answer.' They have to call a recess and Helen sees her lawyer out in the hallway and then she comes back into the grand jury room and the prosecutor says, 'Now, I ask you again. You emptied the contents of the Turnpike Commissioner Callahan's wall safe, did you not?' And she says, 'Yes, I did.' And the prosecutor says, 'Now I ask you what did the contents of the safe consist of?' And Helen Healy said, 'Ten thousand Xerox copies of Elliot Richardson's 1939 drunken-driving record.'" (In Boston they never throw anything away—not even the drunken-driving record of an eighteen-year-old.)

O'Neill's roar rang out through the plane, along with Ford's.

"I'd never heard that one," Ford said.

"Now you have," O'Neill said proudly.

At the golf tournament, Ford and O'Neill walked down the fairway together, arms behind each other's back. Pictures were snapped. The picture ran everyplace. The Republican Vice President and the Democratic House Majority Leader. O'Neill mentioned the picture as being of great humor. As a professional politician, there was no reason for him to mention the unspoken agreements that had caused the picture to be taken. Proper practice is to turn to the humor of the act. The White House, however, regarded the picture as exactly what it was: a final eviction notice.

On Friday, August 2nd, in the White House staff dining room, a small, noisy room in the basement, Leonard Garment, J. Fred Buzhardt, Jr., William Timmons, and Dean Burch had lunch. There was a discussion of what Nixon had to do. There were only two options. Everybody had looked out the windows and saw that by now the flood of paper had the building up on pilings, with the paper eating through the creosote on the pilings and into the wood. One option was for Nixon to see it through to a certain loss. The other was for him to resign. Leonard Garment was in favor of resignation. Buzhardt said nothing to him. After lunch, on the way back to their offices in the Executive Office Building across the alley from the White House, Buzhardt said to Garment, "He's going to have to resign. Some of this new stuff on the tapes we have to turn over to Jaworski is very bad."

Over the weekend, Nixon went to Camp David with Alexander Haig and Raymond Price and Pat Buchanan. It was obvious the last two were there to write something. On Sunday, Dean Burch received a phone call at his home from Haig.

"We've got problems with these new tapes Jaworski is to receive," Haig said. "But it's nothing we can't deal with."

Burch said that was fine. Then at 8:30 on Monday morning, August 5, 1974, he went to his office in the White House. Timmons and Ken Clawson, the deputy communications director, were to be briefed on the weekend by Pat Buchanan.

"Now about this tape," Buchanan said. He went over what was on the tape of June 23, 1972. As Buchanan finished, Burch was getting up and reaching for something.

"All I can conclude," Buchanan said, "is that the Old Man has been shitting us."

Burch now had in hand what he had been reaching for. A bottle of bourbon.

"Let's have a drink," Burch said.

Later that day, later on Monday, August 5, 1974, at a few minutes after three o'clock, there arrived on the floor of the House of Representatives a page girl in white blouse and blue slacks, carrying a sheaf of long paper. The floor was less than a quarter occupied at the time, but among those present was O'Neill. O'Neill's heavy freckled hand reached out to take a copy from the page; two sheets stapled together, letter-spaced typing. Tip O'Neill held the paper away from him and began reading it aloud, a small group standing around his seat and listening to his deep North Cambridge street tones.

"For immediate release. Office of the White House Press Secretary. The White House. Statement by the President: I have today instructed my attorneys to make available to the House Judiciary Committee, and I am making public, the transcripts of three conversations with H. R. Haldeman on June 23, 1972. I have also turned over the tapes of these conversations to Judge Sirica as part of the process of my compliance with the Supreme Court ruling.

"On April 29, in announcing my decision to make public the original set of White House transcripts, I stated that 'as far as what the President personally knew and did with regard to Watergate and the cover-up is concerned, these materials, together with those already made available—will tell it all.' Shortly after that . . ."

O'Neill read on. He kept looking for the word "resign" or a synonym thereof. For many weeks now he had assumed that somebody in the White House would break through the numbness and inform Nixon that he was through. But as he read, the words O'Neill expected to see did not jump at him from the page, the way things of importance are supposed to do. The statement wandered through sentences which became paragraphs of words that were a half-notch off true meaning, and all delayed what had to be said. The preamble to Confession can only make you look worse, which is why Catholics use only one sentence—"Bless me Father for I have sinned, it has been six months since my last Confession . . ." before going right into the account of sin. Nixon attempting to make his first confession straggled about with these dreadful amateurisms: ". . . although I recognized these presented potential problems . . . I did realize the implications. . . ." Sitting in the House O'Neill droned on, turned the page, and now, finally, here it was, on the top of the second sheet:

"The June 23 tapes clearly show, however, that at the time I gave these instructions [to the CIA and FBI] I also discussed the political aspects of the situation, and I was aware of the advantages this course of action would have with respect to limiting the possible public exposure of involvement by persons connected with the Re-Election Committee."

It was over. Richard Nixon's story, his front, his alibi, had lasted for 780 days. He had damn-near proved Lincoln wrong.

When O'Neill finished his dramatic reading, he walked off the floor, took the elevator the one flight down, and ambled into his suite of offices. He held the paper out for anybody who wanted it.

"Well, here it is. Confession is good for the soul, but it doesn't save the body."

He then got down to work that was of high importance to him at a time such as this. He had to call his wife, Milly Miller O'Neill, at Harwichport, on Cape Cod, and tell her to get her clothes together because she was going to see a new President sworn in. When his wife asked him when, O'Neill told her that Nixon probably would be out within forty-eight hours. Milly Miller O'Neill said he could give her a call when the President was finished officially; she was staying at the Cape until then. Under the best of circumstances, she is not too strong on great ceremonies; when O'Neill's own John F. Kennedy was inaugurated, Milly Miller O'Neill said it was too cold for her to sit on a wooden chair on cement steps, and she stayed in a hotel a block away from the Capitol and watched it on television. It would take much to move her to see Nixon under any circumstance. Finally, on Thursday morning, August 8, 1974, daughter Rosemary O'Neill, who works in Washington, stopped at her father's office and he gave her the assignment of getting her mother down to Washington immediately.

"Mother," she said on the phone, "Dad says you better get dressed and come down here. He's got a room for you at the Jefferson."

"A suite," somebody called out.

"A nice suite," Rosemary said.

Rosemary hung up. "Dad, she says she has to drive to Cambridge to get a dress. She doesn't have any dresses with her at the Cape. So she won't be able to drive all the way home and still get a plane tonight. She'll be on the first plane in the morning."

At 2:44 on that Thursday afternoon, Eleanor Kelley, O'Neill's secretary, buzzed him. "The Vice President," she said.

O'Neill was in a long, narrow back office that he uses for eating diet lunches. He punched a button on a green telephone bank. His face broke into a laugh. For months, O'Neill had been saying to Ford on the phone, "Say, Jerry, I heard every time it rains, you call up the White House and tell them to close the windows." This time Ford opened up the conversation by discussing the golf picture of the two that was in the issue of *Newsweek* magazine. In mentioning the picture, Ford talked to O'Neill about it being a funny picture; they appeared to be picking each other's pockets. "Well, we sure had a helluva time," Ford said. He then got down to what he was calling about: Richard Nixon was submitting a letter of resignation to Henry

Kissinger at 10:00 A.M. on the next morning, August 9th. The resignation would be effective at noon. Ford then would be sworn in at noon, and he asked that O'Neill be present.

"Are wives invited, Jerry?" O'Neill said. "The reason I'm asking is that I've already told Milly to pack herself up and get down here."

"Wives were not invited, but they are now," Ford said.

"Now Jerry, I've got a statement prepared and I'll read it for you." He picked up a typed release.

"While we are close personal friends and I have great respect for his honesty, integrity, and ability, our political philosophies are diametrically opposed. I wish him every success in bringing our politically torn country together. He can expect cooperation from Congress and I trust he will cooperate with Congress and most of America in the days ahead."

"That's fine, Tip. And I want to say I'll be relying on you for your advice and assistance."

"I can tell you one thing, Jerry, don't think of a Democrat for Vice President. This country doesn't work that way."

"Thanks for the advice."

"Christ, Jerry, isn't this a wonderful country? Here we can talk like this and you and I can be friends and eighteen months from now I'll be going around the country kicking your balls in."

That Thursday night, Nixon went on television to announce his resignation. He refused to make anything more than a vague acknowledgment that something wrong had occurred. First, he did not want to admit anything to anybody. And second, he did not at this time have a pardon deal worked out, therefore anything he said about himself might have returned to bother him at a later date. Later that night, Nixon called a friend of mine, who had worked for him in the White House, and said good-by.

"He talked about going to jail," my friend tells. "He was saying to me, 'Well, if they want to go all the way with me, I guess it won't be so bad. You can do a lot of political writing in jail. Lots of political books were written in jail. Just give me a table and a pad and pencils and let me go to work. No telephones to bother me. Yes, a lot of heads of state have gone to jail. Gandhi went to prison, you know.'"

It is very common for defendants to spread the belief that prison will kill them. People in Washington, who are unused to everyday life, made Nixon's health the basis for his pardon.

On the following Monday, August 12, 1974, here I was at a few minutes before nine o'clock at night, sitting in a chair on the floor of the House of Representatives. Brown leather, wine-red carpeting with flower patterns, polished brass spittoons, and half-light which suddenly turned into hot white light as the banks of television lights began burning down on us. In the seats to my right were the Kennedys and McGoverns and Liz Holtzmans and Herman Badillos. In the seats directly in front of me were these muscular African diplomats in white dashikis and skullcaps talking high Oxford English; the man in front of me, with shoulders like two brick stoops, sounding like Alistair Cooke, should thank God nightly that he was born in the jungles in Africa. If he was born in Washington, he would speak in unintelligible mumbles from getting slugged around as an underpaid offensive guard with the Redskins.

The television lights, banks of thousand-watt bulbs clamped to the ceiling of the old chamber, were beginning to outrun the air conditioning, first movements of discomfort showing in the crowd lining the walls, this ending immediately upon the sight of William (Fishbait) Miller, the House doorkeeper, stomping down the aisle, calling out in best Southern Baptist voice, "Mister Speaker, the President of the United States." When the doors swung open and everybody in the chamber saw that it was not Richard Nixon walking in, the cheers that went up around me on the floor were merely perfunctory when matched with the feeling of relief, a feeling so intense that it could be felt, almost heard, as it rose from their chests and shoulders to leave them free of Nixon and all the name meant to their careers and their country. Oh, they liked Jerry Ford very much. He had been one of them; his success might mean their success. But for anybody who was standing up with the crowd, watching, listening, feeling, it was obvious that these men, who are in politics for a living, would have cheered for anybody.

Ford stood at the rostrum, stood in the lights and the noise, folded his hands behind his back, just folded them lightly, the thumbs hooked. I watched his hands very closely. They were not clenched in tension. When Ford spoke, he did so effortlessly, he needed no water, there was no throat-clearing, no sudden hand or body motions to break the pressure. The world watched, but Ford seemed to be talking to a small gathering of friends. For this one night anyway, Jim Hartz had just become President.

The next day, the first thing O'Neill and Leo Diehl did was to make reservations on the 6:40 P.M. Delta Airlines to Boston. They would have something to eat at Jimmy's Harborside and then drive down to the Cape for a few days. They discussed the reservations and plans with the same intensity which had gone into the talk of impeachment throughout the preceding weeks.

This was the problem for the day, getting to the 6:40 Delta to Boston, to Jimmy's Harborside, and then on to the Cape and George McCue's piano. Yesterday, the country shook. That was yesterday.

In mid-afternoon, new President Ford's secretary called O'Neill's office. He was having his first state dinner on Friday night, honoring the Shah of Iran. The new President Ford was inviting Congressman and Mrs. O'Neill to the dinner.

"I'll have to see," O'Neill said.

He called Milly Miller O'Neill at Harwichport, Cape Cod. He told her that there was this invitation to the new President's first state dinner, honoring the Shah of Iran, and did she feel like coming down to Washington for it?

"You've got to be kidding," Milly Miller O'Neill said. "A state dinner? I'm at the Cape and I'm staying. Which Delta are you making tonight?"

"We're on the six-forty."

"Well, don't miss it," she said.

The invitation from the new President was respectfully declined.

The Capitol building became empty early that day. At six-fifteen, O'Neill called to Eleanor Kelley, his secretary, "Is Roger ready to go?"

"He's outside already," she said.

"Well, we're off."

Leo Diehl already was out in the hallway. O'Neill stuck a

Daniel Webster cigar into his mouth, said goodnight to Eleanor Kelley, and left.

The long marble hallway was silent and deserted and softly lit for the evening. Leo Diehl was halfway down it, body swinging in the air between his crutches. O'Neill walked slowly. He began to hum. Softly first. He took a breath and hummed louder. Now he took the cigar out of his mouth and started to sing.

> *Some of them write to the old folks at home,*
> *That's their old ace in the hole. . . .*

Up the hallway, Leo Diehl picked it up and now the two sang together as they went down the long marble hallway of the empty Capitol, leaving after the summer of 1974 and singing:

> *The others have girls on the old tenderloin,*
> *That's their old ace in the hole. . . .*

COLUMNS 1976–2004

Two Who Will Watch and One Who Won't

O N A chilly Sunday in 1972, my friend Klein, who was a lawyer in Queens, had another major fight with his wife, which caused him to sulk out of his house and go to his office on Queens Boulevard, across the street from the Criminal Court Building in Kew Gardens. Agitation impaired his ability to work, and he went downstairs to a bar that was crowded with people watching a football game. The only thing Klein the Lawyer disliked more than football on television is a client who is innocent. Klein feels that is too much of a burden.

He was about to leave when he saw, sitting alone, a woman who looked almost exactly like his wife.

"I don't like you," Klein said to her.

"Why?"

"Because," Klein said, speaking as a lawyer.

"If you don't like me, then at least buy a drink."

Klein bought the drink. They exchanged names. The woman's name was Rosalie.

"What game is this, anyway?" Rosalie said.

"Flushing High School," Klein said.

"Did you go there?" she said.

"Sure, that's why I know who it is," Klein said.

"Then I'm rooting for Flushing High," she said. "Which team is it?"

"That one," Klein said. He pointed to the Dallas Cowboys team, which had the ball and was on its way to winning the 1972 Super Bowl over Miami.

As the day went on, the girl brush-blocked Klein. He went for the knee like he was supposed to. And in the final moments of the Super Bowl game of 1972, Dallas was defeating Miami on television and at the bar romance was annihilating Klein the Lawyer. He took his new girlfriend's hand. He never let go.

On each Sunday afternoon since that day in 1972, Klein and Rosalie had sat in the same place at the same bar, holding hands and looking into each other's eyes. At first, to get out of the house on a Sunday, Klein would tell his wife that he was having a big secret meeting with clients in the Mafia. They would cut his throat if he ever disclosed the location of the meeting, he told his wife.

As time went on, Klein grew more brazen and began to give no excuses. And his girlfriend Rosalie began to change. Instead of looking *almost* like Klein's wife, she now looked exactly like Klein's wife. Finally, this year, Klein parted with his wife and took up completely with Rosalie.

Which made many people on Queens Boulevard uneasy. Other wives, hearing the news, were beginning to ask questions about life on the Boulevard. The truth is that life on Queens Boulevard is absolutely sensational. At noontime one day there was a fire in an apartment building across from the courthouse. Rushing out of the apartment building, buttoning and tucking in shirts, were lawyers, judges, prosecutors, politicians—and the undercover cops assigned to check on all the others.

And the undercover cops assigned to check on them.

"You're jamming us," Klein's friends told him. "My wife said she's coming here for lunch today. She never did that before. She's checking up on me."

Klein the Lawyer and Rosalie began to remain clear of the area during the week. But each Sunday they were in the bar on Queens Boulevard, the Part One Bar, having several drinks, holding hands and seeing nothing but each other.

Several weeks ago, in anticipation of Super Bowl X, Shelley Chevlowe, the bail bondsman who also runs the Part One Bar, installed one of these new movie screen-sized television sets. He then invited most of the people he sees all week to come around and watch the Super Bowl on the new screen. As nobody can get out on Sunday without his wife, Shelley the Bondsman planned a buffet in honor of the wives.

"I can't show up," many of the boys told Shelley. "My wife will put one foot into the place, see Klein with his girlfriend and go crazy."

"I'll tell him not to come," Shelley said. "That's easy."

It was not. "I can't help you, I'm bringing Rosalie Sunday," Klein the Lawyer said. "She says it's our anniversary. She remembers one of these teams was playing the day we met. The Cowboys or something."

"You're making everybody we know stay home," Shelley the Bondsman said.

"So let them stay home. I'm in love with my girl," Klein the Lawyer said.

So while Dallas plays the Steelers today, Klein and Rosalie will be at the Bar of the Part One, celebrating their anniversary, and not seeing one play of the game. And all the regulars have to remain at home.

Which proves once more—in the midst of all this consuming interest in a football game—that one turn of a woman's head still is stronger than anything that has happened since man got off all fours and started running off-tackle plays.

January 18, 1976

Dies the Victim, Dies the City

THEY WERE walking along in the empty gray afternoon, three of them, Allen Burnett, Aaron Freeman, and Billy Mabry, Burnett the eldest at seventeen, walking up Bedford Avenue in Brooklyn and singing out Muhammad Ali rhymes into the chill air. As they reached the corner of Kosciusko Street, it was Allen Burnett's turn to give his Ali rhyme: "AJB is the latest. And he is the greatest."

"Who AJB?" one of them said.

"Allen J. Burnett."

They were laughing at this as they turned the corner onto Kosciusko Street. The three wore coats against the cold. Burnett was in a brown trench coat; Freeman, a three-quarter burgundy leather; and Mabry, a three-quarter beige corduroy with a fox collar. A white paint stain was on the bottom at the back of Mabry's coat. Mabry, walking on the outside, suddenly was shoved forward.

"Keep on walking straight," somebody behind him said.

Billy Mabry turned his head. Behind him was this little guy of maybe eighteen, wearing a red sweater, dark pants, and black gun. Aaron Freeman, walking next to Mabry, says he saw two others besides the gunman. The three boys kept walking, although Mabry thought the guy in the red sweater had a play gun.

"Give me the money."

"I don't have any money," Allen Burnett said.

The guy with the gun shot Allen Burnett in the back of the head. Burnett pitched into the wall of an apartment house and went down on his back, dead.

The gunman stood with Allen Burnett's body at his feet and said that now he wanted coats. Billy Mabry handed back the corduroy with the paint stain. Freeman took off his burgundy leather. The gunman told the two boys to start running. "You don't look back!" Billy Mabry and Aaron Freeman ran up Kosciusko Street, past charred buildings with tin nailed over the windows, expecting to be shot in the back. People came onto the street and the guy in the red sweater waved his gun at them.

The people dived into doorways. He stuffed the gun into his belt and ran up Bedford Avenue, ran away with his new coats. Some saw one other young guy with him. Others saw two.

It was another of last week's murders that went almost unnoticed. Allen Burnett was young. People in the city were concentrating all week on the murders of elderly people. Next week you can dwell on murders of the young, and then the killing of the old won't seem as important.

Allen Burnett's murder went into the hands of the Thirteenth Homicide Squad, situated on the second floor of a new police building on Utica Avenue. The outdoor pay phone in front of the precinct house has been ripped out. The luncheonette across the street is empty and fire-blackened. At first, a detective upstairs thought the interest was in a man who had just beaten his twenty-two-month-old child to death with a riding crop. That was unusual. Allen Burnett was just another homicide. Assured that Burnett was the subject, the detective pointed to Harold Ruger, who sat at a desk going through a new manila folder with Burnett's name on it. Ruger is a blue-eyed man with wavy dark-brown hair that is white at the temples. The twenty-four years he has spent on the job have left him with a melancholy face and a soft voice underlined with pleasant sarcasm: "They got two coats. Helluva way to go shopping. Looks like there was three of them. That leaves one guy out there without a coat. I'll look now for somebody who gets taken off for a coat tonight, tomorrow night, the next few days."

In a city that seems virtually ungoverned, Harold Ruger forms the only municipal presence with any relationship to what is happening on the streets where the people live. Politicians attend dinners at hotels with contractors. Bankers discuss interest rates at lunch. Harold Ruger goes into a manila folder on his desk and takes out a picture of Allen Burnett, a young face covered with blood staring from a morgue table. In Allen Burnett's hand there is a piece of the veins of the city of New York.

Dies the victim, dies the city. Nobody flees New York because of accounting malpractice. People run from murder and fire. Those who remain express their fear in words of anger.

"Kill him for nothing, that's life—that's what it is today," his sister Sadie was saying. The large, impressive family had gathered in the neat frame house at 30 Van Buren Street. "He was going into the army in January and they kill him for nothing. That's the leniency of the law. Without capital punishment they do what they want. There's no respect for human life."

Horace Jones, an uncle, said, "The bleeding hearts years ago cut out the electric chair. When the only way to stop all this is by havin' the electric chair."

"We look at mug shots all last night," Sadie said. "None of them was under sixteen. If the boy who shot Allen is under sixteen, there won't be any picture of him. How do you find him if he's under sixteen? Minors should get treated the same as everybody else. Equal treatment."

"Electric chair for anybody who kills, don't talk to me about ages," Horace Jones said.

The dead boy's mother, Lillian Burnett, sat with her head down and her hands folded in her lap.

"Do you think there should be an electric chair?" she was asked.

"I sure do," she said, eyes closed, head nodding. "Won't bring back my son, but I sure do want it. They tied up three old women and killed them. If they had the electric chair I believe they would rob the three women, but I don't believe they'd kill them."

The funeral was held two days later, at the Brown Memorial Baptist Church, on Washington Avenue. A crowd of three hundred of Allen Burnett's family and friends walked two by two into church. Walked erectly, solemnly, with the special dignity of those to whom suffering is a bitter familiarity. Seeing them, workmen in the street shut off pneumatic drills. Inside the church, the light coming through the doorway gleamed on the dark, polished wood of the benches. The casket was brought in by men walking soundlessly on the carpeted floor. The doors were closed, an organ sounded, and the people faced the brutality of a funeral service; a baby cried, a woman rocked and screamed, a boy sobbed, a woman fainted, heads were cradled in arms. The mother screamed through a black veil, "My baby's gone!"

An aunt, Mabel Mabry, walked out of the church with lips trembling and arms hugging her shaking body. "My little nephew's dead," she said loudly. "They find the ones who killed him. I'm tellin' you, they got to kill them too, for my nephew."

The city government, Harold Ruger, just wants to find the killer. Ruger was not at the funeral. "I got stuck in an eighty-floor elevator," he said when he came to work yesterday. "I was going around seeing people. We leave the number, maybe they'll call us. That's how it happens a lot. They call." He nodded toward a younger detective at the next desk. "He had one, an old man killed by a kid. Information came on a phone call, isn't that right, Al?"

"Stabbed eight times, skull fractured," the younger detective said.

Harold Ruger said, "What does it look like you have? Nothing. And he gets a phone call, see what I mean? The answer is out there and it will come." His finger tapped the file he was keeping on the murder of Allen Burnett.

November 1976

On the Hunt for Son of Sam

WE PUT the letter on the table and read it again. In his opening paragraph he writes:

Hello from the gutters of N.Y.C. which are filled with dog manure, vomit, stale wine, urine, and blood. Hello from the sewers of N.Y.C. which swallow up these delicacies when they are washed away by the sweeper trucks. Hello from the cracks in the sidewalks of N.Y.C. and from the ants that dwell in these cracks and feed on the dried blood of the dead that has settled into the cracks.

"He's a pretty good writer," somebody at the table said.

"Yes, he is," I said.

The letter was from the person who calls himself "Son of Sam." He prowls the night streets of New York neighborhoods and shoots at young girls and sometimes their boy friends too, and he has killed five and wounded four. He sneaks up on victims with a .44-caliber pistol. Most of the young women had shoulder-length brown hair.

One of the victims was Donna Lauria, who was 18 last year when the killer shot her as she sat in a car with her girl friend outside the Laurias' apartment house on Buhre Ave. in the Bronx. Donna Lauria was the only victim mentioned by the killer in this letter, which was sent to me at my newspaper in New York, The Daily News. So yesterday, I took the letter up to the fourth-floor apartment of Donna Lauria's parents and I sat over coffee and read the letter again and talked to the Laurias about it.

The killer had sent one communication before this one. He left a note to police after murdering a girl and boy as they sat in a parked car at a place only five blocks from where Donna Lauria had been killed. Both notes were hand-printed.

Yesterday, in the sadness and tension of the Laurias' dining room, I read the letter again. Following the first paragraph, it said:

J.B. I'm just dropping you a line to let you know that I appreciate your interest in those recent and horrendous

334

.44 killings. I also want to tell you that I read your column daily and find it quite informative.

Tell me, Jim, what will you have for July Twenty-Ninth? You can forget about me if you like because I don't care for publicity. However, you must not forget Donna Lauria and you cannot let the people forget her, either. She was a very sweet girl but Sam's a thirsty lad and he won't let me stop killing until he gets his fill of blood.

Mr. Breslin, sir, don't think that because you haven't heard from (me) for a while that I went to sleep. No, rather, I am still here. Like a spirit roaming the night. Thirsty, hungry, seldom stopping to rest; anxious to please Sam. I love my work. Now, the void has been filled.

Perhaps we shall meet face to face someday or perhaps I will be blown away by cops with smoking .38's. Whatever, if I shall be fortunate enough to meet you I will tell you all about Sam if you like and I will introduce you to him. His name is "Sam the Terrible."

Not knowing what the future holds I shall say farewell and I will see you at the next job. Or, should I say you will see my handiwork at the next job? Remember Ms. Lauria. Thank you.

In their blood
and
From the Gutter.
"Sam's Creation" .44

P.S.: J.B., please inform all the detectives working on the slayings to remain.

P.S.: J.B., please inform all the detectives working the case that I wish them the best of luck. "Keep Em digging, drive on, think positive, get off your butts, knock on coffins, etc."

Upon my capture I promise to buy all the guys working on the case a new pair of shoes if I can get up the money.

Son of Sam

Directly under the signature was a symbol the killer drew. It appears to be an X-shaped mark with the biological symbols for male and female, and also a cross and the letter S.

When I finished reading the letter, Mike Lauria, the father, said to me, "What do you think?"

"Want to see for yourself?" the father was asked.

He pushed the letter away from him. "I don't want to see it."

"Let me," his wife, Rose, said.

"You don't want to see it," the husband said.

"Yes, I do. Because I have a lot of cards she used to get. Maybe the printing is the same."

The husband shrugged. "Go ahead then."

We took out the page that mentioned her daughter and gave Rose Lauria the rest. Her large, expressive brown eyes became cold as she looked at the printing. On the wall behind her was a picture of her daughter, a lovely brown-haired girl with the mother's features.

The mother put the pages down and looked up. "He's probably a very brilliant man, boy, whatever he is," she said. "His brain functions the opposite way."

She looked up at the picture of her daughter. "She was a dancer and a half. Every place you went, people used to praise her. Is it possible he saw her some place and she didn't speak to him or something?"

"Who knows?" the husband said. "How can you say anything about a guy you don't even know?"

Nobody knows. The .44 killer appears to be saying that he is controlled by Sam, who lives inside him and sends him onto the streets to find young people to shoot. He does this at close range: One young woman, walking home from college, held a textbook over her face and he put the gun up to the book and killed her.

The detectives, whose shoes he would buy, walk the streets at night and hope for a match with the man with the .44. "He's mine," one of them, a friend of mine, was saying Friday night. "The man is Jack Ripper and I'm makin' a personal appointment with him."

The hope is that the killer realizes that he is controlled by Sam, who not only forces him into acts of horror but will ultimately walk him to his death. The only way for the killer to leave this special torment is to give himself up to me, if he trusts me, or to the police, and receive both help and safety.

If he wants any further contact, all he has to do is call or write me at The Daily News. It's simple to get me, the only people I don't answer are bill collectors.

The time to do it, however, is now. We are too close to the July 29 that the killer mentions in his letter. It is the first anniversary of the death of Donna Lauria.

"She was sitting in the car with her friend Jody Valente," Rose Lauria was saying. Jody Valente was wounded and has recovered. "Mike and I came walking up. We'd been to a wake. I went up to the car and I said, 'Tell me, Jody, what happened tonight.' She always used to tell me about her boy friends. She said, 'It's a long story tonight. Donna'll tell you when she gets upstairs.' Now my husband says to Donna, 'What are you doing here at 1 A.M., you got to work tomorrow.' I said to him, 'What is she doing that's wrong?'

"So we went upstairs. My husband says, 'I'm going to walk the dog.' He goes with the dog to the elevator and I hear Jody's horn blowing downstairs. I called out in the hall to my husband. He says to me, 'Well, go look out the window and see.' I look out and here's Jody screaming that Donna's been shot."

Rose Lauria, nervous now, got up from the table. "You know the last month when he killed the two more around here? My husband and I were at a wedding. We were supposed to meet some people after it. We left the wedding and I said to my husband, 'I don't want to go to meet anybody. Something's the matter. I want to go home.' And we just got inside at the same time the two got killed."

"She was pacing around here like a cat," Mike Lauria said.

He walked me downstairs to the street. He stood in an undershirt, with the sun glaring on his wide shoulders, and he pointed to the spot where his daughter had been shot.

"She was starting to get out of the car when she saw this guy on the curb. Right where we are. Donna said to Jody, 'Who's this guy now?' Then the guy did what he did. Jody, she can't get herself to come near my wife. Forget about it. I saw her a couple of weeks ago. She spoke to me from the car. Told me she got engaged. She couldn't even look at me. I told her, 'All right, Jody, go ahead. I'll see you.' I let her go home."

He turned and walked back into his building. I took my

letter from his daughter's killer and went down the street and out of his wounded life.

June 5, 1977

To the .44-Caliber Killer on His 1st Deathday

IT WAS nearly 6 A.M. and the blue carpet was covered with cigaret butts and gum wrappers from the big crowd of the night that had just ended. Timothy Dowd, a deputy inspector of New York police, stood by himself in the middle of one of the rooms of this discotheque called Elephas, on Northern Blvd. in Bayside, Queens. This was June 26 and, two hours before, the .44 killer had shot two more young people, his 10th and 11th victims, while they sat in a Cadillac parked down the block from the discotheque. And now Dowd, his arms folded, stared at the floor.

His head jerked up. "Think he was in here?" he called to one of the policemen who were using the phones.

"I don't know," somebody answered.

Dowd's eyes gleamed. "You know he wasn't in here," he said. "Can't take pressure like this. Couple of hundred young girls in here. He'd fall apart. Couldn't take it in here. You know he was waiting outside. That's his spot. Alone in the dark."

He stared out the open front door. The first light of morning was washing the empty street outside. Dowd shook his head. "Mean bastard," he said.

Alone and mean. These are the traits of the .44 killer, the one who calls himself the Son of Sam and who, tomorrow, will have been a part of the lives of many of the young people of this city for a full year. He has killed five people with his .44 and wounded six, and has young women with long brown hair afraid to be out at night.

On July 29, 1976, at 1 in the morning, Donna Lauria, 18, sat with her girl friend in a car double-parked outside her apartment house at 2860 Buhre Ave., in the Pelham Bay section of the Bronx. Her father and mother, walking home from a wake, came up to the car and the father, Mike Lauria, complained about his daughter's being out so late.

"You've got to go to work in the morning," he said. Donna was a medical technician.

"What's she doing so wrong?" the mother said. "She's here in front of her own house, she'll be up in a minute."

The father and mother went upstairs. The father was going to come back down and walk the dog. Donna Lauria sat in the car for a couple of minutes more and then she opened the door to get out.

The killer was standing at the curb, two car widths away. Standing alone and staring at her.

Donna Lauria pulled the car door shut. "Now, who the hell is this?" she said.

And now it was his moment, his chance to satisfy the voices inside him. He dropped into a crouch and his two hands came out holding his .44-caliber pistol. He fired two shots into the car, killing Donna Lauria and wounding the girl with her. Then he walked away into the night.

On June 5, the killer wrote a letter addressed to me. It was his second letter. The first was addressed to Capt. Joseph Borelli of the Police Department and was left at the scene of the April 18 killings of Valentina Suriani, 18, and Alexander Esau, 20, on a dark street only six blocks from the place where Donna Lauria was killed.

I have spent hours reading the hand-printed three-page letter. I can recite every line of it. He uses a comma before "and." Whoever he is, he is probably the only killer I've ever heard of who understands the use of a semicolon. Yesterday the letter came out again. Once again, I read the .44 killer, Son of Sam, as he told us about Donna Lauria:

"Tell me, Jim, what will you have for July 29? You can forget about me if you like because I don't care for publicity. However, you must not forget Donna Lauria and you cannot let the people forget her, either. She was a very very sweet girl but Sam's a thirsty lad and he won't let me stop killing until he gets his fill of blood."

At the end, he says: "Remember Ms. Lauria. Thank you."

What do I have for the 29th? I have this, a column about the .44 killer and his victims, particularly the first victim, Donna Lauria. Which is exactly what the killer wanted when he sent me the letter. He who would be God with the lives of young women can also use his great power to direct the newspapers to write what he wants and when he wants it.

And, somewhere in this city, loner, a deranged loner, picks up this paper and gloats. Again he has what he wants. Is tomorrow night, July 29, so significant to him that he must go out and walk the night streets and find a victim? Or will he sit alone, and look out his attic window and be thrilled by his power, this power that will have him in the newspapers and on television and in the thoughts and conversations of most of the young people in the city?

I don't know. Nobody else does either. For we deal here with the night wind. Nobody knows what the .44 killer looks like. Nobody knows what he sounds like. We don't even have a sample of his handwriting: The two letters are printed.

Almost certainly, this is a man who is unable to touch a woman. He says he is not a woman-hater, but in his own hand he refers to them as "Wemon" as in demon. If he cannot function as a man normally, he decides in his deranged mind to prove to the world, and to this voice named Sam, that of course he is a man. He kills to prove it.

He has to be unable to carry on a relationship with other people, also. How else, except by living the life of a recluse, could the killer have lasted a full year without somebody around him noticing him? A person living even semi-normal existence would raise the suspicion of family, acquaintances, people at work. Caressing his .44, going out into the night with it, out on many nights, the .44 killer has gone uncaught because he probably stays to himself so much that nobody in a city of more than 7 million knows him. He could come out of a room in a YMCA or from a rooming house in a transient neighborhood. He could work alone, at night. After 12 months, it seems certain that he does not work where there are other people.

There have been a staggering number of phone calls and letters from people in New York who suspect a person in the family or neighborhood, and every message has been checked. Never in my time in my business have I seen the awareness that people display over the .44 killer. And he has not been found.

So he sits alone someplace in this city, alone with his .44, and only he knows when the voice of Sam forces him out into the night after a victim. This is a killer without a schedule or a face.

He taunts the police and he has me writing what he wants and when he wants it. Remember Donna Lauria, he says. We remember all of it. The blood-soaked pine bushes on Dartmouth St. in Forest Hills where Virginia Voskerichian, shot through the head, fell dead. And JoAnne Lomino of Bellerose, shot on her stoop, sitting paralyzed in a wheelchair and saying, "I'm going to walk again." And the women in the Bronx walking out in the morning with pails of water to scrub the blood from the street where Valentina Suriana and Alexander Esau were shot while they sat in a car. And, a few blocks away, the apartment house on Buhre Ave. where Mike and Rose Lauria sit up most of the nights because they are unable to get over their daughter's being killed by this deranged person nobody knows. A person who, on any night he goes out, could wind up over the hood of a police car, like a deer.

July 28, 1977

Door Opens, It's Always Stacy

AT NIGHT, Pat Violante, whose son lay practically blind from a .44 slug, came to the home of Jerry Moskowitz, whose daughter had just died by the same hand.

"Did you tell your boy that Stacy died?" Jerry Moskowitz said.

"No," Violante said, "what do you think I should do?"

"The boy don't need any shocks," Moskowitz said. "Let him take care of himself. Let him get over this, let him get better."

"And then," Violante said.

"Then the two of us work it out together," Moskowitz said.

Now, yesterday afternoon, Jerry Moskowitz sat on the windowsill of his bedroom in the rear of a second-story apartment on E. Fifth St. in Flatbush and he had the door closed.

"When you have children you go through four or five tortures, the way I figure it," he was saying. "When they're born, when they're first growing up, when they're in school and then when they're old enough and they're getting married. Then of course they have their own children and their own problems and they try to put all that off onto you. Now we're going to miss that phase, I guess."

"I didn't go through the first parts. That was my wife's worry. When Stacy was being born, my wife went to the hospital a couple of times and they sent her home. Then I was at work and they called up and said she had the baby. I said, 'Thank God, already.' The fellow who owns the ice cream plant, he had them make up a big cake, saying, 'Thank God, already.'

"I don't remember much about her being a baby. She slept at night, I know that. My kids always slept through the night. A thing like teething, I don't remember teething. I'm the kind that says: 'I'm going to sleep, don't 'wake me.'

"Kids grow up on their own. I never sat down and told her all about life or anything like that. I wasn't the sitting-down type. My wife does the sitting down. I just had one thing I always wanted: I wanted all the kids from the street to always come to our house. I always wanted kids in my house. Have them all in. How many, what do I care, how many. Just make sure they

343

stay around my house. I open the door. Put your foot up on the furniture. What do I care, just be in my house.

"But after that, then I was in it. Sunday night at 8 o'clock. 'I didn't do my homework.' I'd say, 'What do you mean, you wait this late? Why didn't you do it?' She'd say: 'I don't have a pencil.' That's all I had to hear. OUT I'd go, buy pencils, notebooks, anything. But don't tell me you can't do homework because you have no pencil. Sunday nights, I'd go out in the rain, the cold, what's the difference? Get a pencil for homework.

"Then you come to the part where there's boy friends. Where am I when he comes? Are you kidding? Right there in the living room. You sit and look at him. I mean, how do you really look at him, I don't know. You look at his shoes and then his clothes and then, you know, you can't keep looking at his face because he'll know what you're doing, so you look at the shoes again and you say to yourself: 'Is this kid a junkie? Is this kid a bum? Is this kid going to be nice to my daughter?' You say to yourself: 'Go ahead and ask him something. Ask him if he uses dope.' And then you say to yourself, how can you do that. Besides, he wouldn't tell me, anyway. So I just sit there and look.

"When she went out, I was always up, but I wouldn't let her know. When she'd come home, she'd look in here and I'd pretend I was asleep. You know. Then the next day I'd sort of say to her: 'What time did you get home last night?' And she'd say: 'Oh, about 1:30.' And I'd say: 'One thirty? I think you just made a slight mistake.'

"I think, all those years when she was going out, Stacy thought her father only knew how to say a couple of things: 'Where are you going? Where were you?' That's why I was so pleased when she went out with Pat's son the other night. He was so clean-cut. A gentleman. I didn't even scrutinize when I saw him. He opened the car door for my daughter and I said, geez, look at this, I haven't seen a kid do this in years."

The phone rang and he picked it up. He told the caller that the funeral for his daughter would be at 8:15 in the morning. Then he stood silent, a burly man in a blue polo shirt, and he looked at the floor.

"I'll always see her in my mind," he said. "She went to Mexico on her own money. Went with a girl friend. She'd never flown before. It was such a thrill to her. She was doing it all on her own. Well, if you knew my Stacy, you'd know what happened. She bought so many gifts for her family down there that she ran out of money. In the meantime, I'm dying for a whole week here, wondering how she's doing, what she's doing.

"I met her at the airport when she came back. Eastern Air Lines on a Saturday night. I'm out there waiting and it was taking her so long. I said to the man at the counter, 'Where did they land this plane, in Chicago?' He had to tell me about Customs. I'd forgot all about the Customs. So I go to the doors there, and I'm pacing back and forth, my daughter has never been away before alone in her life, and now when the door swings open I see her inside on the Customs line. She had on white shorts. Everytime the door swung open, I saw her, the white shorts. I just kept looking. The door swings open, there she is. The door swings open again, there she is again.

"Then the door swings open and it's Stacy walking out. She was smiling. Lit up. You should have seen her face. She said to me: 'Dad—boy, what a ball I had. I can't wait to go back.' Then she says to me: 'I didn't forget you.' She gave me dollar-fifty cigars she bought down there.

"I can always sit here and see that door swing open and there's Stacy. The door swings open again and there's Stacy again."

He turned around and stared out the window, out at the hot Brooklyn day.

"At least she had one good time," he said.

August 3, 1977

How I Shot Down the Concorde All by Myself

At a little before 7:00 P.M. in Manhattan, longshoremen of Local 824 walked along the edge of pier 86, unfastened the hawsers that held the *QE2* to the West Side, and threw them out into the oily water of the slip. High up, ten stories up, seamen of the *QE2* began hauling in the rope. When the last hawser was thrown from the pier, hitting the water with a slap, the great ship, free to move, gave three deep blasts of the whistle. The people standing out on Twelfth Avenue began waving handkerchiefs. From the ship, you could see children looking down at their feet because the sidewalk was vibrating.

Once, it was part of the life of this city, the ocean liners of the world announcing their departure for the sea. Now, with the *QE2* the last big one afloat anywhere on the waters of the world, its deep sound becomes an emotion. On this night, when the tugs pushed the ship into the middle of the river, her twin six-bladed propellers first churning while the tugs slid away, the great ship, on her own, going down to the sea, sent three more proud blasts into the evening air.

I love sounds. Taxicab horns coming through an open window from the Manhattan street twenty-five stories down. A subway train's pleasant roar as it breaks out of a tunnel and into a lighted station. And the first sound of a jet plane: a whistle in the cold air, calling the eyes to follow a beautiful silver arrow soaring across the sky.

But then, of course, the jet plane's noise changes. It becomes a blare that blankets the ground and grows louder and louder and just when you are certain that now it must stop, now the sound must diminish, the noise only increases and carries to the beginning of pain and beyond.

In a neighborhood of New York such as Howard Beach, which sits on the edge of runways at Kennedy Airport, people grope for a way to explain the noise. How does a bus driver tell of the feeling of irritability that comes over everyone in his house about ten minutes before the landing patterns are changed? Animals uneasy over an impending storm only they can sense.

And now these people in Howard Beach are asked to accept a plane that makes even more noise, the Concorde plane. Howard Beach fears that someday all overseas flights will be Concordes and turn everyone's ears to stone. Because of this I was on this night standing on the boat deck of the *QE2* as she ran with the tide to the sea. Once, it was the only way to go. Now, I sail the Atlantic to the port of Cherbourg, in France, where I intend to confront these French, who build a machine that makes infernal noise and want Howard Beach to suffer in silence. In Howard Beach, people who must go to work for a living say they will blockade entrances to Kennedy Airport rather than allow the Concorde to send its roar through their roofs. In Paris, the president of the country, Valéry Giscard d'Estaing, has made personal remarks about Howard Beach people, thereby causing an international incident. He has entertained American politicians and paid enormous sums of money to American lobbyists who imitate his sneer when Howard Beach is mentioned. I go to Paris to report on the arrogant and thus defend people who work for a living and live in Howard Beach, which is a neighborhood of Queens, from whence I come.

Howard Beach is a narrow, crowded strip of land with bay water on both sides and a subway line, the A train, to Manhattan. A wide street, Cross Bay Boulevard, runs through Howard Beach to the ocean and forms two areas of Howard Beach. In one, the old side, some of the houses are there from the days it was considered a summer resort. Wash blows on lines strung from wooden houses. In the mornings, there is fresh sawdust on the floor of Sal's Butcher Shop and women customers sit on high stools so they can converse with each other while peering over the counter to watch the butcher make up their order. In the early afternoons, the voice of the track announcer over at Aqueduct Race Track sounds on the streets. In the late afternoons, the streets are empty in the painful noise of airport traffic.

On the other side of Cross Bay Boulevard is the new Howard Beach. Blocks of split-level and ranch houses and attached two-family bricks, all built over the last fifteen years, with small lawns in front, some of the lawns with religious statues on them. Incoming planes skim so low over these houses that people standing in the backyards unconsciously duck. As these people have heavy mortgages and no money to run elsewhere, they have organized to fight the Concorde by forming the Spring Park Civic Association and conducting protest meetings at PS 207. Because of this, the Port Authority, which operates Kennedy, has withheld permission for the Concorde to land.

And so Valéry Giscard d'Estaing called Jimmy Carter and said the French would block all American planes from Paris. Giscard kept saying through his nose, "Oward Beach." Next, British Prime Minister James Callaghan, whose country is a partner in the Concorde, flew to Washington to see Carter personally about these dreadful people in Howard Beach. On the next flight came a British cabinet member, Anthony Wedgwood-Benn. When nothing happened, Giscard and Callaghan recruited American political people to help them. American lawyers so far have been paid over a million dollars to represent the Concorde against Howard Beach.

"What do they think we are, imbeciles?" Mrs. Debby McGuire of Ninety-sixth Street said yesterday. "They're not courtroom lawyers. They're fixers. Everybody in Howard Beach has a hearing problem he isn't even aware of yet. Now some big shots put in a fix so the Concorde can come over my house like a cannon and make us move. I know what's going on."

Charles Goodell, one of the big-name lawyers representing the Concorde, was asked about this. Records show Mr. Goodell's law firm has been paid $195,000 by the Concorde people. Goodell is a former United States senator from Jamestown, New York.

"I represent the minister of transport of France; actually I'm the chief counsel," Goodell said.

"Does a French government ministry always pay such high fees to lawyers?" Goodell was asked.

"Well, I've been in court for them on cases," Goodell said. "One is pending. One is fully briefed."

"You once represented the people of Howard Beach as a senator," I said to Goodell. "Don't you feel there is a conflict here?"

"Oh, yes, I represented that area," Goodell said. "And I've been out there at Kennedy Airport many times. It's very noisy. But the issue here is discrimination against one plane."

"Well, were you chosen by France because you're such a good lawyer or because you're a former United States senator with good contacts?" Goodell was asked.

"Oh, I've done a lot of litigation," he said. "I was a litigator before I went to the Senate, you know."

"Did they used to pay you fees as big as this?" he was asked.

"Oh, well. You have to remember, I was in Jamestown," Goodell said.

When she heard this, Mrs. Debbie McGuire of Ninety-sixth Street sniffed. "What do I do, tell you the wrong things?" she said.

I then showed her that the law firm of William Rogers, the former secretary of state in the Nixon administration, received $701,000 from the Concorde.

"Why do you think he got more than Goodell?" I asked Mrs. McGuire.

"Because a secretary of state costs you more," she said. "You won't see either of them in a courtroom. They do all their work out of sight."

This opposition was discussed one afternoon at Lenny's Clam Bar on Cross Bay Boulevard, only yards away from the Kennedy runways. Everybody was eating calamari and scungilli with sauce so hot it caused the mouths to fly open.

"When they try to stick their foot right down your throat, then you got to get up and fight," Ralph Turchio was saying. Ralph Turchio is built like a front end. Once, he was a shoeshine boy; now he has a house that cost him $58,000. What Ralph Turchio would do to defend his $58,000 house is frightening to think about. And now Ralph was saying that noise from the regular jetliners has him crazy, but if they ever let a Concorde fly 200 feet over his house he would be finished. "When that plane flies way up over the ocean, it wakes up the tuna fish," Ralph says.

"When I first moved in here," Turchio was saying, "the plane comes over my house at night and the floodlights come into my room and I could look out and see people in the seats in the plane. I run under the bed. Now what am I supposed to do, let them blow me right out of the house?"

"What do you think of the French argument that they need the Concorde for their economy?" Turchio was asked.

"My money is more important than theirs," he said. "I got an all-electric house. I had to shut down half the house all winter. The kids doubled up. We couldn't afford the electric bills. And I'm supposed to worry about some plane a hundred big shots can ride in? They think we're a bunch of peasants. Hey! We got all the leadership we need to stop them.

"Do you know how I'm living here now? Plane comes in over my house when I'm on the phone, I can't hear a thing. I got to say to the guy, 'Wait a minute.' Now the plane goes by. So I start talking. But now the plane is over the other guy's house. And he has to say to me, 'Wait a minute.' So we wait. Then here comes another plane and we start all over again."

Turchio stood up to leave. "Let's face it," he said, "I never spoke to important people. I got a small business and a house and that's it. But I tell you, the smarter the people I meet on this thing, the dumber they are. They tell me they're going to bank the plane so it won't make noise. Bank it where? On my roof? This house is all I got. The neighborhood is good. You see what's happenin' to the rest of the city. This neighborhood holds up. I got no place else to go. I'm goin' to stay here, and no plane is going to make me move."

When a report of this conversation was printed in my newspaper, read by French consulate people in New York and transmitted to Paris, the reaction from a man as haughty as Giscard d'Estaing was predictable. He went to the NBC cameras in Paris and spoke to reporter Tom Brokaw. "The airport is on the sea and the sea is crowded by fishes, not people," Giscard said with a sneer.

And that morning, in his bedroom in Howard Beach, Ralph Turchio bounced up and down on the edge of his bed.

"What is he, tough?" Ralph shouted.

"Ralph!" his wife, Eleanor, said.

"Ralph nothing!" he said. He made a fist. "Your plane is a dead lox," he yelled to Giscard on television.

"Ralph, you got to go to work," his wife said.

"I'd like to go to work on this guy," Ralph said.

Later that morning, on behalf of Ralph Turchio, I sat in my office on Forty-second Street in Manhattan and called Giscard, whose number in Paris is 261-5100.

First there was a woman who said, "Ooohh."

"I want to speak to President Giscard d'Estaing, he called my people fish," I said to her.

She put me onto a man who said, "Noooooo." I told him the same thing. Then another man came to the phone who gave his name as Monsieur Arnaud.

"I want to speak to Giscard d'Estaing," I said.

"I am speaking to you for him," M. Arnaud said.

"Why did he call us fish?" I said.

"He never said that," M. Arnaud said.

"Yes, he did. I saw it on the television in Ralph Turchio's house this morning."

"That is a distortion. I was there when President Giscard d'Estaing gave his interview to the television. He did not say that."

"I was in Ralph Turchio's bedroom and he said it there."

"But I was directly with President Giscard and he never said that."

"Did he say fish?"

"Yes, but he said that as a joke. That was a joke by the president."

"Joke? Your president has no humor. If he said something, he meant it. And he has all of Howard Beach upset."

"But they cannot be upset. He never said such a thing."

"Do you know what Howard Beach is?"

"Yes, I have heard this name."

"I am glad you know it, because that's the place that's going to put your Concorde plane into a museum. Where is Giscard? I want to tell him this myself."

"He did not say what you say he said."

"What have I got, a drain in my head? Of course he did. Put him on the telephone."

One or two more shouts into the phone and it was over. But it was disturbing. For the last two weeks now, humorless, demanding French and British politicians and technocrats have been all over New York, seeing politicians and businessmen at expensive luncheons. And every place you go in New York you hear that they are nearing success, that Americans in power are going to see to it that people who live around Kennedy Airport are to have no choice but to suffer under more technology.

It was at this point that the French consulate in New York

asked if they could persuade me to see their president's side. I decided to go to France and fight them on their own grounds. For in America, the tactic of the Concorde now was to delay and postpone hearings, as they understood that time goes on and people get tired, but money is patient. Perhaps diligent reporting would speed things up and force politicians to suddenly say, No, the plane won't land and that is all.

And so I sailed for France on the *QE2*. On the first night out, I sat in my stateroom and wrote a column about the trip. As I typed, I read my notes. They were filled with personal insults to Valéry Giscard d'Estaing. I became so angry that I wrote that I not only would see Giscard but that I was challenging him to a duel. I handed my copy to the ship communications officer and relaxed.

A couple of days later, the glasses on the bar were vibrating from the power of the twin screws, directly underneath, that were driving the ship at twenty-eight knots along the edge of the ice fields of the North Atlantic. I stepped outside and looked down. White water boiled up and spread out into the darkness. I came back inside and went to bed. The room was creaking from the motion of the ship. A low, steady, lulling sound.

At Cherbourg, television crews fought with each other for position on the pier.

"You are here to challenge President Giscard d'Estaing to a duel!" the interpreter for a reporter shouted at me.

"Of course," I said. "He insulted me, and everyone else from Howard Beach."

The interpreter chattered my answer in French into the microphones.

"How do you dare such a thing as challenge our president?" an announcer shrieked.

"He insulted me. I shall avenge these insults," I said.

"You would duel our president?"

"And win," I said.

When this was interpreted, the cameramen and soundmen acted as if they wanted to drop their equipment and assault me. Head high, I walked through this crowd of rabble and took the boat train to Paris.

Where, that night, I sat in my hotel room and watched the

evening news on television. The lead story was on my arrival.
I was a thug from Howard Beach, the anchorman announced.
Then I came on. I thought I was beautiful. Right after me was
a series of interviews with politicians who commented on what
I just had said. The politicians went crazy. I fell asleep happy.

In the morning, I went to the Assemblée nationale, a stone
building made dark by the centuries. It was across a bridge
over the Seine. As arranged from New York, a man waited for
me in the foyer of the Assemblée, a foyer of white pillars and
men speaking in the same low tones as are heard in the backs
of storefront political clubhouses back in Queens.

The man clearly found me distasteful. He threw his head in
the direction of the doorway and snarled something and left.

"What did he say?" I asked the interpreter. He refused to
answer. He led the way through a softly lit room with a desk
of polished wood, pushed a door, and stepped into a large barroom which looked onto a garden with gravel paths. The bar
had a marble top and a great copper rail. Six bartenders were
on duty to serve the politicians, who came off the Assemblée
floor to wash the harangue from their throats.

Waiting at the bar was the deputy from Toulouse, where the
Concorde aircraft is assembled. He was a short, stocky man
in an expensive light-blue pinstripe suit. His name was Alex
Raymond and he was agitated.

The interpreter explained my presence and Raymond nodded
several times. "Oward Beach. Oui. Oward Beach. Oui."

Four members who were drinking whisky at the end of the
bar looked around. You are not an unknown in France, from a
railway station bar in Cherbourg to the Assemblée nationale, if
you are from anywhere near Howard Beach. Deputy Raymond,
who has factories of aircraft workers as constituents, cared only
about the Concorde landing in New York. His blue eyes flashed
and his hand waved.

"He says it's not noisier than a Boeing," the interpreter said.
"He said he knows this because he is in the aerospace section
of the Socialist Party."

"Tell him," I said, "that the teachers have to stop when the
regular planes pass over the schools in Howard Beach. The
Concorde will drive them out of the classrooms."

M. Raymond nodded as he heard this. He spoke. Then

the interpreter said, "He said that this is an issue which is not beyond the genius of both countries if they would cooperate to make planes less noisy. But in the meantime, efforts should be directed at not just the French aircraft."

"Tell him the people in Queens say his plane is too noisy for them," I said.

The interpreter said, "He says that the problem really is a rivalry between aircraft companies, between your Boeing and the French company assembling the Concorde."

"Tell him it is a problem of the ear. We don't want to listen to his noise," I said.

The interpreter said, "He says that a friendship binds France and the United States. It is of vital importance to both of us. It is not in the interests of the United States to tarnish the image of Franco-American cooperation."

I said to the interpreter, "Tell him that a study at Queens College shows that the noise of the Concorde makes people impotent."

M. Raymond's eyes widened as he listened to this. His voice barked.

"He says he is most certainly not impotent," the interpreter said.

"Tell him to prove it," I said.

As the interpreter spoke to him again, M. Raymond's mouth opened. The interpreter said to me, "He says not with you."

M. Raymond turned and went to the end of the bar to speak to the other socialists, who drank whisky and glared.

The interpreter said, "It is a problem no one in this chamber can understand. They do not understand why the United States refuses to recognize this step forward that the Concorde represents."

"It isn't the United States stopping the plane, it's Howard Beach," I said, "and everybody's ears hurt. So they're not going to let the plane land. They'll tie up Kennedy Airport on Sundays for a couple of years."

"Here, too, we are très passionnés," the man said.

Deputy Raymond suddenly stepped into the center of the barroom. He held his fists to his chest. Then one hand came out with two fingers raised. Raymond called out something.

The interpreter said, "He said he will show you that he is

not impotent from the Concorde going over his head, that you are to get him two Blue Bell Girls from the Lido and he will show you."

Raymond's chin came out defiantly. He turned around and walked out of the barroom and went back to the floor of the Assemblée nationale.

Later that day, an air attaché from the American embassy arrived at my hotel with a serious air about him. He said that Giscard d'Estaing, enraged, would not see me. Giscard had informed the agency that he was too dignified to speak to this person who dared to challenge him to a duel. Giscard d'Estaing then was caught live on French television saying, "This Breslin is uncouth. He opposes the Concorde because he is jealous of the French."

I again attempted to reach the man by phone. He refused to speak to me. Big shot. I then dropped off a note at the Elysée Palace. In the note I told Giscard that to me and to people in Howard Beach, he was a veal chop.

Now I decided to go home by Concorde plane. Perhaps I could start something by that. What, I didn't know. But I booked a flight for the next day. When I got up that morning, I went to Mass at the Cathedral of Notre Dame, where three old women prayed while the priest said Mass in the morning chill. The Mass was in French, which seemed wrong, for the cathedral demanded a particular richness of language, a unifying connection with the past, in order to remind the one kneeling of his insignificance. On the way out, I mentioned this to the priest. It is not my doing, he said. Then in a café across a bridge, the porter handed me a newspaper, *France Soir*, which had a headline about me over the story carrying Giscard's personal attack:

OPPONENT OF CONCORDE MAKES EVEN MORE NOISE

Right away, for some reason, I knew that something would happen that would make me a huge winner on this trip.

On the way to the airport, we went through Goussainville, which sits in the midst of fields where flowers are raised. The road is narrow and lined with Lombardy poplar trees. In the town, the car barely fit between buildings. A young man and woman strolled along, ripping off pieces from a giant French bread. At a crossing, a man in a sweater with a wicker shopping basket on his arm was asked about the plane. He put the shopping basket on a wall and clapped his hands to his ears. Then we headed for Charles de Gaulle Airport. Coming up the hill to the airport, there was this slim white needle sitting alone out on the tarmac in the pale evening light. In a special, carpeted area of the departure terminal a bartender served somber-eyed, deep-voiced, chuckling businessmen as they waited for the Concorde.

Which took off on time, with a roar inside the cabin, but only the suggestion of the noise exploding in the air outside. The money inside was, as always, well protected. I thought of Frankie Busycorner in Howard Beach, whose backyard, made entirely of marble, is cracking from the noise of regular jet planes.

Somewhere over the Atlantic, more than fifty thousand feet up, with all of us strapped into this flying bullet, the Concorde acted as if it had been punched in the nose. The plane shook. Five, six, seven times. That was it. An air pocket, I figured. Then there was a vibration as the plane suddenly began to slow down. The computer screen showing the air speed began to blink backward and the supersonic numbers descended to old-fashioned figures: five hundred miles an hour instead of fifteen hundred.

Apparently, one of the engines had started to rock off, or the wings started to drop off, who knows what it was. But here was the pilot announcing, "We are going to land first at Halifax, Nova Scotia. It is one hour and thirty-two minutes to Halifax."

Many people groaned in disappointment. But a man in back, who had looked out his small window and seen something happen to one of the engines, like the thing blew up a little, was biting his lip.

The pilot now said, "It is one hour and eighteen minutes to Halifax."

A short time later, he said, "It is one hour to Halifax."

I said to myself, The pilot in the cockpit is praying that we make it.

At Halifax, the plane came in low over snow and onto an airport that was crowded with emergency trucks lining the runway, their roof lights twirling, and behind them, what seemed to be every Boy Scout, policeman, and hospital worker in Nova Scotia. They stood in the winter air, ready for an international tragedy, and the Concorde bumped down and then used all but a few yards of the runway before it could be stopped.

I got off the plane and went to the bar for a beer. Standing there, over the next five hours, I saw television all over America carrying reports of the plane's accident, and shaken Frenchmen saying to the cameras, Oh, but this is the first time anything like this ever has happened. The embarrassment over the accident spread like the noise the plane makes.

And now this feeling I had earlier, that I would win, was overpowering. That punch in the nose the Concorde took up in the sky was going to last a long time. I went to the phone and called Ralph Turchio in Howard Beach.

"You can forget the Concorde," I said.

"You think so?" he said.

"They'll get over today," I said. "They'll keep a plane or two going around, but they'll never sell the fleets of them they were counting on. They'll go broke with the thing. Put that down," I told him. I went back to the bar and felt terrific.

January 1978

Bella Was Old Hat

AT NOON on Tuesday, Vincent F. Albano, Jr., the Manhattan Republican leader, watched some absentee ballots being counted in Peter Cooper Village on the East Side. There were twenty-eight votes for Bill Green and eight votes for Bella Abzug in the special election for Congress. Albano mumbled something.

"What's that?" a guy with him said.

"I said, I got something going for me," Albano said.

He was on the streets working in elections when he was twelve years old, Vince Albano was, and now, fifty-five years later, he only had to look at a few numbers.

At night, twenty minutes after the polls closed, Albano sat in his office at the Roosevelt Hotel, the radio on, phones ringing. On the radio, the newscaster was conceding the election to Bella Abzug. With 12 percent of the vote in, he said, Bella was so far ahead that we could be expecting her victory statement quite soon.

On the telephone, one of Albano's captains, Joy Tannenbaum, was calling in the arithmetic from the 63rd Election District of the 65th Assembly District.

"Green two sixteen, Abzug ninety-three," she said.

"I love you," Vince said.

"It's terrific, isn't it?" Joy Tannenbaum said.

"I love you," Vince said.

Albano hung up the phone. "We pulled it out," he told everybody in the room.

An hour or so later, the broadcasters started to catch up with his figures.

And, in the morning, the national newscasts were saying that a Republican won a congressional seat in New York and that to do it he had to upset Bella Abzug. The Republican win was spoken of as perhaps the start of a swing around the country. Which could be good for Albano, who has a candidate for governor. But the more important part of the story was that Abzug, by losing, seemed to reveal the weakness of the women's movement.

As Gloria Steinem said after the count, "We no longer can depend on the electoral system. The street is the only place for our movement."

The mathematics seems to support her. In the medieval year of 1962, there were eighteen women in the House of Representatives and two women in the Senate. Now, after the tumult of the late sixties, after the awakening, the raising, and pushing, there are eighteen women in the House and one senator, Muriel Humphrey, who is there on a maneuver we once thought was reserved only for backward Southerners; the wife taking the husband's seat. This tawdriness is nearly enough to force you to recall Hubert Humphrey's cheerleading during the Vietnam war.

"The figures in state legislatures are discouraging too," Gloria Steinem was saying. "Eighty percent of the women elected are from the opposition party, which means that nobody thought they had a chance to win. If an election seems winnable, the man is the candidate. The average age of a woman in the state legislature is much higher than that of a man. The legislature is a woman's ultimate reward for years of civic work, while the male politician normally starts out on his career in this job."

The Equal Rights Amendment, which has been thrown out of many state houses as if it were a disease carrier, appears as more evidence. Yesterday, an intern named Barbara Smith at the National Women's Political Caucus said gloomily, while compiling statistics, "Much of the language used by people against the ERA is the same as was used against women's suffrage. What do we hear? 'Vulgarizing the image of women. Robbing women of their inherent privileges.' These are right out of textbooks about women's suffrage. Nothing ever changes."

So on Tuesday night, when its greatest figure, Bella Abzug, went down to an astonishing upset, the women's movement seemed, to many inside it, to be floundering desperately. Male prejudice has triumphed as surely and as easily as it did when the Iroquois were in charge.

Perhaps not. For Bella Abzug's loss also could be seen as an example that being a woman is not enough to win a national office.

Last week when she could have been on the streets of the district campaigning, Bella Abzug went to Washington and dropped into the office of House Speaker Tip O'Neill. She discussed committee assignments she might be able to get. Bella was uncertain of exactly which committee she wanted to be on, so O'Neill caused the postponement of a meeting of the House Steering Committee, which assigns committee jobs. The Steering Committee was to have met today. Bella did not think she would have her mind made up by this point.

While she was in O'Neill's office, Bella also brought up the number of table reservations she would need in the House dining room for people attending her swearing-in.

Then she came back to Manhattan and she lost.

There might have been reasons other than overconfidence for Bella's defeat. There has come to be a tired quality to Bella's pushiness; even her hats seem boring. Perhaps the real trouble is that she has been in an election or so too many.

Therefore, her loss could have nothing to do with the strength of the women's movement. For on election day, the same day the great woman figure lost, the New York State Court of Appeals, conservative and sluggish, held that a divorced woman can live with another man and still collect alimony from her ex-husband. This is about the largest crack so far in the thick wall of double standards behind which all men live. The climate is being set for women to begin living the same lives, including cheating, that men do.

A political election is much less of an indicator than it is supposed to be. Abzug loses. But talk to your daughter: the past is over. The reason the women's movement has trouble making its expected indent on politics is that the movement is too new, the people in it too young. Politics is, like croquet, a sport for the old. The males who dominate it are either white-haired or bald. The bellies protrude, the eyes weaken, the faces grow flush from even a flight of stairs. A touch of emphysema is the badge of a great political pro.

The women's movement, then, will begin to make it big in politics only when its leaders are a lot of old ladies who have been on ballots for about a half century.

The case of James Earl Carter, Jr., seems to be a contradiction. It is not. Carter is a smart technician who spotted a flaw in the Democrats' system of nominating a president and he took advantage of it and won. Won resoundingly. Terrific.

Good for Jimmy. And then he went to Washington with all his bright people around him, his new faces in town, and they all strode briskly past the old heads of Washington politics. And the old heads looked up and gave a little nod. They had seen it all before. And then one day Carter's best friend, his great new face in Washington, Bert Lance, came into the Oval Office wailing. A bear trap hung from Lance's ankle.

White House rudeness turned to apology, independence into reliance. And Carter, the brilliant technician of primary elections, turns out to be an aimless guy whose latest decision, selling planes to the Arabs and Israelis so they both can be a bit more certain that they are able to kill each other, is a classic.

The Abzug election, then, has nothing to do with either the end or the slowing of the women's movement. It has to do only with the slowest part of life, politics. Nobody suggests that slowness is a sign of health: inability to change is the reason for all the trouble in the country. If a system of old men will not make room for women except over decades, then how long must we wait until blacks get an even chance?

So that election in Manhattan on Tuesday was less significant than women yesterday were saying it was. The movement will make it in politics. Only when it does, the women will be gray-headed and able to tell stories from a lot of years back. Certainly, it's lousy. It has to be. It's politics.

February 16, 1978

Un Occhio's Portrait with a Singer

I N THE summer of 1977, Un Occhio, or One Eye, the leader of all organized crime in New York, and thus the nation, arrived at the Westchester Premier Theatre for a concert by Frank Sinatra. Federal agents and New York City police in the audience were surprised to see Un Occhio, who rarely makes an appearance in public.

With Un Occhio was a slim young man named Polo the Artist. Polo jiggled while he stood and wriggled when he sat. Polo was in that half-place where fear and hunger mix and a man is forced to decide whether a meal is worth risking his life. Polo carried with him a large artist's pad. His pockets were full of charcoal. Polo was going to make a charcoal drawing of Frank Sinatra and Un Occhio after the concert.

A year before, Don Carlo Gambino had gone to the Westchester Premier Theatre and had his picture taken with Sinatra. Un Occhio had disdain for this. Pizza stands have pictures of people with singers. Un Occhio would have an oil portrait of himself and Frank Sinatra. Polo the Artist, his hunger greater than his sense of self-preservation, had agreed to do the portrait.

Polo the Artist had wanted to bring a camera and take a couple of pictures of Sinatra and Un Occhio and use the pictures as he did his portrait. Un Occhio became angry when he heard of this. "No camera," Un Occhio snarled. What was this artist speaking to him of cameras? The police use a camera. Old has-beens like Gambino use cameras. Did not this artist know that he, the artist, was allowed to be in such important company only because Gambino had used a camera and that Un Occhio always must be better than Gambino?

Anger rays came from Un Occhio's body. When Polo the Artist felt them, he said, "I am going to smash every camera I see in this place tonight."

When Sinatra came out to sing, Polo opened his pad and began to chalk in some of Sinatra. Suddenly, Polo's hand was on fire. He had to bite his lip in order to prevent himself from crying out.

Un Occhio, who wears as a ring a metal cutter that newsboys

use to open wired-up newspaper bundles, had brought his ring hand down on Polo the Artist's hand. The wire cutter had taken a bite out of the hand.

"No picture without Un Occhio!" the old man warned.

At the end of the show, Polo was taken backstage and thrown into a jammed hallway. By peering around the shoving mob, he could see Sinatra, who was standing in the doorway to his dressing room. Suddenly, Un Occhio was alongside Sinatra. Un Occhio's wrinkled face attempted to smile, but the man has done this so little in his life that it goes against the lines of his face and makes him appear cockeyed. But the ceaseless glare from Un Occhio's good eye, the right eye, caused Polo's knees to buckle. He never had seen such true evil in his life.

With all the shoving and noise distracting him, Polo tried desperately to capture Sinatra and Un Occhio together and his charcoal worked furiously. But then, when he raised his head, he saw that it was over. And there was Un Occhio saying to him, "Now we go home."

It is known that Un Occhio took Polo into the living room and pointed up to the great cathedral ceiling, three floors up.

"Make a mural," Un Occhio told Polo.

Un Occhio then produced for Polo a copy of a portrait of Enrico Caruso. He wanted the mural to have Caruso and Sinatra, as lesser persons of course, and Un Occhio in the middle, with a glow spreading from his entire body, not just from the top of the head, as they do with the saints in church.

The next day groups of workmen went in and out of Un Occhio's house. They were erecting a scaffold for Polo the Artist to work on. Polo the Artist climbed up the scaffolding and began the job of sanding down the marble ceiling to give it some tooth. Then Polo the Artist put on the first of four coats of prime. When he was finished, he decided to climb down and relax while the paint dried.

Polo the Artist was halfway down when he heard the growl. It was Un Occhio's dog. Un Occhio tells people the dog is a husky, but it really is a timber wolf. Polo the Artist stared at the wolf. Two slanty eyes looked back. Polo decided to test the wolf. He came down and put one foot toward the floor.

Soundlessly, the wolf came into the air. Polo the Artist was not quick enough pulling the foot up. The wolf caught the heel. His fang went right through the Cuban heel and gave the bottom of Polo the Artist's foot a slight tickle.

A few minutes later, Un Occhio came into the room. He patted the wolf. "Hey!" he called up to Polo the Artist. Then he tossed Polo a bottle of iodine. With the wolf standing guard, Polo the Artist stayed on the scaffolding for two days until the ceiling was primed with four coats and was ready to take the great masterpiece of Un Occhio, Sinatra, and Caruso.

To do the painting, Polo worked off the Caruso print and his meager charcoal of Sinatra. But to capture Un Occhio's face, which looks like an old time bomb, Polo the Artist needed a sitting by Un Occhio.

He explained to Un Occhio that he could not work well unless he had the most even light, north light, and in Un Occhio's house this was present only in the early morning. At quarter past seven the next morning, Un Occhio appeared on the living-room balcony dressed in the suit he wore to Tommy Brown's funeral.

"You paint," Un Occhio said.

Polo the Artist began to work. After ten minutes, Un Occhio's voice ruptured Polo's concentration. "You stop painting," Un Occhio said. Un Occhio began to scratch his thigh.

Everybody agrees that it went like this for the next two years. Polo the Artist tried to paint and Un Occhio would be digging at himself like a monkey. Some say that Polo the Artist was allowed to come off the scaffolding at night. Others insist that Polo lived on the boards for the entire time, and that the wolf was taken out of the room and Polo allowed to come down only for washups and, on two occasions, to combat influenza.

At the end, Polo climbed down and Un Occhio came in and stood alongside him and they both stared up at this great masterpiece on the ceiling. Polo the Artist had a bottle of wine. As he swallowed it, he became giddy. I have duplicated Saint Peter's, he told himself.

Un Occhio loved it at first glance. Here on the left was a subdued Caruso, looking respectfully at Un Occhio, who was in the middle and looked like an angry deity. And on the right was a filmy Sinatra. Un Occhio's eye snapped back to Sinatra. Frank Sinatra was looking straight ahead. He was not gazing respectfully at Un Occhio!

Un Occhio snarled. Did Polo see him as somebody like Gambino, who appears in a picture with Sinatra and does not even have Sinatra looking at him? Polo the Artist, his brain paralyzed by wine, disagreed. He did more than disagree, apparently. Some people say that Polo exploded.

Authorities differ on what happened after that. A woman on Pleasant Avenue says she heard a noise in the middle of the night coming from Un Occhio's candy store. The noise reminded her of an oven door slamming. Then a man who was out walking his dog on the East River Drive says that on the same night he saw three men throw what seemed to be a large object, the size of a body, into the water. Authorities think the stories could be conflicting. Their theory is that if Polo the Artist was burned up in Un Occhio's oven, how could there be so much of him left to throw into the river?

After all, detectives agreed, ashes usually can be put in a small urn.

Authorities do agree, however, that Polo the Artist is not anymore.

The other day, Un Occhio was followed downtown, where he was met by three burly men who kissed Un Occhio on the hand and then led him upstairs to a loft that is rented by a young artist.

December 28, 1978

They Always Shoot the Young

JERUSALEM—A panel in the large wooden door opened and the face of a young man appeared. "What it is you want?" he said.

"To come in," he was told.

"Nobody is allowed to wait inside," the young man said. "This is the rule of the hospital. Today is very bad. Everyone must wait outside. Don't you see that the other people are doing this?" The women sat on the steps of the hospital at Ramallah, a Palestinian town on the West Bank, and the men were up on a wall at the end of the building.

"Do you have a person named El Huj in there?" the young man was asked. El Huj was one of four university students shot by Israeli troops during a Palestinian demonstration the day before.

"Oh. That is a different matter." He opened the door and told us to wait while he went upstairs and brought down a young doctor.

"You cannot see him, but he is all right, I think."

"The bullet came in from the back and came out the front."

"He was shot in the back?" a woman said.

"The entrance of the wound is from the back," the doctor said again. "He is sixteen. That is what helped him."

A few blocks away, truck tires had been thrown in the middle of Ramallah's main street and set afire, to both block traffic and announce, by the black smoke rising over the street, that anyone who wished to cause trouble and throw stones at the soldiers should hurry to the place where the smoke was coming from.

The ones throwing the burning tires into the street were in their late teens and early twenties. They were followed by packs of small children. There is a general strike of Palestinian people on the West Bank to protest the peace talks. The military commander then closed all the schools. The streets and alleys of Ramallah were crowded with children all day. If you stood on a street corner for more than a few moments, you became surrounded by children and had to walk in half steps.

Wherever there are Arabs, the numbers stun. In Cairo, after walking the streets and alleys for a couple of days, I fell asleep at night with waves of people coming at me. There are so many people there that the official census figure has to be picked from the sky. And it is similar in these Arab places outside of Jerusalem. There is no pill, and abortion is a word used by university women. And in the alleys there are only small children bumping into your legs as you walk, so many children bumping that you still feel them hours later. The figure is 3 million Palestinians in the Middle East. I hope nobody has to feed the numbers over 3 million.

One of the older boys in the street in Ramallah crouched down and peered through the black smoke and saw an Israeli armored personnel carrier turn the corner. The older boy began to run and everybody followed him, spilling down alleys and across lots where goats grazed.

The armored personnel carrier rolled down the street without stopping. The Israeli soldiers held up automatic weapons and watched fiercely for any sudden motions. After the vehicle went by, the smallest boys rushed out of the alleys and jeered the Israelis.

This was on the day that Jimmy Carter trudged to his diplomatic success in getting Egypt and Israel to agree that their future is not in bleeding. It is a treaty that mentions the Palestinians with words such as linkage and autonomy. But no Israeli leader ever will allow the Palestinians to have a country of their own on Israel's border. And the Palestinian millions appear to be led by Arafat, a terrorist, and he demands land for a country, that vague word in a treaty. So peace is something that Israel probably still must scratch out of the years to come. The great danger, Egypt, has been removed. But the Palestinians remain. Yesterday, the West Bank was heavily patrolled by Israelis, and in the north, artillery fired at Palestine Liberation Organization rocket bases in Lebanon.

"We are only beginning to gather strength," Ramondo Tawhil was saying in the living room of her house in a comfortable residential part of Ramallah. Ramondo is considered the voice of the PLO in the district. She has all the prerequisites of a revolutionary: a banker husband, a daughter in medical school, a son in engineering school, and rhetoric for any occasion.

"There were four boys shot yesterday, not three," she said. "Someday the bullet of the oppression will melt to water in the face of the resistance."

She patted the midsection of a figure that many say causes as much trouble among Arabs as oil. "I must diet," she said. "The best diet is to be in jail. I lost eleven kilos [about twenty-four pounds] in jail last year. I am under house arrest now. If I go out of the house, they claim I am inciting. They will put me in jail. It might be good for my diet. No, I have been last year in jail. Once is enough."

"Have you spoken to Arafat about the peace treaty?" she was asked.

"Why me? It is Carter who should speak to Arafat. Carter should look at Iran and then he would know he should speak to Arafat. Your Mr. Carter, the prophet, should go directly to Arafat. He speaks for all Palestinians."

Which was not thoroughly accurate. Sometimes, the Palestinians do not talk to themselves. Later in the day, in Bethlehem, which was a grim town, with soldiers standing on rooftops in the rain and truckloads of troops at roadblocks, the home of the former mayor of the city was pointed out as an illustration of the troubles among Palestinians.

The Palestinian Christians who live in the town of Bethlehem do not speak to the Palestinian Muslims who live in the refugee camp at Bethlehem. The former mayor, Bandak, a Christian, went beyond this; his animosity toward the Muslims was extraordinary and the Muslims were always eager to return it. Bandak then stole much money as mayor and bought land directly across the street from the entrance to the refugee camp. He built an expensive stone house and atop the house placed a high television tower. Running down the tower, in the kind of letters used to advertise cigarettes, is the name "Bandak." Across the street in the refugee camp, every time a Muslim raises his head he must see Bandak's name. Then, when he left office, Bandak had the city council name the street in front of the refugee camp "Bandak Street." Each time a Muslim leaves the refugee camp, he spits at the sign that says he lives on Bandak Street.

The Bethlehem refugee camp is an old one. The Israelis have provided electricity and water, and most of the men in the camp work at jobs in Israel at Israeli pay. So the conditions of the camp are better than usual and Israel receives credit for the manner in which it handles the camp. But Israel cannot take care of the millions of other Palestinians, and at the same time the Palestinians don't want Israel around them, even if Israel is making sure they have light and can eat.

An old man sat at a table in a hut in the camp where he sells note pads and candy bars. He said his name was Muhammad Abdullah, and when asked for his age, he wrote the number thirty-seven. The number sixty-two was jotted down and shown to him. He shook his head and printed out forty-two. When the figure eighty-four was printed in retaliation, Abdullah became angry and wrote down the number fifty-eight. Finally, after fifteen minutes of bargaining, he admitted to being seventy-one.

When he was asked about the peace treaty, he shook his head. "We are no peace treaty. We are Palestinians. We must wait and we will get our peace."

March 14, 1979

Thousands of People Are Dying to Live in New York

THE FIRST person murdered in New York in 1980 turns out to be Salvadore Vargas, 36, of Fourth Ave., Brooklyn, who was shot at about 8 P.M. on New Year's Eve and then took so long to die that he tumbled clear out of the 1979 statistics and onto the top of the list of 1980. Vargas died at 1 A.M. on New Year's Day, a clear two hours ahead of the next victim.

Statisticians, however, were fighting over Vargas yesterday. I don't know why; Vargas certainly was not needed so desperately for the 1979 figures. In New York last year, there were 1,733 murders. These are the most murders committed in any city in the world at any time, outside of some place like Hue in 1968, where they used gunships to get up the numbers.

Nor was Vargas required to make our murder figures for the first day of 1980 seem impressive. Here in New York on New Year's Day, amidst our grandeur, our mansions in the sky, why, right in the center of our absolute renaissance, we killed 13 people; shot them, stabbed them, strangled them, did everything but chew them to death.

Of all the murders, however, Vargas' was the most controversial. At about 8 P.M. on New Year's Eve, Vargas came running down Washington Ave. in Brooklyn from the general direction of a bar called Reggie's Place. As fast as Vargas ran, he did not go faster than the man behind him. This man carried a gun. He caught up with Vargas in front of a tailor shop at 702 Washington Ave. The man shot Vargas in the head. Vargas fell on his face under a car. His feet were on the curb.

Vargas was alive when taken to Kings County Hospital and the 13th Homicide was called. The case fell to Detective Bob Jones. As Vargas was still alive in the evening, Jones listed the case as an assault. There were about 27,000 assaults in New York last year; the exact figures have not yet been compiled.

As the New Year began, Vargas died. However, when the police called the hospital in the morning, an administrator said, "Vargas is in the operating room."

"How can he be in the operating room when he's on a slab in the morgue?" a detective said.

"I have him in the operating room," the hospital administrator said.

"Then you better go into the operating room and get your doctor off the table, because he's the only one who could be on it; Vargas is in your morgue."

"Well, I have to find that out," the administrator said. He still was listing Vargas officially as an assault case. A short time later, the administrator called the 13th Homicide and said, yes, Vargas most certainly was in the morgue; he now was to be listed as a murder victim.

In the 13th Homicide, Detective Jones then blotted out Vargas as an assault victim in 1979 and put him in the murder column for 1980. The mayor and police commissioner now can proudly claim that assaults are down by one in the city for 1979.

But there still was a question about this record keeping and Jones and the other men of the 13th were debating that yesterday morning.

"In basketball," they were told, "if a man releases a shot before the final buzzer, and the shot is in the air and then it goes into the basket, that basket counts. Now, Vargas was shot in 1979. He was put in the air, so to speak. He remained there right through the final buzzer for 1979. Then, after the buzzer, he died. Doesn't that mean that Vargas was actually a 1979 murder?"

"Good question," one of the detectives said.

"Well, look at the sheet here," another said. "See this? They got him listed as Detective Squad Case No. 232. That's the last number we used for 1979." He pointed to another number. "And here, U.F. 61, No. 16261, that's a '79 number, too."

Jones, the detective in charge of the case, listened to this. Then he said, "No, I had him listed as an assault in 1979. Then, when he died, I listed it as a homicide. That was on New Year's Day. So that makes him a 1980 homicide." I accepted this as the official ruling on the matter.

I also came upon a sheet that showed that Mr. Vargas had almost become a vital statistic last June. He was shot in the stomach in front of a club on Myrtle Ave. and was taken to

Cumberland Hospital. When Vargas woke up, he saw a detective at his bedside.

"What do you want?" Vargas said.

"I'm from Homicide," the detective said.

"What do I need you for, I'm alive," Vargas said.

"I want to know who shot you," the detective said.

"Don't bother me, I'll take care of this myself," Vargas said. "I'm alive, so I'm not telling you anything."

I grabbed this report and sat down at a typewriter and began to copy it off. It was early in the morning, before the day shift for the 13th Homicide came in. While I was typing, the sergeant, Alongi, came in to start his day's work.

"Nice day yesterday?" somebody asked him.

"Nice day," he said. "I took down the Christmas tree. Always do that first of the year."

Then Alongi saw me copying the report. "Who gave you that?" he said.

"Nobody gave me nothing," I said.

This made Alongi mad because I was using Vargas' language on him.

"You're not supposed to have any report on Vargas," Alongi said.

"He's a very famous man," I said.

Alongi grabbed the report from the desk I was using. "Who are you to come in here and take this report on Vargas?" he snapped. He walked into his office and sat there pouting.

I thought that he was mad at me because I was copying down exactly how the detective typed out the interview last June with Vargas. The detective typed out Vargas' statement this way: "I was walking down Myrtle Ave. toward DeKalb and then I was going home. As I was passing the club at 336 Myrtle Ave. *their* was a fight going on . . ."

Maybe, I thought, Alongi figured that I would put down, smart-guy style, about how the detective used "their" when it should have been "there." That shows you how much Alongi knows about the world. For if he knew how well newspaper people know how to spell, then he'd realize that newspaper people don't have the license to look down on anybody in spelling. Across the Daily News newspaper copy desk the other day came a lead sentence saying, "This agreement *flys* in the face of . . ."

So I said to myself, while I was sitting at the desk and listening to Alongi yell at me, that I would get even with this Alongi. I would go back to my office and write in the newspaper that Alongi is built like a pot roast and he isn't in good enough shape to work on any police department supported by public taxes.

But when I got back to Manhattan, I forgot all about this. For our Law and Order Mayor, Koch the Mayor, was in the midst of taking his usual direct, forceful action. He collects a paycheck from a city that has just set the all-time world record for murdering inhabitants. And Koch was proudly saying at City Hall that he was requesting the State Legislature to pass a law making it a greater crime for a citizen to assault a public official than to assault an ordinary fellow. This came because Koch, in one of his usual chin-out, bait-them periods, had a tussle with a doctor on the stage at the Hilton Hotel. After the thing was over, Koch announced that he had had the urge to kill the doctor.

January 3, 1980

For the Love of a Thief

HER NAME is Joan and her nationality is thief. She is dark-haired, exciting, and thoroughly believable.

When she told an old lady in Central Park that she had just found all this money on the walk, the old lady immediately said, "Did you? What are you going to do with it?"

"I'm going to give the money back and get a big reward," Joan said.

"Isn't that wonderful," the old lady said.

"Do you want to get some of the big reward with me?" Joan asked.

Of course the old lady wanted some of the reward. And of course before the week was over, Joan had taken the old lady for $10,000 and the old lady, wailing, was in a police station identifying a picture of Joan.

The old lady, Klein the Lawyer decided, was a greedy old thief herself, one too ignorant to figure out any decent larceny on her own, and therefore her attempt to join in Joan's reward plan brought her exactly what she deserved. Klein the Lawyer formed his opinion when he was called in by Joan's friends to be Joan's lawyer. However, if Klein the Lawyer announced that the old lady was a greedy thief, he would be admitting that his client, Joan, had been doing something wrong too.

Bail was set at $4500. As none of Joan's people came forward with any money—thieves are always broke, which is why they steal—Joan was sent to Rikers Island. Leaving the court, Klein the Lawyer muttered, "If she can't make bail, how can she do something more important, pay me?"

At 6:00 A.M. the next day, he left his bedroom without making a sound. Recently, his woman friend, or second or third wife, or whatever the legal standing is this time, Rosalie, moved into Klein's apartment. When she moved in, she brought her dog with her. The next week, an aunt arrived. Now Klein the Lawyer tiptoed past Rosalie, past the aunt's door, and stepped over the sleeping dog. He did not do this because he is so considerate. He did this because he has decided that he is irritated with Rosalie, hates her aunt, and wants the dog killed.

374

As he was closing the door, Rosalie's sleepy voice called out, "Now it's all right with the party?"

"Do what you want," Klein said. He neither knew nor cared what she was talking about. His mind was on business. By eight-thirty, he was at the women's jail at Rikers Island to talk to his client, Joan, about money. She came into the room in a drab smock and sad face. A beautiful sad face. She took Klein's hand and looked into his eyes and said, "Thank you for coming to save me."

Klein the Lawyer has fallen in love in many places. At the bar watching the Super Bowl; in a dry-cleaning store; in the elevator of his apartment house. This was the first time he ever had fallen in love in a jailhouse.

Joan handed him a bankbook with withdrawal slips made out. "Go to the bank and get all this money and take out your fee and then put up my bail and tonight we will be together someplace," Joan said.

Klein the Lawyer never looked at the bankbook. His eyes remained on Joan.

Later, at a bank in the Bronx, a teller smirked at Joan's bankbook. "She's got eighteen dollars in the account," the teller said.

This woman is trying to make a fool of me, Klein told himself. She doesn't know what she is up against this time.

He drove back to jail, waited an hour for his client to be produced, and had a growl in his throat when she walked in. Joan walked over to Klein and brushed her lips against his.

"I'm sorry I failed and didn't get the money," Klein said.

"Somebody must have forged my name at the bank," Joan said. "Go to my uncle's house tonight. He'll put up all the money we need."

Some hours later, the uncle stood in his doorway and said, "I don't even want to hear her name."

"Her name is Beautiful Joan," Klein the Lawyer said.

At Rikers Island the next day, Joan told Klein the Lawyer, "If you can get me out of here, we'll be together forever."

Klein brought forth all of his instinct and training to solve the matter. All of his life, Klein had seen true love separated by prison bars and he felt it terribly sad, but now that it was his love that was being denied by prison bars, he felt the true agony of such a situation.

And he went to court, in a smashing new suit and with long hours of preparation behind him. He confronted the old lady. Klein looked down at his notes. The detective, hired for considerable money out of Klein's pocket, had done a beautiful job of looking into the background of this greedy old lady.

"How long did you have the money that you say you lost?" Klein asked.

"My husband left it to me," she said, in her best old-lady weak voice.

"I understand your husband was in the banking business," Klein said.

"The trucking business," she said.

"Is a term that your husband always used to use, 'six for five,' part of the trucking business or the banking business?" Klein asked.

The greedy old lady said, "I don't think I lost ten thousand dollars. Maybe it was only a thousand."

No Roman conqueror ever strode through public halls as did Klein the Lawyer as he took Beautiful Joan out of the courthouse and to her freedom in the early evening. She kissed him on the steps. She said she was going home to change and that she would expect Klein at 8:30 P.M. She kissed him again. Klein's heart soared. What did it matter that he wasn't being paid? He was in love. He headed for his apartment. His effort had left him wringing wet and he wanted to change clothes.

When he stepped into his apartment he thought he was getting on a subway train. There in the living room was Rosalie, her aunt, her mother and father, her dog, and nearly everybody whom Klein the Lawyer ever had known on Queens Boulevard.

"What's this?" Klein said.

"The housewarming party for our apartment together," Rosalie said. "I told you about it twenty times." She guided him toward the kitchen. "You're in charge of making the drinks."

Later that night, Klein the Lawyer, an island of silence in a loud room, stood at the picture window of his living room and stared down at the lights of Queens Boulevard. After a while, bars appeared in the window.

"I get her out of jail and I wind up in jail myself," Klein the Lawyer said. He stood at the window and drank until it didn't matter where he was.

May 11, 1980

"Are You John Lennon?"

Writer's note for this book: I was home in bed in Forest Hills, Queens, at 11:20 p.m. when the phone and television at once said Lennon was shot. I was dressed and into Manhattan, to Roosevelt Hospital, the Dakota, up to the precinct, grabbed a cop inside, back to the Dakota, grabbed a cop outside, and to the Daily News. *I wrote this column and it made a 1:30 A.M. deadline. I don't think there is anybody else who can do this kind of work this quickly.*

I particularly like the mistake in it. Moran from Williams Avenue in the Bronx. It is Willis Avenue.

As I can't use a terminal—the keys don't make the noise I need and require too light a touch for me to make them work—a desk clerk put my typewritten copy into the terminal. He made the Williams Avenue error. I sure as hell know Willis Avenue, having had a drink in every bar there when it was Irish and having centered a whole novel on the street now that it is Puerto Rican. The mistake and the reasons for it are testimony to the speed with which it was done.

THAT SUMMER in Breezy Point, when he was eighteen and out of Madison High in Brooklyn, there was the Beatles on the radio at the beach through the hot days and on the jukebox through the nights in the Sugar Bowl and Kennedys. He was young and he let his hair grow and there were girls and it was the important part of life.

Last year, Tony Palma even went to see *Beatlemania*.

And now, last night, a thirty-four-year-old man, he sat in a patrol car at Eighty-second Street and Columbus Avenue and the call came over the radio: "Man shot, One West Seventy-second Street."

Palma and his partner, Herb Frauenberger, rushed through the Manhattan streets to an address they knew as one of the most famous living places in the country, the Dakota apartments.

Another patrol car was there ahead of them, and as Palma got out he saw the officers had a man up against the building and were handcuffing him.

"Where's the guy shot?" Palma said.

"In the back," one of the cops said.

Palma went through the gates into the Dakota courtyard and up into the office, where a guy in a red shirt and jeans was on his face on the floor. Palma rolled the guy over. Blood was coming out of the mouth and covering the face. The chest was wet with blood.

Palma took the arms and Frauenberger took the legs. They carried the guy out to the street. Somebody told them to put the body in another patrol car.

Jim Moran's patrol car was waiting. Moran is from the South Bronx, from Williams Avenue, and he was brought up on Tony Bennett records in the jukeboxes. When he became a cop in 1964, he was put on patrol guarding the Beatles at their hotel. Girls screamed and pushed and Moran laughed. Once, it was all fun.

Now responding to the call, "Man shot, One West Seventy-second," Jim Moran, a forty-five-year-old policeman, pulled up in front of the Dakota and Tony Palma and Herb Frauenberger put this guy with blood all over him in the backseat.

As Moran started driving away, he heard people in the street shouting, "That's John Lennon!"

Moran was driving with Bill Gamble. As they went through the streets to Roosevelt Hospital, Moran looked in the backseat and said, "Are you John Lennon?" The guy in the back nodded and groaned.

Back on Seventy-second Street, somebody told Palma, "Take the woman." And a shaking woman, another victim's wife, crumpled into the backseat as Palma started for Roosevelt Hospital. She said nothing to the two cops and they said nothing to her. Homicide is not a talking matter.

Jim Moran, with John Lennon in the backseat, was on the radio as he drove to the hospital. "Have paramedics meet us at the emergency entrance," he called. When he pulled up to the hospital, they were waiting for him with a cart. As Lennon was being wheeled through the doors into the emergency room, the doctors were on him.

"John Lennon," somebody said.

"Yes, it is," Moran said.

Now Tony Palma pulled up to the emergency entrance. He

let the woman out and she ran to the doors. Somebody called to Palma, "That's Yoko Ono."

"Yeah?" Palma said.

"They just took John Lennon in," the guy said.

Palma walked into the emergency room. Moran was there already. The doctors had John Lennon on a table in a trauma room, working on the chest, inserting tubes.

Tony Palma said to himself, I don't think so. Moran shook his head. He thought about his two kids, who know every one of the Beatles' big tunes. And Jim Moran and Tony Palma, older now, cops in a world with no fun, stood in the emergency room as John Lennon, whose music they knew, whose music was known everywhere on earth, became another person who died after being shot with a gun on the streets of New York.

December 9, 1980

Society Carey

THERE ARRIVED in this office yesterday, and thus prominently, this message that came whizzing through the communications satellite and joined the flood of worldwide news:

CABLES
H (CAREY) DRYDENS 08200: ELEVEN-PERSON CAREY GROUP ARRIVED HERE HONGKONG SATURDAY EVENING FROM TOKYO. DUE LUNAR NEW YEAR'S HOLIDAYS NIGHTCLUBS ETC CLOSED UNTIL TODAY. CAREY STAYING AMERICAN INTERNATIONAL UNDERWRITERS' GUEST HOUSE AND MOST OTHERS AT MANDARIN HOTEL. (ABOUT DLRS 80 MINIMUM.) PLANNED MEETINGS TODAY LEAVE TUESDAY ABOUT NOON. TOKYO ANSWER SEPARATELY. RGDS. ANDERSON-HKG UPI.

Beautiful. We in New York are privileged to have the most marvelous representation by the government for which we pay. Let these other states have governors who slobber around state fairs and supermarket openings. Look at Connecticut. The governor who just died, Ella Grasso, was a dear woman, but she sold the state plane and helicopter and drove around in a Citation. Our governor in New York is different. Our governor is Society Carey. For the last several days, Society Carey and a party of ten, paid for by tax funds out of the money you work for each week, have been sweeping across the Orient.

The object of the trip is to let Society Carey see the Orient, which he never has, and to let the Orient see Society Carey, which it never has. In that way, a whole new part of the world will know that we in New York have a governor, which we have, and his name is Society Carey.

There are many thousands living without heat in Brooklyn who say that they never knew they had a governor until newspapers ran pictures of Society Carey looking out of a helicopter in Japan. But these people living in the cold in Brooklyn are not Society Carey's kind of people, and you can be sure that he will keep the same distance from them that he always has, and that is quite a lot of distance. Tokyo is not that far.

We in New York could be proud of the first picture of Society Carey, the one showing him in a helicopter, because that let all of Tokyo know how our governor lives in New York. Society Carey has a great big million-dollar helicopter that he rides all over New York while we take subways, if you can get on them, and he also has two planes, one of which is so big it can barely fit on a runway, and he uses it every night to go back to Albany from Manhattan and it costs only $750 a night to do this.

The Society Carey party in the Orient includes three advance men. An advance man is a traveling doorman. He sees to it that the right luggage is in each hotel room and that cars are available and helicopters ready on the pad, and that, always, doors are held open for Society Carey. The luggage is much more important than you think. As someone from the governor's office in New York was pointing out yesterday, this trip to the Orient involves dramatic climatic changes. The trip started in Albany, where the temperature drops to the low teens, and went through Hawaii, in the high seventies, to Tokyo, which was in the forties, and on to Hong Kong, which is in the sixties. But this is weather in the winter and is highly unreliable.

Why, here one morning you could have Society Carey arising in Hawaii and the temperature could be in the high seventies. Moreover, if Society Carey ever put on a heavy Albany suit and went out into the street, he most certainly would boil like a cabbage. By noon in Honolulu, Society Carey would keel over. Yet on the other hand, if Society Carey ventured out in his truly tropical suit, his tea planter's white, he might be out and about the whole town and have the temperature suddenly plummet many degrees. Here would be Society Carey in the middle of Honolulu, being attacked by chilblains.

So here is what the three advance men have been doing each day on Society Carey's trip through the Orient:

One advance man stands outside the hotel each morning for a half hour in order to fully acclimate himself to the temperature. Then the first advance man makes a policy decision as to the weight of the suit Society Carey will wear. This outside advance man waves his arm, in coded signal, to a second advance man, stationed inside the hotel lobby. The second advance man grabs a phone and calls up to the third advance man, who is positioned in Society Carey's suite. Upon getting the message, the third advance man pounces upon Society Carey's wardrobe and pulls out the proper suit for Society Carey to wear on this day.

Sometimes this system, which worked beautifully at hotels, had to be modified to fit a change in Society Carey's living quarters. As the UPI cable from Hong Kong indicates, Carey in Hong Kong stayed in the American International Underwriters' guest house. American International Underwriters appears to have some connection to the insurance industry. By staying there, Society Carey placed great hardship on his advance men. They had practiced long hours for hotel duty, but this method of climate control at the American International Underwriters guest house could be done by only two advance men. And the two advance men were able to do the job, and apparently quite well. The trip has gone so smoothly for Society Carey, wearing all his suits in all the different weather, that he has not even taken a Dristan.

Society Carey's party in the Orient also includes two New York State policemen. This causes some people in New York City to say that since there have been 9851 murders in the city in Carey's time as governor, then perhaps any loose cops should be used on Nostrand Avenue instead of Honolulu. Other people say that if Society Carey's trip to Hawaii, Japan, and Hong Kong is so dangerous that he cannot make it without great protection, then perhaps he shouldn't go at all.

You must disagree with those who say such things. It is now official American policy to face up to terrorism wherever it may be. If there is terrorism on Waikiki Beach, or at the American International Underwriters in Hong Kong, then it should be fought vigorously. We in New York State have sent Society Carey and two state troopers to make sure that this national policy is carried out.

These same people squawking about the cost of sending secretaries, advance men, and two state troopers around the Orient—round-trip plane fare is $1600, and that is only the start—are the same ones who made the most noise the other day when Society Carey, before leaving for Hawaii and the Orient, put in an expense voucher of $6400 that was to be paid to

Dr. Philip D'Arrigo. He is the dentist whose house on Shelter Island was seized by the state because it blocked the view of the water from Society Carey's family house. They had to give the house back to the dentist. This switching back and forth caused the dentist to run up bills of $6400. As the problem was part of the governor's personal life, he sat down and, of course, asked the taxpayers to pay the $6400. This is why Society Carey has such great style; he has 14 million people paying for him.

Officially, Society Carey has announced that his trip, his eleven-man sweep of the Far East, has nothing to do with sightseeing. In Japan, Society Carey announced that the great Okuma Machinery works would expand its business and set up a huge production plant on Flatlands Avenue, Brooklyn. The Okuma plant would sit alongside the great new international headquarters of the Mitsubishi Corporation, which will move here on March 3. These announcements of great industries coming here are similar to those made when Society Carey took his last overseas trip, to Germany. Society Carey then announced that the main Krupp plant in Dusseldorf would move to Flushing Avenue, Maspeth, on February 16.

Society Carey's tour of the Orient does make a fool of at least some of his critics. Society Carey has maintained that the state cannot run without the services of his assistant, Robert Morgado. To prove this, Society took Morgado with him all over the Orient and he and Morgado even stopped at Morgado's home in Hawaii. And the state ran just as it always did, which proves how important both Society Carey and Morgado are to us.

Also out of this great, quite costly trip, I personally learned a lesson. Some time back, I noted that Society Carey was unique in government: he had invented the eleven-hour workweek. A person I respect and cherish called me on this. He said I had my figures wrong and should be embarrassed. I can now report to this man that, yes, he was right and I was wrong. By careful addition, I have determined that since January 1 of this year, Society Carey has worked an average of nine and a half hours each week. As this is not the eleven-hour week I said he worked, I stand corrected. Beautiful.

February 10, 1981

Klein Lives

T HE ONE most scurrilous charge in my time in my business came during a call from *Newsweek*, which is a magazine where imbeciles sit in cubicles and say they see the world.

The man first asked about Janet Cooke. She worked on a newspaper in Washington, made up a story about an eight-year-old drug addict and won a Pulitzer Prize. Why she had to make up the story is beyond me. Walk the city streets and you get anything you want; in Brooklyn the other day there was a seven-year-old who took part in a felony homicide. Besides, I saw nothing wrong with her getting the prize because Pulitzer used to fake even the weather reports in his papers.

And then came this underhanded question: "We've been reading your stories about Klein the Lawyer and some of us were wondering whether he was real or not."

I was stunned. I don't mind people being new in this business, but a question like this went beyond inexperience and into stupidity. The last person who doubted the existence of the people I write about was Abe Rosenthal, the editor of *The New York Times* newspaper, who, of a night some years ago, came to the old Pep McGuire's on Queens Boulevard for a personal inspection. When Rosenthal arrived, somebody was cleaning a machine gun in the office. At the bar was the late Norton W. Peppis III, whose Con Edison payment had just bounced off the rim in the final moments of a game at Boston. Also there was Jimmy Burke, Fat Thomas, and a blonde as tall as an apartment house, perhaps the tallest stewardess in Lufthansa airline history. In Rosenthal's presence at the bar that evening a historic conversation took place. It is remembered clearly by everyone who was there and it is repeated here, and thus prominently:

JIMMY BURKE: What airline did you say you work for?

BIG BLONDE: Lufthansa.

JIMMY BURKE: Gee, that's a very good airline.

Now, years later, Mr. Burke is in Danbury Prison because federal prosecutors think he robbed $8 million from Lufthansa. Fat Thomas is still around, although you'd never know it from me; I am not speaking to him for this entire year, and even as I type this out, I am sorry that I am putting his name in the *Daily News* newspaper.

Rosenthal, I'm told, is still around. And he knows. So now, along comes some guy from a cubicle at *Newsweek*, and he wants to know if another of the Queens Boulevard people, Klein the Lawyer, actually exists.

On the day that this question was asked, on the day that Klein the Lawyer's presence on earth was being questioned, here he was sitting in a courtroom, and in great turmoil.

At the defense table next to Klein the Lawyer was a man of ill repute. An extortion trial was going on, and not well; every time the prosecutor spoke, the ears of jurors seemed to prick forward, like those of a Thoroughbred horse. Whenever Klein spoke, the jurors' eyelids slowly lowered.

Nor had the client paid Klein. The client kept saying, "Concentrate on the case. The case is the important thing, not the money."

Klein, however, was under great pressure. For weeks, he had been promising Rosalie that he would take her to Florida on a Thursday-to-Monday weekend. Rosalie is Klein's second or third wife, nobody is quite sure; public figures seem not to tell the truth about matrimony. But one thing was certain: Rosalie was on Queens Boulevard getting clothes out of the dry cleaner for the trip to Florida and Klein was in the courtroom without the money for the trip.

He had one chance. A father had been calling him for weeks about his daughter, who was in danger of being indicted in federal court for her part in a large fraud operation. The father wanted Klein to take over the moment the indictment came down. The father said he understood that it would be an expensive federal case and that he was prepared to pay an immediate retainer.

At the luncheon break of the extortion trial, Klein called his office. He was told that the young woman's father had been calling all morning about the federal case. A band struck up. Klein the Lawyer kept saying "Florida" as he dialed the father.

"I can't tell you how happy I am," the father said. "My daughter agreed to turn over some people to the prosecutor and now he isn't going to indict her. So we won't have to bother you."

"Wonderful!" Klein said. "I'm so busy I truly didn't know how I was going to fit you in. Now, I won't have to go through all the trouble to juggle my schedule to make room for you."

Klein felt like he had diphtheria. In the courtroom, his client stared at him. "Something the matter?"

"Yes, I thought that maybe I could break even today," Klein said.

"I told you. Forget about the money and concentrate on the case," the client said.

Later, after being pummeled by life through another long day, Klein the Lawyer, hopes dashed, had to call Rosalie and tell her that the Florida trip was off. Then he sat at the bar on Queens Boulevard and listened as I told him about the question from the magazine.

He thought for a while. Then he brightened. "Could you get them to put in print that I don't exist?" Klein the Lawyer said. "I'll sue them in Queens."

April 26, 1981

He Bites the Helping Hand

As THIS was the first subway ride in days in which someone's elbow was not in my mouth, I was able to talk to the person alongside me on the train from Queens yesterday morning.

He boarded at Jackson Heights, where people usually rush the doors as if attacking the referee at a soccer match. But rather than assault those in his way, he slid in on the oblique and did harm to none. Nice fellow, I thought.

"What's doing?" I asked him.

"I'm going for a job," he said. He held in his hands a yellow state unemployment booklet. "I signed for three weeks, and they still don't get me a check. It's better to work. The man at the unemployment told me to go to this place." He showed me a slip of paper with an address for Stagelight Cosmetics, 630 Ninth Avenue.

"What kind of a job is it?" I asked him.

"Shipping. The man told me they pay a lot of money, pretty good."

"What's a lot of money?"

"A hundred and ninety dollars."

He took out a pay stub from his last job, at David Goldberg, a swimsuit manufacturer in Long Island City. The stub showed he had earned $150 regular time and $109.48 in overtime.

"I wish I had this money this week," he said.

"What happened to the job?" I asked.

"Got laid off. They closed from May until September. I'm going back there when they open again."

He got off at Thirty-fourth Street, walked over to Ninth Avenue, and started looking for the address, which it turned out was above Forty-second Street. So we walked together up Ninth Avenue. It was only a couple of minutes after 8:00 A.M., so there was no rush.

"By the way, what's your name?" I asked.

"José."

"Where are you from?" I asked.

He gave me an address in Corona. "I was born in Santo Domingo. I came here when I was ten. I'm twenty-three now."

He was a good-looking young man, with close-cropped black hair and a mustache. He wore a red Adidas polo shirt, jeans, and Nike sneakers. Good and neat for a shipping clerk, I thought.

"I hope I get this job," he said. "I got a wife. I don't hang out. I want to work for her. She goes to high school."

"If she doesn't work either, how do the two of you survive without a job?" I asked.

"The last money I got, I got to pay rent. Then I got a thirty-eight-dollar bill for electricity. I hope I get this job. I don't like to work in a place pays a hundred and ten. I don't go for that. Once, I made two hundred and twenty dollars clean. That's a lot of money. That's what I hope this job is like."

"I'll go with you," I said.

"Do you want a job, too?" he asked.

"No, I'll just go with you and see. Maybe I can help out."

It was obvious why I did this. Stagelight Cosmetics is located in one of those film center buildings on Ninth Avenue, and I have been around there maybe a thousand times in my life in this city, doing a voice-over for somebody, or a film spot for somebody else; the last time I was around there, I think it was for the Fresh Air Fund. And I thought I would just walk in with this kid and of course somebody would know me right away and I could say, Here's a nice guy needs a job, why don't you put him on?

Stagelight Cosmetics was on the fourth floor. As José and I walked in, a young blond woman in a striped dress looked up from a curved reception desk.

"Hi!" I said loudly, putting the steam on right away.

"May I help you?" she said.

"My man here needs a job," I said.

"I see," she said.

"Of course, I don't need a job," I said. "I already have a job."

"Well, what he has to do is fill out an application," the receptionist said crisply. "There's nobody here right now from shipping."

"If the boss of the whole place is in, I'd be delighted to say hello," I said.

"Why don't you just be seated next to him?" the receptionist said. How could they hire anyone so unaware, I thought.

"I'll bet the boss would like to see me," I said.

The receptionist handed José an employment application form. "You can put down the person who recommended you on this line here," she said, indicating the back of the form. José nodded.

I turned to José. "Put down Jimmy Breslin as a reference," I said loudly. He shrugged. The receptionist became busy.

"Excuse me, miss . . ." I said. She held up her hand as the phone made a low sound.

"Stagelight Cosmetics," she said. "Hold on a minute." She put the phone on hold. Then she called out to someone in a rear office, "Are you in for Arthur Farmer?"

"No, tell him I didn't arrive yet," a voice called out.

The receptionist relayed this message to Arthur Farmer.

"I'll bet he's in for Jimmy Breslin," I said. She didn't seem to hear me. Dope.

A woman holding a container of coffee strolled out of an office.

"I write myself tons of little notes on Friday so I can remember what I'm doing on Monday," she said to the receptionist.

"That's right," the receptionist said.

I turned to José, who was painfully filling out the application form. He did not fill in the "job desired" or "salary desired" blanks. I don't think English is José's strong game.

"Forget it," I told him. "I know what to do." Of course I did. I would sit down and write a very nice column about this young guy looking for a job and everybody at Stagelight Cosmetics would read it and read it again and, forget about it, José would be working and I could once again assure the only person who counts in my life that I was a hero.

José left the application with the receptionist, and we went across the street for coffee.

"Sometimes life looks tough," I said.

"Like the day the judge get mad at me," José said.

"What judge?"

"The judge in Queens. I don't know his name. He gave me zip-three."

"What for?"

"A robbery. I was only eighteen then. The lawyer says, you going up on appeal. I won the case. I was in Elmira nine months and the guard came to me with the letter and he said you won. That was when there was such a big snowstorm that I had to wait a couple of days before I could get out."

"But you learned your lesson from that, didn't you?" I said.

"Oh, sure I did. I don't get in trouble ever. I want to have babies. I got to have money when I have a little boy, a little girl. Working is the only way to get money."

"What do you want to do with your life?" I asked him.

"Try to be somebody," he said.

The last answer did it. So what if he went to Elmira? A guy like this comes off the streets. What is he going to tell you, that he went to Portsmouth Priory and MIT? I'll take some shot for this kid, I told myself.

I said good-bye, and because I was feeling so good with myself for what I was about to do, I decided to walk for a while. Then, I don't know, for one reason or another as I was passing a phone booth, I ducked in and made a call to David Goldberg, the swimsuit place in Long Island City where José had worked.

"I was just checking," I said. "José was laid off, isn't that right?"

"Oh, yes, he was laid off," the guy at David Goldberg said. "He was laid off after I sat here and looked at him on closed-circuit television as he and the elevator operator were about to take half the place out on me."

"Oh," I said.

I hung up. Stagelight Cosmetics! If it were not for some brilliant office help, José would have had so much Stagelight Cosmetics on Roosevelt Avenue in Queens that people would have been smearing it on their clothes. I then did exactly what I always do on these occasions. I went into a bar and it was only ten o'clock, but that was the end of that day. Maybe tomorrow I will try again.

June 2, 1981

She Said Good-bye with Charm

Jimmy Breslin's wife, the former Rosemary Dattolico, was buried yesterday. She died Tuesday morning after a long illness. Breslin wrote the following eulogy and read it at the funeral services at Our Lady of Mercy Catholic Church in Forest Hills, Queens. We wanted to share it with our readers.

ABOUT A year ago, when she was unwell to the point where even she became unsure, she offered during prayer to her God a suggestion that she thought was quite good.

Her youngest had experienced difficulty through the start of his schooling. Then suddenly, he had expressed great interest in attending one school.

His mother developed great faith in the situation.

And so, she proposed, give me this year while my son goes to this school. Let me try to help him as best I can. Then that should do it. He will be on his way.

And I will be perfectly happy to be on my way.

Providing the school works out.

The year went by and the youngest attended school and she lived despite the gloomy signs given by her body. For a period, she simply willed herself to improve. The mind over a blood count.

And her youngest suddenly grew. A plant nourished.

Whatever she had asked for, she appeared to be receiving.

And now, the other day, from the depths of a hospital bed, with her body in revolt, she looked up and said, "The report card was pretty good. But now I don't feel like keeping my part of the deal."

Which was her notion of fairness. For all of her life, she believed that true evenhandedness meant that those in need always were allowed more.

And now, at the end, she desired to follow her own counsel.

So as she left us, she did so with that most elusive of qualities, a little bit of charm.

We of her family who remain have a special burden. We have lived with nobility.

391

She was a person who regarded life as one long attempt to provide a happy moment or so for another person.

Always, she was outraged by those who rushed about, shouldering past others, their sides lathered with effort, horses in some cheap race, as they pawed for material success.

She knew that life belonged to those who seek out the weary, sit with the defeated, understand the clumsy.

And do this not as some duty. But do it with the cheerful realization that we are a part of it all.

She thought the word "duty" meant that each day there should be a word or a gesture that would cause someone else to smile over the life about them. Her contempt was reserved for those who would not attempt this. Who are you, she would rail, to go through a day, knowing that another day is to follow, and another after that, and knowing that it is all ceaseless, and still you refuse to join with us and help soften the path of those about you?

She was a woman utterly unspoiled. I thank God for the high privilege of having known her so well.

She ran my life and those of her children almost totally. She leaves us with a tradition of decency that we must attempt to carry on. Her strength was such that even if those of us here today stumble now and then, I think the Rosemary Dattolico line of decency will reveal itself time after time in whatever generations there are to come.

As was said of another aristocrat such as this one:

Earth, receive an honored guest.

June 11, 1981

"Por Unas Horas"

ONE DAY in April of 1980, Cibella Borges, then a twenty-two-year-old who earned a little over $100 a week as a police department civilian administrative aide, teaching typing at the Police Academy, met a photographer who offered her $150 for posing for pictures that were supposed to give all men the thought of incredible pleasure.

Not quite. Some men who saw her pictures in a magazine had, rather than boiling loins, a cold wind of fear inside. This has caused Cibella, now twenty-five, great trouble.

She sat at the kitchen table of her steaming apartment and waited for her aunt to bring a copy of the magazine. Cibella's mother, Norma, fifty, making coffee, said, "*Por unas horas.*"

"She is saying," Cibella said, "that all this is just for a couple of hours. That's all I spent posing for the pictures."

The mother said, "Would it be better if she appeared on the front page of a newspaper shot dead or on the last page of a nudie magazine?"

The daughter, wearing a T-shirt and jeans, went to look out the window for her aunt. "*Por unas horas,*" she said. "And now it does not end."

When she had been asked to pose, back in 1980, Cibella, who had been operated on once for a cyst, had just been informed that she needed another operation and this one probably would end her ability to bear children. "What's the difference, I can't have any kids, so who's going to marry me?" Cibella said. She went to a studio on the West Side, posed for the pictures, put on her clothes, and went home to Orchard Street, where her front door is between two stores, one selling baby clothes and the other men's suits. Clothes hung outside the stores and blew in the wind over Cibella's head as she came home. Her apartment was two floors up.

Nobody ever said Cibella Borges was another Brooke Shields. The child pornography pictures of Brooke Shields were so acceptable to the public that Brooke enrolled at Princeton, where, next fall, gallant young men probably will go charging through the line in hopes of gaining her smile. Cibella Borges of

Orchard Street, whose poses had been at least a bit rough, saw neither stardom nor Ivy League schools in her future. She made application to take the police department exam for patrolman.

Her photographer spent many months showing the pictures around town to editors who work in the city's literary underground. Finally, he was able to sell them to a magazine named *Beaver*, which is a publication read with one hand. The *Beaver* editor put the pictures in a file for use sometime. He had no idea of the name of the small Hispanic woman in the pictures.

As months went by, Cibella Borges took the patrolman's exam, passed, attended the Police Academy, and then was sworn in as a police officer late in 1981. At four-foot-eleven and ninety-five pounds, she was the smallest police officer in the department's history. She also spoke Spanish in a city where there are far more Hispanics than there are citizens with Irish names, although the police department is commanded almost entirely by middle-aged Irish Catholics.

Working her job, Cibella, and another officer, stopped a car at Bleecker and Charles, ordered the three occupants out, and found three guns on the front seat. The three previously had committed armed robberies, and for her part in the arrest, Cibella was given a meritorious service medal. She then was transferred to the Nineteenth Precinct on the Upper East Side of Manhattan.

And then on the night of July 27, 1982, nine months after Cibella Borges had started as a police officer, there arrived on the cheaper newsstands in town these stacks of the magazine *Beaver*. A police officer from the Nineteenth Precinct picked up the magazine while going around on his midnight-to-eight tour. There is no record of an arrest being made on a newsstand dealer who forced *Beaver* magazine on the police officer. As the magazine is priced at $2.95, it does not take a cynic to figure out how *Beaver* magazine got from a newsstand to the precinct: the badge beats a grappling hook.

Back at the precinct, the cop went through *Beaver*, whose index listed photo layouts for Sheena, Jackie and Pattie, Corrie, Lisa, and, on page fifty-six, Nina. The cop went through the magazine page by page and, reaching page fifty-six, noticed that not only were the pictures particularly dirty, but the layout starred Police Officer Cibella Borges. The cop took the magazine to his sergeant. The sergeant was aghast. The sergeant gave the magazine to the lieutenant. The lieutenant was shocked. When Cibella was told about the magazine, she went downstairs and found the lieutenant showing the magazine to a whole group of cops. She remembers that as she walked in, the lieutenant shoved the magazine into his desk. Then he took it out as if it were a communicable disease, dropped it on the desk, and allowed her to look.

"This is very serious," he said.

"I posed for these pictures before I came on the force," Cibella said, staring at pictures of her bottom. "I forgot all about them."

Three days later, members of the New York Police Department Internal Affairs Division questioned Cibella. An inspector, captain, and lieutenant, sitting in an office, with *Beaver* magazine in front of them. They hastily shoved it under a pile of papers. They now began to talk to Cibella about pictures taken for the magazine before she even took the test and long before she took the oath as a police officer.

One of the internal affairs men asked Cibella if she ever had thought, while working as a civilian administrative aide in 1980, of the tremendous disgrace she would bring upon the police department by posing for dirty naked pictures. Another wanted to know why she hadn't listed her one-day modeling job in the "previous employment" space on her department application.

The police department should have been proud of the pictures, as they prove that at least one member of the force is in marvelous physical condition; most officers are in such deplorable shape that if called upon to pose for pictures, they would first put on overcoats.

Yet Cibella was in trouble. As an Hispanic, she could not invoke the rules of the Irish-dominated force: the surest way an Irish cop explains away most offenses, and particularly sex offenses, is to claim alcoholism. Misuse of alcohol is acceptable to the Irish; misuse of the body calls for condemnation to a chamber of Hell. If born Irish, Cibella could have walked into the hearing and said, "I drink too much and I don't know what I'm doing. In fact, I'm thirsty right now." Instead, being a dirty Hispanic, she had to admit openly that she had posed for naked pictures. Promoting sins of the flesh!

The most famous defense at a departmental trial was on behalf of a police officer charged with making a Puerto Rican housewife pregnant. The officer's captain appeared as a defense witness at the trial. The captain said it was impossible for the man to make the woman pregnant because the man was a good Irish Roman Catholic with five children at home. If he ever had screwed this Puerto Rican, he would have worn a condom; the officer was too good of a Catholic, the testifying captain insisted, to be unprotected with a Puerto Rican and then go home and sleep with his wife.

One member of the trial board was miserable enough to ask the witness why the officer was in the Puerto Rican woman's apartment to begin with. The captain said, "The man has a drinking problem." The members of the trial board nodded understandingly and the cop was saved.

Cibella Borges, being a dirty Puerto Rican, unable to cry whisky, was dismissed from the force. The police commissioner, who is known as Dead Body McGuire and who has stayed on the payroll longer than any commissioner in memory, who has 9000 murders and 500,000 armed robberies committed while he clings so tightly to his job that the desk squeaks, announced that the pictures were repulsive and he fired Cibella for posing for dirty pictures that were taken nearly a full year before she was sworn in as a cop. These aging Irish Catholics who run the police department are frightened of sex, which is at best the Act of Darkness, and becomes dangerous when it is being committed by some dirty naked Puerto Rican. The Devil in the squad room!

It was at this point that Cibella Borges's mother squalled, "What about the men who are on the police and they take women and they take drugs and they take money?"

There was no answer from the aging Irish. It seemed to me that if we are to have a pure police force, Norma Borges's charges must be confronted. If indeed there was dirty lewd behavior by cops, then the citizens of the city must involve themselves. I volunteered to become an assistant keeper of the morals for the department. For a long time, I had observed police officers ducking in and out of photo-developing shops to pick up sets of photos from private swimming pool parties. And of course I had observed young women out with married police. As an assistant keeper of the morals, I asked every woman who goes out with a married cop to send me the name, shield number, and either the exact location or a description of the place where she meets him. I then would send one copy to the police commissioner, Dead Body McGuire, and the other to the cop's home.

The next mail brought a letter from the Bronx. I immediately wrote in that day's column, "That detective in the Fifty-second in the Bronx who told his girlfriend that he was single and then he got nervous and transferred . . . she knows."

I also read a letter about a summer house at Kennedy Lane, Hampton Bays, where cops and firemen acted like savages with women to whom they were not married. I put that in the paper.

Early, a couple of mornings later, I was having coffee on Third Avenue and was surprised to see a full-page advertisement about me, a direct personal attack on me, in my newspaper, the *Daily News* newspaper. The organization that took the ad, the Patrolmen's Benevolent Association, paid the *News* newspaper, I learned later, exactly $16,240 for the ad.

The writer was guilty of premature semicolons and had the periods outside quotation marks, but the type was nice, the PBA badge at the bottom looked good, and it also was nice to know that the PBA can get mad at something. The problem was, the union was supposed to be representing Borges, who had been paying dues for a year and was a union member in a union city being dismissed for a most minor point. Always, policemen charged with things far more serious, crimes and murders, have a crowd of officers about them in the courthouse and the head of the PBA shouting that the man is innocent. For Cibella Borges, an Hispanic woman who posed for dirty pictures before becoming a police officer, the union did nothing. Instead, they paid over $16,000 for an ad attacking some newspaper writer.

The funny thing about the ad was that, while I could sort of understand it if the head of the union was, like so many of the cops, some fat Irish guy afraid of sex, the guy who is the PBA head now is Italian. They are a people who are supposed to love sex. Still, he refused to help Cibella. The nasty thought arose that the police union did not stand up for a member because in this case she was Hispanic and female.

And Cibella Borges has been suspended from her job, which paid over $400 a week, the most money anybody in her family ever had earned, and she was off the payroll because she posed for dirty pictures before she became a cop.

August 1, 1982

Mix Me a Family

SOME MONTHS ago, I married a woman named Mrs. Eldridge, who has three children; I have six. Therefore, we placed nine children from two marriages under one roof and asked them to get along famously.

Both first marriages had ended with somebody unfortunately passing away. So the nine children had no other parents outside the house to run to with complaints. Similarly, Mrs. Eldridge and Breslin had only themselves to be mad at.

Also, I am the only one in the marriage, and certainly one of the few in Western civilization, who has two mothers-in-law.

Because of this, I today turn from temporal subjects that usually fill this space—politics, urban mayhem, and essays on daily incompetents—and write of a matter that will be here as long as the earth persists: the attempted mixing under one roof of human beings not of the same parentage. Oh, yes, *attempted* is the proper word.

The entire matter started in the face of a culture gap: Mrs. Eldridge of the West Side, on a spring day, standing on the sidewalk outside Costello's on Forty-fourth Street, which is near my place of business, and, not seeing me because the inside of Costello's is as black as a basement, calling through the door: "How can you *stay* there?"

"It tastes good. C'mon in."

"You told me we were going for a nice walk."

"Well, I lied."

And at the outset of the marriage, when we put all the kids together for the first time, daughter K. Breslin whispered to me, "This is making me very unhappy."

"What's the matter?" I asked.

"Them." She was pointing at the three Eldridge children.

"You'll just have to try," I said.

"Oh, yes. Yes, there's one other thing," K. Breslin said.

"What's that?"

"Her." She pointed at Mrs. Eldridge.

I provide dialogue by K. Breslin because at that time I could not hear what the three Eldridge children were saying. They were in a huddle with their mother that resembled a basketball team at a timeout. Once in a while, a head would pop up and glare at K. Breslin. So it was obvious that the Eldridge family huddle was not about the *Essays* of Charles Lamb. Immediately, daughter L. Eldridge went up to her college at 116th Street and Broadway and enrolled in a special study program in France. The program lasts a year.

"The courses they're giving you in France aren't the ones you're supposed to be taking," her mother said.

"I'll take whatever they give. The best thing is that the course takes all year," L. Eldridge said, packing as she spoke.

We have this week religious holidays of great significance to at least a couple of faiths. As Eldridge is Jewish and Breslin is Catholic, this is an excellent time to observe what actually happens when different people are asked to live with each other.

Passover is today and Easter is on Sunday. These are the first holidays we have attempted. We dogged it last Christmas. We had workmen pull the kitchen out and told the nine kids that it was too bad, but there could be no joyous gatherings for Christmas or New Year's because the workmen wouldn't be finished with the new kitchen until at least February and therefore they had best try an aunt's house.

This week, with kitchen installed and holidays here, we took it on.

For Passover arrangements, my wife's mother, which makes the woman one of my two mothers-in-law, arrived at the house and looked at the crowd of Queens Irish Catholics surrounding her daughter. Mrs. Eldridge's mother dropped her head as if suffering from a severe neck injury and stared at the floor.

"What's the matter?" I asked her.

"I came here to see my daughter."

"Well, here she is."

She stared at the Irish about her daughter.

"That's not my daughter."

Meanwhile, in Queens, on Seventy-fourth Street, in Glendale, my other mother-in-law was busy in the kitchen.

"I'd like to invite you to a Passover seder with the Eldridges," I said.

"Is that what you want?" she said.

"Yes."

"Why don't they come here for Easter dinner?" she answered.

As for the children involved at this time of religious holidays, I give this report—Son D. Eldridge, student: "I love big, new families. But I'm pretty busy in school." Daughter E. Eldridge, student: "I won't be able to get home from school in time for the seder." School being two and a half hours outside of New York. What about Easter Sunday? "I don't think you'll see me on Easter." Daughter L. Eldridge, student abroad (by postcard): "Feel terrible that I can't be home for the holidays with all of you."

On the other side—Daughter K. Breslin, student: "A seder? I'm going to my friend's house." Which friend? "My friend." Son C. Breslin, student: "I like everybody a lot but I'm not feeling too good today." What about Sunday? "We'll see what happens then." Son P. Breslin, student: "Is it all right if I go with my friends tonight and spend the weekend?" Daughter R. Breslin, worker: "I'm going to New Jersey." Sons J. and K. Breslin, workers, have not been heard from except a note stating: "Don't count on us."

This, then, is a report on the lengths the parents and children go to to accommodate each other, to work toward achieving the great sense of "we" that stepfamilies are said to love. So far the only "we" that can be found under our roof is: "We don't want to go with them."

The Eldridge-Breslin Passover-Easter will consist of two persons.

March 29, 1983

Light, Then Shadow of a Gunman

THE OTHER defendants left the information booth and pay telephones and ran toward the revolving door yesterday morning as Bernhard Goetz was propelled into the harsh bright light awaiting him in the courthouse lobby. His frail face was without expression and his thin body swayed as the pack of cameramen shoved him. A stranger's eyes peered through large wire-framed glasses.

Goetz never noticed the shadow that covered everything in the building at 100 Centre St. in lower Manhattan. It had been cast by the intensive care unit on the ninth floor at St. Vincent's Hospital, where during the night an alarm went off on a heart monitoring machine and Darrell Cabey, age 19, with one of Goetz' bullets in his back, slipped into a coma.

Nobody in court yesterday morning had been told of this. As Goetz floated across the courthouse lobby, then went up a flight of steps and into a courtroom, he still appeared as a person who had caused many to react in a manner that the most strong-limbed or persuasive of tongue never could achieve. Goetz had people advocating loose fantasy as a new subdivision in law.

A white, sitting in a corner of a subway car, approached by four young blacks, who asked for $5. He shot them all. Left them on the floor and jumped off the train.

Those who thought it was fine for Goetz to shoot a black in the back, even if it paralyzed the guy for life, not conceivably could be asked to raise their cheers for death.

Goetz came into the courtroom yesterday and sat at a table on the left side of the room. He wore a brown leather jacket with a fur collar, a tan shirt open at the collar and Levis. His lawyer, Frank Brenner, a much shorter man, sat next to him.

The railing in front of the spectators' seats was live with artists who sketched Goetz on tan paper. On the other side of the railing, the desks were covered with the pink, yellow, blue and white papers that run the court world. Now the court workers began to assemble. Four court officers in white shirts, then three women around a desk and then two more clerks came in through one door. Another door opened and a man with an eyeglass case in his shirt pocket peered in, then stepped out, and after him were two women. Three corrections officers walked out of another door. Suddenly, there were 16 people in the front of the courtroom.

Goetz, who had tried to handle the law alone, kept talking to his lawyer.

One of the women in the front of the room, a woman in a gray pinstriped suit, walked over to the railing to talk to Enid Gerling, an attorney waiting for another case. She wore a tan hat.

"I was telling my friend in Brooklyn that you are the only polite court officer," Enid said.

The woman in the gray pinstriped suit smiled. Then she shook her head as a court stenotypist came in hurriedly, carrying his machine.

"I've got to say something to him, coming in here late," the woman in the suit said.

At 9:35, court officer Tom Pizzo stood in front of the bench and called for everybody to take seats. The judge, Jay Gold, wearing a tan jacket and no robes, walked out.

"Bernhard Goetz," Pizzo said. "One ten/one twenty-five twenty-five. Two sixty five oh three."

The 265.03 is possession of a gun, the 110/125.25 is attempted murder in the second degree.

As long as the heart monitoring machine and respirator on Darrell Cabey at St. Vincent's Hospital remained steady, the two numbers on Goetz remained the same. A death at the hospital could change this immediately. The penal code number for murder in the second degree is 125.25. On Goetz' sheet, all they would have to do is cross out the "110," which stands for attempted.

An assistant district attorney, a woman in a brown plaid, said that the people requested adjournment. Then Brenner, Goetz' lawyer, said something to the judge that couldn't be heard.

"What did he say?" somebody in the spectators' rows asked.

"He said that he had been assigned by the court at the arraignment, but since then he has been retained by Goetz. He isn't court-assigned any more."

Then the judge gave the date for the next hearing as Jan. 16.

"Clear the well," Pizzo yelled.

Goetz' lawyer left and then a few minutes later, Goetz came out of the room and into the hallway. A woman leaned against the wall and smoked a cigaret. Next to her was a water fountain with a paper bag stuffed under it. Goetz, with court officers around him, moved down the hall, past a door that had "Men" printed on it in Magic Marker.

Then he was going down a flight of stairs with cameramen shoving. A female court officer wearing a white shirt and handcuffs was directly behind Goetz. She elbowed a cameraman out of the way and pushed Goetz out into the 16-degree air. Goetz walked through the sun to a car. He still did not see the shadow of a hospital room that suddenly could cover his sky.

January 10, 1985

Goetz Should Take Mayoralty Shot

SOME MINUTES before eight o'clock yesterday morning, Joseph Kelner, attorney for Bernhard Goetz, walked through the chill air and into the studios of "Good Morning America" on W. 67th St. Shortly thereafter, he was on television all over the country and, most prominently, in the five boroughs of this city.

He was putting the case of Bernhard Goetz into politics.

And then at 9:30 A.M., here was Goetz himself, standing in a second-floor courtroom at 100 Centre St. He wore a three-quarter length sheepskin jacket and a vertical striped shirt with a button-down collar, open at the neck.

Gone was the brown leather jacket with fur collar that we saw on Goetz when he turned himself in to police in New Hampshire, and at his first court hearing a week ago.

At yesterday's hearing, Goetz' posture was different. The shoulders were up, not slouched like some common billy goat. The chest was expanded. And his head was up and there was a glow of strength to a face that once seemed so vulnerable.

Watching him, a keen observer understood immediately. Not only was the case of Bernhard Goetz into politics, but so was Bernhard Goetz himself.

If the public decides to stop mouthing and to put its money and its votes behind Goetz, perhaps it can make this 37-year-old subway rider the Mayor of New York.

One of the four shot by Goetz, Darrell Cabey, 19, went into his ninth day in a coma this morning. His backbone is severed because Goetz shot him in the back. New Yorkers claim they stand ready to cheer Goetz' actions. All right, then, let's go all the way. Cheer for gunfire and make Bernie Goetz the Mayor.

So that people can express their support for Bernie Goetz, who as an expression of law and order shot four young black people on a subway train, two in the back, and didn't even wing a bystander, we print today an important coupon.

If you like what Bernhard Goetz stands for, then let him know. Put yourself on record. You don't even want Bernie Goetz tried. Forget law, lawyers, judge and court. Throw it out. Fill in the blank coupon and say that because Bernie Goetz shot people on the subway, you want him to be Mayor.

Let's draft Bernhard Goetz for Mayor.

No longer will I attack the public will. Instead I print herewith a coupon for the public to show whether we are in a new time, with Bernhard Goetz as your candidate and people applauding the coma of a black he shot in the back.

Many people have suggested this slogan for the campaign— GOETZ: WHAT THEY DESERVE.

We want Bernie Goetz to know how many New Yorkers agree that he should be the next Mayor. The more coupons received from readers, the bigger the response, the more it is possible that a "Draft Bernie for Mayor" movement will gather force and eventually sweep him on to victory.

He seems to be a hero at a time when the city has none. And he enters politics at a time when there is no politician around to challenge a Mayor who, despite his mouth that proclaims his invincibility, is quite weak because he has not done the work assigned to a Mayor.

Who knows more about subway shootings, Koch the Mayor or Bernie Goetz?

Who knows how to get things done, Koch the Mayor with his big mouth or Bernie Goetz with a good compact .38?

There are 26,800 New York City policemen and 5,800 civilian employes at a cost to taxpayers of $1,017,000,000 a year.

Yes, that is over $1,000,000,000 for police. Not including pensions.

Do you get $1,000,000,000 worth of protection?

And there are 3,820 Transit Police, with 338 civilian employes in that department. The cost to taxpayers is $144 million. This doesn't include pensions.

The total cost of these two police forces is $1,161,000,000.

And there was not one policeman on the No. 2 train when the four young blacks approached Bernie Goetz on Saturday afternoon, Dec. 22, and he shot them all, two in the back, and one of them is in a coma and New Yorkers are cheering Bernie Goetz and paying $1,161,000,000 for police not to be on the train.

What are we paying taxes for, to listen to Bernie Goetz' gun go off on the seat next to us?

Everyone knows that the most important part of the City of New York, the people riding the subway system, is largely unprotected.

If there can be a motorman and conductor for every train that runs in this city, night and day, then why can't there be two policemen on the train, too?

There is only one Bernhard Goetz. Where are these thousands of policemen? Who cost billions.

When we have Mayor Goetz in this city, there will be none of these questions any more.

We will have only point-blank answers.

January 17, 1985

They Call It Their Bumpurs Case

THAT MORNING, Paul Fava Sr., remembers, with the temperature rising to the 70s and people walking the Bronx streets without coats, his son Paul, 20, spent the morning washing and waxing the family car.

At 1 P.M. his son came in and got dressed in a gray sweatsuit, and the father drove him from their house on Country Club Road to the home of Dennis DeMartino, who lives in an apartment house on Hobart Ave., a block away from the el on Westchester Ave.

"I told him to have a good time," the father remembers. "He was going into the Navy the next day. The recruiting officer from Yonkers was going to pick him up at 6:30 in the morning."

As Dennis DeMartino, 22, remembers it, Paul Fava came into his bedroom and woke him up. Dennis had been home the night before, but had stayed up late.

"Get up," DeMartino remembers Paul Fava saying. "We're going out."

"Where?" DeMartino said.

"South Street Seaport."

"Why?"

"Because it's great man," he remembers Fava saying. "There are people there that bring radios and they chill out. You walk around and see cafes and things."

DeMartino got up and the two had chicken sandwiches and then they got dressed. Fava borrowed a white tank top from DeMartino and put it on under his gray sweatsuit top. DeMartino wore black levis and a gray and black vest.

DeMartino remembers that he and Paul Fava first started walking over to see a girl named Traci, who lived near Morris Park Ave. They had walked for about 10 minutes when Paul Fava saw two guys he knew who were passing in a car. He whistled and the guy stopped.

"They're two fatties from the neighborhood," DeMartino recalls. "Big overweight guys. Paul knew the names. I don't know the names."

The two drove them to the girl Traci's house and DeMartino

remembers that Paul Fava went in to pick up $20 that the girl Traci had borrowed from him. He came out, and the two fat guys drove them to the Westchester Square station of the No. 6 line.

DeMartino says he remembers hearing an el train passing overhead as they came up to the stop.

Bus routes start at Westchester Square, where there always are several of them parked near the el stop. As it was a sunny day, the benches around the square were filled with the old, who have made it a popular place to sit. It was nearly 4 P.M. when Fava and DeMartino went up the stairs to the change booth.

DeMartino doesn't remember seeing anybody else on the platform. He remembers that he wasn't finished with the Kool cigaret when the cops came.

The police say that they were called by bus drivers who said that somebody was throwing light bulbs from the platform to the street. DeMartino says that he and Fava threw no light bulbs. He scoffs at the idea, saying that both of them were too old. He says whoever threw the bulbs probably got on the train that came into the station while he and Fava were still down on the street.

Robert Francis, 16, a Lehman High School student who also takes weekend courses in art at the Fashion Institute of Technology, remembers that he was standing under the el, in front of a Chinese restaurant, when four or five light bulbs came through the tracks overhead and broke on the street. He is unsure of trains going or coming and he remembers seeing nobody going up or down the stairs. He does remember light bulbs hitting the street. He never heard any other sound. "You can't hear a gunshot," he says. "They're like a firecracker. A gunshot is not like in the movies."

There are only a couple of 60-watt light bulbs hanging from the roof over the el platform at Westchester Square. The rest of the sockets are empty. People in the area say that throwing the bulbs down is not uncommon.

But the first policeman up the stairs, a policeman answering a complaint about light bulbs being thrown, came onto the platform with his gun out. The police officer was Mervin E. Yearwood, 32. Behind him was Officer William Oates, 37.

DeMartino remembers that Oates had his gun out, too, but that it was Yearwood who pointed his gun at DeMartino and then at Fava. Both police officers were black and Fava and DeMartino are white, and in the times in which we live it unfortunately becomes important to say this.

The people who live in Fava's Bronx neighborhood insist that it is their Bumpurs case.

DeMartino heard somebody say, "Get against the wall."

He put his hands against the wall and the officer on him placed a hand flat against DeMartino's back and stood there. DeMartino remembers that he could not see the officer on him, but that he could see Fava and Yearwood.

He remembers hearing nothing. He only remembers that Yearwood's right hand, holding the gun, disappeared behind the right side of Fava's head. He could not see whether the officer had the gun cocked or not. He remembers seeing only Fava. He says he did not hear anybody speak and he did not see Fava move. DeMartino remembers that Fava did not flinch when the officer put the gun to his head and did not make any other movement.

And then Fava's head moved as the gun held to his ear went off. DeMartino saw the head flinch as the life flew out of a 20-year-old.

He remembers that Fava's knees buckled and his body went down and the head flopped forward and slid down the wall.

He remembers that Officer Yearwood suddenly flopped on the platform and appeared in distress.

"I got no sympathy for him," DeMartino said yesterday. He has been interviewed by the Bronx district attorney's office and is scheduled to be a witness in front of the grand jury that will be asked to hear the case. The policeman, Yearwood, is suspended.

Yesterday Fava's mother, Marianne, 45, was disturbed by this.

"What is to prevent this cop from leaving the country?" she said. She was with her husband, Paul Fava Sr., 46, in the rear of the large health foods store they own on Gramatan Ave. in Mount Vernon, a couple of blocks over the city line. She sat with coffee and staring at her hands.

"I want to call Merola up," Paul Fava Sr. said. "Is this guy under arrest? Are his weapons taken away? I don't want him to kill himself."

He showed a letter from Merola's office that congratulated Paul Fava Jr. for his testimony to a grand jury that helped send a burglar away for a four-to-eight-year sentence.

March 3, 1985

Torture Charge Could Prod Cops

A T THE start, it was over nothing, an alleged $10 sale of pot on a street corner in Queens, and now it has turned into a case that could change the system of law enforcement used in this city.

At approximately 7:30 P.M. last Wednesday, Mark Davidson, 18, was talking to Denise Memminger, 21, on the corner of 132d St. and 111th Ave. in South Ozone Park, in Queens.

Both are black. They are from solid New York families. Davidson, in his last year at Martin Van Buren High School, has a mother and brother who work at TWA at Kennedy Airport. His father, a retired postal worker, is in Fort Hamilton Veterans Hospital with bad legs.

Denise Memminger works in the dietary department at Long Island Jewish Hospital. Her father, Raynard, 43, is a night supervisor for United Parcel Service. He has been employed by United Parcel for 19 years. The Memminger name is known in the city's sports history because a cousin, Dean, played for the New York Knicks world championship team in 1973.

As Mark Davidson and Denise Memminger talked last Wednesday, a gray station wagon pulled up and, as both recall, six policemen jumped out, five in uniform and one in plainclothes. All were white.

What six policemen were doing out on an alleged $10 pot buy is one small question. How six policemen could be involved in the sale and then manage to miss making the arrest on the spot is another. These points are quite small, however, compared with the charges about what happened next.

The young woman was sent home. Mark Davidson says he was taken to the 106th Precinct stationhouse. The police had Joseph Patterson, an older man, already at the precinct for being part of the alleged pot sale. Davidson was taken upstairs and says a tall man in a police uniform walked out of an office and demanded to know what Davidson had done with the $10. Davidson again said he didn't have the money because he was not involved in the sale.

Davidson said the tall man, who appeared to be in charge, took him into a room where, the teenager says, he then was punched in the right eye. Davidson had been to an eye doctor earlier that day for an examination, and the doctor now certifies that there was no mark around either eye. Davidson then says that the tall man slammed his head into the wall twice. He says that the tall man then left the room and reappeared in streetclothes and with a can of Budweiser beer. Davidson said the tall man again demanded to know about the $10. The tall man called out the door that he would find out. Davidson says that when he did not answer the man put something on his back which gave him an electric shock. He says that he yelled as loudly as he could when he was shocked.

Davidson says he turned around and saw the tall man holding something that was black and fit in his hand and had two metal prongs about 6 inches long. The man then started to apply the prongs to Davidson's body, front and back, and sent shocks through him repeatedly. Davidson yelled. He says no other policeman entered the room to see what was causing the yelling.

Davidson says that he believes the shocks went on for about 20 minutes. He says he yelled loud enough for anybody in the police station to hear him. He says that he asked to call his mother. The tall man with the instrument shocking his body refused him, saying that they were not part of a television program. Davidson says the cop threatened to put the shock apparatus to his testicles. At that point, Davidson says, he made up the story about spending the $10 in a store.

After many shocks, Davidson shouted that he spent the $10 in a store on the corner of Linden Blvd. and Van Wyck Expressway. Davidson says that he made this up in order to get the cop to stop torturing him.

The store owner, Raphael Duran, 39, says that policemen came to his store about 10 P.M. on Wednesday and checked the $10 bills he had in his cash register. The marked bill was not there. Duran said the police did not ask if a young man fitting Davidson's appearance had been in earlier with a $10 bill.

Denise Memminger's father and mother went to the precinct last Wednesday night to complain about their daughter being searched on the street by male cops twice. Memminger had no pad with him and took down two shield numbers and names on scraps of paper. One was badge No. 17937, the officer's name: Aranda. The other was 31698. Memminger wrote down the name as Baladasa.

Memminger said that then a tall cop in plainclothes, who said he was the superior officer in the narcotics unit, came down and was abusive. Memminger says that the tall cop who argued with him fits Davidson's description of the tall man who tortured him.

"He said that he could do anything that he wanted," Memminger says of the tall cop. "Then he got into a fight with my wife. I told my wife to shut up. I was on their turf and I didn't want any strange accidents happening to me."

At 10 P.M. on last Wednesday, Davidson was taken to Central Booking at the 112th Precinct stationhouse. He was not brought to night court, a half dozen blocks away, until 7 P.M. on last Thursday where he was charged with criminal sale of marijuana in the fourth degree, a misdemeanor. He also was listed as a juvenile offender.

The Memminger young woman had notified Mrs. Davidson of the arrest. Mrs. Davidson went to the precinct at 10 P.M. Wednesday and was unable to see her son. On Thursday, she retained Marvyn M. Kornberg, who is famous in Queens for his aggressive style. Kornberg began squalling about the electric burn marks on his client's body. In court, the assistant district attorney had the body marks videotaped. A call to the Police Department internal affairs division brought the response that a matter such as this should be turned over to something called the police civilian complaint review board.

When Davidson was released after being arraigned, Kornberg took him to an office on Queens Blvd.

"Lift up your shirt," Kornberg said.

Davidson lifted the shirt. On his bare skin there were sets of burn marks, of the size and color of burns made by cigarets, in neat twos, as if put there by prongs. There were 11 sets of burns on his chest. Twenty two burns. He had 10 sets of burns on his back. Twenty burns. Also, one long burn, which suggested that the instrument was dragged over his back.

"He put them on my rear end, too," Davidson said. Then last Friday night, with Queens District Attorney John Santucci overseeing the case, Davidson was examined by a New York City Medical Examiner Manuel Fernando. Assistant District Attorney Greg Leshak was present.

The medical examiner said that the burns were caused by electricity and not stabs or cigarets and had occurred within the last 36 hours. The medical examiner said that one long line on Davidson's back was consistent with a person wriggling his body in an attempt to get away from an electric shock.

Santucci then had a search warrant issued for police lockers in the 106th. His staff supervised the search, which was carried out with Internal Affairs officers.

Apparently, the instrument was not found. Kornberg believes it is a stun gun, or an instrument similar to those illegally used at the race track to shock horses.

There now undoubtedly will be a lineup of cops and a grand jury investigation. And, coming at a time of the Michael Stewart and Eleanor Bumpurs cases, the matter of Mark Davidson allegedly tortured in a Queens precinct, at the least will cause more pressure for a special state prosecutor to be named to handle cases of police brutality. One look at Davidson's body would end most of the opposition to a special prosecutor.

Yesterday in Ozone Park, on a lamppost in front of the 106th, there was a sign for a non-existent cross street. Hill Street, the sign read. On any other day, this would have brought a smile. Seeing the sign in the gray morning yesterday only heightened the impression that the real police and those on television get confused in the minds of both public and police.

A sergeant named Carl Danielson was on duty at the desk of the 106th yesterday.

"Is the captain in?" he was asked.

"No."

"Is there somebody in charge?"

"You're looking at him," the sergeant said.

He said that none of the officers involved in the Davidson arrest was on duty. He said that maybe a lieutenant would be in by 4 P.M.

In the meantime, a precinct that might be involved in a case of torturing an arrested 18-year-old sat yesterday with only a sergeant in charge. Nice guy, but still a sergeant. Superior officers, who are supposed to keep tight order in the department, were nowhere to be found.

April 21, 1985

Putting the Cattle Prod to Justice

MARK DAVIDSON walked along Queens Blvd. yesterday, past the dry cleaners and the Pastrami King and up to an office building across the street from the courts in Kew Gardens. Technically, he was a defendant on his way to see his lawyer upstairs. In reality, of all the people who have walked this patch of ground before taking up business with the law, Davidson could be the one who could cause the most change in our time.

He is 18 and has never been arrested and he says that policemen of the City of New York in the year 1985 tortured him with electricity. There is evidence that appears to back this up.

His mother, Ladell, her eyes tired, and a friend, Denise Memminger, 22, were with him. Denise had an auburn hint to her hair, wore large earrings and blue jeans and sneakers.

"What did you do all day?" Davidson was asked. He wore a light blue warmup suit and sneakers.

"School."

"He just got home from school before," the mother said. "Give him a bite to eat before we came here."

Last Wednesday, Denise and Davidson were standing on the corner of 132d St. and 111th Ave. in South Ozone Park, an old Queens residential neighborhood. Six cops jumped out of a stationwagon, searched the two, found nothing, then let Denise go and arrested Mark for selling two bags of pot. He was taken to the 106th Precinct. There, last Wednesday night, in a second-floor room, Davidson says he was tortured by two cops. He says they used a black electrical instrument that put 42 burn marks on his chest and back. A medical examiner said the burns and the time they probably were inflicted were consistent with Davidson's story.

It is easily the most disturbing story to come out of law enforcement in this city. Torture by electricity represents a collapse into sadism that usually is associated with foreign lands, not a New York City police precinct on a street in Queens.

Davidson was on Queens Blvd. yesterday to look at pictures of policemen to see if he could pick out the two who tortured him with the electricity machine, probably something called a Nova 500, which is a small cattle prod.

Davidson yesterday went up to the second-floor office of his attorney, Marvyn Kornberg. He waited there for a call from a district attorney, who was across the street getting photos together.

"Have you spoken to any police?" Mark was asked.

"They talked to a friend of mine," Mark said.

"They said to him, 'Do you know Mark?' He said no. So they said to him, stop lying. He said that he knew me. They said to him, 'You're a hoodlum, too.'"

"What was your friend's name?" he was asked.

"Chink. Drina's little brother."

Somebody in the office asked him, "How clear did you see the faces of the cops?"

Kornberg interrupted. "That's for a court of law."

"How many times did you ask them to stop?" Davidson was asked.

"I'm not sure. It was a lot."

The questions were being asked by reporters, who leaned against office walls. Now photographers came in and Davidson was asked to stand up and show the burn marks. He stood and took off his shirt. A big strong handsome kid with these evenly spaced burn marks across his stomach and back. Forty-two of them.

"You're a big kid. How did they hold you down?" he was asked.

"I was handcuffed behind the back."

The lawyer took the electrical device and held it to the young man's body to show that each set of burns had the same spacing as the machine. Then somebody took the machine off to the side and pressed the button. There was a sharp crackle and blue electricity appeared.

Then the phone rang and Kornberg answered it, nodded and hung up. He told Davidson to put on his shirt and the two walked out of the office. They went downstairs and out onto Queens Blvd., and were immediately surrounded by reporters and television camera crews. If there is anything that can trivialize torture, it is the form of today's news gathering.

For as Davidson walked across the boulevard, he was in the same position as any cheap politician or singer or chicken stand owner or whatever it is that constitutes a celebrity that day.

But he walked over to a side entrance to Borough Hall, which is a few yards away from the court building. The homicide division of the Queens district attorney's office has a bureau office one flight up. Davidson walked upstairs with his lawyer and was gone. Inside, he would go over the photos of New York City policemen and try to pick out two who were torturers.

It was five o'clock by now, and from the regular offices of Borough Hall, from the sewer department and the real estate taxation offices, women streamed out and headed home.

One group, seeing the crowd following Davidson, stopped and watched.

"I know who that is," one woman, a burly blond, said. "That's the guy that the cops beat up."

"They didn't beat him up, they charged him up with electricity," the one next to her said.

"Could you imagine that?" the blond said. "Whoever heard of a thing like that?"

"And in Queens," her friend said.

Upstairs, Davidson sat at a table and was shown a card on which were eight new color photos of policemen. He looked and immediately pointed at the second picture on the card.

"He put the machine on me," Davidson said. "I don't have to look at anybody else."

He then was shown a second sheet of photos. The finger went to one picture immediately.

An officer from the Internal Affairs Division then pulled out an envelope, vouchered by the property clerk—obviously the result of a search—and took from the envelope a small black electrical device. The device had light fingerprint dust on it. The Internal Affairs officer asked Davidson if he had seen the device before.

"I can't tell you, because I was in pain," Davidson said. "But that looks like it."

In another room, there were the six members of the narcotics team that had arrested Davidson last Wednesday night. And now, a Police Department supervisor stepped into the room and indicated that two of the policemen were to leave and go into another room. Apparently, they either were being suspended or arrested.

Then Mark Davidson walked out into a wet Queens night and went home. He had to get up for school in the morning.

April 23, 1985

In This Scandal, the Buck Stops

I N QUEENS, where once so many were raised as the children
of policemen, perhaps as many as five members of the Police
Department of the City of New York could be under indictment on charges spreading from the alleged torturing with
electricity of a helpless and handcuffed teenager in the 106th
Precinct in Ozone Park.

Always in New York, a police scandal meant payoffs from
bookmakers, prostitutes or the narcotics traffic. Commissions
were established, prosecutors had great careers and there was
always a sort of hero cop who came forward with assorted tales
which enchanted movie producers. But through the Gross
bookmaking scandal and Serpico and the Knapp Commission,
the problem was only over money.

Those policemen expected to be dragged into court in
Queens would be there on charges of torturing citizens, an act
usually associated with another century or continent.

None of the policemen lives in this city. But they have made
us all lousy.

This tale of squalor began last April 18, a Thursday, when at
6:30 P.M. the clerk in Part AR-1 of the Queens courthouse in
Kew Gardens held up a fresh list of prisoners who had been
brought to the courthouse by van from Police Central Booking
at the 112th Precinct.

Marvyn Kornberg, a lawyer who was sitting on one of the
spectators' benches, asked the clerk, "Do you have a Mark
Davidson?"

The clerk nodded. Kornberg walked to the door leading to
the detention pens, one flight over the courtroom. In one of
the pens upstairs, four young men, all blacks, were sitting.

"Which one of you is Mark Davidson?" Kornberg said. He
had never seen Davidson. The night before, Davidson's mother
had reached Kornberg. Her son had been arrested on charges
of selling $10 worth of pot to an undercover policeman. David-
son, who had never been arrested before, was grabbed by a half
dozen cops five blocks away and a half hour after the alleged
sale. He claimed mistaken identity. Davidson automatically

qualified for youthful offender treatment on the charge, and an adjournment contemplating dismissal usually is given in these cases.

When Kornberg called out the name, one tall light kid came up to the cell bars. The others in the cell turned their backs. Among the customs learned by young blacks and Hispanics in this city is one that calls for leaving a man alone when he talks to his lawyer. Any attempt to overhear the conversation is considered a breach of manners.

Mark Davidson had light skin and eyes that were a mixture of green and blue. One of the eyes, the right, was blackened.

"What happened to your eye?" Kornberg said.

"The cops did it," Davidson said. He held out his right wrist to show a burn mark made by handcuffs. "They did this, too."

Kornberg was unimpressed. For years, lawyers have stepped out of holding pens and reported to the judge that their clients inside were scarred from police beatings. These claims usually are met with bored stares. Many defendants lie. And the people who actually have been beaten don't complain too strenuously.

"You're brought up in one of these ghetto neighborhoods to expect a beating when you're arrested," Kornberg said. "I had a guy whose arm was broken by police and he came out for the arraignment with the arm in bandages. Nobody cared."

But the client this time pulled up a T-shirt that said "Greater New York." He showed Kornberg electrical burns that dotted his stomach and lower back. "The cops did this to me, too," Davidson said.

Kornberg stared at the burn marks and left Davidson and went downstairs and found an assistant district attorney, David Everett. He told Everett what he had just seen. Everett said that it should be reported to the Police Department's Internal Affairs Division. Everett called from the courthouse and was told by the division that this was a matter for the Civilian Complaint Review Board. Everett then called a special field Internal Affairs unit. The answer was the same.

"This is insanity," Kornberg said. "If this kid upstairs had paid a lousy $20 bribe to a cop, the Internal Affairs would be all over the case. But they don't want anything to do with police brutality. We're trying to report a torture and all they want to hear is a twenty dollar bill."

Everett decided that the district attorney's office would look into the case without the help of police. As Queens District Attorney John Santucci was born in the 106th Precinct, attended school there, represented it in the state Legislature and still lives there, only a few blocks from the stationhouse, there was no question about how intensive the investigation would be. There also was another dimension: If a case of this magnitude, occurring in his own neighborhood, ever got by Santucci, his present job—a very good job for a guy from Ozone Park—soon would be a memory. His future would be gone. Santucci, who likes both job today and promising future, had flames coming out of the sidewalks in front of the 106th.

At that moment, the most disturbing scandal in the history of the New York City Police Department erupted. Here was a department which allegedly was responsible for an 18-year-old black youth, handcuffed behind his back, being tortured with an electrical device by at least two white cops, with others present, in a precinct in Queens and would not even take a phone call of complaint about it. And the black youth, Mark Davidson, who still was in a cell upstairs in the courthouse, had a story to tell which, in the hours and days that were to pass, never changed, always checked out and always tested the anger of a listener.

Davidson first told the tale to his lawyer, then to me, then to a district attorney, then a day later in open court at a hearing where he was asked questions for three hours, and then, last Tuesday, to a Queens grand jury.

The word on Queens Blvd. last night was that the grand jury, too, had believed Mark Davidson's story.

Last Tuesday, after testifying to the grand jury, Davidson and his mother, Ladell, took the bus home to their two-story frame house at 111-11 135th St. in South Ozone Park, Queens.

"I'm so nervous. I don't know whether to go to work tomorrow or not," the mother said. "I work at Trans World, over at the airport."

"What do they have you doing?"

"In the food department. Tray setups. All the things on the tray. The cake, salad, cup, bread and butter. We set them all up. Then put them in the modules. They told me that I could take off because of this. Maybe I will."

She looked at her son. "He gets his eyes from his grand-father. The girls have been calling. I want him to settle down. He got to get out of school."

"How many days have you missed?" Mark was asked.

"Four."

"He only needs two credits to graduate," the mother said.

"I'll graduate, don't worry about it," Mark said.

One of his teachers at Martin Van Buren High School, David Mead, has said that he expects Davidson to graduate, and that he would encourage Davidson to go on to college.

"What tests do you have to pass?" Mark was asked.

"History is one of them. The history is up-to-date stuff. We learn how the White House runs. How the Capitol in Washington runs. About all different laws."

"Do you talk about law enforcement?"

"We learn the different courts. How someone has the right to go to the State Court of Appeals. Then you got the right to go to Supreme Court."

"Do you discuss the police?"

"No. The only time we talked about them is when the lady officer was killed in the jail. How the guy who killed her took his case to the Supreme Court. We talked about that."

"Nobody mentioned your case?"

"My teacher mentioned about the weapon being outlawed. And everybody else said to me, 'How you feeling?' That's all."

"What do you think about what happened?" he was asked.

"I think the district attorney and everbody is doing a good job. I don't think about the rest of them."

The mother said, "I just worry. That, you know, maybe somebody will try to do something to us on account of this."

"I think you're a little too prominent for anybody to dare," she was told.

"So you think that we're out of trouble?" the mother said.

"You are. Nobody else is, though."

May 2, 1985

Ward Left His Job in San Francisco

I AM TOLD that something like 40 New York police personnel, most of them patrolmen, are to be brought into the
Internal Affairs Division because of their refusal to tell anything
to the Queen's district attorney about alleged torturing by
electricity of a handcuffed prisoner in the 106th Precinct.

The newspapers referred to this as a "blue wall of silence,"
which by the drama of the phrase makes it all seem acceptable.
Actually, the 40 are paid dollars by New York City to enforce
the law, and yet they refuse to solve a most ugly crime in their
own stationhouse.

The 40 are to be read a passage called General Order 15, a
departmental rule that gives immunity from criminal charges
to anybody answering questions in internal affairs. Once GO
15 has been read, however, the police officer must answer any
question, including those about torture in the 106th Precinct,
or be suspended on the spot and face a departmental trial that
would end the officer's employment and pension.

There should be 41 people brought into internal affairs. The
police commissioner, Benjamin Ward, should walk into the
place, read GO 15 to himself, and then suspend himself.

Two weeks ago, this torture broke open on a Thursday night
in Queens court in Kew Gardens. Benjamin Ward was in San
Francisco. I find it hard to believe that he wasn't notified that
night that something was up. If he was not, then we have a
Police Department so dumb that it can't tell the commissioner
what's going on. Ben Ward stayed in San Francisco on Thursday night. All day Friday, April 19, there was the beginning
of a major problem for the police. You had a strong lawyer,
Marvyn Kornberg, screaming, and an 18-year-old client with
marks all over his body. At least a couple of district attorneys
were listening. I was around with a notebook and pen.

Commissioner Ward stayed in San Francisco. I don't know
what he was doing in San Francisco, the guy gets paid for
being in New York and he goes to San Francisco. I am told
to be happy about this, that at least people knew where he
was this time. There was the Palm Sunday of 1984 when there

were 10 killed in East New York and nobody could find Ben Ward. The whole Police Department couldn't locate him. He was out there somewhere. We had 10 dead in East New York and a police commissioner out on a tear. Beautiful. Well, as I say, things were a lot better this time. At least somebody knew where the police commissioner was: He was 3,000 miles away from Ozone Park.

In this recounting, we are now up to Friday afternoon. There are phone calls being made throughout the Police Department. It was known that a newspaper and a district attorney were on to something. That creak was the roof about to fall. If the commissioner's office did not call Ward then his people are guilty of the highest of all treachery, which is incompetence. If they did call Ward and he did nothing, then we are dealing with the subject of this column, which is Ward getting out his job.

Go to Friday night. A medical examiner came into Queens District Attorney John Santucci's office and was asked to look at marks on Mark Davidson's body. The medical examiner purposely was not told anything about the case. He was simply asked what he thought could have caused the marks, and when were they made.

He looked, and then said, "They are electrical burns within the last two days."

An inspector from the Internal Affairs Division appeared out of nowhere in the office. Then there was another. Soon, there were men with braid all over their uniforms rushing about.

"I am in the police tailor shop," Kornberg said.

Lockers in the 106th were searched. Now it was about 9 P.M. in Queens, or 6 P.M. in San Francisco, where there were 10 P.M. flights to New York. Ben Ward stayed in San Francisco.

On Saturday, there was a sergeant, and nobody else in command in the 106th. All day, Ben Ward was in San Francisco. On Saturday night about 7, the New York Daily News newspaper came out with a column about the torture in the 106th. If there ever had been a chance for the investigation to be put aside, it now was gone. The column in The News newspaper caused the biggest and quickest reaction that I have experienced in a couple of decades. Out in San Francisco, Ben Ward could have had his clothes packed, had a farewell drink, and made a plane that would have placed him at Kennedy Airport, less than 5 minutes from the 106th, at dawn on Sunday. He did not move.

Finally, on Monday, with policemen being arrested in Queens on charges most shocking, did Ben Ward get out of San Francisco and return to New York, which pays him his salary.

The newspapers and TV of course did not bother to contact him in San Francisco. Which is a failing that will be dealt with in the next column. In the past, Ward appeared drunk in public and no newspaper, this one most prominent, did anything about it. The public should have been warned, and it was not.

Upon his return to the city late Monday, Ward became a frightened bureaucrat. He protected himself first. He began firing Police Department commanders on the theory that the alleged torture incidents happened while they were in charge.

What Ward neglected to consider was that it all had happened under his command, and that he had not even been in town, and that he didn't show enough interest in his city, or even enough fear of being unemployed, to rush to New York and to be around, simply as a sign that he cared. His Police Department was wounded in Queens and he sat in San Francisco.

For these and other transgressions against the city and its people for allowing a Police Department to fall apart and get involved in torture, Ward should stand up tomorrow and read himself GO 15 and then dismiss himself as a cop. He is a commissioner of police at a time when it is charged that an 18-year-old in handcuffs is tortured in a police precinct. It is at least poor taste for Ward even to think of remaining on the job.

May 5, 1985

His Days Turn to Daze on 8th St.

D AVID COMACHO, who is 27, remembers that it was last February, about 3 o'clock on a Friday afternoon, while he was working in the bookstore where he was assistant manager, that he felt the first fever. At 4 o'clock, he went into the back of the store and told the manager that he was going home. Which is why David remembers the time of day so clearly: It was the first time in his life that he left work early.

He took the bus home to his apartment on the second floor of a building on W. Eighth St. When his lover came home, David was in bed with a temperature of 102.

"Some kind of a flu," David said.

The fever remained all weekend. He got up on Monday to keep a regular appointment with a dermatologist in Greenwich Village. When he stepped out of the shower, he noticed his right side, particularly the arm, had turned scarlet. When the dermatologist saw it, he said it might be scarlet fever. He sent David to a doctor in Chelsea, who mentioned scarlet fever or German measles. The doctor drew blood for tests and David went home. As he remembers it now, the fever was gone when the blood test results came back. "One test showed that the T cells were real low," David says. "I went to see the doctor and he said, 'We have to keep an eye on that.'"

The T cells are the measurements of the immunity system. There are helper cells and suppressor cells. In counting them, there should be more helper cells, 1.6 and up, to each suppressor cell. If the helper cells dip and the suppressor cells rise, so does the suspicion of those reading the results.

David remembers that he felt well through the first part of March. Then one day he noticed a red welt on the base of his right thumb. He found another at the ankle. He wasn't concerned and forgot about them. After work one day, during a visit to his dermatologist, he happened to look at the welt on the thumb. It had grown.

"As long as I'm here, you might as well look at this," he said, holding the hand out.

He remembers the dermatologist looking at the thumb closely, then at the ankle, then picking up his head with this small smile and saying, lightly, "Oh, I think that we better do a biopsy on this." David went for the biopsy to his doctor on Seventh Ave. in Greenwich Village. While awaiting the results, he was at work in the bookstore, again on a Friday, and in mid-afternoon he again had a fever and left. He had more blood tests.

On the day he called the doctor for results, the doctor's secretary said, "Hello. We have the results of your tests."

"How were they?"

"You better come in. He'd like to talk to you."

He knows that as he walked from his house to the doctor's office on Seventh Ave., only a couple of blocks, it was sunny. He doesn't know what he thought about; he had entered the numb confusion of desperate illness.

The doctor told him that he had low T cells and that the welts on his thumb and ankle were Kaposi's sarcoma, which is the name given to a large tumorous lesion; call it anything, it still belongs to the word cancer.

The two, the unbalanced T cells and the tumor, meant that David Comacho, at 27, had AIDS.

In May, they found he had a form of tuberculosis that is rarely seen, for most bodies can throw it off. David Comacho, open to assaults from anywhere, was put into the hospital. His fever shot up to 104 and 105. Then one day the fever was gone and he was home. By now, it was last June. He had two good weeks in July and then the fever returned and he was back in the hospital for half of last August. He got out again and returned to Eighth St. The date this time doesn't count. By now, he measured nothing around him. Week, month, day, night, summer heat, fall chill, the color of the sky, the sound of the street, clothes, music, lights, wealth dwindled in meaning.

The other night, at home, he sat at the table in his large living room and smoked Salem cigarets and drank a container of coffee. The table was covered with medical reimbursement forms. In the last 12 days he said he had received 12 different insurance forms to fill in and mail back.

He has short brown hair and a handsome face. At 139 pounds,

he seems a little thin. He was born in Paterson, N.J., attended Rutgers and then came to Manhattan. Before he was ill, he was going for his master's degree.

He is open, likable and thoroughly brave. From his apartment, people could be heard calling to each other on W. Eighth St. David Comacho neither wails nor hides. He announces his illness for his people of his streets. "I want people to know that you can't get it by shaking hands or riding on the same bus. If you could, the whole city would have it by now. And I'm sure I've woken up other people. I have more meaning than a statistic in the paper or on television." As a member of the Village Independent Democrats, he was chairman of a club dinner at Windows on the World last spring that had the governor as the guest of honor. "I never said anything that night because it was a festive occasion and my illness had no place in it."

Now, sitting in his living room the other night, he had a large welt on the tip of his nose.

"From radiation?" he was asked.

"No. The disease."

"What do you do for it?"

"Nothing."

He held out his right hand. The welt on the right thumb was the size of a thumbnail.

"And for the hand?"

"Nothing."

"They have you waiting for something?"

He shook his head. "I'm not going to let them radiate any more. This was small." He touched his nose. "Now when they radiated, it grew. Look at it now. I'm not going to let them do it any more."

He had five bottles of pills in front of him. "These two are experimental drugs. They come in a box from the disease control center in Atlanta. This is Clofazimine." He touched a white plastic bottle. The other, in a glass bottle, had a label that said it was ansamycin. "This one," he said, holding up the white plastic bottle, "when I signed the release form to let them use this medicine on me, the bottom of the form said, 'The side effects may be permanent skin discoloration from red to purplish black.' I got the tan, which is socially acceptable."

"Do any of the pills do any good?" he was asked.

"They're just guessing. The only thing doctors can do is monitor the thing. And all you really can do for yourself is laugh about it. The days you can't laugh are the worst. When I find I can't make myself laugh, I stay in bed. There's no sense getting up. Other times, I try. I force myself out of bed and do 20 pushups. I used to do 40 while the shower was getting warm in the morning. I used to bound up the steps here two at a time. I don't do that any more, but I still can make it up."

"Can anything happen?" I asked him.

"It's a question of time. They didn't kill polio in six months. Kill is a wrong word. Subdue. If I can last another two years, they'll have something to keep it under control. All those Nobels are hanging out there. Someone will grab one of them."

"What about your lover?"

"I'm sure the fear has passed through his mind. We're relieved that studies have shown that partners do not have a great susceptibility to it. His T-cell count is fine. What do we do now? You don't have much sex with a 104-degree fever. No exchange of body fluids. Nobody knowledgeable would do that, anyway."

"Where is he tonight?"

"He's in Texas. He has a play he wrote opening there. He has to carry almost all the expenses here. I get only $440 a month from Social Security. The rent here, forget it, it's $850. A friend of ours looked at all my bills and at my income and said, 'David, you just can't make it like this.' I said, 'Well, then we're just going to have to have a smash hit on Broadway.'"

David put on a sweater and an Army field jacket and went downstairs. He waved into the open doorway of a clothing store and the two women at the counter smiled and called out to him. Then he went down the front steps and into the life of Eighth St.

And then I called David up Friday to check on a couple of things and he answered the phone with a dull voice.

"You're not laughing," I said.

"No. I just got off the phone with the doctor. He told me the test results came back and he thinks the cancer has spread to the lungs. I just got off the phone with him."

I said nothing.

"I'm trying to keep myself together by washing the windows," he said.

November 3, 1985

Sick with AIDS and Without Real Aid

WHEN HE was in high school, his family moved down from Philadelphia onto a farm a mile outside of this town in southern Georgia, right there by the Alabama line, a town with the old Southern Railway tracks still running through the middle, with the town square and its pre-Civil war courthouse and all the decent folks on the east side of the tracks, the blacks and the white trash on the other. Most everybody not on a farm worked at West Point-Pepperell, making sheets and towels in a nonunion plant. His father liked the town's values. No public drinking, although he took a drink himself, and a whole lot of churches.

On those first nights on the farm, he remained awake for hours listening to the tree frogs and crickets. One of his two sisters jumped into the town life, and was on the football cheering squad at high school. When the others called out, "*Spy*-rit!" and she said, "Sp*ear*-rit!" everybody got mad at her because she couldn't do the cheers *raht*. He and his other sister decided they wouldn't even go to the games because of this. On game nights, they rode around town in a van and got drunk and high.

When he went to the University of Georgia, the big yell in the stands at the football game was, "Go get 'em, *Dawgs*!"

His interest in books instead of admiration for the football team irritated the father, who wanted to hear about get-'em-Dawgs! and not about poetry festivals, and so his son remembers being told by the father, "You're an overeducated, philosophical ass. You got no common sense," and he told his father, "You mean like you, sense real common?" The back of the father's neck turned into a steam iron.

He took out girls, which was just all right, he remembers, and then this girl Debbie told him that the best disco up in Atlanta was a gay place and they went there, drinking and dancing, and while there was no moment when the body suddenly understands, he felt more than comfortable that night. "I went into the grey area right after that," he said. Soon, Debbie, who thought she was going to marry him, realized that the best they were going to have together was friendship.

433

"Every good family has a gay, and I guess I'm the one in mine," he said. He stayed in Atlanta, with other young people who had left small Georgia towns because they didn't want folks to know they were gay. Then he went to New York.

"There was never one time when I said anything to my family or they said anything to me," he recalls. "I lived without words."

He got a public relations job in Manhattan, took an apartment on Seventh Avenue in Greenwich Village and went into the gay bar called "Uncle Charlie's Downtown," where the customers appear to be out of prep schools. "I never went to bathhouses," he says. "But I had more than one partner in the last five years, so I guess I have been exposed to AIDS."

Last spring, he went back to Georgia for the first time in five years. He stopped in Atlanta and saw his friend Debbie, who now is a schoolteacher and still single. "I'm mad at you," Debbie said. "I was counting on you." He told her that he couldn't help. Then he went home to the family farm in the small town which, at this time, was talking about the murders of two transvestites, one in March, the second only two weeks before he arrived. This second gay had been shot three times in the head and thrown in a dumpster. The county sheriff told the Atlanta Constitution newspaper that the murders were being investigated.

As he read the story, he told himself, "This isn't the place for you." He went back to Manhattan early.

Last summer, he had a $500-a-week job in a public relations place, but was not covered by hospitalization insurance. He worked at night as a play reader and through this he was able to join a group health insurance plan on the first of August, the policy to be effective on the 13th of the month.

On August 6th, he met friends and had a vodka in a bar on 43d Street, went to a screening of a film called "Summer Rental," and afterwards went to a restaurant near Lincoln Center. As he stepped inside the door, he felt dizzy. He never had fainted in his life, but he was certain he was going. He stepped outside and took a breath. The dizziness increased. He went to the curb and got in a cab and went home. He went to the toilet and blood poured out of him. He called a friend, who wasn't home, and got the lover, who has AIDS and was having a tough night, but came to the apartment at 10:30 P.M. and helped him to St. Vincent's Hospital. Doctors first thought it was an ulcer. He told himself that it had to be something like that, for there had been none of the usual announcements of AIDS: night sweats, sudden weight loss, swollen glands, lesions on the extremities. They decided to operate the next day.

When he looked up in the recovery room, he saw his mother and one of his sisters. A nun came and took them for a cup of coffee. He was in intensive care when a doctor walked in and began poking at his glands. He remembers saying to himself, "Is he giving me an AIDS exam?" His mother was there the next time the doctor came in.

"You have Kaposi's sarcoma," the doctor said. "One of them was on an artery. That caused your trouble. There are 10 or 12 more in there."

"What does that mean?" his mother said.

He remembers mumbling to his mother, "That is the cancer you get when you have AIDS."

He and his mother looked at each other. Now the life he never talked about was part of the family album.

He remembers hearing a noise and looking up. Debbie was standing in the room.

"I can't believe you're here," he said.

"Hey, where did you expect me to be?" she said.

His father arrived by car the next day. The father was nervous and left the room every couple of minutes and went for something to eat.

On the second day, he was in bed with tubes down his throat and in his nose and he was thinking that maybe he wouldn't heal from the operation because of his weak immunity system, and then his father walked into the room and right away, he could sense what was coming.

He remembers the father saying, "I'm sorry, son, but I can't help but believe that your living this deviate life style is why you're sick. I can't help but believe that God is punishing you for your life style."

The father got up and started pacing. The mother whispered, "I'm so sorry."

On the next day, he remembers the father coming in and saying, "Have you learned your lesson? Maybe if you give up your life style, God will forgive you and you'll get well."

He remembers whispering to his father, "Do you want grandchildren with AIDS?"

Later, when Debbie came in, she became angry. The mother and sister, with an ally, stood up and told the father to go back home, that he was of no use here.

Debbie and the mother stayed in New York until he was out of the hospital. On Aug. 21, the day he was released, he received a letter at home from Blue Cross-Blue Shield. It said that his contract did not cover an admission to a hospital before the effective date of his membership. The effective date was Aug. 13. He was admitted to St. Vincent's on Aug. 6. The letter also said, "Nor does it provide benefits for any condition, disease or ailment which existed on that date (Aug. 13) until your enrollment has been in continuous force for eleven months." He had a hospital bill from St. Vincent's for $18,076.60, nothing to pay it with and no medical insurance for whatever comes next in a disease that lurks outside the limits of science and imagination.

He returned to work at the start of fall. He looks good and says he feels fine. The other day, the owner of his public relations firm announced, "I have to be 'up' all the time to do my job right. He is making me depressed. I don't know if I can have him here any more. I don't have the head for this."

Nor, of course, the heart.

The owner now told him that he could work only half days, and his salary was cut to $325 a week, which barely covers his rent and leaves him still owing a back medical bill and facing more each week. If his life becomes tougher, if he can't make it in New York, he always can go home to his father and the farm in the small town in Georgia.

November 7, 1985

Shooting Script

THE COURTROOM was empty in the morning, and the guard said that the hearing on Bernhard Goetz' motion to have the charges against him dismissed wouldn't be heard until 2:30 in the afternoon.

Goetz, he said, wasn't expected. "The lawyer comes here, not Goetz."

"Are you sure?" I asked him.

"Oh, we'd know. We would've been told to have security ready if Goetz was coming. Only the lawyer is showing."

As it was now only 9:30 A.M., I decided to walk over to St. Vincent's Hospital to see Darrell Cabey, one of the four unarmed teenagers from the Bronx who was shot on the subway train by Goetz on Saturday afternoon, Dec. 22, 1984.

When three of them approached Goetz on the No. 2 train and asked for $5, Goetz jumped up and shot them. He then shot Cabey.

Goetz said he shot because he was defending himself in a robbery. He told police he then walked over to Cabey, looked down at him and then said to Cabey: "You don't look too bad, here's another."

He then shot Cabey in the back.

When all this was presented to a grand jury, Goetz was indicted for attempted murder of all four.

Since last December, Cabey, paralyzed, has been in St. Vincent's Hospital. He was 19 when they carted him into the place and now he is 20. He never has said anything in public during the year because for much of the time he was unable to speak.

Yesterday, I called his mother in the Bronx and told her I would meet her at the hospital and both of us could go up and see her son. Then I walked over to St. Vincent's.

When I got there, an administrator, Dan Sorrenti, was in the lobby. He said that Cabey didn't want to see me.

I called Cabey on the house phone from the lobby.

"What is this, you don't want to see me?" I said. "I'm a very important person."

The voice on the other end of the phone laughed. "You comin' up?" he said.

"Yes."

I took the elevator to his room and went inside with two administrators and a doctor. Cabey was sitting in a wheelchair. He wore a yellow sweater and striped pajama pants.

Tubes showed at the bottom of his pants. He had on gold-framed glasses. His upper torso appeared in fine shape. Flat under the yellow sweater.

Many times over the last few months, I have been told that Cabey remembers nothing about the day of the shooting.

His recollection, everybody said, ends at the point where he walked through the subway turnstiles in the Bronx and got on the train that day.

I thought, then, that any conversation with him yesterday would be unimportant. I asked him how he felt, and he said, in a voice that was a little thick, that he was fine. He told me his favorite soap opera was "Loving."

"So all you can remember is going through the turnstile?" I asked.

"Turnstile on 14th St.," he said.

"You didn't get on at 14th St., did you? I thought you got on in the Bronx."

"We were traveling. I think so."

He seemed confused. The emotion of talking about the day slowed his speech.

"Well, do you remember the shooting?"

"Yes."

"Do you remember Goetz?"

"He had on glasses and a beige coat."

"What else do you recall?"

"I wasn't with them. I know them."

Obviously, he meant the other three.

"I know what they were trying to do. I left them and went one car away. I didn't want to be with them."

"You weren't even in the same car?"

"I came back. I was talking to them. I shouldn't have talked to them. Goetz saw me talking to them. He was down with them. They goin' rob him."

"Who were they going to rob?"

"Goetz."

"Where were you when it happened?"

"I came back to the car. I sat down a couple of seats away. I wasn't with them."

"Why were they going to rob Goetz?"

"They were goin' to rob him. They thought he looked like easy bait."

"That's why they went up to him?"

"He looked like he had money. They ask him for $5."

"Is that all they wanted from him?"

"Five dollars," he said again.

"Did they pull out screwdrivers?"

There were two screwdrivers inside one jacket and a third inside another jacket when police and ambulance workers removed the clothes from the wounded teenagers who had been shot. The popular belief is that the screwdrivers, sharpened, were waved in Goetz' face.

"No. No screwdrivers."

"How were they going to rob him?"

"Just scare him."

He made a motion with his right arm in the air. I didn't know what he meant and I asked him about this a second time and he said: "Scare him."

Then, referring to robbing Goetz, he said: "I could see they were going to do that. I said to myself, I don't want to be involved. It was a train ride on a Saturday. I wasn't looking for no trouble. Mind my business."

Questioning had to be sparse, for Cabey, who was having some trouble in speaking now, became uneasy when I attempted to ask him about something a second time, or when I asked him something too rapidly.

The three hospital people in the room also grew restless when Cabey showed nervousness.

People at St. Vincent's are proud that they have brought Cabey this far. He was in a coma for weeks, then for long months was unable to pronounce a word such as "cat."

"Did you see him shoot?" He nodded.

"How did he shoot you?"

"He turned and he looked both ways."

Cabey now imitated how he remembers Goetz. He looked

right and left in the room. "Then he saw me. He saw me talking to them before. He looked and he saw me. He pointed the gun at me."

Cabey held both hands out as if firing a gun. "He shot me. Right here."

Cabey twisted in the wheelchair and his hand went around to the lower right side of his back. "He shot me right here."

"Did you hear him say anything to you?"

He shook his head no.

"What do you remember him doing?"

"I see him run down the train."

Nobody else in the room talked. Then Cabey said: "There's something in the news about Goetz today?"

"There is a hearing in court later today. Do you want to know what happens with it?"

"Yes."

"What do you think of Goetz?"

Cabey's face became expressive and his body moved in the wheelchair. "He's crazy."

As I walked out, Cabey rolled out into the hall in his wheelchair. He stopped to talk to a nurse halfway down the hall.

The other three with Cabey that day were Barry Allen, 19; James Ramseur, 19; and Troy Canty, 19. The other day, Allen 19, surrendered to police in a mugging of a Bronx man. He is in jail.

As is James Ramseur, who is now awaiting trial on raping an 18-year-old girl in the Bronx last May. Troy Canty is in the Bronx and has no present troubles with the law.

And in court in Manhattan yesterday, the decision was reserved on the motion by Bernhard Goetz' lawyers to have the charges dismissed. I called Darrell Cabey at the hospital, couldn't get him and left the message for him early last night.

November 26, 1985

Life in a Cage

THAT WINTER, when the landlord didn't give any heat because, as people in the building remember him telling them, he simply forgot to do it, Juan Perez would wake up and go right into the shower. All the time that anybody knew him, the little boy started the day with a shower. All that winter it was a shower with icy water, which made all the other people cringe, he couldn't wait to jump in each morning.

"He came to this apartment in the morning," Frances Tamariz was saying yesterday, "with this wet head. And I would say, Bezoki, that was the name we called him, Bezoki, how can you go around with a wet head when we are all so cold? Did you take a shower? And he would say, 'Yes, I love the cold water.' That was what he was like."

Frances Tamariz lives on the second floor and the family of Juan Perez on the first floor of 162 E. 18th St., in Flatbush, a neighborhood of old apartment houses that are packed with people who trace their beginnings from anywhere from south of Virginia to the islands in the last waters of the Caribbean. Frances Tamariz is Peruvian. Just walking along yesterday, on any avenue, down any street, there seemed to be easily more children than can be seen anyplace in the city. Around the corner from the Perez house yesterday, I counted 43 kids on the street and when I turned the corner and got to number 162, where Juan Perez lived, here was a woman walking into the building who had seven children with her.

The name Juan Perez was the special one yesterday, for on Tuesday night, a raw night for the time of year, he slipped into the polar bear cage at the Prospect Park Zoo, a few blocks away, and intended to swim in the partially water-filled bear moat. When the other two kids with him were afraid of the water because it was so cold, Juan Perez took their clothes and threw them in the water to make sure they'd have to go in after them. Then when the two polar bears, aroused and angry, padded toward Juan, the two friends ran, and Juan Perez, in the cold night, stayed and the polar bears caught him in the corner and began to bite him. As Juan Perez did not know how to be afraid, he told his friends to go and get help because the bears were biting him hard.

And so, at age 11, he became a kid living in the middle of teeming Brooklyn who was eaten alive by polar bears. As this was a special death for a young person, the streets of Flatbush were filled with reporters and television people and, everywhere you went yesterday, all along Prospect Park, here were these television microwave trucks with thick cables coiled around light poles, so the signal could be sent clear and strong to stations that cannot wait to get the pictures out. Pictures of anything: the park, the streets, the people. Get them out, get everything out, get anything out, for this was a most startling news story: Boy eaten in the heart of Brooklyn by polar bear.

I guess it was a momentous story because of the manner in which the boy died. But at the same time, perhaps somebody should stop just for a paragraph here this morning and mention the fact that there are many children being eaten alive by this bear of a city, New York in the 1980s. To say many is to make an understatement most bland, for there are hundreds of thousands of young in New York who each day have the hope, and thus the life, chewed out of them in a city that feels the bestowing of fame and fortunes on landlords is a glorious act, and that all energies and as much money and attention as possible be given to some corporation that threatens to move 40 people to Maryland.

We live in a city, in this New York of the '80s, which makes some builder like Donald Trump into a cheap celebrity, and has a mother who lives with her daughter in a shelter on Catherine St., saying, "You can tell anybody living in a shelter. They all stooped over. All you do is just be sitting all day on the edge of the bed, all hunched over. Nothing to do and no place to go. Just sit there with your little girl and try and amuse her."

And each day in the schools of this city, we stack dead chewed bodies of children up to the classroom ceilings and somebody, somewhere is keeping count and also track of those who are supposed to be in charge or there is no justice anywhere.

The two polar bears were shot.

And now, for the day, we go back to the most thrilling death of a young child, that of Juan Perez. Yesterday, Carmen Perez, the mother, was on the couch in her first-floor apartment, a relative cuddling her head. Others sat in an immaculate living room. The mother cannot speak English and she cannot read or write in any language. But maybe she didn't have time for things like that because she had this apartment on the first floor and there was no way to keep Juan Perez under control. If she walked into the front room, he went out the back window and into an alley and was gone. If she sat in the front room on one of her clean, neat couches and her eyes drooped just a little, Juan Perez was out the window and onto the sidewalk and gone.

"She always would chase him," Frances Tamariz was saying yesterday. "But he could run so fast. All he wanted to do was to go out on the street. There was nothing wrong. He always looked nice. The little clothes he had all were clean and pressed. All he wanted to do was run."

"Where was the father?" she was asked.

The father was a drunk. Frances Tamariz, in her proper way of talking, said, "The father was a person who abused alcohol."

"Did he live at home?"

"She got rid of him. He wouldn't work and he lost all hope. He just stayed on the street and drank. When he would come he would try to beat her up. She said to me one day, 'I can take care of myself and my children. I cannot support him.' She threw him out."

"Has he been around today?"

"He died two months ago. He died right out on the street."

"Where?"

"Oh, I don't know. On Church Avenue someplace. By the subway stop. He just died in the street. Then Carmen had to go out and get his body and bury him. He wasn't her husband any more and she had to bury him. I came home that night with my husband. My husband's name is Fidel. He is a painter. We were coming into the building and Carmen heard us and she opened the door and she told me that her husband died and that she needed money for the funeral. My husband gave her $20. The other people in the building collected money so she could bury her husband."

"How did Juan take it?"

"I saw him when the father died. Juan had on nice black

pants and a white shirt. Clean white shirt, all pressed. And he said, 'I saw my father. His face was swollen. But I wasn't afraid. I looked at my father. I wasn't afraid.'"

May 21, 1987

Trump: The Master of the Steal

SUDDENLY, WE have all these prudent, responsible bankers, loan papers crackling in their frightened hands, chasing madly after Donald Trump for money. It seems like great sport, but I must tell you that I believe this to be temporary and that Trump, no matter what kind of a crash he experiences now, will come back as sure as you are reading this. I now will tell you why.

Trump survives by Corum's Law. This is a famous, well-tested theory and is named after Bill Corum, who once wrote sports for the Hearst papers when they were in New York. He had a great gravel voice and did radio and television announcing for the World Series and heavyweight championship fights. He was a round little guy who was the youngest Army major in World War I, and when he came back he announced, "I just want to smell the roses." He read Balzac at the bar, often wrote exciting English, drank a ton of whiskey and lost as much money as he could find at the racetrack. He was a tough guy who understood weakness.

Corum was asked to become the head of the Kentucky Derby by Louisville businessmen who said they had a grave problem. Newspapers all over the world claimed Louisville was a place where Derby visitors were robbed. Prices were tripled, touts were everywhere and women who were supposed to be available and uncommonly glamorous turned out to be nothing more than common thieves.

Corum glanced at the clips and threw them in the air. "This is great. There is nothing better for a championship event than a treacherous woman. If a guy from North Dakota goes home from here after the race and has to be met because he doesn't even have cab fare left, that guy is going to say to himself, 'Wow, I must have had a hell of a time. I can't wait for next year.' But if that same guy goes home and he still has half his money, he is going to say 'I guess I didn't have such a great time at the Kentucky Derby after all.'

"Because, gentlemen, this is the rule. A sucker has to get screwed."

Corum ran the Kentucky Derby on this premise for years, and the game was good for all of Louisville. No sucker ever wept.

Today, Corum's Law runs all of Donald Trump's situation. But instead of horseplayers, the suckers who must get screwed are a combination of news reporters and financial people. It is all quite simple. Donald Trump handles these nitwit reporters with a new and most disgraceful form of bribery, about which I will tell you. He uses the reporters to create a razzle dazzle: There are five stories in the newspapers in the morning papers leading into 11 minutes of television at night. The financial people, who lead such dreary lives, believe what they read and see on television. Trump is larger than life. No, not Trump. Don't use that name. It's Donald! He cannot lose. The financial geniuses can't wait to rush into the glamour and lights. They want to touch Trump's arm. "Here, I'm from Prudential, the rock of Gibraltar. Take our $75 million to build another crap game. Can I ride on your boat?"

During 1989, when Trump announced he was buying the Eastern Shuttle and about to start a building on the West Side that could be seen from Toledo and would park 9,000 cars, he was on the first page of this paper and others as often as the logo. There were four stories about Trump in one day's issue of The New York Times newspaper. He had the joint from front to back. I remember looking at the paper with the four stories in it and saying to myself, "Look at this, all these years later and the Times hires a whole room full of guys who are out on the take." On television that night, all I saw was announcers genuflecting as they mentioned Trump's name. They mentioned it in unrelated conversation, as if Trump were a part of the language. I said, "What kind of a payroll must this guy have?"

But when I started to think about it, I immediately realized I was wrong. Things were even worse. These reporters were doing it for nothing! The scandal in journalism in our time is that ethics have disintegrated to the point where Donald Trump took over news reporters in this city with the art of the return phone call.

Trump bought reporters, from morning paper to nightly news, with two minutes of purring over the phone.

"I just talked to Donald!" I heard somebody say in the place where I work. "Donald called!" somebody at the Times told me they hear various reporters say, enthusiastically, almost every day. "I have to get off. Donald is on the other phone," a friend of mine at NBC said one day. They even put an article in front of his name, as if he were The Bronx.

Donald Trump, who must have been spending about half of each day on the phone with reporters and editors, owned the news business.

From reporters and bankers, the illusion spread. How can one forget the sight of wise businessmen standing at a book-store and buying Trump's book so they could learn something about business. These book buyers were taking a fall without even getting a phone call from Trump. The book was nothing more than safe-cracking by hardcover. Yet here were people working for a living reading and nodding at the sage advice, "Smell blood!"

Trump's next book, scheduled for publication any day now, has been held up. It is being edited with flea powder.

Once, here was healthy dishonesty in the news business in New York. Then, a gossip columnist named Walter Winchell had a nightclub build a personal barbershop for him. If Winchell had Trump, he would have made Trump bigger than the president. Winchell also would have been living on a full floor of the Plaza. But today all of this has been replaced. Not a quarter hits the floor. "I'm going to take over all of Atlantic City and then Los Angeles," Trump announced. It made the front pages. "Donald called!"

But all involved now, particularly the worried bankers, should know that Corum's Law remains. Trump will call and announce his rise. The suckers will write about a heroic indomitable spirit. Redemption makes an even better tale. So many bankers will grab his arm the sleeve will rip. All Trump has to do is stick to the rules on which he was raised by his father in the County of Queens:

Never use your own money. Steal a good idea and say it's your own. Do anything to get publicity. Remember that everybody can be bought.

The trouble with Trump's father was that he was a totally naive man. He had no idea that you could buy the whole news reporting business in New York City with a return phone call.

June 7, 1990

A Master Goes into the Skull

I N THE morning on Nov. 22, I was rolling down the hallway to an operating room at Barrow Neurological Institute in Phoenix, Ariz. A priest had visited me in my room before I was pulled out. Now I stared at the ceiling and kept seeing the faces of people I absolutely despise. I had promised the priest that I most certainly would stop my habit of slandering and backbiting at every chance. But now here was all this temptation up on the ceiling. I said, "Oh, lord, if you just let me call one of these people the name he deserves to be called, I will come out and build you a church."

Pre-Op Notes:
    09:20: *Patient arrived at OR per cart, alert and awake, pleasant and cooperative. No disgust noted.*
    Patient verbalizes understanding of procedure and wishes to proceed.
    Concerned with knowledge deficiency.

Reading this now, I think I was allowed a little anxiety about something happening to the front of my brain where any ability to write begins. Because the young guy back in the room next to me had received a blow on the head and for some time now had been unable to use nouns. If something happened to the curl in my brain that causes verbs I would be one of those home relief cases that people hate so much.

Already, however, I had been given an intravenous solution of Midazolam, a sedative that is a strong Valium. Almost immediately, I lost memory of anything, including the rats on the ceiling. In the operating room, I was given Diprivan and a synthetic narcotic called Sufanty. That was enough to knock out a cow. Certainly, it took care of my senses. I now was the body on a table for brain surgery. But while my brain was there, anything I could do with it was completely out of reach.

All these details from now on, therefore, come from notes that were dictated and placed on a computer by the surgical team. Also, by the recollections of some of the people who work in the operating room. There were seven in the operating room. The surgeon was Robert Spetzler.

The operation was listed as "Right Pterinonal Craniotomy with clipping of unruptured anterior communicating artery aneurysm." The "Right Pterinonal" refers to a ridge that separates the middle and front of the brain.

An aneurysm is a bulge in an artery and it usually is undiscovered and all too often bursts. When this happens, half of the people die on the spot, and of the survivors, half of them wind up as vegetables. The rest escape, although only they know in what condition.

In New York, every prominent name in medicine had told me to go to Spetzler when, by tremendous fortune, the aneurysm was found accidentally in the front of my brain. The State Health Commissioner, Mark Chassin, spent most of a day asking about doctors and at the end he said, "There are three surgeons in New York who can do this operation very well. However, if there is anything unusual, I would go to Spetzler."

I said, "It is a very unusual aneurysm. It is in me!"

I had never seen Spetzler until the day before, when I came to the hospital. He is a tall man with strong looking arms. He is 50 and was born in Wurzburg, Germany. He was at Case Western Reserve and was passed over as head of the neurosurgery department. You do not pass over anybody like Spetzler for any reason. He came to Phoenix and built an unusual center at the Barrow Neurological Institute, which is a seven-story building attached to St. Joseph's Hospital. Out here in the desert he built a reputation that now has people coming to him from all over the world. On this day, the Queen of Saudi Arabia had the whole top floor of the hospital taken. She had 45 doctors from all over the world, but was there because of Spetzler.

Spetzler has a baritone voice and is an old swimmer. He does things like ski out of helicopters. He takes chances for sport, and for a living.

From 9:20 A.M. until 10:30 A.M. on this morning, Nov. 22, they work to set me up properly on the operating table. My head had to be in what Spetzler considered perfect for orientation to the aneurysm. While the body was on the table, the head was hanging off and was held by three pins of a device called a Mayfield clamp. The head had to be rotated to the

precise angle needed to take the skull bone off and go into the
brain. The position of the body required no pressure on the
arms or legs. I was covered with a blue foam that looked like
the inside of a crate of eggs.

The operating room note said: "Patient in supine position
with head on a three-point Mayfield headrest. The right arm
foam padded and tucked onto the side. The left arm on foam
padded armboards. Extra foam padding to all pressure points.
Pillow underneath and lower legs. Carefully taped onto OR
table." While my head was being set, there were intravenous
lines put into the artery in my neck and into the arm. They
ran drugs into me and checked blood pressure and heartbeat.
Now Spetzler made a small exposure of the scalp, cutting the
hair with a thin razor. The skin was covered with a solution
called betadine.

They then isolated my head from the rest of my body and
the rest of the room by using sterilized drapes and sheets. The
room was dim and the temperature as cool as possible. Now
Spetzler sat on a chair that looks like something you'd find in a
barber shop. He operated the height and tilt of the chair with
his feet. In his mouth he had the controls to a microscope. He
kept a hand free to use on the operation itself. Now Spetzler
began by cutting to the bone with a thin scalpel. He ran a
straight line at the hairline to the right temple and then came
down a little.

He then picked up a Midis Rex high speed saw, whose speed
he operated with his foot. The Midis Rex saw looks like a heavy
fountain pen with a line attached to it that goes to a tank of
gas. The high speed saw operates at a thousand RPMs. First,
he drilled a small hole in skull at the top of the head. An entry
point was next. He changed the drill bit to use one that would
make the precise room he needed to go inside to get at the
aneurysm to go under the skin flap and inside. He sawed an
opening in the skull. There are two boney hard surfaces to the
skull, with a soft middle. The Midis Rex drill makes such a loud
sound as it saws the skull bone that many surgeons wear pilot's
earmuffs against the high-frequency sound that often causes
loss of hearing.

Now, in the cool and darkness, the one light coming from
the ceiling picked out the cloud of bone dust as the saw bit into

the skull. The saw had such speed that it turned skull bone into dust instead of splinters that could fly into the brain. The area was heavily irrigated with water that rushed the bone dust away as sludge. It was sucked up by a hose.

Spetzler sawed a three-inch by four-inch oval in the skull. He then took the piece out. The color of the bone was shiny ivory white. He placed the piece of skull in a container. He then removed the dura, which is a light covering of the brain, and peeled it back to the pia, which is a thin film directly covering the brain. The brain was pink on the surface, running to gray coiled vessels underneath.

Spetzler peered through a microscope, which he controls with his mouth. The brain was exposed and he could see down a dark valley to the aneurysm. Which no longer was this compact bulge that was seen on a two-dimensional MRI or angiogram film.

The anesthesiologist Peter Raudzens, put barbiturates into my vein to reduce the oxygen to the brain and, for a time, suspend the blood flow.

The aneurysm that Dr. Spetzler looked at was dark red but the outer part of it was so thin that it changed to purple. It was like a balloon filled to the point of bursting. The blood swirled around inside the aneurysm with each of my heartbeats.

Now, Spetzler said, "All right, no talking please. Only if you have to. Thank you."

Suddenly the room was still and he went into a trance. "You would think that your aneurysm was talking to him," Dr. Raudzens said.

His body still, his concentration total, he held pliers. A silver clip that was six millimeters long was in the pliers. It was just long enough to clip the aneurysm but not too long to obstruct the vessels around it.

And now as they looked at the aneurysm it suddenly moved. It seemed to move right up at him, the blood swirling. This was somewhat more dangerous than advertised on film. And it was at this moment that his life and ability came together. At 50 he has done thousands of these operations. Which is exactly why I was on an operating table in Phoenix. You don't want anybody who hasn't seen one of these things acting poorly before. He has the confidence and daring, based on plenty of experience, to look at the aneurysm and decide the thickness and what surprise could lurk behind it. He worked on the aneurysm for 42 minutes.

Dr. Marcos, the senior neurosurgery fellow, came out to the visiting room and told my wife that the operation was more complicated than expected. The aneurysm was larger, softer, and twisted. That was at 2 o'clock in the afternoon. Inside Spetzler was working at setting the clip at the base of the aneurysm. "That was almost perfect," he said. Which meant he was going to start all over again. Finally, with a twist of his wrist the pliers placed the clip at the base of the aneurysm. The clip closed and choked off the ballooning part of the aneurysm. There were small pieces of cotton around the clip that were to cause a scar tissue in the artery, strengthening the outer wall. The aneurysm now was gone.

Spetzler reached into the container for the piece of white skull. He fitted it back into the skull like the last brick in a wall. It now had miniature plates and screws fastening it to the rest of the skull.

At 4 o'clock, they walked out and told my wife, "He is in the recovery room. You can go and see him."

This was on Tuesday, the 22nd. I did not move a muscle until late in the afternoon of the 23rd. At which time the famous surgeon, Spetzler, walked in and looked at me. He asked me my name.

"J.B. Number 1," I said.

He asked me what city I was in.

"Topeka," I said.

Outside, my wife said, "So far so good. He was like that when he came here."

December 13, 1994

Disaster Below Jolts the City's Spinal Cord

SIRENS PIERCED the Christmas music on the chilly streets of downtown Manhattan. Renee Harris, 39, standing on a traffic island on Broadway was talking quickly, because of the nerves.

"I was going to get on the Number Four."

"For where?"

"Two twenty-seven Schermerhorn. I work at the food stamps."

"Did you get on the train?"

"I got to the stairwell, going to the train, then boom! I lean up against the wall. Then this young Hispanic boy comes running up the stairs. He says, 'The train blew up. I saw a man missing his arm.' He was real upset. He kind of leaned on me. Then there was all this black smoke coming up the stairs. I walk off."

She stopped for breath. "I'm hyperventilating."

Whoever did it, whatever the reason, whether by accident or a deranged act, the subway firebombing yesterday put the smell of burned flesh into the Christmas air and gave us the scene of people in flames running through a subway car.

She had short dark hair and a round expressive face. She wore a button with the picture of a smiling young boy. "That's my Eric. My five-year-old son," she said proudly.

Then she said, "People were burning. The man ran out of the token booth and he covered them with foam."

Somebody asked her where she lived and she said "South Jamaica Houses."

"The Forty Houses" somebody said.

"That's right. I live there 15 years."

"Then you've been around explosions," somebody said.

Right away, she snapped, "Yes. When the cops ran and was shooting at people while we was sitting outside."

She looked around at the metal river of police cars and fire trucks. "Makes me nervous to think of it," she said.

And over in Brooklyn Heights, a man came out of the

453

elevator at the Clark Street stop, trembling, with his face scarlet from fire, his pants legs shredded from flames.

Transit police officers stopped him.

White guy with an Irish name. Edward Leary. Age 49.

They asked him why he was here. He said that he had been burned in the subway explosion over in Manhattan. When they asked him why he had come to Brooklyn, he said it was because his wife was a nurse and she knew how to take care of him.

The transit officers decided that the burn unit at New York Hospital-Cornell was better for treatment and also for keeping Leary in sight.

When Leary was brought uptown, detectives began talking to him. One of their bosses said last night that Leary told them that he had been out looking for a job and that he had been carrying these resumes with him. Then one of the resumes fell and went right into this bag that was sitting there on the floor of the subway car. So, needing the resume, he bent down and pulled the resume out of the bag. The bag now exploded, he said. He raced away from the flames.

"Why did you go to Brooklyn?" he was asked again.

"So my wife could take care of me. She's a nurse. She knows what to do for me."

When Leary left the No. 4 train after the explosion yesterday, he had to run through a tunnel and onto another platform to the train to Brooklyn. Detectives felt this showed a greater concern with getting out of the area than it did caring for his burned legs.

Leary said he had been depressed and was on the drug Prozac. He said he owned a home in Scotch Plains, N.J., that was valued at $280,000. He and his wife, Marge, and son lived for 15 years in one of two co-ops he owned at 10 Plaza St. in Park Slope in Brooklyn. It was 12A.

Last night, his former neighbors said that Leary was a quiet man. People don't remember what he did for a living. "Something with computers in the financial area," one thought. The wife worked in the medical field, although nobody knew her specific job.

Leary and his wife and son moved to Scotch Plains eight months ago. Both co-ops have been up for sale for eight months. Neighbors say each could sell for $120,000, but the market is poor.

A neighbor named Rob was a friend of Leary's wife and he accompanied her to the hospital yesterday. He called his house and left a message for his wife, who said that it was: "I'm here with Marge. She needs me to be here." When Rob returned last night to the co-op, he was accompanied by detectives.

Leary's present marriage sounded all right on tape when a call was put into the Scotch Plains number late yesterday. "Hello. You have reached the home of Edward, Marge and William. Please leave a message."

Now police were on the phone to get somebody to take a look at Leary's house in Scotch Plains, N.J.

And they still were all over the narrow streets of downtown Manhattan in the late afternoon because there is no crime or catastrophe bigger in this city than something that happens on our subways. For they are the iron spinal cord of the city.

December 22, 1994

Mick's Docs Sow Disease of Despair

S HE DIDN'T like it right away. She was walking from the cafeteria and through the waiting room to the treatment rooms to start the day. She passed this man who was always there early. He was older than most of the lung cancer patients she was going to treat today. They are here usually because they started smoking at between 10 and 12 years old and now at 50 the smoke finally has spawned tumors.

She said hello to the older guy and he did not say hello to her. That was bad. His wife was with him as she always was, and she looked anxiously at the nurse.

A few minutes later, he was in one of these high-backed chairs they use in the infusion room of this Manhattan hospital.

"Hello," she said, with great cheer. She knew enough not to ask him how he felt.

"He's going to have treatment today?" the wife said.

"Yes. Coming right up."

"He wants to talk to the doctor about that."

The nurse talked directly to the man. "Did something happen?"

"He read about Mickey Mantle," the wife said. "We were talking last night. He wonders, what's the sense of all this treatment? Maybe he doesn't have that long. Why ruin the time? Look at Mantle."

The nurse resented every word of what she had read about the death of Mickey Mantle. These cheap sobbing uninformed Pekinese of the Press had hurt her patients.

This had nothing to do with Mantle, who went out without an excuse or a whine. But the doctors and the newspaper and television reporters had misrepresented his last days and misled a lot of poor souls.

Mantle had a liver transplant that was a tremendous publicity success for the hospital's program. It was announced that he was free of cancer when he received the transplant.

Immediately, he died and did so rapidly, a month from announcement of a lung cancer to death. Of course he had lung cancer. But in the nurse's world, lung cancer has no history of growing that quickly. It is only fair to believe that Mantle was sick with it before they did a liver transplant on him.

The news reporting made it seem as if Mantle's lung cancer was sudden. This was as bad a job as has been seen. It is one thing to make up a hurricane, as the news people did this week. But poor reporting on something like lung cancer can have hideous consequences. People with lung cancer read these stories and immediately wonder if they are about to die now, and whether it is worth it anymore to go through harsh chemotherapy treatment.

And here, the older guy who was at the hospital early with his wife accompanying him picked up his head and said to the nurse:

"I see this Mantle," the man said finally. "He died in what, a month? Why should I go through all this if it could be over so soon?"

"Who told you a thing like this?" she said.

"It's in the paper. He got lung cancer a month ago and now he's gone."

"I think the paper carried something that wasn't true," the nurse said. "Lung cancer takes a long time. You can do a pretty good job of holding it off. You've got a lot of time with your wife in front of you. Come on now."

"Yeah, but everything I read about Mantle."

"The newspapers," she said.

"Oh, I saw a doctor saying that, too."

"He's from Baylor, isn't he?" the nurse said. "Baylor and Duke. They're famous for plenty of press conferences."

"You don't know what to believe," the man said.

"Believe in God, yourself, the doctor. You've already outlived Mickey Mantle. So keep going. You're certainly not going to change your treatment because of a newspaper story. I'm not going to let you."

"You're always hard on him," the wife said, smiling. That cleared the matter up.

The nurse went out to the pharmacy and came back with pouches of chemotherapy.

Another of her patients sat just inside the door and she paused and greeted him. He was about 30. He sat disconsolately. She knew what it was going to be about.

"Should I begin to save blood?" he asked.

"I don't think you have to."

"I see where Mantle had all these blood transfusions. I mean, if it goes like that I better start saving my own blood, huh?"

"People with lung cancer don't need blood transfusions."

"Why did they say lung cancer then?"

"I can only tell you that it was around a long time with the poor guy. He did not figure to go all at once from lung cancer, like it seems."

In a few minutes, he would be getting adriamycin, which looks like Kool Aid and is hard on the one who takes it and requires all his strength and spirit, and the cheer and compassion of those around him. He needs no disturbing lies about the disease that torments him.

The nurse now took the chemotherapy bags and hooked them to the top of a pole and said to the older guy, "All right, if you can forget baseball long enough for us to preserve your life."

"I didn't start it," he said.

"I know. I wish they'd think of somebody like you when they start putting wrong things in the newspapers."

She took his arm and began pressing on the inside of the elbow to find a place where she could inject the chemotherapy into the vein. It would make him sick and weaker. But it might shrink the tumor in his lung and allow him to live longer.

"Tired," he sighed.

"That's all right," she said to him.

"I sleep a lot. When I wake up I'm tired."

He winced a little bit as she put the needle into him and then watched as the first yellow fluid dripped down the tube to his arm.

"All right," she said, cheerfully.

Now she looked around. Two more people had arrived. Soon, there would be a room full of people getting chemotherapy. And for this day and, she knew, the next set of days to come, the ones with lung cancer all would ask why they had to take chemotherapy when maybe they had weeks left, the way the news reports said it had happened with Mickey Mantle.

August 20, 1995

A Mother's Son Lost and Found

THE BROTHER, Jose, ran through the airport shrieking for Alberto Fermin, who was flying to Paris. Jose gave everybody his name and shouted in all the rooms he went into.

The mother was home on her bed in the dark front room of the ground floor apartment at 208 Barbey Street in East New York. All through the long mean night she wept for her son.

When a news photographer asked to borrow a picture of her son, she shook her head and threw her hands to make him go away.

"Please leave her alone," somebody said. "Her son might be dead."

Alberto Fermin was 28 and he had worked in a clothing store on Columbus Avenue in Manhattan and saved his money so he could fly to Paris for the first time in his life.

The manager of the store was up all night at a computer trying to find the name in the crash news.

He came from Barbey Street in East New York, which is in the 75th Precinct and for the last many years has been the center of violence in the city. Yesterday, they talked about how Alberto got through all the years in East New York only to be blown up on his way to the splendors of Paris. "He is the second one from here who went this way," a woman said. "There was a Marine boy from down the street who stopped to help somebody and he was hit by a hit-run. He died. They never find the one did it."

Barbey Street runs through East New York to its end, where the streets plunge into weeds and marshes that end at Jamaica Bay and across from it, the ocean, where off to the left, many miles off but not that many really, the bodies from the TWA plane floated through the night and into the first light of the morning and then the hot day on the calm surface, with shoes and seat cushions around them.

The mother thought that Alberto was in this ocean.

"Crying all night," a woman on the front steps said.

"Crying all night," another said.

And the mother sat on the bed with her hands to her face and stared at the dimness and waited for the moment when her son Alberto would pick himself up from the water, as if it were a wood floor, and come walking to her, smiling and young and proud. Walking right off the ocean and into her arms in this room. Only she knew this.

Into the frame house the others came, these members of the big wide Dominican family. They went past the mother's bed in the front room and pushed through a dark narrow hallway to a back room which became so crowded that there was no room for seats. There was another son, Jose, and a chubby guy, Star Cartadena.

"She cannot talk," they said of the mother.

When somebody tried to look in on her, a heavy young woman in a pink T-shirt held a hand out and pushed.

Yesterday morning, the woman from upstairs and Annette Evanson, who lives across the street, stood in the heat and talked about a prayer service in her mother's house.

"She has a leg that she can't move about," the woman from upstairs said.

"They are coming to pray in her house," Evanson said. "Reverend Taylor will come and have a prayer service."

Barbey Street was so far from Paris. At the corner, el tracks the color of mustard had sun coming through down to the street in patterns. Under the el, bodegas were at each corner.

"How have things been?" a young guy on the street named David was asked. He was 24 and had his hair in short braids.

"There's been no shooting?" he was asked.

"Nothing on this block. This block's quiet. Oh, I got shot on the next block. I got shot in the back and the leg. I know it was mistaken identity. They didn't want me."

In the house the mother held the phone.

"He is alive!" she shrieked in Spanish.

"Alive!" one of the women around the bed said.

The mother sat up in bed in the dimness and saw her son rising from the ocean. She called out to her son Alberto.

Outside in the street somebody shrugged. "I don't know what happened inside, but I don't believe he is alive," he said.

International tragedy did not stop the life of the street. Now a woman double parked her car and went inside the house. An unmarked police car with license D939WK came along and one cop said they were going to ticket the double-parked car.

David said something about the plane crash and the cop said something about locking him up and now Evanson yelled and the cop said, "EFF you," as the unmarked car drove off and the chubby guy, Cartadena, came running out of the house, shouting to the streets.

"He is alive. She received a call."

"No."

"Yes, I am sure."

"Who says so?"

"She does."

"Then he is alive," Evanson said. She ran across to the Fermin house and then came out in tears.

"We got to barbecue later!"

The woman she spoke to was in tears.

"We goin' thank God," Evanson said.

"I don't know what happened," somebody said. "I don't know how he could be alive."

Later, the manager of Alberto's store on Columbus Avenue said he had spoken to Alberto's roommate and that he was alive. Then Alberto himself called his mother on Barbey Street.

Nobody knew what plane Alberto took or why he wasn't on the TWA flight, but what he had done was to get another flight on another airline without bothering to tell anybody. They all thought he was dead in the water. The reason nobody heard from him right away was that he went shopping yesterday in Paris. But these are only facts. His mother knows there was something more powerful than such a simple explanation. All day, the only two people to know he was alive were Alberto and his mother, who knew he would get up from the water and come home.

July 19, 1996

His Words Will Never Disappear

I ALWAYS WILL remember him in a heavy rain, sitting on his bicycle under my window. Sitting with the rain on his white hair and his ears covered with a Walkman. Listening to Louis Armstrong. A pipe turned upside down stuck from his mouth. Bicycle clips on his pants cuffs and a bag of books and records strapped to the bike.

"I think I'll go down to court today," he called up. "First I'm going to stop on Mulberry Street and have coffee with Boobie. Or Joe Butch."

This is conversation for Brooklyn or Ozone Park, but Kempton was on West 67th Street, calling up to a window, which isn't done, and then talking about hoodlums. Hearing this, people running by in the rain were astounded.

I don't know where Boobie is at the moment, but Joe Butch is in a prison in Minnesota and not enjoying it.

They were Murray Kempton's people. If you had to list his top three prime readers, they would be: Afeni Shakur, mother of the late Tupac; Joyce Persico, wife of Junior Persico, away forever, and Senator Patrick Moynihan.

Now on this morning on his bike in the rain, Kempton swung out into the traffic on Central Park West and headed downtown. It did not matter if you knew the man most of your working life, the sight of his head bobbing to Louis Armstrong in his ears while riding a bike, as thin as a pencil, with a huge bus throwing thick white water over him, with morning traffic pushing by, each car pausing at the sight of him, you had to call to others: "Look at this!"

Of course that was the Kempton in public. But the one with whom I am most familiar sat alone at a typewriter, now a computer terminal, sat for long lonely hours, and fought himself and the air around him for these phrases that people would remember, often be startled by.

He gave people elegance and truth and in doing this he put more honor into the newspaper business than anybody in my time.

He lived for the loser. In writing about the great 1957 World

462

Series perfect game by Don Larsen, he went to the losing pitcher, 40-year-old Sal Maglie. He had pitched a two-hitter and lost. The column said:

"Did he make any mistakes?" Campanella, the catcher, said in the dressing room. "Yes. He made one by pitching today."

My friend Peter Johnson, a Wall Street lawyer now, remembered that he and two other longshoremen, bucking the union, called newspapers for publicity and one person came down to see them. "It was a young Murray Kempton. He met us for lunch. I was a brand new lawyer. He treated me as if I were the attorney general. He called everybody mister. He took one sniff and knew that there wasn't five dollars among us. So he said, 'Before we start. Don't even think of it. I am buying the lunch.' He then became excited when we told we weren't stopping. He said that means labor will never die. He wrote beautifully about us. Just show him an underdog."

The last time I saw him on the street was on a Sunday morning, and he was walking on Broadway with a black prayer book under his arm, heading for Episcopal Church services.

That was one morning. The other religious acts of Kempton are with me forever.

Here he is in Sumner, Miss., in 1958, at a time when federal agents were afraid to go into the place and Kempton, a reporter years before the others, watched littler Mose Wright suddenly stand up and accuse thugs of murdering 14-year-old black, Emmett Till.

"The country in which Mose Wright toiled and which he now is resigned to leaving will never be the same for what he has done. Today, the state will put on the stand three other field negroes who tell how they saw Milam and Bryant near the murder scene. They came in scared; one disappeared while the sheriffs were looking for him. They, like Mose Wright, are reluctant heroes. Unlike him, they had to be dragged to the test. And we owe that sight to Mose Wright, who was condemned to bow all his life and had enough left to raise his head and look the enemy in those terrible eyes when he was 64."

There was one hot spring noon in Alabama, with people sitting on the grass square in front of the old courthouse in Hayneville. The jury was in a second floor room pretending to deliberate in the trial of Ku Klux Klan members charged with killing Ms. Viola Liuzzo after Martin Luther King's march from Selma to Montgomery. The Klansmen had gone to trial with a buffoon as lawyer. So much for your charging us with murder just over some woman driving around Lowndes County with blacks.

At noon, people bought sandwiches from a store on a white corner of the square. It was owned by a man named Kelly Coleman. He also sold souvenir-sized bottles of whisky, and that was good enough for Murray Kempton. He loved Kelly Coleman.

Murray Kempton had been writing in the meanest of the south for 15 years now. He was a full decade ahead of those who were supposed to be telling the country about race. But of course this was only natural, for he regarded these dusty, dreadfully dangerous southern towns as the places that caused him to preserve his ideals.

Now the jury announced it was hopelessly deadlocked, which the locals described as a great advancement. "Used to just acquit without even havin' a smoke." Federal attorneys and marshals stared. They were going to move next and it would be different. One of the Klan guys, a tall man named Thomas, said to Murray, "What do you think?"

And Kempton, hating what the guy had done and stood for, but standing there with a heart that would not go blind, put a hand on Thomas' shoulder and said, softly, "Please get a real lawyer."

In Manhattan in 1970, a dozen Black Panthers were indicted. A fund raiser for their defense was held by Leonard Bernstein and Burton and Lynn Lane. They were mocked in an article called "Radical Chic." The phrase was quite the rage in white Manhattan. But the money raised went for a Panther defense that included a stunning Murray Kempton pamphlet that dealt with the rights of the defendants as opposed to the convenience of the court. There was virtually no case against the Panthers and they were acquitted in record time by a jury. His book on the subject, "The Briar Patch," won a 1974 National Book Award.

It was Kempton's writing in the South, and particularly on the Liuzzo killing, that had so much influence on Lyndon Johnson's Voting Rights Act of 1965. Without it, you do not have a nation. While Kempton only appeared in one paper, he was read by and dominated the thinking of virtually every writer in the nation.

And when Lyndon Johnson got up at a joint session of the Congress and announced "We shall overcome," Murray Kempton wrote the next day:

"Someday we will tell our grandchildren of the heights to which Lyndon Johnson took this nation last night."

Kempton's work will be in print or on a screen in a thousand places for a thousand years. For many forms of life will change but never will the force of a brilliant mind and clear powerful heart when turned on a matter of importance to humans.

May 6, 1997

The Threat Lies Within

THE FIRST patrol car with white paint sat in the space between barricades on Pearl Street, at police headquarters. A van came up with an official sign in the window. The patrol car rolled back several feet to make room. The van passed. The patrol rolled up to block the street again.

Three times more, a car or a van came up and the patrol car rolled back, paused, then rolled forward to block the space again.

"Don't make fun of me," the cop driving said. "This is my job."

Down the block another white patrol car sat between barricades. A car came, the patrol car rolled forward a few feet, stopped, let the car go through, rolled back, stopped.

On the Broadway entrance to City Hall, a patrol car with a cop was in the gap but did not move. But on the Park Row side it was rolling away, back and forth, three times as you watched.

"Don't you get carsick?" the cop was asked.

He shrugged. "Security."

Insanity is more like it.

These three cars are going back and forth like toys for 24 hours a day, seven days.

Three shifts a day, plus days off and vacation, require 42 cops to keep the cars rolling for their seven feet or so.

At an average salary of $50,000 a year, that means these cops in cars rolling like toys cost the city $2,100,000 a year, plus payments to the health and pension plans.

With the one-man car at the City Hall entrance, there is an added dimension.

"Excuse me, where are you going?" the cop asked a woman who squeezed through the barricades and was walking up to City Hall.

"I want to look at the building."

"I'm sorry you can't. City Hall is closed to the public." Only a police force of outlandish size, 40,000, can be used to perpetrate such offenses against the public.

It is now 17 days since an unarmed working man, Amadou

Diallo, of color, was in a vestibule not big enough to hang up a winter coat. Four white police shot 41 times to hit the unarmed Amadou Diallo. Four white cops in a black neighborhood and they call it undercover. Four in a car—Let's hit it!—that good spirit, a softball team with guns.

Giuliani does not even give citizens an outline. Wait for the Bronx grand jury, he says. The Bronx is the place where police were acquitted by judges in non-jury trials for the slaughter of Eleanor Bumpurs and now Anthony Baez. There is no reason to believe the case of Amadou Diallo will be any different.

What Giuliani does attempt to fill your paper and screen with is this utterly cheap prattle about some Senate race against Hillary Clinton. Anything to take attention from Amadou Diallo, dead with 19 or so bullet holes in him. Hillary could shut up, too, out of respect for Amadou Diallo's death.

Stand on a chilly afternoon and watch the dancing cars of a psychotic City Hall and see how life has been altered by this nasty religious right-wing Giuliani. He uses the last refuge of the fearful and domineering—security! He has turned City Hall and the streets around it into a disgraceful junkyard of strewn cement barriers and chain-link fences. He raised the spectre of bomb threats on City Hall. There is nothing in City Hall vital to the citizenry, neither secret paper, nor phone nor politician.

On the day the Senate voted on Bill Clinton's impeachment charges, the most ominous day in 131 years, families and other visitors could be found walking up and down the steps and all through the following: the Supreme Court, the Senate, the Capitol, the House of Representatives. A couple of uniformed cops were off to the side. That is all you need.

Giuliani's excuse for anything is that he brought down crime. He barely had anything to do with it. The last man on the stage of a great success takes the bows. Fine. Crime was going down before Giuliani arrived because people stopped smoking crack and there were many fewer street corners for which sellers would shoot.

And now the big crimes are committed by police. With 40,000 of them, with their rolling cars and night riders, you have a city of so many humiliated citizens, of illegal search and seizures of citizens of color being shot by cops.

The two worst police scandals of our time, the Abner Louima

torture and Amadou Diallo killing, are on Giuliani's hands, and he won't even look down to recognize this.

The lowness of government is revealed by the moral superiority of the people of the city. Walking uptown from City Hall, there was found, on the sidewalk where Diallo sold his goods, in front of a candy store on 14th Street, a few doors west of Second Avenue, a pedestal with a jar of flowers on it and a ledger book. This was first observed by Michael Daly.

It is an altar. The book, thick, opened to the first clear page, becomes the great religious document of our city.

All day, people walk up and write of Amadou Diallo. Their words reveal the beauty and goodness and deep spirituality of people of the city of New York. They take time, while going for a subway or bus, maybe a thousand of them so far, and for page after page this is how their goodness reads:

"Though we never met you, we consider you a neighbor as are all of us who live in this city. We promise to do what we can to stop these atrocities from happening to our neighbors. We are so sorry . . . Shirley Herman and Joan . . ."

And:

"May the Lord embrace you in his arms—your customers who all miss you, Manny, Lisa and Family."

The pages say "Allah be with you" or "God bless you," but it is all the same indescribable beauty. The book shines in the dark of night.

A night that is made up of the paranoid, the psychotic, a municipal government of patrol cars making small rolls forward and backward, like toys. And of other cars bringing death. And the night also is made up of all who allow the beginnings of a police state to flourish.

February 21, 1999

A Smile Gone, but Where?

I STAND on the street corner in the darkness and wait for her, but for another day she is not here.

I don't remember the first time I saw her. I know the hour, between 5:45 and 6 A.M., because I already have finished swimming at this health club and she comes walking along on her way to the gym for her exercise.

The street was West 68th, between Columbus and Broadway, and I am walking down from Columbus and she is walking up from Broadway. In the darkness of the end of winter nights, she kept her eyes fixed straight ahead and her face showed resolve and a little apprehension upon seeing somebody walking toward her.

I stepped into the street and crossed to the other side.

She was young and had short black hair and a face that was delicate and filled with energy. She had a fast stride.

Quick-quick-quick. I never more than glanced at her because I wanted to put her completely at ease. I walked across the street and went home.

This went on for a long time. One morning I was late or she was early and I was still on Columbus Avenue, almost at the corner of 68th Street, when she came around the corner with that fast walk. People who barely recognize each other and suddenly meet at a strange place exhibit warmth. She smiled a little and her lips said hello, but I did not hear her voice. I nodded.

From then on, when we would see each other on the familiar 68th Street, she would smile and I'd nod or smile back. But I still went to the other side of the street.

This went on through so many months of darkness and cold and morning rain, when we both walked with heads down, and then at times when the sky lightened and spring arrived and after it summer heat. Always, a nod and a smile and then I parted and she went on.

I never spoke to her, nor did she ever speak to me. I never got her name or where she was coming from at such an hour and

469

what job she was going to for the rest of the day. She smiled, I nodded. Month after month.

I don't know when I realized that I had not seen her. It was 10 days ago, a week ago, but suddenly in the morning I noticed that she was not walking on the street at about 6 A.M.

I began to look carefully into the morning dimness to see if she was down the block someplace, not yet crossing Broadway, or if she was still coming down Broadway from uptown. I never knew where she came from. She just materialized on the street, walking so quickly. And now I did not see her all last week.

I found myself irritated. "Where is she?" I said aloud.

The days and nights of my working life had become one of hurt women asking in strained voices for lost men, and so many young men in tears standing in a hospital doorway and asking if the woman of their lives might possibly be inside.

And there was nobody. Not in the wreckage at the World Trade Center, nor at the hospitals. The morgue was empty. There were 6,453 listed as missing, all of them in the sky forever from the moment the building blew up.

And this young woman no longer passes me going the other way in the morning.

Not only do I not know her name, but I never saw her with anybody else. I have no one to ask.

Yesterday morning, on the 14th day since the catastrophe, I was around the corner on West 68th Street at the appointed hour. She was not there. She was not in the dimness on the other side of Broadway. When I reached the corner and looked uptown on Broadway, she was not one of those coming through the light of the outdoor newsstand on the corner of 69th.

She was not here in my morning.

I stood on the corner in front of the Food Emporium super-market and looked for several minutes. Maybe she moved, I thought. Maybe she got married to some nice guy. Or maybe some nice guy she is already married to had a new job and they moved. Maybe she has a new job and her hours changed. Maybe she comes to exercise later in the morning. Maybe there is a pleasant reason for her not being here in the morning. Maybe she will simply be here tomorrow and not have the slightest idea why I am upset.

Right now, as I stand on the street corner in the early morning, this young woman, whose name I do not know, whose voice I have never heard, is part of the overwhelming anxiety of the days of my September in the city.

The butcher from the supermarket came out, holding a container of coffee.

"What are you looking for?" he said.

"Somebody."

"They'll come," he said.

"I hope so," I said.

September 25, 2001

Days of Wine and Rosaries

I MUST APOLOGIZE today to William Murphy, whose job for now is bishop of the Rockville Centre diocese on Long Island. He is about one strong voice coming out to lead the betrayed away from being gone. But until then, I correct all errors.

I wrote that the convent at St. Agnes Cathedral that he was taking over for a huge private residence had room for 36 apartments.

That was wrong, and I admit it. It made the bishop mad, and it should have. He said my figure of 36 apartments wasn't fair or just. He is right. I never should have said 36 apartments.

The convent has room for 37 apartments.

A housing specialist, Ed Ward, points out that once 56 nuns lived in the St. Agnes convent and therefore the number of apartments, 37, is correct.

Some months ago, there were only six nuns left and Murphy moved them out in favor of opulence. There were only six nuns left because virtually no young women or young men are entering the religious orders. The people at the top are the cause of it.

This is why he is known as Mansion Murphy and he goes beyond a matter of some local bishop drowning in greed. He is a symbol of why, the land over, this has turned into the rustiest church of all.

The amount of money that Murphy is spending on rooms for himself is an embarrassment. One thing he doesn't have to worry about is feeling ashamed. He is devoid of that. The renovation work the bishop has ordered will cost over $5 million, including the $1.6 million for placing gold plating on the brass pipes of the church organ.

You've got to be crazy to give the place any money. When you go past St. Agnes, clutch your purse or keep your hands in your pockets.

Murphy said the convent was "close to the cathedral, which is my cathedral, and if it makes sense that I could be close to my cathedral, then I should be." In New York, one of the oldest expressions is "the super in my building." It is a way of talk. Murphy appears to believe it. "My cathedral."

The bishop is making three spaces on the third floor of the convent. One is for himself: a bedroom, marble bath, sitting room and large study. In the sitting room are two exquisite armchairs that are in front of a fireplace. Both chairs appear equal to the task of absorbing a direct hit by a big bishop coming straight down.

But some good side to side swaying of the same real avoir-dupois could splinter the arms of the chairs.

There is a dining room with a new table and 12 upholstered chairs. Murphy can sit and tell 11 people at once about himself.

A second suite is for Murphy's secretary. All you have to do is call out from the study and the secretary rushes in ready to do anything. Murphy also is going to have a suite that he refers to as "the cardinal's suite." He must think that he can house Cardinal Law of Boston, who is going to be run out of there for sure, and soon. Law, Murphy and Daily of Brooklyn were in the diocese headquarters in Boston, in charge, when pedophiles like Geoghan and Shanley were being transferred from parish to parish to savage the young.

Murphy can't think of himself becoming a cardinal with his record. But he can see himself and Law observing the evening from the long covered porch of the convent and gazing at the sweeping lawns and toasting each other.

The one part of the renovation that causes concern is the kitchen. He says he spent $120,000 on a Sub-Zero refrigerator and freezer unit and a six-burner Viking professional range. That is reasonable for a single millionaire. But an adjoining pantry has an under-counter temperature-controlled wine-storage cabinet that can hold 50 bottles.

Now that is a lot of wine, even for a church.

The special temperature cabinet has a top shelf set at 45 degrees, for white wine and champagne, and a lower shelf set at 55 degrees for red wine.

By heritage, Irish, even Irish bishops, are not very good at wine. Never have I heard anybody with an Irish name announce, "I'm going to stop for a good glass of wine."

I know that wine is 12 percent alcohol. And if you get into bottles of it, get 10, 12 glasses down, get going good, you have maybe 144 percent alcohol somewhere in there.

Then you have that marble bathroom where a guest who trips can have this head up for grabs.

Mansion Murphy now has this obscene big house in Rockville Centre, and the dizzy judgment to show the place off.

Mike Bloomberg took Gracie Mansion in New York out of the dreams of these grubby politicians whose only reason to run for mayor has been to live in the place. Rather than live in the house, he has turned it into a museum. Mansion Murphy could surpass this. He could get out and turn his convent into 37 apartments instead of living there alone and talking about himself all night.

Once again, keep your money clear of this man.

October 8, 2002

Church Isn't What It Should Be

I DON'T WANT to be a bishop anymore because the bishops of America have given the title such a bad name.

When the Catholic Church bishops and their priests around here stumbled into the open for all to see for the atrocious failures that they are, I decided to run my own parish. Bishop Breslin. I would give tremendous sermons to gatherings, as they do in the west of Ireland where they hold Mass without a priest, for there are no priests left, and "without the magic," or transubstantiation. But they remain faithful.

Suddenly, I actually have to plan the start of services. Read again on this morning, and thus with time to reflect, the report just issued by the State of Massachusetts attorney general entitled, "The Sexual Abuse of Children in the Roman Catholic Archdiocese of Boston."

Large damaging sections were given to Thomas Daily and William Murphy, who were in charge of Boston priests. There were complaints from the families of 800 molested children. For magnificent service they were given promotions: Daily now is bishop of Brooklyn and William "Mansion" Murphy is bishop of Long Island.

How do you like it? How do you like it if you're a Catholic and they make your bishop the central figure in a report on pedophiles? How do you like it if you have kids? If you have kids at home, you ought to read the report twice. It's all over the Internet. It says children have been in danger around the church because of these bishops.

The first thing I have to do is come up with a new title for myself. Bishop Breslin was a terrific title. But now I don't dare use it in legitimate places.

I cannot understand why, today, right now, Mansion Murphy of Rockville Centre dares to remain on church grounds after all he has done to place children in jeopardy.

Nor can I fathom the reason why Bishop Thomas Daily was still in his residence in Brooklyn this morning.

Both bishops belong in the city dump.

They strut around with these big crosses hanging on chains

475

around their necks. Also on that chain they might hang a photo, a new one every week, of a child molested by one of their priests.

One statement reportedly made by Christ, and which I fervently believe, is, "Woe to those who do harm to children. It is better that he tie a millstone around his neck and go off a cliff into the ocean."

From the Massachusetts attorney general's report:

"Bishop Daily had a clear preference for keeping priests who sexually abused children in pastoral ministry and generally followed a practice of transferring those priests without supervision or notification to new parishes rather than removing them . . . Bishop Daily apparently did not believe that a priest who engaged in such misconduct was apt to engage in such conduct in the future. Accordingly, he failed to take any meaningful steps to limit abusive priests' contact with children in the future."

From the report:

". . . And, even with undeniable information available to him on the risk of recidivism, Bishop Murphy continued to place a higher priority on preventing scandal and providing support to alleged abusers than on protecting children from sexual abuse."

He seems the same here. He called a Linda Moraitis at her Farmingdale home one Sunday morning and told her that he saw no reason to ban a priest who she and her son testified had abused the son. "I told him he believed his priest and not my son," the mother said.

What kind of a belief can he have in anything? He lives in an obscene mansion that he had renovated for himself.

The only way to drive these people out is to withhold money. Anybody who puts five dollars in a collection basket approves of what they've done.

And it could have been so different. It could have been the clamor that came up the staircase as I went to the basement auditorium of Our Lady of Mercy church in Forest Hills. I was meeting my friend Arlene D'Arienzo, who sat at a table with Jason Zivkovic as he worked on a papier-mâche house. Her friend Sister Ann Barbara Desiano was up in front of 110 excited children in a summer Bible study class. The wonderfully exuberant nun was in the costume of a Pharaoh, a tall paper hat and a brown smock and silver paper to look like a sword hanging from a belt. The wall behind her was covered with large drawings of camels and Egyptian buildings mounted on large panels of cardboard. Arlene D'Arienzo worked on them in her house across the street from church. Now, the nun was telling the story of Moses trying to get his people out of 400 years of slavery.

"Moses said to the Pharaoh, 'Let my people go!'"

She had them all call, "Let my people go!"

Then Ann Barbara Desiano read of the plagues of Egypt. "Frogs!" the nun called out.

With this, she rushed up the aisle throwing handfuls of small rubber frogs.

And the auditorium turned into more than 100 pairs of scrambling bare legs as boys and girls went diving under the tables to collect the frogs.

She called out the next pest.

"Locusts!"

The nun again pounded down the aisle throwing small rubber locusts. The kids pounced on them all at once.

Then Sister had them call out, again, "Let my people go!"

In the laughing and excitement, Arlene D'Arienzo said, quietly, "Isn't this a sweet moment?" I nodded. "This is probably too homespun for you," she said.

No. It was what the Catholics should be about. One sweet moment after the next. We know it as love. When I start my parish this is all it will be.

July 27, 2003

A Daughter's Last Breaths

As it was with the mother who went before her, the last breath for the daughter was made before an onlooker with frightened eyes.

First, there were several labored breaths.

And here in the hospital room, in a sight not distorted by passion, was the mother sitting on the end of her bed, as the daughter once had sat on the mother's in Forest Hills for a year unto death. They both were named Rosemary. When the mother's last breath told her to go, the daughter reached in fear, but her hand could not stay the mother's leaving.

By now, Rosemary, the younger, is married to Tony Dunne. He knew she was sick when he married her. He then went through 15 years of hospital visits, stays, emergencies and illness at home and all he wanted was for her to be at his side, day and night. His love does not run. And now, in the daughter's hospital room, as it always does, fear and deep love brought forth visions of childhood.

The daughter is maybe 4, sitting on the beach. She wants money for ice cream. The mother's purse had money to pay the carpenter at day's end. Earlier, the mother had tried to pay a carpenter by check and he leaped away, as if the check was flaming. The daughter plunged into the purse and found no change for ice cream. With the determination that was to mark every day of her life, she went through that purse, tossing large bills, the carpenter's money, into the air, digging for ice cream change. She sat there infuriated, throwing money into the sea wind. The mother was flying over the sand trying to retrieve it.

Another labored breath.

Then I could see her later, and with even more determination. Typing a script with tubes in her arms. Writing, rewriting, using hours. Clearly, being attacked by her own blood. She said that she felt great. She said that for 15 years.

I don't know of any power that could match the power of Rosemary Breslin when sick.

Suddenly, the last breath came in quiet.

The young and beautiful face stared into the silence she had created. Gone was the sound of her words.

The mother took her hand, and walked her away, as if to the first day of school.

June 20, 2004

THE SHORT SWEET DREAM
OF EDUARDO GUTIÉRREZ

For
Teresa Gutiérrez Daniel

For
Awilda Cordero

For
Maurice Pinzon

Chapter One

TOMÁS EDUARDO DANIEL GUTIÉRREZ was the firstborn of a fifteen-year-old mother in the town of San Matías Cuatchatyotla in central Mexico, about three hours by car from Mexico City. Daniel is his father's last name and Gutiérrez is the mother's. The baby was familiarly called Eduardo Daniel, but the official records used the formal name, Tomás Eduardo Daniel Gutiérrez. A midwife assisted. He was born on a Sunday morning, which allowed his father to be present. The father was away on the other six days, traveling by truck to sell loads of bricks. Sometimes he was given the wrong address for the customer, and he wound up driving for an entire day around Mexico City, selling the undelivered bricks door to door.

San Matías Cuatchatyotla starts as an alley running from the two-lane highway going to Puebla in central Mexico, forty-five minutes away. The alley is a Third World dirt path that runs straight through the dust with children leaning against walls and young mothers standing aimlessly on street corners holding staring babies, and dogs coated with flies sleeping in the alleys or walking in circles in front of entranceways to shacks. Old women walk bent in the heat and the flies. Their legs are thick and the grandchildren's thin, but this does not matter. All in San Matías, body bowed or lithe, have legs that can walk a thousand miles.

The alley runs into a network of other dusty alleys. They are lined with one-story sheds and lots filled with bricks. At first, the brick piles seem to be unfinished buildings, but then a kiln shows its hot sides to display the town's business, baking bricks.

Papers by archaeologists say that fired bricks used in the construction of a temple in the area disputes the conventional belief that only the Mayans built structures in this region. Fired bricks were not Mayan; they were from the Roman Empire. All these centuries later, archaeologists say the bricks of San Matías are relics not of the Mayans but of people from Europe—you figure out how they reached here. The physical evidence says they did.

The official address of Eduardo's birth was number 8 Calle

Libre, that figure scratched on the wall at the start of the alley that runs to a green tin fence with a door in it. A loud knock, and the door is opened by a child with a dog leaning against its legs. The hour of day, day of week, or time of year doesn't matter, for there is always a child with a dog at the door. The doorway opens to a crowded yard that has a large evergreen tree and is lined with concrete huts of single-room size that have flat roofs and curtains over the doorways. The thirty members of the Gutiérrez family (the next baby makes thirty-one)—uncles, cousins, nephews, nieces, dogs—brush through the curtains. There are no toilets or showers. Water is pulled up from the deep old stone well in a heavy wooden bucket with great effort by women whose mouths contort and whose bare arms throb as their large hands go one over the other in pulling up the bucket. On a long table there is a row of seven plastic buckets for washing dishes and pots and scrubbing clothes. Dogs lap up soapy water in spill buckets on the ground. The women hang wash on lines tied to the evergreen tree. The clothes flap just above rabbits in wood cages. There are chickens in a wire pen, and dogs covered with flies spread out on the ground, peaceful now but not always.

On the day Eduardo was born, the father, Daniel, waited in the courtyard while the women washed dishes and clothes.

"Somebody always washes," he recalls. "When somebody dies, they wash. When somebody is born, they wash."

Eduardo's mother, Teresa, was shy to the point of agony. She spoke to nobody but her family. She left the house only when she heard the church bells up the street ring three times for the start of mass, or to buy something she needed. Each time, she draped a blue scarf over her face, Middle Eastern style. Everybody knew the scarf, but no one knew her, although San Matías is a small place. Eduardo was born with the deep shyness of his mother, but what directed body and life was neither home nor nationality. Mexico is just the name of a country, which comes from Mexica, another name for the Aztecs.

Eduardo's life came from the lines circling a globe.

Latitude rules.

Chapter Two

EDUARDO WAS born in a room off this courtyard with the sky above determining from the instant of his birth who he was and would be and how he would live the rest of his life. He cried into the world on June 15, 1978, at 19 degrees, 3 minutes north of the equator, and 4 degrees below the tropic of Cancer, in a place where the sun strikes the earth and those on it nearly directly. The path of the sun in the sky over San Matías is virtually the same each day of each year. Months are words. Seasonal changes carry the weight of a falling leaf. Each morning the sun rises straight up in the sky, to 80 degrees. For six hours each day in San Matías, for all the days, the burning eye of the sun stares unblinking and straight down. There are no shadows in its remorseless glare. The people at this latitude all have brown skin, often running to black. They must have it or they die in the sun.

All over the earth, the sun strikes from different angles. In Norway the sun gets half as high as over Mexico, 40 degrees, and comes at the earth on the oblique. People can't cast a shadow to equal their height. The sun must be 45 degrees before that can be done. In New York, except for June 21 and the days around it, the sun makes high sweeps across the sky, and the direct burning it does lessens by the day until December.

In the latitudes between 23½ degrees north, the tropic of Cancer, and 23½ degrees south, the tropic of Capricorn, the earth steams eternally, and most inside those lines are born with hues that often cause the whites above the tropic latitudes in the north to be somewhat apprehensive. Mexicans don't cause white foot races so often as the blacks; many Mexicans have slightly lighter skin, which makes them a little less frightening. Therefore businessmen and housewives see the Mexicans as the most worthy of all workers: The Mexicans are cheap labor.

Their heritage is Mexican by map and tongue, but latitude rules their bodies. The largest organ of the body is the skin, 6 percent of the body weight, whose hue originated so many millions of years ago. Color is spread through the skin by pigment that comes in drops so small that they fall beneath our ability to weigh them. Yet you put them together, the skin and the weightless pigment, and they can move the earth more than an earthquake.

In skin of any hue, the major cell population is the basal keratinocytes. There is a lesser group known as the melanocytes, whose effect is eternal. The number of melanocytes is the same in all skin: one melanocyte for every four to ten keratinocytes. Melanocytes contain granules called melanosomes, which carry melanin, the pigment that colors the skin. They bring pheomelanin, a light yellow or auburn, or eumelanin, which is dark brown.

In those latitudes near the equator, the sun blazing straight down for all those millennia has caused the melanocytes to be very active, producing large amounts of eumelanin. As in people of any color, the melanin granules rise to cover the keratinocytes' nuclei, protecting them from the effects of ultraviolet radiation. In so doing, the pigment colors the skin dark brown, or into shades of black. This skin color has nothing to do with intelligence, size, or athletic ability. It has to do with survival.

The dark pigment was first put into the body by nature—and beyond that the hand of God—to darken the skin and pass this hue down and thus protect all who follow against melanoma, a merciless killer. Melanoma starts with a genetic mutation of a cell caused by the ultraviolet rays of the sun. Ultraviolet rays bathe the white skin to death. It provides no defense. Black skin is a fortification. Melanoma, this abnormal growth of tissues, is uncontrolled, has no expected endpoint, and is furiously aggressive; it spreads like splashed acid. Then it kills from all the places of the body that it has touched.

People are born colors from tan to black in order to save them from being white.

Latino or Hispanic identity is as muddied as the waters of the Rio Grande. Color is of so many gradations that it confuses anybody with an official chart trying to count by race and hue. The combination of European and Indian heritage, with skin color thrown in, makes for a complex Hispanic concept of race.

The writer Richard Rodriguez noted, "I used to stare at the Indian in the mirror. The wide nostrils, the thick lips. Such a long face—such a long nose—sculpted by indifferent, blunt thumbs, and of such common clay. My face could not portray the ambition I brought to it. What could the United States say to me? I remember reading the ponderous conclusions of the Kerner Report in the sixties: two Americas, one white, one black, the prophecy of an eclipse too simple to account for the complexity of my face. Mestizo in Mexican Spanish means mixed, confused. Clotted with Indian, thinned by Spanish spume."

At each election, when New York added up ethnic voting, the total of non–Puerto Rican Hispanics was minute and the Chinese were listed as "other." There was only black and white.

Into New York they came, these people of every shade, from African black to Mexican and Indian brown and Chinese yellowish tan, people with dark eyes and straight black hair. They changed the city forever, including strong, proud white Queens, the place of cops and firemen, of the late Carroll O'Connor, who came from under the Jamaica Avenue el to become Archie Bunker. Suddenly the sidewalks were crowded with continents of children running through the gates of schools like P.S. 69 at the end of the day. Then one afternoon, a woman named Quinn who lived in Rosedale, outside Kennedy Airport, complained about the schools and as proof of her lack of prejudice said, "And I'll have you know that my son goes to a school that is ninety-nine percent minority. That's right. He goes with ninety-nine percent minorities." This school has pupils from seventy countries who speak forty languages. On this afternoon, the day before St. Patrick's Day, the kids had on green cardboard hats that they had made in class. Here came a little girl from India, with her Irish green hat tilted over dark hair.

"What's the green for?" she was asked.

"St. Patrick."

"What does he mean?"

"A parade."

"What kind of parade?"

"White people."

She had just identified the New Minority in New York.

As the 2000 census showed, there are now two types of people in the city. There are those of color. And there are those without color. Those of color are a large majority.

The old minority of the city is now the majority. The old majority is now the minority.

Chapter Three

AT AGE four, Eduardo Gutiérrez walked behind his father through the tin gate, out of the alley, and a few yards up to the brickyard. They passed a pit where a small pack of shrieking dogs leaped and clawed the dirt sides, teeth bared, trying to climb straight up and race through the streets and tear somebody to pieces. Each day when the sun rose to the top of the sky, instead of dozing while their fleas leaped, the dogs went heat crazy. Eduardo's father, Daniel, took the dogs from his yard and the alley and any strays and threw them into the pit, where they screamed for revenge until their mouths cooled in the evening shadows and he lifted them out.

Spread out on the dirt brickyard were long rows of gray cement slates used for roofing, called *tabiques* but considered bricks. There were also stacks of regular bricks awaiting a truck. The slates were drying in the sun. There were hundreds of them, arranged like cards in solitaire. Right away, Eduardo's uncle Tomás, sixteen, went up to the lines of slates and grabbed the last one in line, with the top of it under the bottom of the next slate, causing all the slates to slip down, one atop another. Tomás made a stack of ten slates in his hands. He carried them to the shed, where Eduardo's father placed them in stacks for more airing before they would be sold.

Eduardo's twelve-year-old nephew Jaime took four of the slates and, pressing them against his stomach, carried them to the shed.

Behind the older boys, his bare feet causing the dust to rise, came Eduardo with a single slate in his hands, all he could lift.

"You see," the father called out, "this is how you learn. My son is little. He learns so much in bricks."

Three years later, when Eduardo could carry four slates, his father said he had a skill with the slates and bricks that would be with him for the rest of his life.

"Yes, school is very important," the father said. "It is also important that he learns a skill so when he leaves school after the sixth year he can work and help his family."

When he was old enough to carry four slates, Eduardo was asked: "Which do you like, school or work?"

"*Trabajo!*" Eduardo called out.

The school was the one-story Benito Juárez School, a few blocks up Calle Libre. Looking up the street from Eduardo Gutiérrez' alley at number 8, you can see low posts placed permanently to block trucks and horse carts from passing in front of Our Lady of Guadalupe, one of 365 Catholic churches in the Cholula area. There is a plaza and a walk on a path under trees to enter the yellow church with red trim, which has insides of gold. After the church, the street continues through the same dust and flies, and the same children in doorways and young women holding babies, until it narrows to the eyes under the hot sky.

A block up from the church, one large truck, here to haul bricks, raises a cloud of dust that obscures most of the street.

On one desolate street corner there is the school, where Eduardo sat at a scarred white wood desk. The learning was difficult because nearly all the kids in the school knew they would go only as far as the required sixth grade, after which, at age twelve, they would go out to work, as do 90 percent of Mexican grammar school pupils. There are charges for junior high school. Books must be bought. There is a 320-peso bill, about $30 American, for tuition, and then charges for administrative costs and building repairs needed during the school year. The taxes do not cover this because the tax money is openly stolen by politicians in Mexico City. The payments don't seem high, 30 pesos here, another 30 there, but families feel that not only is it intolerable that kids who should be doing some of the heavy lifting at home are wasting the day in a schoolroom, but it is not right that the family has to pay for this injustice. Having a kid come straight home for a big free dinner after school on a day when he didn't even try to lift something is the sacrifice that hardens the heart.

In Eduardo's fourth-grade class, all parents had to appear on the next-to-last day of school to collect report cards. Mostly mothers did this. While Eduardo's mother signed all his report cards at home, she was too shy to go to the school and pick it up. The father showed and was instantly angered when Eduardo's card said he had not been promoted.

The father went home and told Eduardo, whose mood immediately turned dark—but not nearly as much as that of the father, who told Eduardo that instead of finishing school in two years, now it would take him three more years. This meant that the father would have to wait an extra year before he had a son giving full-time help in the brickyard.

It was the start of a life for Eduardo Gutiérrez that was to allow him to see nothing in San Matías other than the dirt and dust and flies. He lived in the end room in the compound with an uncle, two brothers, and various cousins. When he heard older people in town talking about going to America, he thought of going there to get money so he could build a new room in the one space left in the dusty compound. He would build the one room and a second atop it. He saw an iron staircase going up to it. He would paint the outside blue.

Dreaming, he could look to the north, to a sky of many colors billowing with white clouds. Somewhere up there—he knew because everybody said so—was a place of excitement and money. Breathing the sultry air on Calle Libre, he could not smell the air of Brooklyn, of Middleton Street in Williamsburg, with buses and an el, and streets so often cold and wet, and of the sound of creaking building walls.

All his young dreams gave him no idea of the dangerous path ahead. The young dream of everything except death. There was no vision of working alongside Nelson Negrón, for example, who cannot read or write in Spanish or English and who does what he is told, climbing the scaffold until he is chest high to the third level of a construction site on Middleton Street in Williamsburg, in Brooklyn, his right side straining under the fifty-pound sack of cement on his shoulder, looking up at a roof that is being held aloft by virtually nothing. If there are no roof beams, he reasons, what could there be under this third floor he is about to throw his sack onto?

There are twenty workmen crawling over the row of three-story brick condominiums being built. If the builder were legit, the workers would cost him about $15,000 a week. But the builder is Eugene Ostreicher, a man in his middle sixties who fled Hungary in 1944. He hires mainly Mexicans, and they take short money and like it or they're gone and Ostreicher finds somebody else for the same or less. His Mexican payroll is $5,000 a week.

Negrón is looking up at Eduardo, who is standing on a deck that moves when something is dropped on it.

In San Matías, Eduardo could not see himself here on this deck.

"The boss told me he wants it this way," Eduardo says.

Negrón drops the bag from his shoulder and shoves it at Eduardo's feet.

The floor went up and down.

"It's going to go down," he told Eduardo.

Across the street from the Benito Juárez School was an open-air tortilla store. A young woman in black stood at the end of a moving belt, and as a tortilla came off, smoking hot, she grabbed it with her right hand and snapped her wrist as if pitching a baseball, making the tortilla flip over, taking some of the heat off her fingers. She put the tortilla on a stack and immediately, continuing the motion, grabbed the next hot one from the moving belt. Every few moments another young woman took the growing stack of tortillas over to a counter, draped a towel over them, and sold them to people coming down the street.

The two jobs do not change, ever. Neither does the pay. Twenty dollars for a seventy-hour week.

Next to the tortilla store was the tiny box of a store where Silvia Tecpoyotti's mother, Olivia, watched the group of teenagers growing into men, one of whom could be for her daughters. Olivia Tecpoyotti Daniel sat in her store on the dirt street, a crammed closet of a store. She sold socks, packs of crayons and boxes of white paste for children's projects, sodas, and chips and tacos for the young men who came in from the street corner to play the two video game machines—among them, Tomás Eduardo Daniel Gutiérrez, eighteen. Right away, the mother's eye picked him out for her daughter. Silvia Tecpoyotti was only fourteen, but life starts suddenly in the dust.

Olivia had seven daughters, with Silvia the third oldest. Olivia's husband had a brickyard across the street. When Silvia was thirteen and sleeping in a room with three of her sisters, the father had a bedroom added to the house. The father and mother moved into it, and soon Silvia announced that she didn't want to sleep with anybody anymore. She carried clothes into the vacant bedroom that was formerly her parents', shut the door, and the room became hers. Nobody thought of complaining. Silvia was a girl who with one long glance got everything she wanted. To make it permanent, Silvia had a lock put on the door. Such luxury, a bedroom where life can be lived in privacy and thoughts can remain personal and be protected.

She put pictures on the wall of Enrique Iglesias, the singer, and her favorite movie star, Rosa Gloria Chagoyán, an actress who could sing. Silvia's favorite movie of hers was *Lola the Trucker*.

Silvia remembers hearing for the first time, at age nine, the lecture mothers gave to all daughters: "The boy must come after you. You are never to go after the boy. Better the man comes to you and talks. You do not go to them and talk. Never. Remember this all your life." This was mixed with religious instructions so that the daughters believed any act of being forward with a boy was sacrilegious.

Silvia needed no such lecture. If she had any early wild thoughts, only she would know of them and nobody else could even have the slightest notion. As for chasing a boy, that would never be her way, even if she was wounded by her stillness in the end. Who was a boy to expect her to follow him?

As the mother inspected Eduardo, Silvia was next door doing schoolwork in the small house attached to the store.

On the street corner outside Olivia's store was a group of young men. Watching from behind her counter, Olivia could see that Eduardo was not rowdy like the others. He was tall and everybody else was short. He already had a thin mustache and brickyard arms. But he fought with nobody on the corner outside. She knew that he worked for his father in the brickyard right up the street, worked hard, and that spoke for the future more than any other quality that could be found in San Matías.

The mother didn't talk much to Eduardo. She watched and listened. To her, there was no question that he was the best of the bunch outside the store.

She told her daughter Silvia, fourteen but almost fifteen, that Eduardo was good. Silvia was the rare one who made it to junior high school. But it was still time to tell her this. Silvia was old enough to start thinking of marrying and having children. And her bright body would bring the proudest young Mexican male crawling at her feet. Oh, she would attract many young men, the daughter would, just with her eyes alone, eyes that widened in laughter and then crinkled in joy and thrilled a boy at a glance.

Then there were moments when her look reflected wisdom so far beyond a teenager. Even the young men who would have recognized intelligence were unable to sense the wisdom, for their attention was taken up by her long, curving neck, a neck as soft as a cloud. They had to remind themselves to breathe.

Silvia had seen Eduardo before, at town dances. She danced and watched him stay against the wall as if nailed to it. At this time, Teresa Hernández was the girlfriend of José Luis Bonilla. One of her sisters married Gustavo Ramirez, who lived on the dirt street behind Eduardo in San Matías. Her other sister married Alejandro Huitzil, who wanted to be an upholsterer in Puebla. It was Gustavo who started it all by leaving his wife and child and crawling into America where there were construction jobs at the astounding pay of $6 and $7 an hour in Williamsburg, in Brooklyn, where there was a builder, Ostreicher, who was going to build many buildings on streets called Lorimer and, later, just around the corner, on Middleton.

THE CITY OF NEW YORK FIRE DEPARTMENT

IST ALARM—PHONE (STRUCT)
02/06/96 E230 E209 LI02 LII9 BC 35 E216 RES
03 RCOI RSO4
BOX 0341
LORIMER STREET MARCY AVENUE
STRUCTURAL BUILDING COLLAPSE

Found cause to be partial collapse of metal beams and building material at a new construction of homes from uppermost floors to cellar with two construction workers who were not injured, Henry Korl, mw39, and Thadeusz Sokilski, mw56. No further construction was permitted until arrival of Department of Buildings. Inspector Migone, Dept. of Buildings, arrived on the scene later. Richard Ostreicher of Industrial Enterprises which is constructing the buildings was on scene.

John M. Dillon, time arrived 9:01.

Chapter Four

I N SAN MATÍAS, Silvia Tecpoyotti and other young women, like Teresa Hernández, knew that you can get $4 an hour for scrubbing floors in Texas, and even more, as much as $5, for making up beds in a motel. How were they going to stay in San Matías? They were not. They believed in the Job. The young of San Matías lived their lives with pictures of American money in their heads.

One night in San Matías, Eduardo came to the corner by the store. He had his black baseball cap pulled down, but the corners of his eyes had the look of a hungry bird as they seized on Silvia's face. Inside the store, she looked out.

He walked on with his face showing nothing.

For his next visit, he came into the store with three or four of his cousins. He went right to one of the video game machines as if she were not in the place, and began manipulating the knobs.

It gave Silvia a chance to inspect his broad back, which came down in a V, and the arms shaped by carrying all those stacks of bricks for so long now.

He finished playing, and as he left with his cousins, she remembers, he glanced at her, his eyes flicking like a camera shutter, maybe committing the sight to memory forever.

And then immediately his expression turned blank with shyness.

The following night, Eduardo's cousin Rafael came into the store.

"Eduardo thinks you are pretty," he said.

Silvia's expression was impassive.

"He told us that last night when we left here," Rafael said.

"Why doesn't he tell me himself?"

"He is afraid," Rafael said.

Silvia didn't answer, and Rafael left.

Anything Eduardo earned in the brickyard was turned over to his family. He did an adult's work and brought the money home like a kid bringing change back from going to the store. To get money for the dances, he went through the farms on the outskirts of the dusty streets and ripped up tomatoes, apples, corn, and other plants and sold them to housewives for a few pesos. Others began calling him Chato, meaning "pug nose." Afterward, virtually everybody drank fat beers and tequilas. Eduardo drank only a little. Then on the way home he unscrewed all the streetlight bulbs.

On another night, Eduardo was back in the store with two cousins, the brothers Moisés and Rafael. Now and then he would turn and look at Silvia and she would meet his eyes with a steady pleasant gaze but show him nothing more. He finished the game and left with his cousins.

Moisés had a girlfriend and was busy thinking of her. Rafael had nobody and thus became the excited messenger.

When Silvia came home from school the next day, she stopped in the store. In from the dusty street came Rafael.

"Why did you hurt Eduardo last night?"

"What?"

"You didn't talk to him. He went home saying how much he loved you and that it is sad you wouldn't speak to him."

"Why didn't he speak to me?"

"It is very hard for him. He didn't think it would be hard for you. He wants you to be his girlfriend."

By telling this to Rafael, whose brother confirmed the conversations, Eduardo was trying so clumsily to conform to the San Matías custom in which the boy must announce to all he knows that a particular girl is his girlfriend. This is an outgrowth of the old Spanish customs, Mayan suspicions, and the Catholic Church's banns of marriage. Before the boy in San Matías makes such an announcement, he cannot take the girl out alone and most certainly cannot kiss her.

Silvia thought of Eduardo's painfully shy mother walking past the store.

"Tell him to try," she said in a prayer. "Tell him for me that I like him."

Eduardo came back with three or four cousins, and they clustered around the video game machine. He never looked up. As they were leaving, he waited until his cousins were out the door, then stood in the doorway and gave a low whistle.

At first Silvia was irritated and dismissed this whistle with a wave of her hand. Then, deciding that she didn't want to chase him away forever, she smiled at him and turned away, with the long locks of her hair waving. An old woman and a young girl came in to buy crayons, she recalls, and when she finished with them, Eduardo was gone. Instantly, she missed him. The next morning, going to school, she decided that she loved the store when he was in it.

One night the next week, when Eduardo and his cousins came into the store, she suddenly felt a tap on her head. It was Eduardo. He acted as if he hadn't touched her.

"That was you," she said to him.

"No, it wasn't."

"I can tell it was you," she said.

"How could you?"

"I know who it was," she said.

But he could only fool with her when all the cousins were there. When he came in alone, it was as if his mother's blue scarf came out of the air and covered his face. He did not talk.

Then one night when it grew late and Eduardo had not been in, she found herself becoming anxious. She looked out the door and asked Rafael, "Is Eduardo coming?"

He shrugged.

"I thought he would come here," she remembers saying. The next day, another cousin, Rafael, came by. "Eduardo is so happy that you love him," he said.

"Who says that?" she said.

"That you told that to my brother Moisés last night that you love him and will die if he does not come to see you."

"Did I say that?"

"Moisés says you did. He told that to Eduardo. Eduardo is very happy. He is proud that you are his girlfriend and that you love him. He loves you."

"He should come and talk to me himself."

"Eduardo said you know."

"You tell him that I am nobody's girlfriend until I am asked."

She sent Rafael off with that directive and also with a pang in her heart.

She remembers that so well. "I loved it when he was in the store. I felt sad when he was not," she says.

She heard about a job in a hair salon in Cholula, whose streets begin only a walk away from her home. She went to the hair salon and was hired. The hours were from 4 P.M. until 9 P.M., six days a week, at 200 pesos a week, $20 a week. Come back in ten years and the hours and money are the same. She listened to the woman in charge telling everybody what to do, and she did not like it. The job put one ambition in her: She was going to get money from working in America and send it all home for a new house next to her mother's and have her own hair salon on the first floor.

In this vision, she saw Eduardo coming home from work to this house. He climbs out of a huge truck that delivers bricks. He owns the truck and he owns the brickyard. He got the money for his business by working in the United States with her.

She rushed home at day's end, so she wouldn't miss Eduardo.

On one of these nights, after she had left the store, Eduardo and his cousins Rafael and Moisés came to her house. Eduardo asked Silvia's older sister for permission to talk to Silvia.

When Silvia came out, he said, "Color our hair blond." The town style for young men was to have a blond streak in front, a rooster streak. Eduardo and the cousins felt like outsiders without it.

"Why ask me?" she remembers saying.

"Because you know how to do it."

She got out bleach and color and started on Eduardo first. He couldn't wait to look like a blond rooster.

Silvia ran her fingers through his hair. He wriggled at the touch.

"I can't do it if you don't stay still," she said.

He tried to brace himself. She could not resist drawing her fingertips across the nape of his neck. He shivered.

Now she started to bleach his hair. She had the coloring in a cup and she brushed it into his hair.

She ran her fingers lightly over his neck.

He made a sound.

But the most resonant sound came from the doorway where her father, Cristino, was watching with rising apprehension.

"Get me coffee," he said.

Silvia indicated that she was working.

"I want coffee," the father said.

Silvia had to stop and went to the small stove and heated

coffee and gave it to her father, who sat on a chair like it was a guard tower.

"Why does he want his hair like this?"

"All the boys want it."

"Why do you do it for him?"

"He asks."

"Is he going to pay you?"

"No."

He asked Moisés and Rafael, "You pay her?"

They were uncomfortable but said no.

"Then why should you do it?" the father said to Silvia. "*Comida*." He wanted to eat.

She held out her hands to show the bleach and color still on them.

He waved that off. "*Comida*."

She rushed through Eduardo's rooster streak and told the other two that she would be right out. She went to the stove, where earlier she had made chicken and vegetables for her father.

She heard him say to Eduardo, "What time do you have to be home?"

"Eleven," Eduardo said.

"It is late now," the father said.

Eduardo's two cousins grunted. They would go another day without the rooster streak.

That night was the start of the father's fifteen-minute policy.

If Silvia or any of his other daughters was outside at night for more than fifteen minutes, he called out, "What are you doing out there? What are you talking to them about? Come in here and tell me what you are saying to them."

To Silvia, who was openly taken with Eduardo, thus drawing the father's sharpest attention, he said, "Here, you. Come in and make me coffee."

As she served him, she remembers him telling her, "You can talk a little while with a boy. Fifteen minutes. That is the most. Then you come in."

What he didn't know was that her ears were filled only with Eduardo's silence.

Over the months, the father's crossness waned. The desire to have his daughters fluttering around him lessened as he considered their futures and realized what every other family in San Matías did: that while it was sad to have children go away, it still was not as painful as having them all at the dinner table with truncated futures.

Always, a coyote—a smuggler—named Manuel was around the corner like a cab driver, collecting money from somebody who wanted to go to America through the Tijuana border. There were others around, walking the streets of the run-down section and onto the narrow, crowded shop streets. There was Angel, whose connections took you through Sonora to Tucson, and Pedro, whose route was through Matamoros and into Brownsville, Texas. They had unlimited customers. Virtually none of the young in these towns around Puebla thought of any future except going to America. So many people told Silvia that a chambermaid job in America was far better than what she had.

One night, she had a dream in which she was on a bus with her uncle going to the border and America, her hand gripping the back of the seat in front of her to ease the rocking. The next night she had the same dream.

Suddenly her father said to Silvia, "I know you think of going to America."

Of course she had thought of this, but it was for sometime ahead, and here the father was stating it as imminent. As long as he had brought it up, she would start planning. She waved a hand in the air, and it brushed against the new house she was building with the hair salon on the first floor.

Silvia's mother said that her brother, Silvia's uncle, had decided to go to America and if Silvia wanted to go, this would be her only chance for a long time. She would not be allowed to go on such an adventure with strangers. The uncle had arranged with the coyote Pedro to take them on his route through Matamoros and on to Brownsville. Her uncle had a brother and two nieces in College Station, Texas, where there were many motels and fast-food restaurants that needed Mexicans.

The date was set for Sunday.

Immediately, Silvia told Rafael, the messenger of romance, that she was going to America on Sunday. When Eduardo didn't come into the store that night, she shrugged, as if to shuck Eduardo off. She and a sister, Emilia, talked about a farewell outing on Saturday night at a dance concert in the stadium in Puebla. Silvia's favorite group, Bryndis, was appearing. On Friday night, they were talking about this again when Eduardo walked in with his cousins. Hearing the talk about the concert, he said to Emilia, "Can I come with you?"

Emilia said to him, "Okay. You go with her," meaning Silvia.

She never expected him on Saturday night. Her sister had set 8:30 as the time they all were to leave for the dance, and when that time came around and Eduardo was not there, she got ready to go out with her sisters.

She didn't know that Eduardo had been outside for a half hour, walking up the block, talking to people, then coming back nervously.

Finally, he was about to knock on the door just as it opened and the sisters bumped into him.

"It is a good idea that you don't go to the dance alone," her father said.

Silvia remembers that she and Eduardo stood in the doorway with her father, and they were a sentence away from being officially together.

Eduardo did not say it, but it was obvious that he had nothing else on his mind.

"I wore a tiny black blouse, a white jacket over it, and white pants," she remembers. She still can see Eduardo in black pants, a white pullover sweater, and his favorite black baseball cap.

The music the group played was slow and the lyrics romantic, and she was surprised and elated when Eduardo, with no shyness, held her close to him as they danced. She remembers pouring her body over his.

"Are you happy that I'm dancing with you?" he asked her.

"Yes," she murmured.

"I am happy," he said.

Some numbers later, still dancing close, he announced with passion, "I am happy I am dancing with you."

"And I am, too."

She was sure that the next thing he said would be a proposal, at least to be his girlfriend. Instead he fell silent. He held her tight but said nothing. The last dance was at 2 A.M. There was a large crowd and only one exit gate, and it took a long time to get through it. Silvia's sister and her boyfriend and Eduardo and Silvia were up against each other in the big crowd, and now Silvia felt that this would do it—you could see that he was thrilled to be so close to her, as was she.

They got out of the park and into a cab. She sat and waited for him to suggest a stop. The cab went up to her house, next to the store. Her sister and her boyfriend got out. Silvia did not move. Of course he was going to kiss her.

When he did not move for many moments, she got out of the cab.

He waved at her as the cab pulled away.

The next morning, she stood on the street for a moment.

"What are you doing there?" her mother said. "Your uncle won't be here for a half hour."

"I know," she said.

She waited in that dusty street, and when Eduardo did not come up it, she was about to break all the rules of her life and go down to that brickyard and maybe the moment he saw her he would come over and hold her, the way he had when they had danced the night before, and he would tell her that he wanted her to be his girlfriend and then she would say to her uncle, no, you go, I am staying here because I love Eduardo.

"Are you ready?" she remembers hearing her uncle say.

This was on the morning of May 8, 1998.

Chapter Five

S ILVIA WAS going into a world where the two American faiths rule at once, and people like her die because they cannot tell the difference.

There is the American worship of commerce that piles money to the sky and makes all good people rich. This moves in the opposite direction of an older belief, one whose prayer books still carry the smell of cold winter seawater from the wood ships of the Puritans, who came to run the morals of a nation. All these years later, their teachings that dourness is good and laughter is bad still cause Washington to make the control of strangers of great importance. If they are not white, then they come from the devil.

There was an afternoon in the House of Representatives in Washington when Peter King watched warily as Rick Lazio walked toward him.

King, a Republican congressman from Long Island, was standing in the aisle and Lazio, then another Republican congressman from Long Island, came on an errand on behalf of the Speaker of the House of Representatives, Newt Gingrich. It was over a bill that would allow immigrants without papers to be deported, right at the airport if found there, with no hearings. Tackle them in airports and at borders, tie them up, and send them back like packages. No hearing or evidence would be required.

"The Speaker wants to know what we need to do for your support in the future," Lazio said.

"Don't bring around any more bills like this," King said.

The bill was sponsored by Lamar Smith, a Republican congressman from Texas, a state that resents and reviles all Mexicans, although they will hire them for $3 an hour. It was cosponsored by Alan Simpson, then a Republican senator from Wyoming, which had 430,000 residents at the time and enough room for the population of a couple of countries.

One part of the bill said that "secret evidence" was allowed at immigration hearings. The phrase brought on an ancient fury in King, who had been all through this during his struggles to get a travel visa for Gerry Adams, the Catholic leader from Northern Ireland. King wanted him to speak to the American Irish. The State Department said there was "classified evidence" that Adams was a danger. They said that they owed it to the British government to keep Adams out. It took years for King to get the decision overturned, during which time his distrust became permanent. Now, on this day in Washington, King stood in the Congress of the United States and looked at the phrase "secret evidence." He saw it as un-American. He voted no. And he would vote no on any other immigration bill of its kind.

Later, walking back to his office across the street from the Capitol, he was saying, "It comes out to be fear, I guess. The idea of a bunch of Mexicans walking around the country—it frightens them. If you ask any questions about immigration, nobody has an answer. They feel it is something so bad that you don't have to explain it."

Now the names have changed. Gingrich of Georgia made everybody furious. Then his moral purity was slightly marred by one girlfriend and he was out. Suddenly, about to take his place is Robert Livingston from Louisiana, a sure antiterrorist. He wanted executions of immigrant terrorists, and if they weren't caught with a bomb, the gas chamber still would do. Livingston is on the floor of the House, about to be voted Speaker of the House. He decides to display his dislike for President Clinton. He calls over to the Democratic side that President Clinton should resign because he is an immoral pig with a girlfriend, Monica. The Democrats rise and shriek, "You resign! You resign!" They are telling each other the news that Livingston has four girlfriends. He has them in motels. Livingston happens to glance upward. He sees two of his four girlfriends. "Motel Livingston!" people shout. "You resign! You resign!!"

"All right, I will," he says. He walks off the floor. His chief supporters run to the back to pick a successor, Dennis Hastert. This one doesn't know Irish without papers or a Mexican. The whip, Rick Lazio, soon is gone. He is replaced by Tommy Reynolds from New York, whose field of interest is Niagara Falls.

And nothing changes. Peter King still goes to his seat ready to oppose any and all bills. None comes up.

Motel Livingston now stalks Capitol Hill as a lobbyist for Turkey. Somebody in the House is sponsoring a resolution condemning Turkey for slaughtering Armenians in 1915, and Livingston is hired to block it. "Turkey is not for genocide," he says. The trucks running through the border towns, carrying mufflers from Mexico and television sets from California, have superseded visions of terrorists or of most any other deaths in Congress. Money wins again.

And in Mexico a new president is worried about immigrants coming into southern Mexico from Guatemala and Honduras. For the northern border he sees a program of guest workers, and Mexican farm labor groups in the United States squall that under this, a guest worker would not be allowed to join an American labor union. "Ensured slavery!" they shout.

Once, virtually all Mexican immigrants made it into the United States safely. At El Paso, the entrance was made from the *colonias*, the shantytowns as hideous as anything in places like Rio or Rwanda, on the edge of the city of Juárez. This was accomplished by fording the shallow brown water of the Rio Grande. Many coming from Juárez who didn't want to come up the river so far took the "ferry," an inner tube pulled by rope across the river, which was wide at this point. The border agents were up on the bridge between Juárez and El Paso, guarding the United States border.

The largest number took the obvious path through Tijuana. They came off the planes on Rodriguez Field, where the air was filled with the magical sound of the song of America, cars rushing, truck horns blaring, smaller and insistent car horns, all of it on U.S. Highway 35, visible from out there on the runways. You can see the American road! The road ran from the large customs and immigration border inspection station at San Ysidro, just yards away, with twin plaques marking the borders of each country. The border is marked on the roadway pavement by a twin line of small metal nipples running across the twenty-four lanes. A dozen southbound lanes go to Mexico, and another dozen lanes go up the coast to San Diego, only miles away, and on to Los Angeles, to the airports, to all of America, to New York. From Rodriguez Field, they slipped through the bushes and across the sand leading up to the highway. Usually, they gathered at 4 P.M., at the changing of shifts of the American border guards, whose schedule they knew as if it were a town prayer. They had only to go over a weak wire fence with barbed wire at the top, barbed wire that could be nullified by one jacket draped over it. Then the whole pack would go up and over; it could be a couple of hundred, suddenly sprinting across the border line wherever you looked, and with speedy little strides covering twelve lanes to the center divider, a step over that, and another run for life and riches across twelve more lanes to the other side. The Mexicans who made it across the highway were new Americans. They melded in with the residents of the apartments and started walking toward San Diego as if they were heading for a store around the corner.

Frequently there was the shriek of brakes and the bare lights of emergency workers; a Mexican, crumpled like a piece of paper, was dead on the highway. Month after month, the Mexicans came off the airport runways. Night after night, Mexican after Mexican went high into the air as they were hit by a car, a trailer truck. So many that Jesus Garcia, the state of California's transportation director, erected a twelve-foot-high heavy wire fence on the highway divider to make it impossible for anybody to get across and be killed while making their run for America.

This way of crossing a border ended with the wave of a gun. A force of nineteen thousand Border Patrol guards spread across the Southwest, from San Diego through Nogales and Douglas in Arizona and Laredo and Brownsville and Corpus Christi in Texas. The towns carry the names of famous western stories, most of which never happened or, if anything did, one shot in real life became a thousand in cheap western stories or preposterous movies.

At the crossing to San Diego, the records of combined forces showed that they turned back 524,231 Mexicans. About a million made it through. Near the end of 1999, they had for the single year stopped 182,267, which seems like a tremendous victory, except three still got through for every one stopped. Yet it still was a gamble for a Mexican to try without a professional smuggler—a coyote.

Suddenly, and from everywhere, the traffic became overwhelming. The North American Free Trade Agreement of January 1, 1994, erased duties and left customs and immigration people standing at ramparts designed to inspect and impound drugs and keep out Mexicans without papers, trying to block a flood with their feet. All border troops try to ignore being parties to the fiction that you can stop masses of people who want to move. They stand on the border as fierce defenders of the American way of life: paycheck. And as part of the great new law enforcement industry, they understand the need for official statistics. Stop two illegals, the figure becomes five in a government press release in Washington.

This still requires a lot of plain hard, frustrating work. They'll receive a tip that a trailer truck is coming through with illegals. Stop the truck and find sixty Mexicans huddled in back. Send them back. Away goes the truck. Acting on information and belief, agents pull over a van and find many pounds of marijuana. The driver says he has no idea how it got there. He is arrested. And as far as the eye can see there is a line of trucks waiting to cross, eighteen-wheel trailer trucks coming from Tijuana. An average of three thousand trailer trucks brush past the border booths every twenty-four hours like an armored column and head anywhere in America.

And in the southbound lanes, another three thousand trucks head from America to Mexico.

Some American unions said the safety standards of these Mexican trucks and their drivers was so low that they were a rolling threat to America. That never happened. The California Highway Patrol and the local San Diego police could not come up with any records of an uncommon number of trucks from Mexico, or trucks going there, involved in accidents on Highway 35. By May of 2000, the Senate Commerce Committee found that of the 63,000 trucks from Mexico running in the United States, 73 percent were inspected during the year and therefore rated as approved.

The common fear was that trucks from Mexico carrying cheaply produced goods would suck up the American economy.

"I don't see anything sucked up," Rudy Camacho, the customs agent in charge of southern California, said as he stood at the border plaza, the sound of trucks forcing him to keep his voice raised. "One can't do without the other anymore. Twenty billion dollars a year in trade. Southern California can't do without it. What's it done to Mexico? It woke up a sleeping giant."

Ray Kelly, then customs commissioner, in for a visit from Washington, stood at the Tijuana crossing and watched the long lines of trailer trucks. Once he figured out that the ones coming from Mexico were carrying mufflers for America, thousands of mufflers, he knew the idea of stopping Mexico was over. "You get something this commonly used and if you slow it up, you'll have auto dealers calling for your head," he said. "What's happened is we've been overwhelmed. The government agencies can't handle the situation. We all need more people. We're told to forget it. What they want is more roads to handle all this. We seized three hundred eighty-five thousand pounds of drugs this year. Pot. We're burning forty thousand pounds of it tomorrow in Long Beach. I don't care how you feel about drugs or pot, but nobody in Washington is interested in drugs anymore. Whether anybody wants to recognize it or not, we're going to have more and more trouble stopping drugs from coming through. Who knew there would be this many trucks?" Nor a war.

The immigrants don't have the complicated daily life of a drug carrier. The drug carriers risk millions and millions. They could lose their freedom and frequently even their lives. They have enemies when they leave and enemies when they arrive.

Immigrants have to risk danger, and more of them die crossing the border, and the prize is the chance to go to work for below minimum wage and be lonely in America.

Eduardo's father remembers that a most improbable man named Chockaloo was the first to leave San Matías for the United States.

"Why go there?" he remembers asking Chockaloo.

"Trabajo."

"You don't even work *here*," Daniel said.

Reluctantly, many of the men in town donated something and wished Chockaloo great luck. Some even thought he was brave. Nobody they knew had ever done this. Daniel recalls kissing him goodbye. He was off to America, facing a new life with only the clothes he was wearing, a shirt and pants.

The owner of a grocery store on the main road outside of San Matías told Daniel that Chockaloo bought several bottles of beer and drank them on the roadside while waiting for the

airport van. He drank enough beer to allow him to open a
bottle of tequila that he had also bought. Later, off into the sky
went Chockaloo. As he had never been higher than the roof
of a brickyard shack, the alcohol was the only thing that kept
him on the plane.

Some months later, Chockaloo's mother was at the money
order window in the appliance store—stoves, television, sound
systems—in Cholula, asking if anything had arrived for her. She
got what she expected—nothing.

"Mama, Chockaloo is home!" a nephew shouted as she came
back to her house. Here suddenly was her most wonderful son
back in the house.

"He told everybody that the police beat him in New York
and he couldn't work," Daniel says.

He sat on street corners and told everybody of his trip to the
United States. He did not know that daily Tijuana bristled with
more new, young, eager, heavily armed law enforcement agents
and that no longer could you merely run across a highway. The
most expensive coyotes were needed.

Chockaloo had no idea of this. He had gone through
Tijuana. He thought that made him a sage. He told Eduardo
that crossing the border at Tijuana was the same as walking
across Calle Libre. He told Eduardo that he stood on the first
street of Tijuana, at a drugstore painted blue that sold coffee,
and was at the exact edge of the highway, only yards away
from the United States line, and that everybody in front of the
store used the outdoor pay booths to call people and tell them
what they were seeing, that their car just passed through the
inspection plaza, and when there would be a change of shift
for the guards.

There is no way of knowing how many young people listened
to Chockaloo on the street corner, bought him a bottle of beer,
and then went up to Tijuana and were terrorized by the guns
of border guards and thrown back like refuse. Silvia's uncle told
her that if she wished to be eaten by animals in the desert or
thrown in jail in the United States, then she should listen to
Chockaloo or anybody else in town. "I will take you. If they say
Tijuana, we'll go the other way."

The fences at Tijuana were erected by a government that
doesn't know the history of the last twenty minutes.

There was a night in Berlin in 1989 when crowds cheered in the damp night air for each sledgehammer that thudded into the Berlin Wall. And two women who took their first subway ride out of East Berlin in twenty-eight years came up the steps in West Berlin. The commercials of the West had drifted over the wall and into the taste buds of the people on the desolate streets of East Berlin.

They were astonished by the blinding neon of democracy. Right away, one of them said: "Ah, look. Burger King."

And as if Berlin had never happened, the United States government boasts that it has a wall that can keep out millions who have watched since they were first able to see a ceaseless rainfall of American diamond chips on their television.

No matter. The federal immigration people were enthralled by the sight of the highway fence at San Ysidro. Right away, they erected a double corrugated metal fence along the border that was high enough to repel an immigrant trying to cross on a cherry picker. The fence sits like a dreary surprise to somebody turning a corner on the streets of the freight center at Otay Mesa, which is a minute or two from the border gates at San Ysidro. The tan metal has a deadening effect on the commercial street. Light towers like those usually found at a ballpark rise over the fence, and at night their harsh, ominous glare makes a prison wall seem soft. A white Border Patrol car with an agent is on the street. Another car sits on an embankment and is almost flush against the fence. The fence runs for 180 miles with border guards said to be in sight of each other all the way. These are figures that can be checked only by going into the desert.

The Border Patrol is the most untruthful of government agencies after the White House. Even if real, these seemingly impressive statistics are out of a candy store. The border is over two thousand miles long, and enforcement at familiar places, the Tijuana crossing or one at Laredo, Texas, or Nogales, Arizona, only forces so many Mexican immigrants to walk blindly into lonely, dangerous areas where there is a river that takes lives, then miles of thorny, knee-high scrub running up to the mountains and then farther out, into the bare hot lands of Arizona and New Mexico and Texas, a desert that is the basement floor of the earth.

Chapter Six

S ILVIA LEFT San Matías with her uncle and took several buses that crawled to Matamoros, on the Gulf of Mexico, across the Rio Grande from Brownsville, Texas. By now there were five who had paid for the coyote. They checked into the Fontana Hotel for $400 for the one room and remained there a day. Then there was banging on the door and a young guy of about nineteen told them they were leaving immediately. The price for walking from the border with a guide to Houston was $600, and Silvia was told the trip would take fifteen days. They were stacked atop of each other in a taxi like luggage. Piling out at the edge of the town, they followed the coyote into high weeds that turned into hot red dirt with low thorny bushes.

Silvia remembers that the coyote yelled, "Run," and they ran, then "Walk," and when they had their breaths back, they ran again. Silvia congratulated herself for bringing a minimum of clothes in the small suitcase, for there was no way of carrying anything heavy. She thinks they ran and walked for five hours, until suddenly the next step was into a ditch, at the bottom of which was the river, narrow—the water dark and seemingly shallow and seemingly innocent. A stick on the surface was moving quickly enough to indicate a strong current. Silvia took off her sneakers and held them high over her head with the suitcase. Then she went barefoot into the water. At this point in the nineteen-hundred-mile-long Rio Grande, the water is shallow and the current deceptive. Then the river can widen and rise until it is sixty feet deep and cold, with a current strong enough to carry a house away. At all times, it is treacherous for young Mexicans, whose experience with water is usually limited to a bucket in a well.

On this day, Silvia listed herself as sixteen, but she was still a little short of that. She had no experience in water, but went into the river with the nerves of a trained guerrilla. The river bottom was sand. Each small step brought her deeper, until the water was up to her neck. She remembers that the current pushed hard on the back of her ankles and lifted her heels and curled under her toes and tried to yank her feet from the sand, turning her into part of the current. Her uncle remembers the strength of the current taking him by surprise. Silvia had strong and limber legs that secured her footing. She dug her toes in and took one step at a time, holding one foot in the sand as an anchor, and soon each step was firmer and took her upper body out of the water.

Many become paralyzed with sudden fear and go off their feet and drown in three feet of water. Any page of any record of the United States Border Patrol has columns filled with lists such as this:

NAME	COUNTY	CAUSE OF DEATH
Unknown	Maverick	Drowning
Unknown	Maverick	Drowning
Unknown	Uvalde	Unknown
Unknown	Kinney	Drowning
Jeronimo Mendoza Guzman	Zavala	Drowning

Del Rio Patrol Sector

NAME	COUNTY	CAUSE OF DEATH
Raul Martínez Delgado	Maverick	Exposure—Heat
Unknown	Maverick	Exposure—Heat
Raul Albarran	Maverick	Exposure—Heat
Unknown	Maverick	Exposure—Heat
Unknown	Dimmit	Unknown
Jorge Cabrera Tovar	Uvalde	Exposure—Heat
Unknown	Kinney	Unknown

Silvia and the group were now in Kenedy County, Texas, and in fact on the Kenedy Ranch, 230,000 acres of mesquite and sandy soil and emptiness, in whose hollows were sometimes found the bleached bones of those who have tried to hide from the sun. She wore two pairs of jeans to protect against the snakes that coiled across the land. These snakes are mostly diamondback rattlers as thick as a fuel hose.

They walked at night, starting at 9 P.M. These were old trails. Often there would be a warning sound from the coyote leading them, and they would promptly fall onto the dirt and, looking up, see a Border Patrol wagon jouncing along.

Somewhere in the night, Silvia was on the ground when the guy nearest her made a motion with his hand. Silvia heard the snake, a hissing sound as it moved over the dirt. If she stood and ran from it, the Border Patrol would see her and probably all the others, and they would be sent back to Mexico—and she was not here to be in Mexico. If she stayed down, the snake could be on her. It was the same as all the other snakes, but it hissed rather than its tail rattling like a gourd. Was it so much closer? The patrol wagon rocked and roared. Was it ever going to get farther away?

"I got ready to kick at the snake," she remembers. "That is all I could do."

Soon the Border Patrol was gone, and she crawled rapidly away from the snake.

Sometime later they came to railroad tracks that suddenly appeared in the mesquite. There were no signs or gates or poles. Just railroad tracks in the emptiness of the night.

"These are good," somebody said. "Snakes don't go on tracks. We'll stay on these for a while."

Records of the county coroner show that the sixth young man to die in a six-month period in Kenedy County, Texas, stopped on the railroad tracks running through the flat hot land, and he and the guy with him intended to rest with their heads on the rails. Mexicans on the trudge north believe that snakes recoil from steel tracks. Instead of resting, they fell asleep with their heads on the rail. A freight train running fast, with no crossing to worry about, no lights, no horns, roared down the tracks. One of the two on the tracks got up and fled. The other was still asleep as the train engineer tried to stop the freight, but he needed a mile for that and he cut through the young guy on the tracks like a steak knife. On another night, a mile away, on the same tracks, a train came rushing up on three who were sleeping. Two rolled away; one stayed and was left in ribbons. Then six were asleep on the tracks when a 105-car Union Pacific freight train carrying scrap metal and paper came through the night at fifty miles an hour and wiped them out. The engineer thought he saw something on the tracks, but there was no way of stopping.

The record was set at Kingsville, where forty Mexicans were walking north on a railroad trestle in the middle of a Saturday night when a train came around a curve and directly at them. Some jumped into a creek four stories down. Some tried to outrun the forty-three-car freight train. Others flattened themselves against the side of the trestle. Four died.

Silvia went on the railroad tracks, stepping from one tie to another, free of the fear of snakes and with no Border Patrol in sight. They walked that way for an hour, she remembers, and then one of them turned in the darkness. "*Tren!*" They hadn't bothered to look, and they could hear no sound even in the stillness of the night. Silvia remembers that the one big light seemed a long way off. People sauntered off the tracks. She looked as she was getting off and suddenly the light was closer. She jumped off the tracks and went down the embankment just as the train moved through a night that thwarted depth perception. Two engines raced by furiously, and behind them came freight cars whose wheels squealed as if they were being ground. She turned icy as she realized how close the train had been. And now that she was off the tracks, she had to worry about snakes again. Anything you can see that looks different is a snake, she told herself. But mostly she could not make out the ground itself and stepped blindly.

At dawn, the group stopped while the guide looked at his watch and muttered. A truck was supposed to be here, he said. They waited for two hours. Then in the first heat of morning, Silvia walked into a town with her uncle and Moisés, Eduardo's cousin, to buy food. Suddenly a white Border Patrol van came onto the street. The three crouched behind bushes—big bushes that could hide them all day, Silvia thought. Some moments later, she heard a sound alongside her. Next to her now was the polished boot of an immigration agent. Several Border Patrol cops with guns in their hands stood over them. They put Silvia, her uncle, and Moisés into the van and drove them through the border station over the small bridge across the river and threw them out in Matamoros.

"Don't ever come back or we'll put you in jail," they told her.

Chapter Seven

IN SAN MATÍAS and the thousand other Mexican towns where hope sits in a fading light, the young never did consider the idea of danger of going north to the United States. Their destination is the Job, not the town or city. And ahead of them, a country fearful and hateful of them has its fences up at the logical crossing points: Tijuana into San Diego on one coast, and through Nogales and Douglas in Arizona and Laredo in Texas and on into El Paso in the middle of the Southwest, where the Mexicans are pushed into the desert as if they are going through a turnstile. After that, they walk until they make it or die. They walk for the Job. There is no time to the Job. It is before all and after all.

They come across the riverbanks and the dry borderlands, these people who want to work, who want to scrub floors and clean pots, or mow lawns, or live in shacks alongside the farms they work on, or show up every day in the grimmest of factory jobs, or wash dishes in the coffee shops of the country—or work construction in Brooklyn for low wages on jobs on which white union members are paid five times as much.

And trying to get there, in all the dust from the wind and the powdered earth rising from their feet, crystals of air snap and unseen fingers high up in the dust clouds suddenly determine the fate on the ground. Nobody disputes this. It happens too often.

Bleached bones were found in the desert outside of Dateland, Arizona. A birth certificate in the sand alongside the bones identified Oscar Peña-Moreno, who had left Guasave, Sinoloa, in May 1996 with two lifelong friends. Their trip north would logically have been through El Paso, but with that town now heavily patrolled, they must have headed west. The three were married to sisters. They were not heard from again. Agents came upon the bones on December 4, 1997, and brought them to the coroner in Pima County, which is Tucson. Of course the flesh was no more. Desert hogs, coyotes, and birds had eaten all. Oscar Peña-Moreno's wallet, which contained his identification, was found in a pair of pants recovered with the bones. For some reason, the coroner cremated the bones and held them in an urn for the family. The people in Guasave pooled whatever money they had and sent the mother of Oscar Peña-Moreno and his wife, Ramona, to Tucson. She took the urn from the coroner and stood motionless with it. Then she put it down on a counter.

"This is not my son," she said.

The coroner explained that of course it was her son. Here is his birth certificate.

"This is not my son," she said.

She went back to Guasave.

Victor Chacon, who is with the federal public defender's office in Tucson, shrugged when he caught the case. This would not be the first time that something in the sky was right and everybody here was wrong. Later, the widow of Oscar Peña-Moreno, whose name is Ramona Quintero, said that of course the mother was right in refusing the ashes. "She prayed to the saint," she said. "She awaits his return. He is alive somewhere."

After which, in the matter of Peña-Moreno's ashes, he found it unsurprising to receive unrelenting pressure from the mother, who said her son and the two who had been with him were working in a logging camp in Utah.

Victor Chacon mistrusted the identification found in the desert. He stated in his report, "Illegal immigrants are often accosted by bands of robbers in remote areas. The robbers make the victims remove all of their clothing. This way the robbers know that the victims are not hiding anything of value. The coroner stated that because clothing gets mixed up, identifications are lost or wind up in other clothes. He states that he has had two cases recently in which the dead person was carrying someone else's identification."

Before the cremation, an autopsy had showed the victim had sixteen teeth in the upper jaw. Peña-Moreno's mother said that one day he had jumped on a bike and had gone to have a throbbing upper molar pulled. She didn't know the dentist. Chacon called every dentist in Peña-Moreno's area. None kept records. His phone calls and the realization that many were dying unidentified have now caused dentists to begin keeping records. However, a woman dentist said that she remembered taking the molar from Peña-Moreno's upper jaw. There was no evidence of any missing molar in the remains examined in Tucson.

The mother was right. The sky had told her so.

For Silvia and the others from San Matías, their being women didn't hinder them from attempting the crossing. The tragedy of the border could be seen on the television now and then, but not enough to stop them. There were only some distinctions that caused special attention: a pregnancy or a babe in arms. Otherwise, women went walking the same as men under a pitiless sun that raises temperatures to 140 degrees.

The nurse stands in the hospital in Bisbee with a hand on the little boy's shoulder as he sits on the examining table. The boy's feet dangle in muddy ripped little tennis shoes.

A nurse looks at the thin man in the doorway, sees his bleak look, and says nothing. He has on a short-sleeved shirt and tie.

The man has been trying to think of something he can do for this kid, and when he sees these ripped and muddy tennis shoes he tells himself, new shoes.

Now he hears people coming along the hall, and his mind outraces the sound of their feet. He knows exactly what it means, and he doesn't want to deal with it. At sixty-five, Miguel Escobar Valdez, the Mexican consul in Douglas, Arizona, has been everywhere for his government. He was in Chicago when they reassigned him here. He is calm enough to be helpful at a moment like this, in this room in the Copper Queen Hospital in Bisbee, the next town up from Douglas, a town of a few empty streets that are the last ones in America.

He is here because this little boy, Carlos Bacan, five, started out ten days ago with his eleven-year-old sister, Ana-Laura Bacan, and their mother, Rosalia Bacan Miranda, thirty-three, from the town of Coacoalco, outside of Mexico City. At 10:30 in the morning of the tenth day they were walking for the long last day before reaching the border, which was forty miles away. Two days earlier, they were in Agua Prieta, a Mexican town that is on the other side of a fence, and one pace in the sand, across the border from Douglas. The fence and the Border Patrol agents at Douglas force people to walk far out into the desert to go around the fortifications. The mother and children were trudging with two neighbors from their hometown. The boy could not keep up with the adults, and neither could his mother, who moaned as she lifted her foot for another step. The neighbors said they were going ahead to see if any Border Patrol agents were around. They said they would return to Rosalia and her children. Sure they would. When the sand turned to snow. They walked off. They left the mother and two children to suffer through hours of hot dirt and the sweeping bitter fields of unyielding knee-high thorn bushes. In the distance on three sides, dark mountains crowded into clouds. Ahead was a sky the color of heat. The mother, Rosalia, had brought only a large bottle of water; most of it was gone, and though she was dehydrated, she took only tiny gulps of water and gave the rest to her children.

The blood of an adult at all times needs five to six liters of water, and when there is less, the vessels contract, the kidneys become dangerously inactive and simultaneously the heart deals with less blood for all the body. Sometime soon, the problem is solved by either fluid or death.

That day it was about 110 degrees everywhere, but out in the desert, where the land throws off heat that mixes with the rays of the sun, the temperature is measured by what it does to people. Rosalia sat, then tumbled full-length into the red sand. Her breathing came from a strangled throat. The daughter tried to give her water, but the mother said no. Her hand waved weakly. You and the boy take the water. She passed out.

The daughter thought she had fainted. She shook the last drops of water onto the mother's cracked lips. The mother didn't respond and the water dripped from her lips. Ana-Laura told her brother to stay with the mother. She walked through thorn bushes until she came to a brown rutted road. She saw and heard nothing. Suddenly, a gas company truck came along and pulled over. The driver called the Border Patrol.

At the hospital, somebody called the Mexican consul, Miguel Escobar Valdez, in his office in Douglas. Now he is standing in the doorway to this first-floor room at Copper Queen Hospital in Bisbee, gathering himself for the sounds coming down the hall.

The girl, Ana-Laura, walks alongside the doctor. She is short and very dark. Her eyes are dry and fixed straight ahead. She has on a T-shirt and jeans. The tennis shoes are caked with mud.

The consul is going to say something to her as she passes, but he does not. I know this one in my heart, he tells himself. She will do this her way.

Ana-Laura stands in front of the brother, whose legs dangle from the examining table.

"*Mama murio*," she tells the little face.

Escobar sees that the boy doesn't understand.

"*Mama murio*," Ana-Laura tells the boy again.

He shows nothing.

She leans to him and whispers.

The boy moves just this little bit.

She leans forward again and whispers.

Does he nod?

I am not about to get near her, Escobar tells himself. The nurse and doctor keep their distance. They understand that these are sacred murmurings, not for their ears.

The girl steps back and looks steadily and solemnly at Escobar.

She has told her brother that the mother is dead. Now what would you have me do?

She says to the brother, "*Ven para aca*." Come over here.

He slides off the table and stands next to her. She walks over to Escobar. The boy is with her. The boy looks at her, expecting a decision from her. Now she is the mother.

Escobar asks her where she is from and for the names of her relatives, and the girl tells him that he must call her aunt in her hometown. The girl has the phone number memorized.

The nurses show them a table of food in another room. The boy sits down and eats. The girl wants only iced tea and then drinks only some of it.

In the town where they come from, people collected money to send the uncle to Douglas. The consulate paid for the mortuary dressing of the mother, and she is now being shipped home. The uncle and two children go across the border to the shabby bus station at Agua Prieta for the long ride to Hermosillo, and a plane to Mexico City and home.

Escobar stands at the bus as the family gets on. He pats the boy. Now the eleven-year-old girl, with the demeanor of a diplomat, steps up to him and shakes hands. She thanks him for their new tennis shoes.

Escobar throws his arms around the girl and hugs her.

When he lets her go, he is crying.

She is not. Her eleven-year-old face does not change. She gets on the bus.

In Douglas, at the last alley that runs off the last yards of the American side of the Pan-American Highway, there is a tan picket fence, without barbed wire at the top, that separates the last houses of Douglas and the first of Agua Prieta, Sonora. Two kids in T-shirts, twelve years old maybe, climb the fence easily on the Mexican side and then climb down into the first alley of America.

Suddenly a white immigration jeep pulls up, and a woman agent gets out and starts walking purposefully toward the kids, who now are the heart and soul of the danger to America. Illegal Mexican immigrants. Right away, when they see her, they climb the fence back to Mexico.

A second white immigration van pulls up, and another one after that.

There are six officers to answer the call on kids climbing a fence. The female agent, who has caught the case, walks toward the fence.

From the top, one of the kids cackles and gives the woman the arm. One, two, three times. Which is the only reason he went over the fence to begin with.

Now a woman holding a baby walks from a house on the American side and goes up to the fence. A man comes out of the last house on the Mexican side. He stands at the fence and the two talk through the pickets for some time.

Our country spends billions for protection from these most dangerous enemy acts.

Chapter Eight

A T THE heaviest center for border commerce in the country, the narrow river crossing from Nuevo Laredo in Mexico to Laredo in Texas, customs agents estimate trailer trucks account for something like $30 billion in business each year.

Immigration and Border Patrol people in the Laredo area estimate that they catch one of every eleven who scurry across the border illegally.

All those people can barely understand the barbed wire and patrols when they approach American cities in the Southwest. Back in their home villages and towns, they learn in classrooms and at dinner tables that all this land was owned by Mexico, and that the cities and rivers and mountains keep their Spanish names because they are by common law Mexican. The Rio Bravo is the river, the Sierra Madre is the mountains, and the cities are San Diego, Laredo, Nogales, Albuquerque, and El Paso. California once was Mexico. To a traveler from Mexico, these are places that cannot be so far from Mexico; the names tell you that they must be so close that they are merely places that you go to and then return. They are baffled at being hunted at the border by the helicopters and searchlights and jeeps filled with men in uniform with guns. How can you oppose my coming across your line in the sand as I go from Tijuana to San Diego, a place that once was my country and remains that way now by population alone?

The journey to Chicago and New York is the foreign experience for Mexican immigrants. These American cities have far fewer Mexican tones than the Southwest. Much more so in New York, where Mexicans aren't the dominant Hispanic group and have less history and are at the bottom of the Hispanic staircase, the foreigners of the Hispanics. They are more likely to have prominent Indian features than other Hispanics. When they come to Arizona, they feel they are walking on lands they have owned for centuries.

Still, the Border Patrol had a crackdown called Operation Hold the Line that drove people out to places where nobody with sense would dare go, into the worst of the desert.

Margarita Alvarado, thirty-two, and her brother-in-law, Juan

Manuel, nineteen, walked into the plaza at Nuevo Laredo, a couple of short streets from the bridge going over the river to Laredo, Texas. The square has a fountain in the center and benches where common people sit to rest and inspect the air. They are alongside the street royalty, the young men who claim that for cash they can guide you across the river and into the land where money floats through the air.

The streets around the square are lined with open-air drugstores, some of which sell American prescription drugs at the lowest of prices and others proclaiming "Farmacia Express," meaning all you want of what you want.

Strolling into the square are people in dresses and tight jeans, some of whom might be women. The yellow and white church, Santo Niño, is on one side. Through the open door you can read a great banner hanging inside and advertising La Indulgencia Plenaria del Jubileo 2000. For the anniversary, a plenary indulgence is granted somehow. A plenary indulgence sends you through the gates of heaven as if you actually belonged.

The indulgence is believed in by most everybody, and, because of such things, the Mexicans come north with a faith that seems as deep and strict as that of the Irish.

The interior of the church in Nuevo Laredo is painted gold. In San Matías, which is even poorer and thus spends on worship until there is true pain, the pillars have many decorations of heavy gold in the form of wreaths. The gold goes to the ceiling and across it, and candlelight causes the entire church to seem to burst into small fires.

Now in Nuevo Laredo, Margarita Alvarado walked up the steps to the church, said a prayer, and returned to pay the coyote whatever she had and followed him out of town, into the desert of thorn bushes and, after that, great stretches of sand fire. Apparently they had bought one gallon of water in a store off the square. A gallon weighs nine pounds. The woman would actually need five gallons alone, but she couldn't carry forty-five pounds. Margarita risked thirst rather than trudge along with the five gallons she needed.

She got through the desert brush, in heat that made her stagger, and then she collapsed and died on the bank of the shallow narrow river.

She was another name on a roster of people who died looking for the Job.

Chapter Nine

UNTIL THE attack on New York, the United States believed in the word *war* as a vital part of any effort against the things troubling the country.

Lyndon Johnson had a war on poverty.

There is a war on cancer.

There is a war on illiteracy.

There was Jimmy Carter's moral equivalent of war on an oil shortage.

And there is the war on drugs.

There is a peace wing to this war. "Just say no," Nancy Reagan said with a straight face.

"We can get the job done with a helicopter gunship," promised General Barry McCaffrey when he was the nation's official drug czar.

However, the word *crusade* then came into the language and replaced *war*. All the real Crusades did was kill innocent people who believed in a different faith, but the word has lived on to imply Christian valor.

The dates of the Crusades suddenly are eerie. They were held in 1350. Muhammad appeared on or about 650. Now, 1350 years old, Islam produces terrorists who attack America in a crusade that uses another name, just as Rome sent out its Crusaders in the year 1350.

Now we say there is an antidrug crusade.

We also have an antijaywalking crusade, a crusade against overtime in the Department of Sanitation, and personal political crusades: "I am on a crusade to become the state comptroller!"

The late Senator Paul Cloverdell, a Georgia Republican, and Representative Porter Goss, also a Republican from that state, came up with a bill that would have stopped anybody from doing business with any company that might somehow have some financial ties with a Mexican drug lord. No evidence was required. Just the presence of Mexicans.

"How can we be sure that the Mexican company doesn't have drug money invested in it?" Cloverdell was asked.

"So many of these Mexican companies," he sighed. "Well,

you take these people coming across the border. How many of them do you think are carrying drugs?"

He thought the answer was just about all.

Yet for those coming from places such as San Matías, none. "Nobody uses drugs here because they don't have the money to buy them," Eduardo's father, Daniel, said one day. "It is not that we are so much better."

In the brickyard in San Matías, Eduardo was shackled with shyness. He could hardly talk to Silvia when he was in the same room with her. Talking to her on the phone might be easier, he thought. At her mother's store, he played the video machine and after it, offhandedly, he asked how Silvia was. The mother said she had not heard anything from her and that she was worried. All these stories on television about people dying trying to cross. Where was this College Station where she had gone? He had never heard of any jobs there, and that was the only way to determine where he would go. You move to the Job.

Gustavo, who lived behind him and had gone to America earlier, had called several times from Brooklyn and said he had a construction job and that the boss, Ostreicher, could use more workers. The pay was immense: Gustavo said he was making $7 an hour. Seven dollars in one hour! Eduardo carried bricks all day for the equivalent of $5 a day and talked about the money Gustavo was making in America. Hearing this, his father knew that he was about to lose a son. There was a compelling reason. Eduardo and Daniel had started to build a new two-story addition at one end of the courtyard after work, with Eduardo mixing concrete and his father and a couple of relatives digging a foundation, but the money ran out. All these things that go into putting up a building of any size—the lumber, the supports, the ironwork—cost more than they had.

Eduardo began to put money away to pay a coyote who would get him to America. It took eighteen months of saving, but by the spring of 1998 he had enough. He went first to the corner by the store to look for a coyote. Nobody was around. He went two doors from his house and spoke to a neighbor, who knew smugglers. Two days later, the neighbor came into the brickyard and told Eduardo it would cost $1,500 to get him to America. With this much money to be made, Eduardo didn't have to look for coyotes. They found him. Just walk with the money and the smugglers will go over mountains and through water to follow you so they can lead.

Eduardo's father had only one thought for him: that liberty is not the country you are in, but the job you have. "If you do not like the job, then you quit and go to another," he said to Eduardo. "It is your only liberty."

People like Silvia and Eduardo had no idea of growing or selling drugs. Crossing the border was about the Job. Because of the drugs, however, they had to face new and imaginative obstacles in order to reach minimum-wage jobs in the United States.

Those carrying drugs into the United States are in the business from the start. A fellow at the New York Botanical Garden gave a lecture one day on the cepas of Bolivia—peasants named after cepa ants, which move as a chain. The human cepas carry packs of coca leaves strapped to their backs from one side of a Bolivian mountain to the crest and then down the hill to the lowlands, where it is cooked into a paste for shipping through Mexico to be sold in the United States, where the demand on Wall Street and in nightclubs and, in rock form, in crack cellars keeps the chain going. Cepas coming down the hill in an unbroken line, one sandal after the other, cepas coming down, cepas going back up the mountain, cepas in a chain draped on a hillside covered with brush. And far off, in Detroit and St. Louis and New York, the stockbrokers hold out cash for powder or, in poor neighborhoods, cash for crack.

Marijuana is smoked so widely in the United States that U.S. law enforcement believes that Mexicans must be wholly responsible. In New York, most pot smokers get their pot by an organized system of messengers, second in size only to the network delivering ad copy and publicity releases and large packages of letters and memos and legal briefs. The papers are carried to offices by bike messengers who are generally black. And then on the streets are these neat white young men pedaling away, carrying knapsacks full of white envelopes. The envelopes are filled with pot and are delivered to offices around Manhattan like take-out food.

The messengers are from offices that take the orders by phone. A woman answers usually, and the caller gives his code:

"RF for number 7." As he says this, he can hear the woman typing the number into a computer to verify that the caller is a legitimate customer and not a cop. You get on the list by having a friend call and then the woman gets your name and number and calls you back to make sure you're not the police. After that, you are on the customer list.

Now, ordering pot by phone, you tell the woman what you want. One envelope. They deliver from 2 P.M. to 9 P.M. You have to call before five to get it delivered by nine. They do not deliver heroin or cocaine. That is another and smaller business.

The bicycle messenger is white because cops don't stop whites. He wears a helmet and backpack and carries a driver's license. He brings the envelope up to the reception room of a business, the customer comes out and hands him an envelope with the standard $60, and the messenger gives him the envelope of pot. The guy goes back to his work and the messenger goes out to his bike and wheels his way through heavy Manhattan traffic on his way to the next customer.

Marijuana is so widespread that its status seems to be close to that of booze during Prohibition. You can't actually tell because pot smokers don't talk much. Drinkers boast, "I had a thousand beers last night." Pot smokers are home alone. But the reception rooms have people waiting, and the messengers are in the elevators, and somewhere they are bringing it in across the Mexican border.

Out of the attempted sealing of the Mexican border comes a most imaginative and effective drug and illegal immigrant enforcement, and it makes no difference. They find a tunnel of one hundred yards in length between Naco, Sonora, and Naco, Arizona, that has been in use by drug smugglers for twenty years. It was three feet wide and four feet high, and they found about $1.5 million in cash and 2,668 kilos of cocaine. By the time they were through counting the money there was another tunnel.

Stopping illegal immigrants and stopping drug peddlers are two separate and fairly hopeless occupations. In the 280 miles of desert leading to Tucson, authorities intercepted 387,406 people in 1998. The next year, there were 470,449 officially returned Mexicans from this area. The population of Tucson is 460,000. And some people feel a million Mexicans got through, but just enough did not, with 500 dead in the desert, to become an international scandal. Simultaneously, 25 percent of the nation's crime caseload comes from the Mexican border. Federal public defender Sandra Pules sat at her desk one afternoon in early 2000 with case number 3,500. The courtrooms are filled with so many Mexicans, the overwhelming number having to do with illegal crossing. As only one or two guards are available to a courtroom, the Mexicans are always shackled like dangerous animals. All day long, courtrooms are filled with the chiming of chains.

At border crossings like Tijuana and Laredo there are signs up saying that there have been four hundred thousand, five hundred thousand—who knows how many—pounds of pot seized at this location. It is something to be satisfied about, like bridge painting. Upon finishing, you turn and start back, chipping and stroking. With drug arrests and seizures, you catch Mexicans and their drugs; meanwhile the majority of drugs come into the country from Puerto Rico. Drug users are supposedly impoverished and despondent and helplessly addicted, and will steal the nearest silverware. Drug rehabilitation can't possibly be effective with these derelicts. The only thing to do is put a million in prison.

And far away from studies and statistics are the people who use drugs because they are fun. Do I use cocaine? You bet. Am I addicted? Don't be silly. Then why do you use it? I told you. Because it's fun.

The community of Sells, Arizona, sits alone in the border desert on the three-million-acre Tohono O'odham reservation, with its Customs Service patrol. The name Tohono O'odham means "people of the desert." They have been at this place since the sand began. Their ancestors were the Hohokam, who can be traced back to 300 B.C. Agents in this unit must be at least one-quarter Native American.

Here are the two agents from this headquarters pulling up to the three strands of barbed wire that make up the border fortifications. They are Doug Bothof, of the local tribe, and Kevin Carlos, a Sioux from South Dakota. They are here on account of drug smuggling, not illegal aliens. The three strands of wire are the fence that is supposed to be keeping all of Mexico's immigrants and marijuana out. It isn't even government wire. It has been put up by ranchers on the reservation. The top strand has been cut and the end hooked once around the post to hold it up, as if it had not been touched. The second and third strands were the same. Unhook all three and this part of the wire fence becomes a gate.

The two agents watch a van parked just on the other side of the wire, in Mexico. A woman is selling water to the immigrants about to sneak across and whisky to members of the Tohono O'odham tribe who cross over because tribal laws do not allow whisky on their lands.

The agents drive along the wire at five miles an hour, hanging out the windows and training on the ground below the most complex, miraculous technology: eyes that have been trained by their blood since time began to look at the ground and see great pictures and precise diagrams in the empty dirt.

They stop and get out. Bothof looks down at the tire marks of a vehicle that has come right through the wire.

"They're old. You can see people walked across them the next day." The outline of a foot is over that of the tire treads. Then he mutters, "Look at these people. See?" In one spot, a second set of treads suddenly runs over the first set. "They crossed here in two vehicles. Vans, I guess."

"Drugs?" Indicating the footprints.

"Immigrants. The footprints over the treads are too shallow for somebody carrying a heavy pack."

The agents are stocky, with equipment bringing Bothof to about 200 pounds and Carlos up to 260. They carry Steyrs, Austrian rifles with a thirty-round clip, plus another clip on their belts, a radio, receiver, a big Magnum handgun, and a flashlight.

Border areas like this one are speckled with buried sensors that pick up people walking, sometimes even their speech. Any activity lights up on terminals back at the base. But so often the metallic technology isn't worth the air its signals soar through. Whoever passes over the sensor can be gone before anybody gets out to the spot. So the agents track. The depth of the footprints indicates the weight being carried. A person with a backpack of marijuana rubbing, cutting into the shoulders has his feet sinking deeper into the ground than some little illegal carrying only his hopes, who skims across the dust, leaving the imprint of a grasshopper. To desert trackers, the term *backpacker* means a drug carrier, not some Ohio State student on summer break.

Sensors are often made futile by all these centuries of hunting and tracking that run in these border agents. Carlos points out that whether a track is fresh or old can be seen immediately. If the prints of a desert rat are on top of the footprint, it means the footprint is not fresh.

The ones the agents want come across with drugs strapped to their backs. It is usually marijuana, weighing from fifty to seventy-five pounds. The backpackers are usually wrecks who come slogging along until they hit this long stretch of scrub, under a remorseless sky that has them gulping water every few yards. At the start of their trek—back where it was slightly cooler and the paths softer—they can do two miles without stopping. Soon they are down to a mile. Now, outside Sells, they do only a half mile before dropping their packs and collapsing.

They pray to Jesús Malverde, the patron saint of drug peddling: "Let my legs be strong. Let the border guards lose their eyes. Help others know that we carry the good. Nothing that is harmful. Our marijuana causes songs. The Border Patrol kills."

And behind them are the natives with badges, tracking them.

Carlos looks at the bits of branch that have been knocked off bushes by a backpacker lumbering through. He feels the leaves. If they are moist, then somebody just went through. If they're dry, it was a while ago.

The coyotes traveling with the backpackers usually try to cover the track by taking branches and sweeping over the trail, as if they were scrubbing a saloon floor. Always, the sweep marks are a better trail to follow than the footprints.

The coyotes tried tying pieces of carpet to everybody's shoes, causing a smoothness where there was supposed to be footprints. Noticing this, the trackers began to sift the dirt. They found colored fabric strands from the carpet. They followed them. Next, the drug packers used mop rope, with strands the color of sand, but it still showed fresh and bright in the agents' eyes.

The drug haulers left signs where they sat to rest. One time, there were traces leading up to the start of mountains, and then on the rocks they found a small boulder dislodged, another overturned when somebody slipped and kicked it. Soon the agents were on four backpackers sitting with five huge packs of marijuana. Bothof was waiting for them to say they didn't know anything about the extra pack. Instead, one of them said it belonged to a group that was just over the next small slope. Which they were. On that day, there were thirteen arrests, and hundreds of pounds of marijuana were confiscated.

Over the course of a year the unit seizes 640,000 pounds of drugs. They are tremendous. They stop a third of what comes across. Because of his ability, Kevin Bothof was sent to Uzbekistan and Kazakhstan to show the police of these states, once part of the Soviet Union, how to track people trying to smuggle nuclear weapons to terrorists in places like Pakistan. When Bothof arrived, the police thought he was going to have sophisticated technology to show them. Instead he said he worked only with a stick and a knife and a lot of walking and bending. Any day now, his expertise will have him back in Uzbekistan.

Yet with all the history and energy, you still have as much chance of stopping drugs as you do of swimming to China. An hour and a half's drive away, in the Mexican town of Nuevo Nogales, there was a dispute over a dispute, and somebody walked across the street to the border crossing station and announced that there were two bastards coming across in their pickup truck with cocaine. By the time the word was passed along, the two Mexicans were through the desert and into Arizona, driving on Highway 19 in their 1997 Ford Lobo double-cab pickup, the truck's windshield smacked up and its rear license plate hammered around, but not enough to obscure its numbers, which had been reported by the stool pigeon. Here was a lone police officer who had just been advised to be on the lookout for a pickup with two men and a lot of cocaine. The policeman needed no surveillance system shooting data to a satellite near the moon and then back to his machine on earth to identify the pickup. Nor did he need a copy of the Constitution to know that he had a right to stop the vehicle; every car is a violation, even parked in the garage—a certificate is pasted in the wrong part of the window, the license plate isn't attached properly. This vehicle also had over six hundred pounds of cocaine. So a common patrolman with a panting German shepherd in the back pulled the pickup over. The Nogales police had received a phone call about the truck. All the cop had to do was look and press the button for his siren to make them stop.

The cop came out of the car with the dog. The police said that upon sniffing at the pickup, the dog went insane.

"*Él huele el sandwich*," one of the Mexicans said. He smells the sandwich.

He could have been right. No matter how well bred, how strictly trained, a dog's sniff is for fresh liverwurst. Plus, a handler and his dog must be together for some time if they are going to be effective. Smelling is a two-man game. But often you'll have the handler transferred and a new one taking over, and by the time this one and the dog are familiar with each other, the officer is up for a new post, and the next guy not only is new but hates dogs. That means the police dog isn't worth the leash he comes on.

This time, who knows what the dog on the highway outside of Nogales smelled? That didn't matter because the cop knew that there was cocaine on the truck. There sure was. He tugged and pulled out 607 pounds of cocaine. The two Mexicans in the truck shrugged. They didn't know what the cop was talking about.

Usually, figures that police announce as to the value of seized narcotics are fantasy. This time anybody with experience could tell you that in New York you certainly could get $6 million for the packages.

And it was discovered by a local phone call, which is the technology used in the ancient method of informing, not with any skilled trackers. Which is a sign of the hopelessness of fighting drugs. For if one truck with 607 pounds is found this way, you need no imagination to estimate all the organized smuggling that doesn't get stopped. Maybe they stopped half a mountainside of cocaine, which was worth millions and millions in a big city. The trouble was, the other half of the mountain came through the border in another pickup truck. Lawmen on the border learned of this some days later.

On the highways around Nogales, I-92 and I-80, right in the middle of the barren land, suddenly there is a traffic tie-up that seems like the entrance to the Lincoln Tunnel in New York. There are cars and trucks sitting on the highway, and finally up ahead are the flashing red lights of law enforcement. The traffic moves slowly. Now traffic cones push the cars and trucks into one lane. There is a small military green tank trailer, which holds water. There are white Border Patrol vans parked, a large van, and a table with agents around it. Out on the road are many Border Patrol agents. One pokes into a car or truck for a few moments, the vehicles move out of the one lane and onto the highway, and he looks into the next in line. Now you are even with the Border Patrol people. Sunglasses, trim mustache, great big gun on his belt, he looks in. No warrant, no discussion. He just looks in. Then he pulls his head out. "Have a nice day." The hand waves and you drive off.

Twenty minutes later, the traffic is backed up again. A van full of Mexicans is being held on the side of the road. The dog and his handler walk around the van and get nowhere.

But there are Mexicans out on the roadside. The big trucks with white drivers go right on through.

"Good afternoon, folks," the Border Patrol guy says as the next car pulls up.

He starts to put his head in.

"You got a warrant?" he is asked.

"We're within twenty-five miles of the border and we have the right to search," he says.

Now his head comes in, he sees the three whites in the car, and his head comes out.

"Have a good day."

Mexicans come into Nogales like blowing sand. And every step is dedicated to silence. This is a town where the most prominent sound in the still air is made by the warning bells of the railroad crossing gates on the freight tracks that run through the center of the town. When the striped gate arms go down, the cars and a small crowd of mostly women with paper shopping bags wait on the street. Three diesel locomotives hooked to each other—two Southern Pacific and a Union Pacific, with all engines throbbing—run through the crossing. Their red and green sides glare in the sun even through the coating of grime. The engineers sit high over the street with chins resting on arms. In a town of adventurers, they pose as the most exciting. The engines go through the crossing and run down the tracks behind buildings and stop. The bells commence and the crossing gates go up. The drivers cross the tracks, the women shoppers rush to the other side. A whistle sounds from one of the engines. The bells chime and the gates come down, halting traffic. The engines back up through the crossing and run on up the tracks a couple of hundred yards to freight cars with several workmen waiting. The crossing gates remain down as the freight cars are coupled to the locomotives. With a whistle, the locomotives come back to the crossing, pulling their freight cars. Suddenly they stop at the crossing. The engineers stare down. The gates are down and the locals sit frustrated in their cars. Finally the locomotives pull the freight cars out of the way and disappear down the tracks. Citizens of Nogales complain that the engines block the crossing out of insolence, to show the majesty of the rails. This controversy spills over to the local newspaper, whose stories are picked up by Tucson television. This was the major local news in a town that everywhere else, from movies to nightly news, was the stage for the cops and robbers of the international drug trade. It also was the place where the wave of immigrants drew itself up and then cascaded across the sand and into America.

Despite the large numbers of immigrants who came in without danger, for many the crossing turned into torture. So many Mexicans, afraid of the Border Patrol at Nogales, circle into the desert to find their way across the border. Others risk arrest and simply jump a border fence or crawl through sewers.

The business street in Nogales ends at a new coffee shop that is owned by a young woman whose husband is with the Nogales police department. She says that she gets a good trade of police as they come off duty.

A few yards down from the coffee shop, there is the high sheet-metal fence and a border crossing point, a tiny customs station with two passageways. On the left as you walk up, a customs agent sits on a straight-back chair and makes sure that the Mexicans who came through have their border identification passes. The people taking the other short passageway, to Nuevo Nogales, need to show nothing. They take a few steps through the passageway and come out into the riot of the first street of Nuevo Nogales. On one corner is a crowd of men, cab drivers, hangers-on, who gave the appearances of being open to any proposition. On the opposite corner is an old building with a big Times Square sign: Girls! Girls! Girls! Underneath it is the less flamboyant and more comforting Liquor.

From the border crossing station, the fence runs up a hill that immediately becomes steep. At the top there is a house on the Mexican side that is right up against the fence. The front porch of the house is as high as the fence and requires only the easiest of leaps to go from the porch to America.

"Where does the fence end?" the customs agent was asked.

"Right up there a few hundred yards out of town."

"What happens when the fence ends?"

"They all come through," he said, waving a hand. Yet too few realize this and go out into a dangerous desert.

At the top of a hot dirt hill, whose street signs said East East Street, there was a Postal Service jeep parked on the side street, North Short Street. It was a low-level slum of houses that appeared to be empty. The street ended at the border fence a few yards away. On the other side of the fence, at the house with the porch touching the fence, a man stood and watched the mailman, Tom McAlpin. Tom was born in Cabrini Hospital on the East Side of Manhattan and has a distant connection to the old Hotel McAlpin on Thirty-fourth Street. He was opening rows of silver mailboxes on a neighborhood stand outside one of the dry, cracked one-story houses. He said that there were no mixups with letters to Nuevo Nogales, Mexico, and to Nogales, Arizona, because, he said proudly, they handle the mail with great efficiency at the post office.

"The Border Patrol parks here a half hour, then goes off for a half hour, then comes back, but they still come over the fence as if nobody was around," McAlpin said. "They put a baby in a basket and lower him over the fence on a rope. Then the father climbs over the fence after him. Sometimes they ask if they can hand me the baby while they climb over. I'm not against the kid. I was a baby myself. But the least I can do for my country is not help them break the law. Besides, we had some guy take the baby and the Mexican jumped over holding another kid and he breaks his leg. The Mexican with the broken leg gets taken to the hospital and who knows when you see him again. Now the guy here has not only one baby but two."

"Where do they go when they don't break their legs?"

He looked around the street of silent decrepit houses, the fronts overgrown. "The house right behind us. I don't want to look, but you can. Just quick."

The house was boarded up and had a rusted tin roof.

"I bet there's thirty-five of them in there now," he said. "They call this a safe house. Sleep on the floor with rats. Then they get out of here. They go up to Terrace Avenue and catch a van."

On Terrace Avenue, there are two hundred licensed taxis and parking lots filled with vans with signs advertising Nogales-Tucson or Nogales-Phoenix. The taxis are numerous, but they, along with cars, can be confiscated if the Border Patrol finds the back packed with Mexicans. The law states that vans cannot be grabbed no matter how many passengers are yanked out and taken to the detention center. Of course the Greyhound buses are best. Nobody touches them.

The vans are for rushing immigrants away from Nogales and on the way to their American dream. One woman van driver complained to the mailman that it was a slow day. "She says she's made only thirteen hundred dollars so far today," he said.

At 42 Terrace Avenue, five men sit under an umbrella in front of a store. None of them has a job, and all of them are on cell phones. They look over a rail at the thousands of cars coming through the customs plaza from Mexico. They know what they are looking for in the river of metal. A fortune coming through in one car, two cars, three cars, maybe a dozen cars.

The largest number of immigrants coming through Nogales—when overwhelmed, the county sheriff says a million a year, and thus far nobody has refuted him—come by foot. All the sophisticated sensors and night lighting and cameras are in the end useless against a population that starts moving like a glacier. In Nogales the modern technology comes down to two Border Patrol vans parked on the highway going out of town and looking into the mouth of the town's sewer drain. The moment they are not there, out of the sewer, scrambling like crabs, come waves of people from Nuevo Nogales. They spread across the land and head north, crossing the ranches of people like Sara Ann Bailey, who at sixty-eight sits on a tractor somewhere on her five-hundred-acre ranch with a .380 Smith and Wesson pistol in her jeans. She bought it at Wal-Mart for

$150. She also has a sawed-off Mosberg shotgun at her feet. She grows hybrid grass, sudan-sorghum, on seventy irrigated acres for cattle grazing and is out there from 8 A.M. to 4 P.M. every day, driving the tractor alone through acres of bushes and low trees. Sometimes an illegal immigrant suddenly appears a few yards away. She has never shot at a Mexican, nor has anybody on the surrounding ranches. She served as a federal magistrate in Nogales for five years and never heard of a Mexican carrying anything but a knife or club to protect himself from snakes or the four-legged coyotes or an occasional sixty-pound mountain lion. Yet the immigrants scare her. When the Mexicans see that she is armed, they disappear in the brush. She lives her days like this. In 1982, an immigrant named Martínez Villareal broke into her house twice. First he stole art, which he sold at the train station in Nogales, Sonora. Then he stole two hunting rifles. He went to the next ranch and had a run-in with the foreman and a cowboy and he shot them dead with one of her rifles. He is still on death row, and she has never gotten over it.

She lives alone in the ranch house with three dogs inside, three outside in a large run, and three roaming loose. She has sensors in the ground around the house, a siren on the roof, and burglar alarms on the doors and windows. One night, a couple of hundred immigrants came across her property. She had her mother, age ninety-six, with her, and the Mexicans began tapping on her window to see if anybody was home. The woman could no longer take it. She let the dogs loose. And she gave return taps on the window with the barrel of her Mosberg shotgun. While the increases in the Border Patrol have cut the number of people roaming across her grounds to only a dozen or so a night, Sara Ann Bailey still has her shotgun for window duty.

The smoke and sand of the border carries with it something much more dangerous than leaves that make people dizzy and dazed. Over in Texas, almost to San Antonio, there is a Border Patrol stop, but it is just another obstacle to brush past.

At Dixon, Illinois, a trailer truck was stopped on the highway and state police were inspecting it for violations, they said, but they were really going over it for drugs.

In New York, a police commissioner named Howard Safir, who came out of a third-rate drug enforcement agency to pander his way into the New York job, attended several conferences in Washington in which Border Patrol people described their tremendous success in stopping drug peddlers. They gave reasons for search and seizure that would not play in New York, even if the police chief was all for it and his mayor, as sick as they come, would love it. A judge would thwart them. So on the East Side of Manhattan at Thirty-sixth Street, a block short of the entrance to the Queens-Midtown Tunnel, the police had traffic cones set up and cars had to roll slowly through a wall of police. A cop stops you.

"Hi. This a friendly stop," he says.

"Have you got a warrant?" he is asked.

"I said it's a friendly stop." He hands in a flyer. "You can go up to the yard on the West Side and get a free car inspection," he said. "It'll be good for your insurance."

The flyer gave directions to the lot where the police keep towed vehicles. Of course they would look over your car for drugs. They couldn't do it here on the street without a warrant. But if you took the car to the pound, then they could go over it for the least smattering of drugs, top to tires. A catastrophe blots out the Constitution. Streets are closed, pedestrians stopped, and police play martial law by blocking traffic for hours.

The stop is more proof that each puff of powdered dirt coming from Mexican footsteps far away at the border is a smoke signal that you can lose your liberty as it always is lost, a yard at a time, a mile at a time, a stop at a time.

Chapter Ten

AFTER BEING dumped back into Mexico, Silvia, her uncle Rogelio, and her friend Moisés went back to the Fontana Hotel, and all three made small moans when they had to pay another $400 for the room. Silvia bought a phone card at a stand next door, after which she called her cousin Belén in College Station.

"You know what? They sent me back," Silvia remembers calling out over the phone.

The cousin told her, "You'll do it again. Everybody who tries again makes it."

The cousin gave her the name of a coyote who was known for getting people through quicker than the ones Silvia had used. "If you need money, I can give you some," the cousin said.

Silvia, Rogelio, and Moisés went to a small restaurant on the same street as the hotel. Silvia asked the cashier if the coyote her cousin recommended was known. The cashier said sure. Silvia gave the cashier the hotel room number.

They sat down to have tortilla sandwiches.

"I can't wait to cross again," Silvia said.

Moisés lowered his eyes and ate his sandwich. The uncle arched his brows in a questioning look. Silvia remembers telling herself, the two of them want to go home.

"You don't want to go to Texas?" she said to Moisés.

"Why is it better than San Matías?" he said.

"Maybe it isn't," said Rogelio.

"You can make more money in Texas," she said.

"I don't like the river," he told her.

He didn't. He had turned many colors of fear when the cold water came up to his chin on the river crossing.

"Did the river frighten you?" she said to her uncle.

"No, it did not frighten me. It was just that it was cold."

She remembered the same cold as he did, but didn't bring it up. When they came back to the hotel, a burly guy with a wood match in his mouth talked to them. Yes, he remembered Silvia's cousin. He got her to Texas, and she paid. He could trust them

539

and they could trust him. He needed $1,200 from each to get across the border.

The uncle swallowed. He had borrowed money from everyone in the family to get the original $600. Moisés winced. He even had some of Eduardo's money in his pocket. They went up to the room to talk it over. It was late afternoon. Silvia stretched out on the bed. Moisés was on the floor. Her uncle Rogelio sat in a chair and looked at her.

They talked for a half hour, during which she discovered that they had two choices in mind: either get the night bus to Puebla and San Matías, or wait until the morning bus. Silvia told Moisés that she knew Eduardo would try again if he were here, and therefore he should honor Eduardo's loan and try again. Moisés shrugged. She told her uncle that she would not dare call home to tell the family that she couldn't go because her uncle wanted to come home. She told Moisés that her father had told her that the only way he would let her go was with the uncle. If she called him now, he would make her come home. Her uncle said nothing.

Now, after thirty minutes of getting nowhere, Silvia put a slight tremor in her voice and a small sadness in her eyes. She said that she was going to continue. As she had no brothers to protect her, she only had Rogelio, the uncle, and Moisés, the friend. When she had left San Matías with them, she felt like they were her real brothers. She had counted on them and still did. Don't let me go across the border alone, she said. I am afraid. Tears in her eyes. She was still fifteen years old.

This time they were taken on a different path to the river, which was knee deep with a lazy current at the point they crossed.

As they were paying $1,200 each, they were driven in a Honda Accord to a house in the center of nowhere. Silvia's cousin had wired money by Western Union to the coyote at the Fontana. They were the hardest dollars in the land. After a couple of years of work, she was empty. But she was expected to put up the money. Mexican families are large, with cousins usually taking the role of friends. When somebody needs money, especially to get to America, the family pitches in. There she was, an expensive traveler at fifteen and a half years old, but she was sure she would be able to repay the cousin quickly because of the good paying job she was sure to get.

Now, the coyote, with payment for a second trip in his pocket, moved Silvia's party from the house into an auto repair shop next door. Her uncle and Moisés stretched out on the greasy floor. Silvia was awarded an old couch that was about as busted down and filthy as you can get, but she remembers that it felt luxurious. The coyote took a look at the uncle and Silvia in the morning. The men's clothes looked like they had been clawed by a mountain lion. Silvia's clothes were also shredded. The coyote said they could not land in the Houston airport dressed like that. They would be arrested and their plane impounded. He disappeared and returned with new jeans and shirts.

After that, they drove to a private airstrip. A man put five of them into a single-engine plane and flew them to Houston. Silvia and her uncle and Moisés got into a cab and said they wanted to go to College Station. The cab driver said he wanted to see their papers. Silvia's uncle showed him money. Two hours later, she walked into the bare rooms of a ground-floor apartment in College Station, Texas. There was only a table and a couple of chairs, and bedding on the floor inside the two rooms where they would sleep. Silvia would start out by sleeping in one of the crowded rooms. But only for now. A tape player was on the living room floor. Silvia took a cassette out of her suitcase and put it on. The soft music of Bryndis filled the barren room.

Silvia got up on the first morning and went up the block to an Olive Garden restaurant. They hired her as kitchen help. The hours were 4 P.M. to midnight.

Several blocks from there was a barbecue restaurant. She got a job making salads from seven A.M. until noon.

She was fifteen and a half years old and she was in America and she was working sixty-five hours a week and she thought it was glorious. She was earning $420 a week, the salary of a rich person in Mexico. When he hears how much I am making, Eduardo will come to College Station, she told herself.

Chapter Eleven

EDUARDO'S MOTHER didn't like the idea of her son leaving. She had a vision of a place she had never seen, of dark buildings rising from a black volcano. She pointed to the black smoke covering the snow at the top of the simmering volcano that rose out of the struggling land outside Puebla. It was many miles away, but still too close for her. "Something will happen," she told Eduardo. "New York is too big."

The father remembers blessing him at the airport, which was the only show of emotion between them. Eduardo flew to Tijuana.

When Eduardo got off the plane, a young guy wearing a black shirt met him, and Eduardo followed him to a taxi. He asked if they were going to the blue pharmacy that Chockaloo had glorified. The coyote smirked. The pharmacy, he said, faced an army camp. They rode for twenty minutes to an old sprawling ranch house that sat in the dust and scrub. Inside the house was a series of cubicles with twenty-five young Mexicans sleeping on the floor. The place had been set up as a motel, Eduardo thought, but they probably saw it was far better to fill it with Mexicans paying some of their $1,500 here, rather than running a motel renting for $49 a day to people in love. Eduardo gave the coyote $1,000 of the payment due. He'd hand over the remainder when he reached New York. This was a pleasant fiction, as if he could withhold payment somehow. Both he and the coyote knew that he could be killed for $500. The coyotes were smuggling people because they didn't want to risk decades in jail for drug smuggling. A drug smuggler would spit at $500; the immigrant smuggler would kill for it.

Eduardo waited there for eight days. For food, he walked down to a Taco Bell, which stood on the edge of town. He was in Mexico, but if anybody made him for what he was, a young guy with money in his pocket to pay a coyote, they would become so jealous that they would not be able to restrain themselves from going out with a shotgun and robbing him, or rushing to the police to report the presence of somebody about to commit an illegal act by crossing the border. The

Mexican border police had a reputation of snatching anybody they thought was going over the border, issuing a beating, and taking the person's money.

Ted Conover wrote in his book *Coyotes* that he and a Mexican were stopped by Mexican judicial police. They took the Mexican into a room, tilted his head back, covered his mouth, and poured carbonated water up his nose and into the sinuses. The Mexican screamed to God during the torture. Then they took his money.

Eduardo waited for eight days, while the twenty-five Mexicans in the ranch house increased to over fifty. Sleeping was accomplished with somebody's foot in the face.

At $1,500 a head, the cash value of this group was somewhere close to $75,000. The money had to be split among the local steerers back in the Mexican towns, the coyotes on duty at the Mexican border, the owners of the safe houses on both sides of the border, and the drivers, who considered their trips hazardous and demanded real money. They also had to buy airline tickets for those being smuggled all the way to New York. At the end, the money had to be like anything else in crime, something for boasting but not buying, because despite the news reports of $200,000 Bentleys, you can't hand a car dealer a pocketful of dust.

Finally, a truck pulled up outside and a fat man with plaid pants and a black shirt got out, and Eduardo's friend Mariano remembers hearing him call to Eduardo and those around him, "All right. Let's go. Get up. We're going to start walking."

They remember walking for two hours through scrub and up into the first high hills that ran into gloomy mountains that climbed above the highway. The fat man led them to a black van that sat in the bushes. They got into the van, elbows into each other, and the fat man drove them the five hours to Phoenix. In a deserted block of low factories closed for the weekend, they pulled up alongside another van. Eduardo and the others had no idea of whether they were in Mexico or the United States. This time, they were driven all the way back to Los Angeles. The fat man explained that this was the most direct route to Los Angeles from Tijuana. These coyotes were knowledgeable about getting through the desert and rivers to America, perhaps, but they seemed cockeyed whenever they read a map of America. At the Los Angeles airport, the fat driver waved to a guy lounging at the baggage desk in front of the American Airlines section. The young guy walked up and handed Eduardo a ticket to New York.

At Kennedy Airport, Eduardo remembered going up to the New York coyote who awaited him. He started to give the guy the remaining $500, knowing he would be shot dead if he tried to leave the airport without paying. The coyote stopped him, saying it would look like a narcotics transaction. They walked outside the terminal and down to the end of the walkway, where Eduardo handed him the cash. Somebody would come to take him on the subway to Brighton Beach, which is in Brooklyn, in America.

Once, they came in dreadful old ships, from Magilligan in Northern Ireland, from Cobh in southern Ireland, from Liverpool and Naples and Palermo and Odessa. The prow went into gray waves with freezing white foam whipping from them, and sometimes it seemed that the prow would not come up and that it would take the whole ship under the gray water. When it finally came up, the passengers vomited and fell off bunks and cried; an old man died and a woman was unconscious and babies bled. Those able to stand always scoured the horizon, through sleet and snow swirls, for the first look at the city where the streets were decorated, if not paved, with gold.

But this was the spring of 1998, and Eduardo was entering a town whose mayor was Rudolph Giuliani. He would get lucky with a war and become an improbable hero. But now he was merely a strange, sneering man who attracted people equally strange, particularly a chief of staff, Bruce Teitelbaum. Teitelbaum was Jewish and a Republican, and in New York this is as common as a camel train.

Eduardo had never heard of either of them, and Giuliani had nothing to do with him, but unfortunately Teitelbaum did. Teitelbaum covered the distance from City Hall to Williamsburg and was the connection, the pull, the clout, in the city administration. He was the major fund-raiser for Giuliani in the Hasidic communities. The position of fund-raiser is one of the few with power in a government. The word *power* is almost always misused, for most municipal gnomes have none, except in the case of Teitelbaum, who took over something called the

Vacancy Control Board. This is a one-man group hidden from view in the basement of City Hall; it decides who can work in city government, who can be transferred, and who can be pushed out of work. Nobody knows what the Vacancy Control Board is except for those begging for a job and pledging to break any rule, tell any lie, bury any report.

Simultaneously, there were no rules for a builder, particularly in Hasidic neighborhoods, other than putting up money on demand for politicians.

Politicians recall first noticing Teitelbaum at a Giuliani rally in the Hasidic Borough Park section of Brooklyn. He didn't understand what he was doing, but he acted as if he did. Which immediately irritated Dov Hikind, the state legislator who ran the rally. It created an atmosphere of intense dislike that later caused Hikind, on trial in federal court for the totally false charge of stealing, to claim that Teitelbaum had put him there. Hikind went on to say that the day was soon coming when Teitelbaum would cry on the way to prison. This deepest dislike shot up from the platform at that first outdoor rally. It was the usual and understandable procedure for a campaign. In all of them, people hand out leaflets and rumors; many of the faces are crossed with insanity. In this case, the venom lasted beyond normal loathing.

Bruce Teitelbaum turned into a city figure when he rose out of a seat at Lincoln Center, where he sat with Mayor Giuliani at a concert of the New York Philharmonic in honor of the United Nations leaders. In the great hall was the Palestine Liberation Organization's Yasir Arafat, who had received tickets from the United Nations. Immediately, the flames shot ceilingward from Mayor Giuliani and his aide, Teitelbaum. How could this murderer be allowed at your concert? Teitelbaum asked Giuliani. Yes, Giuliani said, I don't run concerts for killers. Get him out of here.

Teitelbaum got up and walked over to Arafat and his two aides. It was during the second movement of Beethoven's Ninth Symphony. Teitelbaum told Arafat and his aides that they had to leave. The mayor didn't want them.

He told this to Arafat and his people while looking to the left and then the right and then up above. At least a few nearby noticed that Teitelbaum displayed such nervousness that it appeared he would collapse. Arafat sat there for a few moments. One of his aides said they had thought about staying because of the mantle of the UN, which was what Giuliani expected. That he had embarrassed them would be sufficient. Then he could say Arafat stayed because of the anti-Israeli UN. But Arafat decided to let them drown in acid. He and his aides stood and walked out in the middle of the performance.

Bruce Teitelbaum, high apprehension subsided, now swaggered like a wild boar. He was indisputably the most important Jewish name in city affairs. He was next to a mayor who did virtually nothing each day except to get into the papers or to meet girlfriends. He was content to have Teitelbaum keep the people in love with him, and if it meant Teitelbaum giving contracts out to Jewish organizations, then let him do all he wants of it. Giuliani was going to run for president or vice president or senator, whatever, and it would cost tens of millions, and Teitelbaum knew how to get the money.

Much of it came from builders, who are crooks with blueprints and are thus at ease with people in City Hall. Teitelbaum handled anything that was needed to keep someone like Eugene Ostreicher, the father, sending in the cash. Joseph Spitzer, who lives in a building on Fifty-ninth Street in Brooklyn's Borough Park along with Richie Ostreicher, the son, is celebrated for bringing $83,000 into Giuliani campaigns. Nothing in New York—no fire chief complaining, and certainly no young Mexican—is allowed to get in the way of that. "How could you say that we gave him the city for his eighty-three thousand?" Teitelbaum said. "We raised eight hundred and thirty thousand dollars from builders. Spitzer gave eighty-three thousand." Spitzer was given a placard that allowed him to park almost anywhere in the city. He usually could be found in the City Hall offices of Teitelbaum and then his successor as the chief of staff of the Giuliani office, Anthony Carbonetti. Whatever Spitzer needed done, they did.

At first, this seems to start in another universe from an obstacle to building in Williamsburg that required help from City Hall. In the 1930s, Louis Carbonetti and Harold Giuliani, the mayor's father, grew up together in East Harlem, on the streets of Tommy (Three-Finger Brown) Lucchese, Joey Rao, and

Trigger Mike Coppola. Harold Giuliani pulled burglaries and holdups. He told the court he did it because of unemployment. He went to Sing Sing prison for sixteen months. Carbonetti did not go to prison. Louis Carbonetti became a second for professional fighters, a bucket carrier who between rounds would lean over the ropes and clean a fighter's cuts. While Carbonetti attended school on First Avenue and in Stillman's Gymnasium on Eighth Avenue, he received a merit appointment as assistant secretary to a new state supreme court judge, Thomas Aurelio. Carbonetti's merit was that he knew Aurelio, and also every mob guy in his district. A wiretap of Frank Costello, prime minister of the underworld, and Aurelio was played in public by authorities hoping to block Aurelio. On it, Aurelio said, "Francesco, how can I thank you?" And Costello said, "When I tell you it's in the bag, it's done."

When he came out of prison, Harold Giuliani married a young neighborhood woman and moved to Brooklyn, where he worked saloons, collecting for bookmakers and loan sharks. His son, Rudy, was born in Brooklyn. Harold took his son to East Harlem on Sundays, where they saw neighborhood friends and then went with the father's friend, Lou Carbonetti, to games at Yankee Stadium. Harold Giuliani then moved Rudy to the Long Island suburbs, taking him away from street life.

Carbonetti wound up being defeated for a Democratic district leadership in East Harlem. That left him jobless; you can't be in a judge's office if you lose your own district. But he had his own cut man, East Harlem's city councilman, the Rev. Louis Gigante. His brother, Vincent (The Chin) Gigante, ran the underworld, but he never as much as served mass for his brother. Father Gigante was to become a true builder of his city, as opposed to a cheap talentless developer. At the most searing, disturbing time in the Bronx, when fires and hopelessness were beyond anybody's capacity to repel, Governor Nelson Rockefeller sent his housing administrator, Edward Logue, to visit Gigante at his parish, St. Athanasius. "Is there some way you could build up here, or are the threats and violence too much?" he asked Gigante.

"We do not tolerate violence. We do not accept threats," Gigante said.

With state subsidies, Gigante took empty buildings and

turned them into new apartments. Over three thousand people lined up for a day and a half to apply for his first apartments.

"God bless Father Gigante forever," Logue announced.

Logue then wrote a famous memo to Rockefeller: "Suppliers and sub-contractors and vandals tend to hesitate before bothering Father Gigante."

Father Lou often could be found in the 115th Street clubhouse of Anthony (Fat Tony) Salerno, who was the second in charge of Vincent Gigante's gang. Tony was the Tip O'Neill of the underworld and would reside forever in Rudy Giuliani's mind. Rudy had to know Tony from early years just by walking the street with his father and Carbonetti. Fat Tony was twelve when he drove a truck for Dutch Schultz. Later, Fat Tony's club, the Palma Boy Club—there is no *s* because there is no *s*—on 115th was around the corner from Lou Carbonetti's Democratic district clubhouse.

The man from around the corner from Fat Tony's old headquarters, Louis Carbonetti, now became the first Carbonetti to work in City Hall. When Abe Beame was the mayor and Father Gigante's friend, and Stanley Friedman was his chief assistant, Father Gigante took Carbonetti down to City Hall and as much as put him in an office and said, "Here's where you work."

He had a son, Lou Carbonetti Jr., who would be the first to follow him onto the city payroll.

Rudy Giuliani went on to become the United States attorney for New York. He made sure he became famous as the zealot who broke the Mafia. Familiarity. At the same time he had a fascination with mafiosi and even imitated Fat Tony Salerno's speech. A Giuliani indictment brought Fat Tony into federal court in a trial of Mafia bosses. Giuliani did not prosecute Fat Tony himself, but it was his indictment. At a break one day, Fat Tony got up and brushed past guards who were supposed to stop him and went to the railing in front of the spectators' rows. A man waiting at the rail handed Fat Tony a cigar. Fat Tony inspected it. The day before, when the same man had brought Fat Tony a cigar, the mobster had exclaimed, "Bring me a thing like this!" and broke the cigar in half and threw it on the floor. This time, the man said, "It's Cuban, Tony."

Salerno grunted and put the cigar in the breast pocket of his suit.

Now he said, loudly enough for the large room to hear, "Did you bring me a gun?" He pointed at the prosecutor. "I want to shoot this prick."

Then he motioned to the judge. "I'd like to fuckin' shoot her, too."

Later in the trial, they played a wiretap of Mafia capital punishment jury deliberations. Fat Tony put on a large yellow headset to listen. It also could be heard on speakers in the courtroom. The tape played for about a half hour, and every voice in crime except Fat Tony's was on it voting to have someone killed. In the spectators' front row, Fat Tony's man brightened. He gave a satisfied nod to Fat Tony. Listening through the earphones in the front of the room, Fat Tony made a face that said, all right.

At this moment there came over the tape the one decisive vote of the mob. It was the unmistakable voice of Fat Tony Salerno calling out, "Hit!"

Fat Tony shrugged. What are you going to do? "Good night, Irene," he muttered to the guys at the defense table.

The Carbonettis—father, son, and eventually grandson and wife—worked in the two mayoral campaigns of Harold Giuliani's son, Rudy. When Giuliani won, he had Lou Carbonetti Jr. helping to hand out city patronage jobs. Then Lou junior had a private copying business that folded and he owed $100,000. It was discovered that he used two driver's licenses. He had to leave the regular city government and take over a private neighborhood organization called a Business Improvement District. His former wife, JoAnna Aniello, received a job in city housing.

The grandson, Anthony Carbonetti, was made the patronage dispenser for the city, under Bruce Teitelbaum. He then was made the chief of staff of the whole administration. Carbonetti's resumé is nonexistent. His last job before City Hall was that of a bartender in Boston. On his 1994 financial disclosure forms he listed a scorching hand at Atlantic City as a source of income.

By 1998, he didn't need slot machines. His salary at City Hall was $115,000. Public jobs are never supposed to give the appearance of impropriety. While gambling in Atlantic City is legal, and you're even entitled to report winnings no matter how preposterous the claim, for somebody in New York's City Hall, it still looks at least lousy.

Carbonetti and the English language were opponents. Some of the most painful moments in City Hall came whenever he sat in his small office and dictated letters. Incidentally, the size and location of a government office is meaningless. Bare and shabby are common. It is the phone or the memo that does it.

Anthony Carbonetti also was as subtle as a thrown brick. On the phone, he told commissioners, "You've got to do this. Just do it. Don't ask me anything. Just do it. This is for a friend of the mayor's." His special interest was the Brooklyn Hasidic community. He didn't have to bother with calls and return calls with Hasidim. Sitting in his office was Joseph Spitzer, who owns a huge four-story house in Borough Park. It has a marble front and a stoop with polished brass banisters. Records show that residents of this house included Chaim Ostreicher, Eugene's son, and Faye Schwimmer, Ostreicher's daughter and Leon Schwimmer's daughter-in-law. It was helpful to find this on record, for Ostreicher and those around him denied the fact that the house even existed. "We don't know Spitzer," one yelled. "He has zero to do with us."

Spitzer talked to Carbonetti, and Carbonetti talked to a commissioner.

If you had building violations or even a building collapse and were Hasidic, City Hall took care of everything. What did a report by a building inspector or a fireman mean? The builder was the mayor's friend, or had relatives raising funds for him.

A Mexican immigrant like Eduardo Daniel Gutiérrez didn't count.

Chapter Twelve

EDUARDO MOVED into a space on an upstairs floor in an attached frame house that was across the street from Grady High School in Brighton Beach. The landlord, who lived on the first floor, was never seen, and the Mexicans were crowded onto the second. There was a kitchen, bathroom, a small bedroom, and a large front bedroom with dark brown paneling and a blue carpet. The large bedroom had two windows looking down at the stoop and street. A television set was in one corner of the room. Eight from Mexico slept and lived there when Eduardo arrived. They slept on the floor on thin pads and pillows. You picked your place to sleep and then it became yours. Eduardo slept between Alejandro and Mariano Ramirez, Gustavo's brother. They had their heads to the wall under the windows. The room was long enough so that their feet did not touch those of the others sleeping with their heads against the opposite wall.

Eduardo was stunned by the bathroom. Never before had he seen one in a house. With nine people and one bathroom, there was an implied agreement that each would take no more than ten minutes. He soon learned that each time somebody slipped past him, it would be ten minutes of listening to running water. Let three get ahead and you lose a half hour. He realized that he had to stand around as if thinking of something and then suddenly jump at first click of the bathroom door opening. He often lost out to a shoulder and a fully slammed door. The most familiar sound in the house was that of someone rapping on the bathroom door to get the occupant to hurry.

In the kitchen there was a stove and a sink; a house with running water in San Matías was at best rare. A turn of the handle brought a flame out of the stovetop. Magic. There was a large round table for the group to eat at. They each paid $95 a month in rent and $25 a week for food. Martha, who was the sister of Gustavo and Mariano, lived in the small bedroom with her husband. She was on the lease and handled the rents and cooking. Martha had three children at home in San Matías with her mother in the rooms right behind where Eduardo's family

551

lived. Her brother Gustavo had left two children in Mexico
with his wife. One day Gustavo's wife left the children with
Gustavo's mother in San Matías and said she was going to look
for work. Instead, she went off with a man and never returned.
This left the grandmother in San Matías with six grandchildren.
All her upbringing and beliefs told her there was something
worse ahead, a catastrophe, a tragedy falling from the sky, and
she never could see it, but now suddenly it was in front of her
at night. In a dream she had, she was in line at the window of
the appliance store for the money order from Brighton Beach
in Brooklyn, and instead of a man with her money order, there
was a skull, a death's head, with eye sockets fixed on her.

In the morning she told this to Eduardo's father at the
brickyard.

He didn't believe her.

"If it happens, what will I do with all these children to feed?"
she asked him.

He doesn't remember what he said, exactly. He knows he just
went to work at bricks. Of course her death's head vision never
materialized. Something worse would: a clerk in the window
shaking his normal head. No, no money order from Brooklyn.

Alejandro lived on the floor next to Eduardo for the same reason as Eduardo: to send enough money home to soften the path
when he returned. But every night he reminded himself that
he'd never thought he would be here living alone and his wife
would be home in Mexico with his children. On most nights he
thought of his marriage. He'd married his wife in a civil ceremony
with his mother and father present. He wore a shirt and he knew
she'd worn a dress, but he couldn't remember what it looked
like—you only wore a white dress for a big church wedding.
He remembered going with her to the clinic for their first baby.
He was there at 6 P.M. and waited with her in one room, where
she was monitored, and then she went into the delivery room
and he stayed outside. They didn't know whether it would be
a boy or girl. Each wanted a *niña*, and that's what they got.

He'd set up an upholstery shop in a room in the house
opening onto the street. He had to rent a compressor because
he couldn't afford to buy one. He had to borrow or rent other
equipment. Air pistols, saws to cut—they would cost another
20,000 pesos.

His biggest job had been for 7,500 pesos. He did the whole room—walls, sofa, love seat, and chairs—in fifteen days, and was very proud of it. Fine. But often he could not get a compressor to rent and he had to tell customers who showed him photos of what they wanted that he couldn't get to them until the week after next.

He had been earning the equivalent of about $150 a week. Alejandro and his wife and her brother talked about Alejandro changing what looked like a bleak future: He was going to earn $150 a week and probably less for all of his life. Alejandro and his wife had been talking of his going to America and had agreed that he could try heartbreak for a year and a half for the money. He could earn enough to buy upholstery tools. Then he could work at home and support a family without sweating blood. But this was not Italy, where the men leave Sicily for seasonal work in desolation and loneliness in the north, in Switzerland even, but return to Sicily at the end of the season. A Mexican going to New York must cross the border like a wanted criminal. No husband could return for a simple visit, and no wife could follow him to New York.

Alejandro's wife, who suddenly realized that she would be alone with the children for a year and a half, had been shaken. Her brother helped make the decision: The only way for Alejandro to give his wife and children a future was to change the order of their living now, and for Alejandro to go to New York.

He'd gotten up at 5 A.M., and his wife went with him on the bus to the Puebla airport. She came inside, kissed him goodbye, and stood alone as he went through the gate to the plane to Hermosillo in Sonora. From there he went across a border that was unexpectedly unguarded that night. Ahead of him was Brooklyn and loneliness.

At Brighton Beach, Gustavo had gotten him a job at $7.50 an hour working construction. His arms soon advertised his work. He has iron bars for upper arms. He is 5 feet 6 inches and 135 pounds or so. He has a mustache and a young smile.

He worked for a builder named Eugene Ostreicher and his son, Richie. They were doing a lot of housing in one section of Brooklyn called Williamsburg.

Chapter Thirteen

MARIANO, WHO slept on the other side of Eduardo in the room at Brighton Beach, came from the house directly behind him in San Matías. His mother and her family kept pigs in pens outside their adjoining cinder-block huts. Anytime they came up short on food, they yanked one of the pigs out of the pen, slit its throat, and went on a steady diet of pig meat. Visitors were happily fed because there wasn't an ice cube in San Matías to keep the carcass unspoiled. If the children became tired of the diet, that was their worry; they could show their ribs. If the pig meat ran out for all, then everybody had rib cages sticking out.

In Brooklyn, Mariano worked at Kentucky Fried Chicken. He didn't know the street it was on, only how to get there. He didn't know what he was going to do when he wasn't working in the afternoon, much less tomorrow. He was single but couldn't go near the topless bars and whorehouses on Fifth Avenue. Lucino Hernández, at thirty-one the oldest in the group, told everybody that the Fifth Avenue bars were dangerous because they get raided by police and anybody without papers could wind up being deported at the flash of a badge.

When they were not out of the house for work, they stayed in their room and watched shows on the Spanish-language stations or talked or slept. On Saturdays they drank. As none of them had a paper to show anything more than name and address, they were inordinately afraid of immigration agents, who in their minds were everywhere. Each day there were reports of a white immigration van on a street somewhere in Brooklyn. When they were walking to work, the impulse was to say something to a pretty young woman, but it was Lucino who always stopped them.

"She might call the police," he said. The police would not bury them in jail for harassing some woman, but they surely would call the immigration agents. And for telling a young woman that you want to get next to her, you would be back in the worst of the dust in Mexico, sent there broke.

It was surer and safer to walk around the corner to Neptune

Avenue and toward Coney Island Avenue and run into one of the many whores who were out there every night.

For his first dinner in the house, Eduardo came to the big kitchen table and sat. Around him, everybody was eating and getting up to go to the stove and then returning to the table. He watched them and wondered when his plate would be put in front of him.

There was a discussion about a group of students who were black and who had come out of the high school across the street. They had called Alejandro "Mexican shit." Alejandro said he pretended not to hear them.

"That was the right thing to do," Lucino said. "The Negro. You get in a fight with them, the police come, and then you are fucked. They don't have anything to worry about. They are citizens. You have no ID. They send you back to Mexico."

Eduardo decided that he would never go out of the house except to work.

At that point, he had not worked for a single day yet. He had barely been around the neighborhood. Yet skin color, which was never an issue in San Matías, now touched everything. Already he was aware of the quick, short glances of the whites as he passed them, particularly the white women. And he was learning that the black people didn't like him, and of course he didn't like the looks of them, either. The Puerto Ricans sneered at the Mexicans. The Puerto Ricans didn't like the Dominicans, either, but they most disliked these Mexicans.

"Incas and Mayans! Little people with straight hair!" said Herman Badillo, the first Puerto Rican elected to Congress and now the head of the City University of New York system. "When they speak of La Raza, they don't speak Spanish, they speak in indigenous languages. They should be in separate classes."

Eduardo looked around again for his food. In his whole life, he had never served himself. The mother's hands were always close: one on his shoulder, the other putting his food in front of him.

"What are you looking for?" Martha said.

Eduardo shrugged.

"You get your own food," Martha said.

He got up. He didn't like it. Eduardo's first Saturday night in

Brooklyn was the same as the ones that would follow. He was in a commune of the lonely. All week, they worked and came home to eat and sleep so they could work tomorrow. On Saturday night, they preferred being drunk. Lucino wanted them to stay in one loud room while they did this. His brow furrowed whenever somebody said they wanted a bar with women. All he could think of was police walking him to the border and throwing him back into Mexico. Stay here, he said. So each Saturday night, everybody stayed in the room and drank big cold beers, Corona and Heineken with lime twists wedged in them. After every third beer they had tequila. The belief of people from Puebla was that three big cold beers caused an indigestion that only tequila could calm. They got good and drunk and talked about going back to Mexico, where they would climb all over the girls.

Eduardo listened and laughed. He drank a couple of beers but not much else, and this left him as the only one in the crowded room able to deride their fantasies. Alejandro, Gustavo, and Miguel were married and had lived faithfully with their wives and families back home. The religion was in them deep enough to keep them out of adulteries.

"How could you do this to these girls?" Eduardo asked them.

They all called out over the alcohol that not only would they do what they said to these girls, but that they would go far beyond that.

"How can you do that if you don't know any girls?" Eduardo said.

As the night grew late, the laughter turned into the silence of homesickness. Alejandro's wife and two children were living with his family at number 29 Avenida Cinco de Mayo in Santa Barbara, Mexico. He told Eduardo that he imagined his children out at a party. A fiesta. The children are playing while he is talking to everybody at the party. The band is playing *cumbia* music, a mixture of Mexican and Colombian. Then he said he was thinking of all the times he went out with his wife and visited relatives. Dropping in. Nothing formal. There are so many cousins in each family that they take the place of friends.

Eduardo thought of his mother and father, and then the store. He told everybody about the store, as if the video game machine was the attraction, not Silvia, the owner's daughter.

* * *

Eduardo lived in local history.

On a larger scale, sociologists first traced Mexican immigration to New York through the Twenty-third Street YMCA in Manhattan, where in the 1920s a small number of people recently arrived from the state of Yucatán established a social club. For some reason, that particular migration ended, but studies of it did not. As there is no way to jump in and out and question some immigrant who doesn't even keep his name on his person, any realistic study must come from a large school, with professors who have a year or two off to work on the project, with papers gathered from everywhere and researchers with the time and funds to travel. Still, it is work done over the longest of hours and you must fall in love with the subject.

The work now is being done by a young professor, Robert Smith, of Barnard College in New York. In a crowded office in Milbank Hall, he writes papers about Mexicans who come to us across the hot sands of an empty desert. On the street outside his window, 116th Street and Broadway, there rise the sounds of New York City traffic at its steadiest and heaviest.

Robert Smith does work that will help so many understand. Others will make a living from his work. He gets a satisfaction that he realizes in the small of the night. He would never trade his life for money.

Two men from a farm south of Puebla live in Professor Smith's studies as the men who started the Mexican migration to New York. They were Don Pedro and his brother Fermin. They had attempted to bribe local Mexican officials and a hungry American bureaucrat to get a contract for the Bracero program that between 1942 and 1964 recruited Mexicans to work in U.S. agriculture. The American sneered at the size of the bribe offer, and the brothers were shut out. They then walked across the border, which at that time, on July 6, 1943, was virtually unguarded. The brothers got on the road and hitched a ride with a man named Montesinos, who was coming from an annual vacation in Mexico City. After talking to them during the long ride to New York, Montesinos thought he could get them started. He put them up at a hotel in Manhattan for two days while they looked for work. At that time, during World

War II, anyone could get a job anywhere, and both brothers did. They started sending money home to Puebla. The arrival of a money order in the town was an event comparable to none other because money describes itself. It is money. Its presence in the hands of the relatives of brothers Don Pedro and Fermin caused others to follow, first in small groups who crossed uncontrolled borders and survived desert and river and, once arrived, ran their palms over the sidewalks of New York, feeling for gold.

By 1980, as many as forty thousand Mexicans had slipped through to New York for the Job. In 1986 there was an amnesty that allowed immigrants to apply for temporary residency, then permanent residency, if they had been living in the United States since 1981. Immigrants who had been unable to leave New York—they had beaten the border once, and most didn't want to try again—suddenly found they could leave the country and return whenever they wanted. They carried messages home about the wonders of New York. Some even told the truth: that it was hard work for higher pay than in Mexico, but low pay for the expensive city of New York.

The number of immigrants rose to 100,000 by 1990. Ten years later, there would be an estimated 2.3 million Latinos living in New York City, with Mexicans the fastest growing of all, at about 275,000. The movement of Mexicans from Puebla and the surrounding towns of San Matías, Atalixco, and Santa Barbara has accounted for 120,000 coming into the city. There is a large Dominican population in the city, as high as 500,000, most in the Washington Heights neighborhood. But there are a mere 8 million people in the Dominican Republic, as compared to 100 million in Mexico. Smith's research showed that Mexico needs between 800,000 and 1 million jobs to support its growing populace. Of course so many would try coming here.

As Smith worked in his office, he did not notice the paper rustling. His pages about the Job came alive on the street below. Five blocks down Broadway, Raymundo Juárez, sixteen, and his father had jobs in a supermarket on Broadway for $6 an hour. They thought it was millions. While the father swept the floor upstairs, his son was crushed to death in a basement compactor. They carried the body out through the basement, and the father never saw the dead son. Now the father stared at a large glass window in the medical examiner's office on First Avenue in Manhattan and a screen over the window went up. The son, Raymundo Juárez, his face swollen, the eyes closed, was on a gurney against a blue cinder-block wall. "*Sí*," the father said, sobbing. Then he and the cousins ran to a car and drove uptown. They were asked where they were going. "To the store. The store owes his pay," a cousin said.

The house Eduardo came to in Brighton Beach is in an old, crowded part of Coney Island. Coney Island is known for roller coasters and midgets and hot dogs and huge crowds on its wide beaches that run into the Atlantic Ocean. The ocean runs up against so much land at its edges, from New Jersey to the miles of Brooklyn and Staten Island, that the waves generally are small and the currents slow. The people duck and swim a few strokes in bays between old jetties. At one end of the island is Sea Gate Village, residences that are behind gates that keep out cheap day bathers. Sea Gate has its own lighthouse. Coney Island proper now runs past public housing, the super rides, hot dogs, and hot corn; the boardwalk ends at the large and famous New York Aquarium. All after that is Brighton Beach. The oceanfront is tighter, the streets lined by a crowd of five- and six-story apartment houses. The main street, Brighton Beach Avenue, is one block up from the ocean. The aorta of New York civilization, an el line, runs over the avenue. It is the last stop on the Brighton line. Also using this station is the F line, which runs as an el through Brooklyn and after that plunges underground to become a subway. It runs for twenty-five miles, under the wealth of midtown Manhattan, through a tunnel under the East River to residential Queens, and out for miles almost to the beginning of suburban Nassau County. There is no ride in the world this far at this price, a dollar-fifty.

Under the el in Brighton Beach, cars are double-parked, often triple-parked, by Russians. At the curbs, the street is a bazaar of Russians selling matryoshka dolls. They begin with a wood peasant woman that unscrews, and inside is a smaller woman, and inside this doll is another, and three or four dolls later, it ends with a peasant woman the size of a thumb.

The sidewalks are under the control of women with shopping carts who stop in the middle of the sidewalk to talk to each other for as long as they feel like it, while people edge by one at a time. The stores sell everything: children's clothing, fruit and vegetables, meats, luggage, shoes. The signs are in Russian, in the Cyrillic alphabet. The stores are crowded and difficult to enter and leave. Push a woman and see what happens.

The streets running north, away from the ocean and the el, have mostly small low wood bungalows that were once summer houses in a resort town. But all this ends suddenly at feature-less streets of brick attached houses sitting between old frame houses. Here is the start of a large colony of Mexicans, with young women who work in knitting factories and young men out on street corners for any manual labor. The first small bare Mexican restaurants are on the avenues. And prostitutes appear, of any race, not necessarily Mexicans. At the last of these streets, across from Grady High School, is the house where Eduardo and the other Mexicans lived. At one corner of the block is a small park that has basketball courts.

After that, on the other side of the high school, is a high-way, and on the far side of that starts the long march through Brooklyn, miles of blocks, miles of people in a borough whose population nears three million.

Since 1970, Brighton Beach was an area of immigrant Jews from Eastern Europe and Russia, mainly from Odessa, which is exactly like Brighton Beach, a city on the shore of waters that do not get stormy. So many Russians came to these streets that in the Russian national referendum of 1993, the Moscow Central Elections Commission declared Brighton Beach an election precinct. The Russian consulate in Manhattan sent representatives to conduct balloting in a crowded room on the second floor of 606 Brighton Beach Avenue, the meeting room of a Russian military veterans organization and the office of an accountant who prepares American income taxes. Only people who were still Russian citizens were allowed to mark paper ballots for an election in which one candidate was Boris Yeltsin. "You cannot vote for Yeltsin. You are an American. You must vote for Clinton," they said to one man.

Five Russian bureaucrats, two women and three men, supervised the balloting. They writhed because they could not smoke. In Moscow, this balloting would be done in cloud banks from cheap Russian cigarettes.

After forty-five years of the two countries testing atom bombs to make sure they could perform as scheduled over Broadway and Red Square, after all these years of hate and fear, with all of it over different political systems, bureaucrats from Moscow sat in Brooklyn and supervised an election in Russia.

Alejandro took Eduardo up to see the avenue and the train station. Alejandro knew his way around by subway. He would tell people, "Just tell me where you want me to meet you, and I can get there."

At first, the subway must have been a marvel to Alejandro, but his face never registered astonishment. Then others were the same. Looking for work, or working, occupied their minds so much that they couldn't capture the enormousness of the difference between their lives in Mexico and their lives in New York. Work and drinking were something recognizable and central. Beyond that, Alejandro was fatalistic about the drudgery of work. The trains were not wondrous, he told Eduardo. They were something you used to go to work. Eduardo, who understood work, agreed.

Alejandro told Eduardo how they took the train to the station called Smith/Ninth Street and transferred to a Williamsburg train. Eduardo tried to memorize what he was being told. But we will be on a different train right now, Alejandro said. We are going to be on the Sea Beach line that takes us up to Fifth Avenue in Sunset Park, where everybody is Hispanic. On the train, Alejandro showed Eduardo the transit map on the wall. The train rocked as Alejandro pointed out the lines: B, D, F, N. On the route map they were long lines—highways—in different colors with the stops noted. Often two and three lines used the same stops for at least a while. The M was dark brown, the F an orange line, the B a darker orange, the Sea Beach a light yellow. On the map the Sea Beach line reaches a fork at the Fifty-ninth Street stop and one yellow line mixes in with the light orange and dark orange and the other remains a single yellow line on a field of white. Eduardo still looked at the map in confusion when Alejandro poked him and they got off at the Fifty-ninth Street stop.

Up on the street, Brooklyn's Fifth Avenue was a two-story street of Hispanic signs and shops and Dominicans and Puerto

Ricans, but the dominant group, more so each day, was Mexicans. Three blocks over, on Eighth Avenue, suddenly there is the city's second Chinatown, the blocks and blocks of people shining and proud of their growing numbers. Eduardo bought a dark sweater with a hood attached.

Back in the house in Brighton Beach, he looked at himself in the bathroom mirror and was so pleased with the sweater that he put it on the next morning and went out in the steamy August day to the el on Brighton Beach Avenue, so he could learn the route to work. It was too hot to wear the sweater, which he put on the seat next to him. He stood up and swayed and tried to read the map. Suddenly the train stopped at the Smith/Ninth Street station. He remembered being told about this one. He jumped out of the train, forgetting his sweater, and went to the other side and took the train back to Brighton.

It wasn't until he walked into the apartment that something felt like it was missing. Immediately Eduardo clutched his shirt. His sweater was gone. In his mind's eye, he saw it on the subway seat where he'd left it.

He turned around and without a word went back up to the el. He would look for the train that had his sweater. Somewhere there would be a terminal where he could find the train he had been on and come upon his sweater. Some 360 trains come in and out of this station each day. His new train moved, the stations went by, the hour passed. At the last stop, with buzzers and a shush of air, the train emptied. He looked outside for a second train. There seemed to be none. Behind him, a motorman walked up to what had been the last car of Eduardo's train and now became the first car. Eduardo asked the motorman about the first train with his sweater aboard, but he couldn't make himself understood. When the train started he rode a couple of stops, got off and waited for the next train. When this one came in, he walked through the cars looking for his sweater. He found nothing and now looked at the map and didn't know what he was looking at. He asked a Puerto Rican for help. The Puerto Rican looked at the map for three stops and then came up with the route. Secure, Eduardo sat down and stared at the wall. Sand poured into his eyes. He had no idea of the time when he woke up. He asked a doubtful Dominican for directions.

The Dominican said learnedly, "Change at Canal Street."

Two people in the conversation hadn't the slightest idea of where Canal Street was: the Dominican and Eduardo. He did remember being on the train with the lone yellow line on the map. He got off at the last stop and walked. He asked Hispanic after Hispanic, and most were unsure of whether they were in Brooklyn or not.

Eduardo got back to the house some thirteen hours after he left.

Chapter Fourteen

THE NEW YORK CITY Department of Health reported that between 1988 and 1999, there was a 232 percent increase in births to Mexican women. The figures fit the life of the first woman to leave San Matías and make it to New York for the purpose of having children. This was Teresa Hernández, who at eighteen and a couple of months carried the strength of all the generations of suffering that had gone before her.

In the middle of the morning of June 21, 1998, with a sister holding her arm, Teresa Hernández of San Matías came out of her one-room Queens Village apartment in the basement of a frame house. Teresa's husband, José Luis Bonilla, was at his job in a fish market over in the Rosedale neighborhood.

The sister drove her in a battered car approximately seventy-five blocks to the Queens Hospital Center, a large, gloomy orange brick complex on 164th Street and the Grand Central Parkway in the center of what was once old Queens, the Irish and German Queens. Teresa walked into the hospital's main entrance as the advance woman for the new Queens.

With the first cries of her first baby later that morning Teresa saw her child held high in the delivery room lights.

She remembers saying a lot of things about the beautiful baby and her love for her husband. Of course, she maintains that she never for a moment considered the advantages of the baby being born in America as a citizen at first squeal. She says the social worker came through the maternity section and told her about the WIC program, which sees that babies receive free milk. Not until then, she states, does she remember looking at the baby and saying, "American."

She named the baby Stephanie. The name, date, and time of birth can be found in the records of the New York City Health and Hospital Corporation. These show that Stephanie Hernández is an American citizen, and each and every one of her children and her children's children and all who come thereafter will be citizens of the United States. Nowhere in the nation, and probably the earth, has such a large, heavily populated, and important place as New York changed with so many spangles and sounds, with the loudest, highest, and most vibrant a sound no great trumpeter can reach: a baby's first cry.

Teresa gave every young person in San Matías great confidence. She could get to America and then do even more than find a job. In San Matías she remembers dancing at parties in halls; Eduardo was "the one who held up the walls." He didn't know how to dance. She tried to pull him off the wall. "You go to his house and he was always working," Teresa says. "He never met a girl." She saw Silvia at dances, but she was with other boys, not Eduardo.

Teresa Hernández, who went as far as the sixth grade, had never seen a picture of New York or heard anything about it from anybody who went up there. A cousin made it to the Bronx and she waited to hear from him, but he never called. Yet as she scrubbed clothes in an overcrowded room in San Matías, she planned life for children and grandchildren she didn't yet have, and understood how she alone knew how to accomplish it.

She wasn't going to live by the countryside rules for a young Mexican woman. If the girl is pregnant and gives birth at age fourteen or fifteen, the boy just takes the girl and baby away to his mother's home. Only rarely do they take the trouble to get married legally after that. But if the girl is eighteen or twenty and not pregnant, the young man asks her father for her hand and they have a church wedding. However, if they can't afford a big wedding or party, then they don't get married.

Teresa decided to marry José Luis Bonilla without ceremony, for she needed no tiara to prove her status. He was in New York, in Queens, with a good job. He cut up fish, leaving the house at 7:30 A.M. and coming back at 9 P.M. He was working six days a week and earned $400. Sometimes this enormous amount became even larger when people tipped him.

Her emblem of young love would be a pregnancy in San Matías that would end with the baby being born in America, which would produce citizenship for the child and free education and medical care forever. Her husband's visit in July took care of that.

Teresa was eighteen and a half, and six months pregnant, when she left for America in January of 1998. She paid a coyote $2,200. For this she received a flight to Tijuana, assistance to

cross the border, and a tourist-class ticket from Los Angeles
to New York. Her husband put up the proceeds from scaling
ten thousand fish. Teresa says the price was worth it, especially
because she was pregnant. She defends the coyotes at each
mention. She says they risk jail and, worse, having their trucks
confiscated by the border guards. If she had a passport, the
journey from Tijuana would consist of stepping across a line
and going on to anyplace in America that she felt like seeing.
Instead, for want of a piece of paper, it became hours of trudging through thorns and up a mountain, following a trail that
was supposed to take them around immigration police and the
Border Patrol.

She was with another pregnant woman, and they stopped
frequently to rest. One rest in plain sight of Border Patrol
agents was interrupted by arrest. She wound up sitting through
the night in the second-floor detention hall at the San Ysidro
border control point. They took a video of her. She and about
two hundred others who had been stopped watched television
they couldn't understand while children ran around and babies
cried.

Early in the morning she told the immigration officer in
charge of the room that she was having her baby right now!
It took about fifteen minutes for them to get her through the
gate and back into Mexico. "They say they would lock me up
in jail if I tried again."

She was back on the trail at nine that night. The coyote told
her to follow him through a dirt tunnel that had been dug in
the desert. Many of the tunnels have been built by Mexican
engineers for money. One tunnel that ended just yards into
America at the Tijuana border was bigger and stronger than
anything they had in Vietnam, and those people won a war with
theirs. Once through, she walked, walked, stopped and wiped
the sand clean of her footprints, and walked on. She knew to
pat the sand gently, rather than just sweep it and leave a wide,
deep track to see from above.

The Border Patrol in their helicopters couldn't see her trail.
She laughs at the boys who don't take the time to sweep carefully behind them and risk getting caught no matter how much
they paid a coyote to cross them safely.

Tijuana to Queens took a week, most of it spent in a shack

that was called a safe house, and her group sat in it for days until somebody came and took them by truck to the airport in Los Angeles and the flight to New York.

She and Stephanie, the first baby, flew home for Christmas in 1998. She found herself pregnant again. Right after the holiday she put her baby, a citizen of America, on the plane to New York with a woman who had papers. Then Teresa joined a group of twenty at the Tijuana Airport, this time paying $1,500. It was hard on her legs, but she was across the border and to the Los Angeles airport without stopping. Even though she was exhausted, there could be no wall, no guard, no storm from the sky that could stop her from getting to her baby in New York.

She paid half the money to the coyote who took her over the border and the last half to one who works out of Queens and who met her at the airport. She will not discuss him, because she knows she will need him several more times.

In Queens, on the morning of July 27, 1999, she asked the landlord upstairs for a ride to the hospital. There, she had her second child, Jocelyn Hernández.

And again, the records of the New York City Health and Hospitals Corporation attest to baby Jocelyn's American citizenship.

She came to this room in a basement of a house in the Queens Village neighborhood, a block off Jamaica Avenue. You walk down an alley and go through the side door and down a short flight of steps to the basement. Her room is in the front of the basement. She is in a room with her children, Stephanie Hernández, one year six months old, and Jocelyn Hernández, four months old.

It is a frame house, like the others on the street, and once was the home of the Queens Irish and Germans. The room has one window high on the wall. There is a small closet. There is a bed that she puts the baby on during the day.

The older child walks around the room. There is a box of toys that she pulls things from. There is a stroller. There are two chairs and a cabinet with a television set on it. In the next low-ceilinged room, a man who rents the space is asleep on a bed against the wall. The rear of the room is a kitchen and refrigerator. On the right is a door to the bathroom. She thinks her single room is a palace.

No matter what happens, she says, I have given them American citizenship.

The song of Williamsburg was played by thousands and thousands of feet on the wood planks of the walkway on the Williamsburg Bridge, one of three gray iron bridges crossing the East River from lower Manhattan to the borough of Brooklyn. The bridges turned Brooklyn into the fourth largest city in the nation.

The Brooklyn Bridge steps out of the sidewalks and streets around City Hall in Manhattan, climbs gracefully over the East River, and descends to Borough Hall and the civic center of Brooklyn.

The bridge on the left, the Manhattan Bridge, starts only blocks away on the downtown East Side, in Chinatown, and spans the river and drops into a Brooklyn of factories that work weekends.

The Williamsburg Bridge is a few blocks farther uptown. It rises gray and is covered with stiffening trusses, steel latticework whose hundreds of strands give the bridge its industrial appearance and its strength. Out of the famous Jewish tenement streets on the Lower East Side, Eldridge and Orchard and Rivington and Ludlow, the dreary bridge breaks into the sky over the river and slopes down to crowded Williamsburg, a place where children used to go to work.

When it started, when there was no bridge, Williamsburg had about a hundred thousand people who lived and labored in the harshest turn-of-the-century conditions. Of course there were the rich Germans, Austrians, and Irish, who had a pillow wherever they sat. There were such grand people as Commodore Vanderbilt, who stole railways, Jim Fisk, and William C. Whitney.

They were in large houses on streets of expensive hotels and clubs. Along the riverfront they established Pfizer Pharmaceutical, Astral Oil (which soon became Standard Oil), and Flint Glass (which turned into Corning Glass). The rich loved to stroll past their big moneymaking plants and enjoy the sight of the river and Manhattan's glorious Wall Street area. Even more, they loved Williamsburg because it encouraged the true American dream, cheap labor.

From the sitting rooms and porches and lawns of the great houses, it was fascinating to watch the bridge rise. Up from these tenements across the river it began its climb on November 7, 1898. Invisible at first, but soon in plain sight, were the first boatloads of workers out on the river, with pile drivers and high stacks of steel floating on barges.

The bridge took five years to build. With two anchors 2,200 feet apart, the length of the bridge and approaches was to become 7,308 feet. The towers grew to 310 feet above high water, the center of the bridge clearing high water by 135 feet. Suspension cables were 18¾ inches thick. The bridge was completed on December 19, 1903, with the cost reaching $30 million.

It was not a handsome bridge, but the idea of bringing together a city yearning to dominate the world was thrilling at first.

And then the song of Williamsburg burst forth.

Here they came across the bridge, thousands and thousands pounding the bridge walkway planks to create a concert, these black hats and beards and anxious dark eyes swathed in babushkas, who rushed in the early-morning darkness to be first to reach the newest of the new land. Soon they would be on trolley cars running across the bridge and immediately after that on subway trains so crowded that choking was part of breathing. The bridge became known as the Jews' Bridge. Those crossing were thrilled by the openness of the streets and the rumors of apartments that were said to be larger than the matchboxes of the East Side. Eyes bulged with astonishment when they saw actual private houses on some of the streets.

Of course they never saw the homes of the rich, but the rich heard their song.

Jews!

The song of Williamsburg came through the air with such force that Commodore Vanderbilt clapped his hands over his ears and swore. No longer would there be a way to maintain his clearing in the social rubble. These people will crush us underfoot! He reached for his walking stick and greatcoat and was out the door with butler and footman, who rushed him by coach out of Williamsburg and home to Fifth Avenue in Manhattan, where he belonged. He would not return. Immediately thereafter the others fled, Whitney and Fisk and such. Williamsburg was left to the grubby commoners in black hats and babushkas who climbed staircases and spilled and shoved into apartments that turned out to be only slightly larger than those they came from, but still allowed perhaps one more pair of shoulders, bunched like a goat's, into the kitchen.

The Vanderbilts, who were the first to flee Williamsburg, became the last family out to buy everything in New York. They lived on Fifth Avenue in a mansion that was big enough to guard the Baltic straits. Partly because of the avalanche of the unwashed in Williamsburg, they wanted Fifth Avenue as a front lawn, and attempted to buy all the land on Fifth Avenue from Fifty-first to Fifty-seventh Streets. When there were complaints from citizens, a Vanderbilt announced, "The public be damned." But the Vanderbilts woke up one morning to find two new hotels going up. Next was a clothing store. They moved farther uptown.

The Williamsburg neighborhood at this time was cut like a map of foreign countries. A neighborhood of Jews ran into one of Italians just off the boat. The Italians had just caused the Germans to move over to the adjacent Bushwick section. Included here was Henry Miller, who was raised for a time on Fillmore Place, off Roebling Street, in Williamsburg, and whose recollections of Ainslie Street were in his writings, which burst forth and shook and shocked the poor constricted authorities of the times. They could not see *Tropic of Cancer* becoming a book that would last forever as a world classic.

Then there were the streets of the Irish Catholics, who were sure that theirs was the only faith and blood, yet the lasting work was done by a daughter of German immigrants, Elizabeth Wehmer, who went to Williamsburg public schools for eight years and left at the age of fourteen. Thereafter, she was described as being autodidactic, which means she taught herself, and at least a generation of newspaper writers who at first thought it meant brain damage used the word to describe her in the ton of stories about her over the many years. In 1943, using her married name, Betty Smith, she wrote *A Tree Grows in Brooklyn*, a novel that pierced the sky over the neighborhood, city, and country as the finest of American letters and emotions.

About that time, there arrived in the harbor a ship with a

glorious figure, a rabbi from Romania named Moshe Teitelbaum. It was he who placed the soul of Jewish survivors forever
into the crowded buildings of Williamsburg. Reunited with
his people, he found only twenty-five of his sect, Satmar, left
from the war. They stood on the dock and waved. He stood
at the rail and waved back. They waved more. He waved back.
It was that way for two days. Teitelbaum made his entrance
to America on the holy day of Rosh Hashanah, but under his
religious laws he couldn't leave the ship until the observance
was over.

The Satmars were people who lived in Romania in the town
of Satu-Mare, which means St. Mary. The Jews called the place
Satmar, which means nothing except they were not going to say
Saint Mary. Before the war, there were several hundred thousand
living in and around Satmar, including Moshe Teitelbaum, the
rabbi so famous in Eastern Europe, he was the Jew the Nazis
wanted first. He disappeared into crowds of his people, and by
the time he was rounded up, he was just another Jew with a
number. They threw him into the Klausenberg concentration
camp. When a man named Kasztner bought a train and then
paid ransom for Jews to fill the train and go to Switzerland,
Teitelbaum, unknown to the Nazis, was one of the first to be
let go for money.

When the war ended, Rebbe Teitelbaum went to Israel, saw
the whole place destitute, and came to New York to raise funds.
He intended to return to Israel, which he saw as a place to live
but not a state. His belief was that there could be no Messiah
until Israel was made up only of Jews. Any Palestinians living
on these lands only delayed the appearance of the Messiah.
Other Hasidic sects in Brooklyn believe that the Torah tells
them there will be no state until after the Messiah arrives.

Once he could leave the ship, Rabbi Moshe Teitelbaum
went first to the East Side of Manhattan and, after that, over
the Williamsburg Bridge. His were the footsteps that sent the
song of Williamsburg highest into the sky. The moment he
arrived in Williamsburg, he was there for good. His group of
twenty-five Satmars had eluded the gas ovens and survived dogs
and guards' clubs and the sound of firing squads and children's
screams. Hundreds of thousands of their sect had died; they
lived. After that, handfuls more came from Europe on old

freighters, these people who had somehow survived, and now were drawn to the leader whose name was a flame through all the nights in all the concentration camps.

Hasidic groups in Williamsburg now included the first of survivors from Hungary and Romania and Poland, members of the Lubavitch, Bobov, Stolin, Ger, Belz, and Puppa orders. Even at its zenith, with every day starting with the incomprehensible fact of freedom, life in Williamsburg was still trying. They first worked in knitting factories for 25¢ an hour and crowded into the sparse apartments for $3 a month.

Each Satmar couple had an average of six children. The original twenty-five Satmars, reinforced by stragglers, grew to fifty thousand in Brooklyn and over thirty thousand in the suburban Orange County town of Monroe. The Satmars created their own schools in Brooklyn with fifteen thousand students. The sight of children walking into school was a far greater monument to the courage and spirit of the Satmars than all the inscriptions placed on all the buildings. Just as Betty Smith's tree grew and multiplied, so the Satmars spread to become a significant population.

Other Hasidic groups grew as rapidly. The average couple had a minimum of five children and more likely ten. The men had side curls and wore black coats and hats, and the women had their heads covered. Only those in one of the neighborhoods could tell one group from another by their dress. The Puppas wore tall, wide hats, homburgs, with no fold in the top. There was an indentation that seemed punched in with a fist. The hat was Hungarian. The Satmar wore flat hats, a flying saucer from Romania. All wore long black coats and black suits.

They place this barrier of custom between their lives and the world outside, and parts of their customs are looked at skeptically, particularly the covered heads at all times, and in the case of women, the wearing of a wig, or *sheitl*; simultaneously, the face of the woman is open for all to see and admire. For the men, the hat is protection against cold.

Hasidic custom forbids them to shake hands with a woman, which causes them to flee from any woman whose hand is outstretched. But their clothes are the armor of any Hasidic political movement. At election time in Williamsburg, they line streets with as many as two thousand, with the sameness of their black hats and coats and side curls making it appear that there are tens of thousands. In Borough Park, Hasidics fill one street for a rally. The politician on the stage thinks the crowd extends for a mile.

"Our voting is massive," Rabbi Shea Hecht announced one night. He alluded to tens of thousands, but the actual number in the Satmar area on election night was thirty-five hundred or so, and in another Brooklyn area, that of the Lubavitch, there were the usual three thousand.

Somebody running for mayor of New York never sees the numbers, just the hats. There is no time to stop and make a campaign promise to the Hasidim. This is not a labor union with a single demand. The Satmars open with schools, hospitals, and police. Nor are they all that anxious to begin bargaining. As a politician is at his most vulnerable in the haze of victory, the thing that stands out most sharply in recollection is all those black hats. Now, one after another, the black hats walk into City Hall or municipal offices where they want something done. If the mayor is a Roman Catholic, like Giuliani, he bows because he thinks anything else will be interpreted as anti-Semitic.

"We feel we are at our strongest when we come to the mayor after the election," Isaac Benjamin was saying one day. Benjamin often speaks to newspapers and television for the Satmars. "Anyone can get a campaign promise. We get government action."

The mayor doesn't know one Hasid from the other, but he throws himself into every set of arms and pledges his love forever. Much more than that. He summons assistants and orders them to handle any contract one of these rabbis—his best friends in the whole world—hands out. Giuliani placed an assistant, Richard Scheirer, into the police department as a liaison to the Jewish community, meaning the Hasidim. He then made a campaign fund-raiser, Bruce Teitelbaum, Chief of Staff, who would be helpful to all the needs of the Hasidic community.

Not once would these politicians, who are supposed to carry the last election figures in their hearts, realize that they picked up the same three thousand or so votes that the guy before them received, and that in their own areas the Hasidim could not defeat a black state assemblyman, Al Vann, and that someday soon the Hispanic vote would bury everybody.

Still, you get a non-Jew—and particularly a Roman Catholic—in office in New York, and here is what he says: What is it that you're talking about? You're trying to tell me that they do not exist, that I can't see all those black hats? If I listen to you and ignore them, every one of them will be an enemy, and you tell me how I get reelected then.

As part of publicity for a Central Park concert, Garth Brooks, the country singer, came to City Hall to meet the mayor. Entering the office, he noticed the most prominent picture, that of Giuliani surrounded by black hats. Brooks' eyebrows went up. "I didn't know you had Amish in New York," he said.

The great temptation of cheap labor rose out of factories that attracted more cheap labor, Puerto Ricans, into the neighborhood. They first came on a ship, the *Marine Tiger*, huddled against the winter cold in the first heavy jackets of their lives. Summer people in winter clothes. Soon they were arriving on late-night flights from San Juan, *kikiri* flights—the flight of the chicken. An expressway was built that cut Williamsburg into two sections and destroyed twenty-two hundred units of low-cost housing. The city's answer was to sweep up all the poor and put them into huge high-rise housing projects. This was first done in ancient Rome when all the poor came in from the countryside and authorities built the first high-rises in the history of the world. After a while, the poor hated them and set fires. As municipal corruption in Rome had no bounds, the firemen wouldn't come unless the chief was paid. The buildings were adjudged a failure, and the high-rises for the poor were no more. In New York, two mayors in a row who had gone to Yale, Wagner and Lindsay, put up more high-rises for the poor than the world had seen. They were supposed to have studied things like this in school.

The projects in Williamsburg started a clash between Satmars and Puerto Ricans over who got the most apartments. In late December of 1970, Satmars boarded yellow school buses and went to City Hall, where three thousand in their black hats and great round fur hats demonstrated. Meanwhile, the

Puerto Rican women rushed the projects and in the lobbies they put up huge Christmas trees. When the Satmars returned and were confronted with this blaze of lighted trees, there was the beginnings of a riot. Somehow, it was established that the Satmars would have apartments on the first three floors because they cannot use elevators on their holy days and the Puerto Ricans would live all the way into the sky. The Satmars and other Hasidim began a thirty-year push to get the land and housing they needed. One of those days in the future was to make a local builder named Eugene Ostreicher an important man in Williamsburg.

Chapter Fifteen

OUTSIDERS, PARTICULARLY anybody nonwhite, assume the Satmars have tremendous wealth. It is at least over-rated. In street talk, most Satmars don't have forty dollars. In Brooklyn, the "economic boom" is something to be read about in the newspapers.

"Am I supposed to be burdened by my fortune of money?" Isaac Benjamin was saying in his hardware store on Church Avenue. Whenever anything happens that puts Satmars in the news, Isaac Benjamin is the one everybody calls. He bought the store by promising the owner, David Kramer, as he was dying, that he would take care of Kramer's son, George, forever. The son is autistic and has a photographic memory. He also yells at people when they walk in. Kramer died, Isaac took over the store, and now he stands behind the counter and Kramer's son, middle-aged, yells as you come through the door. He walks to the window and looks out at Church Avenue's traffic. A truck goes by. "Ralph Avenue!" he calls out. That is the address on the truck.

"If he is here thirty years from now, he will tell you Ralph Avenue," Benjamin says.

Kramer's son comes back from the window.

"Birthdays," Benjamin says. "He knows everybody's birth-day."

"What's your birthday?" George Kramer asks. "October seventeenth? Same as Christine's. Isaac's is November seventh. Same as my friend Etta Wagner. She's in the Hebrew Home for the Aged, the Bronx. Fifty-nine-oh-one Palisades Avenue. Goldfine Pavilion, room one-fifty-seven. Al Wagner lives in Boynton Beach, Florida. Fifteen Victoria Road. His birthday is June tenth."

Benjamin has read of tax breaks to Pergament and Home Depot and vast riches for all big stores. He fights it out in Brooklyn at full taxes and with Kramer's son still yelling at the customers. He tries to keep up with all matters Satmar.

"Nobody knew," he said. He was talking about the builder Ostreicher. This stocky man came here from Hungary in 1951 and became a citizen in 1956. He started by putting in flooring for supermarkets and then went into general construction in Williamsburg and upstate New York Satmar communities.

"We never knew anything about him except that he let himself be giving to charity. Yeshivas were enjoying his fruits. At dinners he was always a sponsor. Rabbi David Neiderman. Herb Siegel of the city Housing Preservation Department. On Hooper Street near the firehouse he built a yeshiva and a shul. In Monroe he did the same thing. How did he begin? I think he started in floor tiles. Construction, his children took him into construction. How do you get into construction? You go in, you learn how to read prints, and then you're in construction, I guess. We didn't know anything except he was a sponsor at dinners."

New York is the only place ever where a landlord receives cheers. Unlike Manhattan, where buildings search the sky and carry the developer's name, Brooklyn buildings are mostly low and carry addresses whose numbers—760 Seventieth Street— immediately mark a person as one who must use a bridge or tunnel to get to Manhattan. The landlord is absolved if he can use the title of builder. In Manhattan, the city of unimaginable riches, it is the land developers, barterers, lawyers, and lenders who live the most lavishly, are regarded as the most important, and have politicians fawning and begging for their money. The Manhattan builders contribute outlandish amounts in public to candidates—brazenly, too, for they will give $250,000 to each candidate and receive no criticism. They are of the preferred class. The finances of Brooklyn builders are usually much less, but for the 1996 campaign of Rudolph Giuliani, an unknown, Joseph Spitzer, showed up at the treasury with $83,000, an amount that caused people to drop to one knee. Mr. Spitzer gave his address as 1446 Fifty-ninth Street in Brooklyn, the same as Chaim or Richie Ostreicher. A man or woman can come to a candidate with a plan to feed hot lunches to orphans, and another can arrive with good big fresh money. Those with the hot-lunch idea remain out by the elevators while the money guy is in the innermost room being worshiped.

Immediately he becomes known as a great builder.

And those known as builders usually can't drive a nail or saw a board.

Especially Ostreicher. In 1993, complaints were received in the offices of the New York State attorney general about the condition of condominiums purchased from Ostreicher. An associate attorney general, Oliver Rosengart, went and inspected the buildings one morning. The buildings were on the Williamsburg streets where Ostreicher did all his construction. The three-story buildings had openings in the walls, with no fire stoppage. There was a vertical column of wood when there was supposed to be steel. Drainage was pumped from the basement out to the sidewalk, and there it ended. Rosengart said to himself that the houses were not good enough for the West Bank. Rosengart, an engineer and a lawyer, wrote a report that said, "These buildings are by far the worst constructed buildings I have seen in ten years in making these inspections."

Eugene Ostreicher was the first to arrive for a meeting.

"If they don't like the houses, I'll pay them back," Ostreicher said.

"How much?" Rosengart said.

"Twenty-five thousand. That's what they paid me."

In an adjoining office were the four families. Already they had sworn that they had paid $180,000 each.

Rosengart stepped in and told them of Ostreicher's figure.

"Liar!" one of them said.

"Robber!" another said.

Rosengart asked for proof. "Have you got evidence? Show me your records."

He knew the answer. Of course they had no papers to show. Hasidic transactions are made in cash, and in full. Other than a sudden outbreak of diphtheria, nothing will empty a room faster than the first flash of a traceable check. Everyone involved here believed deeply that any check would be scrutinized by the chief accountant of the Internal Revenue Service himself. Money to buy a house was tough enough to earn without having to risk prison by being asked to account for it.

"You can't go to civil court without any records," Rosengart said. "You better go to a rabbinical court."

The closest outsiders can compare this procedure to are the Italian mob sit-downs, where one person made important by his murder statistics hears complaints and delivers irrevocable judgments. However, the four purchasers had difficulty finding a rabbi in Williamsburg who would sit in judgment of Eugene Ostreicher. He was one of the few people who could obtain land and build housing for people who were sleeping on floors and in hallways. So what if some things were wrong with some of his houses? That could be fixed. The important thing was that people should have a place to raise families and a place to worship. It takes a great man to build for them. Therefore, Ostreicher was great.

The house buyers went from one rabbi to the next and finally they turned to Rosengart and said that they would go to his *bais din*, or rabbinical court. At first he refused, only to succumb to the ceaseless tugging from the four buyers. So there came a morning when they sat in Rosengart's office and he was behind the desk with the full power given to him by thousands of years of Jewish law.

"How much did you pay?" he asked the four. He looked at them sternly.

"One hundred and eighty thousand dollars."

"Is that true?" he said to Ostreicher.

"They gave me thirty-five thousand," Ostreicher said.

"He lies!"

"How could you lie like that? You are in a sacred court."

"I'll pay," he said.

"How much?"

"What they gave me. Four hundred thousand dollars."

"He lies again!"

"Seven hundred twenty thousand," one of the buyers said.

"I received six hundred twenty-five thousand," Ostreicher said.

"When will he stop deceiving and lying?" another of the buyers said.

"Which is it?" Rosengart asked sharply.

"Seven hundred and twenty thousand," Ostreicher said finally.

The agreement was reached with both sides seething. They finished at an hour reserved for prayer. Anger was suspended. There were nine, including Ostreicher. A tenth man was needed in order to reach a minyan, the number required for prayer. "You?" they said to Rosengart. He nodded. Why, of course. The long day of distrust, deceit, and denunciations ended in prayer.

However, when Rosengart finally got back to his office, he put the details of the unconscionably bad construction into a file, where it would remain for six years. Then one day an investigator for the government's Department of Labor took the file. It would become the start of a clear fact pattern in a case against Ostreicher.

The son, Richie Ostreicher, had spent several years studying the Talmud in a Satmar community in Monroe, New York. Studies in Hebrew schools are at marathon length. His friend Sam Newman, who was there with him, recalls, "We studied fourteen, fifteen hours a day. We got home twice a year. He seemed to like it. I was not too sure. You can see who is going to continue as a scholar. After you come out into the free world, and you still want to study, that shows your desire. Me, I wasn't so much for it. Richie did study once in awhile."

As the sections of the Talmud are thousands of years old, each section must be scoured and discussed and gone over again and again. Newman says that of course he and Richie studied for interminable hours the rules that no one is allowed to take advantage of an employee, that no employer is allowed to eat until he pays his workers. But this refers to day workers, who put in a hard day and should be paid that night. Workers on a weekly or monthly payroll are different. As for day workers, if a man says he needs the job so desperately that he will work cheap, you shouldn't take advantage of him. Still, he is so desperate for work that at times you create a job for him, and this puts it into a gray area. It isn't right to take advantage of him, but the question is, is it the wrong thing to give him this work right away? After all, you're not God. God is God. The man needs work. But does his need mean you're supposed to pay him more than he'll take? On the street, the answer is a distillation of scriptures: Pay the guy enough so that you can have something under your feet when you stand and claim that you're not robbing him.

In their lives and times of living in the most diverse center of population in all the world—a Brooklyn of people driven off the cotton fields of the South by machines, or from the slums of San Juan and Port-au-Prince and Santo Domingo and the sparse living of Cholula—the Hasidim had the most complicated feelings. They didn't like anybody who wasn't white, don't worry about that. But they couldn't do without them, particularly Mexicans, because they were cheap labor and the world has nothing to rival that, nor has it ever. Then, unlike the non-Hasidic Jews and the Irish and Italian and Germans, the Hasidim did not flee from other races. The Hasidim bought land and houses because they were going to remain in Brooklyn. The Lubavitch grand rebbe, Menachem Shneerson, called it a deep moral obligation not to run from blacks. Others, particularly Catholics, didn't know what he was talking about. They were moving out to Long Island to spend three and four hours a day getting to and from work because they loved the Long Island Expressway so much. The Hasidim regarded themselves as morally superior to these people. They stayed in Brooklyn and called 911 on the blacks and Mexicans at night. In the morning they hired them to work off the books, and for minimum wage—maybe.

Walking into the temporal world, Richie Ostreicher went immediately to work in his father's construction company. He also became active in the Ninetieth Precinct community meetings. If a cop was sick or injured, Richie was a visitor. He became a cop buff with a yarmulke. The police at first thought he was a local rabbi, but then Richie, by behavior and speech, magnified this illusion into his becoming a police chaplain, and a man of the cloth with this badge can do just about anything and at all times.

Williamsburg is the neighborhood of the Ninetieth Precinct, which is in a gray cement three-story corner building on Union Street. The precinct shares the front of the building with the Fire Department's Battalion Fifteen. Chief John Dillon, short and stocky, with a crew cut, is in charge. The boss over him is Deputy Fire Chief Charles Blaich, who is a critic of the New York City Buildings Department and of the work they allowed to proceed. Blaich began with a degree in chemistry and a master's in protection management, and then kept taking construction courses because all fire department promotion exams have many building questions.

Blaich married Mary DiBiase, who was the photographer for the New York *Daily News* who climbed a fire escape to get the famous picture of mobster Carmine Galante dead with a cigar in his mouth in the backyard of a restaurant in Ridgewood, Queens. "Don't you look up my dress!" she said to the photographers following her up the ladder. Her photo went all over the world. Now she raises two kids in Staten Island and once in a while gets a call from the *New York Times* and from some Catholic publications. She goes out with her cameras and tells herself, "queen for a day." She bought $6,500 worth of cameras for sports events, and she takes pictures of night baseball games at Yankee Stadium while whatever her family does for dinner, they do it alone.

Around the side of the building is Truck Eight of Police Emergency Services. Upstairs, always on the ready, is Billy Pieszak, out of Our Lady of Czestochowa school, on Thirty-second Street in the Sunset Park neighborhood. During his school days Polish was the first language. His home bar is Snooky's, which everybody in his Brooklyn knows. His best souvenir is a New York City detective badge used to open the show *NYPD Blue*. It was given to him by Bill Clark, who once was a detective in the Ninetieth Precinct and went on to become the producer of *NYPD Blue*.

There was an afternoon when Bill Clark and a television crew were shooting a scene in front of the precinct. A car with police lights and windshield parking placards pulled up, and a heavy guy with a beard and yarmulke got out.

"Bill Clark, *NYPD Blue*? I'm the NYPD Jew," he said.

He introduced himself as Richie Ostreicher. Clark thought he was a Police Department chaplain. If there is one thing that makes an Irish detective back off, it is a Jewish chaplain. Clark, even though retired, did what every Catholic cop ever did, and that was to virtually genuflect. This came from the nights and days of the Satmar's famous Rabbi Wolfe, who was introduced as an untouchable by the Brooklyn commander and who then walked into the squad rooms of the Sixty-sixth and Seventy-first and Ninetieth Precincts and without so much as a grunt of hello went into the confidential files. Detectives typed up notes without looking at him.

Rabbi Wolfe's main need was all accident reports involving Satmars. If, on rare occasions, a Satmar had a criminal matter pending, Rabbi Wolfe studied the complaint, then asked for a match.

After the day's filming, Clark went for dinner at the Old Stand, on Third Avenue and Fifty-fifth Street in Manhattan. Richie followed in his car. As he observed kosher rules, he ate no food. Instead, he had soda and talked incessantly about the police. He said it was "the job," which is how police give their occupation: "I'm on the job." He identified precincts in cop language. It was the "nine-oh," not the Ninetieth. He was engaging and excited about cops. Clark recalls, "He did not have a gun. If he had one, he would have made sure that I was aware of it, that he was carrying. He talked like the construction business was his. But I assumed his father was the show and that Richie just did things for him."

When Clark got back to the Regency Hotel, where he was staying, there were flowers in the room for his wife, Karen, from Richie Ostreicher.

Richie Ostreicher was married on November 25, 1998, and had the reception at the Le Marquis at 815 Kings Highway. The guest list showed Police Commissioner Safir at table fifty-four, Inspector John Scanlon at fifty-five, First Deputy Commissioner Patrick Kelleher at thirty-one, Inspector Vincent Kennedy at thirty-two, Deputy Chief of Patrol William Casey and Chief Tom Fahey at thirty-six, in addition to the mayor's special assistant, Bruce Teitelbaum.

The father had just bought nine lots from the city at an uncontested sale for $345,000. The lots ran the length of a long Williamsburg block, Middleton Street. He intended to build three- and four-story apartment houses.

At the same time the construction work of Eugene Ostreicher was stopped temporarily by the Fire Department, Eduardo Gutiérrez was in and out of stores asking for work. A Korean who had a fruit store on Fifth Avenue in Brooklyn hired him without saying a word. Eduardo knew that the job was seven days a week of twelve-hour days at pay of $250 a week.

Eduardo became another Mexican sitting on a box in front of the flowers and fruit bins outside a market, the immigrant learning that *America* is a word that also means drudgery.

The United States Department of Labor showed in a survey that a Korean immigrant starting work in New York received $500 a week and a Mexican only $270, which is an unrealistically high figure. Down to the bottom, the lightest skin color does best.

One Korean store owner hired a Korean for $500 and two Mexicans for $230 and $270 a week. When his business slowed, he fired the Korean and one Mexican and hired a second Mexican for $170 a week.

The study showed that the usual Mexican earned $170 a week for a seventy-hour week, the equivalent of 1,700 pesos; there was no such salary in dream or reality anywhere in San Matías.

The Mexican population in the United States has reached six million. They wire home $6 billion a year. This amount is counted on by Mexico's banks. Mexico's credit line with American banks is based on the expected national income from Mexicans without papers in America.

They are in the dark dawn doorways of coffee shops and restaurants, the bread delivery next to them, waiting for the place to open for the start of their twelve hours as dishwashers and porters for $170 for a six-day week.

"Why don't you go to school?" Angelo, the owner, asked José, fourteen, when he presented himself for a job in the Elite Coffee Shop on Columbus Avenue. José asked, "Is the school going to pay me?" Angelo shrugged and he motioned the kid to the kitchen, where he would still be ten years later.

They all put their bodies up.

My friend Maurice Pinzon was on an East Side subway when three Mexicans got on at the stop underneath Bellevue Hospital. One held up a hand that had a white hill of bandages. He cursed the job that caused this. He had lost a finger and the doctors in Bellevue couldn't help. "They throw away my finger like garbage," he said. One of his friends said, "Now you cannot work."

"Why not?" the injured one said.

"How can you drive at work?" one of his friends said.

The guy shrugged. "I drive with one hand."

In Brooklyn, the A train on the old dreary el tracks outside drowned out the crying of the women in the second-floor rooms. The body of Iván Martínez, 17, a brother and cousin to the thirteen people in the apartment, had just been taken off the street and carted to the medical examiner. He was here from Puebla, delivering pizza for $150 a week, when three hoodlums from the neighborhood shot him in the head, took $36, and went for chicken wings from a Chinese takeout.

And Brother Joel Magallan sits in the offices of the Asociación Tepeyac de New York on West Fourteenth Street and talks about the trouble of trying to make it better. "They hired census organizers a year before. They hired Mexicans one month before. We had no chance. The new president of Mexico wants to have a guest worker program. You sign up in Mexico. That means none of the people coming here as guest workers can join a union."

He held out his hands. In the far suburbs of Suffolk County, two Mexicans who stood in front of a 7-Eleven store in the town of Farmingville were picked up by two whites who said they wanted them for day work but instead took them to an isolated place and gave them a beating. Some politicians in Suffolk thought that a central hiring hall would stop violence, but the county executive turned down the idea. He said it would be illegal to put a roof over their heads.

In the room next to Magallan's offices, one of his staff was interviewing a young guy who had been working at a store selling accessories in the Bronx. He worked one hundred hours a week for $200. The boss had tables set up outside the store and wanted the Mexican to work them. "I had a bad cold," the Mexican told Magallan's worker. "He fired me." They had the Mexican get a witness and made out papers for $8,800 in back pay. Maybe there would be this one victory. Maybe not. It is so hard to be on the bottom in New York.

Eduardo Gutiérrez became another of the black and brown who stand in the cold darkness of Bedford Avenue in Williamsburg and wait for someone to pick them up for a day's work. It is his first morning here. He had come to Brooklyn for a construction job, but it was shut down for a while, and the Korean market was a bust, so he was on the street to look for work.

There is no street with the past and present of Bedford Avenue, which starts miles away at hamburger stands and bars around Brooklyn College and crosses Nostrand Avenue to form a space where old men, with cheers still in their ears, tell of the day John F. Kennedy drew a crowd of far over a million in his campaign in 1960.

After the college neighborhood, Bedford Avenue runs into streets almost entirely of color. It is here, a few yards up from the corner of Empire Boulevard, that it goes past high gloomy brick public housing known as Ebbets Field Houses, which stand where the old ball field had the Dodgers as a home team. So few know that it is the place where the most profound social change in the country took place. That was on a raw March afternoon in 1947 when Branch Rickey, the owner of the Dodgers, sent a typewritten note to the press box at Ebbets Field during a preseason exhibition game. "The Brooklyn Dodgers today purchased the contract of infielder Jack Roosevelt Robinson from Montreal. He reports immediately." Thus changing baseball, and the nation, whether it realized it or not. Robinson was the first of color ever to play in the majors. This happened while Martin Luther King Jr. was a sophomore in an Atlanta high school, it was before *Brown vs. Board of Education*, before Harry Truman integrated the armed forces, before Little Rock school desegregation, before the lunch counter sit-ins of the South. Before anything here was Jackie Robinson on first base at Ebbets Field as the first black in baseball. Long years later, during a lecture at the New-York Historical Society, Frank Slocum, who had been in the Dodgers office in Robinson's time, was asked how something of such magnitude and complications could have been done with only two sentences, when any decent law firm would compile a foot-high stack of briefs.

"Yeah, but we were really doing it," Slocum said.

Today, the Ebbets Field Houses and the school across the street from it, Intermediate School 232, the Jackie Robinson School, are dreadful proof that one magnificent act becomes just that, one act, when placed against the grinding, melancholy despair of life every day. Cling to the great act that can inspire and give hope. But you can't brush away the effects of the disease of slavery and suddenly make softer the life of thousands of children who come out of the housing project with keys around the neck, latchkey kids, for no one is at home when they return from school. The school has a narrow fenced-in cement yard unworthy of a state prison, a yard with flowers at one end for the young boy who was shot dead while playing basketball. The school is one of the five worst in the city.

Past the housing project, the avenue goes down a long slope, and the color suddenly changes to white and the avenue becomes one of Hasidic Jews, the men with black hats, beards, and long curls, the women with heads covered with kerchiefs.

The four-story brick corner house at number 527 has claws coming out of the foundation. It is the home of builder Eugene and son Richie Ostreicher. On the side is a new addition, a garage for their construction company.

The street goes around a curve and comes up to a park and bodega where Eduardo stands outside, looking for work.

He was in T-shirt, jeans, and sneakers, with his black cap on backward. And he was, like the others standing alongside him, a person of towering dignity. He had put up his young life to come to this curb and look for work to build a house for his future, and to buy book bags for his sisters in San Matías.

He became one of the blacks and Mexicans who waited for people to pull up and beckon to them and take them away for day labor, cleaning lots, emptying trucks, rearranging warehouses. They stand here in their rough clothes and dark skin, mostly unable to speak English, coming from rooms without bathrooms, without kitchens, and if they must walk far to a subway, then they walk far to a subway. In the dimness they may seem like unkempt shadows, but as you watch them, they grow and the features are defined and the heads are raised. They are the aristocrats, descendants of the pure royalty of 1947 of their street. Yes, it happened long ago. And now there still is so far to go. But once you were too far down even to dream. Now, back where Bedford crosses Empire Boulevard, Jackie Robinson hits a single and right away takes a couple of steps off first base and the crowd shouts in anticipation. He is going for second! He is the only player who can cause a commotion just by taking a couple of steps off first. And take the step he does, and take second he does, and when he stands and brushes off the dirt, he becomes the hope for those millions and millions who had gone out each day, as did the generations before them, feeling only the deadliness of despair, believing there was nothing better.

He stood for the dawn people on Bedford Avenue who take a step off the curb and peer at the headlights to see if anybody is slowing down to stop and give them work. Bedford Avenue whispers in their ear. Sure, so much is hideous. But the dream has been handed down to them. They take any insult, suffer any degradation, face every unfairness and injustice, yet never leave, because they are here for others, for wives and children at home, and nothing can make them quit.

Here on Bedford, each time a car or van suddenly pulls up and the driver calls "One" or "Two," the number of workers he needs, the street standers rush blindly to the car and go diving into the backseat. They go off without knowing where they are going or how much they are going to be paid. The word *job* throbs through their bodies unconditionally. Those waiting on the curb can be there for the full day. One or two, or at the most three at a time, jump off the fence and run to get a job without questioning. The jostling on the sidewalk is continual and causes despair among those left at day's end.

For all the valor spent chasing work, the Mexicans also are irresistible temptations, the nearest occasion of mortal sin: cheap labor.

It is blood in the mouth of nearly everybody who hires.

That left Eduardo with only one thing to do. He was on the curb at Bedford Avenue by 6 A.M., one of a pack of people trying to feed a family. One or two remember being there with him. One was Rafi Macias, who had had a job for $7.50 an hour at a luggage factory in Long Island City. One Monday when he climbed the factory steps to his floor, the foreman was in the doorway and told him that there was no work. The place had moved. He remembers that his first thought was of his son on a tricycle on the street in front of the housing project in Coney Island. He came right to the curb at Bedford. He remembers that he caught a job that day, cleaning a yard in Hackensack, New Jersey. The guy gave him $60 and that was all right. He didn't return from the curb empty.

Somebody told Miguel Aquino that Italians paid $10 an hour for construction workers, and so he went to Eighteenth Avenue and Sixty-fifth Street in Bensonhurst only to find so many waiting that he was shut out. After that, he remembers trying Utica and Fulton, where Italians in vans were hiring, but when Miguel started for one van, a Puerto Rican punched him on the side of the head, and Miguel lost his balance and the job.

He, too, did not go home. He came straight to Bedford, though it was too late the first day. But he says he stayed because he couldn't face his wife and children at home knowing that he had quit when he should have kept trying.

On that first day on the street, Eduardo missed out on every chance and went home disgusted. He reminded himself that he had to get the jump on them. He was quicker the next day and was out front for a plumbing truck, and spent the day moving pipes. He came home with $45.

Farther along, the street for work, Bedford Avenue, now becomes Puerto Rican. Flags, loud music, Spanish calling through the air. Then the sidewalks turn old Polish and new Eastern European, a street of people smoking furiously in coffee shops with leather jackets tossed over their shoulders. But so many Polish stand under the Williamsburg Bridge and look for work each morning. At North Eighth Street is a subway that is only one stop to Manhattan's East Side, and it is a thousand miles away.

Eduardo took the room's cell phone into a corner of the kitchen and called Silvia in College Station for the first time. She remembers being surprised to hear from him, for she knew that he hadn't asked her mother or father for her phone number. He told her that he got the number from a brother-in-law of her cousin in the Bronx.

"How is work?" she asked him.

He mumbled. She thought later that he didn't want to admit that he had traveled this far to get hit-or-miss work.

She told him that she worked at the barbecue stand in the morning and the Olive Garden at night.

"I make minestrone soup for four hundred and fifty people," she said. She was aware that he didn't know what minestrone soup was, so she told him about cutting up the vegetables for it.

She asked how many people were in his room. He told her six. She thinks that he didn't want to tell her the exact number, eight, because he knew that she didn't like a crowded bedroom.

He asked her how many were in her house in College Station. She told him five, but it was only a two-bedroom apartment and she was used to her own room. Things would be better soon. Finally, he volunteered something. He had done his own laundry. He had taken all his shirts and underwear to a coin laundry and washed and dried them.

"Make sure you tell that to your mother," she said. "She won't have to do your wash anymore. I won't either."

That got him flustered and the call was over. He said he would call again, and he did. But he made the call when he came home after work and she was just leaving for the night job at the Olive Garden. She could say only a few words. On the next couple of calls, the time difference caused him to miss her. Silvia remembers trying him once on the cell phone and getting no answer.

The next time he called, he said he was working on a construction job. He didn't say much more. He was still strangled by shyness, even when shielded by a phone. By now, everybody in the room at Brighton knew this, and when they all got off the train at Flushing Avenue and walked down the streets to the job at Middleton, they started in on him, did it because he was so easy, just walking there with them.

"Look at the pretty girl, Eduardo," Alejandro remembers saying to him when a woman passed by going to work. "Go up and tell her how pretty she is. Tell her you will die for her."

Eduardo never stopped to think that the others never would do this. They were afraid that the woman would call for the police and get them deported. All he did was look at the sidewalk as he passed the woman. Early on in his days on the job, Eduardo showed that he could not break out of his shyness; nor could he handle the others taunting him about this. One morning he came off the el steps running. He went all the way to the job. He liked the run. It kept them out of his ears. From then on, he ran from the el each morning. Finally, they said that they would stop fooling with him. He did not believe them. Still he ran.

Chapter Sixteen

THE BUILDING business in Brooklyn lives on the eighth floor of the seedy old Municipal Building, upstairs from the Court Street stop of the number 2 train. You come off the elevator on the eighth floor only to be blocked by the back of a large woman in a plaid coat who is on one of the three pay phones on the wall.

"Listen, he thinks that because I work around the corner, I can come in here as a favor for noth—" She listened for half a breath. Then she roared, "Exactly! They think I can do this when I go out for coffee. I'm here an hour alread—"

This time she suffered the other voice for a moment, then snaps, "No. Give me Alex. I'll tell him that I want to get paid for this."

A small man in a leather cap is jammed into the wall by the woman. He talks in a low voice on another pay phone.

Inside a cubicle a step away from the phones, three people sit at old computers that rattle. A sign on the wall says each person is allowed ten minutes. Another says, If You Offer a Bible, It Is Considered a Gift.

Next to each computer, a printout machine that could have carried the news of Truman's victory rattles and grinds as it sends out long pages of building violations. They are printed too faintly for all human eyes except for those of the expediter. Without the expediter, builders couldn't build a doghouse in Brooklyn. These are hallway people who know computer codes, all Buildings Department regulations, and also the offices and members of the Buildings Department. The commissioner for Brooklyn, Tarek Zeid, has a wife who is an expediter. His office was a few yards down the eighth-floor hallway until he took a leave under some fire.

Expediters gather all the paper a builder needs and do it in a tenth of the time he could and then move in and out of hallways and offices and fix anything that has to be fixed. The builder wouldn't know where to begin.

A rabbi spins around and asks, "What do I do?"

"You got to take a number," he is told. "Take a number like it's the butcher's."

Three people sitting on chairs ignore the rabbi. Four others are standing against the wall. Now one person at a computer stands up, clutching his printouts. Two tumble from the wall and try to get there first. But a man gets out of his chair and beats them to it. He starts commanding the computer to find his specific violations. The woman in the plaid coat from the hallway bursts forward. She yells to everybody, "You didn't take a number!" She pushes hard. The man leaving with printouts has to burrow through the people.

One person at the computer, a young law student named Maurice, whose long pointed chin looks as if it could punch a hole in the keyboard, turns around and says, "This doesn't work."

A man with a face of cigarette smoke and wearing a candy store sweater, an old maroon cardigan with pockets for change, jumps off the wall.

"Go back. Punch A. Did you hit A? All right. Hit PUB, then PRM. That's—"

"I already did."

"Then you're in. You're logged on."

"I'm still not."

"Did you hit three?"

"Three?"

"You want Brooklyn, you press three to get into Brooklyn. Every borough got a different code. Three is for Brooklyn. You want Brooklyn, you just press three and you got Brooklyn."

Maurice nods and presses the key. With Brooklyn up, he taps out the name he was doing research on, Ostreicher. His chin comes closer to the keyboard.

His tutor has gone back to leaning against the wall. The young guy is learning the trade of expediter, which is as essential to the building of a building as the roof.

The printer alongside the young guy now begins to grind out page after page of violations for Ostreicher.

34232893K VIOL ACTIVE

43 LORIMER STREET

RESPONDENT INFO: OSTREICHER, CHAIM 527 BEDFORD AVENUE, DESCRIPTION OF VIOLATION:
STAIR ENCLOSURE DOES NOT COMPLY WITH THE REQUIRED FIRE RESISTANCE RATING; IN THAT BUILDING IS BUILT AS A FOUR-STORY OCCUPANCY GROUP—WHICH REQUIRES A TWO-HOUR FIRE-RATED ENCLOSURE AS PER SECTION PFI.

B 5027
STRUCTURAL DEFECTS VIOLATE REFERENCE STANDARD RSIO-5B IN THAT I.—NO STRAP BRACING FOR "C" JOISTS II ANCHORAGE BETWEEN JOIST AND BEARING OR NON-BEARING WALL WAS NOT PROVIDED.

B5C 27
EXISTING APARTMENT DOORS OPEN DIRECTLY INTO STAIR ENCLOSURE CONTRARY TO D 27 373. REMEDY: FILE PLANS TO LEGALIZE IF FEASIBLE AND CONFORM TO CODE.

Every ten minutes the person at the machine is supposed to give it up and let the next person look up all his violations. But when Maurice's ten minutes are up, unseen hands push him back down. As the old violations come out of the printer, one of the expediters is offended by Maurice's inefficiency. "How could you let this go on?" he says. "You are supposed to get certificates of correction."

The large woman in plaid snarls, "The engineer has to write a letter. That's work you should have done. Who are you? What are you doing with such a mess?"

After all, their business is to rectify dangers in a building by means of pieces of paper. All this noise from people on the phone, from the world's only noisy computers, from old printers makes it impossible for a person to think of somebody dying in a building. If somebody dies in a fire in a stairwell or falls off the building, that is a tragedy. But these things do not happen every day, and therefore what is of concern is getting the proper certificate so the builder can build.

One expediter prints out complaint number 4069852, filed on September 8, 1997: "Multiple dwelling fire escape in danger of collapse—all rear." The clerks handling the complaint listed it with priority C, which placed the complaint on a level with a missing shingle. That had to please the expediter. Some 339 days later, the Fire Department inspected the premises. Their report said the fire escape was "in danger of collapse and was a health hazard to both the building's occupants and members of the Fire Department." The owner was ordered to fix the fire escape immediately. But if the clerk in the Buildings Department had listed the complaint as priority A, where it belonged, it would have been targeted for inspection in a day and a half.

That a potentially hazardous condition was placed in the wrong priority category was found in twelve complaints out of a batch of seventeen. The response time in inspecting and ordering repairs for these defects—which ran from a corroded I-beam to an unsafe structure—went from the day and a half of a priority A to the weeks and months of other priority classes.

This could be the result of a department with so few inspectors that it is impossible to inspect even the urgent. The priority category is dropped to protect the department workers, with everyone hoping that the conditions won't worsen and people won't get hurt. The change of categories is also a smashing tactic for expediters. Turn the B into a C and tell the owner he can go on vacation.

The first street on Ostreicher's violations list, Lorimer Street, was empty and sullen when Ostreicher first arrived to build. Old closed factories sat on the edges of empty lots. Up ahead was the old yellow el trestle passing by the red brick Woodhull Hospital. Once, when John Lindsay was mayor and the people running the city were young and full of hope, Woodhull was built as a public hospital with all private rooms. It was Lindsay's belief that if people could have a private room in Lenox Hill Hospital because they had the money to pay for it, then the poor should have a private room because they didn't have the money to pay for it.

Lorimer Street backs onto Middleton, where Ostreicher also planned to build.

His streets of brick condominiums—look-alike, in trouble alike—stood for the worst, and they looked up the street at the best.

* * *

José Daniel, seventeen, Eduardo's younger brother, talked to Eduardo several times on the phone about his coming to New York. In March 1999, Eduardo told José that he could get him a construction job. José immediately left San Matías. The coyote price was $1,600. The entire family in San Matías dug hard and came up with airfare to Tijuana, but that was it. José, following the path of his brother, and the others who had gone before him, went to a small hotel in Tijuana called the Azul, where he met the same coyote who had taken his brother across. José arranged to come to New York as a "collect immigrant." His brother would somehow have the money waiting. But as José had not even made a partial payment, he was considered a risk to flee once he was in America. Therefore, he was treated as a suspect through the entire trip. The coyote would have a man take him to New York, where Eduardo would meet them with the money in his hand. Please be there.

José was one of a crowd of twenty young men who followed the coyote for long hours through a desert of bushes and sand. The coyote pulled away bushes that covered the entrance to a tunnel that had dirt walls and ceiling. There were only a couple of wood supports visible. The tunnel was pitch black and airless. The coyote used a flashlight. The ones with him used their fear. José remembers people calling out that they felt a snake. Some tried to turn and go back, but they were going through the tunnel in a chain, and so this could not be done. One raised his voice to a scream. This stopped nothing. When they emerged from the tunnel, José remembers, they walked in the scrub parallel to a highway for a long time. Two vans then picked them up and drove them to a house in Phoenix. He does not remember how long he stayed there. The immigrants with him were leaving one at a time with a coyote. In the late afternoon, a Mexican who had nothing to say grunted and indicated the door. He was burly with uncut hair and wore a black rain jacket. José and three others went with him. A van took them to the Phoenix airport, where they went through the metal detector while the silent coyote walked around it. A Hispanic working at the metal detector nodded. They got on a flight to New York. When the coyote sat, his rain jacket was open and a shirt showed something beneath, gun or knife. The coyote jammed the ticket receipts into his pocket. He spoke for the first time. He told José in short harsh words that his brother Eduardo had better be right on time for their meeting and have the money. He said no more. He was unconcerned about the other three. When the plane stopped at Chicago, they got off without goodbyes.

The flight to New York brought José and the coyote into chilly darkness at LaGuardia Airport. The coyote, who knew the city, took José on a bus. Then they took a subway for some time. José was excited by the noise and lights and speed. He asked where he was. The coyote told him the Bronx. The train then became an el. José stood up and walked to the opposite side of the car in order to see what was behind a bank of bright lights on the ground below. The coyote immediately stood next to him. When José went back to his seat, the coyote was with him. The train stopped and the doors opened, and suddenly the coyote held an arm in front of José. He acted as if he was stopping José from getting off at the wrong stop. He had not come this far to lose a cash customer. As the train was going to the next stop, the coyote showed some tension. He put a hand on José's arm. At the next stop, he guided José out to a platform that was empty. The coyote had a hand close to whatever he had inside his jacket and under his shirt.

There was a call from the middle of the platform. Eduardo was coming off a staircase and walking excitedly through one station light and into the darkness toward them. The coyote pretended to smile, but José remembered that he kept his shoulder in front of him. Eduardo walked up and put his hand into his pocket to get the money. This caused the coyote to stiffen, and his hand dug into his jacket pocket. Then he saw the cash. It now was a straight exchange, immigrant for cash. Suddenly Eduardo and José were afraid that the coyote would take the money and for some reason kill them. They had never thought of such a thing before, but now it was obvious in the night air on the empty platform. The coyote's right hand held the weapon, showing that he was afraid that the two brothers would kill him and keep their money. There had been a series of dead bodies in the Bronx to validate all their fears. Eduardo counted the money out as fast as he could. He then handed it to the coyote. This was the instant where murder might take place. The coyote snatched the money with his left hand and walked off in one motion, closing his jacket.

There was no construction work because of the weather. José went to the curb on Bedford Avenue and then was told by Lucino in the room in Brighton Beach about a job at a grocery store on Avenue U, which was within walking distance of the Brighton house. He got the job and worked twelve hours a day, seven days a week, and was paid $240. At the end of each day he sat in gloom. Had he known that he would make such little money, had he known that if he kept a job like this it would take him almost a year to repay the $1,600 to his brother, he would have stayed in San Matías.

Then the weather broke and there was excitement in the room at Brighton Beach. They were going to work, and they were sure they could get José on the job. They did.

Suddenly, he was making $340 a week and he could repay the loan and still send money home. He worked three floors up at the back of the site. Lucino was his partner. Eduardo was on the street side. The brothers rarely talked during work. Afterward they went to the corner bodega and sat in the back and had pizza or chicken or tacos. Then they took the train home. Sometimes they went to a store and bought Mexican vegetables and steak and cooked that at home. Otherwise, nothing changed except the date on the calendar. This drudgery each long day consumed their lives just as would an illness.

Everybody working regarded the structure as unsafe. Eduardo and José talked about this during what both felt was their one best day in New York. They took the subway over to Battery Park and stood looking at the Statue of Liberty.

Eduardo posed while his brother took his picture, and then he took pictures of his brother, and after that they asked tourists to take pictures of both of them. They were proud to show their best shoes, dark construction boots with yellow tops.

They wondered if their youngest brother, Miguel Angel, was carrying more than one slate at a time. He must be up to two or even three, they agreed. He was eleven by now and loved the work. When Eduardo had left San Matías, the addition to the house had only the cement work done. There were no walls. The father said he would buy steel beams with the money Eduardo would be sending home. He needed people to help him with it. They had to be friends, as he had no money to pay for help now.

Eduardo mentioned that they should go home to help. It

was a nice thought, except it didn't include directions on how to get money for the construction if nobody was working.

José remembers that they looked at the statue and wondered how the workers had been able to get up to the arm and put on the torch.

"They couldn't do it on our job," the brother remembers Eduardo saying.

"Doesn't anybody look at our job to make sure it is safe?" José asked.

"They say they do, but I never see nobody," Eduardo said. "The floor shakes."

José thought this was because no Mexicans worked on the Statue of Liberty. The ride home on the subway reinforced this idea. Anybody sitting near them left room so they wouldn't be rubbing up against these Mexicans.

Still, the thrill of seeing the statue made Eduardo call Silvia and tell her about it excitedly. She said she would have to come sometime. Eduardo and his brother sent the pictures to her and everybody in San Matías.

All vacant land in New York, from marshes in Staten Island to abandoned junkyards in the Bronx, all these empty lots everywhere, covered with old tires, filthy refrigerators, and stained mattresses bloated by rain, is like a jewelry store window to a builder. Yet his is a slow dream. Possession of unoccupied land is not ruled by time of day or month of year. But when you get it, only a lottery is better.

The city has a series of rules that are designed to make the public feel it is being protected, and at times it actually is. Simultaneously, a land grab can appear honest and sometimes even be honest, while at all times it protects the politicians' right to accept bribes and the builders' right to bribe and cheat and steal while smiling for the public.

The system is the result of ages of politicians who proved that they were not nearly as stupid as they acted. They put together a system where many are paid and few are apprehended. It takes seven months to get permission to build anything in the city.

In Brooklyn, a number of empty lots on Middleton Street were in rem, which means the city and state have taken them over for nonpayment of taxes. An in rem procedure begins in the City Council, where a member lobbies for the return of the property to the one who lost it and has now paid the taxes. In Albany a member of the State Assembly proposes that with taxes paid, the property can be returned to the owner, who in this case received the tax money from Richie and then sold him the property.

The moment a person not in need of a lobotomy hears this antiquated, complicated, and thoroughly suspicious method being evoked, he must go on guard duty. As usual with in rem cases, the facts do not show, and therefore City Councilman Stanley Michels of the Washington Heights section of Manhattan grunted when he saw listed on the voting agenda of this day, "By Council Member Ward: SLR 471. Res. 3245. Assemblyman Genovesi. Reconveyance of block 2242 to Louis Ortiz."

"When this comes up, you abstain," he told two people sitting near him on the floor, new council members. "It's the things you don't vote for that save your life."

Michels had started doing this when he had two children in fine colleges and he preferred not to lose the means of keeping them there.

"What's the matter with it?" he was asked.

"The matter with it is I don't know what it is about. I don't know what any of these things are about. Neither do you. Let's keep investigations far away. Abstain."

At the end of the meeting they had the day's business, all resolutions and bills, together in one package on which the members started to vote.

"You vote yes on all except SLR 471, Resolution 3245," Michels said. "On that you abstain."

"And then?"

"And then you're all right. If it's got to do with buildings, then you're safe to abstain all the time."

Sometimes what appears to be a direct approach by a wounded citizen is made in the land business. The wounded citizen writes as one poor lone person, but when you parse the sentences you find lawyers, lobbyists, and references to phone call after phone call to city officials.

September 12, 1995
The Honorable Rudolph Giuliani
Mayor of the City of New York
New York, New York

Dear Mayor:

I am a registered Republican in the all Democratic neighborhood of Williamsburg, and have never asked for political help. I am deeply involved in community affairs, but I am not a politician!

It took us five years to change the zoning on Block 2240 in our neighborhood, from MI-2 to residential R-5. We own most of the lots in the block, but the City owns five parcels (see diagram attached herewith). Upon the recommendation of Borough President Howard Golden, we have been in contact with HPD regarding the acquisition of these lots. We would like to develop the City's lots in conjunction with our own residential construction on this block, so that the street should be uniformly developed. We are willing to sell or rent these lots for low-income people.

At this point in time, we already have approved plans and building permits (copies attached) ready for our construction. We therefore would need special assistance to obtain these permits from the City in a timely fashion.

We have been advised that you, the mayor, can make this happen.

Respectfully yours,
Eugene Ostreicher

There is no record of any return letter from Giuliani because if it existed, it would have gone to Ostreicher and you would need a crowbar to get it from him.

Immediately after this, a lawyer who knows the political landscape took over. Rosina Abramson has an honorable background as counsel in the office of the old city council president, and her client does not. It is obvious that a contractor trying it alone has as much chance as he would trying to walk in the sky. For it can take the work of the legitimate and illegitimate to get anything done.

Rosina Abramson, Esq.
135 East 57th Street
Suite 1100
New York, NY 10022

December 5, 1995
Phil Dameshek, Esq.
Dept. of General Services, Division of Real Estate
Municipal Building, 20th Floor So.
1 Centre Street

Dear Phil:
   Thank you for your advice regarding my client, Eugene Ostreicher, who is seeking to redeem. . . . He has taken assignments from the former property owners. . . . I'm also enclosing a recent letter he wrote to Mayor Giuliani. I would appreciate your guidance regarding how this matter can be brought to Commissioner Diamond's attention. Thanks.

Dec. 7, 1995
Randal Fong, Assistant Commissioner, Planning
Dept. of General Services
Municipal Building, 20th Floor So.

Dear Randy:
   I certainly understand your concerns regarding competition. I believe we can structure a restricted competition that protects and benefits all parties, particularly the City and the public. . . .

December 8, 1995
Richard J. Schwartz
Senior Advisor to the Mayor
City Hall

Dear Richard:
   First, let me thank you for participating in the panel discussion on Business Improvement Districts, sponsored by the

Municipal Affairs committee of the Bar Association. Your focus on encouraging private enterprise inspired me to think more creatively regarding an interest in a client which should coincide with furthering city policies, both with regard to in rem vacant land and affordable housing. . . .

December 12, 1995
Hon. William J. Diamond
Commissioner, Dept. of General Services
Municipal Building, 17th Floor
1 Centre Street

Re: Privatizing in rem vacant land, fostering private development—a pilot project proposal

Dear Commissioner Diamond:
   . . . I understand that DGS has recently suspended its Adjacent Home Owners Program (AHOP). . . . Rather than eliminate this privatization strategy, I suggest eliminating restrictions and expanding the program, at least on a pilot basis. . . .
   A case in point . . . is presented by the situation in which my client, Eugene Ostreicher, finds himself. Mr. Ostreicher, through his own personal initiative and individual enterprise, has begun to turn an abandoned block in Williamsburg into affordable housing. My client is seeking to redeem in rem properties adjacent to property he is developing on Lorimer and Middleton Streets . . . in the Williamsburg section of Brooklyn. I'm enclosing a recent letter he wrote to Mayor Giuliani expressing his desire to build on the in rem parcels. . . .

                      Sincerely yours,
                      Rosina Abramson

Chapter Seventeen

IT HAPPENED in the morning, and whoever the workers were—Polish from up in Greenpoint, Mexican from Brighton and Sunset Park—they had already gone to the hospital. The fire and police vehicles had pulled out by the time Charles Blaich, a deputy chief of the Fire Department, arrived in a department station wagon. He looked at the construction site as if it were an empty casket. This building job on Lorimer Street was a block of four-story multiple dwellings that the builder stated was to house faculty for Hasidic schools. The first wall on Lorimer Street was a stack of cinder blocks without enough support to stop the wind. Which is not a turned phrase but a precise estimate of the wall's strength: On this February morning at 7:30 in 1996 a wind strong enough to make people pull their coats around themselves came along Lorimer Street, and it simply knocked the wall down.

They had poured concrete and put heavy cinder blocks on the floor. How did they expect that to hold up? Blaich looked at the twisted beams that were the result.

As Blaich looked at the wreckage, Richie Ostreicher showed up. "Those idiots," he said.

Richie Scheirer, liaison between police and the Hasidic community, arrived, took a look, and left. "Be back," he said.

Blaich called in John Humble, the trade representative for the American Iron and Steel institute. Blaich knew him from courses in construction he had taken over a period of twenty years. The steel being used in the buildings here on Lorimer Street was dirt cheap compared to wood, but it still had great strength. That was Humble's opinion until he saw gaps in the building walls.

"What if there had been a fire?" Humble said.

Blaich stiffened. There had been a fire-alarm fire in Bay Ridge, and the C-joists had collapsed with no warning. Later inspection showed they had the appearance of cooked spaghetti.

After this, out of sight and sound in the Bronx, two units of firefighters were working a four-alarm in a building where C-joists were put up for installation on a new story being erected over the original buildings. The C-joists had no fire protection, and touched by flame, they failed immediately and soundlessly. They too were reduced to cooked spaghetti.

Collapses of C-joists became common in the parts of Williamsburg where Ostreicher built.

C-joists are cold-formed steel and were first used in 1973 to rebuild at least some of Bushwick, a neighborhood that, for the most part, was turned into char by arson in the '60s and '70s. Fires had been set for insurance by owners of buildings that were empty when whites fled the arrival of people of color. The fires then were set without the excuse of money.

C-joists are long silver beams that can be from six to twelve inches wide and an inch and a half thick. They come with an open side, thus forming the C, and the joist is then fitted onto tracks of a floor beam or wall beam. There should be sixteen inches between each C-joist. The C-joists can cost as little as a few dollars apiece but can go as high as $20. For builders cutting corners, the less you use, the more money sticks to the pocket, rather than the supplier's bill. The C-joists barely resist the first lick of a fire and become sudden death. To guard against this, contractors supposedly cover the deck C-joists with a concrete spray and the ones on the wall with plasterboard.

Blaich and Humble looked at the basement. The block of Lorimer Street buildings was supposed to have elevators, but instead there were wood staircases to the cellar. Blaich took a look from one end of the cellar to the other. A fire could come through here like it was a wind tunnel.

A firefighter coming into a burning building can gauge how long it will take burning wood beams to give way. It could be five minutes, it could be nine. Experience tells him when to flee. But when the C-joists get ready to give, you have nothing to see and everything to fear.

FIRE DEPARTMENT
2/9/96
1. e-239 responded to reported bldg collapse 49 Lorimer St. Upon arrival found row of new construction in progress. Bldgs are 2-story M/D's.
2. Questionable construction tactics being used. Bldg's experienced a lean-to collapse in early phase of construction.

3. Request review of bldg. dept. permits and architectural plans.
4. Request on site inspection by Building Dept.

Respectfully submitted,
Joseph M. Sweeney Lt. E-230

TO: Edmund P. Cunningham, Chief of Fire Prev.
FROM: Roderick J. O'Connor, Battalion Chief, Bn. 57

Upon receiving the report from E-230 and speaking with Capt. Regan E-230, I performed an on-site inspection. I concur with Lt. Sweeney's opinion and request for an immediate inspection by the building department.

The materials used for this construction appear to be acceptable but the practices putting them to use does not seem appropriate. There have been two incidents of collapse and upon viewing the site today, the floors in place seem uneven and incapable of withstanding the heavy loads they will be expected to carry. I collected two pieces of the metal floor beams used. It seems that if the flooring material (three quarters inch plywood) is not placed on these floor beams immediately, the metal floor beams tend to twist loose from their perch which is a cutout in the concrete block walls.

This construction site should be inspected as soon as possible in order to prevent any possible improper practices of construction. It is open frame now and can easily be evaluated.

Respectfully submitted,
Roderick O'Connor

On February 29, 1996, there was a third collapse, this one in the dark of night. The sound ran down empty streets. At that hour, with no workers on the job, nobody was hurt. At daylight, Chief Dillon of the Fifth Battalion arrived from the firehouse on Union Avenue, alongside the Ninetieth Precinct. Around a corner of the building was Truck Eight of Police Emergency Services. They were not needed—this time.

Dillon arrived at the scene of new rubble and had his men put up yellow crime scene tape. The Mexican workers stood across the street, uncertain. Suddenly Richie Ostreicher got out of a car with police lights and shields and any other placard he had been able to get from police commanders who thought they were dealing with a police chaplain. He called to the laborers, "We go to work."

Dillon said no.

"Forget it," Ostreicher told his crew. "We go to work."

Dillon said, "You don't."

"Who are you?" Ostreicher said.

"I'm Chief Dillon, New York City Fire Department. I closed this place."

"You can't do that."

"Yes, I can. I'm in charge here until I hand over the place to somebody else, the Buildings Department."

"I own this place," Ostreicher said.

"I closed it," Dillon said.

"What do you know?" he asked Dillon.

"I know I'm a fire chief in charge."

"You don't know buildings."

"I went to school for it," Dillon said.

"What degree did you get?"

"GED." (Everybody knew that he got that degree from a high school continuation course.)

"What's that?"

"General Engineering Diploma."

"Oh," Richie Ostreicher said.

Dillon's men stood in a semicircle with him and tried not to smile.

Now Ostreicher said, "Can I talk to you?"

"That's what you're doing," Dillon said.

"No, I mean, alone. Over there." He pointed to the other side of the street.

"All right," Dillon said. He tapped his aide, Chris Steidinger, who walked over with him.

"We can talk alone," Ostreicher said.

"We are alone. He counts as me," Dillon said.

Ostreicher went into his pocket and brought out a gold badge. He had it cupped in his hand and held the hand close to his pants pocket.

"Do you know what this is?"

Dillon looked at it. A gold shield with two stars on it. Some kind of police inspector's badge.

Dillon said nothing.

"This doesn't mean anything to you?" Ostreicher said, pushing the cupped hand toward Dillon.

"Are you a member of the Police Department of the City of New York?" Dillon said.

Quickly Ostreicher put the badge back in his pocket. Once Dillon started making it official, he stepped back.

Dillon drove back to the firehouse.

FIRE DEPARTMENT
ENGINE CO. 230
FEB. 25, 1996

Responded to a structural collapse at 49 Lorimer Street. This was the THIRD COLLAPSE in the past few weeks at this construction site. Fortunately, the workmen were able to escape without injury. The Owner Chaim Ostreicher was given three summons.

I AM REQUESTING A PERMANENT STOP WORK ORDER AND JOINT INSPECTION OF CONSTRUCTION SITE TO DETERMINE STRUCTURAL STABILITY OF EXISTING STRUCTURES.

See attached report dated 2/9/96 from BC O'Connor, fwded after the SECOND COLLAPSE. . . .

Respectfully submitted,
Edward J. Regan, Captain, E230.

Hertzberg & Sanchez
Consulting Engineers
295 Northern Boulevard, Great Neck, NY 11921-4701

Feb. 26, 1996
Department of Buildings, Borough of Brooklyn
Att: Mr. Darryl Hilton
Chief Inspector

RE: *29 Lorimer Street (#300437800)*
      21 Lorimer Street (#300437837)
      41 Lorimer Street (#300437064)

Dear Mr. Hilton:
This will confirm that Hertzberg and Sanchez will be

*observing the construction in progress to assure that the walls
will be properly braced by the installation of the floor joists.*

   *The bricklayers have been instructed to brace the walls
before they close for the day.*

   *We require immediate approval to continue with the work
as vandalism is rampant in the area.*

Very truly yours,
Louis Sanchez, P.E.
Vice-President

The engineers wrote as if they were in charge, which they
were. Because the city Building Department, which sounds
like a massive government bureau, is so small, with only eight
hundred workers, including office maintenance workers, recep-
tionists, and computer workers, there is no way to inspect the
eight hundred thousand buildings in the city, particularly if
City Hall cuts the funds to nothing. Buildings Department
people rarely see any structures. The architects and professional
engineers supposedly put up their reputations and license and
certify each of their construction jobs. If anything falls down,
their licenses flop with it. That never happens. What does happen every day is that the trust of a huge city is given to people
with no official responsibility.

On March 14, 1996, Michael Caterina, a compliance officer
from the Occupational Safety and Health Administration—
which is commonly known as OSHA—received an anonymous
complaint about collapses of Ostreicher buildings on Lorimer
Street. In the building world, an anonymous complaint is too
often a phoned-in stiletto. Business competitors or personal
enemies regard them as a marvelous way to hurt another.
Caterina, then, was wary when he walked down Lorimer Street.

Here, standing in the street, a statue of a biblical character
who suddenly was breathing, was Eugene Ostreicher. He was
short, stocky, and suspicious. He was in black from hat to shoes.
A great white beard billowed at the cheeks. Prominent dark
eyebrows stood out over his pale blue eyes. He had the brusque
movements of someone used to being in charge on the street.
He was impatient when Michael Caterina of OSHA spoke to
him in the middle of Lorimer.

Caterina asked Ostreicher if there had ever been a collapse at the site.

"What collapse? What are you talking about? Do you see a collapse? Tell me. Do you see a collapse?" He waved at his site of attached three-story brick condominiums. "A collapse. Where did you get that from?"

"I heard that," Caterina said.

"Where did you hear that from? Who told you that? You heard a fairy tale from somebody."

"You're stating that there have been no collapses at this site?" Caterina said in official tones.

"Absolutely. There never is a collapse here."

Caterina went back to the OSHA offices on Varick Street in Manhattan and typed up a report with Ostreicher's answer to an official question from a government agent.

If Ostreicher hadn't been so quick and boisterous to hurl out his denials, Caterina might have helped him. OSHA has only civil penalties, and the staff would have been anxious to push Ostreicher away from dangerous practices. He liked loud lying better. And this became obvious, and started Caterina on investigating the building being done on the block. First, there were witnesses who had seen a collapse. Then there were the Fire Department records. Caterina then began to talk about this lying with James Vanderberg, a thirty-two-year-old agent for the United States Department of Labor. This agency could prosecute criminally. The file on Ostreicher now included the results of all this investigating, along with Fire Department reports of collapses on the scene and of Ostreicher's involvement with the buildings. Neither memos nor Fire Department reports would go away. They were written and filed in the time of computers, but the paper lasted and the reports retained their clarity and impact about the three collapses in February 1996.

Joseph Trivisonno, the buildings superintendent for Brooklyn, was in anguish trying to keep his job against stiff interference on the Lorimer Street buildings. Suddenly, Trivisonno was bewildered by the papers about a building being built at 26 Heyward Street, up the block from the brick condominiums being built by Eugene Ostreicher. The more he looked at the papers, the more his eyes narrowed. He was on crazy street. The plans for 26 Heyward were for a building that was 108 feet deep. That allowed room for the building and for a 35-foot-deep backyard as required by law. Trivisonno knew that the lot was only 100 feet deep. Somewhere the builder had to reach into the air and come up with eight feet of Brooklyn land. The owner of the land behind the offending building said he wanted to keep his eight feet and would fight all the way to the Supreme Court for it.

At the end of 1996, two businessmen who were of the Puppa sect of Hasidim bought 26 Heyward and wanted to change the footprint of the building, the floor-to-area ratio, to build nine condominiums in the five-story building to house faculty for a yeshiva. Under the zoning laws, if you put even as little as a rabbi's office in a building, you were allowed to enlarge it. Excavation for number 26, on an empty lot next door to number 18, and the placement of struts between the old and new buildings (which meant the new building was holding up the old one) put cosmetic cracks in the old building. A complaint came in by phone, and Trivisonno had his inspectors stop the job until 18 Heyward was stabilized. No blueprints had been turned in. Another call brought a claim that there was no such religious anchor as a rabbi's office in their five-story building, but there were condominiums that would go for $350,000 each.

The records of the United States Department of Education show that a great college was located in the tan two-story building a few doors up at 105 Heyward Street. Supposedly, it was a converted yeshiva grammar school. It became the most ambitious temporal reach of the Skver Hasidic group, who came out of Russian mud to Williamsburg. They also occupy their own town of New Square, in near upstate Rockland County.

In a bakery on the corner of Heyward, the milk bottles have the labels of New Square Farms, the upstate milk farm of the Skver group. There are about three thousand living in New Square, eleven hundred of them registered voters. All are dedicated to study and the passing of knowledge and wisdom to those who follow. While this is a beautiful way of life, all this studying takes as many as thirteen hours a day, and this leaves no time for a job. Simultaneously, bills must be paid with more than prayer. One day, four of the men of the village sat down and developed a plan that would allow the village to study and still have an income. They announced a university-level school called Toldos Yakov Yosef. The students were not required to attend classes, but regular contact with an assigned mentor was supposedly required. The school was beautiful to run in that it required no start-up fees other than the few dollars for applications for government Pell grants for students. The Pell grants are American government at its most indescribably beautiful. Named after Claiborne Pell, the senator from Rhode Island, they are federal college tuition assistance grants—not loans—awarded to undergraduates and based on income. It gives a student without enough money some help to finish an education. The students receive grants of $1,500 or so, with a maximum of $3,300 a year. The program has some defenses against the stray schemer, but it never envisioned nor threw up breastworks against an organized criminal raid from a place like Heyward Street, Williamsburg. Soon, the new university had 1,544 checks for Pell grants coming in the mail to the school. This made the school more than somewhat profitable. . . .

Because there was no school.

While 105 Heyward grammar school was the address, there were no students. There was no faculty. There were no books.

On streets whose waking hours were dedicated to trimming corners, Eugene Ostreicher looked up from his cinder blocks and bricks a block or so away, and found his shaky buildings produced loud, treacherous candy store money in comparison to 105 Heyward, where they had only to empty the mailbox each day to gain their fortune.

They collected the Pell grants for the first year of their no-show college. There wasn't even a letter asking a question. They went on to the second year and it was better yet: they added a few students and received grants for them. After this, year after year it went on, and the school brought in $40 million of government money. All of New Square studied and prayed, and the bills were paid. Four people ran the school. They spent all of their time cashing checks and evading inspections.

A federal Department of Education group, including agent Brian Hickey, finally moved on Heyward Street, the home of the great university. This time, Hickey came in with a scheduled government inspection, from which there could be neither postponement nor subterfuge. Also, it was scheduled for five days, from the second through the sixth of June, 1992, with a full team of inspectors. The school could not stand the light of a heavy candle.

The inspectors began with the book lists of the college students. They discovered that books bought with Pell grants were high school books for the eleventh and twelfth grades of the yeshiva schools upstate in New Square.

The inspectors found that the chief administrators listed on the Pell grant records were: Chancellor Chaim Berger, the "brilliant thirty-two-year-old nationally known educator," and the registrar, Kalmen Stern.

Hickey found the chancellor in a room on the first floor. He was in fact a ninety-one-year-old man.

"Hello," Berger said.

"Are you the chancellor?" he was asked.

"Hello," the old man said.

Next Hickey met the registrar, Kalmen Stern. Somehow he got Stern to write something for him. "Write down what you think of your job," Hickey said. Stern wrote, "He has a good car." Then he wrote what he thought of America: "A-M-R-I-C-A."

The first floor of 105 Heyward had some old men reading religious textbooks. They had been gathered up from the neighborhood and thrown into a sudden university.

There was a great amount of noise from the second floor, where the student body, preschool and kindergarten kids ages three to six, was running about. They had been dispossessed from their usual first-floor playroom to make room for the university inspection.

The inspection team asked to speak to six college students. The school could produce only four. Registrar Stern presented a man who said he was a college student.

"When did you enroll?" Hickey asked.

"What do you mean by enroll?" the man asked.

A woman had a transcript that showed two years of philosophy courses.

An agent asked her, "Do you know what philosophy is?"

"No."

A woman named Polyna was introduced as an English major.

She needed a Russian interpreter to speak to one of the inspectors.

"Student number 21," the federal report stated, "could not recall when he started at the school, but thought he had attended last year. Student 21 stated that he did not understand most of what went on because he doesn't know the English language.

"Student No. 23 stated he did not have time to discuss education. Student 23 did not respond to questions regarding the subjects studied. He asked the reviewers to put the questions in writing and send them to him."

When the reviewers were leaving, the educational genius, ninety-one-year-old Chaim Berger, looked up from a nap.

"Hello."

Back in the Manhattan offices, the federal education team filed a simple report: "We are requesting emergency action and termination be taken against Toldos Yakov Yosef."

The students and school were an illusion, but the money from government grants was more than somewhat real.

The New Square educators took down $40 million from the government over ten years. In recorded American crime— groups under five members, no weapons—this receives all-time honorable mention.

But then it went further. There were four people sent to prison over this. On the day they went in, Skvers were writing letters to get them out. The Skvers were ceaseless and went from one official to the other until, in the year 2000, they wound up with a president's wife who thought everything she looked at, from trinket to mansion, was hers. Hillary Clinton was running for the Senate. All Hasidic groups voted against her, for good reason: She was a woman. However, at New Square, she willingly walked on the women's side of the street, and did not shake hands with the men. When meeting the wise man, Rebbe Twersky, she sat with the desk between them. The town of New Square alone voted for her, by 1,200 to nothing. After the election, all she saw was black hats. She then made an appointment at the White House for Rebbe Twersky. The date was for a Friday. The rebbe and his people were unsure of where the White House was. One of them called an editor of a Jewish publication in Brooklyn and asked, "Can the rebbe go to Washington and come back in time for sundown?" At the White House, Twersky and Ms. Clinton, now a senator-elect, sat happily as Bill Clinton issued a presidential pardon for the New Square prisoners. That night in Borough Park, Brooklyn, a non-Jew, and therefore one who could answer a phone that day, rushed into a synagogue and told the son of one of the New Square prisoners, "They pardoned your father!"

In February 1997, the mayor was up for reelection, and with the first rustle of campaign money sounding in Williamsburg, the expediter for 26 Heyward Street headed out of the computer room and went down the hall into Joseph Trivisonno's office. Trivisonno remembers the expediter telling him to get a zoning change that would take care of the missing eight feet. Trivisonno said his department did not get zoning changes or grab land out of thin air. Trivisonno says the expediter said to him, "You get approval for us."

Trivisonno remembers saying that he could not.

"We'll get you."

"The next thing was somebody saying I was anti-Semitic," Trivisonno said.

Kenny Fisher, a city councilman from an old, well-known Brooklyn political family, suppressed that quickly.

Afterward Trivisonno felt the first fatigue. "If I had to ask for all this help for nothing, then how am I going to last through something that actually happens?" he said to a friend.

Mayor Giuliani announced a policy of closing X-rated movie houses and bookstores because they hurt children. He ordered seventy-five building inspectors out to do the work. Forty percent of a store had to be legitimate books and videos. The rest of it could be for adults. As the history of censorship could serve as wallpaper for a psychiatric ward, sex shop owners began to stock shelves with biographies of Daniel Boone. Once these hit the required 40 percent, here came all those adult books.

This brought the former Carmella Lauretano, who is the wife of a building inspector on detached duty in sex shops, to see Trivisonno. As Trivisonno recalls it, she said to him, "Make my husband get off that job. My husband is a building inspector. You have him in whorehouses. My husband is a family man. You got to stop this."

* * *

Fire Chief Blaich called a meeting of technical people from the Buildings Department, engineers and experts in construction. They stood on the street in front of the Lorimer Street buildings, and each time Blaich pointed out a dangerous flaw, they all concurred. "Ostreicher should be stopped from doing any building," Blaich said. "We'll put it in writing. We'll all sign it and that should put it over." Suddenly the group with him began to shrink. "You better do that yourself," one of them said. Blaich said, "Why only me?" The guy said, "Because you're civil service."

Blaich wrote the letter and sent it in.

The answer came on August 26, 1998, when the first of eleven certificates of occupancy was signed by Joseph Trivisonno and issued to the owner of the Lorimer Street buildings. A certificate of occupancy means you can move into, rent, or sell the building, which has been certified as legal by the City of New York.

Trivisonno said that the building defects had been cured and that in all other cases such as this the building was allowed to be completed and certificates issued.

Blaich shrugged. He had gone further than anybody had before. He had made charges on paper and signed it. The cave-in this time was Trivisonno. Of course it wasn't enough. Nothing helped Trivisonno, either. In City Hall, they still complained that Trivisonno was obstructing commerce in Brooklyn. Commissioner Gaston Silva wanted him to take a leave. "Teitelbaum is the one who wants to get you," Silva said, "but we hear he may be going. He'll head Giuliani's campaign when he runs for the Senate. When he goes, you can come right back."

Next, Silva asked about the problem with 26 Heyward Street. Trivisonno said the owner had claimed faculty housing that in fact wouldn't be there, and that there was an eight-foot overlap problem. Silva hung up. Trivisonno now heard from a secretary: "They want you out." Trivisonno called the commissioner and asked who wanted him out. Trivisonno resigned in March. He was replaced by Tarek Zeid, whose wife is an expediter. Zeid departed and soon, Commissioner Silva was gone.

Chapter Eighteen

THAT DAY, Eduardo got home by 4:30 and called Silvia, and this time he got her before she left for work. She had spent most of the hours after finishing her morning job at the mall on the other side of Highway 6. She had bought pants and blouses for her sisters back home and Winnie the Pooh toys for her nieces. Her sister Emilia was with her now; she had been stopped twice at the border and frightened several times in the desert, but there was no thought of giving up. Silvia got her jobs at both the barbecue restaurant and the Olive Garden. Between them they were sending home $2,500 a month. They now had a one-bedroom apartment, near where Silvia had first lived. That one had been filled with enough relatives to form the trunk of a family tree.

When Eduardo called Silvia this time, he talked about his job. "He told me he had to climb up on the building," Silvia remembers. "He told me that the work was very hard. Then he said again that he had to climb up on the building. He said the sun was cruel. He had to climb up. He said he didn't like that. It seemed shaky to him. I knew he had never been that high up. I asked him if it was dangerous, and he said it was. I didn't know what else to say. He was there. I was here. What could we do?"

For Eduardo the days had changed only because he was not staying home in the room so much. Now he came to the room in Brighton Beach right after work, took a shower, and went out. He was the youngest of the group by five years, and the age difference with the roommates had become wearing. On Friday night, the others started out at the round table in the kitchen, and Alejandro drank one beer with great gulps, then another and a third, after which he reached for the bottle of tequila. The rest tried to keep up with him. Originally when they did this, Eduardo would sit on the kitchen floor and make fun of them, or he'd go into their room and fall asleep. But over the months he saw that drinking was a morose celebration and that conversation consisted of short bursts of despair. When they needed more alcohol, somebody went down to the store on Neptune Avenue. Later, Eduardo noticed that one of them would leave and wouldn't return for some time, after which a couple of others would leave. After a few months, he figured out they were going with prostitutes in doorways and cars. Once, in one long drunk that went on for a day and a half, Alejandro drank thirty bottles of Corona beer and a bottle of tequila. There were no classic drinking stories told of this episode. Only the number of bottles was cited. Alejandro had a fierce hangover, but neither he nor the others could speak about it with any humor. One sad night of drink in the kitchen became another the next week, and the weeks became months and the months would become years.

Not only did late-night homesickness torture them, but the loneliness became more searing in the sunlight. They sat in the room and told themselves—and then their wives and children on the phone—that they would be home soon. They did not learn English because they were sure of leaving for home forever. They drank at sunrise on weekends and spoke only in Spanish, thus robbing themselves of any chance for better work.

Many times, Eduardo went to watch television in his friend Lucino's room two flights over Kings Highway, a subway stop up from Brighton. Lucino lived with his cousin Julisa and her husband and two children. He was a short, stocky, handsome thirty-two-year-old with a prominent nose. Working in Mexico City as an accountant, he saw there was no future and left. He came unannounced to Julisa's apartment. Why wouldn't he? He was a relative. After a couple of days, it was plain. Why would he ever leave? He lived there.

Following this, one night Lucino's brother Pedro called. "I'm here," he said.

"Where?" Julisa said.

"At the airport. I'm coming over."

Pedro came in, sat down, weary from travel, and went to sleep. Next, a cousin, José, called from the airport. He, too, was coming over. He, too, could not be moved if you put dynamite under his feet. Soon another of Lucino's brothers called from the airport. Julisa couldn't remember his name, but knew he could eat. Lucino mentioned vaguely that Aunt Matilda might be coming in from Mexico. Julisa thought that this would be sometime in the distant future, and in the meantime Aunt

Matilda could get arrested at the border. Two nights later, the
phone rang. "I'm here!" Aunt Matilda cried.

First they put the men in one room and the women and baby
in the other. Finally, Julisa's husband told her that her cousin
had to clear the place. Lucino did. He told all the others to
leave, and he took over a room for himself. Lucino was out
looking for work from the start. He knew one here and another
there and he wound up catching on with a construction job
that was starting on Middleton Street. He worked there with
Eduardo. Lucino had a treasure: a room to himself. Soon Eduardo was walking into the apartment with his head hanging
like a penitent's and he'd slip into Lucino's room without
talking. They usually drank and watched pro basketball. When
he went in there on one night, Julisa heard something slapping
a board and one of them laughing. They were playing some
board game, soccer football probably.

Julisa was nineteen and in the second year of medical school
in Mexico City when she and a couple of students came for a
holiday to her hometown of San José edo de Tlaxcala, which is
near Puebla. She had a twin sister, Lourdes, and seven brothers.

Julisa and her classmates arrived on the one day of the year
that the fair came to town. Her glance took in children's rides
and the booths for games and stopped when she saw the
handsome young guy in the booth with soccer games on the
counter. The guy was putting prizes on a shelf. Of course the
woman is not supposed to be so forward as to walk up alone to
a booth with a man behind it.

No such thing could happen. The young man in the booth,
José J. Eduardo, had his entire attention captured by Julisa,
whose long hair and large beautiful eyes filled with gladness
caused her dignity to evaporate. His mother, who sold lottery
tickets a few booths away, thought she noticed something. He
came out from behind the counter and promptly stumbled. He
then ran up to Julisa and the others and asked if they wanted
to play the soccer game on the table outside the booth. Julisa
answered for everybody. She said yes and she went up to that
strange game and played it as best she could, and played it
for most of the night, her smile so expressive, her shoulders
moving with her words, and all of it for this young man who
was handsome and so attentive.

He could not wait to graze her.

She decided to marry him.

Professors at the medical school in Mexico City said dolefully that she wouldn't be able to finish school if she was married.

"When you fall in love, whatever you say, I still get married," she says. But she stayed in school, although she was studying with one emotion and dying to get married with another.

Two years later, she came to her town to get married in church. The reception was in her home.

She was pregnant in five minutes and was angry with herself and her husband. The couple didn't have enough money, and their families couldn't help. She took a bookkeeping job in a Mexico City bakery. The new husband studied chemical engineering but still had to travel with his family to these one-day fairs. With her last year in school and three years of residency in front of her, Julisa had a miscarriage. She couldn't even pay for books. She dropped out. I'll try next year, she told herself.

Her twin sister, Lourdes, and her husband went with another couple to Tijuana, and Lourdes called to report that they were going across the border on Saturday night. The hospital in Tijuana called on Sunday to say that Lourdes and two others were dead as a result of beatings that were apparently handed out by marauding thieves in the scrub. Julisa had been raised in the same womb and bed with her sister, but she shucked off as much misery as possible and tried to help raise the money to bring Lourdes back for a funeral.

Two years later, she and her husband were living in defeat in Mexico City. She wasn't a day closer to returning to school, and he couldn't get a job in engineering. They saved and borrowed $1,800 for a coyote to cross them at Tijuana. We will make it all up in America, and I'll come back for school, she told herself. Then she and the husband left for Tijuana.

Fear owned her as she walked and ran over the same soil where her sister had died. The coyote had them hide in a garbage dump. Then they were among a group of five who stuffed themselves into the back of a van going to Los Angeles.

The woman who rented them the first room in Brooklyn instructed Julisa and her husband never to go outside except to go to work and back, because the police would arrest them, and the police were everywhere.

Julisa brought two babies home to these rooms but learned

only snatches of English. "We were afraid to go to school at night for English," she remembers. They moved into the rooms on Kings Highway, and her brother Valentine came to live with them, which gave them an extra hand with baby-sitting and the rent. Mostly, the husband watched the babies while she went out and cleaned houses. When she came home, he left to sweep out a beauty parlor. She paid out the toughest thousand dollars for a booklet, "Fast Practical English," put out by the UCEDA English Institute, which counted her thousand in English. She picked up a couple of new words and not much more after listening to the CD sent by the institute. Supposedly, there were classes she could attend in a hall someplace, but she was never able to get there.

While a social worker was complaining about the UCEDA English Institute to Joel Magallan, SJ, the director of the Asociación Tepeyac de New York, he waved a hand.

"The Mexicans already know a second language," he said. "The ones from Puebla were raised on Aztec Indian—we call it Nahuatl. Then in school they had to learn mainstream Spanish. The other Indian language they learn as babies is Tarahumara. That is spoken in the Sierra Nevada mountains. Otomi is the first language of those in Baja. Mayan is spoken first in Chiapas."

One day, Julisa's brother left on his bicycle for his job at a refrigerator manufacturer on Atlantic Avenue, a wide, extremely busy street. A while later, a policeman came to the door to tell Julisa that her brother was dead. There had been a two-car accident, and he couldn't get out of the way and was killed.

Once more, she had to grope through her grief to come up with money for a dead body.

Now here she is, five years after leaving medical school, standing in her room, a baby sleeping on her bed that is covered with a big brilliant red Mexican blanket. Still, energy and enthusiasm fill her eyes and brighten her face and she says that soon, yes, soon, she will be able to leave this place and go back to medical school in Mexico. It is still the reason she does not try to find time to go to school for English. Why should she? She just told you that soon she would be going back.

Never once does she pause to realize that she has no money for any school, and that she is a cleaning woman when she should be a doctor, and that her husband is sweeping up in a beauty parlor when he should be an engineer. And that all around them the lives of the Mexicans are the same. Here in her house right now, Lucino is an accountant, and he was the cheapest of labor. Visiting for the basketball games was Alejandro, an upholsterer who works for perhaps a dollar over minimum wage. Simultaneously you'd look at each week's pay with Mexican peasant eyes—it was rich man's money—and then add their weekly bills in Brooklyn and realize they live at the bottom.

At those moments when Julisa suddenly saw the walls of her room for what they were, a life sentence, she said to herself right away, soon I will go back to school. She says that through each year.

Does she still love the husband she met at the fair?

"For my children I love him."

And Eduardo worked at bricklaying, which he knew, for the lowest money in all of construction. He didn't have the slightest idea that a white in New York gets $23 an hour for the same work. How could he know such a thing? Nobody could speak English, and the only people they knew had jobs as bad or worse. Sometimes Julisa felt sad for Eduardo when he walked past her as if afraid to talk.

When Eduardo went out at other times, he hung out in front of the Mexican store on Neptune Avenue with a kid named El Viejo, which means "the old man." He was twenty. They went to the boardwalk at Coney Island and played video games and talked with others who were their age. Frequently, they now rode the el up to Fifth Avenue in Brooklyn, where one night in a Mexican restaurant the waitress looked at Eduardo and when he put his chin down, she put her hand under it and lifted it. "I like you the best," she told him. His chin went right back down.

When they left the place, everybody was laughing at Eduardo because of his shyness. It was one thing for the older guys back in the room to make fun of him, but these were kids his own age. He told them that he would show them all. He would go back to the restaurant and take the waitress out of there for all to see how much she loved him. A week later, he walked ahead of the others into the restaurant; he didn't know exactly what he was going to do, but for sure they were not going to laugh at him anymore because he was going to talk to that waitress and make her like him and go out with him. Nobody would laugh. He walked in and found another waitress working. He asked for the one he wanted. "She quit," the owner said.

On March 11, 1999, an application for a $2 million general liability insurance policy on Ostreicher property under the name of Faye Industries Corp., 527 Bedford Avenue, was forwarded by a broker to Greg Portnoy, a broker in the Westchester suburb of White Plains who places accounts with the First Financial Insurance Company, which has an Illinois license but conducts business all over, much of it in the state of North Carolina.

The application called for the policy to be in effect on March 17, 1999. It was a simple three-page questionnaire of yes-or-no answers in boxes. There were two questions about background, the first of which appears to be there only to please the religious beliefs of Carolina:

> 7. Any past losses or claims relating to sexual abuse or molestation allegations, discrimination or negligent hiring?

Let no hands commit a sin of the flesh in a lumberyard. (The discrimination and hiring can be considered a throw-in.)

Answer: no.

The next question was at the center of the insurance business:

> 8. During the past ten years has any applicant been convicted of any degree of the crime of arson? The question must be answered by any applicant. Failure to disclose the substance of an arson conviction is a misdemeanor punishable by a sentence of up to one year of imprisonment.

Answer: no.

There is not even a thought of punishment, save loss of this particular policy, for some grubby child molester. Strike one match without admitting it and, according to the piece of paper, leg irons can be clamped on.

As collateral, Faye Industries listed ten vacant lots and two buildings. The lots happened to have buildings on them. Industrial Enterprises listed five vacant lots and one building. Ramon,

Inc., listed four empty lots and a building. Both Ostreichers said they had three empty lots. A cousin, Samuel Newman, was down for three vacant lots. Middleton Street, where everybody worked, had seven addresses that were listed as vacant lots. This could disorient an experienced postman. Later, a lawyer for First Financial thought that the number of addresses for Middleton Street were there to dizzify those looking at the application.

Then on the third page of the application there were three questions, short and easily answered.

12. Any structural alterations contemplated?

Answer: no.

13. Any demolition exposure contemplated?

Answer: no.

14. Has applicant been active in or is currently active in joint ventures?

Answer: no.

One possible explanation for all of Ostreicher's answers was that it was cheaper to insure an empty lot than a building full of workers. Anyway, who was going to check? If there was no catastrophe, the policy would sleep in a file. Who would be dumb enough to list all the work being done and pay those higher premiums?

On the last blank on the application, Ostreicher came up with his personal safety net:

APPLICANT'S SIGNATURE: _____

The space was blank.

Two brokers and an insurance company collected premiums. Therefore, the policy was good. What does it matter if the guy forgot to sign his name? Just an oversight. We'll get it when we get it.

They could not envision Ostreicher sitting at a legal

proceeding and saying, in substance, "It is not my policy. I
never signed it. This policy is full of mistakes made by some
clerk in the insurance company. I have never seen such an
application full of errors. You can see I never signed it. Where
is my signature?"

8/10/99 BF 25 FIRE OPERATION REPORT
58 Middleton Street. On arrival found cause for alarm to
be a partial collapse of a building under construction with
workers trapped. Engine 269 stretched hand lines, stood
fast assisted with first aid and victim transport. Three non-
life-threatening injuries to workers, all taken to Bellevue.
A two story building 20 feet by 40 feet. A phone alarm at
11:17 units here four minutes later 11:21 all hands at 11:23
three engines and two trucks and special units rescue two
squad one. Under control 12:42. Three civilian victims.
Chief Corcoran from 11th division pd 90. Buildings Mr.
Maniscalco on site. Supervisor Leon Schwimmer Industrial, 527 Bedford. Block Foreman Colin Torney.

Since the accident had happened at the far end of the construction site, none of the Mexicans knew about it. Only that
something had happened.

The three workers battered in the collapse of a floor went
out through the building's rear and were taken over the bridge
to Bellevue Hospital on First Avenue in Manhattan, which
is the Yankee Stadium of emergency rooms. Their names on
police aided cards were Herb Lubin, Brian Dubois, and Robert
Jackson. All the Mexican workers were at the other end of the
construction site. They let these three work together because
they spoke no Spanish. The injuries were minor: a sprain, a
bruise. They had no medical coverage from the job. They
walked out of Bellevue and went into the perpetual night of
itinerant workers.

Only Eduardo and his brother José knew about this collapse.
A few days later, the boss, Leo Schwimmer, sent them up to the
building. (Leon Schwimmer, known as Leo, is the father-in-law
of Faye Schwimmer, who is the daughter of Eugene Ostreicher.
Faye and her husband, Ed, who live in Ostreicher's house at 527
Bedford, are part owners of the sites on Lorimer and Middleton

Streets. Including the founding father, Eugene, there are eight Ostreicher relatives on the building company's payroll.) José says now, "The building wasn't level. It didn't have a lot of beams. We wanted to know who was working there but we couldn't ask or we'd be fired."

The cause of the collapse was cinder blocks heaved onto the third level before cement poured on the C-joists as support had hardened. The cinder blocks were put there because the man in charge of the job, Eugene Ostreicher, had ordered them to be.

The day after the accident, Blaich was on the block when Ostreicher drove up.

"The fools!" Ostreicher said of the people working for the lowest money. "I told them not to put anything heavy on the floor. They're fools!"

Someone at the Buildings Department put in papers for violations and went home. His job was done, and he knew the paper would be in a file or on a computer forever because anything to do with Ostreicher, or any other Hasidic builder, was fixed by City Hall in advance.

Blaich, who admits to having had more faith, was at least surprised when the job, which had been closed for three days, suddenly reopened with Ostreicher and his engineers, Hertzberg and Sanchez, standing with one foot on the Mexican workers as usual. The Buildings Department sent no inspectors to see if they were making anything any safer. The Buildings Department issued a statement saying that, under the law, they do not have to inspect such a building until it is completed.

Chapter Nineteen

H IS THIRTY-SECOND birthday was on the twelfth of September, 1999, a Sunday, which is why Nelson Negrón
is sure of most of the things that happened. The day before,
Saturday, he had been out on the curb in front of the bodega
on Bedford, and at eight o'clock a van pulled up and the guy
called out for three people who wanted to work. Nelson and
his friend Miguel got in the van, which took them to a factory
in Long Island City where they spent the day moving sewing
machines. To push a machine was a two-man job. Even so, by
the middle of the afternoon their arms were made of lead. The
guy gave Nelson and Miguel $60 and drove them back to the
bodega. Nelson walked home. His roommate, Tony, had rice
and beans ready. After that, Nelson watched television and fell
asleep.

"My birthday," he said when he woke up at 7 A.M.

"Happy birthday," Tony said. "What are you going to do?"

"To work. I have no choice."

He got dressed and walked to the bodega, the DR, on
Bedford Avenue. He had a pastrami sandwich and coffee and
stood outside on Bedford, eating and hoping for the great job,
a birthday present, a trailer truck from the south coming up
and paying a hundred for the day to unload it. Instead, Leo
Schwimmer pulled up in a green van and asked Negrón if he
wanted to make $50. Put the $50 together with the $60 from
the day before and I got $110 to begin the week, Nelson told
himself. Beauty! If I ever put together five days, including the
weekend, on top of this, then I got the best week I ever had
working.

Negrón enthusiastically went over to the van, which he
remembers had a sliding door. Leo knew from past jobs that
Negrón could speak the language and was a good strong worker.
Nelson had worked on beams, support beams, and taping for
Leo. When Leo got to the Middleton Street site, a full crew was
working. That it was Sunday meant nothing to Leo, and was
not vital to the Mexicans, who believed that work is prayer. Leo
told Nelson to get fifty-pound sacks of cement up to the third

level of the new buildings. The building fronts were wide open. Framing would come later. They were working on a series of four-story brick houses that started at the corner bodega and ran up the street, taking in numbers 40–50 on Middleton Street. Across from the houses was a dreary brick grammar school.

Nelson got a sack on his shoulder and stepped up to the bottom level of the scaffold. That was one. Now he went up another level. Heaving and sweating already, up the scaffold he went, looking up at Eduardo's face and a roof held up by false hope.

"Too heavy!" Eduardo said. By this time, September 1999, he had gone from the curb at Bedford to construction sites all over Brooklyn, one job leading to another. Finally he was part of the crew on this group of buildings being built by Ostreicher. This was the job he had first heard about in Mexico.

"Nothing is too heavy for me," Negrón remembers saying. He weighs 220 and can handle weight.

He threw the sack onto the floor. The wood went up and down. Not a lot, but just enough to give him the idea that the floor where they were working was no good.

Negrón stayed on the scaffold and looked in. There were little cracks in the few beams he could see holding up this top floor. There were only three beams across.

Seeing that Negrón, too, had noticed the floor support, Eduardo asked, "Where's the rest of the beams?"

When Negrón complained, Eduardo's friend, Lucino, knew Negrón was saying the truth, but he didn't know what to do about it.

"We could get hurt," Negrón remembers Eduardo saying.

"You could get more than that," Negrón said.

He remembers that Alejandro then came over and said, "Could we get killed?"

"That's right," Negrón said.

"What are we supposed to do?" Alejandro said.

"I don't know," Negrón said.

"If we say it, the boss fires us," Alejandro said.

"This is how he wants it," Negrón said.

"It's wrong, but he told me to do it this way," Eduardo said.

"Around here," Negrón said, "around Bedford, the guy with the money runs your life."

Leo came back and told Nelson to take beams from a stack of shining aluminum and lug them to the top level. First, Negrón went to the corner bodega to get a bottle of water. They had learned that soft drinks don't do you much good.

Eduardo took Negrón's place with the cement sacks. Eduardo was sopping wet in the hot September afternoon as he made his way up the scaffolding with the fifty-pound sack on his shoulder. Eduardo struggled with the sack and was about to throw it on the third level when he slapped the wood with his hand. He felt it give.

"I could knock this thing down," Alejandro remembers Eduardo saying.

And he remembers saying to Eduardo, "You think so?"

"Sure."

Just inside on the third level, Eduardo had a circle of sand and a water hose and mixed the cement mushy, between dry and wet.

On the sidewalk, Leo looked around, made a phone call on his cell phone, and left.

Nelson Negrón threaded a rope through one of the utility holes in the beam and ran it up to a pulley fastened to the third level. He and a guy called Miguel then pulled the beam up. Miguel clambered up the scaffolding and got on the top level. Nelson came up behind him. Standing on the scaffolding, Nelson began to shove the beam onto the third level. He heard a sound, a screw dropping out of the scaffold. He went to put his right foot firm on the scaffolding, but there was nothing there. He was in the air, going over backward, and fell three stories to the dirt and debris.

He has no idea of how long he was there.

The first thing he saw was a man with no teeth bending over him and lifting him up by the arm. The man had on a long black sweater and good sneakers. Somebody said that the guy's name was Louis. Whoever he was, he had just appeared, and as soon as he got Negrón onto the sidewalk and propped against the base of the building, he went away.

At the same time, Negrón remembers that Leo showed up. When somebody said to call 911, Leo shouted, "No!" They had just finished three collapses around the corner and one on this block. He wanted no record of this one. He slid the door open while a couple of workers carried Nelson Negrón into the van.

When Leo delivered him in front of his apartment house, Nelson couldn't get out. He couldn't move one leg. His back was filled with barbed wire. Somebody from the sidewalk in front of his house had to come out and help him.

Negrón remembers Leo handing him $30.

"You didn't work the whole day."

He made a U-turn and drove off without looking at Nelson.

That was the last time for a while that Negrón saw anybody. Soon he had a cane and long empty days in his apartment.

Chapter Twenty

THAT NOVEMBER of 1999, Eduardo's brother José admitted that he no longer could live away from his mother and father. He also missed a girl in San Matías named Teresa. "Besides," he told Eduardo, "I can help building the house." He sent all his savings, a thousand dollars, home to his father for the building. He went to Delgado Travel under the el and bought a ticket to Puebla. He spent most of his time packing his clothes. There were shirts and caps and jackets with insignias on them. The others in the room wouldn't have minded if he left some of them, but you cannot come back from America in such defeat that you don't even have a big thick Buffalo Sabres zipper jacket.

The little tricks of living with almost nothing were now brought into play. The day before he was to leave, José had to pick up his ticket. The woman in the agency said two identifications were required to get on the plane, and also to get back into Mexico. The Mexicans were copying the United States by having gatekeepers. The woman told José that his birth certificate alone was not enough; he could be sent back from Mexico and arrested upon his arrival in New York. In a Russian gift shop across the street a man in the back took his picture and for $10 quickly made a plastic identification card that said, "Bearer has top security clearance for this company." A handwritten signature was at the bottom. The back of the card contained a brief lecture on the bearer's importance to the company.

His plane was at 4:30 on Saturday afternoon. Two and a half hours early, José and Eduardo carried one huge duffel bag to the travel agency; in his free hand Eduardo struggled with a much smaller but still heavy duffel bag. They threw it into the trunk of the Odessa Car Service livery car that he had ordered. Now on the sidewalk, a tiny woman with an old Indian face peered over the top of an immense box covered with black cloth. She had two young men helping her push it. The Mexicans call it a *muchila*, a knapsack, which she said held a stereo for her family in Cholula, but it was big enough to hold a bandstand. The woman's wrinkled hand held out a clump of bills. The woman wanted José to include her *muchila* as part of his baggage. She put $60 in his hand. She swore that the overweight charge would be thirty dollars, and the rest was his. He took the money, and the woman and the two with her pushed the box to the curb. They pointed to the trunk. The Russian cab driver stared at the cigarette in his hand. They pushed and tugged the black box into the back of the cab. Eduardo and José barely fit in.

At the airport, the line for the Mexican flight was about a block and a half long. Eduardo stayed with the luggage while José went for soda. Then Eduardo wandered over to the waiting room windows that looked out at the great plane with the AeroMexico markings that sat in hope and splendor in the sun. He told his brother that he could see his mother standing in the doorway of the courtyard as he walked toward her, with the dogs jumping onto him in joy. He wanted to get on this plane right now. So what if he couldn't do it? He'd go to the travel agent and get the next one.

The woman at the AeroMexico counter grimaced as she and another agent pulled José's two bags off the scale and threw them onto the conveyor. She told José that the overweight charge was $68. He had to put $8 of his own to the overweight bill. José muttered. He would still have to pay several dollars more or nobody at the Puebla airport would help with his luggage.

Chapter Twenty-One

H E WOKE up slowly. Instead of coming off the floor with a rush to get into the bathroom, Eduardo propped his chin on his fist and watched a pair of feet go by. He was thinking of something, because he didn't move, and another pair of feet whisked by. Ten minutes for each miss. When he heard the door opening, he pulled himself up and started for the bathroom, but someone else went right by him. He waited for the ten minutes and decided to add his banging to the day's confusion. Alejandro came out. "The last," he said to Eduardo. "Your timing is off."

They walked to the el on Brighton Beach Avenue.

Two short blocks over, on Fifth Street, Angel Tlapaltotoli came out of the dungeon of a rear basement apartment in the frame house where he lived with his wife and child. He walked up the alley to the street and turned for the el, which was only a few doors down. Lucino Hernández Robles was up at six o'clock in his room two flights up over Kings Highway and the subway. His cousin, Julisa, was busy with her baby. They said good morning to each other, and Lucino was gone to his job. Blocks away, in an unfurnished first-floor apartment, a block off the el, Juan Sánchez and his brother, Angel, each 5 feet 3 inches, threw on their clothes and left for the job. Juan had been here for seven years, and his younger brother only a few months. All the family was in New York working. The last to arrive, the father, was asleep in a back room. He worked in a restaurant. Juan was often anxious about the entire family barely making it; an uncle who earned $500 a week in a fish market was the greatest wage earner. Still, he knew it was better than the small farm in Mexico where he worked "morning to the sun, even to midnight" and for virtually no money. There also was a brother-in-law far over on Dean Street who was in the subway going to work at this hour.

The ones leaving the house in Brighton Beach rode the train to Smith/Ninth Street. They sat together and as usual had *huaza* talk about the young women on the train. They changed and took the local to Flushing Avenue and came down the stairs onto Middleton Street. In the morning dust ahead was the Job and the bodega next to the last building, 50 Middleton Street.

Eduardo had a container of coffee and one piece of toast in Lupita Bodega. He sat with four others at a small table covered with linoleum and wedged between shelves of jalapeño peppers, sugar, onions, Mr. Clean, Tampax, Pampers, Ziploc bags, and racks of pornographic books. It was a chill day and they wore heavy clothes. Summer people in winter clothes.

Hurshed, one of the Russians, had a can of soda that he held out for Eduardo. The others said Hurshed was taking the place of Eduardo's father.

The large red Speedy Pumping Concrete truck pulled up outside on Middleton Street. Its barrel revolved as the insides of rocks and cement were being mixed. There was a hose running from the truck up the front of the building to the third floor, where a heavy metal stand held up a spout for throwing off concrete. Eduardo held the handle of a machine that looked like a large electric floor waxer.

Somebody called up, and with a roar the concrete truck's engine became loud and the cement came pouring from the spout. Eduardo, on the third floor, pushed with his big spreader; the others working had wood trowels. The noise filled all ears.

Over in a corner in the rear of the floor there were these fingers of light coming through cracks where the right wall of the structure should have been fastened to the rest of the place, including the roof.

Juan Sánchez looked up and was surprised to see the light coming through cracks. He became frightened when he saw the bars of light growing larger. Already, after working four months on this building, he noticed that rainwater was in the bottom part of the building but not up on the third level. He didn't know what that meant. He knew he didn't like that the building shook when they poured concrete.

He says that this time he called out, "*No bueno.*" But the noise from the concrete pump on the third level and the spreading machine Eduardo was pushing were too loud.

There was no swaying or quivering. No time even for a

warning gasp from somebody. One second to the other, Alejandro says. An instant, a shrug of concrete and metal, and the
floor under Eduardo went.

Down Eduardo went, so quickly that he made no sound.

Down went Alejandro and Lucino and Gustavo and two
Angels and Juan.

Down they went so quickly that nobody screamed.

The third floor fell into the second floor and the second fell
into the first and everything fell into the basement. The rear
wall blew out, as did a wall that was supposed to be tied to the
building. There was a cascade of cinder blocks and metal.

What were supposed to be metal beams holding up the floors
were as strong as aluminum foil.

Eduardo fell face first into three feet of concrete on the
basement floor and drowned.

There were shrieks in the basement from the dozen who
were injured and in the concrete.

Above, the cement pump still stood on one part of the floor
that had not snapped. The pump kept pouring concrete down,
the thickest of gray rains. The workers were stuck in it. As it
covered the chests of the workers, it started to flatten them and
stifle their breathing. If one exhaled, the weight of the concrete
on his chest prevented him from inhaling again.

Angel Sánchez fell into concrete, and his brother landed on
top of him. Angel was partially buried, and the concrete came
down in a gray storm. His brother-in-law pulled him up.

Alejandro went under the concrete and would have been
gone forever except Angel Tlapaltotoli caught sight of him.
He is small, this Angel is, and he was hurt and stunned from
the fall, but he saw the spot where Alejandro disappeared, and
somehow he took one leap out of the concrete and landed
in next to Alejandro and stabbed both arms down through it
and onto Alejandro. He yanked Alejandro's head up and was
rubbing the concrete from his mouth and nostrils. Alejandro
was unconscious. But he was alive in Angel's hands.

How many did Gustavo Ramirez grab?

All anybody remembers is the cries for help and Gustavo
grabbing at people. Grabbing for Lucino, who was in shock and
unable to move. Or at Hurshed, the big guy, whose head was

above the concrete, but when he became catatonic, his head had to be held up.

The woman in the bodega called 911.

When Chief Dillon from the Fire Department arrived, he saw the concrete truck on the street oblivious to what was happening. It was still pumping concrete upstairs. Dillon's aide, Chris Steidinger, ran up to the truck and shouted at the driver to stop it.

Now Bill Pieszak of Emergency Services, just off the truck, came through an opening into the basement. Another cop, Dave Kayen, went through the first floor window.

Sticking out of the concrete were arms and legs and the white oval of a mouth. It was strange, Pieszak remembers, but the wet concrete saved a couple of them because they landed on something soft. At the same time, Pieszak and Kayen were in wet concrete up to their thighs and could barely move. They began to try to remove people by first bending forward with their arms stretched out and digging at the wet concrete with their hands.

Dig it and shove it to make a clearing around the body. As they made this clearing, the concrete came back like a heartless tide. They kept pushing the concrete. Pieszak lifted a body. Lifted it four inches. He took a breath, reached into the concrete again, and tried for another four inches.

The concrete parted under Kayen's hands and he saw a prize, a belt with a big buckle. The buckle was covered with concrete, but it had a value greater than any medallion ever struck for royalty. This was a buckle you could grab and pull up, and he raised the body of a mauled human out of the sucking concrete just enough to let him live. With Pieszak tugging at the shoulders and Kayen at the belt, they lifted.

Four inches. Maybe a little more. Lift again. Four inches. Now again. Four inches. Lifting, lifting, lifting. Now slide a board under the body and up comes a mummy able to breathe. Because of the concrete, the worker weighed twice his normal weight.

Now there were firemen and cops everywhere, tugging, heaving, and these voices were calling out, "Angel?" "Juan!" One Mexican, battered, dazed, and bleeding, tried to slip away after they pulled him out. Firefighters grabbed him. They were afraid he was hurt and would collapse trying to walk home. The guy kept trying to get away. He was more afraid of an immigration agent than of an injury.

Eduardo's body was pulled out of the cellar by ropes. He was one hundred pounds heavier with the cement on him. The body was taken to the morgue at Bellevue Hospital.

In Woodhull Hospital, Lucino was in bed in a haze and with his body hurting. José J. Eduardo, the husband of Lucino's cousin Julisa, was allowed in. She had medical knowledge and the husband had none, so of course she remained with the children and he saw Lucino in intensive care. José told him in amazement, "Do you know, somebody died." He told Lucino it was Eduardo. It would be many months before Lucino could say the name without crying. Miguel called Eduardo's father, Daniel, and said that something had happened. The father went into denial and hung up on him. Then Gustavo's sister, Teresa Hernández, who had gotten several calls about the accident, called the father from her basement room in Queens Village. She said that Eduardo had died. The father in San Matías shouted, "No!" and hung up. The father called Brighton Beach and got only Mariano Ramirez, a brother of Gustavo and Teresa who'd slept on the floor with Eduardo and who had two brothers hurt in the collapse. Mariano didn't want to be the one to tell Eduardo's father. He told Daniel that he would find out and call back. Finally, after many calls, Miguel, the husband of Martha, Mariano's sister, called Daniel and told him. This time, Daniel believed the bad news. He closed the cell phone and turned around and told his wife that the first child born to her was dead.

Silvia was surprised that her mother was calling her this late, after she had returned home from the night job at the Olive Garden. It was her mother who called rather than anybody from Brighton Beach, because Eduardo never had informed anybody that she was his girlfriend.

The mother said she did not know how Eduardo died. Silvia remembered him saying he had to climb up the building. In her mind she saw him dead on the ground, sprawled dramatically. Nobody told her mother or her how he actually died. Her mother asked if she was coming for the funeral, and Silvia said of course she would be there. She hung up and sat through part of the night thinking about it. That they had not seen each other in months was suddenly not important. They could get past that and live their lives. But the death left her blank. She had never experienced anything that had a finality to it. This did. At her age, all the days and months were part of looking ahead.

Back in New York, a social worker, Awilda Cordero, drove Angel and Mariano to the morgue. They went into a conference room, and one of the assistants came in with color pictures of Eduardo's corpse. The two looked at the picture, said, "*Sí*," and the identification was through. It took several more days for the body to be released because immigration people had to be notified that the young man was here without papers. This is poor form for a dead body.

That Sunday afternoon, with the sky gray and the wide commercial street outside desolate, Eduardo's body was in a white casket in a closet of grief at the Lopez Funeral Home in Brooklyn. He was in a good white shirt, and the black cap he loved sat atop the casket. Everybody who was not in the hospital came there in rough clothes and sat in silence. Gustavo was angry and kept mopping his forehead, which was still bleeding.

The cost of getting the body to Mexico was paid by the Red Cross and the New York City Central Labor Trades Council, whose members in the construction trades are mostly white and from New Jersey, and whose officers are in their element at cocktail parties in Manhattan with politicians. The labor leaders paused to pay for the funeral and get in the newspapers.

The case was in the jurisdiction of the Kings County District Attorney's office, whose normal tenacity in pursuit of justice slowed to a stroll when faced with the history of the Board of Elections, in whose records are carried no list of winners who attack Hasidim.

At this moment, into the ominous gloom and wet smell of the collapsed building on Middleton Street came James Vanderberg of the Department of Labor. He was another of these people who exude mildness and can destroy you. He was slim and young. His job was to find out how this poor Mexican got killed. But he had to do it with a lightened step. Under the

OSHA rules, a violation of safety rules causing the death of a worker is a misdemeanor. The maximum for the misdemeanor is six months in prison. There is no restitution for the victim. But if a felony could be made out of Ostreicher's lying to the federal agent, Caterina, then there was a chance that something could be gained out of the sourness and misery of the matter. For the felony would be punishable by from zero to six years in prison. Restitution for the Gutiérrez death could somehow be made a part of any plea agreement, and there certainly would be one; Ostreicher could face no jury. The fine could then be substantial and Eduardo's family, which had only been hurt until now, could receive some financial help. Eduardo had drowned in concrete during great arguing on Mount Olympus about world commerce and work. Eduardo had no understanding of the names of the technologies that caused fists to wave on the streets of Seattle and Genoa. Nor could he name the diversities of trade, nor the new merchandise that comes off the shelf not by hand but by a tapping key whose message flies to the sky and back to the shelf. Yet Eduardo represented the most invaluable part of the economy of the world. He was cheap labor.

In a vacant corner of the airport in Mexico City, international trade was represented by the casket of Eduardo, who had died in Williamsburg, in Brooklyn, and was in Mexico to be buried. He was put on a van. Mariano, who had brought the body home, cried as he got into the van, which drove down to Eduardo's house and the funeral.

In College Station, Silvia sat one last night before deciding that she couldn't go to the funeral. Getting to San Matías was simple. But then she would have to sneak across the border again, and that could take days and weeks, particularly if she got turned back. Surely she would lose both her jobs. She thought of the railroad tracks in the night with snakes in the brush. That settled it. She would sob for Eduardo and then live for the living.

The order of grieving in San Matías calls for nine days of prayers before the burial. By the time the body arrived in the yard at Calle Libre, eight days had passed, and the father agreed with the priest that the young man should be buried on the next morning.

The night before the funeral, Eduardo's casket was in a room that had been cleared out and was across from his new blue room. There was no upstairs because there was no money to build. Eduardo's new room shrugs off storms and sun. It is painted blue with white trim. It is a glorious room. The casket was surrounded by candles, and there was wailing and fainting.

Instead of many prayers and drinks, there were only prayers that night. On the morning of the funeral one of his cousins, a woman with a face of the Aztecs, bit her lip and began hauling a bucket of water out of the well. One hand over the other, arms straining as she pulled the rope. Now the large pail came out with the water sparkling in the sun, and some of this reflected onto the wall of the room Eduardo died for.

They carried Eduardo's body through the heat and among the children running with dogs alongside, the large crowd pushing to get closer to the casket of Eduardo Daniel Gutiérrez, who drowned in concrete in Brooklyn at age twenty-one while trying to make money.

They went to the old yellow church with red trim, with candlelight flickering on the gold wreaths and babies crying and the sound of children's feet. The people stood outside the doors and threw rice to symbolize the marriage Eduardo never had.

Then they walked the streets to the cemetery. They were in the middle of the cobblestone walk that went up to the cemetery gates. The walk went past stacked tires and the clotheslines of families living in shacks, and the crowd threw white carnations at the casket.

Nine young women stepped out of the crowd. One, whose name was Sol, wore a white sweater and a heartbreakingly young face. She went up to the casket and took the place of a young man. She held the casket handles underhand. Eight other young women took the places of the young men who had been carrying it.

Now there were nine young women, each of whom held the handles underhand.

A mariachi band at the end of the procession played a song called "Las Flores." As the trumpets sounded in the hot sunlight, the band leader, wearing a powder blue suit and black gloves, began singing the song.

On the left side of the casket, Sol swayed back on her right foot. So did the other young women on her side. The young women on the other side swayed forward with the casket.

Now the young women on the left side stopped going back and swayed forward. All hands gripped the casket handles, and the young faces were determined as they swayed with the heavy box. The young women on the right side stepped back.

As the left side came forward, all the young women caused the casket to dance a couple of feet closer to the cemetery gate.

Young women learn this dance just by living here. It is done only with the caskets of women who die unmarried or a young man like Eduardo Daniel Gutiérrez, who drowned in concrete at age twenty-one in Williamsburg in Brooklyn.

The young women carrying his casket were friends of Eduardo. Their faces were determined. Soon, however, they cried as they made Eduardo's casket dance. Sway forward on the left leg, sway back on the right foot, sway forward, sway back, sway, sway, sway, dance the young man to his grave.

In front of the cemetery, as the mariachi singer cried out the last notes of his song about flowers, the young women had their places at the casket taken by older men. The older men now rocked the casket as if it were a rowboat.

Three young men sat atop the cemetery arch and threw candy down. The kids raced for it.

Inside the graveyard there was a tangle of small graves covered with dead flowers. The grave had been dug by friends of the father, Eduardo Daniel. The cemetery is staffed only by flies.

Before the casket was lowered, Eduardo's mother, Teresa, was at the foot of the casket, and her face, uncovered, held a thousand years of grief. All through her roots, lifetime after lifetime, somebody young had died in every one of the families that came before her. At moments like this, her only emotion was dull acceptance.

Mariano Ramirez Torres tried to bury his round young face into the top of the casket. In the throng pushing forward to be near the grave was his mother, Angelina. With the two sons hurt in Brooklyn and not working, and the other son here to mourn, she said that there were no money orders from Brooklyn. She is raising the four children of one of the injured sons, Gustavo.

At the graveside the grandmother, Angelina, was racked with grief and necessity.

There were at least half a dozen men standing in the fresh dirt at the lip of the grave. Two men in white polo shirts were in the hole. When they pushed and tugged the casket into place, they got on either side of the casket and began slapping new red bricks, baked in this shack town, atop the casket. They wanted a brick wall to protect the top of the casket when the dirt and sand would be thrown down on it.

Eduardo Gutiérrez had already drowned once.

Epilogue

ON JUNE 15, 2001, the New York City Central Labor Trades Council ran a media bus tour of South Eighth Street in Williamsburg, where another Mexican immigrant from Puebla, Rogelio Daze Villaneuva, was crushed to death. He lost his life only blocks away from where Eduardo had perished.

A Hi-Lo forklift caused a ramp to collapse on the demolition job of an old hot dog factory that was uninspected.

In the doorway of a building next door, a gray-haired man wearing a shirt with the words *Kabila's Knishes* on the front pocket said, "No papers."

"The contractor?"

"No, the Mexicans. They have no papers, no green card. No paper, no pay. Cheap pay. Five, six dollar an hour. Nobody looks at the building."

Rogelio, an immigrant with no papers of any sort, had been making about a third of union wages. He had four children.

The union announced that the bus ride was to "shine a bright, public light on violations of basic human rights of workers in New York City."

Eduardo's father, Daniel, arrived in Brooklyn unnoticed at that time. He was here for depositions for lawsuits. The lawyer had sent tickets. He got off the plane with two hundred dollars. Two hundred American, he said to himself. I can stay here for a month.

He was on Lorimer Street, the one behind the ruined buildings on Middleton Street where his son died. This is not using the name Lorimer Street as geography in a story. Rather, the attempt at justice was made on that dull, treeless block.

Daniel crouched and pushed through a narrow, ragged opening in a chain-link fence and trudged through this lot filled with debris that was covered with weeds. He came to the rear of the collapsed buildings where Eduardo drowned in concrete.

The father was forty-six. Suddenly, he seemed so much older. Pain spilled from the dark eyes and ran through the small creases around his eyes and into the ravines and rivulets of his cheeks and mouth. He looked over seventy.

Then the sunlight splashed the brown face and the lines softened and he was forty-six again. A sadness weighs on his eyes, and he looks down to hide this.

The construction site is silent. A metal sign says it is in the hands of a demolition company. On the left, the last two units have wood ladders of four steps leading up to the second level. The one next to last has a basement yawning dark and wet. Daniel looks into the open first floor. He shakes his head, then holds his thumb and forefinger far apart. He points at a space between the wall and the floor above.

At the ruins of the last site, the one that was going to be numbered 50 Middleton, he went up the ladder. For so many nights and days in San Matías he tried to imagine this place. But now there was only a pile of cinder blocks and bricks and twisted metal that has an evil shine.

The sound of a bus idling comes from Middleton Street.

Suddenly, and in a quiet voice, Daniel says that he can see Eduardo at work. "He is talking to the other workers," Daniel says. "He is happy and young."

Now he steps up to the vision that has dissolved. He sees the pile of bricks at the place where the floors caved and his son dropped face first into a lake of concrete covering the basement.

The father's face does not change. He does not talk. The moment causes tongue and face to be frozen. This is where his firstborn son died. Walk up to the place and look at it. Then call the boy's mother in Mexico and tell her what it looked like. What else is there to do? It is your life as a Mexican.

Now tears finally run from the corners of his eyes.

He stays only for a few minutes. Leaving the street, they drive him up a few blocks to Woodhull Hospital, which sits under the el.

"This is where they took Eduardo," somebody told Daniel.

Immediately he twisted to see the building. He took a pencil out of his pocket and tried to write the name down on a scrap of paper. The driver, Awilda Cordero, stopped the car and printed it in large letters.

"Woodhull," he said, reading it.

He put the piece of paper into his breast pocket. "For the mother," he said. The hospital made him cry.

He had six days left in Brooklyn before flying back to San

Matías. He was staying in a blue frame house on a small crooked street in Brighton Beach with Mariano and three others from San Matías, who had moved a few blocks from the one room where everybody slept on the floor.

At 11 A.M. on a Thursday, he was watching an animal show on the Discovery Channel. He was fascinated by a large python at work. The el train ran almost directly over the house, and the noise kept filling the room.

He had no way of knowing that suddenly on this day a year and a half of frustration was coming to an end a few miles away, in downtown Brooklyn, where the clerk in the fourth floor federal courtroom of Judge Leo Glasser called out, "United States of America versus Ostreicher, Criminal Information 01CR717."

Eugene Ostreicher, blocky and decisive of step, walked up to the bench. He had on a black yarmulke and a black suit with a white shirt open at the collar. His beard was two large white puffs coming from his cheeks. He had sharp dark eyebrows over pale blue eyes. He stood motionless.

"Frank Mandel for Eugene Ostreicher," his lawyer, a thin man, said.

"Assistant United States Attorney Richard Faughnan for the government."

Ostreicher was sworn in. He was here to plead guilty to a criminal information. This is different from a grand jury indictment, which causes a full jury trial. A criminal information gives a defendant the chance to slither out of deepest trouble with a plea.

The judge said, "Do you realize that you must tell the truth, that it is a crime to tell a lie after you swear to tell the truth?"

"Yes," Ostreicher said.

Glasser then asked him if he was under any medication that would interfere with his ability to understand what he was doing. Then he asked him to read a copy of the charge against him. The judge then said that rather than plead guilty right here he could stand on his constitutional right to a grand jury. He told Ostreicher that a grand jury is made of between sixteen and twenty-three people, and if at least twelve say there is a probable cause that a crime has been committed, there will be an indictment. Did Ostreicher understand?

He understood too well. For eighteen months he had been twisting and ducking the chances of such a thing, for he understood that the indictment inevitably leads to a trial and the chances for imprisonment would be high.

Now Glasser read the charge. "On March 14, 1996, in the Eastern District of New York you knowingly made a false statement to an OSHA officer by stating that at buildings number 25–49 Lorimer Street there had been no collapse."

Glasser pressed Ostreicher. "You have a right to say not guilty. In that case there will be a public jury trial."

Ostreicher showed no anxiety.

"I do not accept a guilty plea from an innocent man," Glasser said.

(The last time I saw Glasser, he took a guilty plea from Sammy Gravano, not quite an innocent.)

"How do you plead?" Ostreicher was asked.

"Guilty."

After a year and a half of investigations by one agency after another, Ostreicher convicted himself of spitting on the sidewalk.

Right to the end, most thought that the plea agreement was supposed to be for an OSHA civil case only, and therefore there would be no prison time. However, the Labor Department agent, James Vanderberg, had never quit pressing for a felony criminal charge and won out in the back rooms of justice. The civil charge was replaced by a criminal felony charge. It included what Vanderberg wanted: a fine of a million dollars so at least the victims could get something. Usually there is nothing for them.

In court, the judge gave him one part of the sentence. He would never be allowed to build again, which was something the Fire Department's Blaich had called for at least three years ago. Then a million-dollar fine was to be paid to the victims of Middleton Street. He was not charged with the deadly collapse, but he was fined for it because on a plea, you can put in almost anything—write down "Rome burning." There was no way anybody was going to let Ostreicher walk away from Eduardo Daniel Gutiérrez's death with no penalty at all. Glasser said the additional sentencing date would be in October. Ostreicher faced anything from zero to five years, the judge said. The chances were that there would be no prison time. That was to happen.

When the guilty plea was over, Mandel stood in the aisle and said to somebody, "Where did you get the police badge from?"

"From the guys he showed it to."

"Who showed it?"

"Richie the Rabbi."

"Who? There is no such person." Mandel playfully punched one of the people with him. "He says there is a Richie the Rabbi in the family."

Mandel laughed and the guy laughed. Ostreicher shrugged. He was not going to say anything to anybody, because that was what had gotten him in trouble. Of course there is a Richie the Rabbi, proper name Chaim. Only this time there was no federal guy asking an official question.

Richie the Rabbi went to Belgium after the collapse. One day he called Captain Bill Gorta at police headquarters in Manhattan and said, Gorta remembers, "I just had a baby. I have to go to City Hall in Brussels to register him. Do you think you could call them and ask them as a courtesy to the NYPD to let me go right through without having to wait on line?"

Later in the day, Daniel stood on the street outside the house in Brighton Beach. The two hundred American had lasted only a couple of days. Mariano, from the house, had found a temporary job for him, installing floors in a supermarket around the corner. Daniel worked ten hours for $50. He hated it. He realized this was how his son had started here. He wasn't going back to the job. He would sit here until he had to get his plane.

"A million," he was told. "For all the victims."

"All the victims."

"Yes, but your son died so that should be the largest amount."

That was a wrong estimate. The Russian, Hurshed, would have to live with his permanent damages and would need every dollar. He would get the most, $800,000. As Eduardo was gone, his father would receive $100,000.

But now, not knowing this, he shrugged. "I only stayed here to see where the accident was. If they give me something, fine. But I'm going back on Thursday. I don't like it here."

He held up four fingers. "I have four more."

"José is the oldest?" he was asked.

"He is married. I just have my first grandson."

"Who carries the bricks in the yard now?"

"I do. With Miguel. You saw him when he was young. He is grown up."

"Then who are the little ones at the end of the line?"

"The girls. Maria Cruz. Zenaida."

He looked down at the sidewalk. Then he took out a pack of Marlboros. When he lit one, it was the end of his conversation. He had lost too much around here, in Brooklyn, in America, and he wanted to get home.

Chronology

notes that the headline should have been in the present
tense: "Mother Tries Suicide.")

1942–46   Attends John Adams High School "for the full five years,"
           Breslin later writes. Plays football, but is thwarted from
           joining the school newspaper ("I couldn't get on it. That
           was only for the smart kids."). Boxes a little. Caddies for
           gangster Frank Costello, "who gave me 50 bucks to take
           my girl to the junior prom."

1945–46   Begins newspaper career as a copyboy at the *Long Island
           Press*, imagining at first that the copy he urgently ran across
           the newsroom concerned events of historic import; instead,
           it was often "four paragraphs about the Eastern Queens
           Civic Association." Takes courses at Long Island University,
           where he later says he majored in excuses, and eventually
           drops out.

1950   Starts writing career as a sportswriter for the *New York
           Journal-American*. Jobs at other New York newspapers will
           follow, including as the night sports editor for the *Long
           Island Press*.

1952   Meets Rosemary Dattolico (b. 1929) in Brooklyn, when a
           wedding party she is in runs into a bar around the corner
           from the *Long Island Press* offices. Wet from the rain, she
           throws the floral bouquet she caught at the reception to
           Breslin and says, "Now you caught it. Want to get mar-
           ried?" "Who to?" "Me." "Sure."

1953   Marries Rosemary Dattolico in December at St. Pancras
           Roman Catholic Church in Glendale, Queens.

1954   Twin sons, James and Kevin, are born November 17. The
           Breslin family lives in Richmond Hill.

1957   Daughter Rosemary is born March 23. The Breslin family
           moves to Ozone Park.

1959   The family moves to Baldwin on Long Island, where Breslin
           is profoundly unhappy, so much so that he plants a sign
           in the front lawn expressing his displeasure with the place
           and its people—a precursor to his annual "People I'm Not
           Talking To This Year" column later in his career.

1961   Son Patrick is born March 23.

1962   Doubleday publishes Breslin's first book, *Sunny Jim*, a bi-
           ography of the celebrated thoroughbred racehorse trainer
           James Fitzsimmons (1874–1966).

1963   Viking publishes *Can't Anybody Here Play This Game?*, a
            chronicle of the first season of the hapless New York Mets
            baseball team (the title of the well-received book echoes
            the complaint of the Mets' wizened manager, Casey Sten-
            gel, about the team's ineptitude). Writes article for *Life*
            magazine about Early Wynn, a veteran baseball pitcher
            trying to hang on long enough to win his 300th game.
            John Hay Whitney, the publisher of the *New York Herald
            Tribune*, is impressed by Breslin's writing and hires him to
            write a five-days-a-week city column that often focuses on
            ordinary people and characters he knows from the bars near
            Queens Borough Hall. "So with absolutely no direction I
            invented a new form for news pages, a column based on
            something happening right now in this city," Breslin will
            write. Joins Tom Wolfe and other well-regarded journalists
            in writing as well for the *Herald Tribune*'s Sunday sup-
            plement, which has been reworked into what will become
            New York magazine. The Breslin family moves back to
            Queens, this time to a house in Forest Hills. On November
            22, President John F. Kennedy is assassinated in Dallas.
            Two days later, the *Herald Tribune* publishes "A Death in
            Emergency Room One," Breslin's deadline story about Dr.
            Malcolm Perry, the emergency room surgeon assigned to
            attend to Kennedy. Then, on November 26, it publishes
            "It's An Honor," Breslin's column about Clifton Pollard,
            the gravedigger who prepared the president's burial spot
            at Arlington National Cemetery. The column stands in
            contrast to the rest of the international media's coverage
            of Kennedy's funeral, which focuses on its somber chore-
            ography. It will become a classic of its journalistic form,
            the impetus for the so-called Gravedigger Theory of news
            coverage.

1964   Breslin appears in several television commercials for Piel's
            beer with Walt Kelly, the creator and illustrator of the *Pogo*
            comic strip. In the years to come, Breslin's pitch for Piel's—
            "It's a good drinkin' beer"—will become famous. Daughter
            Kelly is born August 3.

1965   On February 21, attends a speech in Upper Manhattan by
            Malcolm X, who is assassinated while Breslin is taking a
            smoking break in a back room. Covers Selma-to-Mont-
            gomery civil rights march led by Martin Luther King, Jr.,
            and files several stories on segregation in Alabama. Briefly
            meets Ronnie Eldridge (b. Roslynn Myers in 1931), a re-
            form Democratic leader from Manhattan's Upper West

Side, at the Carlyle Hotel while interviewing New York
senator Robert F. Kennedy about the Vietnam War, which
Breslin opposes. Leaves the next day for Vietnam, filing
dispatches on the war for the *Herald Tribune*. Has a brief
conversation with Richard Nixon after an informal press
briefing at the Saigon residence of U.S. press officer Barry
Zorthian.

1966   The Newspaper Guild calls a strike on April 25 in opposi-
        tion to a plan by the *Herald Tribune* and two other strug-
        gling New York newspapers to establish a joint operating
        agreement that would allow the three papers to stay alive—
        though at the expense of more than 1,700 jobs. Breslin
        joins other prominent journalists in trying to organize a
        newspaper union strictly for editorial personnel that would
        rival the Newspaper Guild, which included a majority of ad-
        vertising, clerical, maintenance, and circulation employees.
        Son Christopher is born August 8. John Hay Whitney, the
        Herald Tribune publisher, announces to the newsroom on
        August 15 that the newspaper will be going out of business.
        A bitter Breslin turns his attention to freelancing but also
        writes columns for a short-lived hybrid newspaper, the *New
        York World Journal Tribune*.

1967   A collection of his columns, *The World of Jimmy Breslin*, is
        published by Viking.

1968   After protracted negotiations, signs a contract in March
        to begin writing columns for the *New York Post*, while
        also serving as a commentator on local television stations
        in New York City; receives a note from the newspaper's
        publisher and editor-in-chief Dorothy Schiff praising his
        first column. Senator Robert F. Kennedy is shot June 5 at
        the Ambassador Hotel in Los Angeles, and dies the next
        day. Breslin is standing five feet from Kennedy when the
        gunman, Sirhan Sirhan, fires. He files a column that night,
        concluding: "And everybody cried when he was shot down
        within feet of them, all through the night they stood on
        the street in front of the hospital and we always knew, all
        of us, that someday we would be doing this." Files several
        other columns in the wake of the assassination, after which
        he struggles with depression.

1969   Works on *The Gang That Couldn't Shoot Straight*, a novel
        about a group of bungling mobsters in Brooklyn, and
        sells movie rights to Metro-Goldwyn-Mayer before it is

completed. Sends resignation letter to *Post* publisher Schiff on February 18; publicly announces resignation the following day via a front-page advertisement in *The New York Times* addressed to a ne'er-do-well friend he often wrote about: "ROBERT J. ALLEN: You are on your own. I am giving up my newspaper column. Jimmy Breslin." Announces plans on May 1 to run for City Council president, on a "51st State" ticket with the novelist Norman Mailer as candidate for mayor. Their platform includes the secession of the city from New York State and usees the slogan: "Vote the Rascals In." But Breslin becomes increasingly annoyed with outlandish pronouncements by Mailer—who at one point infamously calls his own supporters "spoiled pigs"— and Mailer's failure to engage on serious municipal matters. Both men finish at the back of the pack in the city's Democratic primary on June 17, though Breslin, who was fifth out of six candidates and received about 75,000 votes, takes pride in having received more votes than Mailer. Has first encounter with Irish Catholic activist Bernadette Devlin at a fundraising event on Long Island where Devlin is the speaker. Makes the first of several reporting visits to Northern Ireland to write about the Troubles there. Writes a monthly column for *New York* magazine. *Running Against the Machine: The Mailer-Breslin Campaign*, a collection of speeches and articles from their electoral bid, along with contributions by Peter Manso, Gloria Steinem, and others, is published by Doubleday. *The Gang That Couldn't Shoot Straight* is published by Viking in November.

1970   Planning to write a book on Ireland, moves in March to a rented house in Killiney, outside Dublin, with his family, including his mother-in-law; returns to New York twice for a libel case (soon dismissed) in Brooklyn related to one of his 1963 *Herald Tribune* columns. Continues to conduct reporting in Northern Ireland, visiting Belfast, Derry, Omagh, and Strabane and making connections with several Catholic civil rights leaders, including Bernadette Devlin and Eamonn McCann. Returns to New York City one month early in August after members of the Special Branch of Ireland's national police force come to his house at 11 P.M. while Breslin is out, claiming to be searching for a suspect in the shooting of two American servicemen; outraged, Breslin accuses the Special Branch of harassing him with "Gestapo methods" because of his ties to McCann and others. His return from Ireland prompts a series of internal memoranda within the Federal Bureau of Investigation that focus on him. One describes *The Gang That Couldn't Shoot Straight* as a "somewhat humorous fictional novel portraying a Mafia 'family'" and claims that Breslin "displays a hostile attitude toward the Director and the FBI indicating that the Mafia flourished in the U.S. without interference from the FBI." Another cites a source who had described Breslin in 1965 as "a heavy drinker who had several underworld connections." Others note his outspoken opposition to the Vietnam War and his contact in Ireland with "Bowes Egan, [a Devlin advisor] who is of extremist left-wing views." Joins nine New York congressmen and other prominent figures in signing a petition circulated by New York City politician Paul O'Dwyer in October that calls on the United Nations' Human Rights Commission to investigate the "oppression and discrimination" directed against Catholics in Northern Ireland. On October 10 Lawrence Eldridge, a Manhattan clinical psychologist, dies at forty-two of a heart attack. Breslin, having a habit of reaching out to people who have suffered a loss, repeatedly checks in with his widow, Ronnie Eldridge, at the time a special assistant to Mayor Lindsay; he identifies himself as Al Capone and asks the same question: "Everything all right?"

1971   Addresses graduating seniors at the first combined Harvard-Radcliffe Class Day on June 16. Film adaptation of *The Gang That Couldn't Shoot Straight*, directed by James Goldstone and starring Jerry Orbach and Robert De Niro, is released in December; it is widely panned.

1972   Testifies on February 28 before a House of Representatives subcommittee about the continuing civil unrest in Northern Ireland. Serves as a New York delegate for George McGovern, presidential candidate and U.S. senator from South Dakota, at the 1972 Democratic National Convention in Miami Beach, FL, July 10–13.

1973   Completes novel *World Without End, Amen*, which draws on his time in Ireland; it is published in August by Viking. Continues to write freelance pieces for various publications and to appear on television as a political commentator and talk-show guest.

1974   Breslin's estranged father, a chronic alcoholic, dies March 20 at sixty-eight in a nursing home in Florida. The *Miami*

Herald runs a story saying, "A Father Dies Penniless, Alone, Unmourned." Breslin pays for the cremation. His only previous involvement with his father in adulthood came when a hospital nurse in Florida sent word through a television network that the elder Breslin had suffered a heart attack. Breslin arranged to have his father moved to a heart hospital in Miami Beach, then sent a telegram that read: "NEXT TIME KILL YOURSELF. YOUR SON." Works on book about the Watergate scandal and the Nixon impeachment, centering on Tip O'Neill, the House of Representatives majority leader and John Doar, special counsel for the House Judiciary Committee.

1975   *How the Good Guys Finally Won: Notes from an Impeachment Summer* is published in May by Viking.

1976   Joins the staff of the *New York Daily News* and on November 16, publishes his first column, "Dies the Victim, Dies the City." His wife Rosemary undergoes surgery for breast cancer.

1977   "Son of Sam," the name adopted by a serial killer (first known as the ".44 killer") terrorizing New York City, sends handwritten letter on May 30 to Breslin: "Hello from the gutters of N.Y.C. which are filled with dog manure, vomit, stale wine, urine, and blood. Hello from the cracks in the sidewalks of N.Y.C. and from the ants that dwell in these cracks and feed on the dried blood of the dead that has settled into the cracks." Referring to Breslin as "J.B.," he writes: "I also want to tell you that I read your column daily and find it quite informative." After consulting with the police, the *Daily News* publishes portions of the letter a week later, along with a column by Breslin encouraging the killer to surrender. For safety reasons, he relocates his family to Long Island but continues to write about the case frequently, prompting criticism from *The New Yorker*: "By transforming a killer into a celebrity, the press has not merely encouraged him, but perhaps driven him to strike again—and may have stirred others brooding over their grievances to act. . . . Another journalist might have kept the news to himself, but Breslin did not." Breslin counters in print that he published the letter at the suggestion of detectives, who thought it could encourage the killer to write another note that might bear clearer fingerprints. The postal worker David Berkowitz is arrested on August 10 and is revealed as Son of Sam. Breslin contracts for a substantial advance to write, with Dick Schaap (primarily a sportswriter), a book about the case. Criticizes the *Daily News*'s decision in September to suspend the comic strip *Doonesbury* after it satirizes Breslin and the newspaper's coverage of the Berkowitz murders.

1978   Breslin and Schaap's fictionalized *.44* is published by Viking to negative reviews and poor sales. Has a supporting role in *If Ever I See You Again*, a feature film directed by Joe Brooks (who also wrote and starred) about a composer of advertising jingles who tries to reunite with a former girlfriend. Both the movie and Breslin's performance are ridiculed.

1980   Mother dies on October 18 at the age of seventy-four. Receives a late-night call at home on December 8 that John Lennon has just been shot and killed in front of his apartment building at Central Park West; goes to the scene and writes a column on deadline.

1981   Breslin's wife, known to his readers as "the former Rosemary Dattolico," dies on June 9 from breast cancer at age fifty-one.

1982   Breslin's novel *Forsaking All Others* is published in June. Marries Ronnie Eldridge, now a prominent New York City politician and widowed mother of three adult children, on September 12. They live in her Upper West Side apartment. The combining of their families—his Irish Catholic, hers German Jewish—causes intrafamilial friction, but provides Breslin with plenty of material for his columns. Is approached at Los Angeles International Airport by the Puerto Rican opera singer Graciela Rivera, who tells him she had once worked as a welfare clerk under the supervision of his mother, who had been supportive in her pursuit of a singing career. It leaves him thinking: "Why did this woman, my mother, thrive on tantrums when she had so much to give?"

1983–85   Works on novel *Table Money*, which he had begun in the 1970s but put aside, writing during the day at the apartment of his friend Irving Selbst; the manuscript will run to more than one thousand pages and will be cut down with the help of Breslin's editor at Ticknor & Fields, Corlies Smith. Collection of columns *The World According to Breslin* is published by Ticknor & Fields in the fall of 1984.

1986   Publishes a front-page column on January 23 that reveals a
            municipal corruption scandal centered along Queens Bou-
            levard, his stomping grounds. The exposé, featuring people
            he considered friends, leads to resignations and criminal
            convictions, and taints the administration of New York City
            mayor Edward Koch. In April, wins the Pulitzer Prize for
            Commentary, for columns "which consistently champion
            ordinary citizens." The selected columns include a harsh
            assessment of the public adulation for Bernhard Goetz, a
            self-described vigilante who shot four Black youths on a
            subway train, as well as descriptions of the struggles of a
            man dying from AIDS. Receives the George Polk Award for
            Metropolitan Reporting for revealing allegations that police
            officers had used battery-operated shock devices to torture
            suspects. *Table Money* is published in May by Ticknor &
            Fields. Hosts episode of *Saturday Night Live* on NBC on
            May 16. Agrees in September to a thirteen-week contract
            with ABC for his own twice-weekly late-night television
            show, *Jimmy Breslin's People.* But because of syndication
            commitments, the show is often delayed or preempted;
            even WABC in New York City pushes the program back
            from its midnight slot to 2 A.M., and occasionally airs it only
            one night a week. Takes out a front-page advertisement in
            The New York Times, November 24: "ABC TELEVISION
            NETWORK: Your services, such as they are, will no longer
            be required as of 12-20-86—Jimmy Breslin."

1987   On May 4, announcement made publicly that Breslin will
            leave the *Daily News* at the end of his contract and will join
            Newsday and its New York edition as a columnist.

1988   Novel *He Got Hungry and Forgot His Manners* is pub-
            lished in January by Ticknor & Fields. Wins Distinguished
            Writing Award in February from the American Society of
            Newspaper Editors for outstanding commentary on the
            aftermath of a racial attack in Howard Beach, Queens, as
            well as on "how ordinary citizens cope with life in New
            York." Attends the Humana Festival of New American Plays
            in Louisville, KY, on February 25 for the opening of his
            play, *The Queen of the Leaky Roof Circuit,* commissioned
            by the Actors Theatre of Louisville. Writes first column for
            Newsday on September 11.

1989   On July 25, CBS broadcasts "American Nuclear" on *CBS
            Summer Playhouse,* a pilot episode of a prospective situation

comedy very loosely based on the blended Breslin-Eldridge family, with Breslin in a small role as a newsstand operator. The series is not picked up. Eldridge is elected in November to represent Manhattan's District 4 in the City Council. Breslin demonstrates his support for her political aspirations in part by writing some of the campaign literature.

1990   In May, uses sexual and anti-Asian slurs while arguing with a colleague at *Newsday*, Ji-Yeon Yuh, after she sends him an email saying that a recent column—in which he jokingly described how his wife's election to the City Council had disrupted his home life—was sexist. In response to the ensuing newsroom uproar Breslin is reprimanded by editor Donald Forst and apologizes for the slurs, but then he phones in to Howard Stern's radio show and makes light of the controversy; after initially rejecting calls by its Asian American newsroom employees to fire Breslin, *Newsday* suspends him on May 8.

1991   Two Black children are struck on August 19 by a car running a red light while following the small motorcade of a prominent Hasidic Jewish leader in the Crown Heights section of Brooklyn. One child dies and the other is grievously wounded. On the third day of the ensuing rioting and looting, Breslin is dragged from a taxi by a group of youths who assault and rob him, stripping him of his clothes down to his underwear; two men who recognize the bloodied Breslin stop the beating and lead him to safety. His biography of the journalist and short-story writer Damon Runyon is published in September by Ticknor & Fields.

1994   Undergoes surgery on November 22 at Barrow Neurological Institute in Phoenix for a brain aneurysm discovered after one of his eyes closed. He is soon dictating notes from his hospital bed for a series of *Newsday* columns under the rubric "Breslin's Brain."

1996   Memoir *I Want to Thank My Brain for Remembering Me* is published in September by Little, Brown.

1999   Receives the Thomas Paine Award for Journalism from the Thomas Paine National Historical Association, given to journalists who devote themselves to writing about ordinary or marginalized people. Makes a cameo appearance as himself in Spike Lee's *Summer of Sam*, film about the Berkowitz case.

2002   Crown publishes *The Short Sweet Dream of Eduardo Guti-
            érrez*, about the life of an undocumented Mexican laborer
            who drowns in a pool of cement at a Brooklyn construction
            site, as well as New York City politics, immigration pol-
            icy, workplace exploitation, and corrupt building practices.
            Novel *I Don't Want to Go to Jail*, about a mobster based
            on Vincent "the Chin" Gigante—who famously feigned
            insanity by walking the streets of Greenwich Village in a
            bathrobe, mumbling to himself—is published by Little,
            Brown.

2004   Breslin's daughter Rosemary, a writer, dies on June 14 from
            a rare blood disease at the age of forty-seven. He writes a
            wrenching farewell in *Newsday*. His book, *The Church That
            Forgot Christ*, in which he examines his Catholic faith at a
            time when scandals are rocking the Church, is published
            in July. In early November, on the eve of the presidential
            election, files column predicting with certainty that John
            Kerry, the Democratic nominee, will beat (as he did not)
            the Republican incumbent, George W. Bush. Also writes
            that this will be his last regular column, concluding with:
            "Thanks for the use of the hall."

2006   Staged reading of his play, *Love Lasts on Myrtle Avenue*,
            about the ripple effects of the September 11 attack on the
            World Trade Center, is performed in Falmouth, MA, as part
            of the Cape Cod Theatre Project.

2008   *The Good Rat: A True Story*, account of a Brooklyn gangster
            who testifies against two corrupt New York City detectives
            that also serves as a meditation on Breslin's long history of
            covering mobsters, is published in February by Ecco.

2009   On April 21 Breslin's only living daughter, Kelly, who
            worked in public relations, dies after collapsing at a restau-
            rant a few days earlier. She was forty-four. He writes his
            final *Newsday* column on November 2 and on December 7
            is honored at a celebration organized by New York Univer-
            sity's Glucksman Ireland House. Hundreds attend, many
            journalists speak, Pete Hamill serves as master of ceremo-
            nies, and Tony Bennett emerges from behind a curtain to
            sing three songs.

2011   His biography of Branch Rickey, the baseball executive
            who helped to break the game's color barrier by signing
            Jackie Robinson, is published by Viking in the Penguin

Lives series. Breslin begins writing a weekly column for the *Daily News* on May 8.

2012   Writes his final column, on the capsizing of the French passenger liner *Normandie* after it caught fire in New York harbor in 1942, on January 29.

2017   Dies on March 19 at the apartment he shared with Eldridge in Manhattan, where he had been recovering from pneumonia. Until shortly before his death, he had continued to rise before dawn each morning to write. His funeral is held on March 22 at the Church of the Blessed Sacrament on Manhattan's Upper West Side.

Note on the Texts

This volume contains sixty-seven newspaper columns and six magazine articles written by Jimmy Breslin and published from 1960 to 2004, along with Breslin's books *How the Good Guys Finally Won* (1975) and *The Short Sweet Dream of Eduardo Gutiérrez* (2002).

The first selections included here from Breslin's long career as a journalist are sportswriting articles taken from mass-circulation magazines such as *True*, *Sports Illustrated*, and *Life*. These pieces are followed by a selection of reportage from Breslin's years at the *New York Herald Tribune*. After the *Herald Tribune* folded in August 1966, Breslin continued to write a column, which like his *Herald Tribune* columns was also syndicated, for its short-lived successor, the *World Journal Tribune*, in operation from September 1966 to May 1967. As well as contributing to publications such as *New York* magazine, *The New York Times*, and *Sport* magazine as a freelancer, Breslin wrote a regular column for less than a year at the *New York Post* (none of his columns are included here) and then for the *New York Daily News*, 1976–88, and 2011–12, and *Newsday*, 1988–2009. The texts of his columns are taken from their first periodical publications except when a particular article was gathered in one of two book-length collections of Breslin's newspaper work published during his lifetime—*The World of Jimmy Breslin* (1967) and *The World According to Breslin* (1984)—in which cases the first-edition book publication provides the text. The sources for the texts reprinted here are as follows:

COLUMNS AND OTHER JOURNALISM 1960–1974

Racing's Angriest Young Man. *True*, November 1960.

Worst Baseball Team Ever. *Sports Illustrated*, August 13, 1962.

The Old Indian's Last Stand. *Life*, April 5, 1963.

Whitey Revisited. *New York Herald Tribune*, June 2, 1963.

The Wake for a Newspaper. *New York Herald Tribune*, October 16, 1963.

The Last Gallo Living at 51 President Street. *New York Herald Tribune*, October 22, 1963.

The Talent Hunt. *New York Herald Tribune*, October 25, 1963.

A Death in Emergency Room One. *The World of Jimmy Breslin* (New York: Viking, 1967; hereafter *WJB*).

It's an Honor. *WJB*.

Holiday in Automat. *New York Herald Tribune*, November 29, 1963.

Feat of Clay: TKO in 7th. *New York Herald Tribune*, February 26, 1964.

Fear and Hate—Sputtering Fuse. *New York Herald Tribune*, July 20, 1964.

The Last Great Statue. *WJB*.

Malcolm X Slain by Gunmen as 400 in Ballroom Watch. *New York Herald Tribune*, February 22, 1965.

On Highway 80. *WJB*.

Alabama Schoolhouse. *WJB*.

The Retreat. *WJB*.

The Day I Company Got Killed. *WJB*.

Four Funerals. *New York Herald Tribune*, August 25, 1965.

Warm Air, Light Skin. *New York Herald Tribune*, September 14, 1965.

Stork Club Closes an Era. *New York Herald Tribune*, October 6, 1965.

The One Woman in the Operating Room. *New York Herald Tribune*, October 10, 1965.

Easter Rising, *WJB*.

A Struck Paper, Famous and Needed, Goes Down. *Life*, August 26, 1966.

Hero of '54 World Series Watches '66 Epic from Prison Bench. Syndicated column, text from *Washington Post*, October 9, 1966.

Will All Those Kids Vote for Bobby? Syndicated column, text from *Washington Post*, December 3, 1966.

Home Folks "Treat" a Hero Too Well. Syndicated column, text from *Washington Post*, February 5, 1967.

"Friendly Napalm" Changes Return Address on a Soldier's Letter. Syndicated column, text from *Washington Post*, April 30, 1967.

Namath All Night Long. *New York*, April 7, 1969.

The Baseball Encyclopedia. *New York Times*, October 12, 1969.

The Greatest Article I Read in My Whole Life. *New York Times*, October 9, 1971.

The Coach Who Couldn't Shoot Straight. *Sport*, December 1972.

The Best Short Stories of Ring Lardner. *New York Times*, April 14, 1974.

COLUMNS 1976–2004

Two Who Will Watch and One Who Won't. *New York Times*, January 18, 1976.

Dies the Victim, Dies the City. *The World According to Breslin* (New York: Ticknor & Fields, 1984; hereafter *WAB*).

On the Hunt for Son of Sam. *New York Daily News*, June 5, 1977.

The Threat Lies Within. *Newsday*, February 21, 1999.
A Smile Gone, But Where? *Newsday*, September 25, 2001.
Days of Wine and Rosaries. *Newsday*, October 8, 2002.
Church Isn't What It Should Be. *Newsday*, July 27, 2003.
A Daughter's Last Breaths. *Newsday*, June 20, 2004.

The texts of both Breslin books reprinted here are taken from their first editions: *How the Good Guys Finally Won* (New York: Viking, 1975) and *The Short Sweet Dream of Eduardo Gutiérrez* (New York: Crown, 2002). Neither book was revised by Breslin after publication.

This volume presents the texts of the original printings chosen for inclusion here, but it does not attempt to reproduce nontextual features of their typographic design. The texts are presented without change, except for the correction of typographical errors. Spelling, punctuation, and capitalization are often expressive features and are not altered, even when inconsistent or irregular. The following is a list of typographical errors corrected, cited by page and line number: 41.5, Whitey,; 41.21, *dile tu nonbre*; 42.33, frm; 44.5, the the; 46.38, bigest; 48.10, nonesense; 49.18, this all; 52.11, of theater; 59.14, years, Father; 65.11, cigarettes; 67.23, La Motta; 71.27–28, saw if for; 72.29, ran int; 72.40, hte talk; 73.2, hte heat; 80.11, sidewalk Malcom; 86.9, I though; 98.29, twelves; 110.33, La Mange; 111.30, saying, I'll; 113.20, officers; 114.23, nurses; 115.8, Lndon B.; 115.10, anesthologist; 115.13, Mayor Clinic; 116.6, sreve; 116.6, Miss.; 116.26, anesthiologist; 116.36, th esecond; 117.20, operation. while; 126.23, Schapiro; 128.6, Penetentiary; 128.31, come; 129.18, 1941; 132.19, Kenedy; 135.13, Kennedy.; 138.30 and .31, Peps; 156.1, Rhone; 156.32, huh.; 158.33, homes runs; 174.8, Bleek's; 182.25, show it you, as; 190.36, Valente; 191.29, 1968; 214.19, anyway, He'll; 229.36 and 233.30, Elliot; 232.20, foreward; 238.30, Valdez; 238.34, De Marco; 286.16–17, from Washington; 290.25, Zigarelli; 291.23, Allenwod; 293.33 and 294.3, Hixson; 295.22, H. Howard; 301.14, eight-five; 306.31, *693,696*; 312.14, Rhenquists; 316.8, "Yes, I did.'; 327.25, one, Klein; 327.25–26, Cowboy; 336.32, mine, one; 339.34, "Pou've; 340.39, pickes; 341.15, prove th the; 341.30, leters; 343.29, lept; 367.18, atomatic; 381.40, men; 402.13 and 403.27, Darryl; 414.22, precient; 414.28, Pepartment; 417.34, land; 421.12, gross; 440.4–5, Allen 19; 451.2–3, areas was; 451.17, barbituates; 462.18, Afini; 463.6, Streeet; 477.19, tabes; 510.9, nothing,; 520.36, Pietra; 549.18, defense table,; 571.1 (and *passim*), Moseh; 571.20, Kastner; 573.32 and 603.22, Schairer; 593.10, for for "c"; 596.38–39, handed it the; 606.39, looked at. A; 625.15, Building; 631.22, Jose.

Notes

In the notes below, the reference numbers denote page and line of this volume (line counts include headings but not section breaks). No note is made for material included in standard desk-reference books or comparable internet resources such as Merriam-Webster's online dictionary. Foreign words and phrases are translated only if not translated in the text, not clear from context, or if words are not evident English cognates. Biblical quotations are keyed to the King James Version. Quotations from Shakespeare are keyed to *The Riverside Shakespeare*, edited by G. Blakemore Evans (Boston: Houghton Mifflin, 1974). For more biographical information than is contained in the Chronology, see Jimmy Breslin, *I Want to Thank My Brain for Remembering Me* (Boston: Little, Brown and Company, 1996) and the documentary film *Hamill and Breslin: Deadline Artists* (2018), directed by John Block, Jonathan Alter, and Steve McCarthy.

COLUMNS AND OTHER JOURNALISM 1960–1974

5.2   Murder, Inc.] Network of hired killers founded by the New York gangsters Louis "Lepke" Buchalter (1897–1944) and Jacob "Gurrah" Shapiro (1899–1947); it committed hundreds of contract killings for organized-crime organizations in the 1930s and '40s.

5.30   Felix Bocchicchio] Colorful sports character (1906–1975) involved in gambling, horse racing, and boxing, most notably as manager of world heavyweight champion Jersey Joe Walcott.

7.19–20   Ted Williams . . . only to sportswriters and spectators] Williams (1918–2002) was a Hall of Fame baseball player who spent his entire nineteen-year career with the Boston Red Sox. His relationship with the press and with fans could be contentious.

11.17   Eddie Arcaro] Jockey (1916–1997) widely considered the greatest in the history of American thoroughbred horse racing, with a career spanning from 1932 to 1962. Inducted into the United States Racing Hall of Fame in 1987.

11.18   Willie Shoemaker] Racing Hall of Fame jockey (1931–2003) whose career lasted from 1949 to 1990.

14.13   Idlewild Airport] Former name of John F. Kennedy International Airport in New York City.

14.14   Sammy Boulmetis] Racing Hall of Fame jockey (1927–2021) whose career lasted from 1948 to 1966.

14.19   Walter Blum] Racing Hall of Fame jockey (b. 1934) whose career lasted from 1953 to 1975.

15.35   Khrushchev] Nikita Khrushchev (1894–1971), first secretary of the Communist Party, 1953–64, and chairman of the Council of Ministers, 1958–64, of the Soviet Union.

18.24–25   Floyd Patterson fight Ingemar Johansson] The heavyweight boxers Patterson (1935–2006) and Johansson (1932–2009) fought for the world championship title on June 26, 1959, at Yankee Stadium, the first of their three fights; in the 1959 match Johansson defeated Patterson, the reigning champion, on a technical knockout.

20.17   Cho Choo Coleman and I only have him for two days] Coleman (1937–2016), a weak-hitting catcher, was called up from Syracuse in the International League and played his first game as a Met on July 27, 1962.

20.21–22   the Mets played the St. Louis Cardinals in a doubleheader] On July 29, 1962, in St. Louis.

21.25–33   Bill Veeck . . . Eddie Gaedel] Veeck (1914–1986) was a Major League Baseball executive who at various times owned the Cleveland Indians, the St. Louis Browns, and the Chicago White Sox; he was known for his baseball acumen and gift for promotions that increased fan attendance. On August 19, 1951, Veeck hired the 3-foot-seven stage performer Eddie Gaedel (1925–1961) to make a single plate appearance for the Browns in a game against the Detroit Tigers; wearing the number 1/8, he walked and was replaced by a pinch runner.

22.25–29   Brooklyn Dodger . . . Ebbets Field] Ebbets Field, in the Flatbush section of Brooklyn, was home to the Brooklyn Dodgers baseball team, 1913–57, before the franchise moved to Los Angeles.

22.34   the Houston Colt .45s] Renamed the Houston Astros in 1965.

23.24   the fabled Rogers Hornsby] Hall of Fame infielder, manager, and coach (1896–1963) who played for the St. Louis Cardinals, the New York Giants, the Boston Braves, the Chicago Cubs, and the St. Louis Browns during his twenty-three-year career as a player.

23.38   Red Smith] Sportswriter (1905–1982), a columnist for the *New York Herald Tribune* and later *The New York Times*. He was awarded the Pulitzer Prize for Commentary in 1976.

26.26–28   stories . . . Babe Herman or Dizzy Dean] Herman (1903–1987), gifted hitter and poor fielding outfielder of the 1920s and 1930s, often remembered for his comical mental lapses on the field. Dean (1910–1974), Hall of Fame pitcher for the St. Louis Cardinals, 1930–38, and Chicago Cubs, 1938–41, who beguiled the public with his on-field antics.

28.5 a second-division team] Team in the bottom half of a league's end-of-season standings in Major League Baseball before the introduction of East and West Divisions within the National and American Leagues in 1969.

28.6 New Haven club] The New Haven Profs in the Eastern League, a minor league active from 1916 to 1932.

29.19–20 "Once when I had Ford . . . with the Yankees] Casey Stengel (1890–1975) managed the Yankees from 1949 to 1960. The Hall of Fame left-hander Whitey Ford (1928–2020) pitched for the Yankees from 1950 to 1967, a span in which the team won eight World Series championships. Gene Woodling (1922–2001) was on the Yankees under Stengel before being traded to the Baltimore Orioles; he finished his career as a player with the Mets in 1962.

34.18 Bill Veeck] See note 21.25–33.

34.37–38 Finley, the man who owns Kansas City] Businessman Charlie Finley (1918–1996), owner of the Kansas City (later Oakland) Athletics.

35.4 Goose Goslin] Hall of Fame outfielder (1900–1971) and exceptional hitter who played for the Washington Senators, the St. Louis Browns, and the Detroit Tigers during an eighteen-year professional career that ended in 1938.

40.3 Stillman's Gymnasium] Renowned boxing gym in Manhattan where champions such as Jack Dempsey, Joe Louis, and Rocky Marciano trained. It was run by Louis Ingber, also known as Lou Stillman (1887–1969).

40.15 Bobby Gleason's Gymnasium] Gleason's Gym, legendary boxing gym then located in the Bronx.

40.17 Lucius Benson] Middleweight boxer (b. 1937) who fought professionally from 1959 to 1964, finishing with a 13–1 record.

40.29 Billy Graham and Rocky Graziano] Graham (1922–1992), welterweight boxer who fought from 1941 to 1955, finishing with a 102–15–9 record; Graziano (1919–1990), middleweight world champion boxer who ended his career, 1942–52, with a 67–10–6 record.

40.33 Doug Jones, who lost to Cassius Clay] On March 13, 1963, Jones (1937–2017) lost a heavyweight bout to Clay (later Muhammad Ali, 1942–2016) by a unanimous but controversial decision at Madison Square Garden in New York City.

41.22–28 "Benny Paret," . . . fight in the Garden] The Cuban welterweight champion Benny Paret (1937–1962) died ten days after injuries he sustained in a televised boxing match at Madison Square Garden against Emile Griffith (1938–2013) on March 24, 1962.

42.11 "Brennan on the Moor"] Irish folk song about an outlaw; the version referred to here is likely the 1961 recording by the Clancy Brothers.

42.37 Iona] Iona College (now University) in New Rochelle, NY; the other schools mentioned are Fordham University in the Bronx, a Jesuit institution, and St. John's University in Queens, a Catholic university.

45.30   Valachi story in Queens] Grand jury testimony given by the New York mobster Joseph Valachi (1904–1971) at the Queens County Courthouse in relation to several underworld murders and other illegal activity. Valachi, imprisoned first for a narcotics conviction and then sentenced to life imprisonment for killing another inmate in a federal prison in Atlanta, had testified as a cooperating witness before a U.S. Senate subcommittee investigating organized crime. His testimony, broadcast on television, provided the first public confirmation of the existence of the Cosa Nostra by one of its members.

46.25   Walter Winchell] Influential New York *Daily Mirror* gossip columnist (1897–1972) and radio personality known for his broad network of sources and his penchant for trying to destroy the reputations of those he disliked or disagreed with.

46.30   the big one with Lepke,"] Louis Buchalter, also known as Louis Lepke, was a New York mobster and the head of Murder, Inc. (see note 5.2). In 1939, worried about being targeted by other gangsters, Lepke—in hiding after jumping bond on federal antitrust charges in 1937—decided to turn himself in to federal authorities and take refuge in prison, envisioning a relatively mild federal sentence. Through an intermediary he contacted Walter Winchell, who, with FBI director J. Edgar Hoover (1895–1972) by his side, offered during his radio broadcast on August 9 to negotiate surrender. On the night of August 23, Lepke got into Winchell's car on a Manhattan street corner, as arranged, and was handed over to Hoover a few blocks away. Convicted of a federal charge, as well as murder charges brought by New York State, Lepke was executed at Sing Sing state prison in Ossining, New York.

46.39–40   Hitler . . . Danzig] The Baltic port of Danzig (now Gdańsk, Poland) was made a free city under League of Nations supervision by the Treaty of Versailles in 1919; Poland was given free use of its port and railways and control of its foreign relations, while its internal affairs were conducted by a government elected by Danzig's majority German population. Hitler demanded Danzig's "return to the Reich" in October 1938, and the city was annexed to Nazi Germany following the German invasion of Poland in September 1939.

48.15–16   Joey, Larry, and Albert Gallo] "Crazy Joe" Gallo (1929–1972), New York City gangster known for his violent, unpredictable nature, reflected in part by his pet lion, Cleo, which he kept in the basement of his apartment on President Street in Brooklyn. He was at the center of an internecine Mafia war and was assassinated at Umberto's Clam House in Manhattan's Little Italy. He oversaw a crew that included his brothers Larry (1927–1968) and Albert Gallo (b. 1930).

48.21–22   the Profaci gang, the Gallo rivals . . . Carmine Persico] The criminal organization now known as the Colombo crime family, one of the so-called

Five Families of the Cosa Nostra in New York City, was led by the Sicilian-born Joseph Profaci (1897–1962) from the 1940s until his death in 1962. (Names now designating the other syndicates are the Gambino, Genovese, Lucchese, and Bonnano crime families.) The Gallo brothers led an internal revolt against Profaci, starting in 1960; the Brooklyn gangster Carmine Persico (1933–2019) initially aligned with the Gallos but then switched sides, later rising to become the organization's head.

49.23   Valachi] See note 45.30.

49.24   *Genowaysee*] I.e., the Genovese crime family.

49.25–27   Sidney Slater . . . lies about Joey] Slater was a businessman and crime associate of the Gallo brothers who became a police informant. Among his claims was that members of the Gallo gang had murdered Albert Anastasia (1902–1957), the head of what is now known as the Gambino crime family.

52.34–35   Cort Theater] Cort Theatre, Broadway theater that opened in 1912, now the James Earl Jones Theatre.

53.5   Fanny Brice] Comedian, singer, and actor (1891–1951).

53.34–35   "If Ever I Should Leave You,"] "If Ever I Would Leave You," song with music by Frederick Loewe (1901–1988), words by Alan Jay Lerner (1918–1986), from the Broadway musical *Camelot* (1960).

53.38–39   Bensonhurst] Neighborhood in Brooklyn.

60.21   Ford's Theatre] Theater in Washington, D.C., where President Abraham Lincoln (1809–1865) was fatally shot on April 14, 1865.

65.1   *Automat*] Horn & Hardart's Automat, a self-service restaurant chain founded in 1902 in Philadelphia, serving patrons inexpensive dishes via vending machines. There were numerous Automat restaurants in New York City into the 1960s.

66.8–12   "This thing they say they're going to build across the street . . . Penn Station] New York City officials revealed plans in 1962 to demolish Pennsylvania Station, a Beaux Arts railroad station completed in 1911, prompting heated public opposition; its demolition led to the establishment of the city's Landmarks Preservation Commission in 1965. It was replaced by a complex that included a train station, Madison Square Garden, and offices.

67.2   Cassius Clay] Later named Muhammad Ali. See note 40.33.

67.4   Big Willie Reddish] American heavyweight boxer (1912–1988) from 1933 to 1944, after which he became a boxing trainer.

67.22–25   the late Marcel Cerdan . . . Jake LaMotta . . . plane crash prevented] Marcel Cerdan (1916–1949), a French boxer born in Algeria, won the middleweight title against Jake LaMotta (1922–2017) in Detroit on June 16, 1949, in a fight in which Cerdan dislocated his shoulder. A rematch in New

York on September 28 was postponed until December 2 because LaMotta injured his right shoulder in preparation for the fight. Cerdan died when his Air France plane crashed in the Azores on October 28, 1949, killing all forty-eight people on board.

67.25–27   Willie Pep . . . Sandy Saddler . . . rematch] Featherweight champions and rivals Willie Pep (1922–2006) and Sandy Saddler (1926–2001) fought four times, with Saddler victorious in all but the second. In their third fight, on February 11, 1949, Pep dislocated his shoulder.

68.18   history right along with Frankie Carbo] Testimony before a Senate subcommittee in 1960 established that the International Boxing Club, 1949–59, which had enjoyed a virtual monopoly over boxing promotion in the United States, had been largely controlled from behind the scenes by Paul (Frankie) Carbo (1904–1976), a reputed former contract killer. In 1961 Carbo was convicted of extortion and sentenced to twenty-five years in prison.

68.19–20   the night Jake LaMotta lost to Billy Fox at the Garden] On November 14, 1947, Fox (1926–1986), a light heavyweight, defeated the heavily favored middleweight LaMotta by technical knockout in a bout lasting four rounds at Madison Square Garden, immediately raising suspicions and prompting the New York district attorney to investigate whether LaMotta had thrown the fight, which he denied. In 1960 LaMotta admitted to a Senate subcommittee that he had intentionally lost the match.

68.20–21   the night Ray Robinson collapsed from the heat against Joey Maxim] At Yankee Stadium on June 25, 1952, with the temperature exceeding 100 degrees Fahrenheit, Ray Robinson (1921–1989) lost the light heavyweight title bout against Joey Maxim (1922–2001) when Robinson, delirious from the heat, was unable to fight the fourteenth round.

73.11–13   A 15-year-old boy . . . shot to death by an off-duty police lieutenant] Fifteen-year old James Powell was fatally shot in Harlem by the off-duty police officer Thomas Gilligan on July 16, 1964, setting off several days of unrest resulting in one death and more than one hundred injured.

73.29   Bayard Rustin] Civil rights activist and organizer (1912–1987).

74.3   No. 28 Hyde Park Gate] London residence of Winston Churchill.

74.17–18   Lord Nelson . . . Trafalgar Square] Trafalgar Square, in London's Westminster section, is the site of a large statue and pillar honoring Vice-Admiral Horatio, Lord Nelson (1758–1805), and commemorating the 1805 British naval victory in the Napoleonic Wars near Cape Trafalgar, off the Spanish coast, in which he was killed.

74.18–20   Duke of Wellington . . . plaza] Hyde Park Corner is the location of an equestrian statue of the British general and statesman Arthur Wellesley, 1st Duke of Wellington (1769–1852).

74.22–23   from Gladstone . . . Church] The Gladstone Memorial, in front of St. Clement Danes church in Westminster, honors the English statesman William Gladstone (1809–1898).

75.14   Admiralty Board] Administrative body overseeing the administration of the Naval Service of the United Kingdom.

75.19   Lamson tube] Pneumatic tube through which objects, particularly letters and documents, could be quickly transported via suction or compressed air, named for the American entrepreneur William Stickney Lamson (1845–1912), whose company popularized their use.

75.23–24   "Winston is back,"] Message signaled to Royal Navy ships and installations on September 3, 1939, the day Britain declared war on Germany, to announce Churchill's appointment as First Lord of the Admiralty, an office he had held from August 1914 to July 1915.

78.25–26   Thomas Hagan . . . ones who were with him] Hagan, also known as Talmadge Hayer (later Mujahid Abdul Halim, b. 1941), was a member of the Newark temple of the Nation of Islam, a Black separatist religious group founded in 1930 and led by Elijah Muhammad (1897–1975) from 1934 until his death. Its members are commonly known as Black Muslims. Halim was indicted for the murder of Malcolm X (born Malcolm Little, 1925–1965) on March 11, 1965, along with two Black Muslims from New York, Thomas 15X Johnson (later Khalil Islam, 1935–2009) and Norman 3X Butler (later Muhammad Abdul Aziz, b. 1938). All three men were found guilty on March 10, 1966, and were sentenced to life terms. In an affidavit filed in 1977, Halim admitted his involvement in the murder and stated that his accomplices were four men from New Jersey. In 2021, the convictions of Islam and Aziz were dismissed after an investigation by the Manhattan District Attorney's office and lawyers for Islam and Aziz revealed that the FBI and the New York Police Department had withheld evidence that would have exonerated them.

79.4–5   fight against . . . Black Muslims] Malcolm X had broken with Elijah Muhammad in March 1964. He then made a pilgrimage to Mecca and converted to Sunni Islam.

82.22   CORE] Congress of Racial Equality, a civil rights organization.

85.37   White Citizens' Council] A white supremacist organization founded in 1954 to oppose desegregation by political, legal, and economic means.

85.39   Alabama A & M] Alabama Agricultural and Mechanical University, a historically Black public university in Huntsville, AL.

86.25   Tobacco Road] I.e., white southerners. *Tobacco Road* (1932), popular novel by Erskine Caldwell (1903–1987) adapted as a Broadway play and film, centered on a family of Georgia tenant farmers.

87.1–2   John Doar, the Justice Department's man in charge of civil rights] Doar (1921–2014) served in the Justice Department's Civil Rights Division as first assistant to the assistant attorney general, 1960–65, and headed the division as assistant attorney general for civil rights, 1965–67. In 1974, he also served as special counsel for the House Judiciary Committee during proceedings that led to the impeachment of President Richard M. Nixon (1913–1994).

91.26   Bobbs-Merrill reader] One of a series of books for young readers produced by the Bobbs-Merrill publishing company.

91.27   *Conrad's Magic Flight*] Children's book (1939) fostering music appreciation by the music educator and composer Hazel Gertrude Kinscella (1893–1960).

93.6   Tony Bennett] Popular American jazz and pop singer (1926–2023).

93.14   Governor of the State of Alabama] George Wallace (1919–1998), governor of Alabama, 1963–67, 1971–79, 1983–87, and third-party and Democratic presidential candidate known for his slogan "Segregation now, segregation tomorrow, segregation forever."

94.2   Fat Thomas] Fat Thomas Rand (b. 1931), bookmaker and actor who was a recurring character in Breslin's columns.

94.4   Jefferson Davis Hotel] A former hotel in Montgomery, AL, that remained segregated into the 1960s.

98.8   Camp Pendleton] Marine Corps training base in San Diego County, CA.

98.11   Da Nang] Large port city in central Vietnam lying on the South China Sea; its airport was used as an air base by U.S. and South Vietnamese forces during the Vietnam War.

108.25   Phan Thiet] Capital of Bình Thuận province, on the southeastern coast of Vietnam.

108.33   Binh Duong] Vietnamese province in the southeastern region of the country.

110.1–2   *Stork Club* . . . SHERMAN BILLINGSLEY] On East 53rd Street off Fifth Avenue, the Stork Club, owned and operated by the former bootlegger Sherman Billingsley (1900–1966), was New York's preeminent nightclub, 1929–65.

110.5   Connie Bennett] Constance Bennett (1904–1965), socialite and movie star whose films included *Born to Love* (1931) and *What Price Hollywood* (1932).

110.7   Walter's] Walter Winchell (see note 46.25).

110.10   Morton Downey] American singer, entertainer, and radio personality (1901–1985).

110.10   Brenda Frazier] Glamorous debutante and socialite (1921–1982) whose 1963 memoir in *Life* magazine recorded her dissatisfaction with her wealthy lifestyle; in a poem she had written as a young woman she noted: "I grit my teeth and smile at my enemies; / I sit at the Stork Club and talk to nonentities."

110.10 Gene Tierney] American film and stage actor (1920–1991) known for her beauty, with starring roles in *Laura* (1944) and *Leave Her to Heaven* (1945).

110.11 Doris Duke] Heiress and philanthropist (1912–1993) whose social life frequently provided fodder for the gossip pages.

110.33 gunmen Owney Madden and Frenchy DeMange] Owen "Owney" Madden (1891–1965) was a gangster, bootlegger, nightclub owner, and boxing promoter; as Breslin had written after Madden's death in Arkansas in April 1965, "Owney left the city in 1935 [. . .] But Owney Madden is still a known name in New York City. He came off the West Side and ran Prohibition breweries and owned heavyweight champions and always had guns around him." His business partner George "Big Frenchy" DeMange (1896–1939) was a gangster whom Owney had freed via a ransom when DeMange had been kidnapped by a rival gangster.

111.9–10 Dick Conlon . . . Gallagher says] Conlon (1915–1975) was the Stork Club's general manager, 1950–1957, and later ran Gallaghers Steak House, 228 West 52nd Street, New York City.

114.3 Rolla, Mo.] Small city in south-central Missouri. Its population in the mid-1960s was about twelve-thousand.

118.1 *Easter Rising*] A six-day armed uprising in Dublin by Irish rebels opposed to British rule beginning on April 24, 1916, the day after Easter. The rebels took control of the city's General Post Office and issued a proclamation of Irish independence from Britain. Over the course of the rebellion 458 were killed and approximately two thousand were wounded. Sixteen rebel leaders were executed by the British, fifteen in May and one in August.

118.14 Eamon De Valera] American-born Irish revolutionary, politician, and statesman (1882–1975), prime minister (*taoiseach*) of Ireland, 1937–48, 1951–54, 1957–59. A death sentence for his involvement in the Easter Rising was commuted to a life sentence; he was released in 1917 when the British government granted amnesty to hundreds of nationalists who had taken part in the rebellion.

120.31–32 a movie with Richard Burton in it] *The Spy Who Came in from the Cold* (1965), film directed by Martin Ritt (1914–1990) and starring Burton (1925–1984), an adaptation of the 1963 novel by John le Carré (1931–2020).

121.2 Watts] Unrest triggered by a police traffic stop in the mainly Black neighborhood of Watts in Los Angeles, August 11–16, 1965, resulted in thirty-four deaths.

121.5–6 Kilmainham Prison, where the British executed sixteen of the Irish leaders] Fourteen of the Rising's leaders were executed on the grounds of Dublin's Kilmainham Prison, May 3–12, 1916. Thomas Kent (1865–1916), who had planned to travel from County Cork to Dublin to take part in the Rising but mistakenly believed that the rebellion had been postponed, was arrested after a gunfight and executed at Cork Detention Barracks. Roger Casement (1864–1916) was hanged at Pentonville Prison in London on August 3, 1916.

123.3 John Hay "Jock" Whitney] Diplomat, philanthropist, and newspaper publisher (1904–1982), a member of the prominent and wealthy Whitney family. He became owner of the *Herald Tribune* in 1958 and was its publisher, 1961–66.

123.13–14 John O'Hara] American novelist and short-story writer (1905–1970) who worked for about six months as a *Herald Tribune* reporter and rewrite man in 1928.

123.14 St. Clair McKelway, Don Skene and Joel Sayre] McKelway (1905–1980), longtime writer and editor for *The New Yorker* who had worked for the *Herald Tribune* in the 1920s. Skene (1897–1938), sportswriter and author of the novel *The Red Tiger* (1934) who covered boxing as a staff writer on the *Herald Tribune*, 1927–31, 1934. Sayre (1900–1979), a novelist, war correspondent, and screenwriter who was a reporter for the *Herald Tribune* in the 1920s.

123.15–16 Joe H. Palmer's] Palmer (1904–1952) was a sports columnist for the *Herald Tribune*, 1946–52, known for his coverage of horse racing.

123.29–30 Red Smith] Smith (see note 23.38) wrote for the *Herald Tribune* from 1945 to 1966.

123.35–36 Walter Lippmann, Joseph Alsop, Art Buchwald] Lippmann (1889–1974) wrote his syndicated "Today and Tomorrow" column for the *Herald Tribune*, 1931–62. Alsop (1910–1989), with his brother Stewart, wrote a syndicated column, "Matter of Fact," for the newspaper, 1945–58. Buchwald (1925–2007), a popular American syndicated columnist and humorist, began writing for the *Herald Tribune* in its European edition in 1949.

124.24 Doug Kiker] Author and journalist (1930–1991) who was White House correspondent for the *Herald Tribune*, 1963–66.

124.26 Andrew J. Glass] Polish-born American author and journalist (b. 1935) who was chief congressional correspondent for the *Herald Tribune*, 1963–66.

125.5–6 James G. Bellows] Bellows (1922–2009) was editor of the *Herald Tribune*, 1961–66.

126.23 Fred Shapiro] Fred C. Shapiro (d. 1993 aged 62) worked on the *Herald Tribune*'s rewrite desk, 1962–65, before becoming a staff writer for *The New Yorker.*

126.38 Walter Kerr] Pulitzer Prize–winning Broadway theater critic, writer, and director (1913–1996).

127.2 Jean Kerr] Author, playwright, and screenwriter (1922–2003), best known for *Please Don't Eat the Daisies* (1957), a collection of humorous essays about parenthood and living in the suburbs, adapted for the screen (1960) and the basis of a television sitcom on NBC, 1965–67.

128.34   10-year sentence] Convicted of armed robbery in 1963, Thompson (1925–1969) was paroled in December 1966. He became a playground director in Fresno, CA, and died following a seizure at the age of forty-three.

129.7   "Did you see Willie Davis make all those errors?"] Davis (1940–2010), the Dodgers center fielder, committed three errors in the fifth inning of Game 2 in the 1966 World Series.

129.19   great pennant finish of 1951] The 1951 National League pennant race, determining the league champion that would advance to the World Series, concluded in a best-of-three playoff due to the New York Giants and the Brooklyn Dodgers ending their seasons with identical records. The Giants won the pennant in Game 3, October 3, 1951, when third baseman Bobby Thomson (1923–2010) hit a home run off Dodgers relief pitcher Ralph Branca (1926–2016), which came to be known as the "Shot Heard Round the World."

132.6   Schrafft's] Chain of moderately priced restaurants that grew out of William G. Schrafft's Boston candy company.

132.13–14   his Newfoundland sheepdog messing the late Sen. Harry Byrd's office rug] In March 1965, shortly after beginning his term as U.S. senator, Kennedy took his Newfoundland dog, Brumus, to meet the cocker spaniel of Virginia senator Harry F. Byrd, Sr. (1887–1966) at Byrd's office; Brumus urinated on a new rug in the office.

140.34–36   Goodson-Todman . . . "To Tell the Truth."] The television game show *To Tell the Truth*, created in 1956 and airing on CBS when this column was published, was one of several successful game shows produced by the company founded by Mark Goodson (1915–1992) and Bill Todman (1916–1979).

142.13–14   the Ed Sullivan Show] Long-running television variety show on CBS, 1948–71, hosted by newspaper columnist Ed Sullivan (1901–1974).

143.35   Gen. Omar Bradley] American military leader (1893–1981) who was field commander of American ground forces in the 1944 Normandy invasion; chairman of the Joint Chiefs of Staff, 1949–53.

143.40   the jerk] Dance craze that began in 1964.

145.14   Toots Shor's] Toots Shor's Restaurant at 51 West 51st Street, renowned for its celebrity clientele; it was named for its owner and proprietor, the businessman Bernard "Toots" Shor (1903–1977).

145.35–36   flag picture from Iwo Jima] *Raising the Flag on Iwo Jima* (1945), by the Associated Press photographer Joe Rosenthal (1911–2006), a widely reproduced Pulitzer Prize–winning photograph taken on February 23, 1945, showing a group of five marines and a navy corpsman raising an American flag on Mount Surabachi.

152.4–5   last season . . . the only lift the city has had] As quarterback for the American Football League's New York Jets, Namath (b. 1943) led the team in an upset victory against the National Football League's Baltimore Colts in Super Bowl III, January 12, 1969.

153.14   Dustin Hoffman in *The Graduate*] Hoffman (b. 1937) starred in *The Graduate* (1967), comedy-drama film that won an Academy Award for its director, Mike Nichols (1931–2014).

153.24   In college] At the University of Alabama.

153.28–29   *Penn-syl-va-nia* kid] Namath grew up in Beaver Falls, a town northwest of Pittsburgh.

155.40–156.1   All-American quarterbacks . . . Tulsa . . . Jerry Rhome] Rhome (b. 1942) was an All-American quarterback for the University of Tulsa in 1964; among the professional teams that drafted him out of college was the New York Jets, but he signed with the Dallas Cowboys.

156.9   Paul Newman and Joanne Woodward are doing a film] Newman (1925–2008) and Woodward (b. 1930), husband and wife, were in sixteen films together over the course of their careers; the film alluded to here is possibly *WUSA* (1971).

156.25–28   Pensacola." . . . new college] The University of West Florida, founded in 1963.

159.5   Mel Ott] Hall of Fame outfielder (1909–1958) for the New York Giants, baseball team 1926–47.

159.18   Pete Reiser] "Pistol Pete" Reiser (1919–1981), Brooklyn Dodgers outfielder, 1940–42, 1946–48, known for the numerous injuries he sustained on aggressive fielding plays.

159.35   Ring Lardner's "You Know Me Al"] Comic epistolary novel (1916) by Ring Lardner (1885–1933) about baseball, featuring error-riddled letters by the unsophisticated ballplayer Jack Keefe.

160.3   Joe Namath] See Breslin's profile of Namath in this volume, pp. 151–57.

160.11   Woodstock] Music festival held on a farm in Bethel, NY (forty miles southwest of the town of Woodstock), August 15–18, 1969.

160.37–39   Josh Gibson . . . not allowed into the major league] A power-hitting catcher, Gibson (1911–1947) spent most of his seventeen-year professional career in the Negro League but never played in the Major Leagues because of the league's racist exclusion of Black players until 1947. He was inducted into the Baseball Hall of Fame in 1972.

161.2   two Yogi Berras] Berra (1925–2015), a Hall of Fame catcher and outfielder, spent all but the last of his nineteen seasons as a player with the New York Yankees, then went on to serve for many years as a manager and coach. He was inducted into the Baseball Hall of Fame in 1972.

161.2   Bill Veeck] See note 21.25–33.

161.7   Dixie series in 1937] Minor league series pitting the champions of the
Texas League and the Southern Association against each other; in 1937, the
Fort Worth Cats (Texas League) defeated the Little Rock Travelers (Southern
Association).

162.3   Attica] A five-day riot by twelve hundred inmates at Attica State
Correctional Institution in Attica, NY, ended on September 13, 1971, when the
prison was retaken on the order of Governor Nelson Rockefeller (1908–1979)
after negotiations with the prisoners broke down. Thirty-three inmates and ten
of their hostages were killed in the action and another eighty persons wounded.

162.10–11   Rockefeller has a family background . . . Ludlow massacre]
Governor Nelson Rockefeller's grandfather, the business magnate John D.
Rockefeller, Sr. (1839–1937), owned a controlling interest in the Colorado Fuel
and Iron Company, which operated coal mines in Colorado. The United Mine
Workers organized a strike in September 1913 in which the striking miners
abandoned the company's camps and established their own tent encampments,
including the site in Ludlow dubbed White City, occupied by about twelve
hundred miners and their families. The Colorado National Guard was brought
in to quell the strike in fall 1913, skirmishing sporadically with armed strikers
over the next several months. On April 20, 1914, shooting broke out between
the Guard, which had mounted a machine gun atop a hill overlooking the
encampment, and the strikers. In the evening guardsmen set tents in White
City on fire, killing two women and eleven children who had taken refuge in a
pit. Over the next week and a half, the strikers attacked mines in the area and
clashed with the Guard; federal troops were called in to restore order. More
than seventy-five people died in the Ludlow violence.

162.18–26   a real bum named Barabbas . . . revolutionary movement, the
Zealot Movement.] In the Gospels, Barabbas is released from custody after
Pontius Pilate, the governor of Judea, offers the crowd the choice of freeing
either him or Jesus; see Matthew 27:15–26, Mark 15:6–15, Luke 23:13–25, and
John 18:39–40. In the latter three versions Barabbas is said to have been an
insurrectionist against Roman rule; the account in Matthew refers to him only
as a "notable prisoner."

162.23   Lepke] See notes 5.2 and 46.30.

163.2–10   two thieves . . . in paradise."] See Luke 23:32–43.

163.6   top hoodlum like Bumpy Johnson] Johnson (1905–1968) was a powerful
crime boss in Harlem.

163.26–27   the three really good prayer people . . . Cooke] Billy Graham
(1918–2018), American evangelical minister and internationally recognized
Christian leader who counseled several U.S. presidents, most notably Lyndon
B. Johnson (1908–1973) and Richard M. Nixon; Norman Vincent Peale (1898–
1993), American minister and author best known for his popular book *The
Power of Positive Thinking* (1952); Terence Cooke (1921–1983), Roman Catholic
cardinal, archbishop of New York, 1968–83.

165.32   Bob Cousy] Basketball player (b. 1928) who was one of the sport's first superstars, a point guard who played most of his professional career for the Boston Celtics.

167.34–35   Malcolm X day] Here celebrated in February, though annual commemorations honoring Malcolm X have come to be celebrated on May 19, his birthday.

170.36   Adolph Rupp, Henry Iba, Phog Allen] Highly successful college basketball coaches: Rupp (1901–1977), who led the University of Kentucky team for forty-two years; Iba (1904–1993), coach of Oklahoma A&M, 1934–70; and Allen (1885–1974), who spent most of his coaching career with the University of Kansas.

170.37   Dick, probably one of the best backcourt men] Dick McGuire (1926–2010), standout guard for the New York Knicks, 1949–57, and the Detroit Pistons, 1957–60, and later coach of both the Pistons and the Knicks.

170.39   oldest brother, John] John McGuire (d. 2016), a police officer and later the proprietor of Breslin's preferred Queens saloon, Pep McGuire's.

172.3–4   House Un-American Activities Committee] Or HUAC, investigative committee of the U.S. House of Representatives best known for its inquiries into alleged communist influence in government and the motion-picture industry in the late 1940s and early 1950s.

172.5   J. Parnell Thomas] Republican U.S. congressman (1895–1970) from New Jersey who in 1947 headed HUAC hearings on communist influence in Hollywood. In 1950, ten uncooperative witnesses—who had been cited for contempt of Congress—were sent to prison. Convicted of corruption that same year, Thomas spent nine months in prison in Danbury, CT, where among his fellow inmates were two of the men cited by his committee.

172.5–6   Reps. John McDowell, Richard Vail and Richard Nixon] McDowell (1902–1957), Republican congressman from Pennsylvania, 1931–1941, 1947–49; Vail (1895–1955), Republican congressman from Illinois, 1947–49, 1951–53; Nixon, later U.S. president, served as a Republican congressman from California, 1947–50.

172.9   Ring Lardner Jr.] Award-winning screenwriter and journalist (1915–2000), son of the fiction writer and journalist Ring Lardner (1885–1933). Lardner Jr. was one of the Hollywood Ten, ten screenwriters who refused on First Amendment grounds to answer questions about their membership in the Communist Party when they were subpoenaed by HUAC in 1947. They were subsequently convicted of contempt of Congress and served prison terms of up to one year.

173.10   movie called M*A*S*H] Lardner Jr. wrote the screenplay for the 1970 adaptation of *MASH: A Novel About Three Army Doctors* (1968), by Richard Hooker (pseud. H. Richard Hornberger Jr., 1924–1997), based on the latter's service as an army surgeon in South Korea during the Korean War. Directed by Robert Altman (1925–2006), the film starred Donald Sutherland (b. 1935) and Elliott Gould (b. 1938).

174.4–6   David Lardner . . . World War II.] Breslin here has confused the deaths of two of Ring Lardner, Jr.'s brothers. James Lardner (1914–1938) covered the Spanish Civil War as a journalist for the *New York Herald Tribune*'s Paris bureau and then enlisted in the Abraham Lincoln Brigade, a unit of American volunteers who fought on the Republican side against the Nationalists; he was killed in action in September 1938. David Lardner (1919–1944), war correspondent for *The New Yorker* and a film critic, was killed near Aachen, Germany, on October 19, 1944.

174.6–8   John Lardner . . . killed in Bleeck's by drinking with Walt Kelly] Lardner (1912–1960) died of a heart attack suffered at his home. His *White Hopes and Other Tigers* (1951) is a book on boxing. Bleeck's (pronounced "Blake's," after its founding proprietor, Jack Bleeck) was a restaurant and bar popular with journalists at 213 West 40th Street, founded during Prohibition as the Artist & Writers' Club. Walt Kelly (1913–1973), artist who drew the syndicated satirical comic strip *Pogo*, 1949–73 (see Chronology, 1964).

174.38–39   I could be a Swanson and get myself a marquis] The third husband of actor Gloria Swanson (1899–1983) was the French film director and producer Henry de La Falaise, Marquis de La Coudraye (1898–1972).

176.12–19   in front of the H.U.A.C. . . . Danbury Correctional Institute] See notes 172.3–4, 172.5, and 172.5–6.

HOW THE GOOD GUYS FINALLY WON

179.23   Mardian] Robert Mardian (1923–2006), lawyer and Republican Party official, assistant attorney general, 1970–72, and coordinator of the Nixon campaign's Committee to Re-Elect the President. Mardian's 1975 conviction for conspiracy to obstruct justice in connection with the Watergate political scandal was overturned the next year on appeal.

183.31   Weathermen] Members of Weatherman (later called the Weather Underground), a violent splinter faction of the leftist Students for a Democratic Society (SDS).

185.31   Larry O'Brien] Longtime Democratic Party official (1917–1990) who served as postmaster general, 1965–68, and as Democratic National Committee chairman, 1970–72. On June 17, 1972, his office in the Watergate building complex in Washington, D.C., was broken into, sparking the political scandal that led to the resignation of President Richard M. Nixon.

190.36   Rip Valente] Anthony "Rip" Valenti (1901–1986) was a prominent boxing promoter from Boston.

191.28–29   Hough at the time of the riot in 1966] Race- and poverty-related riot in Cleveland's Hough neighborhood, July 18–23, 1966. Four people were killed and fifty others injured.

195.4–5   Watergate investigators, Dave Dorsen for one] David M. Dorsen (b. 1935) served as assistant chief counsel of the Senate Select Committee to Investigate Campaign Practices, better known as the Senate Watergate Committee.

195.36   Fred Malek] Business executive, philanthropist, and longtime Republican political adviser (1936–2019); he served as special assistant to the president, 1970–73, and as deputy chief of the Committee to Re-Elect the President.

195.38   John Connally's Democrats for Nixon] Connally (1917–1993), who as a Democrat had been secretary of the navy, 1961, and governor of Texas, 1963–69, headed this Republican-funded group in 1972; he switched parties and became a Republican the following year.

197.24   a friend, Charles U. Daly] Daly (b. 1927) was an aide to President John F. Kennedy and, later, the director of the John F. Kennedy Presidential Library and Museum.

198.6   one of the trips this Cora Weiss takes."] The activist Cora Weiss (b. 1934) traveled to North Vietnam several times, beginning in 1969.

198.25   Ervin committee] The Senate Watergate Committee, chaired by Sam J. Ervin, Jr. (1896–1985), Democratic U.S. senator from North Carolina, 1954–74.

198.33   *Jeb Magruder*] Jeb Stuart Magruder (1934–2014), businessman, Republican Party official, aide to President Nixon, and deputy director of the Committee to Re-Elect the President. He pleaded guilty in 1973 to conspiracy charges and served seven months in prison.

198.34   *Gordon Strachan*] Lawyer (b. 1943) and White House aide during the Nixon administration, including a brief term as chief of staff; he was the White House liaison with the Committee to Re-Elect the President.

199.2   *John J. Caulfield*] Caulfield (1929–2012), a former New York City police detective who worked as a security operative for the Nixon administration, engaged in various dirty tricks, including surveillance work against perceived enemies of the president. He testified before the Senate Watergate Committee but avoided prosecution.

199.26   August Busch] August Anheuser "Gussie" Busch, Jr. (1899–1989), executive and chairman of the Anheuser-Busch company, 1946–75.

200.3   Kenny O'Donnell] Political consultant (1924–1977) and a close associate of the Kennedy family, serving as special assistant and appointments secretary to President John F. Kennedy and as an adviser to the 1968 presidential campaign of Robert F. Kennedy.

201.13–16   Ford . . . had called for the impeachment of Supreme Court Justice William O. Douglas] At the behest of President Nixon, who had been angered by the defeat of two southern nominees to the Supreme Court in 1969–70, Gerald Ford (1913–2006), then House minority leader, gave a speech on the House floor on April 15, 1970, calling for the impeachment of Supreme Court justice William O. Douglas (1898–1980). A six-month investigation by the Judiciary Committee concluded that there were no grounds for Douglas's impeachment.

203.19–20 a candidate for citywide office] See Chronology, 1969.

203.25–26 "The reputation of power is power." From *Leviathan* (1651), pt. I, ch. 10, by the English political philosopher Thomas Hobbes (1588–1679).

206.21 judge named Whipple] Lawrence A. Whipple (1910–1983), judge of the United States District Court of New Jersey, 1967–78, including as chief judge, 1974–78; served as senior judge, 1978–83.

207.35–36 a Cambridge politician named Chick Artesani] Charles J. Artesani (1911–1992), Massachusetts state representative, 1939–58, and a municipal court judge in Brighton.

208.1–2 committed to Mike Neville] In 1946 Neville (1899–1962), formerly a Massachusetts state legislator and the mayor of Cambridge, was defeated in a Democratic congressional primary in an election won by John F. Kennedy.

208.24 picture of a PT boat] PT 109, the patrol torpedo boat Kennedy commanded during World War II, was sunk after it was struck by a Japanese destroyer in the early morning hours of August 2, 1943, in the Blackett Strait south of the Solomon Islands. The story of the ordeal faced by Kennedy and his surviving crew members before their rescue several days later circulated widely via newspaper accounts and magazine stories such as "Survival" by John Hersey (1914–1993), published in *The New Yorker* on June 17, 1944, and in abridged form in *Reader's Digest* the following month.

215.5 Derek Bok] Lawyer and educator (b. 1930), president of Harvard University, 1971–91, and acting president, 2006–7.

215.6 John Silber] Educator (1926–2012), president of Boston University, 1971–96.

215.12 Raoul Berger] Constitutional scholar (1901–2000), a law professor at the University of California, Berkeley, and at Harvard University School of Law. His well-known criticism of "executive privilege" was considered damaging to President Nixon.

215.29 Sumner Prize for Originality] Harvard University awards its Charles Sumner Prize not for originality but for a written work "dealing with any means or measures tending toward the prevention of war and the establishment of universal peace."

217.38–39 Sam Rayburn's old "Board of Education"] Twenty-four–term Texas congressman Sam Rayburn (1882–1961) was Speaker of the House of Representatives, 1940–47, 1949–53, 1955–61, and hosted "Board of Education" meetings, where powerful House members would gather for drink, poker, and off-the-record conversations about politics.

217.39   John McCormack] Politician (1891–1980), a Democratic congressman from Massachusetts, 1928–71, and Speaker of the House, 1961–70.

219.38–39   from grocery store] As a teenager Nixon worked for his family's grocery store in Whittier, CA.

220.11–12   stepped into the helicopter on the lawn] Boarding a military helicopter on August 9, 1974, Nixon, having just resigned as president, waved and made the V-for-victory sign with both hands in front of a crowd assembled on the South Lawn of the White House.

220.13   Dean Burch] Lawyer, lobbyist, and prominent Republican (1927–1991), chairman of the Federal Communications Commission, 1969–74, and counselor to the president, 1974–75, in the Nixon and Ford administrations.

220.35   Kissinger, Mansfield, Scott, Griffin, Rhodes, Byrd] Henry Kissinger (b. 1923), who for the Nixon and Ford administrations was both national security advisor, 1969–75, and secretary of state, 1973–77. Montana U.S. senator Mike Mansfield (1903–2001), a Democrat, 1953–77, Senate Majority Leader, 1961–77. Pennsylvania U.S. senator Hugh Scott (1900–1994), senator, 1959–77, Senate minority leader, 1969–77. Michigan U.S. senator Robert P. Griffin (1923–2015), a Republican, senator, 1966–79, minority whip, 1969–77. Republican Arizona congressman John Jacob Rhodes (1916–2003), representative, 1953–83, minority leader, 1973–81. Robert Byrd (1917–2010), Democrat from West Virginia, U.S. senator, 1959–2010, the longest Senate tenure in history, during which he held several positions, including Senate majority leader, Senate minority leader, and Senate president pro tempore.

221.31   the Israeli war] The Yom Kippur War, October 6–October 25, 1973, in which Egypt and Syria, with support from other Arab states, fought Israel.

222.14–18   "There is," wrote Kierkegaard . . . deeds."] From *Fear and Trembling* (1843), treatise by the Danish philosopher Søren Kierkegaard (1813–1855).

222.36–37   George Beall] Lawyer and public official (1937–2017, pronounced "bell") who, as United States attorney for Maryland, prosecuted Vice President Spiro Agnew in 1973 on charges of conspiracy, bribery, extortion, and tax fraud stretching back to Agnew's tenure as Baltimore County executive in the 1960s. Agnew resigned the vice presidency and pleaded no contest to one count of tax evasion, for which he was fined $10,000. (He later paid the state of Maryland $268,482, the amount he was known to have taken in bribes.) Beall's brother and father were both U.S. senators from Maryland.

223.26–28   part of the letter . . . precedents, involving the case of John C. Calhoun] Agnew's letter cited a December 1826 letter by John C. Calhoun (1782–1850), then vice president, requesting that the House of Representatives investigate a newspaper's allegations that Calhoun had benefited from a stone contract for the building of a fort given in 1818 to Elijah Mix, the brother-in-law of Christopher Van Deventer (1789–1838), the chief clerk under Calhoun as secretary of war. A House commission met for forty days and found no wrongdoing on Calhoun's part.

224.28   Barry Goldwater] Republican politician (1909–1998), U.S. senator from Arizona, 1953–65, 1969–87, and Republican nominee for president in 1964.

229.36   Eliot Richardson] Lawyer and Republican politician (1920–1999) who served in the cabinets of Presidents Nixon and Ford. On October 20, 1973, in what became known as the "Saturday Night Massacre," Richardson resigned as attorney general rather than fulfill Nixon's order to fire Special Counsel Archibald Cox (1912–2004), the lawyer Richardson had appointed to oversee the independent investigation of the Watergate scandal. Cox had subpoenaed secret recordings of Oval Office conversations from the president, which Nixon claimed were protected by confidentiality. After the resignations of Richardson and the deputy attorney general, William Ruckelshaus (1932–2019), who likewise refused to dismiss Cox, the acting attorney general, Robert Bork (1927–2012), carried out the firing.

230.39–231.1   general named Sherman Miles . . . also in politics] Miles (1882–1966), a military officer in Army Intelligence, served as a representative in the Massachusetts House of Representatives, 1947–52. He was the grandson of Civil War general William Tecumseh Sherman.

231.1–2   in the Ardennes Forest] Region of Belgium, France, and Luxembourg, site of German offensive campaign in the Battle of the Bulge, December 16, 1944–January 28, 1945, a victory for the Allies.

231.23   Dwight Chapin] Political operative and businessman (b. 1940) who served as special assistant to President Nixon, 1968–71, and deputy assistant, 1971–73, responsible for the president's appointments schedule. Convicted in 1974 of lying to a grand jury investigating the Watergate scandal, he served eight months in federal prison.

231.29   of Colfax] Schuyler Colfax (1823–1885), vice president of the United States, 1869–73, was accused of accepting a bribe while serving as Speaker of the House, 1863–69; the House Judiciary Committee determined that he could not be impeached because the alleged bribe had not taken place while he was vice president.

231.29–30   of Andrew Johnson] The House of Representatives voted to impeach President Andrew Johnson (1808–1875) on February 24, 1868, and approved eleven articles of impeachment on March 2–3. On May 16 the Senate acquitted Johnson of the most comprehensive article of impeachment, 35–19, one vote short of the required two-thirds majority to remove him from office.

He was acquitted of two further articles of impeachment on May 26 and his trial was adjourned indefinitely.

231.30   the Journal of James Madison] The meticulous report by Madison (1751–1836) of the proceedings of the Constitutional Convention of 1787, including discussions of impeachment among the delegates.

234.20–21   There would be no Caldwell Butlers or Tom Railsbacks] Republican congressmen on the House Judiciary Committee who worked with Democrats in what they called an "unholy alliance" to advance the impeachment process against Nixon. Butler (1925–2014), from Virginia, serving 1973–83, and Railsback (1932–2020), from Illinois, serving 1967–83, helped draft and voted for two of the three articles of impeachment against the president that the House Judiciary Committee referred to the full House of Representatives in July 1974.

235.1–2   Charles Colson] Lawyer and Republican political operative (1931–2012), special counsel to President Nixon, 1969–73, with a reputation as Nixon's "hit man." In 1974 he pleaded guilty to obstruction of justice in the espionage case of Daniel Ellsberg (1931–2023), a former U.S. government official who had given the "Pentagon Papers," a secret Defense Department study of the Vietnam War, to the press. Colson served seven months of a one- to -three-year sentence in federal prison, where he underwent a religious conversion, going on to a second career as an evangelical minister and champion of various causes, including prison reform.

236.37–38   John Wayne, even when he was in the middle of it all at Wake Island] Japanese forces captured Wake Island in the Pacific on December 23, 1941; their first attempt had been repulsed by U.S. Marines on December 11. The battle was dramatized in *Wake Island* (1942), starring tough-guy actor Brian Donlevy (1901–1972). Wayne (1907–1979) starred in numerous World War II movies, including several set in the Pacific Theater. Breslin may have been poking fun at Wayne, a war hawk, who never served in the military, and saw combat only on movie-studio lots.

236.40–237.1   Leonard Garment of the White House staff.] Garment (1924–2013) was White House counsel at the time.

237.14–15   *Marbury* v. *Madison*] U.S. Supreme Court decision (1803) establishing the principle of judicial review, which assigns to the judiciary the power of determining whether laws are constitutional.

238.14   Elizabeth Holtzman] U.S. congresswoman (b. 1941) from New York 1973–81, later Brooklyn district attorney and comptroller of New York City.

238.30–31   Joe McFadden and Nino Valdés . . . Sunnyside Gardens] The fight between heavyweights McFadden (1927–1990) and the Cuban-born Valdés (1924–2001) took place at the Sunnyside Garden Arena in Queens on January 4, 1952, with Valdés victorious by knockout in the seventh round of an eight-round bout.

238.34–35   when Tony DeMarco fought Carmine Basilio?] DeMarco (1932–2021) was defeated by Carmine Basilio (1927–2012) in a welterweight title bout in Syracuse, NY, on June 10, 1955, and in their rematch on November 30, 1955, at the Boston Garden, the fight referred to here by O'Neill.

239.1–2   Rocky Marciano] Heavyweight boxing champion (1923–1969) from Brockton, MA, who won all forty-nine of his bouts in his professional career, 1947–55.

239.14   on the *Sequoia*] The *Sequoia* was a yacht used by American presidents since Herbert Hoover; Nixon used it frequently, on eighty-eight occasions.

241.12   Father Berrigan] Daniel Berrigan (1921–2016), American Jesuit priest, peace activist, and poet who was one of the Catonsville Nine, nine Catholic activists who on May 17, 1968, extracted 378 draft files from the draft board office in Catonsville, MD, and burned them; found guilty of the destruction of U.S. property and of Selective Service files, he served eighteen months of a three-year sentence in federal prison.

243.11–12   my own Congressman, Benjamin Rosenthal] Lawyer and politician (1923–1983), a Democratic U.S. congressman who represented the Eighth and then the redrawn Seventh District in Queens, 1963–83.

243.16   if Manny Celler were still in charge."] Celler (1888–1981), Democratic congressman from New York, 1923–73, was Rodino's predecessor as chairman of the House Judiciary Committee, a position he had occupied since 1955.

246.9   Thomas Hale Boggs, Jr.] Lawyer and lobbyist (1940–2014), the son of powerful Louisiana congressman Thomas Hale Boggs (1914–1972) and Lindy Boggs (1916–2013), congresswoman and ambassador.

247.23–24   Meade Esposito, the Democratic leader of Brooklyn] Political boss (1907–1993) and longtime leader of the Democratic Party in Brooklyn. He was found guilty of a federal bribery charge in 1988 and received a suspended sentence and a $500,000 fine.

249.36–37   What was it Macbeth said . . . done right away.'"] See *Macbeth*, I.vii.1–2: "If it were done, when 'tis done, then 'twere well / It were done quickly."

252.5–8   indictments of three . . . James Chaney] On August 4, 1964, the bodies of three civil rights workers—Michael Schwerner (1939–1964), James Chaney (1943–1964), and Andrew Goodman (1943–1964)—were found near Philadelphia, MS. They had been murdered by Ku Klux Klansmen who had buried their corpses under an earthen dam. Among the eighteen men indicted on January 15, 1965, by a federal grand jury on conspiracy charges related to the murders were Neshoba County sheriff Lawrence Rainey (1923–2002) and Cecil Price (1938–2001), a deputy sheriff. (Patrolman Otha Neal Burkes had been charged in December 1964 but was not included in the indictments.) A federal district judge dismissed the indictments against all the accused except

Rainey and Price on February 24, 1965, but in March 1966 the Supreme Court unanimously reversed his decision. The defendants went on trial in Meridian, MS, on October 9, 1967, with John Doar, then assistant attorney general for civil rights, leading the prosecution. On October 20, 1967, an all-white jury convicted Price; Rainey was acquitted.

253.22   the late Philip J. Philbin] Democratic U.S. congressman (1898–1972) from Massachusetts, 1943–71.

255.1   MR. WIGGINS] Charles E. Wiggins (1927–2000), Republican from California who served in the House of Representatives from 1967 to 1979. Initially a staunch defender of Nixon, he supported impeachment proceedings after more facts emerged.

256.21   GAO] Government Accounting Office.

258.39   Melvin Laird] Politician and cabinet official (1922–2016), secretary of defense, 1969–73; he had served in Congress as a Republican representative from Wisconsin, 1953–69.

259.9–11   Justice Department . . . Selma to Montgomery.] Martin Luther King, Jr., (1929–1968) led a march from Selma to Montgomery, AL, March 21–25, 1965, that was protected by federal troops. Earlier that month, on March 7, civil rights demonstrators attempting to march from Selma to Montgomery had been severely beaten by state troopers after crossing the Edmund Pettus Bridge. King had led a second march across the bridge on March 9, but then had the marchers stop and return to Selma in order to avoid further violence.

264.15   San Clemente] Site of La Casa Pacifica or the "Western White House," beachfront mansion in Orange County, CA, that served as President Nixon's office when living and working away from Washington, D.C.

268.22–23   John Dean informed him of the "cancer growing on the Presidency."] Phrase repeated by Dean (b. 1938) in his televised testimony before the Senate Watergate Committee on June 25, 1973: "I [told] the president there was a cancer growing on the presidency, and if the cancer was not removed, the president himself would be killed by it."

269.21–22   McCord . . . the Re-Election Committee] The former CIA official James W. McCord, Jr. (1924–2017) was security director for the Committee to Re-Elect the President and one of five men arrested for breaking into the Democratic National Committee headquarters at the Watergate office complex on the night of June 17, 1972. After his conviction on six counts of conspiracy, burglary, and eavesdropping on January 30, 1973, he wrote Judge John J. Sirica (1904–1992) that White House officials had pressured him and the other defendants to plead guilty, allegations that spurred further investigation into the Watergate break-in and its cover-up.

269.23   Liddy] G. Gordon Liddy (b. 1930), special counsel to the Committee to Re-Elect the President in 1972; with the former CIA official E. Howard

Hunt (1918–2017), he planned the Watergate burglary. Liddy served a four-and-a-half-year prison sentence for his involvement in the break-in.

269.31–32   like Maureen Barden working in the library] Barden (b. 1948) was a member of the U.S. House of Representatives impeachment staff who oversaw many of the paralegals working on the case.

272.10   Eastward Ho] Eastward Ho!, a country club in Chatham, MA.

273.33–35   *I'll be with you . . . mine*] From the song "I'll Be With You in Apple Blossom Time" (1920), music by Albert von Tilzer (1878–1956), lyrics by Neville Fleeson (1887–1945).

275.38–39   vote for Al Smith for President] Smith (1873–1944) was the Democratic presidential nominee in 1928, the first Catholic to win a major-ticket nomination for the presidency; he was defeated in a landslide by Herbert Hoover.

276.26–27   John Sirica (scholastic background at best vague)] Sirica was never an undergraduate; he received his law degree from Georgetown University in 1926.

276.29–30   Mary McGrory, the writer] McGrory (1918–2004) was a political columnist for the Washington *Star* and the *Washington Post* who was awarded the Pulitzer Prize for Commentary in 1975 for her columns about the Watergate scandal.

282.31   James Michael Curley] Curley (1874–1958), a Democrat, was a Massachusetts congressman, 1911–14 and 1943–47, governor of Massachusetts, 1935–37, and mayor of Boston, 1914–18, 1922–26, 1930–34, and 1946–50. Under constant scrutiny for political corruption, he was convicted of mail fraud in 1947 and spent five months in federal prison before his sentence was commuted by President Harry Truman (1884–1972).

282.34–35   Roosevelt offered Curley the post of United States Ambassador to Poland] According to Curley, President Franklin D. Roosevelt (1882–1945) had informally promised him the post of secretary of the navy, but Curley was later informed that he would not be named to a cabinet position. Roosevelt met with Curley and proposed an ambassadorship to Italy but at a subsequent meeting offered him the ambassadorship to Poland instead.

282.36   Polish corridor] Or Danzig corridor, a strip of land established by the post–World War I Versailles treaty connecting Poland to the Baltic Sea and separating the German territory of East Prussia from the rest of Germany. See also note 46.39–40.

283.4–5   the political people, Anne Armstrong, Dean Burch, and William Timmons] Armstrong (1927–2008), counselor to the president, 1973–74, serving under Presidents Nixon and Ford; Dean Burch (1927–1991), counselor to the president, 1974, under Nixon and Ford; Timmons (b. 1930), Republican lobbyist and consultant, assistant for legislative affairs, 1970–75, under Nixon and Ford.

287.37–288.2   Joseph Moakley . . . Louise Day Hicks] Moakley (1927–2001), U.S. congressman from Massachusetts, 1973–2001, had won his seat in 1972 running as an Independent, defeating the one-term incumbent Democrat Louise Day Hicks (1916–2003), prominent local politician best known for fighting against the desegregation of Boston's public schools, including court-ordered busing, in the 1960s and 1970s. Moakley was unopposed in both the Democratic primary and the general election in 1974.

288.4–9   James Burke . . . run against him in the primary] Burke (1910–1983), U.S. congressman from Massachusetts, 1959–79, defeated Boston city councilman Joseph M. Tierney (1941–2009) in the September 1974 Democratic primary; there was no Republican candidate in the general election.

290.7   Egil Krogh of the Watergate case] Krogh (1939–2020) was an aide in the Nixon administration who with David Young (b. 1936) headed a clandestine group of operatives known as "the Plumbers" until December 1971. He pleaded guilty in 1973 to conspiring to violate the civil rights of psychiatrist Lewis Fielding by approving the burglary of Fielding's office to gather information on Daniel Ellsberg (see note 235.1–2); Krogh was not involved in the Watergate break-in.

290.25   Joseph Zicarelli] Nicknamed "Bayonne Joe," a capo in the Bonnano crime family who was publicly linked to Gallagher (1921–2018) in an August 9, 1968, *Life* magazine article.

291.38   John Murphy] U.S. congressman (1926–2015), 1963–81, a Democrat from New York.

292.16–17   Patrick Buchanan of the White House staff] Buchanan (b. 1938) was a special assistant and speechwriter in the Nixon administration.

293.33   Vernon Hixon] Television writer and producer.

295.22–23   E. Howard Hunt] See note 269.23.

298.19   Rayburn Building] Rayburn House Office Building, congressional office building for the U.S. House of Representatives.

299.32   Fort Custer] There is no Fort Custer in Cheyenne or its vicinity. Breslin is referring to Francis E. Warren Air Force Base, formerly known as Fort D.A. Hill.

300.1   "Pershing lived in that house,"] General John J. Pershing (1860–1948), commander of the American Expeditionary Forces in Europe during World War I, was married to Helen Frances Warren (1880–1915), who lived at Fort D.A. Hill with the family's three children while Pershing was stationed elsewhere, 1913–15.

300.13   Sandhill massacre] I.e., the Sand Creek Massacre. On November

29, 1864, the 3rd Colorado Volunteer Cavalry attacked an encampment of Cheyenne and Arapaho at Sand Creek in southeastern Colorado and killed more than 150 people, mostly women and children.

300.14 "Where was Custer massacred?"] Lt. Col. George Armstrong Custer (1839–1876) led troops of the U.S. Army's 7th Cavalry Regiment against Lakota, Northern Cheyenne, and Arapaho forces at the Battle of Little Bighorn, in southern Montana, on June 25–26, 1876; he was killed during the battle and his troops were overwhelmingly defeated.

301.6 William Hamilton] Political consultant for the Democratic Party and pollster (1939–2000).

301.34–36 "Justice Brandeis said, 'Decency, security, and liberty . . . matters.'"] Cf. U.S. Supreme Court justice Louis D. Brandeis (1856–1941) in his dissenting opinion in *Olmstead v. United States* (1928): "Decency, security and liberty alike demand that government officials shall be subjected to the same rules of conduct that are commands to the citizen. [. . .] To declare that, in the administration of the criminal law, the end justifies the means—to declare that the Government may commit crimes in order to secure the conviction of a private criminal—would bring terrible retribution. Against that pernicious doctrine this Court should resolutely set its face."

303.22 LaRue] Fred LaRue, Sr. (1928–2004), Republican from Mississippi and aide in the Nixon White House who, in 1974, became the first administration official to plead guilty to crimes related to the Watergate scandal. He personally delivered more than $300,000 in hush money to participants in the Watergate burglary.

303.23–24 L. Patrick Gray III of the FBI] Gray (1916–2005) was acting director of the FBI, 1972–73, following the death of longtime FBI director J. Edgar Hoover. During his Senate confirmation hearings for the directorship he disclosed that he had passed the bureau's files on the Watergate inquiry to the White House; his nomination was withdrawn in April 1973 and he resigned from the FBI.

304.17–18 Alexander Butterfield] Retired military officer (b. 1926) who served as deputy assistant to President Nixon, 1969–73.

307.18–19 the Mexican money or the Florida bank account] In April 1972 cashier's checks from Mexican and Florida banks, totaling $124,000 in contributions to the Committee to Re-Elect the President, were deposited in an account at the Republic National Bank of Miami in the name of the real estate firm of Bernard L. Barker (1917–2009), one of the Watergate burglars. Over several weeks Barker withdrew a large number of $100 bills from this account, fifty-three of which were found on the burglars when they were arrested on the night of the Watergate break-in.

309.32 Hamilton Fish, Jr.] Liberal Republican and scion of a prominent New York political family, Fish (1926–1996) was a U.S. congressman, 1969–93.

309.34   Harold Froehlich] Republican congressman from Wisconsin (b. 1932), 1973–75.

312.13–14   Blackmuns, Rehnquists] The Supreme Court justices Harry Blackmun (1908–1999), associate justice, 1970–94, and William Rehnquist (1924–2005), associate justice, 1972–86, chief justice, 1986–2005.

313.4   followers of Sun Myung Moon] Members of the Unification Church, religious sect led by its Korean founder and self-proclaimed messiah, Sun Myung Moon (1920–2012).

313.24–25   *A Star Is Born.* James Mason going into the ocean while Judy Garland sings] Toward the end of the 1954 film *A Star is Born*, directed by George Cukor (1899–1983), the English actor James Mason (1909–1984), playing a former matinee idol whose career is in decline, drowns himself while on the soundtrack Judy Garland (1922–1969), as a young singer on the verge of stardom, sings "It's a New World," music by Harold Arlen (1905–1986), lyrics by Ira Gershwin (1896–1983).

316.28–29   J. Fred Buzhardt, Jr.] Lawyer from South Carolina (1924–1978), special White House counsel for Watergate matters, 1973, special White House counsel, 1974.

316.29   William Timmons] Republican lobbyist (b. 1930) and consultant who managed the Republican conventions that nominated Richard M. Nixon for president in 1968 and 1972; he was assistant for legislative affairs to Presidents Nixon and Ford.

317.4   Raymond Price] Journalist and author (1930–2019), Nixon's campaign aide, chief speechwriter, and loyal friend.

320.40   Gandhi went to prison] Mahatma Gandhi (1868–1948), who led the Indian movement for independence from British rule, was imprisoned several times.

321.10   the Kennedys and the McGoverns] Massachusetts U.S. senator Edward Kennedy (1930–2009) and his first wife, Joan Bennett Kennedy (b. 1936); South Dakota U.S. senator from South Dakota, George McGovern (1922–2012), the Democratic Party candidate for president in 1972, and his wife, Eleanor McGovern (1921–2007).

321.11   Herman Badillos] Herman Badillo (1929–2004), Democratic U.S. representative from New York, 1971–77, Bronx borough president, 1966–69, and frequent candidate for New York City mayor; and his second wife, Irma Badillo (1917–1996).

321.15   Alistair Cooke] British writer and journalist (1908–2004) known for his work on radio and in television, including serving as the longtime host of the *Masterpiece Theatre* program broadcast on PBS.

322.6   Jim Hartz] Television journalist (1940–2022), at the time the cohost of NBC's *Today* show.

323.8–14   *Some of them write . . . ace in the hole*] From the traditional song "Ace in the Hole."

COLUMNS 1976–2004

327.2   my friend Klein] A longtime character in Breslin's columns, an ever-hustling courthouse denizen known for his problematic love life and struggles to collect legal fees. Based on Melvin M. Lebetkin (1928–2006), a Queens lawyer who in 1989 pleaded guilty to mail fraud and served seventeen months in prison for his role in a municipal scandal involving parking fines.

334.13–14   the person who calls himself "Son of Sam."] The pseudonym of David Berkowitz (b. 1953), a postal employee from the Bronx who, from July 1976 to July 1977, terrorized New York City with a series of deadly shootings; in all, he killed six people and wounded seven others. Before he was caught, Berkowitz sent a handwritten letter to Breslin signed "Son of Sam." See Chronology, 1977.

346.1   *Concorde*] A French-British supersonic airliner in service from 1976 to 2003. Because of complaints about sonic booms, the Concorde was temporarily banned from use at John F. Kennedy International Airport, but scheduled service to and from London and Paris began in November 1977.

346.4   *QE2*] *Queen Elizabeth 2*, transatlantic ocean liner and cruise ship, 1969–2008, now a floating hotel in Dubai.

348.13–14   Anthony Wedgwood-Benn] British Labour Party MP (1925–2014) also known as Tony Benn, the U.K.'s energy minister, 1975–79, among other cabinet appointments over the course of his career.

348.27–28   Jamestown, New York] Small city in the southwestern corner of New York, about three hundred miles from Howard Beach.

348.35–36   "You once represented the people of Howard Beach as a senator,"] Goodell (1926–1987) had been a Republican U.S. senator from New York, 1968–71.

350.26   Tom Brokaw] Longtime television journalist (b. 1940), host of NBC's *The Today Show*, 1976–81, and anchor of *NBC Nightly News*, 1982–2004.

355.2   Blue Bell Girls] Members of the Bluebell Girls, a glamorous, scantily clad chorus line that performed at the Lido cabaret on the Champs-Élysées in Paris.

358.1–5   *Bella Was Old Hat . . .* Bill Green] Bella Abzug (1920–1998) was an outspoken feminist activist and Democratic congresswoman from New York, 1971–77; she was often seen wearing a hat. She was defeated in a special election for the 18th Congressional District in an upset win by William Green (1929–2002), a liberal-leaning Republican who served in the U.S. House of Representatives, 1978–93.

358.2   Vincent F. Albano, Jr.] Republican politician (1914–1981), a power broker in Manhattan and the chairman of the New York County Republican Committee, 1962–81.

359.1   Gloria Steinem] Journalist and activist (b. 1934) best known as a leader of the American feminist movement during the late 1960s and early 1970s.

359.9   Muriel Humphrey] Humphrey (1912–1998) was the wife of Hubert H. Humphrey (1911–1978), vice president of the United States, 1965–69. When he died in 1978 while serving as a U.S. senator from Minnesota, she was appointed to his seat. She did not run in the special election for the Senate seat later that year.

359.22–23   Equal Rights Amendment . . . a disease carrier] The Equal Rights Amendment, forbidding the denial or abridgment of rights on account of sex, was proposed to the states by Congress on March 22, 1972, with a seven-year deadline for its ratification. After thirty-five states had ratified the amendment, Congress voted on October 6, 1978, to extend the deadline to June 30, 1982, but there were no further ratifications and the amendment did not go into effect.

361.6   Bert Lance] Businessman and politician (1931–2013) from Georgia who served as director of the Office of Management and Budget in 1977. He resigned amid allegations of corruption related to his previous role as the chairman of a Georgia bank, about which he was questioned by the Senate Governmental Affairs Committee. He was later indicted on conspiracy and other charges but was acquitted of all counts.

361.9–11   Carter . . . Arabs and Israelis] In the face of opposition at home, the Carter administration's plan to sell advanced fighter jets to Israel, Egypt, and Saudi Arabia was ratified by the Senate in May 1978.

362.15   Don Carlo Gambino] The mobster Carlo "Don Carlo" Gambino (1902–1976), the longtime head of the Gambino organized crime family in New York City.

363.23   Enrico Caruso] Legendary Italian opera tenor (1873–1921).

364.17–18   Tommy Brown's] "Tommy Brown" was a nickname for Thomas Lucchese (1899–1967), gangster and longtime head of the Lucchese organized crime family in New York City.

364.33–34   Saint Peter's.] St. Peter's Basilica at the Vatican.

366.33   the peace talks] Continued Egyptian-Israeli negotiations following the peace agreements negotiated at Camp David, MD, in September 1978; a peace treaty between Egypt and Israel was accepted by the leaders of both countries in mid-March 1979 and formally signed on March 26.

370.13   Hue in 1968] North Vietnamese and Viet Cong forces captured much of Huế, the former imperial capital of Vietnam, on January 31, 1968. The city was retaken by American and South Vietnamese troops on February 25 after heavy fighting.

373.10 Law and Order Koch, Koch the Mayor] Ed Koch (1924–2013), a Democrat, was elected mayor of New York City, running on a law-and-order platform. He was mayor from 1978 to 1989. He and Breslin did not get along.

374.16 Klein the Lawyer] See note 327.2.

377.2 *this book*] This note was added by Breslin when a selection of his columns was collected for *The World According to Breslin* (1984).

377.5 *the Dakota*] Co-op apartment building on the corner of 72nd Street and Central Park West, where John Lennon (1940–1980) lived with his second wife, the artist and performer Yoko Ono (b. 1933), and their son Sean (b. 1975).

377.16 *a whole novel*] *Forsaking All Others* (1982).

377.25 *Beatlemania*] Revue featuring the music of The Beatles that ran on Broadway from 1977 to 1979.

378.11–12 Tony Bennett] See note 93.6.

380.1 *Society Carey*] Breslin's nickname for Hugh Carey (1919–2011), a Democrat from Brooklyn who served as the governor of New York, 1975–82, as well as in the U.S. House of Representatives, 1961–74.

383.1–2 Shelter Island] Island at the eastern end of Long Island, with a large summer population.

383.23–24 Robert Morgado] Businessman (b. 1942) and Carey's chief aide while Carey was governor of New York; he later served as chairman of Warner Music Group.

384.1 *Klein*] See note 327.2.

384.5–7 Janet Cooke . . . Pulitzer Prize] Cooke (b. 1954), as a reporter for the *Washington Post*, won a Pulitzer Prize in 1981 for "Jimmy's World," a front-page profile of an eight-year-old heroin addict. Cooke later admitted that the story was "in essence a fabrication" and resigned from the newspaper; the award was rescinded.

384.21 Pep McGuire's] See note 170.39.

384.26 Jimmy Burke] Criminal (1931–1996) with organized-crime affiliations who is believed to have been the mastermind behind the Lufthansa heist of 1978, in which $5.8 million in cash and jewels was stolen from a vault in the Lufthansa Airlines cargo terminal at John F. Kennedy International Airport. Several of the supposed participants in the robbery were later murdered. Burke served prison sentences for other crimes but was never charged in the Lufthansa case.

384.26 Fat Thomas] See note 94.2.

387.36–37   Santo Domingo] The capital of the Dominican Republic and its largest city.

388.22   Fresh Air Fund] A nonprofit organization that provides free summer vacations in the country to children from economically challenged communities in New York City.

389.40   Elmira] The Elmira Correctional Facility, a maximum-security prison in Elmira, NY (about 240 miles northwest of Manhattan), that, until the 1990s, focused primarily on younger offenders.

390.12   Portsmouth Priory] Former name (before 1969) of Portsmouth Abbey School, Catholic boarding school on Rhode Island's Narragansett Bay.

392.26–27   As was said of another aristocrat . . . Earth, receive an honored guest.] From "In Memory of W. B. Yeats" (1939) by the English poet W. H. Auden (1907–1973).

393.33–34   Brooke Shields. The child pornography pictures] Shields (b. 1965) posed at the age of ten for a series of nude photographs with the consent of her mother. Portraying a child prostitute, Shields appeared nude in *Pretty Baby* (1978), directed by Louis Malle (1932–1995), filmed when she was eleven.

396.18   who is known as Dead Body McGuire] Breslin's nickname for Robert J. McGuire (b. 1936), New York City's police commissioner, 1978–83.

397.18   Patrolmen's Benevolent Association] Police union representing the majority of the members of the New York City Police Department.

398.1   Cibella Borges has been suspended from her job] Suspended from the police department in August 1982, Borges (b. 1957) was fired on May 11, 1983. On April 9, 1985, a New York state appeals court ruling ordered her reinstatement to the NYPD with back pay. An out-of-court settlement in her case against *Club* magazine, which had published photographs of her after her reinstatement, awarded her control of the photographs.

399.2–3   Mrs. Eldridge] Ronnie Eldridge (b. 1931) is a New York activist, television host, and Democratic politician who represented Manhattan's Upper West Side in New York's City Council from 1989 to 2001. She was married to Breslin from 1982 until his death in 2017.

399.20   Costello's] Literary haunt of a saloon on the East Side of Manhattan.

400.3–4   the Eldridge family huddle was not about the *Essays* of Charles Lamb] The English essayist Charles Lamb (1775–1834) is known for *Tales from Shakespeare* (1807), children's adaptations, with his sister Mary Lamb (1764–1847), and *Essays of Elia* (1823).

402.4   Bernhard Goetz] On December 22, 1984, Goetz (b. 1947), a white man, shot four Black teenagers with an unlicensed pistol after one of them approached him on a New York City subway and demanded $5 from him. After fleeing Manhattan, he turned himself in to police officials in Concord,

NH, and was arraigned on four charges of attempted murder in New York City. In late January 1985 a federal grand jury indicted Goetz on three counts of illegal gun possession but refused to indict him on murder, assault, and reckless endangerment charges. Two months later a second grand jury indicted Goetz on ten murder, assault, and other charges. In a six-month trial, December 1986– June 1987, Goetz was acquitted of the attempted murder and assault charges against him but was found guilty in the third degree of criminal possession of a weapon. He served eight months in prison and was fined $5,000.

402.10   100 Centre St.] The Lower Manhattan address for the New York City Criminal Court.

402.13   Darrell Cabey] Cabey (b. 1965), who suffered brain damage and was paralyzed from the waist down due to the shooting, filed a civil suit against Goetz and in 1996, Goetz was ordered to pay $43 million in damages, after which he declared bankruptcy.

405.1   *Goetz Should Take Mayoralty Shot*] Goetz later ran for mayor of New York City as a fringe candidate in 2001.

408.1   *Bumpurs Case*] Eleanor Bumpurs (1918–1984), a Black woman with a history of mental illness, was shot dead by an NYPD officer in her Bronx apartment on October 29, 1984, when police were summoned by New York City's Housing Authority after she had refused to accept an eviction notice from city officials. The incident, among others, led to changes in police protocol for dealing with people with emotional issues or other disabilities.

410.30–32   grand jury . . . The policeman, Yearwood, is suspended.] Yearwood was charged with criminally negligent homicide and acquitted. He was dismissed from the NYPD on April 6, 1987, for his role in the shooting.

410.39   Merola] Mario Merola (1922–1987), district attorney of Bronx County in New York City, 1972–87.

415.18–19   Michael Stewart and Eleanor Bumpurs cases] In the early morning of September 15, 1983, the Black artist Michael Stewart (1958–1983) was arrested by New York Transit Police while allegedly writing graffiti on the wall of a Manhattan subway station. When he arrived in police custody at Bellevue Hospital, bound and bruised, he had no pulse. He was revived but remained in a coma until his death on September 28. Six transit police officers were acquitted in 1985 of manslaughter and perjury charges related to the case. For Bumpurs, see note 408.1.

415.25   Hill Street] A reference to *Hill Street Blues*, a groundbreaking television police drama on NBC, 1981–87.

421.12–13   Gross bookmaking scandal] Hundreds of New York City police officers retired, were demoted, or were convicted of criminal charges emerging out of the Brooklyn district attorney's investigation, launched in 1949, of the gambling empire of bookmaker Harry Gross (1916–1986).

421.13 Serpico and the Knapp Commission] In 1967 the New York City police officer Frank Serpico (b. 1936) alerted his superiors to corruption within the police ranks. When his reports were ignored, he became a whistleblower, contributing to a front-page exposé in *The New York Times* that led to several investigations and the establishment in 1970 of the Knapp Commission, a five-member investigatory body that confirmed the existence of systemic corruption and issued several recommendations for how to change police culture. Breslin's "enchanted movie producers" makes reference to *Serpico* (1973), a film starring Al Pacino (b. 1940) as the titular whistleblower.

423.34 Trans World] Trans World Airlines (TWA), a major airline carrier from 1930 to 2001 with a hub at John F. Kennedy International Airport.

425.1 *Ward Left His Job in San Francisco*] Benjamin Ward (1926–2002) was a New York City police officer who rose to become New York City's first Black police commissioner, 1984–89. The title is a play on the popular song "I Left My Heart in San Francisco" (1953), music by George Cory (1920–1978), words by Douglass Cross (1920–1975), and associated with the singer Tony Bennett, who recorded the song in 1962.

427.3–4 policemen being arrested . . . charges most shocking] NYPD officers Richard Pike and Jeffrey Gilbert were convicted of felony assault and misdemeanor charges in 1986 and sentenced to two to six years in prison for their role in the Davidson case.

429.18 Kaposi's sarcoma] A form of cancer often associated with HIV/AIDS. Symptoms can include dark-colored lesions developing on the skin and in the mouth and respiratory and gastrointestinal tracts.

430.13 Windows on the World] A restaurant that anchored other venues on the top two floors of the north tower of the World Trade Center.

433.22 *Dawgs*] Nickname for the University of Georgia Bulldogs sports teams, particularly its football squad.

437.1 *Shooting Script*] For the Goetz case, see notes 402.4 and 402.13.

438.18 "Loving."] Television soap opera that aired on ABC, 1983–95.

445.16 Balzac] Prolific French realist novelist and playwright Honoré de Balzac (1799–1850), author of the Human Comedy cycle of novels.

446.19–20 buying the Eastern Shuttle] An air shuttle service of the now-defunct Eastern Airlines that linked Washington, D.C., New York City, and Boston. The ground rights and seventeen aircraft of the shuttle were sold in 1988 to Donald Trump (b. 1946) to create the short-lived Trump Shuttle.

447.11 Trump's book] *The Art of the Deal* (1987), credited to Trump and Tony Schwartz (b. 1952).

447.20 Walter Winchell] See note 46.25.

447.33–34   his father in the County of Queens] Fred Trump, Sr. (1905–1999), a real estate developer in Queens.

449.29   the Queen of Saudi Arabia] Princess Anoud bint Abdel Aziz (1923–1999), the first wife of Saudi king Fahd (1921–2005), arrived at Barrow in October 1994 for treatment of a spinal condition and stayed two years.

453.27–29   "South Jamaica Houses . . . Forty Houses"] Also known as "40 Projects," or "The 40s," a subsidized housing development in the South Jamaica section of Queens known in the 1980s and '90s for its persistent drug-related violence.

455.12–13   police . . . Leary's house] Leary (b. 1945) was convicted in 1996 of carrying firebombs onto two Manhattan subway trains in December 1994, injuring forty-eight people, more than a dozen of them seriously. He was sentenced to ninety-four years in prison.

456.1   *Mick's*] Mickey Mantle (1931–1995), Hall of Fame baseball player who spent his entire eighteen-year Major League career with the New York Yankees. An outfielder and first baseman, he hit 536 home runs.

459.29–30   the bodies from the TWA plane] TWA Flight 800, en route from New York to Paris, accidentally exploded and crashed into the Atlantic Ocean off eastern Long Island shortly after taking off from John F. Kennedy International Airport on July 17, 1996, killing all 230 passengers and crew aboard.

462.4–5   Louis Armstrong] American trumpeter, singer, actor and composer (1901–1971), one of the most important figures in the history of jazz.

462.10   Joe Butch] The mobster Joseph Corrao (1936–2001), known as "Joe Butch," was a member of the Gambino crime family.

462.11–12   Kempton] Murray Kempton (1917–1997), newspaper columnist and author, known for his baroque writing style and incisive social commentary. A longtime columnist for *Newsday*, he was awarded the Pulitzer Prize for Commentary in 1985.

462.18–19   Afeni Shakur, mother of the late Tupac] Afeni Shakur (born Alice Faye Williams, 1947–2016), activist and member of the Black Panther Party in the late 1960s and early 1970s. In his National Book Award–winning *The Briar Patch* (1973), Kempton wrote about her trial in 1970–71, with other Black Panthers, on attempted murder and conspiracy charges related to an alleged plan to bomb two police stations and an education building; Shakur acted as her own lawyer and was acquitted, as were the other twenty defendants. Her son, Tupac Shakur (1971–1996), was one of the premier rappers of his era. He died in Las Vegas after the car in which he was a passenger was sprayed with bullets. His assassination remains unsolved.

462.19–20   Joyce Persico, wife of Junior Persico, away forever] "Junior" Persico is the mafia boss Carmine Persico (see note 48.21–22), who spent much of his life in prison, where he continued to direct the operations of the Colombo crime family. Two separate 1986 convictions resulted in combined prison sentences of 139 years. Kempton once said of Carmine Persico: "I have tremendous admiration for Carmine Persico. There's just a dignity about him. Of course, he is a killer, a real killer. But I love him because of his wiretaps. They are just wonderful."

462.20   Senator Patrick Moynihan] Daniel Patrick Moynihan (1927–2003) was U.S. senator from New York, 1977–2001.

462.37–463.1   World Series perfect game by Don Larsen] Pitching for the New York Yankees in Game 5 of the 1956 World Series against the Brooklyn Dodgers, Larsen (1929–2020) became the only pitcher in Major League history to throw a perfect game (a game in which none of the opponents' players reach base) in World Series play.

463.24–26   Mose Wright . . . Emmett Till] Fourteen-year-old Emmett Till was murdered on August 28, 1955, while visiting Leflore County, Mississippi, from Chicago; he was beaten and shot to death after he allegedly whistled at a white woman. His murder and the acquittal on September 23 of Roy Bryant and J. W. Milam, the two white men charged with the crime (both of whom later admitted to a journalist that they had killed Till), attracted widespread public attention. Till's great-uncle Mose Wright (1892–1977), a sharecropper and preacher, testified against Bryant and Milam at their trial.

464.1   Viola Liuzzo] Civil rights activist from Michigan (1925–1965) murdered by the Ku Klux Klan after participating in the freedom march from Selma to Montgomery, AL. See pp. 259–60.

464. 27–29   A fund raiser . . . "Radical Chic."] "Radical Chic: That Party at Lenny's," published in *New York* magazine on June 8, 1970, sardonically described the fundraiser for the Black Panthers at the Park Avenue apartment in Manhattan of the conductor and composer Leonard Bernstein (1918–1990) on January 14, 1970. Burton Lane (1912–1997) was a composer and lyricist; Lynn Lane was his second wife.

465.3–4   Lyndon Johnson got up at a joint session of the Congress and announced "We shall overcome,"] On March 15, 1965, making reference to a protest folk song often sung at civil rights demonstrations.

466.37–467.1   Amadou Diallo] An immigrant from Guinea (1975–1999) who was shot and killed by four plainclothes New York City police officers who mistook him for a suspect from a year-old rape case in the Bronx. The four officers were later acquitted of second-degree murder, but the shooting death of the unarmed man sparked protests over police brutality and racial profiling.

467.9   Eleanor Bumpurs and now Anthony Baez] Bumpurs, see note 408.1. Anthony Baez (1965–1994) was a security officer involved in an altercation with New York City police officers after a football he was throwing with his brothers accidentally hit a squad car. He died after being subdued in a chokehold (prohibited by NYPD rules) by Officer Francis Livoti, who had been the subject of prior brutality complaints. The city's chief medical officer determined asphyxiation to be the cause of Baez's death. Acquitted in a judge-only state trial of criminally negligent homicide in October 1996, Livoti was dismissed by the NYPD in 1997 and convicted in a 1998 federal trial of violating Baez's civil rights and sentenced to seven-and-a-half years in federal prison.

467.12–13 utterly cheap prattle about some Senate race against Hillary Clinton] It was widely speculated at the time that Rudolph Giuliani (b. 1944), then mayor of New York City, would run against Hillary Rodham Clinton (b. 1947) in the 2000 U.S. Senate race for the seat vacated by Daniel Patrick Moynihan, who had announced his retirement in 1998. Giuliani did not run and Clinton won the seat in a race against Republican Rick Lazio (b. 1958).

467.24–25 On the day the Senate voted on Bill Clinton's impeachment charges] February 12, 1999, the day the Senate voted to acquit President Bill Clinton (b. 1946) of both impeachment articles against him, accusing him of perjury and obstruction of justice. "The most ominous day in 131 years" refers to what had been the only presidential impeachment, that of Andrew Johnson in 1868.

467.40–468.1 the Abner Louima torture] Louima (b. 1966), a Haitian immigrant, was arrested outside a Brooklyn nightclub in 1997, then brutalized and sodomized with a broom handle in a holding cell by New York City police officers. Officer Justin Volpe (b. 1972) was later convicted on various charges related to the assault and sentenced to thirty years in federal prison; he was released in 2023.

468.8 Michael Daly] Journalist and author (b. 1951), a former columnist with the New York *Daily News.*

472.2 William Murphy] Roman Catholic prelate (b. 1940) who served as the bishop of Rockville Centre on Long Island, 2001–17. He served as auxiliary bishop in the Archdiocese of Boston from 1995 to 2001, and since has been accused of helping to shield abusive priests there, allegations that he has denied. Murphy was also criticized for his managerial style as archbishop, reflected in part by his decision to convert the third floor of a convent into his private residence at considerable expense, forcing several nuns to relocate.

473.18 Cardinal Law of Boston] Bernard Francis Law (1931–2017) was archbishop of Boston from 1984 until his resignation in 2002, following revelations that he had failed to remove sexually predatory priests in his archdiocese from the ministry despite prior knowledge of their behavior.

473.19 Daily of Brooklyn] Thomas Daily (1927–2017), Roman Catholic prelate who served as the bishop of the diocese of Brooklyn from 1990 to 2003, but who was also vicar general of the Archdiocese of Boston from 1976 to 1984, a time when archdiocesan priests suspected of or identified as sexual abusers were allowed to remain in the ministry.

473.20–21 pedophiles like Geoghan and Shanley] Predatory priests John J. Geoghan (1935–2003) and Paul R. Shanley (1931–2020), whose sexual assaults against children were covered up by officials in the Boston archdiocese at the highest levels. Geoghan was convicted of child sexual abuse in 2002 and was murdered in prison while serving his sentence. Shanley was convicted of child rape in 2004 and served twelve years in prison.

476.4   One statement reportedly made by Christ] See Mark 9:42.

478.12   Tony Dunne] A builder of movie sets who was married to Jimmy Breslin's daughter Rosemary.

THE SHORT SWEET DREAM OF EDUARDO GUTIÉRREZ

488.37   The writer Richard Rodriguez noted] In the memoir *Days of Obligation: An Argument with My Mexican Father* (1992) by the American writer Richard Rodriguez (b. 1944).

489.1–3   conclusions of the Kerner Report in the sixties: two Americas, one white, one black] The National Advisory Commission on Civil Disorders was led by Illinois governor Otto Kerner, Jr. (1908–1976), appointed by President Lyndon Johnson on July 27, 1967, following major riots in Newark, New Jersey, and Detroit. On March 1, 1968, the commission issued its report, warning that "the nation is moving toward two societies, one black, one white—separate and unequal."

489.14–16   Carroll O'Connor . . . Archie Bunker] The actor Carroll O'Connor (1924–2001), raised in the Elmhurst and Forest Hills sections of Queens, portrayed Archie Bunker, the bigoted, conflicted patriarch of a blue-collar Queens family depicted in the popular CBS television sitcoms *All in the Family*, 1971–79, and *Archie Bunker's Place*, 1979–83.

505.1–6   travel visa for Gerry Adams . . . King wanted him to speak to the American Irish . . . decision overturned.] Beginning in 1980, King (b. 1944) traveled to Northern Ireland and met with Gerry Adams (b. 1948), the leader of the Sinn Féin political party, 1983–2018, and someone long suspected to have been a leader of the paramilitary Provisional Irish Republican Army, an allegation Adams has denied. Adams had been refused a visa to travel to the United States eight times before the Clinton administration, over the objections of the British government and the U.S. State Department, Department of Justice, and FBI, authorized the issuing of a forty-eight-hour temporary visa for Adams to travel to New York City to speak at an event in February 1994. King, Adams's chief supporter in the House, met Adams at John F. Kennedy International Airport.

505.19–20   his moral purity was slightly marred by one girlfriend and he was out] House Speaker Newt Gingrich (b. 1943), a Republican from Georgia, resigned from Congress on November 6, 1998, in the wake of his party's poor electoral results and a reprimand from the House ethics panel over his use of tax-exempt funds. In the period of Clinton's impeachment there were rumors about Gingrich having an extramarital affair, which Gingrich admitted to in 2007.

505.27–28 because he is an immoral pig with a girlfriend, Monica] A sex scandal involving President Bill Clinton and White House intern Monica Lewinsky (b. 1973) broke in 1998. It led to impeachment proceedings against Clinton (see note 467.24–25).

505.29–30 the news that Livingston has four girlfriends] On October 4, 1998, Larry Flynt (1942–2021), publisher of the pornographic magazine *Hustler*, placed an advertisement in the *Washington Post* offering up to $1 million for proof of "infidelity, sexual impropriety, or corruption concerning a current United States senator, congressperson or prominent government official." On December 19, 1998, after Flynt announced he was looking into claims that Republican Louisiana congressman Bob Livingston (b. 1943), just named Speaker-elect of the House, had four extramarital affairs, Livingston stepped down from the speakership and announced he would give up his seat in six months. He had admitted two days earlier that "on occasion I have strayed from my marriage."

505.34 a successor, Dennis Hastert] Hastert (b. 1942), Republican politician from Illinois, was Speaker of the House, 1999–2007.

506.2–4 a resolution condemning Turkey . . . Livingston is hired to block it] The Livingston Group, the lobbying firm Livingston formed after leaving Congress, represented the Turkish government among its major clients. In 2000 it lobbied against a House of Representatives resolution acknowledging the Turkish genocide of Armenians in 1915–23; the resolution was withdrawn shortly before a scheduled vote. (The Livingston Group also lobbied against proposed Armenian genocide resolutions in 2004 and 2007. In 2019 both houses of Congress passed a resolution acknowledging the genocide.)

506.9 a new president] Vicente Fox (b. 1942), president of Mexico from 2000 to 2006.

509.1 Ray Kelly, then customs commissioner] Kelly (b. 1941), a marine and a New York City police officer and police commissioner, 1992–94 and 2002–13, served as commissioner of the U.S. Customs Service, 1998–2001.

524.5 war on poverty] In his first State of the Union address in January 1964, President Lyndon B. Johnson called for a federal response to a national poverty rate near 19 percent: "This administration, here and now, declares an unconditional war on poverty." Subsequent legislation created various anti-poverty initiatives, including Medicaid and Medicare, as well as programs for job training, food stamps, legal services, community action, and early childhood education.

524.8–9 Jimmy Carter's moral equivalent of war on an oil shortage] In a televised speech to the nation on April 18, 1977, President Carter characterized efforts to reduce oil and energy consumption as a "moral equivalent of war," a phrase now often used to refer to the speech as a whole. It was taken from the title of a lecture delivered in 1906 by the American philosopher and psychologist William James (1842–1910).

524.11–12   "Just say no," Nancy Reagan said] Slogan for the anti-drug campaign that had First Lady Nancy Reagan (1921–2016) as its chief spokesperson, part of the Reagan administration's War on Drugs initiative.

524.14–15   General Barry McCaffrey when he was the nation's official drug czar] McCaffrey (b. 1942), a professor, consultant, news commentator, and much-decorated soldier during the Vietnam War, served as the director of the Office of National Drug Control Policy, 1996–2001.

530.19–20   Jesús Malverde, the patron saint of drug peddling] Jesús Malverde is the hero of some Mexican folktales, said to have been a good-hearted bandit—a Robin Hood–like figure—who roamed the Mexican state of Sinaloa during the late nineteenth and early twentieth centuries. The character is considered to be a kind of saint by some Mexican drug traffickers, and its likeness appears in spiritual supplies, including statues, candles, and lithographs.

537.18   still on death row] Ramon Villareal-Martínez's death sentence was vacated due to intellectual disability in 2002, and he was released from prison in 2006.

537.39–40   a police commissioner named Howard Safir, who came out of a third-rate drug enforcement agency] A former assistant director of the U.S. Drug Enforcement Agency, Safir (b. 1942) served in the administration of New York City mayor Rudolph W. Giuliani, first as fire commissioner, 1994–96, and then as police commissioner, 1996–2001.

543.4   Ted Conover wrote in his book *Coyotes*] *Coyotes: A Journey Across Borders with America's Illegal Migrants* (1987) by the American writer Ted Conover (b. 1958).

544.34–37   Williamsburg . . . Hasidic communities] Brooklyn's Williamsburg neighborhood has a substantial population of Hasidic Jews.

545.13–15   Dov Hikind, the state legislator . . . on trial in federal court] Dov Hikind (b. 1950), a longtime power broker in Brooklyn's Orthodox Jewish community who served as a Democrat in the New York State Assembly from 1983 to 2018, was indicted in 1998 by a federal grand jury on corruption charges related to money he received from Rabbi Elimelech Naiman of the Council of Jewish Organizations of Borough Park, a social services organization, in exchange for state grant funds. Hikind was acquitted, though Naiman was convicted on a charge of making corrupt payments to him.

546.11–12   to meet girlfriends] While mayor and still married to Donna Hanover (b. 1950), Giuliani was romantically involved with Judith Nathan (b. 1954), later his third wife. Giuliani's estrangement from Hanover, leading to their divorce in 2002, was acrimonious and highly publicized. When Hanover announced her separation from Giuliani in May 2000, she claimed Giuliani had also had an affair with a member of his staff.

546.21   Joseph Spitzer] Brooklyn developer (b. 1950) who enjoyed unusual access to the Giuliani administration, due in part to his generous campaign contributions. In addition to receiving two of eleven special mayoral parking permits, allowing him to park anywhere in the city, Spitzer appeared in Giuliani's "Godfather" musical number during a City Hall–centered charity event in 2001.

546.39   Tommy (Three Finger Brown) Lucchese] See note 364.17–18.

546.39–547.1   Joey Rao, and Trigger Mike Coppola] Gangsters Rao (1901–1962; rhymes with "mayo") and Coppola (1900–1966) were both based in East Harlem and were ranking members of the underworld organization now known as the Genovese crime family.

547.9   Thomas Aurelio] New York State Supreme Court judge (c. 1892–1973) who was dogged by allegations of mafia links, including suspicion that mobster Frank Costello (1891–1973) helped him to get elected to the bench in 1943.

547.11–12   Frank Costello, the prime minister of the underworld] Italian-born American gangster, boss of what is now called the Genovese crime family. Breslin claimed to have caddied for Costello as a teenager and to have received a large tip.

547.27   Rev. Louis Gigante] Roman Catholic priest (1932–2022), community activist in the South Bronx, city councilman, and the younger brother of two New York gangsters, Mario (1923–2022) and Vincent (the Chin) Gigante (1928–2005).

547.28   Vincent (The Chin) Gigante] American gangster who began as an enforcer and rose to become the boss of the Genovese crime family. Best known for feigning insanity for decades, in part by wandering the streets of Greenwich Village in a bathrobe, muttering to himself. While pleading guilty to racketeering charges in 2003, he admitted that it had all been a ruse to avoid prosecution.

548.9   Tip O'Neill] Thomas P. O'Neill, Jr. (1912–1994) a Democrat, represented North Boston in Congress, 1953–87, and served as Speaker of the House of Representatives, 1977–87. He is a central figure in Breslin's *How the Good Guys Finally Won*, included in this volume.

548.13   Dutch Schultz] Born Arthur Flegenheimer (1901–1935), a Prohibition-era mobster and bootlegger with considerable influence in New York City.

548.19   When Abe Beame was the mayor . . . Stanley Friedman was his chief assistant] Beame (1906–2001) was New York City's mayor from 1974 to 1977, with Friedman, hailing from the Bronx, serving as deputy mayor, 1975–77.

560.34–35   Boris Yeltsin] Soviet and Russian politician (1931–2007), the first president of the Russian Federation, 1991–99.

568.29–31   Commodore Vanderbilt, who stole railways, Jim Fisk, and William C. Whitney.] Vanderbilt (1794–1877) made his fortune, among the largest in American history, in railroads and shipping. Fisk (1835–1872), was a stockbroker, businessman, and robber baron of the Gilded Age who was shot to death by a former business associate trying to extort him. Whitney (1841–1904), descended from a prominent American family, was a capitalist, thoroughbred enthusiast, and political leader who opposed the corrupt Tammany machine in New York; he served as secretary of the navy under President Grover Cleveland, and at the time of his death had amassed one of the largest landholdings in the eastern United States.

570.22   Henry Miller] American writer (1891–1980) who often pushed the limits of propriety regarding sexual subject matter in semi-autobiographical novels such as *Tropic of Cancer* (1934), which were banned from the United States for decades.

571.1–4   Moshe Teitelbaum . . . only twenty-five of his sect, Satmar] Teitelbaum (1914–2006) was a rabbi and world leader of the Satmar, a Hasidic sect founded by his uncle, Rabbi Joel Teitelbaum (1887–1979), in Satu Mare in what is now Romania, in 1905.

571.19–20   Klausenburg concentration camp . . . Kasztner] The German name for the city of Cluj, now in Romania, is Klausenburg (Hungarian: Kolozsvár). When the Nazis occupied Cluj in 1944, Jews from the city and the surrounding area were forced into a ghetto before the vast majority of them were transported to Auschwitz and murdered. Rudolf Kasztner (1906–1957), a Hungarian Jewish journalist from Cluj, negotiated with SS officials, including Adolf Eichmann (1906–1962), to allow a train carrying 1,686 Jews to travel from Budapest to Switzerland in exchange for money and assorted valuables. (The train's passengers were detained at the Bergen-Belsen concentration camp before they were permitted, in two departures months apart, to continue on to Switzerland.) In 1952 Kasztner became an official in the Israeli government; the following year he was accused of collaborating with the Nazis and having personally benefited from his negotiations with the SS. His accuser was then sued for libel. Judge Benjamin Halevy (1910–1996) upheld most of the accusations and said Kasztner had "sold his soul to the devil" in the affair. On March 4, 1957, Kasztner was attacked in Tel Aviv by three members of the underground militia Lehi and died twelve days later. In January 1958 the Supreme Court of Israel overturned most of the judgment against Kasztner, ruling that the lower court had "erred seriously."

572.14   Orange County town of Monroe] Monroe in Orange County, NY, about fifty miles north of New York City. For many years it included a large Hasidic Jewish community called Kiryas Joel, which became its own town, Palm Tree, in 2019.

573.6   Rabbi Shea Hecht] Lubavitch rabbi and community leader (b. 1954) in Brooklyn, known for working to ease racial tensions. He was appointed by Mayor Rudolph W. Giuliani to both the Commission on Human Rights and the Police Task Force Committee.

573.32   an assistant, Richard Scheirer] Scheirer (1946–2012), formerly an official of New York City's Fire Department, was a longtime aide to Mayor Rudolph W. Giuliani who most notably served as director of the city's Office of Emergency Management from 2000 to 2002, in charge of rescue and cleanup efforts after the 9/11 terrorist attacks; he also served as deputy police commissioner.

574.2   Al Vann] A longtime political leader (1934–2022) of the African American community in central Brooklyn who served in the New York State Assembly, 1975–2001, and the New York City Council, 2002–2013.

574.10–11   a Central Park concert, Garth Brooks, the country singer] Brooks (b. 1962), among the biggest-selling musical act of the 1990s, performed in a free concert in Central Park on August 7, 1997, to 980,000 people, according to New York Fire Department estimates.

574.32   Wagner and Lindsay] Robert F. Wagner, Jr. (1910–1991), New York City mayor, 1954–65; John V. Lindsay (1921–2000), New York City mayor, 1966–73.

576.32   Pergament] Pergament Home Centers, regional chain store that went bankrupt and shuttered in 2001.

581.8–9   Lubavitch grand rebbe, Menachem Shneerson] Longtime leader (1902–1994) of the Lubavitcher Hasidic movement, so prominent a leader that he was known simply as "the Rebbe" (rabbi).

582.1   famous picture of mobster Carmine Galante dead] Widely known photograph by Mary DiBiase (later Blaich) first published in the New York Daily News, July 13, 1979, an overhead shot of the dead body of Carmine Galante (1910–1979), onetime boss of the Bonanno crime family, who was shot to death while finishing lunch on the backyard patio of an Italian restaurant in Brooklyn. The photograph shows Galante's bullet-riddled body, a cigar jutting from his mouth.

582.18   NYPD Blue] Popular police-procedural television series that aired on ABC from 1993 to 2005, centered on a detective squad in a fictional Manhattan police precinct.

585.6–7   Asociacion Tepeyac de New York] Nonprofit organization that advocates for Latino immigrants and promotes the cultural heritage of Mexicans and Mexican Americans in New York.

585.14   Suffolk County] Mostly suburban New York county covering the eastern two-thirds of Long Island.

586.19   Brown vs. Board of Education] In Brown v. Board of Education (of Topeka, KS), decided on Monday, May 17, 1954, the Supreme Court unanimously ruled that segregation in public schools violated the equal protection clause of the Fourteenth Amendment and that the doctrine of "separate but equal" set forth in the Plessy v. Ferguson railway segregation case (1896) had "no place" in public education.

586.20–21   Little Rock school desegregation] After a federal district court ordered nine Black students to be admitted to Little Rock's all-white Central

High School, Arkansas governor Orval Faubus (1910–1994) used the Arkansas National Guard to prevent them from entering the school on September 3, 1957. The Guard was withdrawn after the district court ordered Faubus to end his interference on September 20. After a large mob attacked the nine students three days later, President Dwight D. Eisenhower (1890–1969) placed the Arkansas National Guard under federal control and sent more than one thousand paratroopers of the 101st Airborne Division to enforce the desegregation order.

591.22   Truman's victory] In the 1948 presidential election.

608.24   Occupational Safety and Health Administration] A federal agency created in 1970 to enforce standards that ensure safe and healthful working conditions.

630.12–13   Buffalo Sabres] Professional hockey team from Buffalo, NY, that competes in the National Hockey League.

639.36–37   a song called "Las Flores."] The traditional Mexican folk song "Flor de las Flores" ("Flower of the Flowers").

Index

*This book is set in 10 point ITC Galliard, a face designed
for digital composition by Matthew Carter and based
on the sixteenth-century face Granjon. The paper is acid-free
lightweight opaque that will not turn yellow or brittle with age.
The binding is sewn, which allows the book to open easily and lie flat.
The binding board is covered in Brillianta, a woven rayon cloth
made by Van Heek–Scholco Textielfabrieken, Holland.
Composition by Gopa & Ted2, Inc.
Printing by Sheridan, Grand Rapids, MI.
Binding by Dekker Bookbinding, Wyoming, MI.
Designed by Bruce Campbell.*